Sexuality and Gender

BLACKWELL READERS IN SOCIOLOGY

Each volume in this authoritative series aims to provide students and scholars with comprehensive collections of classic and contemporary readings for all the major sub-fields of sociology. They are designed to complement single-authored works, or to be used as stand-alone textbooks for courses. The selected readings sample the most important works that students should read and are framed by informed editorial introductions. The series aims to reflect the state of the discipline by providing collections not only on standard topics but also on cutting-edge subjects in sociology to provide future directions in teaching and research.

Sexuality and Gender

Edited by

Christine L. Williams
and
Arlene Stein

First published 2002

2 4 6 8 10 9 7 5 3 1
Blackwell Publishers Inc.
350 Main Street
Malden, Massachusetts 02148
USA

Blackwell Publishers Ltd
108 Cowley Road
Oxford OX4 1JF
UK

Library of Congress Cataloging-in-Publication Data has been applied for.

ISBN 0–631–22271–5 (hardback); 0–631–22272–3 (paperback)

British Library Cataloguing in Publication Data

A CIP catalogue record for this book is available from the British Library.

Typeset in 9.5 on 11.5 pt Sabon
by Kolam Information services Pvt. Ltd, Pondicherry, India

Printed in Great Britain by Antony Rowe Ltd., Chippenham, Wiltshire

This book is printed on acid-free paper.

Contents

Contributors

John P. Bartkowski is Associate Professor of Sociology at Mississippi State University. Much of his research examines the relationship between religious involvement, social inequality, gender, and sexuality. His most recent published works include the book *Remaking the Godly Marriage: Gender Negotiation in Evangelical Families* (2001), along with articles in journals such as *Social Forces*, *Sociological Quarterly*, and *Gender & Society*.

Evelyn Blackwood is Associate Professor of Anthropology and Women's Studies at Purdue University. She is co-editor with Saskia E. Wieringa of *Female Desires: Same-Sex Relations and Transgender Practices Across Cultures* (1999) and editor of *The Many Faces of Homosexuality: Anthropology and Homosexual Behavior* (1986).

Lionel Cantú is an Assistant Professor of Sociology (with affiliations in Latin American and Latino Studies and Women's Studies) at the University of California, Santa Cruz. His research interests include international migration, HIV/AIDS, Latino/a Studies, Feminist Studies and Queer Theory. The essay in this volume is drawn from his dissertation research, *Border Crossings: Mexican Men and the Sexuality of Migration*, which examines how sexuality influences migratory processes among Mexican men in the United States and Mexico.

Wendy Chapkis is an Associate Professor of Women's Studies and Sociology at the University of Southern Maine. She is the author of many articles and two books on gender and sexuality, including "Power and Control in the Commercial Sex Trade," in *Sex For Sale* (2000), *Live Sex Acts: Women Performing Erotic Labor* (1997), and *Beauty Secrets: Women and the Politics of Appearance* (1986).

Patricia Hill Collins is Charles Phelps Taft Professor and Head of the African American Studies department at the University of Cincinnati. She is the author of *Fighting Words: Black Women and the Search for Justice* (1998) and *Black Feminist Thought: Knowledge, Consciousness, and the Politics of Empowerment* (2000).

Julia O'Connell Davidson is Professor of Sociology at the University of Nottingham. She has been researching prostitution, sex tourism, and child sexual exploitation in various parts of the world since 1993. She is the author of *Prostitution Power and Freedom* (1998).

Dorothy Dinnerstein, now deceased, is the author of *The Mermaid and the Minotaur: Sexual Arrangements and Human Malaise* (1999).

Meenakshi Gigi Durham is an Associate Professor in the School of Journalism and Mass Communication at the University of Iowa. She has published widely in the area of feminist media studies, with a focus on representations of the female body in the media and issues of adolescent gender and sexuality. She is the co-editor, with Douglas M. Kellner, of the anthology *Media and Cultural Studies: KeyWorks* (2000).

Steven Epstein is an Associate Professor at the University of California, San Diego, where he teaches classes on the sociology of science, medical sociology, sexuality, LGBT studies, social movements, and social theory. His book, *Impure Science: AIDS, Activism, and the Politics of Knowledge*

(1996) analyzes the "politics of credibility" in scientific debates about AIDS and emphasizes the roles played by laypeople in these debates.

Susan Faludi is a Pulitzer Prize winning journalist. She is the author of *Backlash: The Undeclared War against American Women* (1992) and *Stiffed: The Betrayal of the American Man* (1999).

Anne Fausto-Sterling is Professor of Biology and Women's Studies at Brown University. She is the author of *Myths of Gender: Biological Theories About Women and Men* (1992) and *Sexing the Body: Gender Politics and the Construction of Sexuality* (2000).

John H. Gagnon is Distinguished Professor of Sociology Emeritus at the State University at Stony Brook. He is the author or coauthor of several articles and books, including *The Social Organization of Sexuality* (1994) and *Sex in America* (1994). In addition he has been the co-editor of a number of books, most recently *Conceiving Sexuality* (1995) and *Encounters with AIDS: Gay Men and Lesbians Confront the AIDS Epidemic* (1997). He is now an Associate at the HIV Center for Behavioral and Clinical Research, Columbia University and the New York State Psychiatric Institute and lives in New York City.

Joshua Gamson is Associate Professor of Sociology at Yale University, author of *Freaks Talk Back: Tabloid Talk Shows and Sexual Nonconformity* (1998), *Claims to Fame: Celebrity in Contemporary America* (1994), and a participating author of *Ethnography Unbound: Power and Resistance in the Modern Metropolis* (1991). His work on social movements, media and culture, and sexuality has been published in *Social Problems, Gender & Society, Sexualities,* the *Journal of the History of Sexuality, Critical Studies in Mass Communication,* and elsewhere, and he has written about television, popular culture, and lesbian and gay

politics for *The Nation, The American Prospect, Tikkun, The Utne Reader,* and *The New Yorker.*

Anthony Giddens has been the Director of the London School of Economics and Political Science since 1997. Previously he was a Fellow and Professor of Sociology at King's College, Cambridge. He is the author of 35 books, published in 29 languages, and numerous articles and reviews. His most recent book is *The Global Third Way Debate* (2001).

Patti A. Giuffre is an Assistant Professor of Sociology at Southwest Texas State University. Her research interests include sexuality in organizations and sexual harassment. Her most recent publication in *Gender & Society* regarded sexuality in relationships between healthcare professionals and their patients.

Lynn Jamieson teaches sociology at Edinburgh University and is the author of *Intimacy: Personal Life and Social Change* (1998).

Elaine Bell Kaplan is Associate Professor of Sociology at the University of Southern California. Her book *"Not Our Kind of Girl": Unraveling the Myths of Black Teenage Motherhood* (1997) won the 2000 Distinguished Contribution to Scholarship Book Award from the Race, Gender and Class Section of the American Sociological Association. She has published various articles on adolescent issues using a gender, race, and class perspective, including "'It's Going Good:' Inner-City Black and Latino Adolescents' Perceptions About Achieving An Education" (1999) and "Using Food as a Metaphor for Care: Middle-School Kids Talk about Family, School, and Class Relationships" (2000).

Debra Renee Kaufman is the Director of Jewish Studies, a Matthews Distinguished Professor, and Professor of Sociology at

Northeastern University. She was the former coordinator and founder of the Women's Studies Program there as well. Her published articles and chapters range widely across feminist and gender issues both in the family and in the workplace. Her books and edited volumes include *Achievement and Women* (with Barbara Richardson, 1981), *Public/Private Spheres: Women Past and Present* (1989), and *Rachel's Daughters: Newly Orthodox Jewish Women* (1991).

Gina Kolata is a science reporter for *The New York Times* and the author of *Flu: The Story of the Great Influenza Pandemic of 1918 and the Search for the Virus that Caused It* (1999) and *Clone: The Road to Dolly, and the Path Ahead* (1999).

Roger N. Lancaster is Director of Cultural Studies at George Mason University. His previous books include *Life is Hard: Machismo, Danger, and the Intimacy of Power in Nicaragua* (1994), which won the C. Wright Mills Award and the Ruth Benedict Prize. He edited (with Micaela di Leonardo) *The Gender/Sexuality Reader: Culture, History, Political Economy* (1997).

Edward O. Laumann is the George Herbert Mead Distinguished Service Professor in the Department of Sociology and the College at the University of Chicago, Chairman of the Department of Sociology, and Director of the Ogburn Stouffer Center for Population and Social Organization. His research interests include social stratification, the sociology of the professions, occupations and formal organizations, social network analysis, the analysis of elite groups and national policy making, and the sociology of human sexuality. He has written twelve books and numerous articles. Three volumes on human sexuality were published in the fall of 1994: *The Social Organization of Sexuality, Sex in America*, and *Sex, Love and Health in America*.

Lauraine Leblanc is the author of *Pretty in Punk: Girls' Gender Resistance in a Boys' Subculture* (1999). In addition, she has published on the topics of media representations of deviance, women in cyberpunk fiction, and teaching research methods. She is the coordinator of the Quebec Public Interest Research Group at McGill University.

Meika Loe is a doctoral student in sociology and women's studies at the University of California, Santa Barbara. Her research exploring the intersections of gender, sexuality, culture, and consumption has been published in *Gender & Society, Sociological Inquiry*, and *Berkeley Journal of Sociology*.

Zella Luria is a Professor of Psychiatry at Tufts University. She is the author of *The Psychology of Human Sexuality* (1978).

Catharine A. MacKinnon is the author of *Feminism Unmodified: Discourses on Life and Law* (1988), *Toward a Feminist Theory of the State* (1989), and *Only Words* (1993).

Karin A. Martin is an Assistant Professor of Sociology and Women's Studies at the University of Michigan, Ann Arbor. Her research on gender, bodies, and sexuality has appeared in *Gender & Society* and the *American Sociological Review*.

Chet Meeks is a graduate student at the State University of New York, Albany. He is working on a dissertation on the sexual politics of normalization and antinormalization.

Fatima Mernissi is a Moroccan feminist writer and the author of *Beyond the Veil: Male–Female Dynamics in a Modern Muslim Society* (1987), *The Veil and the Male Elite: A Feminist Interpretation of Women's Rights in Islam* (1992), *Dreams of Trespass: Tales of a Harem Girlhood* (1995), and *Women and Islam* (1998).

Michael A. Messner is Associate Professor of Sociology and Gender Studies at the University of Southern California, where he teaches courses on sex and gender, men and masculinities, sexuality, and gender and sport. His most recent books are *Politics of Masculinities: Men in Movements* and *Masculinities, Gender Relations and Sport*.

Robert T. Michael is the Eliakim Hastings Moore Distinguished Service Professor in the Irving B. Harris Graduate School of Public Policy Studies at the University of Chicago. He is the co-author of *Sex in America: A Definitive Survey* (1994) and *The Social Organization of Sexuality* (1994).

Ken Plummer is Professor of Sociology at the University of Essex, UK and the editor of the journal *Sexualities*. He has published many books and articles, including *Sexual Stigma* (1975), *Telling Sexual Stories* (1995), and *Documents of Life-2* (2001). He is also the editor of *The Sociology of Sexuality: Critical Assessments* (2001).

Beth E. Schneider is the chair of the Department of Sociology at the University of California, Santa Barbara. She is the co-editor of *Social Perspectives on Lesbian and Gay Studies* (with P. Nardi, 1998) and *Women Resisting AIDS: Feminist Strategies of Empowerment* (with N. Stoller, 1994).

Steven Seidman is a Professor of Sociology at the State University of New York, Albany. His books include *Embattled Eros: Sexual Ethics and Politics in Contemporary America* (1992), *Queer Theory/Sociology* (1996), and *Contested Knowledge* (1998).

Judith Stacey is the Streisand Professor of Contemporary Gender Studies and Professor of Sociology at the University of Southern California. Her research and teaching interests focus on the relationship between social change and the politics of gender, family, and sexuality. Her publications include *In the Name of the Family: Rethinking Family Values in the Postmodern Age* (1996) and *Brave New Families: Stories of Domestic Upheaval in Late Twentieth Century America* (1998). She is a founding board member of the Council on Contemporary Families, a group committed to public education about research on family diversity.

Jacqueline Sanchez Taylor is Lecturer in Sociology at the University of Warwick, UK. She has been involved in research on sex tourism for six years, and is particularly concerned with theoretical and empirical questions about sexual–economic exchanges between local men and tourist women in tourist resorts in the Caribbean.

Barrie Thorne is Professor of Sociology and Women's Studies at the University of California, Berkeley, where she is also Co-Director of the Center for Working Families. She is the author of *Gender Play: Girls and Boys in School* (1993) and co-editor of *Feminist Sociology: Life Histories of a Movement* (1997) and *Rethinking the Family: Some Feminist Questions* (1992).

Francie Traschen is a graduate student at the State University of New York, Albany. She is working in the area of social movements.

R. Stephen Warner is Professor of Sociology at the University of Illinois. His research centers on the significance of increasing religious diversity in the United States, including the religious institutions of post-1965 immigrants. He is co-editor, with Judith G. Wittner, of *Gatherings in Diaspora: Religious Communities and the New Immigration* (1998) and, with Ho-Youn Kwon and Kwang Chung Kim, of *Korean Americans and Their Religions: Pilgrims and Missionaries From a Different Shore* (2001). He currently directs the Youth and Religion project at the University of Illinois at Chicago.

Kath Weston is Director of Studies in Women's Studies at Harvard University and a member of the National Writers Union. A sociocultural anthropologist, she is the author of *Families We Choose* (1991), *Render Me, Gender Me* (1996), and *Long Slow Burn: Sexuality and Social Science* (1998). Her research focuses on political economy, ideology, and kinship, with an emphasis on how gender and race articulate with sexuality and class under conditions of globalization.

Christine L. Williams is Professor of Sociology at the University of Texas, Austin, and co-editor of this volume.

Acknowledgments

Bartkowski, John P., "Breaking Walls, Raising Fences: Masculinity, Intimacy, and Accountability among the Promise Keepers," *Sociology of Religion* 61 (2000), Association for the Sociology of Religion, Inc.

Blackwood, Evelyn, "Sexuality and Gender in Certain Native American Tribes: The Case of Cross-Gender Females," *Signs* 10 (1984), reprinted by permission of the author and the University of Chicago Press.

Cantú, Lionel, "A Place Called Home: A Queer Political Economy: Mexican Immigrant Men's Family Experiences" from *Queer Families, Queer Politics: Challenging Culture and the State*, ed. M. Bernstein and R. Reimann (Columbia University Press, forthcoming).

Chapkis, Wendy, "The Meaning of Sex" from *Live Sex Acts: Women Performing Erotic Labor* (Routledge, New York, 1997).

Collins, Patricia Hill, "The Sexual Politics of Black Womanhood" from *Black Feminist Thought: Knowledge, Consciousness and the Politics of Empowerment* (Routledge, New York, 1991).

Davidson, Julia O'Connell and Taylor, Jacqueline Sanchez, "Fantasy Islands: Exploring the Demand for Sex Tourism" from *Sun, Sex and Gold: Tourism and Sex Work in the Caribbean*, ed. Kamala Kempadoo (Rowman and Littlefield Publishers, Lanham, MD, 1999).

Dinnerstein, Dorothy, "Higamous-Hogamous" from *The Mermaid and the Minotaur: Sexual Arrangements and Human Malaise* (Other Press, New York, 1999).

Durham, Meenakshi Gigi, "Girls, Media, and the Negotiation of Sexuality: A Study of Race, Class, and Gender in Adolescent Peer Groups," *Journalism and Mass Communication Quarterly* 76 (1999); reprinted by permission of the Association for Education in Journalism and Mass Communication.

Epstein, Steven, "A Queer Encounter: Sociology and the Study of Sexuality," *Sociological Theory* 12: 2 (July 1994).

Faludi, Susan, "The Naked Citadel," *The New Yorker* September 5, 1994.

Fausto-Sterling, Anne, "The Five Sexes: Why Male and Female are Not Enough," *The Sciences* (March–April 1993) and also from *The Meaning of Difference*, ed. Karen Rosenblum and Toni-Michel Travis (McGraw Hill, New York, 2000).

Gamson, Joshua, "Publicity Traps: Television Talk Shows and Lesbian, Gay, Bisexual, and Transgender Visibility," *Sexualities* 1: 1 (1998).

Giddens, Anthony, "Intimacy as Democracy" from *The Transformation of Intimacy: Sexuality, Love and Eroticism in Modern Societies* (Stanford University Press, Stanford, CA 1992 and Polity Press, Cambridge, 1992).

Giuffre, Patti A. and Williams, Christine L., "Boundary Lines: Labeling Sexual Harassment in Restaurants," *Gender & Society* 8: 3 (September 1994).

Jamieson, Lynn, "Intimacy Transformed? A Critical Look at the 'Pure Relationship'," *Sociology* 33: 3 (1999), © by BSA Publications

Limited, published by Cambridge University Press.

Kaplan, Elaine Bell, "Tough Times: Susan Carter" from *Not our kind of Girl: Unraveling the Myths of Black Teenage Motherhood* (University of California Press, Berkeley, 1997).

Kaufman, Debra Renee, "Sex-Segregated Living: Celebrating the Female" from *Rachel's Daughters: Newly Orthodox Jewish Women*, © 1991 by Debra Renee Kaufman. Reprinted by permission of Rutgers University Press.

Lancaster, Roger N., "Subject Honor and Object Shame: The Construction of Male Homosexuality and Stigma in Nicaragua," *Ethnology* 27: 2 (April 1988). Reprinted courtesy of Department of Anthropology, University of Pittsburgh.

Leblanc, Lauraine, "'The punk guys will really overpower what the punk girls have to say': The Boys' Turf" from *Pretty in Pink: Girls' Gender Resistance in a Boys' Subculture*, © 1999 by Lauraine Leblanc. Reprinted by permission of Rutgers University Press.

Loe, Meika, "Working for Men: At the Intersection of Power, Gender, and Sexuality," *Sociological Inquiry* 66 (1996).

MacKinnon, Catharine A., "Pleasure under Patriarchy" from *Theories of Human Sexuality*, ed. J. Geer and W. O'Donohue (Plenum Publishing Corporation, 1987, reprinted by permission of Kluwer Academic Publishers/Plenum Publishers).

Martin, Karin A., "'I couldn't ever picture myself having sex...': Gender Differences in Sex and Sexual Subjectivity" from *Puberty, Sexuality and the Self Girls and Boys at Adolescence* (Routledge, London, 1996).

Mernissi, Fatima, "The Muslim Concept of Active Female Sexuality" from *Beyond the Veil: Male–Female Dynamics in Modern Muslim Society* (Indiana University Press, Bloomington, 1987).

Messner, Michael A., "Becoming 100 Percent Straight" from *Inside Sports*, ed. Jay Coakley and Peter Donnelly (Routledge, London and New York, 1999).

Michael, Robert T., Gagnon, John H., Laumann, Edward O., and Kolata, Gina, "Sex and Society" from *Sex in America: A Definitive Survey* (Warner Books, New York, 1994). © 1994 by CSG Enterprise Inc., Robert T. Michael, Edward O. Laumann, and Gina Kolata. By permission of Little, Brown and Company (Inc.).

Plummer, Ken, "Symbolic Interactionism and Sexual Conduct: An Emergent Perspective" from *Human Sexual Relations*, ed. M. Brake (Pantheon Books, New York, 1982; Penguin Books 1982). © by Ken Plummer, 1982.

Schneider, Beth E. and Jenness, Valerie, "Social Control, Civil Liberties, and Women's Sexuality" from *Women Resisting AIDS: Feminist Strategies of Empowerment*, ed. B. Schneider and Nancy E. Stoller. Reprinted by permission of Temple University Press, © 1995 by Temple University. All Rights Reserved.

Seidman, Steven, Meeks, Chet, and Traschen, Francie, "Beyond the Closet? The Changing Social Meaning of Homosexuality in the United States," *Sexualities* 2: 1 (1999).

Stacey, Judith, "Gay and Lesbian Families are Here; All Our Families are Queer: Let's Get Used to It!" from *All Our Families*, ed. Mary Ann Mason (Oxford University Press, New York).

Thorne, Barrie and Luria, Zella, "Sexuality and Gender in Children's Daily Worlds,"

Social Problems 33 (1986), © 1986 by the Society for the Study of Social Problems, reprinted from *Social Problems* 33: 3, February 1986, pp. 176–90 by permission.

Warner, R. Stephen, "The Metropolitan Community Churches and the Gay Agenda: The Power of Pentecostalism and Essential-

ism" from *Religion and the Social Order*, vol. 5 (Jai Press, 1995).

Weston, Kath, "Copycat" from *Render Me, Gender Me: Lesbians Talk Sex, Class, Color, Nation, Studmuffins,* © 1996 by Columbia University Press. Reprinted by permission of the publisher.

Introduction

There is probably no area of social life today that is more explosive than sexuality. Every day seems to bring new questions about the meaning and place of sexuality in our lives. Open any newspaper or magazine and you are likely to encounter heated debates about teen pregnancy, sex education, pornography, abortion, AIDS, lesbian/gay rights, sexual harassment, and the adulterous affairs of politicians. Tabloid talk shows and popular "reality" programs like *Temptation Island* and MTV's *The Real World* regularly push the limits of socially acceptable sexual expression.

Our public preoccupation with sexual diversity is a relatively new phenomenon. Until quite recently in Western history, most people believed that human sexuality came in only one flavor: adult heterosexuality, in marriage, for reproductive purposes. Anything else was considered deviant, sick, antisocial, immoral, or criminal. Today, however, the norm of the heterosexual married couple is no longer quite so taken for granted.

We are clearly living in a time of rapid social change regarding sexuality. What society considers reasonable or tolerable regarding sexual practices is undergoing remarkable transformation. Sociologists are today trying to understand these changes in the context of changes in the wider society.

In this volume we have gathered together some of the best articles about sexuality from a sociological perspective. The sociology of sexuality is an emerging area of research and courses on this topic are growing in popularity. Unlike courses entitled "Sexuality" or "Human Sexuality," which have been taught for years in psychology and human development departments, the sociology of sexuality does not focus on biological and developmental processes, sexual behavior, and sexual function and dysfunction. Instead, sociologists are interested in how society shapes the expression of sexual desire through cultural images and social institutions. We seek to understand how organizations like the family, religion, and the state shape and encourage some forms of sexual behavior and not others. We examine how society privileges or discriminates against members of different groups on the basis of their sexual practices, and also how groups defend, resist, and/or challenge their treatment. Sociologists are particularly interested in how a person's race, gender, and social class are related to their beliefs and values relating to sexuality. Finally, we are interested in how and why norms about appropriate and inappropriate sexual behavior change over time.

The tremendous volatility of the subject matter makes the sociology of sexuality an exciting field for research, but it also presents several challenges. Since the very meaning of sexuality is debated today, basic terminology is often difficult to define. In general, the term "sexuality" refers to sexual behavior (what people do) and sexual desire (what people want to do and what they fantasize about doing). The term "sexual" in everyday speech refers almost exclusively to genital activity and its associated fantasies, but it can include any sensual experience that has erotic meaning for the individual. "Sex" can refer to two things: (1) sexual behavior, consisting of the acts that people engage in to achieve pleasure. (2) Sex also refers to the anatomical and reproductive differences that men and women are born with, or develop. Thus, people often talk about "sex differences" referring to the typically dimorphous characteristics of our biology: men's penises and testicles; women's vaginas and ovaries. As many of the articles in this collection suggest, however, our understanding of sex differences is shaped in part by "gender." Gender refers to the cultural meanings, social roles, and personality traits associated with sex differences. This is the social (as opposed to the biological) aspect of being a man or a woman. Our society traditionally has insisted that there are only two "sexes" – male and female – and only two corresponding "genders" – masculine and feminine. Today, however, there is a greater recognition that these terms (sex and gender) do not necessarily overlap in reality. Men can be feminine and women can be masculine, and most people do not conform entirely to either designation. Nevertheless our expectation that men should be masculine and women feminine sometimes obscures the variation that occurs in nature, and limits our collective ability to recognize and imagine alternative possibilities.

The final term important for the sociological study of sexuality is "sexual orienta-tion," sometimes called sexual identity. This refers to a person's preferred sexual partner: a man or a woman, or either. The terms homosexual, gay, lesbian, bisexual, queer, and heterosexual all refer to categories of sexual identity. Not surprisingly, these are also contested terms. They each have different meanings, historical connotations, and political implications. Some people argue that sexual identity is a fixed feature of our personality, and others maintain that it is more fluid and changeable. Exploring the connections between sexual identity and gender identity is one of the central goals of this book.

The articles in this collection explore these themes from a variety of perspectives, but they all share a common respect for tolerance and diversity. Society will always shape sexuality, but we hope that greater awareness of the patterning of sexual life will inspire efforts to achieve more equality and social justice in our collective pursuit of sexual happiness.

Part I

Thinking about Sexuality

How do men and women differ sexually? Where do our notions of what is normal and natural and what is not come from? For most of the twentieth century, scientific approaches dominated sexual knowledge. This book, in contrast, begins with the belief that sexuality is socially constructed. To know how men and women experience their sexual selves, we need to consider the worlds in which they live. A case in point: heterosexuality is a social institution. It transmits certain notions of how we should act, and how love and reproduction should occur.

The heterosexual romantic ideal dominates our cultural imagination. And it shapes social practices in the family, and also outside, in the workplace, for example. In Part I of the book, we explore different ways of thinking about sex and sexuality as social phenomena. We begin with psychoanalytic theory (Dorothy Dinnerstein) and symbolic interactionism (Ken Plummer), and then explore radical feminism (Catharine MacKinnon). We end with a look at an emerging body of sexual thought, queer theory (Steve Epstein).

1 Higamous-Hogamous

Dorothy Dinnerstein

Higamous hogamous, woman's monogamous.
Hogamous higamous, man is polygamous.

Folk rhyme

A central rule under a strikingly widespread range of conditions is, first, that men act sexually more possessive than women, and second, that women act less free than men to seek "selfish" sexual pleasure.

The reason for this rule can seem deceptively simple. Wherever we look common sense offers us glaringly visible explanations. And the presence of these common-sense explanations – the existence of obvious *external* supports for the double-standard rule – makes it easy to overlook the presence of vital, but less obvious, *internal* supports. The rule will not be understood, or centrally changed, until people see that it rests not only on brute force, practical pressure, societal coercion, but also on something subtler and harder to defy: it is supported within each person on that stubborn wordless level of adult feeling which is continuous with infant feeling and with the emotional realm of early childhood.

The "practical" bases for asymmetric human sexual privilege have clearly started to crumble, and if advanced industrial civilization survives they will clearly crumble further. What remains very much intact, however, is its deepest emotional basis: a central psychological asymmetry between the sexes, laid down in the first months, and consolidated in the first years, of life, is built into the primary-group arrangement that Washburn describes as the "fundamental pattern ... [of human] social organization." This central asymmetry, which drives men to insist on unilateral sexual prerogative and inclines women to consent to their insistence, will endure as a powerful force until the "fundamental pattern" is outgrown – until, that is, the female monopoly of child care is broken.

To see how this complex asymmetry develops and ramifies, one must examine it aspect by aspect. (And the necessity, I must warn the reader, makes a certain amount of repetition inevitable.) Let us look first at the special sexual possessiveness of men; then at the special muting of women's erotic impulsivity; and then at a third tendency which is – in our own culture at least – a close relative of these two: the tendency for sexual excitement to be more tightly tied to personal sentiment in women than in men.

My discussion here is in one sense frankly ethnocentric; it is mainly couched, in its literal details, in terms of the nuclear family of contemporary white middle-class America. *Its central points are meant, however, to be usefully translatable to any human situation in which women preside over life's first stages and men are at the same time present as emotionally significant figures for young children.*

Unilateral Sexual Possessiveness

The human male's tendency to claim one-sided access to a female, and the human female's tendency to consent to this claim, are rooted first of all in infancy, in the differing relationships of boy and girl to the parent who has so far always dominated the beginning of life. On this initial set of differences another set is overlaid in early childhood. These two layers of experience (along with later ones) fuse, to be sure, in the formation of adult emotional proclivities;

they are considered separately here only in order to help clarify their nature.

Roots in infancy

At the outset, for the infant it is in the relation with the mother that all joy is centered, and it is largely through body contact that this joy comes. Other people with a claim on the mother's intimate concern, and especially on her body, are resented competitors for a vital resource. Boy or girl, one wants her for oneself; on the most primitive level of feeling, one remains unreconciled to sharing her: to possess a woman (more precisely, to possess a creature of the kind who later, as our perceptions develop, turns out to belong to the category "woman") is under present conditions every child's early wish. What happens to this wish – which survives throughout life in what used to be called the heart – depends on whether its original object is later reincarnated partially inside, or primarily outside, one's own skin. And this later reincarnation, of course, is inevitably a different matter for the girl than for the boy.

The pleasure that lures animals into procreative activity has an additional function on the human level: it allows us to relive some of the original life-giving delight of infancy. When the boy, as an adult, finds this delight in heterosexual lovemaking, he finds it outside himself, as before, in a female body. And if the inhabitant of this female body feels free to bestow its resources on a competitor, she is re-evoking for him the situation in which mother, unbearably, did not belong to baby.

The girl grows up into a heterosexual situation significantly more complex. She has – at least partially – become the mother. She now lives in the female body that was once the vital source of nourishment, entertainment, reassurance. It is true, to be sure, that a man – despite his male physique – can provide for her, as she provides for him, a direct opportunity for reliving the original embrace. There are momentous physical

facts to support this emotional opportunity: he is corporeally large, warm, and strong, as the mother was; and his penis, taken into a yearning orifice of the body as the nipple once was taken, can provide a comparably miraculous joy. To the extent that he has this meaning for her, she is vulnerable to something like the simple, direct distress that he feels in the face of sexual competition. And yet their distress is not wholly the same. Hers is apt to be modulated in several ways.

First, despite the man's size, and his penis, the physical differences that are likely to exist between a man and the early mother – in shape and skin texture, in voice quality, gesture, rhythm – are important ones. His bodily presence typically cannot in itself call up the atmosphere of infancy for her in these respects so literally as hers can call it up for him. In the sense and to the extent that this is the case, his physical infidelity cannot revive the grief of infancy for her so graphically as hers can for him: its shock value for her is apt to be less concrete, more purely symbolic.

What may be more important, however, is the fact that even the *symbolic* shock value of the other's physical infidelity is far less absolute for her than for him. The mother-raised woman is likely to feel, more deeply than the mother-raised man, that she carries within herself a source of the magic early parental richness. In this sense – even if not in others – she is more self-sufficient than the mother-raised man: what is inside oneself cannot be directly taken away by a rival.

The tranquillity that goes with this conviction typically rests, of course, on external confirmation of the woman's feeling of inner richness; she requires evidence that somebody else depends on access to what she has. It is not unusual for her to accept a man's infidelities – even to enjoy them, for reasons discussed below – so long as she is sure he would be desolate to lose possession of her. If this is how she feels, it is only by making him give her up altogether that a rival can shake the foundations of her confidence in herself as a being equipped with an internal supply of what is most basically needed. The fact that this attitude is far less usual in a man stems not just from the pressure of convention. More basically it stems from the mother-raised boy's sense that the original, most primitive source of life will always lie outside himself, that to be sure of reliable access to it he must have exclusive access to a woman.

Roots in early childhood

There is another way in which female-dominated childhood tends to make jealousy more complex for women than for men, less continuous with the infant's imperious, monolithic rage at maternal infidelity, less likely to arouse sharp impulses of self-assertion. To understand it, one must consider not only the relation between the pre-verbal infant and its mother, but also the shape of the small child's situation as it starts to enter a wider world. During this period, formal sex-role education – learning what is expected of a girl and of a boy – is of course going on. The importance of this process is by now well understood; it is a process that deserves, and is currently getting, detailed attention from writers oriented to the project of reorganizing our sexual arrangements. Here, however, we are concerned with a set of emotional facts whose significance is much less widely recognized, facts which have so far been discussed mainly in the conservative psychoanalytic spirit of understanding why things must be the way they are, not in the revolutionary psychoanalytic spirit of thinking out how they can be changed.

Under prevailing conditions the little girl, if she is to develop the early orientation to gender that will later allow her to feel heterosexual passion, must overcome an initial handicap. What is required of her is a central shift of erotic allegiance: it is to this shift that Freud and his students point, more unanimously than to the shaky theory of penis envy, as a basis for their working assumption that woman's sexual disadvantage

is inevitable. (And in fact this assumption would be a wholly reasonable one, if female-dominated childhood were inevitable. There is nothing wrong with the logic behind it. The error is in its tacit initial premise.) The girl's original love, they remind us, was, like the boy's, a woman. Upon this prototypic erotic image, the image of man must be superimposed.

This emotional feat is typically in progress during the two- or three- to five-year-old period that Freud – naming it from the viewpoint of the boy – called Oedipal. During these years, the child's worldly awareness expands dramatically. The father becomes a more distinct figure, and as he does so it becomes clear that there are two sexes, with physical and social differences between them that are crucial for one's own present and future privileges, obligations, and opportunities. It becomes clear also that there exists a special and exclusive relation between the parents, the nature of which has sharp bearing on one's own place in the affections of each.

"*Oedipal*" *jealousy*. The little boy's concern about his own position in the relation with the two parents is apt to be focused mainly on the father's rival claim to the mother: she is the parent with whom the boy has been physically intimate from the outset, and to whom he is likely still to be much more attached, in this way, than to his newly vivid father; and now his growing awareness of bodily and social maleness tells him that she is a member of the sex for whose affections he is destined to compete with other males.

In the girl's case, this jealous concern about one's place with the parents is typically much more deeply two-edged. The father's animal allure is likely to be more powerful for her than it is for the boy. (This may be simply because he acts more seductive with her: he can treat her openly as an attractive little female; he is less free to flirt on an animal-poetic level with his son. It may also be – we do not know – that even in the small child some central neural basis for a specific interest in the opposite sex is already operating.) At the same time, the mother is for the girl, as for the boy, the parent around whom bodily based tender passion was first organized. This means that for her, love of this kind is more evenly directed toward both parents than it is for the boy, and rivalry with the mother for the father's love is more evenly balanced against rivalry with the father for the mother's. The growing insight that this balance is scheduled to tip mainly in the father's direction is on some level wounding. To realize that one is a female, destined to compete with females for the erotic resources of males, is to discover that one is doomed to renounce one's first love.

In the jealous woman, the emotional atmosphere of this childhood discovery is apt to be reactivated: she can feel at the same time pained by the other woman's access to the man and excited by the man's access to the other woman, through which she is offered vicarious re-access to a female erotic figure. The eruption of this more or less buried early erotic interest can distract or humiliate or baffle her, taking the sharp edge off jealous anger. She may find herself helpless in the throes not only of masochistic satisfaction at being forced to accept the painful presence of a rival but also of bisexual pleasure in simultaneous contact with a man and – vicariously – a woman. (There are, of course, many women in whom no such feelings erupt, and whose jealousy is as fierce as any man's.)

In the jealous man, two-edged feeling of this kind (though it does in fact often occur) is less typical. A certain degree of straightforward animal-poetic attraction toward the same-sex parent is likely to have been part of his, like the girl's, childhood Oedipal dilemma. The likelihood that this factor will later work to take the edge off heterosexual jealousy is less in his case, however, because his attraction to his father is apt to have differed in two crucial ways from the girl's attraction to her mother. One difference – to which I have referred just above from the father's point of view – is that the boy's

erotic pull toward his father is apt to have been more ego-alien, less compatible with his own self-image and the expectations of the people around him, than the girl's toward her mother (which had to be accepted as an expression of the young child's still lively physical dependence on parental – a word that under prevailing conditions means maternal – care). Another, related, difference between these two early homoerotic pulls is that the onset of his was later. The father under present conditions tends to be a far less distinct figure than the mother until the child is verbal and mobile, and relatively knowledgeable and rational. The attraction to him is thus inevitably less primitive, more modulated from the beginning by the abstract considerations that language carries. It is an attraction, moreover, far less deeply tied up with sheer survival: bodily contact with him can be exhilarating and playful (he typically carries the child, and tosses it in the air), or threatening (he may administer corporal punishment, or show terrifying anger, or figure in violent sexual fantasies), but it does not ordinarily have to do, as contact with the mother does, with the basic maintenance of life.

What has been said above about the difference between the boy's "Oedipal" jealousy and the girl's, as these bear on one-sided male possessiveness in adult sex life, can be summed up as follows.

First, the young child's ties to its mother are earlier born, more continuous with the passions of helpless pre-verbal infancy, than those to its father. This means that in the mother–father–child triangle the heteroerotic side of the child's feeling has more primitive weight for the boy than for the girl, while the homoerotic side has more primitive weight for the girl than for the boy. The adult consequence of this difference is that a woman's heterosexual jealousy is apt to be more deeply complicated than a man's by homoerotic excitement, her rage more blurred, her impulse to get rid of the intruder less pure.

Second, not only is the homoerotic side of the boy's feeling in this early triangle later born and less primitive than the girl's; it is also more disgraceful. The adult consequence is that even where homoerotic excitement *is* strong enough to complicate a man's heterosexual jealousy, this excitement is likelier to be suppressed, since it is too shameful to be admitted into awareness. Suppressed erotic feeling toward a rival does not defuse jealous rage as it can when it comes closer to the surface of consciousness. Indeed, it is apt to have the opposite effect: suppressed, its energy can feed into the rage, making the latter even more primitive and self-righteous.

But the boy's relation to the parents contrasts with the girl's in a way that goes far beyond these intimate strains within the original threesome.

The "Oedipal" dilemma and the wider human realm. It is true that both son and daughter in these early years feel – and handle somewhat differently for the reasons discussed above – the pull between an old love and the possibility of adding a new one. A momentous additional difference between his case and hers, however, lies in the human–social nature of this new possibility, its implications for one's future place in the world beyond the parent–child triangle.

In the son's case, what is apt to be salient is that resentment of the father's claims upon the mother threatens to interfere with a crucial opportunity that is now opening before him: attachment to his newly interesting and powerful male parent represents solidarity with his own sex, a solidarity upon which much of his thrust toward worldly competence is starting to depend. His main task is to find a balance between two contrasting varieties of love, one that provides primitive emotional sustenance, and another that promises – if rivalry over the first can be handled – to offer membership in the wider community where prowess is displayed, enterprise planned, public event organized. His old tie to his mother starts at this point

to be felt as an obstacle to new and more grown-up ties with his own sex. These are the ties upon which – in the world he is beginning to know, the world as it now is – the opportunity will rest to exercise some of his most important human capacities.

This new difficulty in the boy's relations with his mother is now likely to coalesce with certain longer-standing grievances, rooted in the inevitable frustrations of infancy, that had been part of his feeling for her from the beginning. (What these grievances are, and how they bear on the atmosphere between men and women, is one of the questions to which chapters 6, 7, and 8 [of *The Mermaid and the Minotaur*] are devoted. At this point, let me assert merely that they exist, and that they are formidable.) Together, these older and newer difficulties help form the basis for the eventual adult feeling that love for women must be kept in its place, not allowed to interfere with the vital ties between men.

Ideally, the little boy manages to find some provisional balance between the old, jealous, aggrieved erotic tug toward the mother and the new feeling of friendship with the father. Later on, he will have an opportunity to resolve this conflict more decisively. He will discover that authority over a woman or women is a mark of status, respected by men. This discovery will help him reconcile what were once competing wishes: the wish for secure access to certain essential emotional resources, which in his experience reside in females, and the wish to take part in certain essential human activities, which in the world he now enters are defined as male.

What is reflected in man's unilateral possessiveness, then, is not only the original, monolithic infant wish for ownership of a woman but also a second, more equivocal feeling, rooted in early boyhood: that attachment to a woman is emotionally bearable, consistent with the solidarity among men which is part of maleness, only if she, and one's feelings toward her, remain under safe control.

For the girl, this aspect of the "Oedipal" conflict takes a different form and its resolution is likely to have the opposite outcome. To her, too, the father is an interesting, powerful figure through whom one reaches out toward the wider world. But he does not normally invite her, as he invites the boy, to follow him out into this fascinating world, and take on its challenges in recompense for the impossibility of owning the mother. Instead he offers the more direct recompense of a second erotic tie, excitingly, but not so sharply as in the boy's case, different from the first one. This second love at its outset valuably supplements the first (for the daughter, like the son, needs another relation to help her achieve perspective on the relation with the mother). And in the girl's situation, the new love for man – unlike the boy's new love for man – is expected gradually to supplant the original love for woman. Her jealousy of the parents, as I said earlier, is more two-edged than the boy's; and at the same time, neither parent is likely to contest her erotic claim on the other as directly as the father contests the boy's claim on the mother. All in all, then, she is under less urgent pressure than the boy is to find some clear-cut way of reconciling the second love with the first.

It will nevertheless turn out to be true in her case, as in the boy's, that ties to the opposite sex and solidarity with one's own sex will pull in opposite directions. But the nature of this pull – as she feels it in childhood, and as she acts on it later – is different for her than for him. For her the deepest obstacles to solidarity with one's own sex first appear not in the mother–father–baby triangle, where the boy first meets them, but in the deep ambivalence of the earlier mother–baby pair. Once the triangle forms, both the "truly masculine" boy and the "truly feminine" girl use its existence to help handle the formidable tensions inherent in the original pair. But they do so in contrasting ways; and the outcome is that women are on the whole far less able than men to balance dependence on each other against dependence on the opposite sex.

When the father first emerges to offer the girl a tie that can supplement (and in part substitute for) the tie to the mother, he makes available to her a new way of handling – a way, that is, of side-stepping the task of resolving – the ambivalence at the heart of the infant–mother tie. What he offers is a fatefully tempting (pseudo) solution to this central dilemma: positive feelings toward the mother are normally split off from negative ones in early life in order to preserve the possibility of feeling, at least sometimes, a sense of unqualified oneness with this central source of all that is good. What the girl can now do is transfer to the father – who starts out with a clean slate, so to speak, innocent of association with the inevitable griefs of infancy – much of the weight of these positive feelings, while leaving the negative ones mainly attached to their original object. She thus gains a less equivocal focus for her feelings of pure love, and feels freer to experience her grievances against her mother without fear of being cut off altogether from the ideal of wholehearted harmony with a magic, animally loved, parental being.

This opportunity comes at a particularly timely point in her development since a new grievance against the mother is just adding itself to those already stored up: just as the boy, during this period, is learning that outside the family an arena exists in which he can exercise some central human capacities, the girl (who possesses these same capacities, and is too young to have been persuaded that she does not) also learns of this arena and begins at about the same time to grasp the strange fact that she is unwelcome to enter it. This misfortune she is apt to blame on her omnipotent mother, who has so far been responsible for every misfortune – as well as every delight – in her young life. The father, if she is to become a "truly feminine" woman who contents herself with motherhood and the maintenance of family life, is typically absolved of blame for her exclusion from this vital extrafamilial arena. Indeed, he is all the more glamorous and newly needed because he provides the only access to it – vicarious access – that she can expect to have. He is glamorous also because the special compensation that she will be offered for keeping the home fires burning and forgoing the rewards of effort in the wide world – the compensation that lies in a certain kind of erotic attention, in exemption from certain risky challenges, in safety from certain possible humiliations – is foreshadowed in the special homage that he has begun to express toward her as a little female: the deprivation for which she feels her mother is to blame is repaired, so far as it can be, by her father.

Early rage at the first parent, in other words, is typically used by the "masculine" boy during the Oedipal period to *consolidate* his tie with his own sex by establishing a principled independence, a more or less derogatory distance, from women. And it is typically used by the "feminine" girl in this same period to *loosen* her tie with her own sex by establishing a worshipful, dependent stance toward men. Just when that boy is learning to keep his feelings for the mother under control, that girl (precisely because her first emotional problems also centered on the mother) is learning to over-idealize the father. This contrast, of course, heavily supports asymmetry of sexual privilege. For without comparably strong, well-defined ways of counterbalancing feelings for the opposite sex with a sense of human identity based on solidarity with each other, women are far less free than men to set their own terms in love.

The nature of the rule

In sum, then: unilateral male sexual possessiveness rests on strong old feelings, both in men and in women. And so long as the care of the very young remains in female hands these feelings – in which echoes of infancy and of early childhood are fused – will persist.

But before turning to the next part of the higamous-hogamous rule, let me emphasize again the dual sense in which unilateral male possessiveness is in fact a "rule." What I have been offering is a *description* of psychological forces, rooted in mother-dominated childhood, which are widespread enough to make it possible for society to enforce a *prescription* about male and female adult behavior. When I say, for example, that a certain emotional situation, or frame of mind, "as a rule" characterizes father-emulating little boys, or jealous women, I am describing a tendency, a probability: there are many little boys, and many jealous women, whose experiences are quite different from the ones I describe. And it is very lucky that this is so, for if the tensions inherent in the "normal" human situation led uniformly to the same outcome for everyone we would have little hope of out-growing what is maiming in our sexual arrangements. As a code of conventionally accepted comportment, on the other hand, the double standard of sexual possessiveness is a "rule" that, whether obeyed or defied, exerts some real coercive force on *every* person. To survive as this kind of rule, it need not have powerful emotional roots in all of us: just in most of us.

The same is true for the rule – to which I now turn – that female erotic impulse must be curbed: it is a societal prescription, fed psychologically by an amalgam of very early and slightly later experience in enough mother-dominated childhoods to make it generally enforceable.

The Muting of Female Erotic Impulsivity

Roots in infancy

Suppression of female sexual impulse has an obvious practical congruence with one-sided male possessiveness: a woman with a strong sexual will of her own may defy a man's wish to keep her for himself. But on the more covert emotional level that we are considering here, there is not only this practical, realistic concern; there is also a different, non-rational kind of fear, a deep fantasy-ridden resentment, directed against her impulsivity itself. Her own bodily pleasure in sex, independent of the pleasure she gives her partner, is the essential threatening fact. It is threatening, first of all, because it resonates with the distress of a very early discovery, a distress that antedates jealousy since it is felt while the infant is still too young to notice the existence of competitors for the mother's resources. This discovery is simply that the infant does not own or control the mother's body: because this body has needs and impulses of its own, its responsiveness to the infant's needs is never totally reliable. (A mother's milk, for example, may sometimes flow faster or slower than is comfortable for the infant. She may be sleepy, distracted, or sluggish when it wants to play; she may alarm it or disturb its peace with over-avid caresses.) The very same spontaneous, impulsive, autonomous erotic spirit in the first parent which – as the baby will later find out – allows her to turn at will to others makes her from the outset imperfectly subject to its desire even when they are alone.

The significance of this awareness on the infant's part goes far beyond the purely sexual matters now under discussion. Some broader consequences of the trouble we have in coming to terms with the early mother's inconveniently human autonomy are explored in chapter 6 [ibid.]. And much of the rest of this book has to do with the trouble we have in handling the more general problem of which this autonomy of hers is just one manifestation: as Freud pointed out, the fact that human infants receive such nearly perfect care seduces them into fantasies which are inevitably crushed, fantasies of a world that automatically obeys, even anticipates, their wishes. The loss of this infant illusion of omnipotence – the discovery that circumstance is incompletely controllable, and that there exist centers of

subjectivity, of desire and will, opposed or indifferent to one's own – is an original and basic human grief.

All of us, male and female, feel this grief. To some degree, it is irreparable. We manage in part to console ourselves for it indirectly, through mastery, competence, enterprise: the new joy of successful activity is some compensation for the old joy of passive, effortless wish-fulfillment. This indirect way of handling the grief is central to the pathology of civilized life, a pathology to which our male–female arrangements contribute in a way that will be discussed in chapters 7, 8, and 9 [ibid.]. At the same time, for the sexual situation with which we are concerned here, the important fact is that we also attempt to undo the grief *directly*. Indefatigably, we go on trying to recover what has been lost: we try it first-hand by seeking out situations in which we can reexperience personally, at least for a moment, the infant sense of omnipotence. And we try it second-hand by acting as nurturers, pleasure-givers, empathic wish-granters, by recreating the mother–infant atmosphere so as to relive vicariously some part of the lost delight.

In lovemaking, both man and woman make this direct attempt to repair the old loss. Each of them does so both first-hand, by taking bodily pleasure, and vicariously, by providing pleasure for the other person. But the balance tends not to be symmetrical. She is the one whose physique more closely resembles the physique of the first parent, and who is likely to have incorporated this parent's attitudes more deeply; he is therefore apt to be the one who can more literally relive the infant experience of fulfilling primitive wishes through unqualified access to another body. For her, the vicarious version of this reliving – providing the body through which the other's wishes are perfectly granted – is likely to be a more prominent feature of the interplay. If this symbiotic arrangement is to succeed, the woman's own sexual impulsivity must not be freely unleashed. Unleashed, it can disrupt the recreated harmony; it can revive – in a first-hand way for him and vicariously for her – the first intimations of isolated, non-omnipotent selfhood; it can reactivate in both of them the malaise that originated in the nursling's discovery of the mother's separate, uncontrollable subjective existence.

The arrangement, of course, is an unstable one. Vicarious bliss has some advantages over direct bliss (imagination fills in gaps, glosses over blemishes), but no vigorous person willingly makes do with it as his or her whole portion. The infant in every adult wants pleasure unlimited and uninterrupted by the ebb and flow of another creature's impulses. On some level woman, like man, resents the other person's uncontrollable erotic rhythm. This resentment is softened in the mother-reared woman by her greater emotional access to vicarious delight. On the other hand, it is sharpened by the crucial physical fact that in coitus she is far more dependent on the man's erection than he is on her vaginal responsiveness. Men have doubtless always sensed the explosive potentialities of this fact: it feeds into their archetypal nightmare vision of the insatiable female, and deepens their feeling that the unleashing of woman's own erotic impulses would disturb the precarious heterosexual peace.

The independent sexual impulsivity of the female, then, is feared because it recalls the terrifying erotic independence of every baby's mother. To soothe the fear, we subordinate Eve's lust to Adam's, but this cure only makes the sickness worse: subordinated, Eve's lust is more frightening still.

Woman's sexuality is under doubly explosive pressure. Her physical situation in coitus, as compared with man's, has in it much more of the infant's dependence on an imperfectly reliable source of fulfillment. Yet it is she who must make reparation to him for what both endured as babies. Coital satiety (to be fucked as the baby would like to be fed: on demand and at the rate one chooses and as long as one wants) is for

anatomic reasons a chancier matter for her than for him; and in addition she is for social and emotional reasons less free to seek it out. Inevitably, like any other suppressed force, her sex impulses come to seem boundless, ominous. And inevitably, this makes it more urgent to suppress them.

Roots in early childhood

The feelings discussed in the preceding section are primarily male feelings. Women share them only vicariously. But there are factors working to mute female lust that stem from a peculiarly female emotional situation. This situation takes shape not in infancy but in very early girlhood.

To repeat what I pointed out above in connection with sexual possessiveness, the mother–father–child triangle that Freud has called Oedipal is apt to arouse much more symmetrically balanced feelings in the girl than in the boy: since the homoerotic side of this triangle is older and more openly acceptable in her case than in his, she is not so purely the rival of the mother as the boy is the rival of the father. (Not only is her own jealousy more ambiguous than the boy's; her same-sex rival is herself more mildly, ambiguously jealous than the boy's is. The mother, to be sure, is an earlier, less rational authority, and in that sense a more formidable competitor than the father; still, competition with her is less apt to feel acutely risky since she is likely to feel less resentful than the father of the claims her child makes on her spouse.)

What is salient for the girl at this stage is not so much rivalry as another, more primitive problem: the realization that she must now, in some basic way, start to renounce, let go of, her first, life-giving love. To yield wholeheartedly to the charm of the opposite sex, she – unlike the boy – must shift a large portion of her early animal-poetic passion away from the parent to whom it was at first exclusively attached. The boy faces a clear crisis of nerve. She must handle a more diffuse, pervasive guilt, a vague sense of disloyalty, an ancient, primal fear of loss.

The sacrifice of sexual spontaneity, the curbing of sexual willfulness, that men will require of her in adult life can serve her own purposes, too, then: it can serve as a penance for this pervasive guilt. In turning toward man, but forgoing the vigorous pursuit of "selfish" body pleasure with him, she can achieve some of the heterosexual rapport that her love for her father taught her to want, and at the same time allay this primal fear of loss.

Woman's need for penance and her sense of primal loss are complicated, moreover, by the other large fact about the girl's Oedipal situation that was discussed above: the fact that the infidelity to her first love that began in this period typically went far deeper than her shift toward the second actually required. The sacrifice of full bodily pleasure with man, which I have heard described as "the gift to the mother," atones for something more than the partial desertion of her that the girl's growth toward heteroerotic susceptibility would in itself inevitably entail. What the girl has been guilty of is lavishing upon her father – that is, upon man – not only the erotic recognition, and the warmth and trust, that he on his own could inspire in her, but also much of the physical affection and filial-romantic gratitude that would have remained attached to her mother – that is, to woman – if they had been integrated with the child's inevitable antagonisms toward her. What she has done is to give away to someone else love that a part of her knew belonged rightly to the mother, in order to spare herself an emotional effort that seemed – but was not really – unnecessary. The result is that she has cut herself off from a continuity with her own early feeling, for which she now mourns. It is in part to propitiate her fantasy mother, to punish herself, and thereby to regain some of this inner continuity that she holds back the final force of her "selfish" carnal passion for man. She holds it back out of love for

him too, out of unwillingness to alarm him and pleasure in acceding to his wishes; but also out of anger at herself and at him: anger at a gratuitous betrayal of her oldest root in life, a betrayal for which she was responsible but of which he (in the form of his original parental predecessor) was the instrument.

But feelings of guilt and loss connected with her first love are not the only preoccupations that work to take the edge off woman's sensual passion for man. She tends also to feel more preoccupied than he does, while they are making love, with the opportunity to achieve vicarious homoerotic contact, and in this way to steal back some of what life has taken away from her: she is apt to be busier than he is imagining herself in the other person's situation, more engrossed in the other person's access to her own body and thus less engrossed in her own access to the other person's body. And in the meantime this holding back, this abstention from full use of the male body as a source of direct pleasure for herself, can also express another, related, feeling: a grudge against the male, her rival for her first, female, parent. The grudge is not normally strong enough to make him unattractive to her. But she can reconcile resentment and attraction by embracing him and at the same time vengefully using the embrace for an ulterior purpose: to get access to the mother again after all.

The mother-raised woman, then, submits to the mother-raised man's demand that she mute her own adult lust; and in submitting she consoles herself by betraying him and going back to her first, infant, love. She avenges herself on him by making him her instrument of re-access to what she has renounced. But it is a weak consolation and a poor revenge. For her re-access is only second-hand, and her old feelings of guilt and loss only feebly assuaged. What she is giving up is the right to use her body's sensuous capacities as directly, concretely, immediately as she did in the original embrace.

Sexual Excitement and Personal Sentiment

Closely related to the two aspects of the double standard of sexual behavior discussed above (at least in our own culture) is a third psychological sex difference: that carnal excitement tends to be more firmly tied to strong personal feeling in women than in men.

This tendency, like some others discussed just above, is supported by a fact that follows inexorably from our prevailing child-care arrangements: since the first parent is female, heteroerotic feeling has deeper roots in infancy for men than for women.

A male disability and a female one

What these deeper roots mean is that in intimate relations between a man and a woman he is in one very important respect more vulnerable than she is: she can more readily re-evoke in him the unqualified, boundless, helpless passion of infancy. If he lets her, she can shatter his adult sense of power and control; she can bring out the soft, wild, naked baby in him.

Men try to handle this danger with the many kinds of sex-segregating institutions that they seem always and everywhere driven to create. Secret societies, hunting trips, pool parlors, wars – all of these provide men with sanctuary from the impact of women, with refuges in which they can recuperate from the temptation to give way to ferocious, voracious dependence, and recover their feelings of competence, autonomy, dignity.

But they need other safeguards too. Short of avoiding women altogether, the best safeguard is to renounce the opportunity for deep feeling inherent in heterosexual love. One way to do this is to keep heterosexual love superficial, emotionally and physically. Another is to dissociate its physical from its emotional possibilities.

Woman is less vulnerable to this danger: in the sexual recapitulation of the infant–mother interplay, she has more of a sense than he does of embodying the powerful mother within herself; a greater part of her than of his reliving of the infant role is vicarious, through the other person. This makes her less afraid of being plunged back into the atmosphere of helpless infancy, and therefore typically better able to fuse intense emotional and intense physical intimacy.

Unfortunately, however, she is also typically less able to *separate* these two feelings when it would be appropriate to do so. Indeed, the gentlest hint that such separation may sometimes be appropriate is obnoxious to many women. To give way to bodily lust for a man without a sense of magical personal fusion with him seems to them unworthy, or dangerous, or degrading; incapacity to do this seems to them a mark of human dignity, rather than the disability which in fact it is. For this disability, there are many well-known practical reasons (women's economic and social dependence makes them emotionally clingy; sex is a more serious matter for them because it can make them pregnant; etc.). But there are also other reasons, less widely understood and at least as important.

I said above that a woman can assuage guilt about betraying her first, homoerotic, love in sex with a man by renouncing the pursuit of "selfish" bodily pleasure with him. But there is also another way for her to assuage this guilt: she can find that she is unable to give way to sensual delight except when romantic love – love shot through with the flavor of the original blissful mother–infant union – has flooded her being. This solution allows her to reap the joy of heterosexual carnality while keeping some magical, loyal connection to her earliest tie. (In her case, unlike his, the sense of catastrophic helplessness that return to the atmosphere of the old union can rekindle is kept within bounds by her own gender continuity, and her partner's gender discontinuity, with the first parent. And to the extent that she does feel painfully helpless with him, her pain [see chapter 8, ibid.] redresses for both of them an old imbalance: now it is mama who cries for baby and baby who lets mama cry.)

The hapless tendency of many women to melt into a feeling of emotional closeness with any man who manages to excite them sexually is related to still another factor: the mother, as a number of writers point out, is likely to experience a more effortless identification, a smoother communication, with a girl baby than with a boy baby. With him, there is more difference and separateness, more of a barrier to be bridged. This means that girls and boys are likely to be treated differently in the prototypic adult–infant situation in which bodily intimacy first occurs. The nature of this difference helps account for the differing degrees of ego-distinctness that they later bring to sex. The girl, as she did at the beginning, melts more easily into the personality of the person to whose flesh she is drawn. Infancy has not taught her, as surely as it has taught him, to feel simultaneously the boundaries of herself and the current between herself and what attracts her.

A male "solution"

For reasons that so far as I know remain to be explored, the degree to which men and women differ in their need and/or ability to dissociate personal love from sex feeling varies from one historical or cultural situation to another. (The present account does not explain this variation: clearly, it depends upon factors that have not been considered here.) But to the extent that it is in fact emotionally feasible for him to maintain such a dissociation, there is one further function, not yet mentioned, that it can always serve for a mother-raised man: it can help him to cope with the problem of ambivalence toward the first parent.

For this problem, as I have been pointing out, the Oedipal triangle offers the girl, but

not the boy, a solution of sorts. (To repeat: she can dodge the work of healing the split between bad and good feelings toward the first parent by shifting a substantial portion of the magically good ones onto the second, so that her love for the opposite sex comes to be infused with the infant's grateful passion toward the mother while most of the hostile, derogatory attitudes remain attached to their original object.) The boy cannot use his father in this way without giving homo-erotic attraction a dominant place in his love life. If woman is to remain for him the central human object of the passions most deeply rooted in life's beginnings, his relation to her must embrace, at a primitive level, *both* the worshipful and the derogatory, the grateful and the greedy, the affectionate and the hostile feeling toward the early mother.

(Before going further, it seems best to stop and acknowledge a question that may well, by now, be irking the reader so seriously that a digression which articulates it – even an arbitrarily timed digression – will be felt as a relief: what makes me think that any conceivable child-care arrangement could magically dispel the problem of infantile ambivalence? What good would it do, after all, if fathers were as actively parental from the beginning as mothers and ambivalence therefore extended impartially to all our relations with people instead of focusing mainly on women? Trial readers of this chapter have asked this question with levels of indignation ranging from gentle to vituperative.

To return, then, to our discussion of male heterosexual ambivalence: one way a man can handle this fundamental difficulty is to sort out the conflicting ingredients into two kinds of love, tender and sensual. Lust then carries all the angry, predatory impulses from which the protective, trusting side of his love for woman must be kept insulated. He may keep tender and sensual love separate by expressing them toward different women, or toward the same woman in different situations or moods. Or he may largely bury one side of his heteroerotic feeling, giving direct expression mainly to the other.

Another way he can handle the difficulty is to mute all animal-poetic feeling for other people. In this case, romantic and sexual interest play such a minor role in his life that women can remain the central object of such interest without causing any serious inner tumult. The result may or may not be a general constriction of the emotional flow between the man and his world. If not, what happens often enough to color the whole climate of history is that his passion can flow into work – that is, into the exercise of competence in the public domain – while his heteroerotic affection stays absent-minded and tepid, his sex life perfunctory. A man like this need not be literally polygamous: his wife is still apt to feel that he is "married" to his business, to the army, to the sea, to science as much as to her, or more so, while she is married only to him. A sex relation that he finds quite adequate to his needs is apt to leave her dissatisfied in one of two ways: either it engages her deepest feelings, which she then finds unreciprocated, since his are engaged elsewhere; or it does not, in which case she feels centrally restless, her personal depths untapped, stagnating. It has often been pointed out that women depend lop-sidedly on love for emotional fulfillment because they are barred from absorbing activity in the public domain. This is true. But it is also true that men can depend lopsidedly on participation in the public domain because they are stymied by love.

*Consequences for the atmosphere
between the sexes*

The tendency of the sexes to differ in their ability to integrate, or separate, sensuality and sentiment has the same early origins, then, as the double standard. It also has the same worldly outcome. It originates in mother-dominated childhood and it contributes to the overall subordination of women. A woman's lust for a man is likely to tie her to him emotionally more closely than his lust ties him to her. Affection is likelier to keep her physically faithful to him than him to her. If he has a strong animal passion for her, his human loyalty and protectiveness may well be reserved mainly for another woman. If she is the one he tenderly loves, she may well have to make do with a sexual pittance. If he has not split off affection from lust – and sometimes even if he has – the chances are that he has muted both, turning most of his passion into realms from which she is excluded. His trouble fusing tender and sensual feeling, and her trouble separating them, enslaves and/or castrates her. She is typically dealing with a partner in some way heavily calloused, and he typically lives in an atmosphere of some kind of reproach: he is heartless; she nags and complains.

The Upshot

The higamous-hogamous adult consequence of mother-dominated childhood maims both sexes. It makes women – for internal, not only external reasons – normally less able than men to defend their interests against rivals; or to give free rein to erotic impulse; or to enjoy sex (in the special way that it can be so enjoyed) without deep personal involvement. And at the same time, it makes men – for complementary internal reasons – normally less able than women to accept the fact that it is impossible wholly to monopolize the erotic interest of another person without crushing the untameable part of that person which makes her/him erotically interesting; or the fact that the other person's sexual impulses and rhythms are by no means automatically synchronized with one's own. It also makes them more frightened than women of the crucial realm of personal feeling to which sex offers access.

The maiming of men under higamous-hogamous conditions is in some respects more cruel than the maiming of women. The truth of emotional experience – their own and others' – tends on the whole to be more threatening to them. As a result their freedom to feel emotional intimacy – with themselves and with others – tends on the whole to be more constricted, hemmed in by the massive denial which is necessary to keep so much truth at bay. And their physical sex pleasure – though wider-ranging than women's and much less likely to be plumb thwarted – is likelier to be impoverished by dissociation from deep personal feeling.

Nevertheless, both sexes see the double standard – quite correctly, I think – as more damaging to women. Men are on the whole content with it, and women on the whole pained by it, for the simple reason that it is women who bear the brunt of the crudest, most primitive constriction to which the double standard gives rise: our sexual arrangements make for a head-on clash between a fact of human anatomy and the emotional constraints that stem inevitably from what Washburn calls the "fundamental pattern" imposed by evolutionary pressures "on the social organization of the human species."

Anatomically, coitus offers a far less reliable guarantee of orgasm – or indeed of any intense direct local genital pleasure – to woman than to man. The first-hand coital pleasure of which she is capable more often requires conditions that must be purposefully sought out. Yet it is woman who has less liberty to conduct this kind of search: the societal and psychological constraints inherent in our "fundamental pattern" leave her less free than man to explore the erotic resources of a variety of partners, or even to affirm erotic impulse with any one partner. These constraints also make her less able to give way to simple physical delight without a sense of total self-surrender – a disability that further narrows her choice of partners, and makes her still more afraid of disrupting her rapport with any one partner by acting to intensify the delight, that is, by asserting her own sexual wishes.

The bodily bind in which this contradiction puts women – less leeway to pursue a primitive goal which is itself more elusive – is part (not the main part, but a vital part) of the reason why it is mainly women, not men, who are urging upon our species the terrifying task of reorganizing its technologically obsolete gender arrangements. As everyone on some level really understands, the issue at stake is not only freedom to seek out genital pleasure but something more as well: the sexual realm under dispute is a wildlife preserve in the civilized world, a refuge within which inarticulate, undomesticated private creative initiative is protected from extinction.

What the double standard hurts in women (to the extent that they genuinely, inwardly, bow to it) is the animal center of self-respect: the brute sense of bodily prerogative, of having a right to one's bodily feelings. A conviction that physical urges which one cannot help having are unjustified, undignified, presumptuous, undercuts the deepest, oldest basis for a sense of worth; it contaminates the original wellspring of subjective autonomy. Fromm made this point very clearly when he argued, in *Man for Himself*, that socially imposed shame about the body serves the function of keeping people submissive to societal authority by weakening in them some inner core of individual authority.

Antagonism to the body is not, of course, simply imposed by society. It does not stem solely from external constraints designed to foster social obedience. It is an attitude with deep spontaneous roots in the psychological situation of our species. It is often used, moreover, to express not compliance, but defiance, independence, strength of will: fleshly ordeals such as fasting – and celibacy – are typically undertaken by humans in a spirit of willful, autonomous personal choice. But the burden of sensual self-abnegation imposed on women by the double standard is not undertaken in a willful spirit. It is passively accepted; and for this reason it does work as Fromm indicated that sensual self-abnegation can work: it helps make women in a special way humble, dependent, malleable.

The chronic bodily muting accepted by "feminine" women is the opposite of dramatic and self-assertive: it wholly lacks the brightness and clarity of a hunger strike or a religious vow of abstinence from sex. Occasionally women flare up a bit and use it vengefully, affirming it as a sign of their own moral superiority to, and power over, the abjectly lust-ridden male. On the whole, however, the female burden of genital deprivation is carried meekly, invisibly. Sometimes it cripples real interest in sexual interaction, but often it does not: indeed, it can deepen a woman's need for the emotional rewards of carnal contact. What it most reliably cripples is human pride.

2 Symbolic Interactionism and Sexual Conduct: An Emergent Perspective

Ken Plummer

Three main traditions of sex research have dominated inquiries into human sexuality until very recently. The first – symbolized by Freud – is the clinical tradition which examines the emotional development of the individual person by means of intensive analytic work on childhood memories and the unconscious. The second – symbolized by Kinsey – is the social book-keeping approach which examines the frequency and social distribution of sexual behaviours by means of interviews, questionnaires and statistical computation. The third – symbolized by Masters and Johnson – is the experimental method which examines the physiology of sexual arousal by means of controlled laboratory observation. There are of course now many interconnections between these traditions but their broad collective 'control' over the field is without dispute.[1]

In contrast to the traditions mentioned above there is a fourth which has a long but undeveloped history in anthropology and a comparatively short one in sociology. Unlike the clinical, book-keeping and experimental traditions, it lacks a symbolic great name with which it can be clearly identified, as well as the generalized influence of these traditions. It consists of a growing number of disparate, small-scale, modest, often apparently trivial, primarily descriptive excursions into the minute world of contemporary contrasting varied sexual experiences. Its channels have led it firstly into exotic and simpler cultures, for example the Trobriand Islanders or the Melanesians, and latterly into the subcultures of urban life: the world of strippers, drag artists, transvestites, transsexuals, homosexuals, prostitutes, and nudists, as well as into pornographic bookstores, gynaecological examinations, massage parlours, lovers' lanes, nude beaches, abortion clinics, public conveniences, sauna baths, brothels and university bathrooms.[2] In each case, the researcher has brought back a limited focused account of life in a small realm of experience gathered through close conversation with and observation of these worlds. Now this tradition – widespread as it is slowly becoming in sociological circles – lacks a coherent, grand and systematic scheme such as the other traditions possess. Its epistemology is one which generally eschews the search for universal truths about sexual matters and shuns abstract conceptualization and grand theorization. Instead its concern pushes it towards the multiple truths of limited contexts. Its task is the relaying – and hopeful comprehension – of focused patterns of sexual experience. In contrast to the clinicians, whose prime focus is the unconscious, the bookkeepers, whose prime focus is behavioural frequency, and the experimentalists, whose prime focus is sexual physiology, the concern of this tradition is with sexual meaning and the way it is socially constructed and socially patterned.

But description without theorizing is empty, and it is only in the past decade that the broad affinity between ethnography and symbolic interactionism has been detected and elaborated. Interactionism, of course, is no new theory; developing out of the pragmatist and formalist strands of thought at Chicago University in the 1920s, it sees the central features of human life as residing in socially produced, interactionally negotiated and personally sustained symbo-lizations.[3] Whilst humans invariably inhabit restraining material worlds (including or-ganic ones), such worlds have to be inter-preted and given sense through a dense web of negotiable symbols which are themselves historically produced. Likewise, humans come to give meaning to themselves, to the groups they identify with, to their own pasts and indeed to everything else they encounter in the world. Such meanings are never given and fixed; they are precarious and ambigu-ous and have to be constantly negotiated and worked at in the ceaseless stream of social interaction. Meaning thus arises in interaction, and the emergent meaning makes human life possible as we distinct-ively know it.

Many sociological theories have broadly similar concerns (phenomenologists, with their focus on the description and constitu-tion of consciousness; existentialists, with their concern to study 'human experience-in-the-world'; ethnomethodologists, with their concern to investigate the procedures by which everyday life is composed) and there are affinities with other disciplines ('construct theory' and 'cognitive theory', for example, in psychology, and linguistic relativity in social linguistics),[4] but it is the interactionists who seem to have focused their general theory most forcefully on human sexuality. Not that the early interac-tionists showed much concern: neither Mead nor Park paid much attention to it,[5] and although one forerunner of Mead's at Chi-cago – W. I. Thomas – did produce a number of papers on sex, as well as a book, they are limited to idiosyncratic (and now greatly superseded) discussions on gender.[6] A few of the Chicago ethnographers provided rela-tively crude thumbnail sketches of sexual conduct in selected areas, but such work made little contribution to theoretical ad-vance.[7] Likewise, the work of the Chicago 'family sociologist' Burgess (with Locke) was essentially eclectic (though acknowledging indebtedness to Cooley and Mead). Burgess also produced a short paper in 1949 – in the

wake of the Kinsey turbulence – highlighting seven rather arbitrary contributions which sociology could make to the study of sex (sexual conduct, sexual roles, role inversion, change and values, extra-marital sex, change and society, research) but most importantly stressing the need to study sexuality as con-duct:

> The sex behaviour of animals is motivated by instinct, that of man by his attitudes and values which reflect those of his intimate groups and of the environing society. . . . The various forms of sexual outlet for man are not behaviour, they are conduct. Conduct is behaviour as prescribed or evaluated by the group. It is not simply external observable behaviour but behav-iour which expresses a norm or violation.[8]

A few years later – this time in the wake of the female Kinsey volume – Kuhn (Blumer's major theoretical rival at Iowa) produced a critique that contained the clearest state-ment of interactionism and sexuality up to that time. For example, he wrote:

> Sex acts, sexual objects, sexual partners (human or otherwise) like all other objects towards which human beings behave are *social objects*; that is they have meanings because meanings are assigned to them by groups of which human beings are members for there is nothing in the physi-ology of man which gives a dependable clue as to what pattern of activity will be followed toward them. The meanings of these social objects are mediated to the individual by means of language just as in the case of all other social objects. That the communicators which involve these defin-itions are frequently – at least in our soci-ety – surreptitious and characterized by a huge degree of innuendo does not in any wise diminish the truth of this assertion. In short, the sexual motives which human beings have are derived from the social roles they play; like all other motives these would not be possible were not the actions physiologically possible, but the physiology does not supply the motives,

designate the partners, invest the objects, with performed passion, nor even dictate the objectives to be achieved.[9]

Important as Kuhn's statement was, it was never developed and it remains 'lost' in the pages of the first volume of *Social Problems*.

The most important contemporary exponents of this perspective are John Gagnon and William Simon; both trained in Chicago in the late 1940s, going on to be senior research sociologists at the Kinsey Institute in Indiana. Since that time, in the mid sixties, they have produced a series of path-breaking papers on the interactionist approach, culminating in their important book *Sexual Conduct*. It is their approach which has provided the litmus for much recent research – though it should be recognized that a number of other interactionists have presented similar statements.[10] Nevertheless, their account is the most innovative and distinctive. It heralded the view that sexuality should not be seen as a powerful drive but rather as a socially constructed motive; the adoption of the metaphor 'sexual script' as a framework for analysing the social construction of sexual meaning; the directive to study the social sources from which human sexualities were constructed; the need to view sexual development not as something relentlessly unwinding from within but as something constantly shaped through encounters with significant others; the need to see the importance of wider socio-historical formations in generating the meanings which people in society assumed in their identities; and the importance of stigmatic labelling in the creation of separate worlds of sexual deviance.

One of the central ideological thrusts of the work of Gagnon and Simon is the wish to take the study of human sexuality out of the realm of the extraordinary and replace it where it belongs: in the world of the ordinary. Sexuality is not to be seen as something special; it is not to be seen as a powerful drive shaping the universe or the personality; it is not to be studied by special theories

which endow it with a further added significance. Instead it should be seen as an unremarkable phenomenon which can be studied in unremarkable ways using unremarkable theories.

John Gagnon summarizes this perspective in the following way:

> In any given society, at any given moment in its history, people become sexual in the same way they become everything else. Without much reflection, they pick up directions from their social environment. They acquire and assemble means, skills, and values from the people around them. Their critical choices are often made by going along and drifting. People learn when they are quite young a few of the things that they are expected to be, and continue slowly to accumulate a belief in who they are and ought to be throughout the rest of childhood, adolescence and adulthood. Sexual conduct is learned in the same ways and through the same processes; it is acquired and assembled in human interaction, judged and performed in specific cultural and historical worlds.[11]

Sexual conduct then is learnt conduct and can be studied just like any other conduct: it is only because – in the past – we have invented such a special importance for human sexuality that we have also needed to invent special theories to deal with it. Theorizing about sex has been shaped by the culture which generated it and this in turn has served to structure and fashion – indeed 'construct' – sexualities (a position arrived at more recently and from a different theoretical angle in the work of Foucault). The interactionist account of human sexuality is hence isomorphic with interactionist accounts of other everyday life phenomena. Its central project is to unravel the social construction of meaning – in history, in interaction, and in biographies; its root metaphor for performing such a task is that of the drama; its key research tools are those which embrace 'intimate familiarity'.[12]

In order to convey something of the novelty and differentives of this approach to sexuality it is instructive to contrast it with an account of the more prevalent views. At many critical points, interactionism subverts the orthodox line, and I will briefly discuss six below.

Changing Metaphors: 'Drive' or 'Script'?

Theories are usually guided (often only implicitly) by some metaphorical image enabling something to be seen from the 'viewpoint of something else'.[13] With sexuality, the prevailing imagery has been drawn from the worlds of biology and technology – portraying it respectively as either an animal-like 'natural' eruption or a machine-like activity: hydraulic flows, orgasm mapping, energy systems. The root image is that of a *powerful biological drive*.[14] The powerful image suggests significance, importance, even centrality to life; the biological image suggests a universal essence – variability is possible only within finite organic limits; the drive image suggests driveness and determinism – sometimes, as in notions of sublimation and repression, closely linked to ideas of hydraulic pressure. This, then, is the metaphor that captures a great deal of thinking about sexuality – an imperious, insistent and often impious force that presses universally for release and satisfaction from within the human body. All shades of thought conspire to use this metaphor: from the libertarian left of Wilhelm Reich to the authoritarian right of 'traditional' Christianity, from the scientific thought of Freud and his followers to the contemporary legion of sex therapists, from the literature of Lawrence to the everyday thought of Everyperson. Variations on a theme abound; but who would challenge the 'naturalness', the significance, the bodily truth of sexuality? Even the sociologists – usually the first to stampede towards a cultural account over a biological one – have traditionally maintained the biological bedrock while merely superimposing cultural variation upon it.

The heretical task of challenging this pervasive orthodoxy has been one of the prime accomplishments of interactionism. The imagery of drive is seen to fail to do justice to either human communication or human creativity: human beings harbour the potential to *create* a diverse array of sexualities through communication with each other. For such a constructive process, the metaphor of the theatre – especially that of the script – thus becomes a crucial building block.

This dramaturgical metaphor has a long history both in sociology and out of it.[15] Despite many difficulties, it has been applied to a wide variety of phenomena: sexual scripts are merely a subset of these, 'formulated in the same ways and with the same purposes.'[16] Following on from Burke's dramatism, the metaphor directs the researcher to ponder the processes by which people come to piece together activities which are identifiable as 'sexual': the scene, the act, the agency, the agent, the purpose.[17] Human sexuality – as opposed to biological functioning – only comes to exist once it is embroiled with partners (real or imagined), activities, times, places and reasons *defined* as sexual.

This general imagery of 'script' is a vivid one in highlighting the relativity of sexual meanings, their humanly constructed nature, and in correcting biological and mechanical imagery, while a number of fruitful studies have emerged within it. But it is only a general imagery, and many problems remain.[18] In the hands of some researchers, it has become a wooden mechanical tool for identifying uniformities in sexual conduct: the script determines activity, rather than emerging through activity.[19] What is actually required is research to show the nature of sexual scripts as they *emerge* in encounters. Such encounters may be seen as stumbling, fragile and ambiguous situations in which participants gropingly attempt (through such processes as role taking, role making, altercasting and self-presentation)[20] to make 'sexual sense' of selves, situations and others.

In assembling sexual meaning, there will always be elements of novelty, unpredictability and inderminateness as actors piece together lines of action. But there will also be elements of regularity, loose 'scripts' which 'name the actors, describe their qualities, indicate the motives for the behaviour of the participants, set the sequence of appropriate activities – both verbal and non-verbal'. Regularities flow partly from personal commitments and self-lodging, partly from the existence of abstract sexual meanings, and partly from the routinization of perspectives with others. The study of the construction of the sexual is an enterprise which has only begun in recent years, and even then has primarily been restricted to areas of the unconventional. Thus there exist studies of the game manoeuvres employed in developing (often unpredictable) sexual roles in public conveniences; of the disembodied and 'work-like' properties of sexual encounters in whorehouses; of the rules employed by boy prostitutes in structuring their money-making sexual activities; of the strategies employed by nudists to render their potentially sexual conduct into non-sexual conduct; and of the emerging 'sexual' perspectives in sex-dominated occupations like striptease and taxi-cab driving.[21] Such studies as the above need to be taken seriously and extended. But the point still remains that very little is known (except by implication) about the construction of more conventional ('non-deviant') sexual encounters. While there now exist clear behavioural accounts of the unfolding of sexual acts, such as that of Masters and Johnson, social description appears to remain taboo. How, for example, do husband and wife piece together lines of conduct into a co-ordinated sexual act? How does an encounter come to be recognized as a 'romantic' one, or as a 'transient', 'commodity' one? How does a solitary individual build up a routine sexual phantasy, and how does she/he shape her/his masturbatory world?

One of the few discussions of these sorts of problems is by Gagnon.[22] In a cursory and anecdotal manner, not using empirical materials, he evokes his central concept that sexuality can be viewed as 'scripted behaviour' and presents a simple, yet telling, account of a sexual encounter between a late-adolescent, fairly inexperienced couple. He describes the settings chosen, the preliminary talk, the confused expectations and effects on self-conceptions, the kissings, the problems in undressing, the merger of public worlds with private worlds, the distractions that intrude, the taking of other's roles and the presentation of appropriate self-images, the balance sought between gaining one's own pleasure and meeting the needs of other, the 'coital mess', the feeling of 'doneness', the re-entry into the non-sexual world, and the transformed relationship. Gagnon's analysis is elementary and verges on the literary; but through the notion of script rather than drive he has placed such work at the centre of sexual analysis.

How these 'scripts' come about – historically, socially and personally – is of prime concern to the interactionist. At once, the concept is made to bridge the most intimate human need and the boldest historical sweep. For *historically* it addresses matters such as the sources of our various cultural constructions of sexuality, and when and how we came to invest so much importance to sexuality in our general scripts.[23] *Socially* it ponders how people came to use sexual scripts for social ends, and how they come to scan their past lives, current moments and anticipated futures in order to hook them on to the available but selected sexual scripts.[24] More *personally* (and more classically) it investigates the psychic needs for individuals to gain excitement from some scripts but not others.[25] All these concerns are interdependent.

Changing Meanings: Essence or Emergent?

The metaphor of 'script' immediately suggests a composed, orchestrated construction – as something unfolding through interaction

– whereas the metaphor of 'drive' suggests an essence awaiting release. A core contrast of the two views, therefore, is the way in which for drive theorists sexual meaning is relatively unproblematic: it is a given, an absolute, an essence. For interactionists this is not so; indeed their central task is to describe and theorize the *processes by which sexual meanings are constructed.* At the outset, it invariably means that all the categorizations and meanings that are routinely taken for granted by scientists and lay-persons alike have to be rendered problematic: 'sex' and 'gender' – along with their myriad derivatives – become objects of investigation. The category 'homosexual', for example, cannot be simply used as a resource to gather a sample, devise a theory or impute a personality type – as it is with other theories; rather, here, the category itself becomes the research focus. When – and for what reasons – did the category emerge? What part does it play in the wider social order? How do people come to impute such a label – to others and to self? And why can so much experience potentially capable of being so labelled escape or defy such categorization?[26] On an even grander scale, the divide between 'men' and 'women' has to be put through this analytic mill.[27] And so too, of course, must the very notion of 'sexuality'. What is this thing called 'sexuality', how do we construct it, why do we sometimes attach so much importance to it?[28]

Of course to those who view sex as a given biological force such questions may seem absurd: we know what all these things are. Naively, perhaps, the interactionists do not. In a striking passage, Simon reveals the relativity of sexual meaning:

> Imagine, if you will, a panel of matched penises entering an equal number of matched or randomized vaginas: the penises all thrust the identical number of thrusts, all simultaneously achieve orgasms of equal magnitude, and all withdraw at the same time, leaving all vaginas in an equal state of indifference. What can we possibly know about the character of any of these

acts? Or any of the involved actors? Let me suggest, if I may, some reasonable candidates for this panel: (a) a lower-class male, having a mild sensual experience, though glowing with the anticipation of the homosocial acknowledgement he will receive as long as the vagina did not belong to his wife; (b) an upper-middle-class male crushed by his inability to bring his partner to orgasm; (c) a male achieving unusual orgasmic heights because his partner is a prostitute or someone else of equally degraded erotic status; (d) a stereotyped Victorian couple 'doing their thing' – or is it 'his thing'? – or possibly, natives of contemporary rural Ireland; (e) a husband fulfilling his marital obligations while dreaming dreams of muscular young truck drivers; (f) a couple performing an act of sexual initiation in the back seat of a VW; and (g) a Belgian nun being raped by a Hun.[29]

In a similar vein, I have remarked elsewhere:

> When a child plays with its genitals, is this 'sexual'? When a person excretes, is this sexual? When a man kisses another man publicly, is this sexual? When a couple are naked together, is this sexual? When a girl takes her clothes off in public, is this sexual? When a lavatory attendant wipes down a toilet seat, is this sexual? When a morgue attendant touches a dead body, is this sexual? When a social worker assists her client, is this sexual? When a man and woman copulate out of curiosity or out of duty, is this sexual? The list could be considerably extended; but the point I hope is made. Most of the situations above could be defined as sexual by members; they need not be. Sexual meanings are not universal absolutes, but ambiguous and problematic categories.[30]

Society and Sex: Contest or Continuity?

The notion of a powerful, 'essential' drive leads to the view that sexuality has an important role to play in the construction of social order – either as a key dynamic in the formation of stable personalities or because of its imperative claim for regulation. Unlike interactionists, who would argue that it is through social scripting that sexuality is channelled, drive theorists suggest that it is through sexuality that social order is channelled. There is both a 'right-wing' and a 'left-wing' version of this view. The former holds that the all-powerful demon of sex needs strong societal regulation for order to be maintained: any chink in the armoury of control leads to rapid moral decay, sexual anarchy, disordered personalities, and the decline of civilization. In the academic literature, such a view is to be found in Freud, Unwin and Sorokin.[31] It is also evidenced in the contemporary moral crusades in England of Whitehouse.[32] The 'left-wing' view holds that the powerful drive could be a means of creative self-fulfilment if it was not twisted and repressed by an oppressive state for its own ends: the state regulates the powerful drive through the family in order to rigidify the personality structure and render it subservient to the needs of the rulers. In the academic literature, such a view is found in the writings of Marcuse, Reich and Reiche,[33] and more popularly in the contemporary ideologies of the Gay and Paedophile Liberation Movements.[34]

While the right-wing view sees sexuality as the demon within and the left-wing sees sexuality as the great liberator, both credit sexuality with enormous – almost mystical – powers in contributing to social order. Sex becomes the central force upon which civilizations are built up and empires crash down. Interactionists remain suspicious of the empirical validity of such a view, and suggest an alternative interpretation of powerful drives and social order: that social needs for survival and replacement have led many societies to attribute great power to sexuality – either by deification or by negation. In the latter case, a combination of sexual meanings which simultaneously encourage sexuality ('it's a powerful drive') and prohibit it ('it's sinful' etc.) lodges the sexual experience in a contradiction which may generate guilt

and anxiety, and bestow an exaggerated importance on sexuality. In this view, therefore, there is a continuity between the cultural meanings and the personal experience of sexuality, and where conflicts exist in the culture they are mirrored in the person.

Sexuality as Determiner or Determined?

A further argument of drive theorists is that sexuality shapes our social conduct. Not only have we become adept at interpreting all manner of social artefacts – from chocolate flakes to motor cars – as sexual symbols; we also treat much social behaviour – collecting, neurosis, stealing, humanitarianism, artistic creation, drinking and eating – as expressions of masked sexuality. Sexual structures come to inhabit asocial worlds. Interactionists argue that instead of sexuality determining the social, it is the other way round: social meanings give shape to our sexuality. Sexuality has no meaning other than that given to it in social situations. Thus the forms and the contents of sexual meanings are another cultural variable, and why certain meanings are learnt and not others is problematic. One important implication of this perspective is the need to analyse sexual activity in our culture for its social origins, the ways in which social experiences become translated into sexual ones. Much sexual behaviour may have 'non-sexual' sources: the health-food faddist may take sex at prescribed regular intervals in the same way as health foods and for the same purpose; the married couple may regularly have sexual activity, even when neither wants it, because each believes the other expects it; the prostitute employs sex as a means of earning a living as does the stripper; the man may seek a flow of regular sexual partners in the belief that this may sustain his public image of masculinity; and the student may masturbate out of habit or out of an association with tension-reduction.[35] In each case, sexual experiences are constructed from social motives and settings.

Gagnon and Simon in one discussion on homosexuality in the prison setting suggest that:

> What is occurring in the prison situation for both males and females is *not a problem of sexual release, but rather the use of sexual relationships in the service of creating a community of relationships for satisfying needs for which the prison community fails to provide in any other forms.* For the male prisoner homosexuality serves as a source of affection, as a source of validation for masculinity, or a source of protection from the problems of institutional life.[36]

Here, sex is not merely a release used to structure experience; rather, the sexual world is itself fashioned by the social needs of the individual. These needs may centre on many issues – and it is but a short step from here to Foucault's view that 'sexuality' is 'used' as a channel for the negotiation of power.

Sexuality: Necessary or Contingent?

A related argument of drive theorists is that sex is seen as an energy which needs release – very often located within a closed reservoir system subject to the laws of the conservation of energy. The argument, in its crudest terms, suggests that the sexual energy is an absolute force which if not allowed to manifest itself in its 'natural' state will break out into other areas of life. Two key concepts here are *repression* and *sublimation*. Thus, if 'absolute sexuality' does not develop 'naturally', the energy may be *repressed*, in which case deviations and neurosis are likely to occur through the damming up of libidinal energy, or *sublimation* may arise, in which case libidinal energy may become the source of extra energy in work, especially in benevolent and artistic occupations. There are other mechanisms by which the energy may be diverted from its original sexual goal. Freud and others thereby encourage a search for the underlying sexual basis of much social behaviour; one becomes very sceptical of the apparently sexless person and imputes to him or her all manner of sublimation techniques.

Now the concepts of repression and sublimation (along with their recent counterpart 'repressive desublimation') are unproven assumptions, which have been absorbed into contemporary 'taken-for-granted' notions of sexuality. Two simple hypotheses may be deduced from the broad assumption of an energy system: (1) if people have little sexual outlet they must be repressing or sublimating their desires in some manner – and consequently, most likely, exhibiting some form of neurosis; (2) if people have much sexual outlet their energy must be sapped away from other things – they are unlikely to be creative, active or productive. In the first case one wonders what such persons can be doing with their sexuality, where it is being sapped to; and in the second case one becomes concerned with the person's ability to perform well in other spheres of life. For both hypotheses, there is little evidence. The work of Kinsey, however, does suggest that individuals with a high degree of sexual activity can be 'of considerable significance socially' – one of his most sexually active respondents was a 'scholarly and skilled lawyer' who 'averaged over thirty [orgasms] a week for thirty years'[37] – and others have suggested that 'no genuine tissue or biological needs' are generated by a lack of sexual activity.[38]

For the interactionist, then, sex *per se* is not an absolute necessity – unlike food, one can live without it, and some societies do[39] – but neither is it ruinous if one enjoys it very often. One might of course learn to become addicted to it, and that could be damaging. But a great deal of sexual experience is not intrinsically harmful.

Becoming Sexual: Orientation or Construct?

Closely allied to this contrast is the way in which sexual development is viewed. For the 'drive' theorists the emphasis is placed upon the evolution of identities and orientations through fairly regular phases in the earlier years of life: sexuality is in a broad sense determined either by birth or by childhood. For the 'script' theorists, sexual development is a life-long learning process which is historically malleable: sexuality is in a broad sense assembled from the cultural categories currently available.

Again it is the drive view that is most common in both social science and common sense. Biology, Freudianism and behaviourism lend support to it by tracing out the sequences of sexual development found in childhood and by suggesting the ultimate 'fiedness' of what happens there. John Money puts this view in its most flexible form:

Each person's turn-on has rather fixed boundaries which are set before puberty. Whether the boundaries are orthodox or unorthodox, conventional or unconventional they were established in childhood as part of the differentiation of gender identity, by the coding of the schemers, and by any quirks or oddities that were incorporated into the schemers. Boundaries may first show themselves at puberty, but they are not set in puberty and they don't change much at puberty or later. Their relative unchangeability helps to explain such phenomena as why second spouse so often resembles the first. Their persistence also explains why adult obligative homosexuals can be fond of and behave affectionately towards a member of the other sex especially if the other is older, but can never fall in love with him or her. Tales of sex degenerates who go from one form of depravity to another, sampling everything, are only fiction; even so-called sex degenerates stick to their particular preferences.[40]

Side by side with this view of the development of sexual orientation is the view that identity emerges simultaneously. This means that either the identity emerges unproblematically, so that the child en route to becoming a heterosexual *being* also learns the heterosexual *identity*, or, alternatively, it means that there is a disjunction between the orientation that is built up in childhood and the identity that develops in adulthood. Thus, in this latter case, one may develop into a 'latent homosexual', where the orientation – that of 'a homosexual' – is set up in childhood but the identity acquired – that of 'a heterosexual' – is inappropriate. This model assumes that the category of heterosexual identity is here inappropriate: the person's *actual* identity is that of a homosexual. The task for some clinicians therefore would be to bring into the consciousness of that individual his or her *real* identity. It hence presumes there may be a real and essential identity – fixed in childhood – independent of members' awareness of it.[41]

In contrast, the interactionist suggests that such schemes generally *impose* taken-for-granted adult images of sexuality upon experiences that are generally incoherent, ill-formed and ill-defined while believing they are *uncovering* the true and essential nature of sexuality.

Thus, for example, studies of childhood sexuality generally fail to record shifts at the level of meaning. While there is now considerable evidence of children being involved in 'adult-defined' sexuality, these studies generally impose adult interpretations upon the behaviour rather than analysing the definitions which the child builds up. It is well documented that in other cultures children may become engaged in copulatory activities from early ages, and that in this culture children are capable of orgasms before even reaching the age of one. Likewise, it has been well established that children 'do' many 'sexual things', conjure up 'sexual fantasies' and have 'sexual things' done to them.[42] But in all of these cases it is naive to assume that children automatically 'feel' and 'recognize' these experiences in the ways that adults do. Genital play and indecent assault may both be experienced by the child in a 'non-sexual' way, because the child has not yet developed competency in the motives and feelings that adults routinely come to associate with sexuality: thus the child is merely 'playing', 'being attacked' or 'playing with an adult'. As one correspondent wrote to me:

> At about the age of eight I was coerced by a stranger to masturbate him. My chief understanding at the time was that the stranger urinated. That is, I did not understand either the ejaculation or the sexual meaning of the encounter. It struck me as bizarre, but the sexual meanings were retrospectively imposed when I learnt about orgasms.

It thus becomes clear what the thrust of the interactionist research programme on becoming sexual is.

The focus turns to the way in which individuals throughout their life cycle come to be defined by themselves and others as sexual beings, how they come to hook themselves on to the wider cultural meanings, and how these are renegotiated or stabilized. Gone is the view that socialization is concerned with the management of some inner pre-existing sexual 'condition' or 'motive'; gone is the view of 'latent' sexual conditions; gone is the view of people 'essentially being' that of which they are unaware. In its place comes a concern with the way 'sexual motives' are fashioned out of existing 'motivational ideologies'; with the ways in which individuals' self-conceptions as sexual beings shift and change through the life cycle; with the ways in which the past is constantly recast through the present. Blumstein and Schwartz have been the most ardent advocates of this view and pose the major research question as: 'What is the formula by which an actor arranges information in order to construct a sexual essence for him or herself?'[43]

Perversion or Variation?

A final significant point of contrast concerns the issue of perversion and deviance. It is the drive theorists who have primarily been responsible for establishing a new rogues' gallery of sexual perverts since – roughly – the middle of the nineteenth century: homosexuals, transvestites, transsexuals, sado-masochists, urolagniacs, paedophiles, fetishists and the rest.[44] In each case the 'type' has largely been discovered by clinicians, their characterization laid out, their aetiologies designated, and suggestions for remedies proposed. At the core of all this endeavour ultimately is a strong – indeed absolute – conception of what sexuality really means: coital procreation in the service of families. To the extent that sexuality has strayed a little from this purpose, it becomes worrying; to the extent that it has strayed far from it, it becomes downright perverted. In any event, most drive theorists do not merely study the pervert – they also attempt to control him.

The interactionist, yet again, moves off in a full-blown alternative direction. Given that sexuality is relative and used for different social purposes, given that it is historically constructed and bound up with specific times and places, and given that society plays an important formative role in all sexualities, then 'the pervert' loses its universal character and becomes a curious invention of our contemporary culture. It becomes, indeed, a specific category to be investigated in itself – but it cannot be clearly taken to reflect a real phenomenon. The general argument thus highlights the view that all humans are initially open to enormous sexual variations; that cultures – through their categorization systems – may restrict and narrow the seeming options to one major route and a number of minor ones; that such categorizations belie the reality of experiences which are in effect much more complex (the term 'homosexual' – like the term 'heterosexual' – hurls together an assortment of people with so little in common that it becomes perniciously misleading); and that finally through stigmatizing some of these diverse experiences, the foundation is laid for elevating their importance and centrality in individual lives. In this last idea there is clearly a strong affinity between interactionism and the ideas of labelling theorists who have highlighted the way in which stigma has the power to transform 'ordinary' experiences.[45]

Conclusion

Much of what has been said of the interactionist image in this article should have raised minor alarms in many readers. For its starting point in the study of human sexuality challenges much of our contemporary wisdom about sex; whereas many presume to know what sex is, interactionists do not; whereas it is commonly sensed as something special, interactionists put it on a par with everything else; whereas it is commonly sensed as being either in need of repression or as a potential source of liberation, interactionists see it as merely reflecting cultural expectations; whereas it is commonly seen as being the motive force for much human behaviour, interactionists invert this wisdom and suggest that sex is engaged in far wider social reasons; whereas 'too much' or 'too little' sex are frequently seen as problems, interactionists see no reason for this; whereas sexual development is usually seen to be determined by childhood experience, interactionists see it as much more fluid and changing; whereas certain patterns of sexual development can be *assumed* as 'perversions', the interactionists see these critically as social constructions. The interactionist is a stranger to contemporary cultural meanings and concocts a heretical view.[46]

My presentation and argument has been clearly overstated. I have lumped together many disparate views under the rubric of 'drive theorists', have performed a great injustice to the subtleties and complexities of their views; and I have polarized the differences of 'drive' and 'construct' too sharply.

All of this I acknowledge. There are, I am sure, ways in which the two views can be bridged and elsewhere I have started to suggest these.[47] But before an adequate synthesis – or *didactical* revision, if you like – can be made, the logic of the counterposed position of interactionism needs to be much more thoroughly explored, empirically and theoretically. As an approach to sexuality, it is markedly different from most that have dominated thinking in the past century; it is itself scarcely a decade old in its developed form, and its more extreme arguments need careful scrutiny before it is watered down into the reigning orthodoxies.

NOTES

1 For a good general introduction to the field of 'sex research', see P. Robinson, *The Modernisation of Sex* (Elek, 1976); E. Brecher, *The Sex Researchers* (Andre Deutsch, 1969); M. S. Weinberg (ed.), *Studies from the Kinsey Institute* (Oxford University Press, 1976). An overview of the current state of the art is to be found in 'Sex Research: Future Directions', *Archives of Sexual Behaviour*, vol. 4, no. 4 (July 1975).

2 Examples of such ethnographic work abound. As illustrative, see E. W. Delph. *The Silent Community: Public Homosexual Encounters* (Sage, 1978), and J. Douglas and P. Rasussen, *The Nude Beach* (Sage, 1977).

3 The nature and origins of symbolic interactionism are now widely discussed, but two contrasting statements of great value are Blumer's *Symbolic Interactionism: Perspective and Method* (Prentice-Hall, 1969) and Rock's *The Making of Symbolic Interactionism* (Macmillan, 1979).

4 For theories that are closely allied to symbolic interactionism, see D. Wright, 'Sex: Instinct or Appetite', in P. Nobile (ed.), *The New Eroticism* (Random House, 1970); K. R. Hardy, 'An Appetitional Theory of Sexual Motivation', *Psychological Review*, 71 (1964), pp. 1–18; and many articles in the *Journal of Social Issues*, 33: 2 (1977).

5 Mead does write of the 'sexual impulse', and describes it as the impulse 'which is most important in the case of human social

behaviour, and which most decisively or determinately expresses itself in the whole general form of human social organization': see G. H. Mead, *Mind, Self and Society* (University of Chicago Press, 1962), p. 228.

6   See W. I. Thomas, *On Social Organization and Social Personality*, ed. M. Janowitz (University of Chicago Press, 1966); W. I. Thomas, *Sex and Society – Studies in the Social Psychology of Sex* (University of Chicago Press, 1907), and various papers mentioned herein and published between 1898 and 1909. On Robert Park, see H. Matthews, *Quest for an American Sociology: Robert E. Park and the Chicago School* (McGill–Queens University Press, 1977).

7   For example, see N. Anderson, *The Hobo* (University of Chicago Press, 1923), ch. 10.

8   See E. W. Burgess, 'The Sociologic Theory of Psychosexual Behaviour', in P. Hoch and J. Zubin (eds), *Psychosexual Development in Health and Disease* (Grune and Stratton, 1949).

9   See M. Kuhn, 'Kinsey's View on Human Behaviour', *Social Problems* (1954), pp. 119–25.

10   Their work can be found in many papers, but their key books are J. Gagnon and W. Simon, *Sexual Conduct* (Aldine, 1973), and J. Gagnon, *Human Sexualities* (Scott, Foresman and Co., 1977). Other writing in this field includes I. Reiss, *The Family System in America* (Holt, Rinehart and Winston, 1971); J. Henslin, *Studies in the Sociology of Sex* (Appleton Century Croft, 1971); K. Plummer, *Sexual Stigma* (Routledge, 1975); J. DeLora and C. A. B. Warren, *Understanding Sexual Interaction* (Houghton-Mifflin, 1977); J. Petras, *The Social Meaning of Human Sexuality* (Allen and Bacon, 1978).

11   See Gagnon, *Human Sexualities*, p. 2.

12   The term 'intimate familiarity' is derived from John Lofland's *Doing Social Life* (Wiley, 1976). It leads to an advocacy of rigorous field work and qualitative research. For a recent overview of this see Howard Schwartz and Jerry Jacob, *Qualitative Sociology: A Method to the Madness* (Free Press, 1979).

13   On the use of metaphor in sociology, see Richard Brown, *A Poetic for Sociology* (Cambridge University Press, 1977), ch. 4, p. 77.

14   Gagnon and Simon refer to this as 'the drive reduction model'.

15   See S. Lyman and M. B. Scott, *The Drama of Social Reality* (Oxford University Press, 1975).

16   See J. Gagnon, *Human Sexualities*, p. 6. A text that uses the script view throughout is Judith Long Laws and Pepper Schwartz, *Sexual Scripts: The Social Construction of Female Sexuality* (Dryden, 1977).

17   See K. Burke, *A Grammar of Motives* (George Braziller, 1955).

18   For a recent set of appraisals see J. Ditton (ed.), *The View from Goffman* (Macmillan, 1980); for an earlier one, see D. Brissett and C. Edgley, *Life as Theatre: A Dramatizical Source Book* (Aldine, 1974).

19   See Jay Ann Jemail and James Geer, 'Sexual Scripts', in Gemme and Wheeler (ed.), *Progress in Sexology* (Plenum, 1977).

20   For a clarification of such terms, see G. McCall and J. Simmons, *Identities and Interactions* (Free Press, 1966).

21   Amongst these studies are Laud Humphrey's *Tea Room Trade* (Aldine, 2nd edn, 1976); J. M. Henslin and M. A. Biggs, 'Dramaturgical Desexualization: The Sociology of the Vaginal Examination', in Henslin, *Studies in the Sociology of Sex*; G. L. Stewart, 'On First Being a John', *Urban Life and Culture*, vol. 1, no. 1 (1972), pp. 255–74; M. S. Weinberg, 'Sexual Modesty and the Nudist Camp', *Social Problems*, 12: 3 (1965).

22   See John Gagnon, 'Scripts and the Co-ordination of Sexual Conduct', in *Nebraska Symposium on Motivation* (University of Nebraska Press, 1972). For an extension of this argument, see J. S. Victor, 'The Social Psychology of Sexual Arousal: A Symbolic Interactionist Interpretation', in N. K. Denzin (ed.), *Studies in Symbolic Interaction*, vol. 1 (1978), pp. 147–80, and K. S. Rook and C. L. Hammer, 'A Cognitive Perspective on the Experience of Sexual Arousal', *Journal of Social Issues*, 33: 2 (1977), pp. 7–29.

23   For an introduction to historical research on sexuality, see *Radical History Review*, 20, spring/summer 1979. The (now classic) statement of a history of sexuality is to be found in Michel Foucault's *History of Sexuality*, vol. 1 (Allen Lane, 1978).

24   For an introduction to both the social uses of sexuality and sexual socialization, see

Plummer, *Sexual Stigma*, especially pp. 32–6, 56–62 and ch. 7.

25 On this, see R. Stoller, *Sexual Excitement* (Pantheon, 1979).

26 On this, see K. Plummer (ed.), *The Making of the Modern Homosexual* (Hutchinson, 1981).

27 See S. J. Kessler and W. McKenna, *Gender: An Ethnomethodological Approach* (Wiley, 1978).

28 See Foucault, *History of Sexuality*, and also his Introduction to *Herculine Barbin: Being the Recently Discovered Memoirs of a Nineteenth Century French Hermaphrodite* (Pantheon, 1980).

29 William Simon, 'The Social, the Erotic, and the Sensual: The Complexities of Erotic Scripts', in *Nebraska Symposium on Motivation* (1973), p. 64.

30 See Plummer, *Sexual Stigma*.

31 E.g. S. Freud, *Civilization and Its Discontents* (Hogarth Press, 1975).

32 See D. E. Morrison and M. Tracey, *Whitehouse* (Macmillan, 1979).

33 E.g. H. Reiche, *Sexuality and Class Struggle* (New Left Books, 1970).

34 E.g. Tom O'Carroll, *Paedophilia: The Radical Case* (Peter Owen, 1980); Dennis Altman, *Homosexual: Oppression and Liberation* (Outerbridge and Dienstfrey, 1971).

35 See J. Marmor, 'Sex for Non-sexual Reasons', in *Medical Aspects of Human Sexuality*, June 1969.

36 See Gagnon and Simon, *Sexual Conduct*, p. 258.

37 See A. Kinsey et al., *Sexual Behavior in the Human Male* (W. B. Saunders, 1948), p. 195.

38 Beech, quoted in Wright, 'Sex', p. 233.

39 On 'low drive', see K. Heider, 'Dani Sexuality: A Low Energy System', *Man*, vol. II, no. 2 (July 1976), pp. 188–201.

40 See J. Money and P. Tucker, *Sexual Signatures* (Abacus, 1977), p. 123.

41 I discuss this issue in 'Going Gay: Life Styles and Life Cycles in the Male Gay World', in D. Richardson and J. Hart (ed.), *The Theory and Practice of Homosexuality* (Routledge, 1981).

42 The literature on child sexuality is now considerable. A recent overview – though certainly polemical – is O'Carroll, *Paedophilia*. See also F. M. Martinson, 'Eroticism in Infancy and Childhood', *Journal of Sex Research*, vol. 12, no. 4 (1976), pp. 251–62.

43 Although Blumstein and Schwartz have published several papers on bisexuality, at present their two most significant papers remain unpublished. These are 'The Acquisition of Sexual Identity' (American Sociological Association Annual Conference, 1976) and 'The Elements of a Sexual Identity' (American Sociological Association Annual Conference, 1980).

44 See Foucault again, *History of Sexuality*.

45 See Plummer, *Sexual Stigma*.

46 A useful commentary on the 'Stranger' in sociology is S. C. Jansen, 'The Stranger as Seer or Voyeur: A Problem with the Peep-show Theory of Knowledge', *Qualitative Sociology*, vol. 2, no. 3 (1980), pp. 22–55.

47 See Plummer, 'Going Gay', and Plummer, *The Making of the Modern Homosexual*.

3 Pleasure under Patriarchy

Catharine A. MacKinnon

then she says (and this is what I live
through over and over) – she says; *I do
not know if sex is an illusion*

I do not know
who I was when I did those things
or who I said I was
or whether I willed to feel
what I had read about
or who in fact was there with me
or whether I knew, even then
that there was doubt about these things
Adrienne Rich, "Dialogue" (1972)

Male dominance is sexual. Meaning: men in particular, if not men alone, sexualize hierarchy; gender is one. As much a sexual theory of gender as a gendered theory of sex, this is the theory of sexuality that will be advanced as feminist here. It is supported by recent work, both interpretive and empirical, on rape, battery, sexual harassment, the sexual abuse of children, prostitution, and pornography. These practices, taken together, express and actualize the distinctive power of men over women in society; their effective permissibility confirms and extends it. If you believe women's accounts of sexual use and abuse by men; if the pervasiveness of male sexual violence against women substantiated in these studies is not denied, minimized, or excepted as deviant or episodic; if the fact that only 7.8 percent of United States women are *not* sexually assaulted or harassed in their lifetimes is considered not ignorable, inconsequential, or isolated; if violation of women is understood as sexualized on some level – then sexuality itself can no longer be regarded as unimplicated. The meaning of practices of sexual violence cannot be categorized away as violence not sex, either. The male sexual role, these studies taken together suggest, centers on aggressive intrusion on those with less power. Such acts of dominance are experienced as

sexually arousing, as sex itself. They therefore are. The evidence on the sexual violation of women by men thus frames an inquiry into the particular place of gender in sexuality as such.

A theory of sexuality that is feminist in my sense here locates sexuality within a theory of gender inequality; gender inequality is a critical term for the social hierarchy of men over women. To make a theory feminist, it is thus not enough that it be authored by a biological female. Nor that it describe female sexuality as different from (even if equal to) male sexuality, or as if sexuality in women ineluctably exists in some realm beyond, beneath, above, behind – in any event, fundamentally untouched and unmoved by – a sexist social order. For my purposes here, a theory of sexuality becomes feminist to the extent it treats sexuality as a construct of male power – defined by men, forced on women, and constitutive in the meaning of gender. Such an approach centers feminism on the perspective of the subordination of women to men as it identifies sex, that is, the sexuality of dominance and submission, as crucial, as a fundamental, as on some level definitive, in that process. Feminist theory becomes a project of analyzing that situation in order to face it for what it is, in order to change it.

Focusing on gender inequality without a sexual account of its dynamics, one could criticize the sexism of existing theories of sexuality and emerge knowing that men author scripts to their own advantage, women and men act them out; men set conditions, women and men have their behavior conditioned; men develop developmental categories through which men develop, and women develop or not; men are socially allowed selves, hence identities with personalities into which sexuality is or is not well integrated, women being that which is or is not integrated, that through the alterity of which a self experiences itself as having an identity; men have object relations, women are the objects of those relations, and so on. Following such critique, one could attempt to reverse or correct the premises or applications of these theories to make them gender neutral, even if the reality to which they refer looks more like the theories – once their gender specificity is revealed – than it looks gender neutral. Or, one could attempt to enshrine a distinctive "women's reality" in sexual theory as if it really is permitted to exist in reality as something more than a dimension of women's response to a condition of powerlessness. Such exercises would be revealing and instructive, even deconstructive, but to limit feminism to correcting the sex bias in existing explanatory schools by acting in theory as if male power did not exist in fact, including by valorizing in writing what women have had little choice but to be limited to becoming in life, is to limit feminist theory the way sexism limits women's lives: to a response to terms men set.

A distinctively feminist theory, however provisionally advanced, would conceptualize social reality, including sexual reality, on its own terms. The question is, what are they? If women have been substantially deprived not only of our own experience but of terms of our own in which to view it, then a feminist theory of sexuality that seeks to understand women's situation in order to change it, must first identify and criticize the construct "sexuality" *as* a construct that has circumscribed and defined experience as well as theory. In feminist terms, then, the fact that male power *has power* means that the interests of male sexuality construct what sexuality as such means, including the standard way it is allowed and recognized to be felt and expressed and experienced, in a way that determines women's biographies, including our sexual ones. Existing theories, until they grasp this, will not only misattribute what they call female sexuality to women as such, as if it is not

imposed on us daily; they will participate in enforcing the hegemony of this construct "sexuality," hence its construct "woman," on the world.

What is taken to be "sexuality," what sex means and what is meant by sex, when how and by whom and with what consequences to whom, is the issue. Such questions are almost never systematically confronted, even in discourses that purport feminist awareness. What sex *is* – how it comes to be attached and attributed to what it is, embodied and practiced as it is, contextualized in the ways it is, signifying and referring to what it does – is taken as given, except when explaining when it is thought to have gone wrong. It is as if "erotic," for example, can be taken as having an understood referent, although it is never defined, except to imply that it is universal yet individual, ultimately variable and plastic and essentially indefinable. But overwhelmingly positive. "Desire," the vicissitudes of which are endlessly extolled and philosophized in culture high and low, is not seen as fundamentally problematic or calling for explanation on the concrete, interpersonal operative level, unless (again) it is supposed to be there and isn't. To list and analyze what seem to be the essential elements for male sexual arousal, what has to be there for the penis to work, seems faintly blasphemous, like a pornographer doing market research. It is supposed to be both too individual and too universally transcendent for that. To suggest that the sexual might be continuous with something other than sex itself – something like culture, something like politics – is seldom done, is treated as detumescent, even by feminists. It is as if sexuality comes from the stork.

Sexuality, in the approach to be argued as feminist here, is not a discrete sphere of interaction or feeling or sensation or behavior in which preexisting social divisions may or may not be played out. It is a pervasive dimension throughout the whole of social life, a dimension along which gender pervasively occurs, at least in this culture. Dominance eroticized defines the imperatives of masculinity, submission eroticized defines femininity. So many of the distinctive features of women's status as second class – the restriction and constraint and contortion, the servility and the display, the self-mutilation and requisite presentation of self as a beautiful thing, the enforced passivity, the humiliation – are made into the content of sex for women. This is to identify not just a sexuality that is shaped under conditions of gender inequality, but this sexuality itself as the dynamic of the inequality of the sexes. This is to argue a sexual theory of the distribution of social power by gender, in which this sexuality that *is* sexuality is substantially what makes the gender division be what it is, which is male dominant, wherever it is, which is nearly everywhere. In this view, the feminist theory of sexuality is its theory of politics, its distinctive contribution to social and political explanation. To explain gender inequality in terms of "sexual politics,"[1] is to advance not only a political theory of the sexual that defines gender but also a sexual theory of the political to which gender is fundamental.

In this approach, male power takes the social form of what men as a gender want sexually, which centers on power itself as socially defined. Masculinity is having it, femininity is not having it. Masculinity precedes male as femininity precedes female and male sexual desire defines both. Specifically, "woman" is defined by what male desire requires for arousal and satisfaction and is socially tautologous with "female sexuality" and "the female sex." In the permissible ways a woman can be treated, the ways that are socially considered not violations but appropriate to her nature, one finds the particulars of male *sexual* interests and requirements. In the concomitant sexual paradigm, the ruling norms of sexual attraction and expression are fused with gender identity formation and affirmation, such that sexuality equals heterosexuality equals the sexuality of (male) dominance and (female) submission.

Post-Lacan, more accurately post-Foucault, it has become customary to affirm that sexuality is socially constructed. Seldom specified is what, socially, it is constructed of. When capitalism is the favored social construct, sexuality is shaped and controlled and exploited and repressed by capitalism; not, capitalism creates sexuality as we know it. *Constructed* seems to mean influenced by, directed, channeled, like a highway constructs traffic patterns. Not: Why cars? Who's driving? Where's everybody going? What makes mobility matter? Who can own a car? Is there a pattern that makes all these accidents look not very accidental? Although there are partial exceptions, but disclaimers notwithstanding, the typical model of sexuality that is tacitly accepted remains deeply Freudian and essentialist: sexuality is an innate primary natural unconditioned drive, centering on heterosexual intercourse, that is, penile intromission, full actualization of which is repressed by civilization for its own survival. Even if the sublimation aspect of this theory is rejected, or the reasons for the repression are seen to vary, sexual expression is implicitly seen as the expression of something that is to a significant extent presocial and socially denied its full force. Sexuality is always seen as to some extent precultural and universally invariant, social only in the sense that it needs society to take what are always to some extent socially specific forms. The impetus itself is a hunger, an appetite founded on a biological need; how it is satisfied is then open to endless social and individual variance, like cooking.

Allowed/not allowed are this sexuality's basic ideological axes. That sexuality is ideologically bounded is known. That these are its axes, central to the way its "drive" is driven, is not. Its basic normative assumption is that whatever is considered sexuality should be allowed to be "expressed." Whatever is called sex is attributed a normatively positive valence, an affirmative valuation. This *ex cathedra* assumption, affirmation of which is indispensable to credibility on any subject that gets near the sexual, means that sex as such, whatever that is, must be "good" – typically natural, healthy, pleasurable, wholesome, fine, one's own, and should be approved. This, sometimes characterized as "sex-positive" is, rather obviously, a value judgment.

Kinsey and his followers, for example, clearly thought (and think) the more sex the better, trivialize even most of those cases of rape and child sexual abuse they discern as such, decry women's sexual refusal as sexual inhibition, and repeatedly interpret women's sexual disinclination as "restrictions" on men's natural sexual activity, which left alone would emulate (some) animals'. Followers of the neo-Freudian derepression imperative have similarly identified the frontier of sexual freedom with transgression of social restraints on access, with making the sexually disallowed allowed, especially male sexual access to anything. The struggle to have everything "sexual" allowed in a society we are told would collapse if it were, creates a sense of resistance to, and an aura of danger around, violating the powerless. Taboo and crime may serve to eroticize what would otherwise feel about as much like dominance as taking candy from a baby. The point is, allowed/not allowed become ideological categories within which sexuality is experienced when and because sex is about power.

One version of the derepression hypothesis that purports feminism is: civilization having been male-dominated, female sexuality has been repressed, not allowed. Sexuality as such still centers on what would otherwise be considered the reproductive act, on intercourse: penetration by the erect penis into the vagina (or appropriate female substitute orifices) followed by thrusting to male ejaculation. "We had sex three times" thus typically means the man entered (penetrated) the woman three times and orgasmed three times. Female sexuality in this model refers to the presence of this theory's "sexuality," or the desire to be so treated, in biological females; "female" is somewhere

between an adjective and a noun, half possessive and half biological ascription. Sexual freedom means women being allowed to behave as freely as men to express this sexuality, to have it allowed, that is, to (hopefully) shamelessly and without social constraints initiate genital drive satisfaction through heterosexual intercourse. Hence, the liberated woman. Hence, the sexual revolution.

The pervasiveness of such assumptions about sexuality throughout otherwise diverse methodological traditions is suggested by the following comment by a scholar of violence against women:

> If women were to escape the culturally stereotyped role of disinterest in and resistance to sex and to take on an assertive role in expressing their own sexuality, rather than leaving it to the assertiveness of men, it would contribute to the reduction of rape. . . . First, and most obviously, voluntary sex would be available to more men, thus reducing the "need" for rape. Second, and probably more important, it would help to reduce the confounding of sex and aggression.

Somebody must be assertive for sex to happen. Voluntary sex – sexual equality – means equal sexual aggression. If women freely expressed "their own sexuality," more heterosexual intercourse would be initiated. Women's "resistance" to sex is an imposed cultural stereotype; it is not a form of political struggle. Rape is occasioned by women's resistance not by men's force; or, male force, hence rape, is created by women's resistance to sex. Men would rape less if they got more voluntarily compliant sex from women. Corollary: the force in rape is not sexual to men.

Underlying this quotation I sense the view, as common as it is tacit, that if women would just accept the contact men now have to rape to get – if women would stop resisting or (in one of the pornographers' favorite scenarios, too) become sexual aggressors – rape would wither way. On one level, this is a definitionally obvious truth. When a woman accepts what would be a rape if she did not accept it, what happens is sex. If women were to accept forced sex as sex, "voluntary sex would be available to more men." It is a mystery, if such a view is not implicit in this text, how women equally aggressing against men sexually would eliminate, rather than double, the "confounding of sex and aggression." Without such an assumption, only the confounding of sexual aggression with gender would be eliminated. If women did not resist male sexual aggression anymore, the confounding of sex with aggression would be so epistemologically complete that it would, indeed, be eliminated. No woman would ever be sexually violated, because sexual violation would be sex. The situation might resemble that evoked by a society Sanday categorized as "rape-free" in part because the men assert there is no rape there: "our women never resist."[2] Such pacification also occurs in "rape-prone" societies like the United States, where some force may be perceived as force, but only above certain threshold standards.

Although intending the opposite, some feminists have encouraged and participated in this kind of analysis by conceiving rape as violence not sex. While this approach gave needed emphasis to rape's previously effaced elements of power and dominance, it obscured its elements of sex. Aside from failing to answer the rather obvious question, if it's violence not sex, why didn't he just hit her, this approach made it impossible to see that violence *is* sex when it is practiced *as* sex. To say rape is violence not sex crucially leaves the "sex is good" assumption intact by distinguishing forced sex as "not sex." Rape can thus be opposed by those who would save sexuality from the rapists while leaving the sexual fundamentals of male dominance intact. Whatever is sex, cannot be violent. Whatever is violent, cannot be sex. Don't we wish.

Although such prior work on rape has analyzed it as a problem of gender inequality but not as a problem of sexuality, other contemporary explorations of sexuality that purport to be feminist fail to comprehend either gender as a form of social power or the realities of sexual violence. For instance, the editors of *Powers of Desire* begin by taking sex "as a central form of expression, one that defines identity and is seen as a primary source of energy and pleasure."[3] This may be how it "is seen" but it is also how they, operatively, see it. As if women choose sexuality as definitive of identity. As if it is as much a form of women's "expression" as it is men's. As if violation and abuse are not equally central to sexuality as women live it. Expanding on the "pleasure" trope, the *Diary* of the Barnard Conference on sexuality pervasively equates sexuality with pleasure. "Perhaps the overall question we need to ask is: how do women... negotiate sexual pleasure?"[4] As if women under male supremacy have power to; as if "negotiation" is a form of freedom; as if pleasure and how to get it, rather than dominance and how to end it, is the "overall" issue sexuality presents feminism. Maybe we do just need a good fuck. Taboos are treated as real restrictions – as things that really are not allowed – instead of being, some of them, guises under which hierarchy is eroticized. The domain of the sexual is divided into "restriction, repression, and danger" on the one hand and "exploration, pleasure and agency" on the other.[5] This division parallels the ideological forms through which dominance and submission are eroticized, variously socially coded as heterosexuality's male/female, lesbian culture's butch/femme, and sadomasochism's top/bottom. To speak in role terms, the one who pleasures in the illusion of freedom and security within the reality of danger is the "girl"; the one who pleasures in the reality of freedom and security within the illusion of danger is the "boy." That is, the *Diary* adopts as an analytical tool the central dynamic of the phenomenon it purports to be analyzing.

The terms of these discourses preclude or evade the following questions, which I take to be crucial and feminist: What do sexuality and gender *inequality* have to do with each other? How do dominance and submission become sexualized, or, why is hierarchy sexy? How does it get attached to male and female? Why does "sexuality" center on intercourse, a reproductive act by physical design? Why is masculinity the enjoyment of violation, femininity the enjoyment of being violated, and why is that the central meaning of intercourse? Why do "men love death"?[6] What is the etiology of heterosexuality in women? Is its pleasure women's stake in our own subordination?

Taken together and taken seriously, feminist inquiries into the realities of rape, battery, sexual harassment, incest, child sexual abuse, prostitution and pornography suggest a theory of the sexual mechanism – its script, learning, conditioning, developmental logos, imprinting of the microdot, its *deus ex machina*, whatever sexual process term defines sexual arousal itself. It is force. Force is sex, not just sexualized; force is the desire dynamic, not just a response to the desired object when desire's expression is frustrated. Pressure, gender socialization, withholding benefits, extending indulgences, the how-to books, the sex therapy are the soft end; the fuck, the fist, the street, the chains, the poverty are the hard end. Hostility and contempt, or arousal of master to slave; awe and vulnerability, or arousal of slave to master: these are the emotions of this sexuality's excitement. "Sadomasochism is to sex what war is to civil life: The magnificent experience,"[7] writes Susan Sontag, illustrating this ethos. "It is hostility – the desire, overt or hidden, to harm another person – that generates and enhances sexual excitement,"[8] writes Robert Stoller, speaking for his gender. Speaking for many of hers, "It seems less demeaning to give one's self, than to submit to compulsion,"[9] writes a slave of her systematic rape by her master. Looking at the data, the force in sex and the sex in force is a matter of simple empirical description – unless one accepts that force in sex is not force anymore, it is just sex; or,

unless prior aversion or sentimentality substitutes what one wants sex to be, or will condone or countenance as sex, for the force that is actually happening.

To be clear: what is sexual is what gives a man an erection. Fear does; hostility does; hatred does; the helplessness of a child or a student or an infantilized or restrained or vulnerable woman does; revulsion does; death does. Whatever it takes to make a penis shudder and stiffen with the experience of its potency is what sexuality means culturally. Violation, conventionally through penetration and intercourse, defines the paradigmatic sexual encounter. Transgression, for which boundaries must first be created, then violated, is necessary for penetration to experience itself. All this suggests that what is called sexuality is the dynamic of control by which male dominance – in forms that range from intimate to institutional, from a look to a rape – eroticizes as man and woman, as identity and pleasure, that which maintains and defines male supremacy as a political system. Male sexual desire is thereby simultaneously created and serviced (but never satisfied once and for all) while male force is romanticized, even sacralized, by submersion in sex itself. Women embrace the standards of our place in this regime as "our own" to varying degrees and in varying voices – as our affirmation of identity and right to pleasure, in order to be loved and approved and paid, in order just to make it through another day. Thus the question Freud never asked is the question that defines sexuality in a feminist perspective: What do men want? Pornography provides an answer.

Pornography permits men to have whatever they want sexually. It is their "truth about sex." From its testimony what they want is women bound, women battered, women tortured, women humiliated, women degraded and defiled, women killed. Or, to be fair to the soft core, women sexually accessible, have-able, there for them, wanting to be taken and used, with perhaps just a little light bondage.

Show me a violation of women – rape, battery, prostitution, child sexual abuse, sexual harassment – I'll show it to you made *sexuality*, made sexy, fun, and liberating of women's true nature in the pornography. Show me a specifically victimized and vulnerable group of women – Black women, Asian women, Latin women, Jewish women, pregnant women, disabled women, retarded women, poor women, old women, fat women, women in women's jobs, prostitutes, little girls – I'll show you what distinguishes pornographic genres, classified according to diverse customers' favorite degradation, as well as everpresent subthemes across genres. We also have women made into and coupled with anything considered lower than human: animals, objects, children, and (yes) other women. Show me anything women have claimed as our own – motherhood, athletics, traditional men's jobs, lesbianism, feminism – I'll show it to you made specifically sexy, made dangerous, provocative, punished, made *men's* in the pornography.

If pornography tells its consumers what they most want to hear, men desperately want women to desperately want possession and cruelty and dehumanization. Inequality itself, subjection itself, with self-determination ecstatically relinquished, is the apparent content of women's sexual desire and desirability. "The major theme of pornography as a genre," writes Andrea Dworkin, "is male power."[10] Women are in pornography to be violated and taken, men to violate and take them, either on screen or by camera or pen, on behalf of the viewer. Not that sexuality in life or in media never expresses love and affection and all that: it is only that love and affection are not what are sexualized in this society's actual sexual paradigm. Violation, transgression, intrusion on women is. The milder forms of it, possession and use, the mildest of which is visual objectification, are. Sex becomes so deeply a spectator pursuit, a spectacle, an entertainment, that observation, visual intrusion, and visual taking is a central feature

of having it. If pornography has not become sex to and from the male point of view, I want to know why the pornography industry makes at least eight billion dollars a year selling it as sex mostly to men; why it is used to teach sex to child prostitutes, recalcitrant wives and girlfriends and daughters, and to medical students; why it is nearly universally classified as a subdivision of "erotic literature"; why it is protected and defended as if it were sex itself, as if there could be, would be, no "sexuality" without it. And why a prominent sexologist fears that enforcing the views of feminists against pornography in society would make men "erotically inert wimps."[11] No pornography, no male sexuality.

Andrea Dworkin's *Pornography: Men Possessing Women* advances a feminist critique of sexuality through an inquiry into pornography. Building on her earlier identification of gender inequality as a system of social meaning, an ideology lacking basis in anything other than the social reality its power constructs and maintains (the analysis describes a *reality* that is circular), she argues that sexuality is a construct of that power, given meaning by, through, and in pornography. In this perspective, pornography is not harmless fantasy or a corrupt and confused misrepresentation of otherwise natural healthy sex, nor is it a distortion, reflection, projection, expression, representation, fantasy, or symbol of it. Through pornography, among other practices, gender inequality becomes socially real and sexual. Pornography "reveals that male pleasure is inextricably tied to victimizing, hurting, exploiting."[12] "Dominance in the male system is pleasure." Rape is "the defining paradigm of sexuality,"[13] to avoid which boys choose manhood and homophobia.[14]

Women, who are not given a choice, are objectified, or, rather, "the object is allowed to desire, if she desires to be an object." Psychology sets the proper bounds of this objectification by terming its improper excesses "fetishism,"[15] thus distinguishing the abuses of women from our uses. Dworkin shows how the process and content of the way women are defined as women, an underclass, are the process and content of their sexualization as objects for male sexual use. The mechanism is (again) force, imbued with meaning because it is the means to death and death is the ultimate sexual act. Why, one wonders at this point, is intercourse "sex" at all? In pornography, conventional intercourse is one act among many; penetration is crucial but it can be done with anything; the penis is crucial but not necessarily in the vagina. Actual pregnancy is an absolutely minor subgeneric theme, about as important in pornography as reproduction is in rape. Thematically speaking, intercourse *per se* is utterly incidental in pornography, especially when compared with force, which is utterly primary. From pornography one learns that the essential of sex is the forcible violation of women. Whatever is that and does that is sex. Everything else is secondary. The reproductive act, one senses, is considered sexual because it is considered an act of the forcible violation and defilement of the female distinctively as such, certainly not because it "is" sex *a priori*.

To be sexually objectified means having a social meaning imposed on your being that defines you as to be sexually used, according to your desired uses, and then using you that way. Doing this *is sex* in the male system. Pornography is a sexual practice of this because it exists in a social system in which sex in life is no less mediated than it is in representation. There is no irreducible essence, no "just sex." If sex is a social construct of sexism, men *have sex* with their image of a woman. Pornography creates an accessible sexual object, the possession and consumption of which is male sexuality, to be possessed and consumed as which is female sexuality. This is not because pornography depicts objectified sex, but because it creates the experience of a sexuality which is itself objectified. The appearance of choice or consent, with the attribution to inherent nature, are crucial in concealing the reality of force here – political systems typically legitimize themselves by concealing the force they are based on – so that love of violation, variously termed female masochism and consent, defines female sexuality.

A victim is "never forced, only actualized."[15] Women fake vaginal orgasms, the only "mature" sexuality, because men demand vaginal penetration and demand we enjoy it. Women whose attributes particularly fixate men – such as women with large breasts – are seen as particularly sexually desirous. Women men want, want men. Women who are raped are seen as asking for it: if some man wanted her, she must have wanted him. Men force women to become sexual objects, "that thing which causes erection, then hold themselves helpless and powerless when aroused by her."[16] Men who sexually harass, say the woman sexually harassed them. They mean that she turned them on and then turned them down. This elaborate projective system of demand characteristics – taken to pathological pinnacles like fantasizing a clitoris in our throat so that men can enjoy forced fellatio in real life, assured that women do too – is surely a delusional structure deserving of serious psychological study. Instead, it is women who resist it that are studied, seen as in need of explanation and adjustment, stigmatized as inhibited and repressed and asexual. The assumption that in matters sexual women really want what men want from us, makes male force against women in sex invisible. It makes rape sex. Women's sexual "reluctance, dislike, and frigidity," women's puritanism and prudery in the face of this sex, is "the silent rebellion of women against the force of the penis," – "an ineffective rebellion, but a rebellion nonetheless."[17]

Each structural essential of the sexuality that is male supremacist, as revealed in pornography, is professed in recent defenses of sadomasochism, described as that sexuality in which "the basic dynamic...is the power dichotomy."[18] Exposing the prohibitory underpinnings on which this violation model of the sexual depends, one advocate says, "We select the most frightening, disgusting or unacceptable activities and transmute them into pleasure." Paradigmatically, the relational dynamics of sadomasochism conform precisely to those of male dominance: the ecstacy in domination ("I like to hear someone ask for mercy or protection"); the enjoyment of inflicting psychological as well as physical torture ("I want to see the confusion, the anger, the turn-on, the helplessness"); the expression of belief in the inferior's superiority belied by the absolute contempt ("the bottom must be my superior... playing a bottom who did not demand my respect and admiration would be like eating rotten fruit"); the consumption of women through sex ("she feeds me the energy I need to dominate and abuse her"); the health rationale ("it's a healing process"); the antipuritan radical therapy justification ("I was taught to dread sex, to fight it off, to provide it under duress or in exchange for romance and security.... It is shocking and profoundly satisfying to commit this piece of rebellion, to take pleasure exactly as I want it, to exact it like tribute"); the bipolar doublethink in which the top enjoys "sexual service" whereas "the will to please is the bottom's source of pleasure." And the same bottom line of all top-down sex: "I want to be in control." The statements are quoted from a female sadist. The good news is, it isn't biological.

As pornography connects sexuality with gender in social reality, the feminist critique of pornography connects feminist work on violence against women with our inquiry into gender roles. It is not only that women are the principal targets of rape, which by conservative definition happens to almost half of all women at least once in our lives. It is not only that over a third of all women are sexually molested by older trusted male family members or friends or authority figures as an early, perhaps initiatory, interpersonal sexual encounter. It is not only that at least the same percentage are battered in homes by male intimates. It is not only that about a fifth of American women have been

or are known to be prostitutes, and a lot can't get out of it. It is not only that 85 percent of working women will be sexually harassed on the job, many physically, at some point in their working lives. All this documents the extent and terrain of abuse and the effectively unrestrained and systematic sexual aggression of one half of the population against the other half. It also suggests that it is basically allowed. But it does not by itself show that availability for this treatment defines the identity attributed to that other half of the population; or, that such treatment, all this torment and debasement, is socially considered not only rightful but enjoyable, and is in fact enjoyed by the dominant half; or, that the ability to engage in such behaviors defines the identity of that half. Now consider the content of gender roles. All the social requirements for male sexual arousal and satisfaction are identical to the gender definition of "female." All the essentials of the male gender role are also the qualities sexualized as "male" in male dominant sexuality. If gender is a social construct, and sexuality is a social construct, and the question is, *of what* is each constructed, the fact that their contents are identical – not to mention that the word "sex" refers equally to both – might be more than a coincidence. The fact is, at least as to gender, much of what is sexual about pornography is the same as what is unequal about social life.

I have argued that gender is sexual; pornography constitutes the meaning of that sexuality. Men's power over women means that the way men see women defines who women can be. Pornography is that way. Reading the data on sex roles and the documentation on sexual violence in light of each other, through the lens of the feminist critique of pornography, each element of the female gender role, the standard women are held to, now emerges as specifically sexual in the same sense in which pornography is sexual. Vulnerability means the appearance and reality of easy sexual access, access that no longer has to be forced. (In simple sex role terms, this can become concrete and almost unbelievably literal: why is *women's* distinctive apparel, cross-culturally, open between the legs? Why does women's make-up typically, cross-culturally, imitate a sex flush?) Passivity means receptivity and disabled resistance, enforced by trained physical weakness and learned helplessness. Softness means pregnability by something hard. Incompetence seeks help as vulnerability seeks shelter, inviting the embrace that becomes the invasion, trading exclusivity of access for protection from more of that same access, settling for one man over many. Domesticity nurtures the resulting progeny, proof of potency among other things, and either cultivates a blasphemous sexuality or tacitly acquiesces in having a prostitute or a daughter absorb what it is a relief no longer to have visited upon oneself. Female narcissism insures that women identify with the image of ourselves held up to us by men. The success of our lives depends upon it. Masochism insures that pleasure in violation defines women's sexuality, so women lust after self-annihilation. The infantilization of women would be seen as paedophilic; fixation on parts of women's bodies would be seen as fetishistic; the animalization of women would be seen as zoophilic; idolization of death-like vapidity would be seen as necrophilic – were they not all so normalized. The point is, the sexualized subordination of women to men *is* the sex–gender system. In a dual motion, gender becomes sexual as sexuality is gendered, and pornography is central to the process through which this occurs.

To say that pornography sexualizes gender and genders sexuality means that it is a concrete social dynamic through which gender and sexuality become functions of each other. Gender and sexuality, in this view, become two different shapes taken by the single social equation of male with dominance and female with submission. Being this as identity, acting it as role, inhabiting and presenting it as self, is the domain of gender. Enjoying it as the erotic, meaning when it elicits genital arousal, is the domain of sexuality. Inequality is what is sexualized through pornography; it is what is sexual about it. The more unequal, the more sexual. The violence against women in pornography is an extreme of gender hierarchy, the extremity of the hierarchy expressed and created through the extremity of the abuse, producing the extremity of the male sexual response. Pornography's multiple variations on and departures from the male dominant female submissive sexual/gender theme are not exceptions to it. Their capacity to stimulate sexual excitement is derived precisely from their mimicry or parody or negation of it, including prohibited reversals, thus affirming rather than undermining or qualifying it *as* the standard sexual arrangement, that in which sexuality as such inheres.

Such formal data as exists on the relationship between pornography and male sexual arousal does tend to substantiate this connection between gender hierarchy and male sexuality. Normal men viewing pornography over time in laboratory settings become more aroused to scenes of rape than to scenes of explicit but not expressly violent sex, even if (especially if?) the woman is shown as hating it. As sustained exposure perceptually inures subjects to the violent component in expressly violent sexual material, its sexual arousal value remains or increases. "On the first day, when they see women being raped and aggressed against, it bothers them. By day five, it does not bother them at all, in fact, they enjoy it."[19] Sexual material that is seen as nonviolent, by contrast, becomes less arousing over time, after which exposure to sexual violence is sexually arousing. Viewing sexual material containing express aggression against women makes normal men more willing to aggress against women. It also makes them see a woman rape victim as less human, more object like, less worthy, less injured, and more to blame for the rape. Sexually explicit material that is not seen as expressly violent has not been found to produce subsequent aggressive behavior; it also produces less sexual arousal over time.

However, sexually explicit material in which subjects see no violence nevertheless does make them see women as less than human, as good only for sex, as objects, as worthless and blameworthy when raped, and as really wanting to be raped. As to material showing violence only, it might be expected that rapists would be sexually aroused to scenes of violence against women, and they are. But many normal male subjects, too, when seeing a woman being aggressed against by a man, *perceive* the interaction to be sexual even if no sex is shown.

Male sexuality is apparently activated by violence against women and expresses itself in violence against women to a significant extent. If violence is seen as occupying the most fully achieved end of a dehumanization continuum on which objectification occupies the least express end, one question that is raised is whether some form of hierarchy – the dynamic of the entire continuum – is currently essential for male sexuality to experience itself. If so, and gender is understood to be a hierarchy, perhaps the sexes are unequal so that men can be sexually aroused; or, to put it another way, perhaps gender must be maintained as a social hierarchy so that men will be able to get erections; or, part of the male interest in keeping women down lies in the fact that it gets men up. Maybe feminists are considered castrating because equality is not sexy.

NOTES

1 K. Millett, *Sexual Politics* (New York: Doubleday, 1970).
2 P. R. Sanday, "The Socio-Cultural Context of Rape: A Cross-Cultural Study," *Journal of Social Issues*, 1981, 37 (4), p. 16. See also M. Lewin, "Unwanted Intercourse: The Difficulty of Saying no". *Psychology of Women Quarterly*, 1985, 9, 184–92.

3 A. Snitow, C. Stansell, and S. Thompson, "Introduction," *Powers of Desire: The Politics of Sexuality* (New York: Monthly Review Press, 1983), p. 9.
4 C. Vance, "Concept Paper: Toward a Politics of Sexuality," in H. Alderfer, B. Jaker, and M. Nelson, *Diary of a Conference on Sexuality*, record of the planning committee of the Conference, the Scholar and the Feminist IX: Toward a Politics of Sexuality, April 24, 1982, p. 27.
5 Ibid, n. 23 *supra*, p. 38.
6 A. Dworkin, "Why So-Called Radical Men Love and Need Pornography."
7 S. Sontag, "Fascinating Fascism," *Under the Sign of Saturn* (New York: Farrar, Straus & Giroux, 1980), p. 103.
8 R. Stoller, *Sexual Excitement: Dynamics of Erotic Life* (New York: Pantheon, 1979), p. 6.
9 Harriet Jacobs, quoted by Rennie Simson, "The Afro-American Female: The Historical Context of the Construction of Sexual Identity," in Snitow, Stansell and Thompson. *Powers of Desire*, p. 231.
10 A. Dworkin, *Pornography: Men Possessing Women* (New York: Perigee, 1981), p. 24.
11 John Money, Professor of Medical Psychology and Pediatrics, Johns Hopkins Medical Institutions, letter to Clive M. Davis, April 18, 1984.
12 A. Dworkin, *Pornography: Men Possessing Women*, p. 69.
13 Ibid, p. 136.
14 Ibid, p. 69.
15 Ibid, p. 146.
16 Ibid, p. 22.
17 Ibid, p. 56.
18 This and the rest of the quotations in this paragraph are from P. Califia, "A Secret Side of Lesbian Sexuality," *The Advocate* (San Francisco), December 27, 1979, pp. 19–21, 27–8.
19 E. Donnerstein, "Testimony," *Public Hearings on Ordinances to Add Pornography as Discrimination Against Women*, Minneapolis, Minnesota; Dec. 12 and 13, 1983, p. 36.

4 A Queer Encounter: Sociology and the Study of Sexuality

Steven Epstein

In just the past few years in much of the English-speaking world, the term *queer* – formerly a word that nice people didn't use – has escaped the bounds of quotation marks. Its growing currency reflects three roughly congruent, yet uneasily related, developments: the emergence of new repertoires of political mobilization in groups such as Queer Nation, ACT UP, and (in England) Outrage; the foothold gained by new programs of lesbian and gay studies within the academy; and – partially in response to both of the above – the rise of an intellectual enterprise explicitly calling itself queer theory.

Queer theory and sociological theory confront one another with some suspicion, and more profoundly with misrecognition. No doubt to many sociological theorists, queer theory suggests this month's trendiness, just the latest progeny spawned by the Foucauldian Revolution and adopted by overeager literary critics and proponents of cultural studies. To practitioners of queer theory, sociology perhaps is often seen as irrelevant or, at the very least, a bit stuffy. My point is not to call for some warm and fuzzy rapprochement, but to emphasize the queerness (in the so-called "original sense of the word") of this particular impasse.

In the 1960s and 1970s, sociologists (along with anthropologists and others) contributed significantly to a fundamental shift in the theorization of sexuality and homosexuality. Against naturalized conceptions of sexuality as a biological given, against Freudian models of the sexual drive, and against the Kinseyan obsession with the tabulation of behavior, sociologists asserted that sexual meanings, identities, and categories were intersubjectively negotiated social and historical products – that sexuality was, in a word, *constructed*. Though sexuality never became institutionalized as a formal subfield of sociological study, the "social constructionist" perspective on sexuality drew much of its theoretical firepower from important currents within sociology at the time, particularly symbolic interactionism and labeling theory. Without seeking to minimize the importance of other disciplines, I would suggest that neither queer theory nor lesbian and gay studies in general could be imagined in their present forms without the contributions of sociological theory.[1] Yet to some recent students of sexuality working outside sociology, the concept of social construction is assumed to have sprung, like Athena, fully formed from the head of Michel Foucault; meanwhile the analyses presented by queer theorists, expressed in their own particular, often postmodern, vocabulary, confront sociologists as an alien power, unrecognizable as anything related in any way to the product of their own labor.

Exactly how this pattern of relationships between intellectual fields (Bourdieu 1988) took shape – and how its contours relate to developments in politics and elsewhere – would be a worthwhile topic for an extended study in the sociology of knowledge. My objectives in this article are more modest: I will explore the continuities and discontinuities in the theoretical understandings of sexuality offered by contemporary queer theory and by an earlier generation of sociology. First, I describe how a durable conceptualization of the social construction of sexuality was developed on the basis of mainstream theoretical currents within the discipline, and how this framework then fueled early work in lesbian and gay studies. Next, I analyze the emergence of "queerness" as both a political and an intellectual current. With reference to some contemporary exemplars and manifestos of queer theory, I argue that there are fundamental similarities with the sociological approaches because of the reliance on the guiding principle of social construction. Yet I also analyze the break with earlier work that queer theory seeks to make by asserting, in paradoxical fashion, the *centrality of marginality* to the study of society and culture, broadly conceived. I conclude by suggesting potential ways in which sociology could usefully complement, contribute to, and challenge such a project.[2]

The Critique of the Natural

In the eyes of sociologists who turned to the study of sexuality in the 1960s and 1970s, sex was both an obvious domain of investigation and the last great frontier resistant to the sociological enterprise. "At no point is the belief in the natural and universal human more entrenched than in the study of sexuality," wrote John Gagnon and William Simon (1973: 3–4) in *Sexual Conduct*. Sexuality was "naturalized" in two senses: first, in the dominant assumption that human sexuality should be understood as a biological function rooted in evolutionary imperatives which are then translated straightforwardly into social institutions and cultural norms; second, in the acceptance of the corollary that certain expressions of sexuality are "natural," while others are therefore "unnatural." With few exceptions, sexuality had not been seen as an important topic for sociological theorization.[3] Yet even a moment's reflection suggested that the domain of sexuality – a domain of elaborate and nuanced behavior, potent and highly charged belief systems, and thickly woven connections with other arenas of social life – was deeply embedded in systems of meaning and was shaped by social institutions.

The primary obstacle to a sociological understanding of sexuality was the restricted emphasis on the mechanics of sex and its link to reproduction:

> Rarely do we turn from a consideration of the organs themselves to the sources of the meanings that are attached to them, the ways in which the physical activities of sex are learned, and the ways in which these activities are integrated into larger social scripts and social arrangements where meaning and sexual behavior come together to create sexual conduct. *(Gagnon and Simon 1973: 5)*

Central to this reinterpretation, as noted by Ken Plummer (1982) [chapter 2, this volume], another of its principals, was a certain dethroning of sexuality. Sexuality should not be placed in the "realm of the extraordinary" as something at a remove from ordinary human behavior that obeyed a logic all its own. Instead, "in any given society, at any given moment in history, people become sexual in the same way they become everything else. Without much reflection, they pick up directions from their social environment" (Gagnon, quoted in Plummer 1982: 226). If the domain of the erotic at times has come to appear as something "estranged" from everyday life – symbolized concretely by disjunctive acts, like turning off the lights, that signal the entry into some other order of experience – this is not because of anything inherent in sexuality. Rather, it has served certain purposes, in western societies, to construct "a realm in which the laws and identities governing everyday life could be suspended and the self be organized in ways that include aspects and qualities otherwise exiled or expressed through muted disguises and/or contrary uses" (Simon and Gagnon 1984: 55).

This was a complex critique with multiple explicit targets. First, the new theorists of sexuality took aim at Freud's (1962) "metapsychology" of drives, with its "hydraulic" metaphors of libido as a primal force that, when dammed up, pressed inexorably for discharge. In the Freudian (1961) view, "sexuality" and "society" stood, in a sense, opposed: libido was an individual possession, rooted in one's biological makeup, and social order was made possible only through the restriction of direct sexual expression and the sublimation of sexual energy into work.[4] By contrast, sociologists assumed that human sexuality was "always already" social in its organization and manifestations.[5] Rather than speaking of drives or instincts, Gagnon and Simon offered the metaphor of "sexual scripts" as a conceptual tool for understanding the drama of sexual conduct, thereby placing emphasis on the dimensions of learning, performance, and revision.[6]

Freudian drive theory, however, was not the only object of critique. For sociologists who believed that (to cite a recent commonplace) the most important sexual organ is the one between the ears, an equally important target was sexological research in the empiricist tradition of Kinsey.[7] Kinsey's (1953; Kinsey et al., 1948) famous studies of male and female sexuality – with his claim that homosexuality and heterosexuality lay on a continuum rather than being discrete categories, and with the noteworthy finding that 37 percent of the men in his sample reported having had at least one homosexual encounter leading to orgasm in their lifetimes – had done much to challenge conventional notions of normality and pathology in sexuality. Yet the exclusive focus on bodies, organs, and acts lost sight of the crucial question: What do these behaviors *mean* to their participants? How are such meanings generated and negotiated? (Gagnon and Simon 1973: 6). Indeed, as Plummer has noted, without attention to the subjective attribution of meaning, it becomes impossible even to tell what is "sexual" and what is not:

> When a child plays with its genitals, is this "sexual"? When a person excretes, is this sexual? When a couple are naked together, is this sexual? When a girl takes her clothes

off in public, is this sexual? ...Sexual meanings are not universal absolutes, but ambiguous and problematic categories. *(Plummer 1982: 231)*

The emphasis on meaning as an emergent product of social interaction marked the reliance of these authors upon the core concepts of symbolic interactionism (Blumer 1969): the social construction of sexuality was simply an insurance of the more general "social construction of reality" (Berger and Luckmann 1967). Related currents of Meadian sociology, such as labeling theory, were equally important in the development of the constructionist perspective. Indeed, the article often cited as the foundation stone of contemporary lesbian and gay studies, Mary McIntosh's (1968) "The Homosexual Role," explicitly applied labeling theory to the understanding of sexual categorization.

McIntosh rejected the notion that homosexuality was a "condition" which one either had or didn't have – that it was invariant in expression across societies and over time, that it could be diagnosed by the appropriate professional, and that its etiology could, in principle, be excavated by science. Just as anthropologists emphasized cultural variability in sexuality by examining different societies, McIntosh turned to historical examples to argue that modern western conceptions of sexual identity were a recent development even in those countries.[8] In her view, the search for the "causes" of homosexuality reflected a category mistake; "one might as well try to trace the aetiology of 'committee chairmanship' or 'Seventh Day Adventism' as of 'homosexuality'" (ibid: 261). Instead McIntosh claimed that "the homosexual" has come to occupy a specific social role in modern societies. Because homosexual *practices* are widespread but socially threatening, McIntosh argued, a special, stigmatized category of *individuals* is created so as to keep the rest of society pure. By this means, a "clear-cut, publicized and recognizable threshold between permissible and impermissible behaviour" (ibid) is constructed; anyone who begins to approach that threshold is immediately threatened with being deemed a full-fledged deviant.

A homosexual identity, in this view, is created not so much through homosexual activity *per se* (what labeling theorists [Lemert 1975] would call "primary deviance") as through the individual's reactions to being so labeled, and through the internalization of the imposed categorization ("secondary deviance"). Other authors writing in the "deviance" tradition conducted studies of the local organization of sexuality, focusing (for example) on boy prostitutes and their customers (Reiss 1978) or on the practitioners of anonymous sex in public restrooms (Humphreys 1978). Goffman's (1963) work on stigma, with its fine-tuned analysis of how potentially "discreditable" individuals sought to manage the disclosure of information about themselves, or sought to "pass" as normal, also influenced analysts of sexuality, who were writing at a time when alternative expressions of sexuality were still, for the most part, "in the closet."

As the emphasis shifted away from the question of etiology, analysts eschewed the related concept of sexual *orientation* and focused increasingly on how social actors negotiated the vicissitudes of forging a sexual *identity*. In these analyses, identity was conceived as standing "in a dialectical relationship with society": "Societies have histories in the course of which specific identities emerge; these histories are, however, made by men with specific identities" (Berger and Luckmann 1967: 173). Barbara Ponse (1978), in one such study, explored the manifold processes by which lesbians organized a lesbian identity – how they drew links between their gender identity, politics, and sexuality; how they negotiated the unsettling periods in which identity seemed to be in flux; and how they retrospectively reinterpreted their personal biographies to conform with present self-understandings and to achieve a consistent sense of self. The frame of identity became increasingly

salient in the study of gays and lesbians in particular. It mirrored the ascendancy of the lesbian and gay movement as a specific instance of "identity politics," one in which the personal trajectory of "coming out" was wedded to the public construction of a group identity and to a political strategy for social change (Escoffier 1985).

The publication in English of Foucault's short yet dazzling first volume of *The History of Sexuality* (1980) consolidated the emergent constructionist perspective, even as it provoked new controversies and suggested critiques of some of the sociological approaches within that perspective (see Stein 1989: 10). Whereas symbolic interactionism often risked eliding history and social structure in its emphasis on concrete social interaction, Foucault trained his attention on the big picture: sexual and erotic desire encompassed a diverse set of practices, strategies, discourses, institutions, and knowledges that were historically contingent and were played out on a dispersed field of power.

In Foucault's account, sexual categories – homosexual, heterosexual, and the like – are themselves products of particular constellations of power and knowledge. The recent historical emergence in western societies of "the homosexual" and other sexual types, Foucault claimed, reflected a shift in the tactics of power from an emphasis on sexual behavior to one on sexual personhood: in place of the opposition between natural and unnatural *acts*, sexual experience would be divided into normal and abnormal *identities*. Sexuality therefore became a central site for the construction of subjectivity.

One implication of this analysis that would attract growing attention in coming years was that the organization of an oppositional politics around the given categories of identity was a necessarily limited strategy in challenging the regime of "normalization" itself, though perhaps it was a necessary starting point, and potentially productive at that (see Weeks 1958: 244). Parallel concerns about the political emphasis on identity were voiced by writers with multiple salient identities, such as Latina and African-American women, who perceived lesbian and gay identity politics as a politics of sameness, within which other forms of diversity were suppressed (Moraga and Anzaldúa 1981; Smith 1983).

With the rise, in the early 1980s, of the lesbian and gay movement (Adam 1987) – a prominent political expression of a politics organized around sexual expression and identity – the academic study of sexuality increasingly became the study of *homosexuality*. By the early 1980s, writers in an array of academic disciplines were engaged in the production of a nascent lesbian and gay studies (Altman 1982; Blackwood 1986; Boswell 1980; Chauncey 1982–3; D'Emilio 1983; Faderman 1981; Freedman et al. 1985; Plummer 1981; Rubin 1984; Vance 1984; Weeks 1985); so were a substantial number of nonacademic "organic intellectuals," many of them affiliated (along with some of the academics) with community-based lesbian and gay history projects (Escoffier 1990).[9] As a rule, theory and empirical research adopted a constructionist perspective, derived from Meadian currents in sociology,[10] from parallel developments in anthropology, from Marxist and feminist theory, and increasingly from the work of Foucault.[11] As a rule, such work also repudiated various traditional approaches summed up under the rubric of "essentialism" – though precise definitions of these opposing terms generated considerable debate as the decade wore on.[12] Broadly speaking, whereas essentialism took for granted that all societies consist of people who are either heterosexuals or homosexuals (with perhaps some bisexuals), constructionists claimed that such typologies are sociohistorical products, not universally applicable, and deserve explanation in their own right. Also, whereas essentialism treated the self-attribution of a sexual identity as unproblematic – as simply the conscious recognition of a true, underlying "orientation" – constructionism focused attention on identity as a complex developmental outcome, the consequence of an interactive process of social labeling and self-identification.[13]

In subsequent years, with the formal establishment of lesbian and gay studies programs in a number of colleges and universities in the United States (Escoffier 1990), with the organization of annual conferences attracting more than a thousand participants to prestigious institutions such as Harvard and Yale, with the emergence of new publications such as the *Journal of the History of Sexuality* and *GLQ*, with the increasing tendency for senior faculty members to come out of the closet and for junior faculty members never to have been in, and with an outpouring of interest by undergraduate and graduate students, lesbian and gay studies, in the face of considerable opposition, has received substantial institutional legitimacy as an academic growth area.[14] Yet – despite the hegemony of social constructionism – the involvement of sociologists in the study of sexuality has diminished over the past decade, as has the visibility of explicitly sociological perspectives within lesbian and gay studies.[15]

Accounting for such a shift is beyond the scope of this article, and I can only hint at possible explanations. The relative decline in prominence of the larger theoretical currents that had given birth to the sociology of sexuality, such as symbolic interactionism and labeling theory, certainly may have made it less likely that the work of people such as Gagnon and Simon, Plummer, and McIntosh would be carried on by a younger generation of sociologists. Meanwhile new scholars, particularly in the humanities, often came to the study of sexuality directly from the work of Foucault, bypassing the social sciences entirely. Finally, as gays and lesbians underwent a dramatic conversion in status from a "deviant subculture" to a "minority group," a "community," and a "movement" (Altman 1982), the "nuts and sluts" approach of the sociology of deviance increasingly seemed misplaced, if not offensive, even to those who understood that "deviance" was not intended as a pejorative term. As Connell (1992: 737) has noted, deviance studies tended routinely to group homosexuals alongside "alcoholics, mentally disordered persons,... and systematic check forgers." Yet by the 1980s, with the rise of a quasi-ethnic self-understanding within well-defined and institutionally elaborate lesbian and gay communities, the most relevant sociological metaphors were no longer that of deviance but of ethnic group formation and social movement mobilization (Altman 1982; Epstein 1987).[16] Applied to lesbians and gay men, the sociology of deviance was the sociology of the closet. The emergence of an affirmative politics organized around sexual identity simply eluded its grasp, no matter what epicycles the deviance scholars tacked onto their theories.[17]

Deciphering Queerness

The late 1980s marked the adoption, in various circles, of the word *queer* as a new characterization of "lesbian and gay" politics and, indeed, as a potential replacement for the very terms *lesbian* and *gay* (Bérubé and Escoffier 1991; Duggan 1992; A. Stein 1992). The term was explicitly associated with the activist group Queer Nation, which sprang up in dozens of cities around the United States; more generally, it reflected new political tendencies and cultural emphases, particularly in a younger generation of migrants to the established lesbian and gay communities. It is a term rife with connotations, some of them contradictory:

- The invocation of the "Q-word" is an act of linguistic reclamation, in which a pejorative term is appropriated by the stigmatized group so as to negate the term's power to wound. (This sometimes has the effect of reinforcing an insider/outsider division: self-styled queers can use the word freely, while sympathetic straights often do so only nervously.)

- Queerness is frequently anti-assimilationist; it stands in opposition to the inclusionary project of mainstream lesbian and gay politics, with its reliance on the discourses of civil liberties and civil rights. In this sense, queerness is often a marker of one's distance from conventional norms in all facets of life, not only the sexual.

- Similarly, queerness describes a politics of provocation, one in which the limits of liberal tolerance are constantly pushed. Yet while confrontational politics (for example, a same-sex "kiss-in" held in a bar frequented by heterosexuals) may work to affirm one's difference, it also seeks to overturn conventional norms. This transformative impulse (an "outward-looking" focus) coexists with the emphasis on anti-assimilation and self-marginalization (an "inward-looking" focus).

- Use of the term also functions as a marker of generational difference within gay/lesbian/queer communities. Younger queers may speak with resentment of feeling excluded by the established "lesbian and gay" communities, while older gays and lesbians sometimes object bitterly to the use of the term *queer*, which they consider the language of the oppressor.[18]

- "Queer" speaks to the ideal of a more fully "co-sexual" politics, within which men and women participate on an equal footing. To some, the use of "queer" to describe both men and women is preferable to "gay" (which includes women in much the same way as "man" used to include women), or to "gay and lesbian" (which emphasizes gender difference).

- "Queer" offers a comprehensive way of characterizing all those whose sexuality places them in opposition to the current "normalizing regime" (Warner 1991: 16). In a more mundane sense, "queer" has become convenient shorthand as various sexual minorities have claimed territory in the space once known simply,

if misleadingly, as "the gay community."
As stated by an editor of the defunct
New York City queer magazine *Out-
week* (quoted in Duggan 1992: 21),
"When you're trying to describe the
community, and you have to list gays,
lesbians, bisexuals, drag queens, transsexuals (post-op and pre), it gets un-
wieldy. Queer says it all."

- The rise of queerness reflects a postmodern "decentering" of identity (A. Stein
1992). As formerly paradigmatic patterns of identity construction (such as
"the lesbian feminist") lose sway, they
are replaced by a loosely related hodge-
podge of lifestyle choices. Collectively
these offer more individual space for
the construction of identity, but none
provides a clear "center" for the consolidation of community.

- Queer politics are "constructionist" politics (Duggan 1992), marked by a resistance to being labeled, a suspicion of
constraining sexual categories, and a
greater appreciation for fluidity of
sexual expression.

- At times, however, queer politics also
can be "essentialist" politics: in these expressions, the new moniker is simply re-
ified into yet another identity category
understood in separatist or nationalist
terms, as the name *Queer Nation* itself
can imply (Duggan 1992).

Clearly, the burdens of connotation
would appear to be heavier than any single
word might be expected to bear. At present,
"queer" has been appropriated to describe a
considerable range of political projects as
well as individual and collective identities.
Yet the meaning of the term is complicated
further by its simultaneous employment by
academics. Sometimes "queer" is put forward simply as the new and concise coinage:
"gay studies," or "lesbian and gay studies,"
or "bisexual, lesbian, and gay studies," or
"multicultural, bisexual, lesbian, and gay
studies" should – for convenience, if for no
other reason – be named "queer studies."[19]

Sometimes, however, the invocation of
"queer" signals important shifts in theoretical emphasis. In this reading, said Teresa de
Lauretis, one of the organizers of a "queer
theory" conference at UC-Santa Cruz,
"queer" is intended "to mark a certain critical distance from the . . . by now established
and often convenient, formula" of "lesbian
and gay" (de Lauretis 1991: iv).

Although many works are emblematic of
the "queer turn" (Butler 1990, 1993; Cohen
1991; de Lauretis 1991; Dollimore 1993;
Edelman 1989, 1992; Goldberg 1991;
Miller 1991; A. Parker 1991; Patton 1993;
Sedgwick 1993; Seidman 1993; Terry 1991;
Warner 1993), Eve Kosofsky Sedgwick's
Epistemology of the Closet (1990) is perhaps most often cited as a canonical text
(even though the term *queer theory* does
not appear there). Basically a critical reinterpretation of specific works of English literature, the book opens with a strong claim:

> *Epistemology of the Closet* proposes that
> many of the major nodes of thought and
> knowledge in twentieth-century Western
> culture as a whole are structured – indeed,
> fractured – by a chronic, now endemic
> crisis of homo/heterosexual definition, in-
> dicatively male, dating from the end of the
> nineteenth century. (Ibid: 1)

Furthermore (as if, perhaps, that weren't
bold enough for an opening paragraph):

> The book will argue that an understanding
> of virtually any aspect of modern Western
> culture must be, not merely incomplete,
> but damaged in its central substance to
> the degree that it does not incorporate a
> critical analysis of modern homo/hetero-
> sexual definition. (Ibid)

All too often, studies of gays and lesbians, or
of other "sexual minorities," have been cast
as studies of "marginal" experience. By contrast, an "epistemology of the closet" seeks
to analyze how various ways of construing
sexual marginality shape the self-understanding of the culture as a whole. For

example, Sedgwick argues, the very notion of the "closet" (as well as the metaphor of "coming out of the closet," now somewhat widely diffused) reflects the influence of the homosexual/heterosexual dichotomy on broader perceptions of public and private, or secrecy and disclosure (ibid: 72). In this sense, as Michael Warner (1993: xiv) suggests, "Sedgwick's work has shown that there are specifically modern forms of association and of power than can be seen properly only from the vantage of antihomophobic inquiry."

Though Sedgwick rejects many of the terms of the so-called "essentialist–constructionist debate" (Sedgwick 1990: 40–1), her work in an important sense continues the tradition of the social constructionist perspective. "Homosexuality" and "heterosexuality" do not describe transhistorical cultural forms, despite the universality of specific sexual practices. Rather, such practices come to *mean* very different things in a society which insists that each individual, just as he or she possesses a gender, also must necessarily occupy one or the other category of sexual orientation. "It was this new development," which Sedgwick and other authors (Halperin 1990) locate around the turn of the century in western societies, "that left no space in the culture exempt from the potent incoherences of homo/heterosexual definition" (Sedgwick 1990: 2).

In constructing a genealogy of the homosexual/heterosexual divide, Sedgwick's work draws on Foucault. In general, the mark of Foucault is broadly apparent in works of this kind – in their emphasis on power and "normalization," in their understanding of the constitutive role of discourse in the construction of subjectivity, in their poststructuralist critique of conceptions of coherent selfhood (Butler 1990, 1993), and in their postmodern suspicion of identity as a totalizing construct that subsumes difference (Cohen 1991). Whereas queer *politics* often seem divided in their approach to identity politics – at times subverting popular notions of stable identities, at times fashion-

ing a new queer identity with their own enforced boundaries – queer *theory* is more consistent on this point. Indeed, the terrain of queerness provides a meeting point for those who come to the critique of identity from many different directions: those who believe that identity politics mute internal differences within the group along racial, class, gender, or other lines of cleavage (Montero 1993; Mort no date; Seidman 1991); those who believe that subjectivities are always multiple (Ferguson 1991; Seidman 1991); and those who are simply suspicious of categorization as inherently constraining. The point (at least as I read it) is not to stop studying identity formation, or even to abandon all forms of identity politics, but rather to maintain identity and difference in productive tension, and to rely on notions of identity and identity politics for their strategic utility while remaining vigilant against reification.[20]

In subject matter, queer studies emphasize literary works, texts, and artistic and cultural forms; in analytical technique, deconstructionist and psychoanalytic approaches loom large. Yet however marked these tendencies, none of them is necessarily definitive of queer theory, whereas the assertion of the centrality of marginality is the pivotal queer move. Just as queer *politics* emphasize outsiderness as a way of constructing opposition to the regime of normalization as a whole, so queer *theory* analyzes putatively marginal experience, but in order to expose the deeper contours of the whole society and the mechanisms of its functioning.

In some sense, this idea is not altogether new: a presumed goal of the sociology of deviance, for example, was to study the processes by which people become labeled deviant, so as to reveal, by contrast, the ideological construction of "the normal." In practice, however, sociologists have tended to relegate the study of "sexual minorities" to the analytical sidelines rather than treating such study as a window onto a larger world of power, meaning, and social organization. The challenge that queer theory poses to sociological investigation is precisely in the strong claim that no facet of social life is fully comprehensible without an examination of how sexual meanings intersect with it. In no way does it disqualify such a claim to recognize it as serving a certain strategic function within the intellectual "field" (Bourdieu 1988): queer theorists are seeking to situate their work as an "obligatory passage point" (Latour 1987) through which other academics must pass if they want to fully understand their own particular subject matters. In this sense as well, queer theory, like queer politics, is locating itself simultaneously both on the margins and at the center.

Perhaps the clearest analogy, as the editors of the *Lesbian and Gay Studies Reader* note (Abelove, Barale, and Halperin 1993b: xv–xvi), is with feminist theory and women's studies programs; they have sought to argue that gender is not a "separate sphere," but rather is partially constitutive of other institutions such as the economy and the state. The goal therefore should not be to restrict concerns with gender to a bounded domain called "sociology of gender," but to introduce gendered understandings into sociological scrutiny across the board. The challenge for queer studies will be to demonstrate the links concretely in the case of sexuality – to identify the precise ways in which sexual meanings, categories, and identities are woven into the fabric of society and help give shape to diverse institutions, practices, and beliefs.

A Return to Sociology?

It should go without saying – but unfortunately needs to be said – that there is considerable space within such an enterprise for the perspectives and approaches of disciplines such as sociology, and indeed substantial need for sociological contributions, both theoretical and empirical. On the one hand, by tracing their lineages back no further than Sedgwick and Foucault, practitioners

of queer theory risk reinventing the wheel. On the other hand, to the extent that queer studies focus overwhelmingly on discourses and texts, crucial questions about social structure, political organization, and historical context are investigated in only partial ways. As noted by Steven Seidman (1993: 132, 135), the poststructuralist reduction of complex cultural codes into "binary signifying figures" in much of queer theory, and the corresponding tendency to abstract discourses from their institutional contexts, verge unhappily on a kind of "textual idealism."

For sociologists, the potentially fruitful lines of investigation are manifold:

Sexual meanings and social categorizations. How are complex, often internally contradictory, and ambiguous systems of sexual meaning constructed and challenged in different cultures (e.g., R. Parker 1991: 172–3)? What is the relation between "macro" patterns of social organization and "micro" negotiations of sexual definition? Which institutions are central to the reproduction or contestation of sexual codes and beliefs? How do sexual belief systems and patterns of sexual conduct and identity formation intersect with other markers of social difference and systems of oppression, such as class, race, and gender (e.g., Almaguer 1993; Connell 1992; Connell, Davis, and Dowsett 1993; Gutiérrez 1991; Mumford 1992)?[21]

Social movements. That so many different and even contradictory meanings have consolidated around the word *queer* is itself suggestive of the richness of queer politics as a case study of the dynamics of collective action within "new social movements." Recent studies of social movements, such as the articles in Morris and Mueller (1992), have emphasized the critical importance of collective identity as something whose existence cannot simply be assumed by the analyst of a social movement.[22] Yet queer politics raise perplexing questions about the relation between identity and action. How are politics possible when actors insist upon the fluidity of identity and resist the very notion of categorization (Gamson no date; Seidman 1993)? Still other questions about movements are suggested by queer politics: How do queer politics differ from the gay rights politics of the late 1970s and early 1980s, the gay liberationist politics of the early 1970s (Duberman 1993), and the "homophile" politics of the 1960s (D'Emilio 1983)? How do these different models relate to the political strategies of other groups? In what ways are the unique rhetorical and dramaturgical styles of queer activist groups influencing other "new social movements" (Kauffman 1993)? How have AIDS activists managed so effectively to link an expressive politics of disruptive street theater (Gamson 1989) with an institutional politics of consensus building with medical experts, pharmaceutical companies, and government officials (Epstein 1991b; no date)?

Other social institutions. How does the state intervene in sexual politics, and how are such politics constitutive of state institutions (e.g., Connell 1990)? How is scientific knowledge about sexual identity constructed by experts? What is the role of the mass media in the dissemination of sexual meanings? How do gender and sexuality structure the shop-floor relations between workers and management, and how do such relations in turn affect patterns of gender and sexuality (Salzinger no date)?

Though such questions may (and should) be addressed from the vantage point of many fields, they are fundamentally sociological questions, bound up with important theoretical currents and ignored to the detriment of the profession. Unfortunately, as Warner has noted, "it remains depressingly easy to speak of 'social theory' and have in mind whole debates...in which sexuality figures only peripherally or not at all" (Warner 1991: 4). One can identify occasional, recent exceptions (such as Giddens 1992), but the basic point remains. Although sociologists will not and should not go about queer studies in precisely the same ways as others have done it, the recent and impressive flurry of activity

under that rubric still might provide a needed wake-up call.

NOTES

1 One can also trace a parallel, and equally influential, lineage in anthropology, beginning perhaps with the cultural relativist perspective of Margaret Mead (1935) and proceeding through more recent work on the "sex/gender system" (Rubin 1975) and on the cultural construction of gender (Ortner and Whitehead 1981) and sexuality (Blackwood 1986; Caplan 1987; Lancaster 1988; Newton 1988; R. Parker 1991).

"Origins stories" are always problematic. My point here is neither to say that "it all started with sociology" nor to argue that sociology's early role entitles it to special respect. Rather, I seek to highlight the curious case of a discipline whose contributions have been forgotten, both within and without.

2 I will confine my analysis almost exclusively to intellectual and political currents in the United States.

3 In Parsons's work, for example, questions of sexuality tended to be subsumed within the study of sex roles and the institution of the family.

4 To be sure, the formal Freudian "metapsychology" was never followed widely outside psychoanalytic circles. Yet in watered-down form, the notion of sex as an overwhelming drive demanding release (a notion that owes much to Freud, even if it preceded him) has permeated popular culture in many western societies. It has also found expression in radical social theory, such as Marcuse (1966).

5 In this sense, the constructionist sociology of sexuality would be far more compatible with some particular post-Freudian strands of psychoanalytic theory. Elsewhere I explore the unappreciated congruences between the sociology of sexuality and the "object relations" strand of psychoanalytic theory (Epstein 1991a).

6 In a useful update to their scripting theory, Simon and Gagnon (1984: 53) have proposed that scripting proceeds along three interconnected levels: *cultural scenarios,* "the instructional guides that exist at the level of collective life"; *interpersonal scripts,*

which the actor must invent and elaborate when there is a "lack of congruence between the abstract scenario and the concrete situation"; and *intrapsychic scripts*, the "internal rehearsals" that become necessary whenever interpersonal scripting becomes so complex that actors become cognizant of, and focused upon, their own script writing in dealing with others and others' script writing in dealing with them.

7   Gagnon and Simon themselves had both been researchers at the Kinsey Institute.

8   McIntosh's important invocation of historical evidence set her apart from most other labeling or deviance theorists (thanks to Kevin Mumford for pointing this out to me).

9   For additional important works from this period, see the articles collected in Duberman, Vicinus, and Chauncey, and, more generally, the articles published in the *Journal of Homosexuality*.

10   For example, Weeks (1977: 239) identifies the main influences on his thinking as Plummer, McIntosh, and Gagnon and Simon; in later essays, he testifies to the importance of Foucault. D'Emilio (1983: 4) cites the same writers with a few additions, such as Jonathan Katz and Estelle Freedman.

11   Historians, however, often criticized Foucault for what they considered to be inaccurate accounts. They also took issue with his nominalist overemphasis on the role of professionals and their normalizing discourses in bringing sexual categories into being. Historians argued, for example, that homosexual subcultures and even certain forms of homosexual identity already had come into existence in large western cities well before the sexological classification of "homosexuality" was created.

Gay and lesbian history (which was particularly important during this period) was also influenced greatly by Thompsonian notions of social history, which stressed writing a "history from below" (thanks to Chris Waters for emphasizing this point to me).

12   See, for example, Epstein (1987) and the other articles reprinted in E. Stein (1992). The so-called "essentialist–constructionist debate" mirrored a profound confusion both within gay and lesbian communities and in the general public about the ontological status of homosexuality – a confusion that seems only to have heightened in the 1990s. It is noteworthy that of the two great debates about gays and lesbians which have been played out recently in the mass media in the United States, one of them – the discourse on the biological or genetic roots of homosexuality – seeks to fix and stabilize sexual categories as discrete states of being, while the other – the brouhaha concerning "gays in the military" – betrays intense fears of the "contagious" nature of homoerotic desire. Thus, although Seidman (1993: 105) argues that "the arcane polemics between constructionists and essentialists has evolved into a sterile metaphysical debate devoid of moral and political import," the underlying concerns at stake in this debate continue to spark passions and reveal deep-seated social anxieties.

13   These critiques of sexual essentialism paralleled constructionist critiques of gender and racial essentialism; see, for example, Chodorow (1979) and Omi and Winant (1986).

14   The recent publication by Routledge of a 600-page *Lesbian and Gay Studies Reader* (Abelove, Barale, and Halperin 1993a) is both suggestive of the kinds of work being produced and indicative of the further institutionalization of the project by means of constructing a canon. On homophobic challenges to lesbian and gay studies, see Nussbaum (1992). On the question of the relation between lesbian and gay studies programs and the grassroots movement, see Escoffier (1990) and Duggan (1992).

15   There are, of course, any number of noteworthy individual exceptions; see, for example, Connell, Davis, and Dowsett (1993), Greenberg (1988), Seidman (1988, 1992), A. Stein (1992), and Taylor and Whittier (1992). A glance at the programs of the annual Lesbian, Bisexual and Gay Studies conferences, however, would easily demonstrate the overwhelming predominance of scholars in the humanities and the relative paucity of contributions from the social sciences.

AIDS prevention is one area where sociological (and anthropological) constructionism has gained a certain niche, both as a theoretical critique of behaviorist or narrowly interpersonal models of safe sex education and as the grounding for the development of concrete health education strategies that acknowledge the problematic, variable, and culturally specific relations between behavior and identity (Connell, Davis, and Dowsett 1993; Davies et al. 1992; Parker, Herdt, and Carballo 1991).

For a (now outdated) review of sociological contributions to the study of homosexuality, see Risman and Schwartz (1988).

16 At least some segments of the profession continue to miss the point, as demonstrated by the *American Sociological Review* in its publishing of this very article by Connell in 1992. Though his article (on the dynamics of gender formation among Australian gay men) owed little to the sociology of deviance beyond his brief critique of it, the journal's cover advertised "Three Studies of Deviant Careers" and listed Connell's article, an article on criminals, and an article on misconduct by lawyers.

Similarly, a 1989 sociology textbook (Preston and Smith 1989) was blasted by the Gay and Lesbian Alliance Against Defamation (GLAAD 1992: 3), a media watchdog group, for "[placing] its information on homosexuality between 'prostitution' and 'alcoholism' under the heading of 'Deviance.'" "Sociology textbooks need to present a more comprehensive and balanced picture of research on homosexuality," the organization advised. (On the treatment of homosexuality and the "hegemony of heterosexuality" in introductory sociology textbooks, also see Phillips 1991.)

17 I have in mind Kitsuse's (1980: 9) attempt to broaden the scope of deviance studies so as to encompass identity politics. Kitsuse conceptualized "tertiary deviance" as "the deviant's confrontation, assessment, and rejection of the negative identity imbedded in secondary deviation, and the transformation of that identity into a positive and viable self-conception."

18 On the heated debates in US "lesbian and gay" communities over whether to identify as "queer," see Gamson (no date).

19 This move, however, remains tentative and controversial. Indeed, the editors of *The Lesbian and Gay Studies Reader* noted in their introduction to the volume (Abelove, Barale, and Halperin 1993b: xvii): "It was difficult to decide what to title this anthology. We have reluctantly chosen not to speak here and in our title of 'queer studies,' despite our own attachment to the term, because we wish to acknowledge the force of current usage."

20 For different approaches to the maintenance of such a "productive tension" in identity politics, see Clarke (1991), Gamson (no date), and Seidman (1993). For the view that "the temporary totalization performed by identity categories is a necessary error," see Butler (1993: 230).

21 Although queer theorists have emphasized the analytical irreducibility of different forms of oppression (Butler 1993: 18–19; Sedgwick 1990: 31–5), in practice there has been inadequate attention to the interweavings of race and class with sexuality, as a glance at the table of contents of the *Lesbian and Gay Studies Reader* (Abelove, Barale, and Halperin 1993a) would suggest.

22 On collective identity in lesbian politics, see Taylor and Whittier (1992) and A. Stein (1992). I am indebted to Josh Gamson for discussion of the points in this paragraph.

REFERENCES

Abelove, Henry, Michèle Aina Barale, and David M. Halperin, eds. 1993a. *The Lesbian and Gay Studies Reader*. New York: Routledge.

——— 1993b. "Introduction." Pp. xv–xviii in *The Lesbian and Gay Studies Reader*, edited by Henry Abelove, Michèle Aina Barale, and David M. Halperin. New York: Routledge.

Adam, Barry D. 1987. *The Rise of a Gay and Lesbian Movement*. Boston: Twayne.

Almaguer, Tomás. 1993. "Chicano Men: A Cartography of Homosexual Identity and Behavior." Pp. 255–73 in *The Lesbian and Gay Studies Reader*, edited by Henry Abelove, Michèle Aina Barale, and David M. Halperin. New York: Routledge.

Altman, Dennis. 1982. *The Homosexualization of America*. Boston: Beacon.

Berger, Peter L. and Thomas Luckmann. 1967. *The Social Construction of Reality*. New York: Anchor.

Bérubé, Allan and Jeffrey Escoffier. 1991. "Queer/Nation." *Out/Look* 11: 14–16.

Blackwood, Evelyn, ed. 1986. *The Many Faces of Homosexuality: Anthropological Approaches to Homosexual Behavior.* New York: Harrington Park Press.

Blumer, Herbert. 1969. *Symbolic Interactionism: Perspective and Method.* Berkeley: University of California Press.

Boswell, John. 1980. *Christianity, Social Tolerance, and Homosexuality.* Chicago: University of Chicago Press.

Bourdieu, Pierre. 1988. *Homo Academicus,* translated by Peter Collier. Stanford, CA: Stanford University Press.

Butler, Judith. 1990. *Gender Trouble: Feminism and the Subversion of Identity.* New York: Routledge.

—— 1993. *Bodies That Matter: On the Discursive Limits of "Sex."* New York: Routledge.

Caplan, Pat, ed. 1987. *The Cultural Construction of Sexuality.* London: Tavistock.

Chauncey, George, Jr. 1982–3. "From Sexual Inversion to Homosexuality: Medicine and the Changing Conceptualization of Female Deviance." *Salmagundi* 58/59: 114–46.

Chodorow, Nancy. 1979. "Feminism and Difference: Gender, Relation, and Difference in Psychoanalytic Perspective." *Socialist Review* 46: 51–69.

Clarke, Stuart Alan. 1991. "Fear of a Black Planet: Race, Identity Politics, and Common Sense." *Socialist Review* 21: 37–59.

Cohen, Ed. 1991. "Why are 'We'? Gay 'Identity' as Political (E)motion (A Theoretical Rumination)." Pp. 71–92 in *Inside/Out: Lesbian Theories, Gay Theories,* edited by Diana Fuss. New York: Routledge.

Connell, R. W. 1990. "The State, Gender, and Sexual Politics." *Theory and Society* 19: 507–44.

—— 1992. "A Very Straight Gay: Masculinity, Homosexual Experience, and the Dynamics of Gender." *American Sociological Review* 57: 735–51.

Connell, R. W., M. D. Davis, and G. W. Dowsett. 1993. "A Bastard of a Life: Homosexual Desire and Practice among Men in Working-Class Milieux." *Australian and New Zealand Journal of Sociology* 29: 112–35.

Davies, P. M., P. Weatherburn, A. J. Hunt, and F. C. I. Hickson, 1992. "The Sexual Behavior of Young Gay Men in England and Wales." *AIDS Care – Psychosocial and Socio-Medical Aspects of AIDS/HIV* 4: 259–72.

de Lauretis, Teresa. 1991. "Queer Theory and Lesbian and Gay Sexualities: An Introduction." *Differences: A Journal of Feminist Cultural Studies* 3: iii–xviii.

D'Emilio, John. 1983. *Sexual Politics, Sexual Communities: The Making of a Homosexual Minority in the United States, 1940–1970.* Chicago: University of Chicago Press.

Dollimore, Jonathan. 1983. "Different Desires: Subjectivity and Transgression in Wilde and Gide." Pp. 624–41 in *The Lesbian and Gay Studies Reader,* edited by Henry Abelove, Michèle Aina Barale, and David M. Halperin. New York: Routledge.

Duberman, Martin. 1993. *Stonewall.* New York: Dutton.

Duberman, Martin, Martha Vicinus, and George Chauncey Jr., eds. 1989. *Hidden from History: Reclaiming the Gay and Lesbian Past.* New York: Meridian.

Duggan, Lisa. 1992. "Making It Perfectly Queer." *Socialist Review* 22: 11–31.

Edelman, Lee. 1989. "The Plague of Discourse: Politics, Literary Theory, and AIDS." *South Atlantic Quarterly* 88: 301–17.

—— 1992. "Tearooms and Sympathy, or the Epistemology of the Water Closet." Pp. 263–84 in *Nationalisms & Sexualities,* edited by Andrew Parker, Mary Russo, Doris Summer, and Patricia Yaeger. New York: Routledge.

Epstein, Steven. 1987. "Gay Politics, Ethnic Identity: The Limits of Social Constructionism." *Socialist Review* 93/94: 9–54.

—— 1991a. "Sexuality and Identity: The Contribution of Object Relations Theory to a Constructionist Sociology." *Theory and Society* 20: 825–73.

—— 1991b. "Democratic Science? AIDS Activism and the Contested Construction of Knowledge." *Socialist Review* 21: 35–64.

—— No date. "Impure Science: AIDS, Activism, and the Politics of Knowledge." Doctoral dissertation, University of California at Berkeley.

Escoffier, Jeffrey. 1985. "The Politics of Gay Identity." *Socialist Review* 82/83: 119–53.

—— 1990. "Inside the Ivory Closet: The Challenges Facing Lesbian & Gay Studies." *Out/Look* 10: 40–8.

Faderman, Lillian. 1981. *Surpassing the Love of Men.* New York: Morrow.

Ferguson, Ann. 1991. "Lesbianism, Feminism, and Empowerment in Nicaragua." *Socialist Review* 21: 75–97.

Foucault, Michel. 1980. *The History of Sexuality*, vol. 1, translated by Robert Hurley. New York: Vintage.

Freedman, Estelle, Barbara C. Gelphi, Susan L. Johnson, and Kathleen M. Weston, eds. 1985. *The Lesbian Issue: Essays from Signs*. Chicago: University of Chicago Press.

Freud, Sigmund. 1961. *Civilization and Its Discontents*. New York: Norton.

—— 1962. *Three Essays on the Theory of Sexuality*. New York: Basic Books.

Gagnon, John H. and William Simon. 1973. *Sexual Conduct: The Social Sources of Human Sexuality*. Chicago: Aldine.

Gamson, Joshua. 1989. "Silence, Death, and the Invisible Enemy: AIDS Activism and Social Movement 'Newness.'" *Social Problems* 36: 351–67.

—— No date. "Must Identity Movements Self-Destruct? A Queer Dilemma." Unpublished manuscript.

Gay and Lesbian Alliance Against Defamation (GLAAD). 1992. *Update*. San Francisco: GLAAD.

Giddens, Anthony. 1992. *The Transformation of Intimacy: Sexuality, Love and Eroticism in Modern Societies*. Stanford, CA: Stanford University Press.

Goffman, Erving. 1963. *Stigma: Notes on the Management of Spoiled Identity*. Englewood Cliffs, NJ: Prentice-Hall.

Goldberg, Jonathan. 1991. "Sodomy in the New World: Anthropologies Old and New." *Social Text* 29: 46–56.

Greenberg, David F. 1988. *The Construction of Homosexuality*. Chicago: University of Chicago Press.

Gutiérrez, Ramón A. 1991. *When Jesus Came, the Corn Mothers Went Away: Marriage, Sexuality, and Power in New Mexico, 1500–1846*. Stanford, CA: Stanford University Press.

Halperin, David. 1990. *One Hundred Years of Homosexuality*. New York: Routledge.

Humphreys, Laud. 1978. "A Typology of Tearoom Participants." Pp. 270–82 in *Deviance: The Interactionist Perspective*, 3rd edn., edited by Earl Rubington and Martin S. Weinberg. New York: Macmillan.

Kauffman, L. A. 1993. "Is Queerness Dead?" *SF Weekly*, April 21.

Kinsey, Alfred C. 1953. *Sexual Behavior in the Human Female*. Philadelphia: Saunders.

Kinsey, Alfred C., Wardell B. Pomeroy, and Clyde E. Martin. 1948. *Sexual Behavior in the Human Male*. Philadelphia: Saunders.

Kitsuse, John I. 1980. "Coming Out All Over: Deviants and the Politics of Social Problems." *Social Problems* 28: 1–13.

Lancaster, Roger. 1988. "Subject Honor and Object Shame: The Construction of Male Homosexuality and Stigma in Nicaragua." *Ethnology* 27: 111–25.

Latour, Bruno. 1987. *Science in Action: How to Follow Scientists and Engineers through Society*. Cambridge, MA: Harvard University Press.

Lemert, Edwin M. 1975. "Primary and Secondary Deviation." Pp. 167–72 in *Theories of Deviance*, edited by Stuart H. Traub and Craig B. Little. Itasca, IL: Peacock.

McIntosh, Mary. 1968. "The Homosexual Role." *Social Problems* 17: 262–70.

Marcuse, Herbert. 1966. *Eros and Civilization*. Boston: Beacon.

Mead, Margaret. 1935. *Sex and Temperament in Three Primitive Societies*. New York: New American Library.

Miller, D. A. 1991. "Anal Rope." Pp. 119–41 in *Inside/Out: Lesbian Theories, Gay Theories*, edited by Diana Fuss. New York: Routledge.

Montero, Oscar. 1993. "Before the Parade Passes By: Latino Queers and National Identity." *Radical America* 24: 15–26.

Moraga, Cherríe and Gloria Amzaldúa, eds. 1981. *This Bridge Called My Back: Writings by Radical Women of Color*. Watertown, MA: Persephone Press.

Morris, Aldon D. and Carol McClurg Mueller, eds. 1992. *Frontiers in Social Movement Theory*. New Haven, CT: Yale University Press.

Mort, Frank. No date. "Essentialism Revisited? Identity Politics and Late Twentieth Century Discourses of Homosexuality." Unpublished manuscript.

Mumford, Kevin J. 1992. "Lost Manhood Found: Male Sexual Importance and Victorian Culture in the United States." *Journal of the History of Sexuality* 3: 33–57.

Newton, Esther. 1988. "Of Yams, Grinders, and Gays: The Anthropology of Homosexuality." *Out/Look* 1: 28–37.

Nussbaum, Martha. 1992. "The Softness of Reason." *New Republic*, July 13, pp. 26–35.

Omi, Michael and Howard Winant. 1986. *Racial Formation in the United States: From the 1960s to the 1980s.* New York: Routledge.

Ortner, Sherry B. and Harriet Whitehead, eds. 1981. *Sexual Meanings: The Cultural Construction of Gender and Sexuality.* Cambridge, UK: Cambridge University Press.

Parker, Andrew. 1991. "Unthinking Sex: Marx, Engels and the Scene of Writing." *Social Text* 29: 28–45.

Parker, Richard G., Gilbert Herdt, and Manuel Carballo. 1991. "Sexual Culture, HIV Transmission, and AIDS Research." *Journal of Sex Research* 28: 77–98.

Parker, Richard S. 1991. *Bodies, Pleasures and Passions: Sexual Culture in Contemporary Brazil.* Boston: Beacon.

Patton, Cindy. 1993. "Tremble, Hetero Swine!" Pp. 143–77 in *Fear of a Queer Planet: Queer Politics and Social Theory*, edited by Michael Warner. Minneapolis: University of Minnesota Press.

Phillips, Sarah Rengel. 1991. "The Hegemony of Heterosexuality: A Study of Introductory Texts." *Teaching Sociology* 19: 454–63.

Plummer, Ken, ed. 1981. *The Making of the Modern Homosexual.* London: Hutchinson.

—— 1982. "Symbolic Interactionism and Sexual Conduct: An Emergent Perspective." Pp. 223–41 in *Human Sexual Relations: Towards a Redefinition of Sexual Politics*, edited by Mike Brake. New York: Pantheon.

Ponse, Barbara. 1978. *Identities in the Lesbian World: The Social Construction of Self.* Westport. CT: Greenwood.

Preston, Frederick W. and Ronald W. Smith. 1989. *Sociology: A Contemporary Approach.* New York: Allyn & Bacon.

Reiss, Albert J., Jr. 1978. "The Social Integration of Queers and Peers." Pp. 436–47 in *Deviance: The Interactionist Perspective*, 3rd edn., edited by Earl Rubington and Martin S. Weinberg. New York: Macmillan.

Risman, Barbara and Pepper Schwartz. 1988. "Sociological Research on Male and Female Homosexuality." *Annual Review of Sociology* 14: 125–47.

Rubin, Gayle. 1975. "The Traffic in Women: Notes on the 'Political Economy' of Sex." Pp. 157–210 in *Toward an Anthropology of Women*, edited by Rayna Reiter. New York: Monthly Review Press.

—— 1984. "Thinking Sex: Notes for a Radical Theory of the Politics of Sexuality." Pp. 267–319 in *Pleasure and Danger: Exploring Female Sexuality*, edited by Carole S. Vance. Boston: Routledge.

Salzinger, Leslie. No date. "Producing Gender, Engendering Production." Unpublished manuscript.

Sedgwick, Eve Kosofsky. 1990. *Epistemology of the Closet.* Berkeley: University of California Press.

—— 1993. *Tendencies.* Durham, NC: Duke University Press.

Seidman, Steven. 1988. "Transfiguring Sexual Identity: AIDS and the Contemporary Construction of Homosexuality." *Social Text* 19/20: 187–205.

—— 1991. "Postmodern Anxiety: The Politics of Epistemology." *Sociological Theory* 9: 180–90.

—— 1992. *Embattled Eros: Sexual Politics and Ethics in Contemporary America.* New York: Routledge.

—— 1993. "Identity and Politics in 'Postmodern' Gay Culture: Some Historical and Conceptual Notes." Pp. 105–42 in *Fear of a Queer Planet: Queer Politics and Social Theory*, edited by Michael Warner. Minneapolis: University of Minnesota Press.

Simon, William and John H. Gagnon. 1984. "Sexual Scripts." *Society* 22: 53–60.

Smith, Barbara, ed. 1983. *Home Girls: A Black Feminist Anthology.* New York: Kitchen Table/Women of Color Press.

Stein, Arlene. 1989. "Three Models of Sexuality: Drives, Identities, and Practices." *Sociological Theory* 7: 1–13.

—— 1992. "Sisters and Queers: The Decentering of Lesbian Feminism." *Socialist Review* 22: 33–55.

Stein, Edward, ed. 1992. *Forms of Desire: Sexual Orientation and the Social Constructionist Controversy.* New York: Routledge.

Taylor, Verta and Nancy E. Whittier, 1992. "Collective Identity in Social Movement Communities: Lesbian Feminist Mobilization." Pp. 104–29 in *Frontiers in Social Movement Theory*, edited by Aldon D. Morris and Carol McClurg Mueller. New Haven, CT: Yale University Press.

Terry, Jennifer. 1991. "Theorizing Deviant Historiography." *Differences: A Journal of Feminist Cultural Studies* 3: 55–74.

Vance, Carole S., ed. 1984. *Pleasure and Danger: Exploring Female Sexuality.* Boston: Routledge.

Warner, Michael. 1991. "Introduction: Fear of a Queer Planet." *Social Text* 29: 3–17.

—— 1993. "Introduction." pp. vii–xxxi in *Fear of a Queer Planet: Queer Politics and Social Theory*, edited by Michael Warner. Minneapolis: University of Minnesota Press.

Weeks, Jeffrey. 1977. *Coming Out: Homosexual Politics in Britain, from the Nineteenth Century to the Present.* London: Quartet.

—— 1985. *Sexuality and Its Discontents: Meanings, Myths & Modern Sexualities.* London: Routledge.

Part II

Gender and Sexual Identities

Sexuality is bound up with gender identity. People's sense of who they are sexually is very much connected, in complicated and varied ways, with their understandings of masculinity and femininity. Dominant conceptions of sexuality imagine sexuality in terms of binaries: male versus female, heterosexual versus homosexual. Deviations from "proper" gender are sexualized, leading to the popular notion of the "effeminate gay man" and the "masculine lesbian." Such individuals certainly exist, but the relationship between gender and sexuality is much more complicated than binary conceptions would suggest. A repressed homosexuality lurks beneath the hypermasculine exterior of many heterosexual men, suggests Susan Faludi, drawing upon Freudian thinking. Roger Lancaster's study of Nicaraguan men shows, too, that the boundary between homosexuality and heterosexuality is often blurry; in many cultures gender is a much more salient identity than sexuality. Evelyn Blackwood's article about Native American sexuality gives us a glimpse of a time when women's gender non-conformity was an institutionalized part of tribal life. Kath Weston brings us up to date, examining the diverse gender practices of lesbian-identified women today.

5 The Naked Citadel

Susan Faludi

Along the edges of the quad, in the gutters, the freshman cadets were squaring their corners. The "knobs," as they are called for their nearly hairless doorknob pates, aren't allowed to step on the lawn of the broad parade ground, which is trimmed close, as if to match their shorn heads. Keeping off the grass is one of many prohibitions that obtain at The Citadel, a public military college on Charleston's Ashley River. Another is the rule that so many of the cadets say brought them to this Moorish-style, gated campus: Girls keep out.

The campus has a dreamy, flattened quality, with its primary colors, checkerboard courtyards, and storybook-castle barracks. It feels more like an architect's rendering of a campus – almost preternaturally clean, orderly, antiseptic – than the messy real thing. I stood at the far end of the quad, at the academic hall's front steps, and watched the cadets make their herky-jerky perpendicular turns as they drew closer for the first day of class. They walked by stiffly, their faces heat-blotched and vulnerable, and as they passed each in turn shifted his eyes downward. I followed one line of boys into a classroom, a Western Civ class – except, of course, they weren't really boys at all. These were college men, manly recruits to an elite military college whose virile exploits were mythicized in bestselling novels by Calder Willingham and Pat Conroy, both Citadel alumni. So why did I expect their voices to crack when they spoke for the first time? Partly, it was the grammar-schoolish taking of attendance, compulsory at The Citadel. Multiple absences can lead to "tours," hours of marching back and forth in the courtyard with a pinless rifle over one shoulder; or to "cons," confinement to one's room.

But mostly it was the young men themselves, with their doughy faces and twitching limbs, who gave me the urge to babysit. Despite their enrollment in a college long considered "the big bad macho school" (as a former ROTC commander, Major General Robert E. Wagner, once put it), the cadets lacked the swagger and knowingness of big men on campus. They perched tentatively on their chairs, their hands arranged in a dutiful clasp on their desktops, as if they were expecting a ruler slap to the knuckles. A few dared to glance over at the female visitor, but whenever they made eye contact they averted their gaze and color stained their cheeks.

"As many of you probably know," their teacher said, "this was almost the day the first woman joined The Citadel." The cadets continued to study their polished shoes. "How do you, in fact, feel about whether women should be allowed to attend?"

Silence reigned. Maybe the cadets felt the question put them in an awkward spot. Not only was their teacher in favor of admitting women to The Citadel's Corps of Cadets, the teacher *was* a woman. Indeed, Professor Jane Bishop seemed to be in the strange situation of calling in an air strike on her own position. It was the first day of fall classes in the 1993–4 academic year at The Citadel, and she was broaching the question of the hour. But this incongruity wasn't limited to her classroom. From the moment I stepped onto the school's campus, I had been struck by an unexpected circumstance: though an all-male institution – an institution, moreover, whose singular mission was "making men" – The Citadel was by no means free of women. Female teachers were improving cadets' minds, female administrators were keeping their records, and an all-female (and all-black) staff served the meals in the mess hall. There was also the fact that female students made up 77 percent of the enrollment of the evening school, and many other female students attended summer school with the cadets. What about them? Of course, summer school and evening school aren't part of the military college proper. Cadets don't attend the evening school; and as Major Rick Mill, The Citadel's public-relations director, notes, those cadets who attend the summer school "aren't wearing their uniforms."

Today they were, and so was their teacher. All permanent instructors, regardless of their sex (about 15 percent are women), wear uniforms as part of their required affiliation with a largely ceremonial outfit once known as the South Carolina Unorganized Militia, and still called by the unfortunate acronym SCUM. Bishop wore hers with what seemed like a deliberate air of disarray.

The cadets' uniforms were considerably tidier – testament to the efficacy of the famous cadet shirt tuck, a maneuver akin to hospital-corners bedmaking and so exacting a cadet cannot perform it without assistance. Even so, the gray cadet uniform, with the big black stripe down the side of the pants and the nametag above the left breast, is the sort more often seen on high-school band members than on fighting soldiers.

"Remember," Bishop prodded them, "speech is free in the classroom."

At last, a cadet unclasped and raised a hand. "Well, I'd have no problem with her in the day program, but she can't join the Corps."

"She," as everyone there knew, was Shannon Faulkner, the woman who had challenged the school's hundred-and-fifty-year-old all-male policy by omitting reference to her sex from her application and winning acceptance to the Corps of Cadets earlier that year – acceptance that was rescinded once the administrators discovered their error. Faulkner's attempt to gain entrance then shifted from the admissions office to the courts. She was allowed under court order to attend day classes during the spring semester of 1994, the first woman to do so. On July 22, a United States District Court ruled that The Citadel must admit Faulkner into the Corps of Cadets proper; three weeks later, the Fourth United States Circuit Court of Appeals granted The Citadel a stay pending appeal.

Yet why shouldn't she be permitted into the Corps, Bishop pressed. One of her students recited the fitness requirement – forty-five pushups and fifty-five sit-ups in two-minute sets, and a two-mile run in sixteen minutes. But the administration made passing the fitness test a requirement for graduation only *after* Shannon Faulkner filed suit. An alumnus recounted in court that many upperclassmen he knew who had failed the test skipped the punitive morning run and "sat around and ate doughnuts." Another of Bishop's students cited the shaved-head rule. But this, too, seemed a minor point. A woman cadet could conceivably get a buzz cut. Sinéad O'Connor had done it, Bishop pointed out, without undue injury to her career. And, anyway, after freshman year the men no longer get their heads shaved. Other deprivations of freshman year were invoked: having to "brace" on demand – that is, assume a stance in which a knob stands very erect and tucks in his chin until it puckers up like a rooster's wattle – and having to greet every upperclassman's bellowed command and rebuke with "Sir, yes sir!" or "Sir, no sir!" or "Sir, no excuse sir!" But women, obviously, aren't incapable of obeisance; one might even say they have a long history of it.

Weighing heaviest on the cadets' minds, it turned out, was the preservation of the all-male communal bathroom. The sharing of the stall-less showers and stall-less toilets is "at the heart of the Citadel experience," according to more than one cadet. The men bathe as a group; they walk to the shower down the open galleries, in full view of the courtyard below, and do so, one cadet said, in "nothing but our bathrobes" or "even without any clothes." Another cadet said, "I know it sounds trivial, but all of us in one shower, it's like we're all one, we're all the same, and – I don't know – you feel like you're exposed, but you feel safe. You know these guys are going to be your friends for life." His voice trailed off. "I just can't explain it, but when they take that away, it's over. This place will be ruined."

"If women come here, they'll have to put up window shades in all the rooms," a cadet said. "Think of all the windows in the barracks. That could be eight thousand, nine thousand dollars. You've got to look at the costs."

At the end of the hour, the cadets filed out and resumed their double-time jog along the gutters – and their place in the "fourth-class system." This "system" is a nine-month regimen of small and large indignities intended to "strip" each young recruit of his original identity and remold him into the "Whole Man," a vaguely defined ideal, half Christian soldier, half Dale Carnegie junior executive. As a knob explained it to me, "We're all suffering together. It's how we bond." Another knob said, "It's a strange analogy, but it's almost like a POW camp."

One cadet dawdled, glancing nervously around, then sidled up to me. He spoke in a near whisper, and what he had to say had nothing to do with lavatory etiquette or military tradition. "The great majority of the guys here are very misogynistic," he said. "All they talk about is how girls are pigs and sluts."

I asked him to explain at greater length. He agonized. "I have to keep quiet," he said, but he finally agreed to meet me later, in an out-of-the-way spot on the upper floor of the student-activities center. He rejoined his classmates with that distinctive knob march, "the march of the puppets," as a professor described it to me later. It was a gait caused in some cases, I was told, by the most conscientious cadets' efforts to keep their shirts perfectly straight with the help of garters – one end of the garter clipped to the shirttail, the other end to the socks.

As I waited for my cadet informant, I decided to kill an hour on the vast parade ground, where the Corps of Cadets marches every Friday afternoon in full dress uniforms, and where, according to an old school brochure, "manhood meets mastery." This is a paramilitary display, not a military one. Despite the regalia and officer ranks, and despite its notoriously fierce military discipline ("To discipline is to teach" is the motto emblazoned on one of the school's books of regulations), this is a military academy by self-designation only. Unlike the federal service academies – West Point, Annapolis, the Air Force Academy – The Citadel has no connection with the United States Armed Forces (other than its ROTC program and its employment of some active and retired officers). Its grounds are adorned with dusty and decommissioned military hardware – a Sherman tank, a submarine's torpedo-loading hatch, a Phantom jet named Annette, two cannons named Betsy and Lizzie. In most cases, the weapons, including the pinless M-14s the cadets carry, are inoperative. The mouths of the various cannons are stuffed with cement – all except those of Betsy and Lizzie, which are fired during parades, but carefully aimed high enough so that their powder does not dust the crenellated barracks. The over-all effect is that of a theme park for post-Cold War kids.

The hokeyness and childlike innocence of the scene – the stage-prop artillery, the toy-soldier clip-clop of the cadets as they squared their corners – were endearing, in a Lost Boys sort of way, and I strolled over to the student-activities center for my rendezvous with my cadet informant thinking that The Citadel's version of martial culture was not so menacing after all. The cadet was not in evidence. I spent the next thirty minutes prowling the halls, which were lined with portraits of stern-faced "generals" (I couldn't tell which were United States military and which were SCUM), and examining ads on the student bulletin board for items like "Save the Males" bumper stickers. I tried to reach the cadet's room by phone –

women aren't admitted into the barracks – but he was not there. A bit thoughtlessly, I left a message with an upperclassman and headed toward town.

At my hotel, the receptionist handed me a message from my vanished cadet. "Please, don't ever call here again!" it read. The phone clerk peered at me curiously. "Sorry about that exclamation mark, but he seemed quite distraught," she said. "His voice was shaking."

What brought a young man to an all-male preserve in the last decade of the twentieth century, anyway? What was going on outside the academy gates that impelled thousands of boys, Southern and Northern alike (about a fifth of its student body of about two thousand are Yankees), to seek refuge behind a pair of corroding cannons?

"The forces arrayed against us," an attorney named Robert Patterson declared in a February, 1994, court hearing, consider his military academy to be "some big-game animal to be hunted down, tracked, caught, badgered, and killed so that some lawyer or some organization can go back up and hang a trophy on a wall in an office." Patterson was defending not The Citadel but the Virginia Military Institute, which is the only other public military academy in the United States that does not admit women, and which was involved in a similar sex-discrimination suit. (Three months later, Patterson, a VMI alumnus, returned to court to defend The Citadel.) "I will say this, Your Honor," he went on. "This quest by these people constitutes the longest and most expensive publicly financed safari in the annals of big-game hunting."

The Citadel's administration has fought the female hunters with a legal arsenal of nearly a million dollars and with dour, tight-lipped determination, which has only increased with time. The Citadel's president, Claudius Elmer (Bud) Watts III, who is a retired Air Force lieutenant general and a second-generation Citadel alumnus, views Shannon Faulkner's legal efforts as an enemy invasion, placing his young troops

"under attack." "The Citadel is in this to the end," he pronounced at a press conference held in the spring of 1994 on the parade ground, his feet planted between Betsy and Lizzie, his uniform decked with ribbons, and his chin tucked in, as is his custom, as if in a permanent brace position.

Later, in his living room, surrounded by coffee-table books on football, Watts told me firmly, "You cannot put a male and a female on that same playing field," though he couldn't say exactly why. Of his own Citadel years he conceded, "I've not the foggiest notion if it would have been different" had women attended. He was just glad there were no female cadets then; otherwise, he said, the cadets would have faced "a different form of intimidation – not wanting to be embarrassed in front of a girl."

Faulkner has been opposed not only by many Citadel staff and alumni but – at least, publicly – by almost all the current cadets. They say that her presence in the Corps would absolutely destroy a basic quality of their experience as Citadel men. She would be what one Citadel defender called in his court deposition "a toxic kind of virus." Tellingly, even before the United States District Court judge enjoined The Citadel to admit Faulkner to the Corps of Cadets for the fall of 1994, and before the injunction was set aside, the administration announced its selection of her living quarters: the infirmary.

Cadets cite a number of reasons that women would have a deleterious effect on the Corps of Cadets, and the reasons are repeated so often as to be easily predictable, though their expression can be novel. "Studies show – I can't cite them, but studies show that males learn better when females aren't there," one cadet explained to me (a curious sentiment at a school where a knob motto about grades is "2.0 and Go"). "If a girl was here, I'd be concerned not to look foolish. If you're a shy student, you won't be as inhibited." Another cadet said, "See, you don't have to impress them here. You're free." From a third: "Where does it end?

Will we have unisex bathrooms?" But among the reasons most frequently heard for repelling Faulkner at the gate is this: "She would be destroying a long and proud tradition."

The masculine traditions of West Point and Annapolis were also closely guarded by their male denizens, but the resistance to women joining their ranks was nowhere near as fierce and filled with doomsday rhetoric as The Citadel's efforts to repel feminine interlopers. At Norwich University, a private military college in Northfield, Vermont, that voluntarily opened its barracks to women in 1974, two years before the federal service academies, the administration actually made an effort to recruit and accommodate women. "There was no storm of protest," said a Norwich spokeswoman, Judy Clauson. But then, "it was a time when there were so many rules that were being loosened." The Air Force veteran Linnea Westberg, who was one of the eight women in Norwich's first coed class, recalled, of her integration into its corps, that "95 percent of the male cadets were fine, especially the freshmen, who didn't know any different." Westberg said she was baffled by the intensity of The Citadel's opposition to women in its corps. "It's hard for me to believe it's still an issue."

"The Citadel is a living museum to the way things used to be," John Drennan, a Citadel graduate and a public defender in Charleston, told me one day during The Citadel's legal proceedings. But how, exactly, did things use to be? The cadets and the alumni of the school, along with those protesting against its exclusionary policies, envision its military tradition above all. And The Citadel once did have a strong military aspect: it was formed as an arsenal in 1822 in response to a slave revolt purportedly planned by the freed Charleston slave Denmark Vesey, which, though it was foiled, aroused widespread alarm in the region. Yet twenty years later the guns and the gold braid became mere adornment as The Citadel turned into an industrial school of

domestic and practical skills. Union troops shut down The Citadel at the end of the Civil War, but it was reinvented and reopened in 1882, after the Union's Reconstruction officials had thoroughly stripped the school of all military muscle. Its new mission was to reinvigorate the masculinity of the South by showing its men how to compete with the business and industrial skills of the Yankee carperbaggers, who were believed to be much better prepared than the sons of Dixie to enter the Darwinian fray of modern commerce. John Peyre Thomas, who ran The Citadel from 1882 to 1885, wrote of the need to teach spoiled plantation boys the rudiments of self-reliance. "It must be admitted that the institution of African slavery, in many respects, affected injuriously the white youth of the South," he wrote. "Reared from infancy to manhood with servants at his command to bring his water, brush his shoes, saddle his horse, and, in fine, to minister to his personal wants, the average Southern boy grew up in some points of character dependent, and lazy, and inefficient. He was found, too, wanting in those habits of order and system that come from the necessity, in man, to economize time and labor."

What makes the school's Reconstruction-era mission important is that in so many ways it remains current; the masculine and industrial culture of our age and that of the conquered South may have more in common than we care to imagine. Again, we are at a psychic and economic crisis point for manhood. And, again, the gun issues hide the butter issues: the bombast masks a deep insecurity about employment and usefulness in a world where gentleman soldiers are an anachronism and a graduate with gentleman's C's may find himself busing tables at Wendy's.

The uncertain prospects of Citadel graduates are worsened by military downsizing. Only about a third of recent graduates entered the military – a figure that has fallen steeply since the mid-seventies, when half of The Citadel's graduating class routinely took a service commission. News of Shannon Faulkner's court case competed in the Charleston *Post & Courier* with news of the shutting down of the local shipyards and decommissionings from the local military installations.

The night before the closing arguments in Faulkner's suit, I had dinner at the on-campus home of Philippe and Linda Ross, who have both taught at The Citadel. Philippe, the head of the Biology Department, had just completed his first round of moonlighting as a "retraining" instructor at the Charleston Naval Shipyard. He had been prepping laid-off nuclear engineers to enter one of the few growth industries in the area – toxic-waste management. Facing a room filled with desperate men each day had been a dispiriting experience, he said. He recalled the plea of a middle-aged engineer, thrust out of the service after twenty-six years: "All I want to do is work." Linda Ross, who was then teaching psychology at The Citadel, looked across the table with a pained expression. "That whole idea that if a young man went to college he could make a decent living and buy a house, and maybe even a boat, just does not hold anymore," she said softly. "There's a Citadel graduate working as a cashier at the grocery store. And the one thing these young men felt they could count on was that if things got hard they could always go into the military. No more. And they are bitter and angry."

In the fall of 1991, Michael Lake, a freshman, decided to leave The Citadel. He had undergone weeks of bruising encounters with upperclassmen – encounters that included being knocked down with a rifle butt and beaten in the dark by a pack of cadets. Incidents of hazing became so violent that, in a school where publicly criticizing the alma mater is virtually an act of treason, several athletes told their stories to *Sports Illustrated*. Much of the violence was aimed at star freshman athletes: a member of the cycling team was forced to hang by his fingers over a sword poised two inches below his testicles; a placekicker had his

head dunked in water twenty times until he was unconscious; a linebacker was forced to swallow his chewing tobacco and tormented until, he said later, "I was unable even to speak clearly in my classes." It was a time when the Churchill Society, a literary club reportedly containing a white-supremacist faction, was organized on campus. It was a time when the local chapter of the National Association for the Advancement of Colored People urged a federal investigation into a pair of racial incidents on the school's campus: the appearance of a noose over the bed of a black freshman who had earlier refused to sing "Dixie," and the shooting and wounding of a black cadet by a sniper who was never identified. (A few years earlier, upperclassmen wearing Klan-like costumes left a charred paper cross in the room of a black cadet.) And it was a time when a leader of the Junior Sword Drill, a unit of cadet sword-bearers, leaped off a five-foot dresser onto the head of a prostrate cadet, then left him in a pool of blood in a barracks hall. According to one cadet, a lacrosse-team member returning from an away game at three in the morning stumbled upon the victim's unconscious body, his face split open, jaw and nose broken, mouth a jack-o'-lantern of missing teeth.

One night, at about 2 a.m., high-ranking cadets trapped a raccoon in the barracks and began to stab it with a knife. Beau Turner, a student at the school, was awakened by the young men's yelling. "My roommate and I went out there to try and stop it," Turner recalled, "but we were too late." Accounts of the episode vary. In a widely circulated version (which was referred to in a faculty member's testimony), the cadets chanted, "Kill the bitch! Kill the bitch!" as they tortured the raccoon to death.

In October, 1993, two upperclassmen burst into the room of two freshmen and reportedly kneed them in the genitals, pulled out some of their chest hair, and beat them up. They were arrested on charges of assault and battery, and agreed to a program of counselling and community service, which would wipe clean their records. They withdrew from The Citadel, in lieu of expulsion, the spokesman Major Rick Mill said.

One of the offending cadets, Adrian Baer, told me that he and the other accused sophomore, Jeremy Leckie, did indeed come back from drinking, burst into the knobs' room after 10 p.m., and "repeatedly struck them in the chest and stomach" and bruised one of them in the face, but he denied having kicked them in the groin and yanked out chest hair. He said that what he did was common procedure – and no different from the "motivational" treatment he had received as a knob at the hands of a senior who came into *his* room. They entered the freshmen's room, Baer explained, because they viewed one of the occupants as "a problem" knob who "needed some extra motivation." Baer elaborated: "His pinkie on his right hand wouldn't completely close when he went to salute. He caught a lot of heat for that, of course, because it's a military school; it's important to salute properly." The strict rule that upperclassmen not fraternize with knobs, he said, meant that they couldn't simply counsel the freshman kindly. "If we just sat down and said, 'Listen, guy, we have a little problem,' that would be fraternization. And more important, knobs would lose respect for upperclassmen. It's a lot of denial on the part of officials at The Citadel about hazing," Baer said. "They don't want to believe it goes on." Leckie's father, Timothy Rinaldi, said that while he believed his son "was definitely in the wrong," he felt The Citadel's fourth-class system bred such behavior. "They help build this monster," he said of The Citadel, "the monster gets up off the table and starts walking through town – and now Dr. Frankenstein wants to shoot it."

Needless to say, not every cadet embraces the climate of cruelty; the nocturnal maulings likely frighten as many cadets as they enthrall. But the group mentality that pervades The Citadel assures that any desire on the part of a cadet to speak out about the mounting violence will usually be squelched

by the threat of ostracism and shame. While group rule typifies many institutions, military and civilian, that place a premium on conformity, the power and authoritarianism of the peer group at The Citadel is exceptional, because the college gives a handful of older students leave to "govern" the others as they see fit. (A lone officer provided by the military, who sleeps in a wing off one of the dorms, seldom interferes.) This is a situation that, over the years, an occasional school official has challenged, without success. A former assistant commandant for discipline, Army Lieutenant Colonel T. Nugent Courvoisie, recalled that he "begged" the school's president back in the sixties to place more military officers – and ones who were more mature – in the barracks, but his appeals went unheeded. Discipline and punishment in the dorms is in the hands of the student-run regimental command, and ascendancy in this hierarchy is not always predicated on compassion for one's fellow-man. In consequence, the tyranny of the few buys the silence of the many.

This unofficial pact of silence could, of course, be challenged by the Citadel officialdom. On a number of occasions over the past three decades – most recently when some particularly brutal incidents found their way into the media – The Citadel has commissioned "studies." But when the administration does go on the offensive, its animus is primarily directed not at miscreant cadets but at the "unfair" media, which are "victimizing" the institution by publicizing the bad behavior of its boys.

In recent years, enough bad news leaked out locally to become a public-relations nightmare, and the school appointed a committee of Citadel loyalists to assess the situation. Even the loyalists concluded, in a January, 1992, report, that the practice of physical abuse of freshmen, along with food and sleep deprivation, had got out of hand. As a result, Major Mill told me, The Citadel ordered upperclassmen to stop using push-ups as a "disciplinary tool" on individual cadets. "That was the most important one" of the reforms prompted by the report, Mill said. Other reforms were adopted: for example, freshmen would no longer be compelled to deliver mail to upperclassmen after their evening study hours, thus reducing opportunities for hazing; freshmen would – at least officially – no longer be compelled to "brace" in the mess hall. At the same time, the report declared that it "wholeheartedly endorses the concept of the fourth-class system," which it called "essential to the attainment of college objectives and the development of the Citadel man."

Institutions that boast of their insularity, whether convents or military academies, are commonly pictured in the public imagination as static, unchanging abstractions, isolated from the ebb and flow of current events. But these edifices are rarely as otherworldly as their guardians might wish; indeed, in the case of The Citadel, its bricked-off culture has functioned more as a barometer of national anxieties than as a garrison against them. The militaristic tendencies within the Corps seem to vary inversely with the esteem in which the American soldier is held in the larger society. In times when the nation has been caught up in a socially acceptable conflict, one in which its soldiers return as heroes greeted by tickertape parades, The Citadel has loosened its militaristic harness, or even removed it altogether. Thus, during perhaps the most acceptable war in American history, the Second World War, the fourth-class system of knob humiliation was all but discontinued. Upperclassmen couldn't even order a knob to brace. The changes began largely in response to the demands of the real military for soldiers they could use in a modern war. "The War Department and the Navy Department were asking ROTC to do less drilling, more calculus," Jamie Moore, a professor of history at The Citadel and a former member of the United States Army's Historical Advisory Committee, told me. "The Citadel dismantled its fourth-class system because it was getting in the way of their military training." The changes didn't seem to interfere with the school's production of Whole Men; on the contrary, an extraordinary percentage of The Citadel's most distinguished graduates come from these years, among them United States Senator Ernest (Fritz) Hollings; Alvah Chapman, Jr., the former chief executive of Knight-Ridder; and South Carolina's former governor John C. West.

The kinder, gentler culture of the Second World War-era Citadel survived well into the next decade. Although a new fourth-class system was soon established, it remained relatively benign. "We didn't have the yelling we have today," Colonel Harvey Dick, class of '53 and now a member of The Citadel's governing body, recalled. "They didn't even shave the freshmen's heads."

The postwar years also brought the admission of women to the summer program, and without the hand-wringing provoked by Shannon Faulkner's application. "WOMEN INVADE CITADEL CLASSES FIRST TIME IN SCHOOLS HISTORY," the Charleston daily noted back on page 16 of its June 21, 1949, edition. "Most male students took the advent of the 'amazons' in their stride," the paper reported cheerfully. "Only the younger ones seemed at all uneasy. Professors and instructors were downright glad to see women in their classes."

The Vietnam War, needless to say, did not inspire the same mood of relaxation on campus. "The fourth-class system was very physical," Wallace West, the admissions director, who was an undergraduate at The Citadel during the Vietnam War years, said. "When I was there, there was no true emphasis on academics, or on positive leadership. It was who could be worked to physical exhaustion." Alumni from those years recounted being beaten with sticks, coat hangers, and rifle butts. That was, of course, the era that inspired Pat Conroy's novel *The Lords of Discipline*, a tale of horrific hazing, directed with special virulence against the school's first African-American cadet. "They just tortured us," Conroy recalled from his home, in Beaufort, South Carolina. "It taught me the exact kind of man I didn't want to be," he added.

In 1968, the administration appointed a committee to investigate the violence. The committee issued a report that, like its 1992 successor, concluded "there have been significant and extensive abuses to the [fourth-class] system." And, with its strong recommendation that hazing result in expulsion, the report seemed to promise a more pacific future on campus.

In the past decade and a half, however, the record of violence and cruelty at The Citadel has attracted increasing notice, even as the armed forces have been racked by downsizing and scandal. The Citadel president during much of this era, Major General James A. Grimsley, Jr., declined to discuss this or any other aspect of campus life during his tenure. "I don't do interviews," he said. "Thank you for calling, young lady." He then hung up. Others have been less reticent.

Thirteen years before Vice-Admiral James B. Stockdale consented to be Ross Perot's running mate, he took on what turned out be an even more thankless task: fighting brutal forms of hazing at The Citadel. In 1979, Stockdale, who had graduated from Annapolis, was chosen to be The Citadel's president because of his status as a genuine military hero: he had survived eight years as a POW in Vietnam. This hero failed to see the point of manufactured adversity. In an afterword to the book *In Love and War*, a collaboration between Stockdale and his wife, Sybil, he wrote that there was "something mean and out of control about the regime I had just inherited."

On his first day in the president's office, Stockdale opened a desk drawer and discovered "what turned out to be Pandora's box," he wrote. "From the top down, what was written on the papers I took out of the desk drawers – and conversations with some of their authors – was enough to break anybody's heart." Among them was a letter from an infuriated father who wanted to

know what had happened to his son "to change him from a levelheaded, optimistic, aggressive individual to a fatigued, irrational, confused and bitter one." He also found copies of memos from The Citadel's staff physician complaining repeatedly of (as Stockdale recalled) "excessive hospitalization" – such as the case of a knob who had suffered intestinal bleeding and was later brought back to the infirmary, having been exercised to unconsciousness. Stockdale sought to reform the system, but he was stymied at every turn. He clashed with The Citadel's powerful Board of Visitors, an eleven-member committee of alumni that sets school policy. The Board of Visitors overruled his expulsion of a senior cadet who had reportedly been threatening freshmen with a pistol. A year into his presidency, Stockdale submitted his resignation. After he left, the board reinstated an avenging friend of the senior cadet who, according to Stockdale, had attempted to break into his house one evening. (The then chairman of the Board of Visitors maintains that the cadet was drunk and looking for the barracks.)

"They thought they were helping people into manhood," Stockdale recalled, from a more serene post, in Palo Alto, California, where he is a scholar at Stanford's Hoover Institution on War, Revolution, and Peace. "But they had no idea what that meant – or who they were."

After Watts became president, in 1989, some faculty members began to observe a creeping militarization imposed by the administration upon the Corps's already drill-heavy regimen. Four special military days were added to the academic year. At the beginning of one semester, President Watts held a faculty meeting in a room above the mess hall. "Watts had these soldiers standing around the room with their hands behind them," Gardel Feurtado, a political-science professor and one of only two African-American professors, recalled. Watts, he said, lectured the faculty for about three hours. "He didn't talk about academics or educational goals. He just talked about cadets' training, and he showed us a film of it," Feurtado told me. According to Feurtado, Watts told the faculty to line up in groups behind the soldiers for a tour of the barracks. "I said, 'Enough of this,' and I started to walk out. And this soldier stopped me and said, 'Where do you think you're going, sir?' and I said, 'You do realize that I am not in the military?'" Feurtado had to push by him to leave.

When Michael Lake looked back on the abuse he suffered during his abbreviated knob year of '91, he could now see before him, like the emergence of invisible ink on what appeared to be a blank piece of paper, the faint outlines of another struggle. What he saw was a submerged gender battle, a bitter but definitely fixed contest between the sexes, concealed from view by the fact that men played both parts. The beaten knobs were the women, "stripped" and humiliated, and the predatory upperclassmen were the men, who bullied and pillaged. If they couldn't recreate a male-dominant society in the real world, they could restage the drama by casting male knobs in all the subservient feminine roles.

"They called you a 'pussy' all the time," Lake recalled. "Or a 'fucking little girl.'" It started the very first day they had their heads shaved, when the upperclassmen stood around and taunted, "Oh, you going to get your little girlie locks cut off?" When they learned that Lake would be playing soccer that fall, their first response was "What is that, a girl's sport?" Another former cadet said that he had withstood "continual abuse," until he found himself thinking about jumping out the fourth-story window of the barracks – and quit. He reported an experience similar to Lake's. Virtually every taunt equated him with a woman: whenever he showed fear, they would say, "You look like you're having an abortion," or "Are you menstruating?" The knobs even experienced a version of domestic violence. The upperclassmen, this cadet recalled, "would go out and get drunk and

they would come home and haze, and you just hoped they didn't come into your room."

"According to the Citadel creed of the cadet," Lake said, "women are objects, they're things that you can do with whatever you want to." In order to maintain this world view, the campus has to be free of women whose status might challenge it – a policy that, of course, is rarely enunciated. The acknowledged policy is that women are to be kept at a distance so they can be "respected" as ladies. Several months before Faulkner's lawsuit came to trial, I was sitting in the less than Spartan air-conditioned quarters of the senior regimental commander, Norman Doucet, the highest-ranking cadet, who commanded the barracks. Doucet, who was to be The Citadel's star witness at the Faulkner trial, was explaining to me how excluding women had enhanced his gentlemanly perception of the opposite sex. "The absence of women makes us understand them better," Doucet said. "In an aesthetic kind of way, we appreciate them more – because they are not there."

Women at less of a remove fare less well. In The Citadel's great chain of being, the "waitees" – as many students call that all-black, all-female mess-hall staff – rate as the bottom link. Some upperclassmen have patted them on their rear ends, tried to trip them as they pass the tables, or hurled food at their retreating backs. Cadets have summoned them with "Come here, bitch," or addressed one who dropped a plate or forgot an order as "you stupid whore." The pages of the *Brigadier*, the school's newspaper, bear witness to the cadets' contempt for these women. Gary Brown, now the editor-in-chief of the *Brigadier*, once advised fellow-cadets to beware of "waitee" food contamination – "the germ filled hands, the hair follicles, and other unknown horrors." Not only was he dismayed by "wavy little follicles in my food" but he found the women insufficiently obedient. "Duty is certainly not the sublimest word in the Waitee language," he wrote. In a letter to the editor, Jason S. Pausman, class of

'94, urged fellow-cadets to demand "waitees without chronic diseases that involve sneezing, coughing or wiping of body parts.... The reality is simple, we CANNOT sit by and let the waitees of this school control us."

Some women faculty members report similarly resentful responses to their presence, despite – or because of – their positions of authority. Angry messages on a professor's door are one tactic. When Jane Bishop recently posted on her office door a photocopy of a *New York Times* editorial supporting women's admission to the Corps of Cadets, she found it annotated with heated rejoinders in a matter of days. "Dr. Bishop, you are a prime example of why women should not be allowed here," one scribble read. Another comment: "Women will destroy the world."

The Citadel men's approach to women seems to toggle between extremes of gentility and fury. "First, they will be charming to the women to get their way," Linda Ross said. "But if that doesn't work they don't know any other way. So then they will get angry." It's a pattern that is particularly evident in some cadets' reaction to younger faculty women.

December Green joined The Citadel's Political Science Department in 1988, the first woman that the department had ever hired for a tenure-track position. She was twenty-six and attractive – "someone the cadets might fantasize about," a colleague recalled. They were less enchanted, however, by her left-leaning politics. She soon found herself getting obscene phone calls in the middle of the night. Then obscenities began appearing on her office door. "Pussy" is the one that sticks in her mind.

Though Green's work at The Citadel was highly praised – she received an award for teaching, research, and service – she said that no one in the administration tried to stop her when she left in 1992, in despair over her inability to contain the cadets' fury. Nor, apparently, had anyone responded to her appeals to correct the situation. "A lot of

terrible things happened to me there," Green, who is now teaching in Ohio, said, reluctant to revisit them. The hostility ranged from glowering group stares in the hallway to death threats – some of which appeared on the cadets' teacher-evaluation forms. The male faculty offered little support. Green recalls the department chairman instructing her to "be more maternal toward the students" when a cadet lodged a complaint about her (she had challenged his essay in which he praised apartheid). And a professor who stood by one day while his students harassed her and another woman informed her, "You get what you provoke."

Green said she eventually had to get an unlisted number to stop the obscene calls, and also moved, in part out of fear of the cadets' vengeance. The last straw, however, came when she submitted the written threats she had received to her chairman, who passed them on to the dean of undergraduate studies, in hopes of remedial action. The dean, she said, did nothing for some months, then, after she inquired, said he had "misplaced" the offending documents.

The dean, Colonel Isaac (Spike) Metts, Jr., told me he didn't recall saying he misplaced the documents but "I might have said it's not on my desk at that time and I don't know where it is." He added that Green was a "very valuable" professor. "I don't know what else we could've done," Metts said. In any event, soon after submitting the threatening notes to the dean Green gave up. At her exit interview, she recalled, President Watts told her he didn't understand why she had been upset by the cadet harassment. "It's just a bunch of kid stuff," another male colleague said. (Lewis Spearman, the assistant to the president, said that, because of federal privacy law, Watts would have no response to Green's version of events.)

The remaining category of women that cadets have to deal with is "the dates," as the young women they socialize with are generally called. (There are no wives; Citadel policy forbids cadets to marry, and violators are expelled.) In some respects, these young women are the greatest challenge to the cadet's sense of gender hierarchy. While the "waitees" can be cast as household servants and the female teachers as surrogate mothers, the dates are more difficult to place. Young women their age are often college students, with the same aspirations as the cadets, or even greater ones. The cadets deal with young women's rising ambitions in a number of ways. One is simply to date high-school girls, an option selected by a number of cadets. Another strategy, facilitated by The Citadel, is to cast the young women who are invited on campus into the homecoming-queen mold. The college holds a Miss Citadel contest each year, and Anne Poole, whose husband, Roger, is the vice-president of academic affairs and the dean of the college, has sat on the judging panel. Each cadet company elects a young woman mascot from a photograph competition, and their faces appear in the yearbook.

The school also sends its young men to an in-house etiquette-training seminar, in which the Citadel "hostess," a pleasant woman in her forties named Susan Bowers, gives them a lecture on how "to act gentlemanly with the girls." She arms cadets with "The Art of Good Taste," a do's-and-don'ts manual with a chapter entitled "Helping the Ladies." The guidebook outlines the "correct way of offering an arm to a lady...to help her down the steps," and the best method for assisting "a lady in distress." (The example of distress provided involves an elderly woman trying to open a door when her arms are full of shopping bags.) Such pointers are illustrated with pictures of fifties-style codes sporting Barbie-doll hair flips and clinging to the arms of their cadets, who are escorting them to "the Hop." The manual's preface states emphatically, "At all times [ladies] must be sheltered and protected not only from the elements and physical harm but also from embarrassment, crudity, or coarseness of any sort."

Susan Bowers explained the duties of her office: "At the beginning of the year, we do 'situation cards' for the freshmen. And we'll bring in cheerleaders and use them as props. ... We show cadets how to go through the receiving line, how to introduce your date, and what to say to them. In the past, we didn't have the cheerleaders to use, so they dressed up some of the guys as girls." Bowers said she felt bad for the cadets, who often come to her seeking maternal consolation. "They are very timid – afraid, almost," she said. "They are so lost, and they need a shoulder."

"The Art of Good Taste" is silent on the subject of proper etiquette toward women who require neither deference nor rescue. And, as Linda Ross observed, when the gentlemanly approach fails them cadets seem to have only one fallback – aggression. Numerous cadets spoke to me of classmates who claimed to have "knocked around" uncompliant girlfriends. Some of those classmates, no doubt, were embellishing to impress a male audience, but not always. "I know lots of stories where cadets are violent toward women," a 1991 Citadel graduate named Ron Vergnolle said. He had witnessed cadets hitting their girlfriends at a number of Citadel parties – and observed one party incident in which two cadets held down a young woman while a third drunken cadet leaned over and vomited on her. Vergnolle, a magna-cum-laude graduate of the Citadel class of '91, recounted several such stories to me, and added that bragging about humiliating an ex-girlfriend is a common practice – and the more outrageous the humiliation, the better the story, as far as many cadets are concerned. Two such cadet storytellers, for example, proudly spread the word of their exploits on Dog Day, a big outdoor party sponsored by The Citadel's senior class. The two cadets told about the time they became enraged with their dates, followed them to the Portosans, and, after the women had entered, pushed the latrines over so they landed on the doors, trapping the occupants. The cadets left them there. Another cadet told Vergnolle that he had tacked a live hamster to a young woman's door. There was also the cadet who boasted widely that, as vengeance against an unco-operative young woman, he smashed the head of her cat against a window as she watched in horror. "The cat story," Verg-nolle noted, "that was this guy's calling card."

Something of these attitudes shows up even in the ditties the cadets chant during their daily runs. Many of the chants are the usual military "jodies," well known for their misogynistic lyrics. But some are vintage Citadel, and include lyrics about gouging out a woman's eyes, lopping off body parts, and evisceration. A cadence remem-bered by one Citadel cadet, sung to the tune of "The Candy Man," begins, "Who can take two jumper cables / Clip 'em to her tit / Turn on the battery and watch the bitch twitch." Another verse starts with "Who can take an ice pick . . ." And so on.

The day after last Thanksgiving, the phone rang at one-thirty in the morning in the home of Sandy and Ed Faulkner, in Powdersville, South Carolina, a tiny com-munity on the outskirts of Greenville. The caller was a neighbor. They had better come outside, he said – a car had been circling their block. Sandy and Ed, the parents of Shannon Faulkner, went out on their front lawn and looked around. At first, they saw nothing. Then, as they turned back to the house, they saw that across the white porch columns and along the siding of the house, painted in gigantic and what Sandy later recalled as "blood-red" letters, were the words "Bitch," "Dyke," "Whore," and "Lesbo." Ed got up again at 6 a.m. and, armed with a bucket of white paint, hurried to conceal the message from his daughter.

A few days after the judge ordered The Citadel to admit Faulkner to the Corps of Cadets, morning rush-hour drivers in Charleston passed by a huge portable sign that read "Die Shannon." At least this threat wasn't home delivered. In the past year, in-stances of vandalism and harassment have mounted at the Faulkner home. Someone crawled under the house and opened the

emergency exhaust valve on the water heater. The gas tank on Sandy's car was pried open. Someone driving a Ford Bronco mowed down the mailbox. Another motor-ist "did figure-eights through my flower bed," Sandy said. "This year, I didn't even plant flowers, because I knew they would just tear them up." And someone with access to Southern Bell's voice-mail system managed, twice, to tap into their voice mail and change their greeting, both times to a recording featuring rap lyrics about a "bitch" with a "big butt." Callers phoned in the middle of the night with threatening messages. Sandy called the county sheriff's department about the vandalism, but in Anderson County, which has been home to many Citadel graduates, the deputy who arrived was not particularly helpful. He told them, Sandy recalled, "Well, if you're going to mess with The Citadel, you're just going to have to expect that."

Every trial has its rare moments of clarity, when the bramble of admissibility argu-ments and technicalities is cut away and we see the actual issue in dispute. One such moment came toward the end of the Faul-kner–Citadel trial, when Alexander Astin, the director of the Higher Education Re-search Institute at the University of Califor-nia at Los Angeles, took the stand. Astin, who is widely viewed as a leading surveyor of college-student performance and atti-tudes, found no negative effects on male students in nineteen all-male colleges he had studied which had gone coeducational.

"Can you tell me what kind of woman you would think would want to attend a coeducational Citadel?" Robert Patterson, the Citadel attorney who had previously represented VMI, asked Astin, his voice full of unflattering insinuation about the kind of woman he imagined her to be.

ASTIN: I suppose the same as the kind of men who want to go there.
PATTERSON: Would it be a woman that would not be all that different from men?
ASTIN: Yes.

To Patterson, this was a triumphant moment, and he closed on it: he had forced the government's witness to admit that a woman like Shannon Faulkner would have to be a mannish aberration from her gender. But in fact Astin's testimony expressed the precise point that the plaintiff's side had been trying to make all along, and that The Citadel strenuously resisted: that the sexes were, in the end, not all that different.

"I was considered the bitch of the band," Shannon Faulkner said, without embarrassment, of her four years in her high school's marching band – just stating a fact. She was lounging on the couch in her parents' living room, comfortable in an old T-shirt and shorts, one leg swung over an arm of the couch. "That's because I was the one who was mean and got it done." The phone rang, for the millionth time – another media call. "I'm not giving statements to the press right now," she said efficiently into the phone, and hung up. She did not apologize for her brusqueness, as I was half expecting her to do, after she put down the receiver. There is nothing of the good girl about her. Not that she is disagreeable; Shannon Faulkner just doesn't see the point in false deference. "I never let anyone push me around, male or female," Faulkner said, and that fact had been exasperatingly obvious to reporters who covered the trial: they found that all the wheedling and cheap flatteries that usually prompt subjects to say more than they should didn't work with Faulkner.

One could scrounge around in Faulkner's childhood for the key to what made her take on The Citadel. You could say that it was because she was born six weeks premature, and her fierce struggle to live forged a "survivor." You could cite her memory that as a small child she preferred playing outside with the boys to playing with certain girls, whom she deemed "too prissy." You could point to her sports career in high school and junior high: she lettered in softball for four years and kept stats for three of the schools'

four basketball teams. You could note her ability to juggle tasks: she edited the yearbook, wrote for the school paper, and graduated with a 3.48 grade-point average. And you could certainly credit the sturdy backbone and outspokenness of both her mother and her maternal grandmother; this is a family where the women talk and the men keep a low profile. Her father, Ed, owns a small fence-building business. At thirty, a few years after Shannon's birth, Sandy returned to college to get her degree, a double major in psychology and education, and became a high-school teacher of psychology, sociology, United States history, and minority cultures. When a male professor had complained about certain "older women" in his class who asked "too many questions," Sandy hurled one of her wedge-heeled sandals at him. "I said, 'I'm paying for this class, and don't you ever tell me what I can ask.'" Shannon's maternal grandmother, 67-year-old Evelyn Richey, was orphaned at six and worked most of her life in textile factories, where, she noted, "women could do the job and men got the pay." Of her granddaughter's suit she said, "Women have got to come ahead. I say, let's get on with the show."

But there's little point in a detailed inspection of family history, because there's no real mystery here. What is most striking about Shannon herself is that she's not particularly unusual. She reads novels by Tom Clancy and John Grisham, has worked in a local day-care center, is partial to places like Bennigan's. She wants a college education so she can support herself and have a career as a teacher or a journalist – she hasn't yet decided which. She might do a stint in the military, she might not. She is in many ways representative of the average striving lower-middle-class teenage girl, circa 1994, who intends to better herself and does not intend to achieve that betterment through a man – in fact, she has not for a moment entertained such a possibility.

Throughout the trial, cadets and Citadel alumni spoke of a feminist plot: she is "a pawn" of the National Organization for Women, or – a theory repeatedly posited to me by cadets – "Her mother put her up to it." Two Citadel alumni asked me in all seriousness if feminist organizations were paying Shannon Faulkner to take the stand. In truth, Shannon makes an unlikely feminist poster girl. She prefers to call herself "an individualist" and seems almost indifferent to feminist affairs; when I mentioned Gloria Steinem's name once in conversation, Shannon asked me, "Who's that?" After the judge issued his decision to admit her to the Corps, she told the *New York Times* that she didn't consider the ruling a victory "just for women" – only a confirmation of her belief that if you want something, "go for it." Shannon Faulkner's determination to enter The Citadel's Corps of Cadets was fueled not so much by a desire to trailblaze as by a sense of amazement and indignation that this trail was barricaded in the first place. She had never, she told the court, encountered such a roadblock in all her nineteen years – a remark that perhaps only a young woman of her fortunate generation could make without perjuring herself.

Shannon Faulkner got the idea of attending The Citadel back in December of 1992. She was taking a preparatory education course at Wren High School, the local public school. Mike Hazel, the teacher, passed out articles for them to read and discuss, and Faulkner picked the article in *Sports Illustrated* about hazing at The Citadel. "It was almost as accidental as Rosa Parks," Hazel recalled. "I just held up *Sports Illustrated* and asked, 'Who wants to do this?'"

Faulkner told me she'd selected the article because "I had missed that issue." During the ensuing discussion, the class wandered off the subject of hazing and onto the question of what, exactly, a public state institution was doing barring women from its classrooms. After a while, Faulkner got up and went down to the counsellor's office, and returned with an application form from The Citadel. "I said, 'Hey, it doesn't

even say 'Male/Female,'" she recalled. While she was sitting in class, she filled it out. "I didn't really make a big to-do about it."

Two weeks after Faulkner received her acceptance letter, The Citadel got word she was a woman and revoked her admission, and in August of 1993 she went off to spend a semester at the University of South Carolina at Spartanburg while the courts thrashed out the next move. As the lawyers filed papers, The Citadel's defenders delivered their own increasingly agitated personal briefs to the plaintiff herself. Faulkner worked evenings as a waitress in a local bar called Chiefs Wings and Firewater until the nightly tirades from the many drunk Citadel-graduate customers got to be too much. Actually, Faulkner said, she wouldn't have quit if some of her male college friends hadn't felt the need to defend her honor. "I didn't want them getting hurt," she said. Her manner of dealing with the Citadel crowd was more good-humored. One day at the bar, she recalled, "a guy came up to me. 'Are you Shannon Faulkner?' he asked, and I said 'Why?' – very casual. Then he got real huffy-puffy, madder and madder." Finally, she said, he stuck his ring in her face, then slammed his hand down on the table. "You will never wear *that!*" he yelled. Shannon saw him a few times in the bar after that, scowling at her from a far table. To lighten the mood, she once had the bartender send him a beer. He wouldn't drink it.

"I never show my true emotions in public," Shannon said, "I consider that weak." She can laugh at the cadets' threats, even when they turn ugly, because she doesn't see the reason for all the fuss. Whenever she is asked to sign the latest T-shirt inspired by the controversy, which depicts a group of male bulldogs (The Citadel's mascot) in cadet uniforms and one female bulldog in a red dress, above the caption "1,952 Bulldogs and 1 Bitch," Faulkner told me, "I always sign under the 'Bitch' part."

The first day that Shannon Faulkner attended classes, in January, 1994, the cadets who had lined up by the academic building told the media the same thing over and over: "We were trained to be gentlemen, and that's what we'll be." But in Shannon's first class, biology, all three cadets assigned to sit in her row changed their seats. The teacher, Philippe Ross, had to threaten to mark them absent to get them to return to their places. (More than twenty unexcused absences a semester is grounds for failure.) Shortly thereafter, a rumor began to circulate that Faulkner was using a fake ID in the local bars. This summer, talk of a plot against Faulkner surfaced – to frame her, perhaps by planting drugs in her belongings. The threat seemed real enough for Faulkner to quit her summer job, in the Charleston area, and return home.

The *Brigadier*'s column "Scarlet Pimpernel" took up the anti-Shannon cause with a vengeance. The columnist dubbed her "the divine bovine," likening her to a plastic revolving cow at a nearby mall (the mounting of which is a cadet tradition). The "Pimpernel" comments on an incident that occurred on Faulkner's first day were particularly memorable. An African-American cadet named Von Mickle dared to shake her hand in front of the media and say, "It's time for women," and compared the exclusion of women to that of blacks. For this lone act, he was not only physically threatened by classmates but derided in the "Pimpernel." "The PIMP doth long to tame the PLASTIC COW on this most wondrous of nights," the anonymous author wrote, with the column's usual antique-English flourishes and coded references. "But it seems that we will have a live specimen, a home grown DAIRY QUEEN from the stables of Powdersville. Perhaps NON DICKLE will be the first to saddle up. He is DIVINE BOVINE's best friend after all."

More disturbing were cadet writings on Faulkner that were not for public consumption. Tom Lucas, a graduate student in The Citadel's evening program, told me about some "very harsh" graffiti that he'd found all over one of the men's rooms in The Citadel's academic building. The inscription that

most stuck in his mind: "Let her in – then fuck her to death."

On the whole, the Citadel administrators to whom I spoke were defensive, evasive, or dismissive of the cadets' hostile words and deeds toward Faulkner. When I asked Citadel officials to respond to reports of barracks violence, harassment of women on staff, or verbal abuse of Faulkner, the responses were dismaying. Cases of violence and abuse were "aberrations"; cadets who spoke up were either "troublemakers" or "mama's boys"; and each complaint by a female faculty member was deemed a "private personnel matter" that could not be discussed further.

Certainly the administrators and trustees themselves are less than enthusiastic about Faulkner's arrival. William F. Prioleau, Jr., until recently a member of the Board of Visitors, implied on a radio talk show that abortions would go up as a result of the female invasion, as he claimed had happened at West Point. Meanwhile, in The Citadel's Math Department, all that was going up as a result of Shannon Faulkner's presence was the grade-point average. Faulkner's highest mark at the semester's end was in calculus, where she earned an A (prompting a surprised Dean Poole to comment to her that she was "certainly not the stereotypical woman"). The Math Department has in recent years invited A students to an annual party. But, rather than include Faulkner, the department limited its guest list to math majors. Math professor David Trautman, who was in charge of invitations to the party, explained in an e-mail message to colleagues, "Her presence would put a damper on the evening."

Linda Ross, then a professor at The Citadel, was speaking one day with a 76-year-old alumnus, and the talk turned to Faulkner's lawsuit. He asked her if she thought it possible that this young woman might prevail. "Well, it's probably an inevitable turning of the tide," Ross said, shrugging. To her amazement, the alumnus began to cry.

"I have the worst chance in society of getting a job, because I'm a white male," William H. Barnes, the senior platoon leader, shouted at me over the din in The Citadel's mess hall, a din created by the upperclassmen's tradition of berating knobs at mealtime. "And that's the major difference between me and my father." In a society where, at least since the Second World War, surpassing one's father has been an expected benchmark of American manhood, Barnes's point is a plangent one. But it's hard to say which Citadel generation is more undone by the loss of white male privilege – the young men who will never partake of a dreamed world of masculine advantage or the older men who are seeing that lived world split apart, shattered.

"I was in Vietnam in '63, and I'll defy you or Shannon or anyone else to hike through the rice paddies," the usually genial Colonel Harvey Dick, 67, a Board of Visitors member, an ex-marine, and an Army lieutenant colonel, was practically shouting from his recliner armchair in his Charleston home. He popped a Tums in his mouth. "There's just no way you can do that. ... You can't pick up a 95-pound projectile. There are certain things out there that are differences." On the wall above his head were seven bayonets. He was wearing his blue Citadel T-shirt, which matched the Citadel mementos that overwhelmed his den – Citadel mugs, hats, footballs, ceramic bulldogs. It was a room known in the Dick household as "Harvey's 'I Love Me' Room." Dick treated it as his command post – whenever the phone rang, he whipped it off the cradle and barked "Colonel Dick!" – but what he was commanding was unclear; he retired in 1993 from a sixteen-year stint as The Citadel's assistant commandant. Still, he at least knew that he was once in charge, that he once enjoyed lifetime job security as a career military man. This was something his son couldn't say: Harvey Dick II, a nuclear pipe fitter, had recently been laid off at the Charleston Naval Shipyard.

Colonel Dick wanted it known that he wasn't "one of those male-chauvinist pigs"; in fact, he believes that women are smarter than men. "Women used to let the men dominate," he said. "Maybe we need a male movement, since evidently we're coming out second on everything." He slipped another Tums from an almost empty roll. The sun was dropping as we spoke, and shadows fell across the Citadel hats and figurines in his room. "Go back and look at your Greek and Roman empires and why they fell," he said.

His wife cleared her throat. "This doesn't have anything to do with male–female," she said.

"I see a decline in this great nation of ours," Dick said. He crossed his arms and stared into the gathering darkness of the late summer afternoon. After a while, he said, "I guess I sound like a buffoon."

Unlike the cadets, the older male Citadel officials often have to face dissent from wives or daughters whose views and professional aspirations or accomplishments challenge their stand on women's proper place. Lewis Spearman, the assistant to the president, recently remarried, and his wife is a feminist paralegal who is now getting her master's degree in psychology. She says she engaged for more than a year in "shriekfests" with him over the Shannon Faulkner question before she halfheartedly came around to the Citadel party line on barring women. And, while the wife of Dean Poole may have sat on the Miss Citadel judging panel, their daughter, Mindy, had loftier ambitions. Despite the fact that she suffered from cystic fibrosis, she was an ardent skier, horseback rider, and college athlete, rising at 5 a.m. daily with her crew-team members at the University of Virginia. And, despite a double lung transplant during her junior year, she graduated in 1991 with honors and won a graduate fellowship. "She was an outstanding young lady," Poole said. "I was very proud of her." His eyes clouding over at the memory, he recalled that she had made him promise to take her to the big Corps Day parade on The Citadel's sesquicentennial. The day the father and daughter were to attend the parade was the day she died. "Sort of an interesting footnote," he said, wiping at his moist eyes. What if she had wanted to go to The Citadel? Well, actually, Poole said, she *had* talked about it. If she had persisted he would have tried to change her mind, he said, but he added, "I would never have stopped her from doing something she wanted to do."

One of the biggest spousal battles over Shannon Faulkner is waged nightly at the home of a man who might seem the least likely figure at The Citadel to wind up with a feminist wife. Probably The Citadel's most legendary elder, thanks to Pat Conroy's thinly veiled and admiring portrait of him in *The Lords of Discipline*, is Lieutenant Colonel T. Nugent Courvoisie, who, as an assistant commandant in the sixties, oversaw the admission of the first African-American cadet to The Citadel. A gravelly-voiced and cigar-chomping tender tyrant, Courvoisie – or the Boo, as he is known, for obscure reasons – was a fixture at the school for more than two decades. There are two Citadel scholarships in his family name, and his visage peers down from two portraits on campus.

A courtly man, and still dapper at 77, the Boo, who has since given up cigars, insisted on picking me up at my hotel and driving me to his home, though I had a rental car sitting in the parking lot. On the drive over, he ticked off the differences between the sexes which he believed made it impossible for The Citadel to admit women – differences such as that "the average female is not as proficient athletically as the average male." When we were settled in the living room, the Boo on his recliner and his second wife, Margaret, who is also 77, in a straight-back chair, the subject of Shannon Faulkner was revisited. The first words out of Margaret's mouth were "The Citadel wants to chop the head off women." A low growl emanated from the Boo's corner. He lowered the recliner a notch. "We don't talk about it here," Margaret said – an obvious untruth. "We haven't come to blows yet, but –"

The Boo interrupted, "I have the correct view."

She retorted, "No one has the *correct* view." She turned and addressed me. "You have to understand him," she said of her husband of nine years. "This is a man who went to military prep schools and a church that was male-dominated, naturally."

The Boo interrupted. "J. C. picked twelve *men* as his disciples," he said.

Margaret rolled her eyes. "See? He even takes it into the church – and he's on such familiar ground with Christ he calls him J. C."

The Boo said, "J. C. never picked a woman, except his mother."

Margaret said, "Oh God, see, this is why we don't go into it."

But, as usual, go into it they did. As the words got batted back and forth, with Margaret doing most of the batting, the Boo levered his recliner progressively lower, until all I could see of him were the soles of his shoes.

MARGARET: You had plenty of good women soldiers in Saudi Arabia.

BOO: Plenty of pregnant ones...

MARGARET: What, do you think [the cadets] didn't get girls pregnant before? There've been plenty of abortions. And I know of a number of cases that, by the time [a cadet] graduated, there were four or five kids.

BOO: That's an exaggeration. Maybe two or three.... With women, there's going to be sexual harassment.

MARGARET: Oh, honey, those cadets are harassing each other right now, all the time.

BOO: That's different. That's standard operating procedure.

In the 1960s, Margaret worked in the library at The Citadel, where she would often see Charles Foster, the first African-American cadet (who died a few years ago) alone at one of the library desks. "He would just come to the library and sit there a lot. It's hard to be the only one, to be the groundbreaker. That's why I admire this girl."

Boo's voice boomed from the depths of his recliner: "But there's no need for her. She's ruining a good thing."

Margaret gave a mock groan. "This is the last vestige of male bastionship," she said, "and it's going to kill 'em when it crumbles." Boo raised his chair halfway back up and considered Margaret. "She has a good mind," he told me after a while.

Margaret smiled. "I'm a new experience for him. He's always been military. People didn't disagree with him."

The Boo showed the way upstairs, to the attic, where he has his own "Citadel room" – a collection of Citadel memorabilia vaster than but almost identical to Dick's. Around the house, there were sketches of Boo at various points in his Citadel career. He told me that, before he retired, the cadets commissioned a portrait of him that hangs in Jenkins Hall. "Man, I looked good in that," he said. "Like a man. A leader."

Margaret didn't think so. "No, it was horrible," she said. "It didn't look like you."

"If Shannon were in my class, I'd be fired by March for sexual harassment," Colonel James Rembert, an English professor, was saying as we headed toward his classroom. He had a ramrod bearing and a certain resemblance to Ted Turner (who, it happens, sent all three of his sons to The Citadel – Beau Turner among them – and donated 25 million dollars to the school earlier this year). The Colonel identifies himself as one of "the last white Remberts" in South Carolina, the Remberts being a Huguenot family of sufficiently ancient lineage to gain him admission to the St. John's Hunting Club, of South Carolina – an all-male society chaired by a Citadel alumnus. Rembert,

who has a Cambridge University doctorate and wrote a book on Jonathan Swift, said he preferred the company of men, in leisure and in learning. "I've dealt with young men all my life," he went on. "I know how to play with them. I have the freedom here to imply things I couldn't with women. I don't want to have to watch what I say."

The literary work under discussion that day was *Beowulf*, and the cadets agreed that it was all about "brotherhood loyalty" and, in the words of one student, "the most important characteristics of a man – glory and eternal fame." Then they turned to their papers on the topic.

"Mr. Rice," Rembert said in mock horror. "You turned in a single-spaced paper." This was a no-no. Rembert instructed him to take a pencil and "pen-e-trate" – Rembert drew the syllables out – the paper with the point. He shook his head. "What a pansy!" Rembert said. "Can't catch, can't throw, can't write." Another student was chastised for the use of the passive voice. "Never use the passive voice – it leads to effeminacy and homosexuality," Rembert told the class. "So next time you use the passive voice I'm going to make you lift up your limp wrist." Literary pointers concluded, Rembert floated the subject of Shannon Faulkner. The usual objections were raised. But then the class wandered into more interesting territory, provoked by a cadet's comment that "she would change the relationship between the men here." Just what is the nature of that relationship?

"When we are in the showers, it's very intimate," a senior cadet said. "We're one mass, naked together, and it makes us closer. . . . You're shaved, you're naked, you're afraid together. You can cry." Robert Butcher, another senior, said that the men take care of each classmate. "They'll help dress him, tuck in his shirt, shine his shoes." You mean like a mother–child relationship? I asked.

"That *is* what it is," another cadet said. "It's a family. Even the way we eat – family style." A fourth cadet said, "Maybe it's a Freudian thing, but males feel more affection with each other when women are not around. Maybe we're all homosexuals."

The class groaned. "Speak for yourself, buddy," a number of cadets said, almost in chorus.

Rembert said, "With no women, we can hug each other. There's nothing so nurturing as an infantry platoon."

The hooted-down cadet weighed in again: "When I used to wrestle in high school, we had this great tradition. Right before the game, the coach, he'd slap us really hard on the butt."

Rembert, a onetime paratrooper, said he and his skydiving buddies did that, too, right before they jumped. "First man out gets a pat right there."

Over lunch, Rembert returned to the theme of manly nurturance among Citadel men. "We hug each other," he said. One of his colleagues "always kisses me on the cheek," he went on. "It's like a true marriage. There's an affectionate intimacy that you will find between cadets. With this security they can, without being defensive, project tenderness to each other."

Months later, I was sitting in court watching Norman Doucet, the cadet regimental commander, testify. He was showing the judge a video of the Citadel experience and explaining the various scenes. First we were shown "one of the great parts" of a knob's first day – the mothers looking weepy at the gate as their sons were led away. Doucet lingered over the head-shaving scene. "This is what does it, right here," he said. "Mothers can't even tell their sons apart after this." Thus shielded from the prying maternal eye, the cadets began their new life, and the video action shifted to a typical day in the life of the Corps. But the editing made it a day as heavy on early-morning domestic chores as it was on martial activity. Much of the film was devoted to housekeeping: scenes of cadets making beds, dressing each other, sweeping, taking out the trash, all of which Doucet described as "like some

kind of a ballet or dance that's going on." This was a dance where the most important moves took place before the show, in the dressing room. "What they are doing here is the Citadel shirt tuck," Doucet said. The tuck requires that a cadet unzip his pants halfway and fold down his waistband, then stand still while his helper approaches him from the back, puts his arms around the cadet's waist, pulls the loose shirt material firmly to the back, jams it as far down in the pants as he can, and then pulls the cadet's pants up. "If you watch closely right here, this is what the fourth-class system is all about," Doucet continued. "In order to get a proper shirt tuck, you can't do it yourself – you need your classmates to do it for you. There's really a lot of dependence upon your classmates." But, as Doucet's account suggested, cadets can experience that dependence only in concealment, away from mothers, away from all women.

When a Citadel attorney asked Doucet why female cadets would pose a problem on the campus, the only issue he raised was the humiliation that cadets would feel if women observed the cadets' on-campus interactions. He spoke of the shame that knobs felt when, on occasion, a woman happened to be on the parade ground while upperclassmen were disciplining them. The cadets observing in the courtroom nodded in agreement.

It may seem almost paradoxical that the fourth-class system should be so solicitous of the emotional vulnerability of its wards – the same wards it subjects to such rigors. And yet the making of Whole Men evidently requires an initial stage of infantilization. Indeed, the objective of recapitulating childhood development is plainly spelled out in The Citadel's year-book, known as "The Sphinx." The 1990 "Sphinx" explained, "As a freshman enters, he begins to release his childhood and takes the first steps to becoming a 'Citadel Man.'...As a 'knob,' every aspect of life is taught, a new way to walk....Knobs are told how, where, and when to walk." Reentrance into manhood for the toddling knobs occurs on Recognition

Day, when the upperclassmen force the knobs to do calisthenics until they drop, then gently lift up their charges and nurse them with cups of water. At that moment, for the first time in nine months, the older cadets call the knobs by their first names and embrace them.

The relationship between knobs and upperclassmen following Recognition Day, as they are integrated into the Corps, shifts from maternal to matrimonial. The yearbooks of the last several years picture Citadel men spending a lot of time embracing and kissing. Of course, this impulse, when it is captured on film, is always carefully disarmed with a jokey caption.

One afternoon, a group of cadets recounted for me the campus's many "nudity rituals," as they jokingly called them. There's "Senior Rip-Off Day," a spring rite in which three hundred seniors literally rip each other's clothes off, burn them in a bonfire, and hug and wrestle on the ground. There's "Nude Platoon," in which a group of juniors, unclad except for their cross-webbing, run around the quad yelling, "We love the Nude Platoon!" And there's the birthday ritual, in which the birthday boy is stripped, tied to a chair, and covered with shaving cream, while his groin is coated in liquid shoe polish.

During the fall semester before graduation, the seniors receive their "band of gold" (as it is called) in the Ring Ceremony. The chaplain blesses each class ring. (Receiving the ring, which I was constantly reminded is "the biggest class ring of any college," is a near-sacrament, and the yearbooks are filled with pictures of young men holding up their rings with fervor, as if clutching a crucifix before a vampire.) Then each senior walks through a ten-foot replica of the class ring with his mother on one arm and his "date" on the other. In a sort of reverse marriage ceremony, the mother gives the cadet away. Mother and date accompany him through the towering ring; then he kisses Mother farewell and marches under the arched swords of the

Junior Sword Drill, a new bride of the Corps. Several cadets and alumni told me that when a Citadel graduate marries, it is a tradition to slide the class ring over the wedding band. Indeed, I saw such an ordering of priorities on the fingers of a number of Citadel men in the courtroom.

In the late-twentieth-century setting of The Citadel, in a time when extreme insecurity and confusion about masculinity's standing run rampant, the Corps of Cadets once again seeks to obscure a domestic male paradise with an intensifying of virile showmanship and violence. The result is a ruthless intimacy, in which physical abuse stands in for physical affection, and every display of affection must be counterbalanced by a display of sadism. Knobs told me that they were forced to run through the showers while the upperclassmen "guards" knocked the soap out of their hands and, when the knobs leaned over to retrieve it, the upperclassmen would unzip their pants and yell, "Don't pick it up, don't pick it up! We'll use you like we used those girls!" A former Citadel Halloween tradition, of upperclassmen dressing up – mostly in diapers and women's clothes – and collecting candy treats from knobs, has given way to "tricks" of considerable violence. (One upperclassman told me of cadets who knocked dressers over on candy-dispensing cadets and then walked on top of them.) The administration tried, unsuccessfully, to put a stop to the whole affair; too many freshmen were getting injured. And the playful pat on the butt that served to usher cadets into the brotherhood has degenerated into more invasive acts. According to a recent graduate, one company of cadets recently devised a regimen in which the older cadets tested sophomores nightly with increasingly painful treatments – beatings and stompings and so forth. The process, which they dubbed "Bananarama," culminated on a night in which an unpeeled banana was produced – and shoved into a cadet's anus.

Given this precarious dynamic, it is not surprising that in the past few years at

The Citadel social rage has been directed toward any men who were perceived to be gay. Several young men who were suspected of homosexual inclinations were hounded out of the school. One cadet, Herbert Parker, who said that he was falsely accused of having a sexual encounter with a male janitor, recalled a year of total isolation – cadets refused to sit near him in the mess hall or in classes – and terror: incessant threatening phone calls and death threats. The cadets and the administration – which had responded to the report of his encounter by sending out a campus-security police car with lights flashing to question him – acted "like I had murdered someone."

The scapegoating reached such brutal proportions that the counselling center recently set up a sort of group-therapy session for the targeted young men, who are known as It, as in the game of tag.

One evening after the trial, I went over to the Treehouse, a "mixed" bar in Charleston, with an upstairs gay bar and nightly drag shows on the weekends. My intention was to ask about cadet violence against gay men. I presumed that on a campus where every second epithet was "faggot" such hate crimes were all but inevitable. There were indeed a few such cases, I learned, but the circumstances were different from what I had imagined. Nor were those cases the essence of my findings that evening.

"The proper terminology for The Citadel," a customer at the bar named Chris said, "is The Closet." Up and down the bar, heads bobbed in agreement. "They love faggots like me." What he meant by "like me," however, was not that he was gay. That night, he looked like a male model – sleek black hair and a handsome, chiselled face. But on the nights he was dressed for a performance he could pass for a woman. Arching an eyebrow, Chris said, "The cadets go for the drag queens."

Chris's observation was echoed in ensuing conversations in the bar. There are thousands of cadets, presumably, who have not dated drag queens, but in two visits to the Treehouse I could find only two drag queens, out of maybe a dozen, who did not tell me of dating a cadet – and that was only because these two found Citadel men "too emotional." Cadets can also occasionally be dangerous, Chris told me. "You can get the ones who are violent. They think they want it, then afterwards they turn on you, like you made them do it." Nonetheless, a drag queen who called himself Holly had been happily involved with a cadet for three years now. Marissa, another drag queen, the reigning "Miss Treehouse, 1993–94," had gone out with one cadet, broken up, and was now in the throes of a budding romance with another. A third drag queen, who asked to be identified as Tiffany, was known to be a favorite of cadets.

As Chris and I were talking that first night, a drag queen called Lownie wandered in and settled on a bar stool. Lownie delighted in the Corps of Cadets pageantry – especially the Friday dress parades. "The parades are a big thing with the queers in Charleston," he said. "We'll have a cocktail party and go over and watch the boys. It's a very Southern 'lady' thing to do." Years ago, Lownie had been a student at the College of Charleston when he met *his* Citadel lover, and they had begun covert assignations – communicating through notes slipped in little-used books in the Citadel library. The only drawback, Lownie said, was dealing with his lover's constant emotional anxiety over making the grade at The Citadel. He was, in fact, a model macho cadet: a Junior Sword Drill member, a regimental officer, and a "hang king," who could dangle interminably from a closet rack by his fingertips. Lownie, who found such records more amusing than impressive, grinned, and said, "I used to make him wear his shako" – The Citadel's military cap – "when we were having sex. It's manhood at its most."

Lownie said he could begin to fathom his cadet's intense attachment to The Citadel

– an emotion that he likened to a love affair – because he himself had spent four years in the Air Force. "The day-to-day aspect of being in a military environment is that you run around in a little bit of clothing and you are being judged as to how good a man you are by doing women's work – pressing pants, sewing, polishing shoes. You are a *better* man if you have mastery of womanly arts....The camaraderie doesn't get any stronger than when you are in the barracks, sitting around at the end of the day in your briefs and T's and dogtags – like a bunch of hausfraus, talking and gossiping." The military stage set offers a false front and a welcome trapdoor – an escape hatch from the social burdens of traditional masculinity. Behind the martial backdrop, Lownie said, "you don't have to be a breadwinner. You don't have to be a leader. You can play back seat. It's a great relief. You can act like a human being and not have to act like a man."

"You know what the [cadet] I'm seeing now said to me?" Tiffany said. We were sitting in the dressing room a couple of hours before the night's performance, and as Tiffany spoke he peered into an elaborate mirror set illuminated with miniature movie-star lights, applying layer after layer of mascara and eyeliner with expert precision. "He said, 'You're more of a woman than a woman is.' And that's an exact quote." Tiffany stood up and struck a Southern-belle pose by way of illustration. "I overexemplify everything a female is – my breasts, my hair, the way I hold myself." And who could better complete the hoopskirts picture than a fantasy gentleman in uniform?

Marissa, Miss Treehouse, looked up from his labors, painting row after row of fake nails with pink polish. "I love how they wear their caps slung low so you can't quite see their eyes," he said. "It's like all of us are female illusionists and they are male illusionists. A man in a uniform is a kind of dream."

Tiffany said, "For Halloween, you know what my cadet boyfriend wanted to dress as? A cadet."

The dressing-room scene before me, of a group of men tenderly helping each other get ready for the evening – an elaborate process of pinning and binding and stuffing – was not very different, in its way, from the footage in Norman Doucet's video of the cadets tucking in each other's shirts. As the drag queens conversed, they tossed stockings and Ace bandages and cosmetic bags back and forth. "Has anyone seen my mascara wand?" "OK, who has the blush?" There was a homey comfort that reminded me of slumber parties when I was a girl, where we would put big pink spongy rollers in each other's hair and screech with laughter at the results. And suddenly it became obvious to me what was generating that void, that yearning, in the cadets' lives – and maybe in the lives of many American men. What was going on here was play – a kind of freedom and spontaneity that, in this culture, only women are permitted.

No wonder men found their Citadels, their Treehouses, where the rules of gender could be bent or escaped. For the drag queens of the Treehouse, the distinctions between the sexes are a goof, to be endlessly manipulated with funhouse-mirror glee. For cadets, despite the play set of The Citadel and the dress-up braids and ribbons, the guarding of their treehouse is a dead-serious business. Still, undercover at The Citadel, the cadets have managed to create for themselves a world in which they get half the equation that Lownie described: They can "act like human beings" in the safety of the daily domestic life of the barracks. But, in return, the institution demands that they never cease to "act like a man" – a man of cold and rigid bearing, a man no more male than Tiffany's Southern belle is female, a man that no one, humanly, can be. That they must defend their inner humanity with outer brutality may say as much about the world outside The Citadel walls as about the world within them. The cadets feel called to defend those walls. Never mind that their true ideal may not be the vaunted one of martial masculinity, just as their true enemy is not Shannon Faulkner. The cadets at The Citadel feel that something about their life and routine is worthy on its merits and is endangered from without. And in that they may be right.

6 Subject Honor and Object Shame: The Construction of Male Homosexuality and Stigma in Nicaragua

Roger N. Lancaster

The Social Construction of Sexual Practices

In Nicaragua one encounters a folk category, the *cochón*. It can be given as either a male (*el cochón*) or female (*la cochón, la cochóna*) noun; either case typically refers to a male. This term is loosely translated as queer or faggot by visiting English-speakers. Educated Nicaraguans, if they are fluent in international terminologies, are apt to freely translate the term in the same fashion, giving gay or homosexual as its English equivalents. It becomes clear on closer inspection, however, that the phenomenon in question is markedly different from its Anglo-American counterparts of whatever shade. In the first place, the term is less clearly derogatory, although it can be derogative and usually is. It can also be neutral and descriptive. I have even heard it employed in a particular sort of praising manner by ordinary Nicaraguans; *viz.*, "We must go to *carnaval*[1] this year and see the cochones. The cochones there are very, very beautiful."

Second, and more important, the term marks and delimits a set of sexual practices that overlaps but is clearly not identical to our own notion of the homosexual. The term specifies only certain practices, in certain contexts, and in certain manners. Some acts that we would describe as homosexual bear neither stigma nor an accompanying identity of any special sort whatsoever; others clearly mark their practitioner as a cochón.

If North American homosexuality is most characteristically an oral phenomenon, at least nowadays, Nicaraguan homosexual practice is decidedly anal in preference. The lexicon of male insult clearly reflects this anal basic route of intercourse in Nicaragua, even as the North American lexicon reflects the oral route. But more is involved here than a mere shifting of the sites of erotic practice. With the exception of a few well-defined contexts (e.g., prisons), where the rule may be suspended, homosexual activity of any sort defines the North American homosexual. In Nicaragua, it is passive anal intercourse that alone defines the cochón. Oral or manual practices receive little social attention, and at any rate, non-anal practices appear far less significant in the repertoire of actually practiced homosexual activities.

The term cochón itself appears indicative of the nature of that status and role. None of my informants was certain about the origin of the term; it is a *Nica*, or a word peculiar to Nicaraguan popular Spanish. Moreover, one encounters different pronunciations in various neighborhoods, classes, and regions, so there can really be no agreed-upon spelling of the word:[2] I have heard it rendered *cuchón*, and even *colchón*. The last suggests the probable origin of the word: colchón, or mattress. That is, as one of my informants suggested when prompted to speculate on the origin of the word, "You get on top of him like a mattress."

This summarizes the nature of that status as well as any phrase could but it also points to the question: "Who gets on top of him like a mattress?" The answer is not, "Only other cochones." Indeed, this type of relationship is relatively rare, and, where it occurs, is generally a short-term affair. It is typically a non-cochón male who plays the active role in sexual intercourse: a *machista*, or *hombre-hombre*, a manly man. Either term designates a masculine man in the popular lexicon; cochones frequently use either term to designate potential sexual partners. Relationships of this type, between cochones and hombre-hombres, may be of any number of varieties: one-time only affairs; purchased sex, with the purchase running in either direction (although most typically it is the cochón who pays); protracted relationships running weeks or months; or full-scale emotional commitments lasting years.

The last sort is preferred but carries its own type of difficulties, its own particular sadness. As one of my cochón informants related:

> I once had a lover for five continuous years. He was a sergeant in the military, an hombre-hombre. During this period of time he had at least fifteen girlfriends but I was his only male lover. He visited me and we made love almost every day. You have asked me if there is love and romance in these relations; yes, there is. He was very romantic, very tender, and very jealous. But he is married now and I rarely see him.

The actual range of sexual practices employed by cochones may be wider than sexual ideology would suggest. Many tell me that they are only really comfortable in the anal-passive position. Others alternate between active and passive roles, depending on whether they are having relations with an hombre-hombre (always passive) or with another cochón (passive or active). Very few report practicing oral sex at all and several of my informants – cochones and non-cochones alike – denied having any knowledge of such techniques. Many Nicar-aguans express repulsion at the idea of either homo- or heterosexual intercourse of the oral sort. A series of (not necessarily sexual) aversions and prohibitions concerning the mouth seems to be involved here. The mouth is seen as the primary route of contamination, the major path whereby illness enters the body, and sex is quintessentially dirty (*sucio*). This conception is socialized into children from infancy onward. Parents are always scolding their small children for putting things in their mouths. This anti-oral outlook militates against the possibilities of oral intercourse.

The resultant anal emphasis suggests a significant constraint on the nature of homoerotic practices. Unlike oral intercourse, which may lend itself to reciprocal sexual practices, anal intercourse invariably produces an active partner and a passive partner. If oral intercourse suggests the possibility of an equal sign between partners, anal intercourse most likely produces an unequal relationship. But this anal emphasis is not merely a negative restraint on the independent variable (homosexuality); positively, it produces a whole field of practices and relations.

The Specific Routes of Stigma

There is clearly stigma in Nicaraguan homosexual practice but it is not a stigma of the sort that clings equally to both partners. Rather, it is only the anal-passive cochón that is stigmatized. His partner, the active hombre-hombre, is not stigmatized at all and, moreover, no clear category exists in the popular language to classify him. For all intents and purposes, he is just a normal Nicaraguan male. The term "heterosexual" is inappropriate here. First, neither it nor any equivalent of it appear in the popular language. Second, it is not really the issue. One is either a cochón, or one is not. If one is not, it scarcely matters that one sleeps with cochones regularly or irregularly.

Indeed, a man can gain status among his peers as a vigorous machista by sleeping with many cochones in precisely the same manner that one gains prestige by sleeping with many women. I once heard a Nicaraguan youth of nineteen boast to his younger friends in the following manner: "I am very sexually experienced. I have had a lot of women, especially when I was in the army, over on the Atlantic coast. I have done everything. I have even done it with cochones." No one in the group thought this a damning confession and all present were impressed with their friend's sexual experience and prowess.

For that matter, desire is not at issue here and it is irrelevant to what degree one is attracted sexually to members of one's own sex. What matters is the manner in which one is attracted to other males. It is expected that one would naturally be aroused by the idea of anally penetrating another male.

This is not to say that active homosexual pursuits are encouraged or even approved in all social contexts. Like adultery and heterosexual promiscuity, the active role in homosexual intercourse is seen as an infraction. That is, from the point of view of civil-religious authority, and from the point of view of women, it is indeed a sin (*pecado* or *mal*). But like its equivalent forms of adultery and promiscuity, the sodomizing act is a relatively minor sin. And in male–male social relations, any number of peccadillos (heavy drinking, promiscuity, the active role in same-sex intercourse) become status markers of male honor.

Nicaraguans exhibit no true horror of homosexuality in the North American style; their responses to the cochón tend rather toward amusement or contempt. The laughter of women often follows him down the street – discreet derision, perhaps, and behind his back, but the amusement of the community is ever present for the cochón. For men, the cochón is simultaneously an object of desire and reproach but that opprobrium knows tacit limits, community bounds. A reasonably discreet cochón – one

who dresses conservatively and keeps his affairs relatively discreet – will rarely be harassed or ridiculed in public, although he may be the butt of private jokes. If he is very discreet, his status may never even be acknowledged in his public presence and his practices will occupy the ambiguous category of a public secret.

The stigma involved here is not at all the same as the stigma implied in the western or North American concept of "the perverse," meaning "mis-use." It is certainly not the stigma of the fully rationalized, medicalized system of sexual meaning that elaborates a category, the homosexual, to identify both practice and identity. Rather, it is anal passivity alone that is stigmatized and it is anal passivity that defines the status identity in question. Moreover, the social definition of the person and his sexual stigma derive from culturally shared meanings of not just anal passivity and penile activity in particular but passivity and activity in general. "To give" (*dar*) is to be masculine, "to receive" (*recibir, aceptar, tomar*) is to be feminine. This holds as the ideal in all spheres of transaction between and among the genders. It is symbolized by the popular interpretation of the male sexual organ as active in intercourse and the female sexual organ (or male anus) as passive.

Cochones are, therefore, feminine men, specifically, feminized men, not fully male men. They are men who are used by other men. Their stigma flows from this concept of use. Used by other men, the cochón is not a complete man. His passive acquiescence to the active drive of other men's sexual desires both defines and stigmatizes his status. Consequently, when one uses a cochón, one acquires masculinity; when one is "used" as a cochón, one expends it. The nature of homosexual transaction, then, is that the act makes one man a machista and the other a cochón. The machista's honor and the cochón's shame are opposite sides of the same coin. The line that this transaction draws is not between those who practice homosexual intercourse and those who do not (for this is not a meaningful distinction at all in Nicaragua's popular classes) but between two standardized roles in that intercourse. Machistas make cochones out of other men and each is necessary to the definition of the other in a dynamic sense that is very different from the way North American categories of the hetero- and homosexual define each other. While each is defined by his exclusion from membership in some normative category, the cochón is defined by his inclusion in the sexual practices of ordinary men, albeit in a standardized and stigmatized role, and the homosexual by his exclusion from the sexual practices of ordinary men.

This inclusive aspect of sex also has implications for the nature of the cochón status as a political concept, for that category lacks the theoretical independence attributed to western homosexuality as a distinct category of activity and personal identity. A cochón requires ordinary men and his activity and identity can never be quite independent of them. Defined by its passivity, the status is ever a dependent one.

The Making of a Cochón

During my fieldwork in a working-class barrio of Managua, I had the opportunity to observe over a period of several months the interaction of boys in the neighborhood with a boy, "Miguel," already labeled a cochón. This label was in very common use. Other children, including his older brother, teased him with the name and, on occasion, even adults would taunt him as such.

At the age of twelve, Miguel bore few characteristics that would distinguish him from other boys his age. He was unusually small, giving the impression of being a much younger child of perhaps eight or nine. He was also quite intelligent, and received good marks in school but not to such a degree that one could say he had thereby marginated himself from his peers. Quite mischievous

and always getting into trouble, Miguel was by no means what one would think of as a sissy or "mama's boy."

A typical interaction between Miguel and the other boys would go as follows. They are all playing some game on the sidewalk out front or in the yard behind the house. The competition becomes acute and an argument develops. The argument eventually centers on Miguel versus some other boy or group of boys. Miguel's claim in the dispute is answered by the charge that he is a cochón. He insists, "*Yo no soy cochón*" ("I am not a cochón"), and fighting ensues, with Miguel typically throwing the first punches. The other boys eventually subdue Miguel and mimic sodomizing him.

In public, Miguel resists the label, in private he is less adamant. It is premature to say whether Miguel will in fact grow up to be a cochón. It appears that public opinion in the neighborhood is attempting to socialize him in that direction. But note that, unlike a North American counterpart labeled homosexual, the boy Miguel, labeled a cochón, is not thereby completely marginated from social activities among boys his age. He plays games and sports with them, fights with them, and at this stage the only thing that distinguishes him from the others is the fact that they call him cochón and pile on top of him in mock intercourse.

Of course, other readings of these actions are possible. Perhaps, seeing that he is small, and vulnerable, and fearing that he might grow up to be a cochón, the community is attempting to avert him from that dishonorable fate by punishing him whenever he shows signs of weakness, dependence, or passivity. It seems to me, however, that he was most likely to be punished by his peers when, as a small person, he attempted to assert his equality with much larger boys. At any rate, the argument is not that this particular case will indeed go on to become a cochón but that it exemplifies something of the rules of that status and its production.

We see this same sort of ambiguous status – stigmatized, yet not fully marginated – concerning adults. One incident in particular illustrates this. I was sitting in front of his repair shop and talking with "Carlos" one afternoon when a young man passed by on the street, riding in the back of a pickup truck that was hauling mechanical equipment. Carlos made obscene gestures at the other man, in effect offering to sodomize him. The man answered with his own gesticulations as the truck drove away. Carlos grinned and said, by way of explanation, that the man in the truck was a cochón, that he had fucked the man before, and that he would probably soon fuck the man again.

These obscene gestures, offers, and childhood games provide insight into the nature of the sexual practices in question and throw light on the social creation of the cochón. The cochón is but a necessary precipitant of the culture of machismo, or aggressive, competitive masculinity. One man offers to sodomize another, in effect, to make of him a cochón, or if he already is one, to use his services. Thus men desire to sodomize other men and fear being sodomized by them (Suarez-Orozco 1982). In the same manner, they desire to claim status and prestige and avoid being stigmatized. The routes of sexual use and pleasure thereby illuminate the pathways of male status and sexual power. Boys likewise exhibit their virility by labeling one of their members and mimicking anal intercourse with him. The object of sex/power is the same in either case. Those who consistently lose out in the competition for male status, or who can be convinced to dispose themselves to the sexual urges and status plays of other men, or who discover pleasure in the passive sexual role or its social status, are made into cochones.

It is most difficult to get reliable long-range material on the life cycles of cochones. Wrapped in an ambiguous public secrecy, they are both protected and maligned by community gossip. In practice, at the level of neighborhood rumors, this lends itself to both admissions and denials, accusations and defenses. Some men are clearly defined by that status, others are only slightly tainted with suspicion. Some apparently live out their entire life in that status, others successfully masculinize themselves by taking a wife and rearing children – though, in practice, they may (or may not) continue having covert affairs with men. Some develop longstanding covert relationships with particular men. Others become known in male gossip as someone to visit for sexual favors.

Rules in the Social Construction of Sexuality

These processes in the production of sexuality do indeed bear some resemblance to North American practices, where male power and status are bound around sexual themes but the resemblance holds only up to a point. Both the homosexual and the cochón are objects in a sexual discourse whose real subject is sexual power. But the structure of that discourse, the meaning of its categories, and the language in which it speaks are decidedly different in each case. To the extent that these processes may be seen at work in our own culture, we may summarize that the object is to label without being labeled, but not to use without being used, for it is the homosexual act itself that is prohibited and not any particular role within the act. Some males, especially adolescents, in our own milieu do in fact attempt to label without being labeled and also use without being used. The difference is that in Anglo-American contexts this is seen as a breach of the rule (or, sometimes, an adolescent suspension of the rule), since homosexual desire itself, without any qualifications, stigmatizes one as a homosexual.

The nature of homosexual transaction in Nicaragua's popular classes seems to bear much greater resemblance to the sexual economy of North America's prison populations (Blake 1971) and, by extension, to the milieu of truckstops (Corzine and Kirby 1977) and public toilet (Humphreys 1970) encounters, where, for purposes of a deviant subculture, one may indeed both label without being labeled and use without being used. Similar rules seem to be in play in either context: passive partners are labeled and stigmatized; active partners are not. The act of intercourse assigns honor to one man, shame to the other. In North American prisons, sex between men becomes a means of exchange because it signifies simultaneously pleasure and power in the absence of access to either by other means. But while suggestive, this comparison should not be overstated or underqualified. Whereas the rules of prison sexuality represent a deviant and stigmatized subculture – that is, a suspension or even inversion of the normal rules – the rules of sexuality and stigma in Nicaragua represent the dominant culture of the popular classes, a normative rather than deviant set of rules and categories.

Thus, the dominant North American rule would read as follows. A man gains sexual status and honor among other men through and only through his sexual transactions with women. Homosexuals appear as the *refuseniks* of that system. In Nicaragua, the rule is built around different principles. A man gains sexual status and honor among other men through his active role in sexual intercourse (either with women or with other men). Cochones are (passive) participants in that system.

Again, similar to Northern stereotypes of the homosexual, the cochón is commonly ascribed (and frequently exhibits) such personal characteristics as effeminacy and flamboyance. Feminized by more masculine men, some cochones act out their role in the more extreme form of transvestism. Many more appropriate semitransvestic forms of dress: a shirt just a little too blousy, or pants slightly too feminine in color, fit, or texture. As a normal rule, transvestism and near-transvestism receive the reproach of the

community. (I once saw a Nicaraguan girl throw out the dishwater on a cochón who passed by her house in just such a state of near-transvestism.) However, on the special occasions of certain popular religious celebrations, cochones may publicly exhibit their cross-dressing with the good will and even encouragement of the whole community.

These festivities represent a special niche in the religious life of the lower classes: like Bakhtin's (1984) carnival, they project the image of a libidinous popular insurrection (Davis 1978) through a spree of stylized rule-breaking. For these ritual occasions, the feminization of men semiotically corresponds to the themes of inversion and reversal that are the core of several popular religious festivities; men dress as women, people take on the costumes of animals, animals challenge human authority, lower classes challenge elite authority, and so on (Lancaster in press). In Masaya's *carnaval*, Managua's *Santo Domingo*, and other such rituals, the cochón is granted a reprieve from his secrecy and surreption, given a political voice, and cast in a central role in popular religious festivities.

The popular imagination, then, takes up the cochón in an ambiguous way that imbues him with two different meanings. On the one hand, he is usually an object of amusement and contempt, a passive participant put to the use of others. On special occasions, though, the cochón becomes a subject who offers his parodical commentary on a whole array of social and sexual relations. Frequently taunting *machistas* and mocking civil-religious authority along the way, the transvestic cochón becomes the polysemic voice of discontent in these processions. In his inversion, object becomes subject, and silence bursts out with a voice that discerns the real powers of the powerless and the used. Through the alchemy of popular ritual, the cochón represents the larger point of view of the dispossessed classes in revolt against established authority.

Again, this points to a striking contrast with the North American homosexual. At his most politically conscious, the homosexual organizes himself into a subculture, a subeconomy, a single-issue politics, all of whose logic is quite singular. The cochón, at his most political, represents a very different sort of thing: through the polymorphousness of metaphor, *carnaval* speaks to a multiplication of meanings and social entanglements, not to their compartmentalization and impoverishment.

Where Nicaragua's folk categories and sexual transactions most strikingly parallel Western European/North American rules is not in any deviant subculture of the present but, rather, in sexual categories and practices widespread in the past, before progressive rationalization in the institutions of religion, law, medicine, and psychiatry had refined a category – the homosexual – out of traditional folk constructs (Boswell 1980; Trumbach 1977; Weeks 1977). Like its traditional Western parallels of whatever shade (e.g., bugger, sodomite, faggot, etc.), the cochón represents a stigmatized sexual identity, as yet still minimally administered by the institutions of rational sexual categorization and control, still more or less under the rule of popular categories and controls. But even here the cultural tradition in which we encounter the cochón is different from its Anglo-European counterparts, whose folk-terms often designate the active, not passive, category of practice, identity and stigma. Even as a traditional or nonrationalized construct, the cochón lives in a different cultural stream than "buggers" and "sodomites."

Cochones and the Revolution

The Sandinista Revolution and its accompanying changes have clearly introduced a variety of contradictory changes in the culture's understanding of sexual practices. It may be that the image of *carnaval* captures and perpetuates the image of revolt so necessary in the imagination of the populace that would be revolutionary, but the consolidation of a revolutionary state is anything but an extended carnival. Certainly, the revolution has produced a constraining effect on homosexual practice. The nature of socialist revolution, and perhaps particularly that variety influenced by liberation theology, entails a strong normative or corporatist component. The "New Man" and the "New Society" are envisioned as hardworking, diligent, and studious; pure and without corruption. The aspect of machismo that the New Man embodies is the self-sacrificing side, not the hedonistic one. The cult of the New Man, then, produces a cultural atmosphere in which homosexual practice (and sexual transgression in general) is at least publicly regarded as more suspect than before, tainted with the image of indulgence or corruption, and is perhaps even somewhat less readily available.

More concretely, the revolution has everywhere tried to strengthen the moral force of the community, especially through the Comites de Defensa Sandinista (CDS), the neighborhood defense organizations. Through such organizations and through the sensibility of revolution generally, the gaze of the community is particularly strong and the semiprivate, semipublic status of the cochón is rendered more problematic. Especially in areas of public morality and public order, a variety of activities, such as prostitution, have been actively curbed by the Sandinista Police and the CDS. On a much smaller scale than Havana, Managua once sported an elite and tourist-oriented night-life, including perhaps a dozen total assorted homosexual bars, exclusive gay clubs, drag shows, and male stripper acts. These serviced Managua's middle-class homosexuals, some of its lower-class cochones, and gay tourists from other countries. They are gone now and what remains is a small handful of much more discreet bars.

Such closures have affected the traditional cochón much less than the Western-oriented gay or homosexual of professional or middle-class origins. As one Sandinista activist from a working-class barrio (who alternately and in his mind synonymously described himself as a cochón, homosexual, or gay) put it, "It is true that there are fewer bars now but most of the ones that existed before served only the affluent, not the poor. You had to be rich to get into those nightclubs. It is not so much that they have been closed down by the police or the CDS, as that they have moved to Miami with the rich people."

Not all of the effects of the revolution on cochones have been restrictive. While maintaining a discreet sexual profile, many have participated in the revolutionary process, some rising to positions of great authority in the CDS, the FSLN (Frente Sandinista de i Liberación Nacionál), and even the government proper. The informant cited above, for instance, had been elected Barrio Director, the highest position in the local CDS. Having fewer family responsibilities and dependents appears to have freed up the time of many politically conscious cochones to work for the revolution. In the process some have gained recognition and stature in the community in a manner not unlike the charisma that priests derive from a life of celibacy and service.

In Nicaragua, the traditional categories remain the dominant popular ones but they are now coexisting and competing with a Western perception of homosexuality. Sexual education in the schools, social contact with internacionalistas from the United States and Western Europe, and greater access to international ideas and philosophies all facilitate the acquisition of Western sexual models, especially in elite segments of the populace; i.e., the urban, middle-class sectors that look to the United States and Western Europe for educational and cultural values.

In some sections of Managua one now hears such terms as "homosexual" and "heterosexual." For certain members of that narrow stratum of urban elites, these terms

are not so misleading. But many of Managua's sexually active youth, even some of working-class origins (like the Dirigente del Barrio cited above), also now call themselves "homosexual," "bisexual," or "gay." New syncretisms are indeed slowly emerging but in practice the dominant logic of the sexual system remains traditional, native, and popular. The casual importation of scientific and even political sexual terminologies serves to confuse casual foreign observers in much the same way that the casual use of those terms in social science confuses issues and assimilates real differences. What a Nicaraguan means when he calls himself "gay" is very different from what a North American has in mind when he uses the same term, even though the two may find themselves in broad agreement on certain particulars. New words like "homosexual" and "gay" typically enter the popular vocabulary as synonyms for familiar categories and practices, rather than as new concepts in themselves. This is especially true in the popular classes; and many Nicaraguans, even in Managua, remain quite unfamiliar with these newly introduced words.

The remarkable conservatism of culture lies precisely in its ability to animate new words with old ideas. While it is doubtful that one could speak of a pure folk model anymore in Managua, it is clear that the traditional logic of sexuality remains intact for the massive lower classes. What would mark a real change in Nicaragua's sexual culture is not the importation of a new sexual lexicon – which might just as easily be imbued with archaic as with modern meanings – but, rather, the introduction of new terms, along with the proliferation of specialized bureaucratic instruments of sexual regulation to which those terms correspond (e.g., psychology) and the development of a homosexual subculture based on a wider variety of less stereotyped roles and practices. But these conditions clearly have not been met.

What is a Homosexual?

Strathern (1981: 682) uses the phrase "No such thing as a woman" to stress certain theoretical points on the nature of gender studies. Here, I follow her lead and attempt to make similar points in treating the nature and construction of the traditional Nicaraguan folk category, the cochón. We may speculate that this category is the result of a syncretism between Iberian and indigenous sexual role systems. Moreover, based on my conversations with other Latin Americanists, it seems that the cochón exemplifies something of the sexual rules that are generally found in most Latin American countries, where the essential elements of the cochón appear under different names and with somewhat different definitions (Carrier 1976; Parker 1984, 1985; Williams 1986: 147–51).

Labels such as homosexual or heterosexual, along with Northern European/North American presumptions about stigma, fail to account for the Nicaraguan sexual constructs that ultimately produce the cochón. Theoretically, this sort of difficulty crimps attempts at writing a general history or anthropology of homosexuality, for such projects must be hedged from the outset with a myriad of qualifications and circumlocutions. At every turn we are always running up against the unintelligibility of foreign practices to our concepts and categories.

But the cochón is by no means as exotic a phenomenon as the cross-gendered (Whitehead 1981) or gender-mixed (Callender and Kochems 1983) native North American berdache, nor are his practices as far from Northern European notions of homosexuality as are the homosexual initiation rites reported for parts of Melanesia (Herdt 1981, 1982). Indeed, it is his very similarity to the North American homosexual that makes the cochón appear at first glance readily interchangeable with him: both are adult males with a stigmatized sexual iden-

tity. Only on close inspection can we see that the process of identity- and stigma-production in each case is radically different, governed by different rules, producing a markedly different existential state. We could say, in Wittgensteinian terms, that machismo is a different game, governed by different rules; or we could say, in Marxian terms, that it represents a different sexual economy, a different mode in the production of sex/gender; or, in Foucauldian terms, we could say that Latin sexuality represents a radically different discursive practice than Anglo sexuality.

The necessity of drawing such distinctions is far from settled in the current literature. Herdt (1981: 3, 321) finds "heterosexual adults" in the highlands of Papua New Guinea and Williams (1986) has more recently reiterated the old thesis that the berdache is an Amerindian gay in native drag. Nonetheless, anthropology has been becoming more or less sensitive to phenomenological differences when they exist at these great distances. Until now, though, the nuances that distinguish such phenomena as the cochón from the homosexual typically have been glossed under the misleading terminologies of the latter. Nash (1979: 141) identifies persons who appear to be the Bolivian equivalents of Nicaraguan cochones as "men with homosexual tendencies" and Cuba's Santeria cult is sometimes given as a native niche for an otherwise unproblematic Cuban homosexuality (Arguelles and Rich, 1984–5: 688). At best, modifications of that terminology have suggested themselves; e.g., "selective homophobia" to identify the stigmatization of the "passive homosexual" (Murphy 1984). (See also Brandes's [1981: 232–4] discussion of the passive role in homosexual intercourse in Andalusia.)

Such terminology, even when modified, obscures more than it clarifies. Nicaragua's cochones are ontologically different creatures of culture than are Anglo-American homosexuals. Both are clearly stigmatized but they are stigmatized in different ways, according to different rules. Nor is it, as it is often maintained, that in Latin America homophobia is of substantively the same sort that one encounters in Northern Europe and North America, only more severe in its operations. It is not that homophobia is more intense in a culture of machismo but that it is of a different sort altogether. Indeed, the word "homophobia," meaning a fear of homosexuals or homosexual intercourse, is quite inappropriate in a milieu where men desire and actively seek homosexual intercourse. An altogether different word is necessary to identify the praxis implicit in machismo, whereby men may simultaneously desire to use, fear being used by, and stigmatize, other men.

If this criterion allows us to distinguish various systems of sexual signification and power, it may also allow us to generalize a limited number of systems based on the operation of similar rules. Nicaragua's sexual system, with its active-honor/passive-shame dichotomy, exemplifies rules governing male sexual relations not only for Latin America generally but also for cultures throughout the Mediterranean and the Middle East. Numerous and widely variegated subtypes no doubt obtain[3] in what we might provisionally call peasant sexuality, but with its series of dichotomous distinctions – penile–anal, active–passive, honor–stigma – it clearly stands opposed to what we might call the bourgeois sexuality predominant in Northern Europe and its offspring cultures, especially in the Anglophone world. While this latter type has undergone successive degrees of intensification and rationalization, its original peculiarity seems to rest on its blanket condemnation of all same-sex practices and, perhaps, especially active ones (Trumbach 1977). In general, bourgeois sexuality is susceptible to greater or lesser degrees of rationalization in sociosexual control, whereas peasant sexuality is susceptible to greater or lesser degrees of severity in its prohibitions, constraints, or stigmas.

This active-honor/passive-shame dichotomy recalls something of the logic of homosexual activity for the ancient Greeks, who divided appropriate roles into two age classes, adult activity and youthful passivity, as Foucault (1985: 221) observes.

> Hence the problem that we may call the "antinomy of the boy" in Greek ethics of aphrodisia. On the one hand, young men were recognized as objects of pleasure – and even as the only honorable and legitimate objects among the possible male partners of men: no one would ever reproach a man for loving a boy, for desiring and enjoying him, provided that the laws and proprieties were respected. But on the other hand, the boy, whose youth must be a training for manhood, could not and must not identify with that role. He could not of his own accord, in his own eyes, and for his own sake, be the object of that pleasure, even though the man was quite naturally fond of appointing him as an object of pleasure. In short, to delight in and be a subject of pleasure with a boy did not cause a problem for the Greeks; but to be an object of pleasure and to acknowledge oneself as such constituted a major difficulty for the boy.

Arguably, the same-sex initiation practices employed in certain Melanesian societies appear to represent a special instantiation of these active–passive rules: (oral or anal) adolescent passivity, (penile) adult activity. But in this case it makes little sense to speak of stigma and Melanesia clearly represents an independent type. The boy's social–sexual status is an absence of manhood; insemination is practiced to correct that, not to perpetuate or reinforce it. And these relationships, as in ancient Greece, ultimately take the form of generalized reciprocity; passive youths become active males vis-à-vis new youths.

Degrees of stigma may vary in both bourgeois and peasant contexts and the practice of labeling may or may not be stringent, depending on historical conditions. But it seems probable that all societies, save those in the Northern European cultural stream, elaborate some passive–active dichotomy for male homosexual practices and that the active role escapes both label and stigma. In none of these cases would we be justified to speak of a homosexual, although there is undoubtedly homosexual activity. In this model, transvestism appears, not as a separate type, as Trumbach (1977) argues, but as a residual one. It may be arrived at in either sexual system by different means or it may constitute a "third gender" (Whitehead 1981) belonging not to sexuality proper but to gender/labor relations more specifically. Unstigmatized and nonstereotyped reciprocal homosexual relations between adolescents may be informally countenanced in all systems save the most rationalized (bourgeois) modes or the most severe (peasant) ones.

The provisional models offered here say little about female same-sex practices. In Nicaragua, as throughout the peasant world, there is little folk interest in categorizing or regulating female same-sex relations and little exists in the popular lexicon to account for it. Surely, Nicaraguans can express censure over female same-sex improprieties but without the refined and specialized vocabulary through which they speak of the cochón. The culture of machismo, which speaks so directly to male practices, can only speak indirectly or inversely of female ones.

Conclusion

This essay differentiates apparent similarities in two sexual systems; it diagrams the rules that define the stigmatized Nicaraguan sexual category, the cochón, and contrasts it with the North American homosexual. The cochón is not just one refraction of a larger, universal homosexual category (embedded in nature – or perhaps, in unnature), nor is the English term "homosexual" an appropriate translation of that concept – which must, indeed, remain fundamentally untranslatable. This method of semiotic differentiation is in keeping with prevailing deconstruction-

ist and Marxist (D'Emilio 1983: 4) approaches in sexuality studies, but it also represents a straightforward application of basic Boasian principles on the terrain of sex: *viz.*, that what is meaningful about culture is internal, not external, and that cultural meaning rests in specific milieux, not in aggregations of cultures assembled in the light of unproblematic commonsense categories. Thus, to study the cochón is also to deconstruct our own universalized category, the homosexual; an act may be called homosexual that involves two men, but what is significant and meaningful about that act lies beyond any *a priori* assumptions about the nature of homosexual activity.

Seen in these terms, the specific configuration of sex, power, and stigma traced in Nicaragua's popular classes is indeed jarringly dissimilar to the predominant North American configuration. But it is not dissimilar to other configurations. Our critical method need not lend itself only to the endless production of distinctions; it can also elaborate typologies based on the operation of similar rules. I have provisionally proposed: (1) Anglo-Northern European or bourgeois sexuality and (2) Circum-Mediterranean/Latin American or peasant sexuality.

This analysis of the cochón and the concomitant typology it draws differ from previous typologies on one significant account. Earlier typologies have classified same-sex practices in terms of simple variations on the repressive principle. For instance, Bullough (1976: 25) accounts for the stark presence of role-differentiated homosexual activity in the Mediterranean by the relative absence of available heterosexual outlets. His logic is very simple: sexuality, like water, is an *a priori* force; dammed up in one outlet, it will invariably seek out another. In contrast to such simple hydraulic models of sexuality, our analysis of the cochón, and our elaboration of a broader cochón type, flows from our emphasis on a productive (not repressive) paradigm (Foucault 1978: 3–13). That is, something in machismo other than scarcity of women (and certainly other than extreme homophobia) precipitates the cochón (as opposed to masturbation or abstinence), shapes his behavior, defines his identity. That something is a configuration of sex/power along the active/passive dimension. It renders certain organs and roles "active," other body passages and roles "passive," and assigns honor/shame and status/stigma accordingly.

This mapping of the body, its accesses and privileges, is at once a map of pleasure and power. And the relationship of the cochón to power, as to the grammar of sex, constitutes a different cultural ensemble than that configuration which we call the homosexual. The object-choice of the homosexual marginates him from male power, except insofar as he can serve as a negative example and thus mark off the circuitry of power; a breaker of rules, he is positioned outside the operational rules of normative (hetero)-sexuality. That of the cochón casts him in the role of object to machismo's subjectivity; that is, it puts him in a stigmatized but by no means marginated relation to sex/power. Each is defined by a play of sex/power but the homosexual is a marginated subject, divested of power, around whom power flows, while the cochón-type is an object through whom power flows and who is therefore, paradoxically, the locus of power's investment in itself.

NOTES

1   Called "the festival of disguises," *Carnaval* is a religious celebration held annually in the large agricultural market town of Masaya. It marks the climax of a series of religious festivals in that town, not the approach of Lent. An important presence among the elaborate masks and disguises of *Carnaval* is that of the cochones, who don female attire and parade alongside other participants in the day's procession.

2   My spelling throughout conforms to the only spelling I have ever seen in print, in a *Nuevo Diario* (December 6, 1985) editorial.

3   For instance, some Middle Eastern cultures cast these active–passive rules in terms of active adults and passive youths (Trumbach 1977: 8).

REFERENCES

Arguelles, L. and B. R. Rich. 1984–5. "Homosexuality, Homophobia, and Revolution: Notes Toward an Understanding of the Cuban Lesbian and Gay Male Experience." *Signs* 9: 683–99 and 11: 13–21.

Bakhtin, M. 1984. *Rabelais and His World*. Bloomington, IN.

Blake, J. 1971. *The Joint*. New York.

Boswell, J. 1980. *Christianity, Social Tolerance, and Homosexuality*. Chicago.

Brandes, S. 1981. "Like Wounded Stags: Male Sexual Ideology in an Andalusian Town." In *Sexual Meanings: The Cultural Construction of Gender and Sexuality*, ed. S. Ortner and H. Whitehead, pp. 216–39. Cambridge.

Bullough, V. L. 1976. *Sexual Variance in Society and History*. Chicago.

Callender, C. and L. M. Kochems. 1983. "The North American Berdache." *Current Anthropology* 24: 1–76.

Carrier, J. J. 1976. "Family Attitudes and Mexican Male Homosexuality." *Urban Life* 5: 359–75.

Corzine, J. and R. Kirby. 1977. "Cruising and Truckers: Sexual Encounters in a Highway Rest Area." *Urban Life* 6: 171–92.

Davis, N. Z. 1978. "Women on Top: Symbolic Sexual Inversion and Political Disorder in Early Modern Europe." In *The Reversible World: Symbolic Inversion in Art and Society*, ed. B. A. Babcock, pp. 147–90. Ithaca, NY.

D'Emilio, J. 1983. *Sexual Politics, Sexual Communities: The Making of a Homosexual Minority in the United States, 1940–1970*. Chicago.

Foucault, M. 1978. *The History of Sexuality, Volume One: An Introduction*. Trans. R. Hurley. New York.

—— 1985. *The Use of Pleasure: The History of Sexuality, Volume Two*. Trans. R. Hurley. New York.

Herdt, G. H. 1981. *Guardians of the Flutes: Idioms of Masculinity*. New York.

—— 1982. "Fetish and Fantasy in Sambia Initiation." In *Rituals of Manhood: Male Initiation in Papua New Guinea*, ed. G. H. Herdt, pp. 44–98. Berkeley, CA.

Humphreys, L. 1970. *Tearoom Trade: Impersonal Sex in Public Places*. New York.

Lancaster, R. N. in press. *Thanks to God and the Revolution: Popular Religion and Class Consciousness in the New Nicaragua*. New York.

Murphy, M. D. 1984. "Masculinity and Selective Homophobia: A Case from Spain." Anthropology Research Group on Homosexuality (ARGOH) Newsletter 5: 6–12.

Nash, J. 1979. *We Eat the Mines and the Mines Eat Us: Dependency and Exploitation in Bolivian Tin Mines*. New York.

Parker, R. 1984. "The Body and the Self: Aspects of Male Sexual Ideology in Brazil." Paper presented at the 83rd annual meeting of the American Anthropological Association in Denver, Colorado.

—— 1985. "Masculinity, Femininity, and Homosexuality: On the Anthropological Interpretation of Sexual Meanings in Brazil." *Journal of Homosexuality* 11: 155–63.

Strathern, M. 1981. "Culture in a Netbag: The Manufacture of a Subdiscipline in Anthropology." *Man* (N.S.) 16: 665–88.

Suarez-Orozco, M. M. 1982. "A Study of Argentine Soccer: The Dynamics of Fans and Their Folklore." *Journal of Psychoanalytic Anthropology* 5: 7–28.

Trumbach, R. 1977. "London's Sodomites: Homosexual Behavior and Western Culture in the Eighteenth Century." *Journal of Social History* 11: 1–33.

Weeks, J. 1977. *Coming Out: Homosexual Politics in Britain, from the Nineteenth Century to the Present*. London.

Whitehead, H. 1981. "The Bow and the Burden Strap: A New Look at Institutionalized Homosexuality in Native North America." *Sexual Meanings*, ed. S. Ortner and H. Whitehead, pp. 80–115. Cambridge.

Williams, W. L. 1986. *The Spirit and the Flesh: Sexual Diversity in American Indian Culture*. Boston.

7 Copycat

Kath Weston

Scratch a lesbian couple, and you'll find a couple of heterosexuals. Or, more precisely, heterosexual wannabes. After all, somebody must be "the man." For the better part of a century, that's been the prevailing wisdom about lesbian relationships. The best efforts of the "women-loving-women" of the 1970s to eliminate gendered differences from their relationships through the look-alike, act-alike stance of androgyny didn't do much to shake this misconception. Too often, ambiguity just paved the way for harassment and interrogation. The bottle thrown from a passing car sailed toward its target on the back of a question: "Who's the guy?"

The belief that gay relationships mirror straight relationships is the stuff of fantasy, fiction, and stereotype. Almost to a person, lesbians say it's not that way. Some fight back against this simple-minded claim with the argument that same-sex relationships are about shared gender, not gendered differences. Women-loving-women, right? Of course, that leaves the little matter of so-called "roles."

When it comes to femme and butch, charges of imitation reappear, this time in the mouths of gay women. Perhaps, some speculate, butch/femme is just another form of male/female worming its way into gay relationships. Like many lesbian-feminists of the 1970s, they see butch/femme as a practice that takes heterosexuality as the standard for measuring all things queer.

The second-hand clothes of a borrowed gender are almost sure to come up second-best, given the premium placed on originality in the United States. Where's the pride in mimicking someone else? But imitation is itself a vexed subject. Exactly who, or what, are lesbians supposed to be imitating? Individual heterosexuals? People who may be as deviant as your mother, as law-abiding as your Uncle Frank (who never did get around to applying for that green card), as fun-loving as the family down the hall, as quiet as the couple with the cement deer on the lawn before the police arrived to arrest the man of the house and carry his wife's shattered body away?

If imitation does not set its sights on individuals, then what? Too many *I Love Lucy* reruns? How about something more abstract, like gender roles? But what are roles, anyway? A white, middle-class model for gendering? Then wouldn't your relationship to imitation differ, depending upon whether you yourself are white or well-off? Could there be as many ways of gendering heterosexuality as homosexuality? Does it even make sense to talk about a prepackaged "woman's role" or "man's role" (much less femininity and masculinity) apart from race and class?

The flip side of the imitation argument contends that gay women have created relationships without the benefit of models. Their partnerships represent forays into uncharted territory, completely set apart from heterosexuality. So what if one partner always takes out the garbage? Why does that have to have anything do with heterosexuality, much less gender? In this interpretation, butch/femme appears to carry forward a uniquely lesbian "tradition."

Some of the women in this chapter think imitation whenever they think butch/femme. They wonder why anyone would bother incorporating gendered contrasts into lesbian relationships. Isn't the point of being queer to get away from all that mess? Yet they voice questions and desires that testify to a lingering ambivalence, even attraction, to forms of gendering they associate with heterosexuality.

Later chapters feature women who argue just as strongly that it is possible to have gendered differences in a lesbian relationship without casting that relationship in a straight image. These women are more inclined to ask why people so easily equate femme with femininity, or butch with masculinity. Isn't there anything distinctive that sets lesbian gendering apart from heterosexual relationships?

Cynthia Murray: "The Dads Always Drive the Boat"

"It's something that I never did quite understand: the why. Why women are extremely butch, or why women are extremely femme. My perception of it has always been, if I wanted to go out with a guy I'd go out with a guy. I wouldn't go out with a butch woman. And I can't understand the mountains of makeup. But I can understand the feeling glamorous part of it.

"I lived in Los Angeles before I moved up here, for eleven years, and I met a lot of older women that were gay. I saw photographs of them when they were young and one of them looked like Rory Calhoun. He was an actor. He did a lot of Westerns in the 1950s and early 1960s. Really dark hair and really blue eyes; quite the ladies' man. This one woman [who] showed me the pictures of her looking like Rory Calhoun – she looked so femme when she was in her fifties! She just died a couple of years ago. She was telling me that she went through so much inner turmoil because that was the only way she could get to go out with the women she wanted. Because the femme women liked butch women.

"A lot of the women that I met in LA that were butch were like that: in one way or another, they all acted like my dad. And some of them dressed like my dad. He was a hunter, a kind of rednecked street kind of guy. He was a party guy. So he was fun but he was very macho and had his opinions. He had my mother on this pedestal; that's where

she should be. He installed swimming pools, so [he wore] everything from coveralls to Levis to man-pants and man-shoes. Shoes made out of petroleum products!

"My initial thought, I suppose, when I was a kid was that I wanted to be a man, not that I wanted to be gay. I wasn't content being a woman. I waterskied and liked driving the boat. The dads always drive the boat – the mom never got to drive the boat. I did things that women just didn't do when I was really young. Like most girls wouldn't walk into a bar by themselves. I would walk into a bar anywhere. I never cared. If I wanted a cocktail, I'd go into a bar! And that was unheard of. Things that it was okay for men to do but it wasn't okay for women to do.

"[Then those things] became more socially acceptable among people in general, among the masses. You saw women going to the moon and they weren't gay. You saw women driving cars and there wasn't someone in Arkansas saying, 'Oh my god, she's queer!' That's one of the good things I think the women's organizations have done. And I'm not on the feminist bandwagon, either.

"A lot of the so-called feminists, they've come a long way, they've accomplished a lot for women, but they've also made it very difficult for women, especially in the corporate atmosphere. Because a lot of times now men will automatically think, 'She's an executive, so she's a bitch. It just goes hand in hand, because she had to fight twice as hard to get where she is.' And that's not true, so it's harder to deal in business now.

"Being gay has never been a major thing for me. No, the butch/femme thing is what confused me. I was fine with being gay; it seemed very natural to me. My parents were very good about it, very understanding, and it didn't break their hearts or anything. But before I knew what gay was, I thought, 'Why do I want to sleep with women? I must want to be a man.' I used to fantasize about being butch and actually about being male. So I took that and ran with it, and that was what made it hard.

"But then when I got older and became more aware of my sexuality, I was really glad that I was a woman. I became more confident with myself. So that is what led me to be more femme than butch. I'm getting a little too old to be active enough to be that butch! As far as being the truck-driving type mama, I don't know! Since I'm calmer now it doesn't make me so aggressive. When I think of butch I think aggressive."

Given what Cynthia described as a change from butch to femme over the course of her 34 years, I was curious about how she thought others perceived her. "First impressions mean a lot. That's why I think how I'm dressed would have a lot to do with it. If it's on one of those days where I just climbed off of a motorcycle, I think I'm going to look more butch than femme! But women that know me think of me as more femme than butch.

"I used to hate it, when I was a little kid, being called a boy. It still pisses me off on the telephone if someone calls me 'sir.' But I think it's for different reasons now. Now it's because I like my voice and I'm comfortable with my voice and I don't feel that it sounds like a man's voice. I feel that they're not paying attention to what they're doing. (You'll listen to this [on tape] and go, 'She *did* sound like a man'!) But when I was a little kid it was because I was afraid of my thoughts, of what I was thinking about wanting to be a boy. And so when they called me that by mistake, I would feel that they knew my deepest, darkest secret. So it was much more sensitive for me then.

"I don't think the butch women are going femme because of their careers. I just think that many more feminine women are coming out of the closet. Especially on the West Coast, because it's so much more socially acceptable here. When I was in a job position that I had to dress up every day, I really resented wearing skirts and femme clothes and lace. I really resented it, because I dressed up every day, so it wasn't special. But now I don't have to and it's more fun to dress up and go out. I get more looks when I'm dressed like that than when I'm dressed more butch. From men *and* women.

"When I flew to New Orleans [on business] recently, I had a layover in Texas. All the guys in Texas were like, 'Oh, let me get your bag! Let me get the door!' They were such gentlemen in that respect. It was real different, because I wasn't accustomed to that in LA. And I do that for men, too. I don't think that courtesy should stop at whether you're butch or femme or male or female. It's just common courtesy.

"I've always thought people should capitalize on their talents. So I feel I should accentuate being a woman. Not trying to change it but trying to accentuate it and make it better."

Charlyne Harris: "You Act Like a White Girl"

"A lot of black males, they don't know that I'm a lesbian. I have a good relationship with them. And it's how I treat them, too. I'm not real aggressive with them. I think men in general have a real strong ego, but black men, especially, their egos need to be acknowledged. You know: 'I am the man and you are the woman.' So it's very few black men that I have a good relationship with that *know* I'm a lesbian. I can't think of one.

"Right now I'm pretty much involved in the black community. But they don't know that I'm a lesbian, too, see. It would dampen our relationship. There would be less trust. Most of them are Muslim, and they *really* believe that homosexuality is bad. Who I sleep with would change their whole ideas about me, when yet and still, my personality is the exact same with them. But just saying that I was a lesbian, I'd be a degenerate! I'd be a degenerate, that's what I would be. And they would try to change my mind.

"When I moved to the Bay Area [as a child], it was really something different for me. I had never lived where it was all blacks, or a majority of blacks. I had a little trouble there. Because my slang was a little different, and just my whole character was different. And you know they noticed it right away. They said, 'Aw, you talk like a white girl. You act like a white girl.' Because the schools I went to [before] was majority white. There was not a lot of racial problems. Kids played together and you never tripped. Well, you know you're black and you know they're white, you know the skin color's different, but mentally you don't really know. It was never like, 'Oh, you're different than I am.' None of that ever came up until I got older.

"[Growing up, we] never really suffered, as far as financially. We always had. My mom made her way. And my grandmother had a little money. I mean, not too many black kids take tap dance. [My mom] always made a little bit of money go a long ways." As an adult, Charlyne made her living in the trades. She was amused to discover that "some women find that real romantic. I don't. It's money. The money's good, and I like what I'm doing, working with my hands.

"I had a boyfriend tell me that I would end up sleeping with women. I don't know what made him think that I will. I know I was real aggressive with him. He couldn't tell me what to do. It was always, 'We are equal!' And I was always making that known. 'There's nothing a woman can do for me.' I remember telling him that.

"I was messing with older men, and they would want to be the aggressor. You know, 'Do what I say.' I started coming out of that shit – I couldn't take that. Then the real me started coming out: 'Uh-uh, buddy, wait a minute! No, no, no.' And then we started clashing. My relationships with men changed, became bad relationships. I remember with my ex-boyfriend, he wanted me to be home at a certain time, wear certain clothes. I couldn't wear this, I can't wear that. 'You're not my father! Shit!' We'd get into arguments like that. I couldn't take that 'I'm the man, you're the woman.' This kind of a relationship [where] you're down here.

"I go to church. Baptist churches are real, real dramatic. They leave a heavy impression on you. When they preach, it's kind of scary. People start shouting. I don't know who said it, but it stuck in my head that if you're bad you go to hell. You know, God is watching you! At all times! I had to come to believe that God, as I understood God, is a loving God. It doesn't matter who you sleep with, just as long as your heart's good.

"If I'd have stayed in my neighborhood, I probably would have never came out. Never. But here there's so much support to be who you are, not to deny yourself. [My mother and I] talk about men. I'd say, 'Well, you know, I *am* attracted to men physically, just not emotionally.' And I said, 'Well, I could get married and see women on the side.' And she's saying, 'No, you got to make up your mind. You can't go back and forth. You got to make up your mind.' She thinks it would affect my relationships, and it would. It would. So I just decided for right now that I enjoy being with women and that's who I'm going to be with.

"I think, being a woman, I'm a woman, and women have certain moods. I don't think that I should put myself in a category and say, 'Well, I'm butch,' and deny myself to feel certain things. I like wearing dresses sometimes. Sometimes I like wearing makeup. I couldn't do it every day – I wouldn't want to do it every day. But yeah, sometimes I get in real feminine moods. Some of [the men at work] might not even believe me [if I told them I was gay]. Because they have such stereotyped ideas about how lesbians are supposed to be. Real aggressive at all times, and real, real butch."

When she first moved to San Francisco, Charlyne had tried to change her style. "A certain [butch] way of talking, a certain walk and dress. Until I learned that, no, I'll just be myself. [It helped] seeing different, other lesbians. Experience." In the beginning, though, "the [racial] prejudice thing threw me off guard. I didn't think I would have to deal with that [in the gay community]. Prejudice is something that no one has to say to you. You *feel* it. You would think that, because being gay you know what that feels like to be discriminated against, that you would not want to make anybody else feel that.

"And this butch female thing, I stereotyped that to the max, [until] I found out different. Just because a woman seem like she's real feminine doesn't mean she doesn't have butch qualities. And that doesn't mean that they don't come out. I'd rather come up to a female than for them to come up to me. It makes me nervous or uncomfortable when a woman approaches me. When women do come up to me, I find that I'll switch it around real fast where I'm the aggressor. I think that's my part in being butch! I like being the aggressor. Not in bed, though, all the time.

"You pick up male-orientated things from being around males, and I try to watch it that I don't have male-orientated ideas. Like I went to a strip show once, a female strip show. That's male-orientated, and I had to really check out why, why was I going?" "So why were you going?" I asked Charlyne. "Women were taking off their clothes," she replied. "Women were taking off their clothes, that's why I was going! I had to let that be okay, and not really trip off [by telling myself], 'Well, this is male-orientated.'"

Paula Nevins: "I Never Knew There Were Feminine Lesbians"

"I didn't give a shit about being a lesbian. I wanted to sleep with Stephanie. If that meant that I was a lesbian, fine. So one day when we were having lunch – we were having a tunafish sandwich in Union Square – I told her that I was interested in having a relationship with her, and I wasn't real picky about what it looked like. It could look like friends if she wanted it to look like that, but it felt like more.

"Stephanie was really the first woman that I knew [who] was up front and gay.

[The first] that I had an opportunity to be with and talk to and not be afraid. Because the only lesbians that I really knew were the – how can I say? – the obvious, very butch type. I never knew there were feminine lesbians. Stephanie was a prom queen." Ironically, Stephanie had always assumed that Paula, as the veteran of a heterosexual marriage, was straight. The two women embarked upon what turned out to be a five-year relationship.

Although Paula considered butch/femme "role-playing" and "a trap," she thought she could understand its attractions. "The roles have sort of been cast, so you don't have to worry about who's butch and who isn't, who should do the asking and who should wait to be asked, who should make the first move. You know, all of the 'shoulds' that go on with women that make women kind of crazy."

As a small business owner with a large lesbian clientele, Paula said, "I've talked to a lot of women and [butch/femme] comes up consistently around this whole dating/sexual issue. They have a hard time with it. Also, it's not easy to find women who are very interested in being casual and not wanting to bond to you. I mean, you can talk about 'I just would like to be sexual or see you once in a while.' Most women don't want to go for that. They really don't. It may be just a three-month period of time, but they basically want to eat, drink, and sleep you. I don't want to do that, and so what I want may be difficult for me to have at this point. I'm going to try and have it, though.

"I'm not sure that the only way to have a casual affair in the lesbian community isn't to get somebody who has a primary relationship but wants to sleep around. So then you're safe. But I think that with women, the bonding issue comes up much stronger than with men. I have very close, intimate relationships with men that are not sexual, but I have never had the real intense, intimate relationship with a man that I have with women.

"Although I've been very, very sexual in my life with men, I was never into it. It was always like paint-by-numbers. I never did anything from an emotional place; I was always absolutely detached from the person. I always felt there was something wrong with me, because I never liked to go to the drive-in and make out. And the interesting thing is, men never had any trouble getting into it. I always wondered, well, can't they sense that I'm not really into this? But I don't think they could, because I think their own needs were primary."

Sometimes Paula wondered if she were moving into bisexuality. "There are times when I don't feel like a lesbian at all. There are times when I do. Certainly relationships with men are a lot simpler. Men are very simple beings." A few months earlier Paula had met a teenage boy while hiking at Yosemite. She described him as "this very beautiful, innocent being. I can't really consider him a man." Contrasting him to "a street-smart nineteen-year-old from San Francisco," Paula found him "lovely, small-town, virginal," with hair to his shoulders. After the two made love on a rock with the river waters swirling around them, Paula decided that "in a sense it wasn't really about sex for me. [It was about] opening up to a very innocent, masculine, young part of myself."

Since she was a child, Paula said she had always "identified with the Superman archetype, or the Mighty Mouse archetype, or the young boy that slays the dragon and saves the princess. I feel that I'm really kind of androgynous. [Yet] I'm definitely more on the masculine side of the scale. There's no doubt about it, because I'm very attracted to the other side of the scale: blonde, blue-eyed Renaissance maidens."

Jeanne Riley: "All These Women Were Throwing Themselves at Me"

"I was a very awkward, gawky straight woman. Somebody said, 'Yes, sir,' to me once when I was wearing a dress! I didn't walk right, I didn't talk right. I was never very comfortable in the classic female role. And I went from a very awkward straight woman to realizing at a certain point, when I was younger, that I was a gorgeous dyke. I used to be able to walk into a social scene or a bar or whatever and women would be immediately interested in me. I was very used to being looked at, and sought after. So I became conscious of feeling that I was quite nice looking and quite attractive. [Coming out] really did change my sense of self-esteem."

On the other side of the room Jeanne's young children played with a block set, thoroughly engrossed in the construction of towers, ramps, and bridges. Over what Jeanne called "leftover kid food" – macaroni and cheese and hot dogs – we sat talking about the process that had led to Jeanne's self-definition as a lesbian and her distaste for the categories "butch" and "femme." She had grown up white in an area of the Western United States with a predominantly American Indian population. "When I was twelve, we started working in the fields. Then, any money we made went to the family, so we worked *for* the family.

"All of my friends were Indians. There was a real different orientation towards money. You get your Indian money, go down to the city and blow it. And you wear it. You drive it. People were very conscious about clothes and dressing. So I think by the time I went to high school, wearing my mother's clothes cut down to fit me was not exactly socially acceptable. I was very conscious of being poor. Now everyone [in that area] was poor, so it was relative. But there were people that spent money and people that didn't. Like my parents felt that it was wasteful to spend money on things like glasses. So I was blind when I was a very small kid. Probably the most phenomenal experience I've ever had in my life is the first time I was able to see. To look at a tree and know that it has leaves on it."

Jeanne began dating after she left home, over her parents' strenuous objections, to attend college on a scholarship. "Southern

Baptism does not lend itself to romance," she smiled ruefully. "The rule was there about [not] dating, but I went to an Indian high school. So it was mixed up with racism."

Unlike many women who first defined themselves as lesbians during the 1970s, Jeanne did not come out in the context of the women's movement. "The community's gone through different phases. I think at one time, to be a real lesbian, you had to wear a vest and write poetry. And it helped if you worked as a printer, too." Speaking of her own employment history, she added, "I think that a lot of the women who have gone into the trades have been seen as butch. Not all of them are, in a classic sense. But because it is definitely a woman doing a *man's* job, then you sort of take on the clothes, the attitude. You're around men a lot. It's hard for women who are separatist to be in the trades, because you have to survive with men.

"Some people say, 'Oh, you're going into the trades. You just want to be a man.' I think that there are some women that do that. But that isn't why *I* do it. I like the work. But in that you're doing what's considered man's work, you're seen more in terms of those masculine kinds of things. If you say you can fix a car, people are like, 'Oh, well, that's a male thing.' You get some, 'What do you do?' 'Oh, I'm an accountant.' Or, 'Oh, I'm a nurse.' 'Oh, I'm a teacher.' All of those have sex roles that are attached to them. So when you say, 'Oh, I'm in the trades' – you *have* to be butch! There's nothing left.

"In my teaching [vocational education classes] I really try to get people to not feel they have to do that. In fact, it's *easier* if you don't act on all that stuff. I have a woman in my class right now who's into wearing leather. She went on an interview for UPS in a leather vest, a leather tie, and leather pants, and wondered why she didn't get the job. I says, 'Eh, uh, let me tell ya! Next time you're gonna go looking like a Catholic schoolgirl!'

"I think the most awkward time I ever had was [when] there was a James Dean party. I love James Dean! We all had to go in fifties things, so of course I went as James Dean, with the engineer boots and the rolled-up pants. Put Dixie Peach in my hair. What was really interesting that evening was [how] all of these women were throwing themselves at me. I really became conscious of there are women in the lesbian community that want a woman to look like a man. And so it bothered me, the whole butch/femme thing.

"I like women who are strong and independent and very much who they are. But they don't have to look like a man or a femme fatale. I went through a period where I had girlfriends who were like Miss Arizona. They were all classically gorgeous. After going through that, I really got more of a sense of looking at people for who they are, rather than for what they look like.

"At that James Dean party, where people were interested in me, we went out and we toured all the bars, of course, because that's what you were supposed to do in those days [ca. 1975]. And because I looked like a man, it was interesting. I really became sensitive to that: people *wanting* me to be butch, or wanting me to be this male person. That *that's* what was attractive.

"People consider Diana, who I've been with for the past twelve years, to be very butch. And so it's real confusing to people, because people that know *me* consider *me* to be very butch. We've played on ball teams before, where we've both been on the team. We played for this one black team in Oakland. There were three white women on the team: me, the pitcher, and Diana. And the role of girlfriend on that team, which was much more segregated into butch/femme kinds of roles, was to sit on the bench and yell! It was real confusing that we were *both* playing and that we were *both* good players.

"Diana had a better social context with them, because I'm sort of country. In the black community, being sort of rural, I don't make the urban connection that Diana does. I'm too polite or something. So they decided, all right, Diana's the *real* butch. And they started treating me like I should be on the bench! Like, 'What's your problem? Don't you know your role? You're not supporting your woman,' and all this. Including me with the girls.

"I've been in contexts where people have wanted me to be the femme and people have wanted me to be the butch. When you go into the trades, it's considered to be not exactly feminine stuff. And I've never been considered feminine, when I was straight or a lesbian. I was always the person asking people to dance. I think that some people would characterize me as butch, but that in my own sense, I see myself as more androgynous. I enjoy confusing people."

Copycat: Double Takes

What is it about fluff and stud – but particularly stud – that bothers people like Jeanne Riley? Above all, they wonder why anyone would go to great lengths to live as something she's not. If you're so enamored of "boy" things, why not become a man? Improved surgical techniques, hormones, and the support of a growing transgender movement make the female-to-male move an increasingly viable option. A related objection, directed toward women who choose butches as partners, asks why they don't get themselves a "real one" if that manly swagger turns them on. Wouldn't it make more sense to "stay straight" (much less hassle) than go through life as a femme?

These commonplace reactions make few, if any, distinctions between man and mannish, between regendering your style and transgendering your body, between masculine and stud, between feminine and femme, between wholesale replication and playful impersonation, between becoming male and passing for male, between passing for male and presenting as butch. "If I wanted to go out with a guy I'd go out with a guy,"

insisted Cynthia Murray, momentarily collapsing "butch" into "man." Yet Cynthia didn't reject butch/femme out of hand. Only its "extremes."

Jeanne tended to use "butch" interchangeably with "masculine." Shocked by the number of women attracted to her gelled, jeaned, and booted character at a James Dean party, Jeanne concluded that some lesbians want a woman who looks like a man. Melissa Simpson, in contrast, claimed she had never known a butch who had actually wanted to *be* a man: "In fact, most of them didn't *like* men very much."

Raye Porter had spent years controlling anger and shame when people mistakenly called her "sir." For Raye, this kind of oversight produced a gendered invisibility compounded by the invisibility she often experienced as a woman of color. Neither Raye nor Melissa considered transgender a logical extension of butch. Reconstructing anatomy was something else, although women who went the transgender route may once have thought of themselves as studs.

Then there was Cynthia, who said she used to "want to be a man." What did those words mean to her? As a child, she thought being a man would give her the freedom to walk into a bar by herself, the authority to pilot a boat. In retrospect, she described her youthful longing to "switch sexes" as the product of a particular time and place. By 1990 it had become more acceptable for white women of her class to frequent clubs and other public spaces without a male escort. As social conditions changed, what Cynthia wanted and her reasons for wanting it changed. Her desire to go boy disappeared, having had as much to do with power and the historical moment as with anatomy. Over the years and the changes from aspiring male to butch to femme-loving-femme, Cynthia's deep voice remained untouched. In her current reincarnation as femme, did those bass tones make her sound "like a man" or, rather, "sultry"?

"Like a man" occupies a key position in the meager vocabulary available for talking about gender and power. It is a phrase thrown around all too lightly, never designed to bear the weight of complex negotiations or to cover such a multitude of situations. What is this notion of "like a man," if not that old bugaboo, imitation?

When Charlyne Harris entered the trades, she did it for money, not because she thought she could attract women by looking "like a man" or because of any romanticized notions about joining the working class. Growing up with enough, but not much, had made her very pragmatic about the importance of a steady income. Jeanne first applied for a blue-collar job because she thought she would like the work. Even though she acknowledged that she had gradually assumed the clothes and "the attitude" that came with a "man's job," Jeanne maintained that her work boots had nothing to do with imitation, transgender, butch identity, or aspirations toward anything male.

Jeanne resisted the idea that crafting things from wood or metal made her "like a man," just as she resisted people's attempts to label her butch on the basis of occupation. Yet Jeanne herself could not completely separate the embodied effects of working in the trades from matters of gender. Remember, this is the same woman who once got called "sir" in a dress.

Problems begin when you try to reduce elaborately gendered effects to terms such as "male-identified." ("What was all that 'male-identified' stuff about?" younger women who had missed the heyday of lesbian-feminism repeatedly asked me.) Charlyne discovered the inadequacy of this particular concept at a strip show. The performance, which some of her friends dubbed "male-orientated" by definition, did not reproduce heterosexual relations in any simple sense. Charlyne attended the show as a woman fully conscious of her desire for other women. ("Women were taking off their clothes, that's why I was going!") Her gaze lingered on performers who gendered themselves butch on stage, as well as more "traditional" acts in feathers and lace. Did stripping by women for women set the venerable heterosexual institution of striptease on its head? The infamous dildo debates that rocked coastal lesbian communities several years later posed a similar set of questions. Must a dildo necessarily signify as a "penis substitute," or can it be, when harnessed by a lesbian, an erotic experience in its own right?

Butch-identified or not, most gay women in the Bay Area had no intention of passing for a man, much less becoming one. Faking out the boys for laughs as a twentysomething baby dyke was one thing; carrying through with the impersonation day after day was another. On the rare occasions when women had tried to pass in a serious way, they explained passing as a response to restricted economic opportunities or dangerous city streets. If passing was what it took to get a decent job at certain points in history, especially for a mannish woman, so be it.

The figure of "the butch" haunts discussions of passing, just as she does tomboy stories. Paula swore she had never suspected that lesbians could be femme, much less dazzling like the women in Jeanne's tales of her younger years. In fantasy the male-identified copycat stands in for all lesbians by taking "the" heterosexual male as her object of imitation.

Does this make the topics of passing and imitation irrelevant to feminized lesbians? Hardly. Women perceived as femme had to deal with gays and straights alike who treated them as forever on the verge of passing over into heterosexuality. This reading of femmes as a threat to "authentic" lesbianism collapses gender into sexuality in some remarkable ways. Why would anyone regard them as likely to turn bisexual or straight? Because femmes are not marked as gender rebels in the same way as butches, or even androgynous dykes. But femmes do not necessarily imitate heterosexual women, any more than butches imitate heterosexual men. Femmes can wear their gender(ing) very differently than straight girls. And they often make highly conscious decisions about how to handle the privilege that comes with passing (for white, for heterosexual, for male). Witness Cynthia, who hated to dress in frills when her job required it but rushed to don those heels for weekend wear.

The train of associations that leaves passing to the boy-girls never stops to consider what it costs a femme to go out with women who are regularly, or even erratically, slid into "male," whether or not they wannabe. And it ignores the potentially disruptive effects of gender fuck. Put that dildo on a woman with Scarlet Sunset on her lips, and who's imitating whom?

Butch/femme derives much of its appeal from an erotics of juxtaposition. Sweet-talking with silence, muscles with breasts, tenderness with bravado, a rock-hard clit under brushed cotton denim. What makes a stud is the boyish figure who remains recognizable *as* a woman. Ah, there's the excitement, and there's the rub. To anticipate a later interview with Sarah Voss: "You're presenting as a man to the most naive heterosexual from Indiana, maybe, but in the city where you probably live, you're presenting as butch. You're a slap in the face of heterosexuality. You're putting yourself in a position where you may at any time be killed by the nearest man, and his woman would probably applaud, if she doesn't go home with you."

But there's something else besides mimicry that alternately puzzles and annoys detractors of butch/femme. Many are disturbed by the apparent rigidity of "roles." They say gendered contrasts incarcerate you, hedge you in, narrow down the possibilities for what two people can build together under the auspices of a relationship. They depict butch/femme as light on creativity, heavy on prescriptions for how to behave. Studs do thus-and-such, femmes do the other. Set aside for a moment the many ways in which the practice of butch/femme has changed

over the years. What sense does it make to put two women together in a household, only to legislate who orders from the menu, who paints the apartment, who asks the other out on a date, or who makes the overtures in bed? Why not celebrate instead the flexibility of an arrangement with the potential to bridge any and every gendered divide?

Paula disdained butch/femme as "a prison" and "a trap." What exactly were femmes and butches supposed to be trapped inside? The same thing they were supposed to be imitating: a "role." Accordingly, Paula emphasized sexuality over gendering in her account of coming out lesbian. In place of a tomboy story, listeners got a narrative about a woman who merely "wanted to sleep with Stephanie." Paula believed that femmes and butches had passed up a unique opportunity to break with straight ways of doing things. Sure, roles fixed the "problem" of who would make the first move. They told partners who should take responsibility for what. But they also seemed to limit the options available to women who chose other women as partners.

If jail is the dominant metaphor in discussions that fix butch/femme as a copycat maneuver, its flip side is escape. Attempts to rescue the prisoner of gender don't always target butch/femme. Sometimes they seek to purge gender from the familiar and the mundane. When Cynthia argued that holding open a door for someone is only common courtesy, she emptied an everyday gesture of gendered significance. No power relations here! (Then why are the guys in the story still the ones getting the door?)

Role theory never did much to illuminate the straight relationships it was invented to explain. Why should it be anything but a disaster when applied to same-sex relationships? The concept of "roles" freezes time and paves right over differences with homogenized terms such as "manhood" or "womanhood." If role theory is to be believed, people have little choice but to shoehorn themselves – more or less successfully – into boxes of prescribed be-haviors marked "woman" and "man." Too cut-and-dried, say its critics.

Fitting all the complexities of gender into a couple of boxes requires you to ignore most of life's ambiguities and contradic-tions. Forget the cultural differences that made sports peripheral to Jewish concep-tions of masculinity. Forget the historical changes that saw middle-class lesbians of the 1980s adopt and modify gendered styles developed in working-class neighborhoods. Forget the oversimplification entailed in re-ducing gender to a glittering array of two – mark that, two – choices (femme *qua* woman, butch *qua* man). For role theory to work, you need lots of consistency, no troubling glitches like the compounding of gender with race or class, and an implicit theory of motivation (the assumption that most people wannabe, or at least wanna-model, these mass-produced parts).

People tend to imagine roles as things outside the individual that tolerate no sudden deviations and brook no un-announced departures. The very idea of a role feels confining because it demands con-formity to a scarcely changing script. A person has to hold the object of imitation steady in order to go about the process of reproduction, right? But is this how gender-ing works? How many heterosexuals would be happy with Paula's facile dismissal of their sex lives as a picture out of a paint-by-number set?

"Just because a woman seem like she's real feminine," Charlyne remarked, "doesn't mean she doesn't have butch qualities." The one who waits for another woman to ask her to dance may prefer to lead in bed. Likewise, it doesn't take an appearance in a skirt for a butch to rattle the prison bars of gender. Every butch who remains recogniz-able as a woman – however streetwise her posture, however close-cropped her hair – highlights inconsistency, not consistency. And inconsistency is anathema to roles.

When people talked about butch/femme as roleplaying, they often had in mind a

"daddy goes to work while mommy plays house" scenario derived from reruns of 1950s television shows. Cynthia tended to view gay history through the prism of family: older gay women "all acted like my dad." But in her story of the woman who changed from butch to femme to get the stud she wanted, the reference point for "femme" may well have been an ex-lover or the femmes from the bars, rather than heterosexual relatives. Even imitating rela-tives could have produced queerness. If a femme's straight mother can ride and shoot with the best of them, you have to wonder which particular form of heterosexuality her daughter is presumed to be copying.

To castigate butch/femme for confining people to inflexible "roles" is to set ablaze a straw woman. Why? Because there is no single idealized, timeless, shrink-wrapped "woman's role" or "man's role." No color- and class-blind prescription for the way (gendered) things are supposed to be. Not even for heterosexuals. Jeanne grew up working in the fields for wages. Why should she ever have expected to assume the stay-at-home position of TV's Donna Reed? Charlyne's boyfriend once predicted that Charlyne would end up sleeping with women because she was aggressive. Yet "ag-gressive" is not a stand-alone trait. "Aggres-sive" is the way a have-not tends to look if she reaches for something.

When Charlyne moved to a predomin-antly African-American neighborhood, she faced accusations that threatened to turn her white. First there was her speech ("You talk like a white girl!"). Then there were after-school activities. Her new neighbors may have perceived tap dance lessons as a middle-class luxury with a complicated his-tory in which black entertainers often per-formed for whites. For Charlyne charges of imitation were as raced and classed as they were gendered.

As an adult Charlyne tended to socialize primarily with other African Americans, and more specifically with black Muslims. She was quick to deride African-American men for getting stuck in an "I am the man and you are the woman" position. Does her statement simply apply two universal gender roles (man + woman) across racial lines? Not in light of the repeated attempts to emasculate African-American men. Not in light of the lynchings, both literal and metaphorical, that brought the defense of "African-American manhood" to the forefront of black nationalist politics. There's no doubt that "I am the man and you are the woman" had spelled oppression to Charlyne and many African-American women before her. Even so, "I am the man" means something different in response to a racist demand to bow and scrape and shuffle than if Cynthia's Euro-American father had voiced the same sentiment as he took over the wheel of the boat.

Jeanne was the rare white girl who actually talked about having a racial identity. Nevertheless, she tended to perceive herself as white in relation to people constructed as Other: classmates who spent their "Indian money" on fine clothes when her own parents would not buy her glasses; Native Americans her parents had forbidden her to date; African-American teammates who searched for gendered contrasts in order to divide Jeanne and her partner into butch and femme.

Embedded in Jeanne's narrative about the softball team are intricacies of gender and race, class and place that exceed the simplistic concepts of roles or imitation. Although Jeanne played a mean game of softball and worked in the trades, African-American women on the team eventually dubbed her partner "the butch." This calculation seemed to have involved a series of associations of (black) masculinity with street smarts, urban location, verbal repartee, and the skill to "play" at things other than sport. Where did that leave Jeanne, with her hard-shell white Baptist country roots? "Too polite or something." And, for once in her life, pegged as femme.

In a complex world, no one creates relationships, much less "traditions," in a vacuum. Because gay people pursue their relationships within a larger world, you can pretty much expect things to be mutually affected and connected. Call it the "lesbians have TV, too" theory of cultural innovation. So maybe what's at stake when lesbians gender themselves is neither mimicry of a mythical heterosexual standard nor a uniquely lesbian way of doing relationships, but something else. Could it be that queers have borrowed from heterosexuality to gender themselves in ways that are of it without being contained within it? Even – perhaps especially – in the case of butch/femme, the form most often dismissed as imitation?

Besides, there's no way to tell a copy from a model unless the copy is somehow different in its own right. Imitation is as much about divergence and distortion as a faithful, point-by-point reproduction of whatever you have in your sights. Add to this the endless possibilities raised by working with "found" materials to create something new that plays off the old. Rumor has it, writes Debbie Bender, that butch women of the 1960s used Kotex to create that unseemly bulge in their jeans. Appropriating and transforming as they went, they took the ultimate piece of "woman's" gear to fashion the genital signifier of "man." In the process, they ended up spoofing biological explanations for gender well before the era that officially gave butch/femme over to playfulness and irony.

If there is no such thing as "mere" imitation, then who knows where transformation may lead. A number of things set lesbian couples apart from the most prevalent kinds of straight relationships. Perhaps the most famous example is that of stone butches: untouchable women who derive their own satisfaction from the satisfaction of their partners. Stone butches constitute only a small segment of the women who identify as studs. But when was the last time you saw a representation of heterosexual masculinity in which a man got his pleasure by getting his partner off? Period?

There were also less dramatic contrasts, evident in Louise Romero's sense that gay women, however butch, are more likely than straight men to take "no" for an answer. If Carolyn Fisher had been interested in men, she probably would have had less difficulty finding someone older to date. Relatively few gay women in the United States support their partners financially. Femme/femme relationships such as Cynthia's tend to unsettle the whole idea of butch/femme as a heterosexuality manqué. Likewise when butches pair up with other butches.

Are there other ways to think about gendering than as a glorified color Xerox of straight relationships? Cynthia thought so. Arguing that "people should capitalize on their talents," she used a concept of accentuation to explain her decision to play up "the feminine." In an interesting way, Cynthia

also ended up putting gender into motion. Her shift from butch to femme raised the possibility of regendering over the course of a lifetime. And the looks she garnered from both men and women after she styled herself femme cut right across the lines drawn by sexual identity.

The movement in Jeanne's chronicle of gender didn't even require a new wardrobe. By changing the way she saw herself in the process of changing her sexual identity, Jeanne transformed herself from an "awkward, gawky straight woman" into "a gorgeous dyke." Fluidity was something Jeanne cultivated on an everyday basis. The joy she took in "confusing people" made gender over into an expandable resource. Buy it, sell it, play with it, get lost in it, decorate and defend yourself with it. Gender for pleasure, gender for hire, gender for self-protection . . . what next?

8 Sexuality and Gender in Certain Native American Tribes: The Case of Cross-Gender Females

Evelyn Blackwood

Ideological concepts of gender and sexuality arise from cultural constructions and vary from culture to culture. The female cross-gender role in certain Native American tribes constituted an opportunity for women to assume the male role permanently and to marry women.[1] Its existence challenges Western assumptions about gender roles. Some feminist anthropologists assume that it is in the nature of sex and gender systems to create asymmetry in the form of male dominance and female subservience and to enforce corresponding forms of sexual behavior.[2] Because kinship and marriage are closely tied to gender systems, these social structures are implicated in the subordination of women. The existence of female cross-gender role, however, points to the inadequacies of such a view and helps to clarify the nature of sex and gender systems.

This study closely examines the female cross-gender role as it existed historically in several Native American tribes, primarily in western North America and the Plains. It focuses on western tribes that shared a basically egalitarian mode of production in precolonial times,[3] and for which sufficient data on the female role exist. Although there were cultural differences among these groups, prior to the colonial period they all had subsistence-level economies that had not developed significant forms of wealth or rank. These tribes include the Kaska of the Yukon Territory, the Klamath of southern Oregon, and the Mohave, Maricopa, and Cocopa of the Colorado River area in the Southwest. The Plains tribes, by contrast, are noteworthy for the relative absence of the female cross-gender role. Con-

ditions affecting the tribes of the Plains varied from those of the western tribes, and thus analysis of historical–cultural contexts will serve to illuminate the differing constraints on sex and gender systems in these two areas.

Ethnographic literature has perpetuated some misconceptions about the cross-gender role. Informants frequently describe the institution in negative terms, stating that berdache were despised and ridiculed. But ethnographers collected much of the data in the twentieth century; it is based on informants' memories of the mid- to late 1800s. During this period the cross-gender institution was disappearing rapidly. Thus, twentieth-century informants do not accurately represent the institution in the precontact period. Alfred Kroeber found that "while the [berdache] institution was in full bloom, the Caucasian attitude was one of repugnance and condemnation. This attitude... made subsequent personality inquiry difficult, the later berdache leading repressed or disguised lives."[4] Informants' statements to later ethnographers or hostile white officials were far different from the actual attitude toward the role that prevailed in the precolonial period. An analysis of the cross-gender role in its proper historical context brings to light the integral nature of its relationship to the larger community.

Cultural Significance of the Female Cross-Gender Role

Most anthropological work on the cross-gender role has focused on the male berdache, with little recognition given to the female cross-gender role. Part of the problem has been the much smaller database available for a study of the female role. Yet anthropologists have overlooked even the available data. This oversight has led to the current misconception that the cross-gender role was not feasible for women. Harriet Whitehead, in a comprehensive article on the berdache, states that, given the small number of cross-gender females, "the gender-crossed status was more fully instituted for males than for females."[5] Charles Callender and Lee Kochems, in a well-researched article, base their analysis of the role predominantly on the male berdache.[6] Evidence from thirty-three Native American tribes indicates that the cross-gender role for women was as viable an institution as was the male berdache role.[7]

The Native American cross-gender role confounded Western concepts of gender. Cross-gender individuals typically acted, sat, dressed, talked like, and did the work of the other sex. Early Western observers described the berdache as half male and half female, but such a description attests only to their inability to accept a male in a female role or vice versa. In the great majority of reported cases of berdache, they assumed the social role of the other sex, not of both sexes.[8] Contemporary theorists, such as Callender and Kochems and Whitehead, resist the idea of a complete social role reclassification because they equate gender with biological sex. Native gender categories contradict such definitions.

Although the details of the cross-gender females' lives are scant in the ethnographic literature, a basic pattern emerges from the data on the western tribes. Recognition and cultural validation of the female cross-gender role varied slightly from tribe to tribe, although the social role was the same. Among the Southwestern tribes, dream experience was an important ritual aspect of life and provided success, leadership, and special skills for those who sought it. All cross-gender individuals in these tribes dreamed about their role change. The Mohave *hwame* dreamed of becoming cross-gender while still in the womb.[9] The Maricopa *kwiraxame* dreamed too much as a child and so changed her sex.[10] No information is available for the development of the female cross-gender role (*tw!nnaek*) among the Klamath. It was most likely similar to the male adolescent transformative experience, which was accomplished through fasting or diving.[11] Dreaming provided an avenue to special powers and also provided sanction for the use of those powers. In the same way, dreams about the cross-gender role provided impetus and community sanction for assumption of the role.

The female candidate for cross-gender status displayed an interest in the male role during childhood. A girl avoided learning female tasks. Instead, as in the case of the Cocopa *warrhameh*, she played with boys and made bows and arrows with which to hunt birds and rabbits.[12] The Mohave *hwame* "[threw] away their dolls and metates, and [refused] to shred bark or perform other feminine tasks."[13] Adults, acknowledging the interests of such girls, taught them the same skills the boys learned. Among the Kaska, a family that had all female children and desired a son to hunt for them would select a daughter (probably the one who showed the most inclination) to be "like a man." When she was five, the parents tied the dried ovaries of a bear to her belt to wear for life as protection against conception.[14] Though in different tribes the socializing processes varied, girls achieved the cross-gender role in each instance through accepted cultural channels.

Upon reaching puberty, the time when girls were considered ready for marriage, the cross-gender female was unable to fulfill her obligations and duties as a woman in marriage, having learned the tasks assigned to men. Nonmarriageable status could have presented a disadvantage both to herself and to her kin, who would be called upon to support her in her later years. But a role transfer allowed her to enter the marriage market for a wife with whom she could establish a household. The Mohave publicly acknowledged the new status of the woman by performing an initiation ceremony. Following this ceremony she assumed a name befitting a person of the male sex and was given marriage rights.[15] At puberty, the Cocopa *warrhameh* dressed her hair in the male style and had her nose pierced like the men, instead of receiving a chin tattoo like other women.[16] These public rites validated the cross-gender identity, signifying to the community that the woman was to be treated as a man.

In adult life cross-gender females performed the duties of the male gender role. Their tasks included hunting, trapping, cultivating crops, and fighting in battles. For example, the Cocopa *warrhameh* established households like men and fought in battle.[17] The Kaska cross-gender female "dressed in masculine attire, did male allocated tasks, often developing great strength and usually becoming an outstanding hunter."[18] The Mohave *hwame* were known as excellent providers, hunting for meat, working in the fields, and caring for the children of their wives.[19] Cross-gender females also adhered to male ritual obligations. A Klamath *tw!nnaek* observed the usual mourning when her long-time female partner died, wearing a bark belt as did a man.[20] Mohave *hwame* were said to be powerful shamans, in this case especially good at curing venereal disease.[21] Many other cross-gender females were considered powerful spiritually, but most were not shamans, even in the Southwest. Cross-gender females did not bear children once they took up the male role. Their kin considered them nonreproductive and accepted the loss of their childbearing potential, placing a woman's individual interests and abilities above her value as a reproducer.[22]

In most cases ethnographers do not discuss the ability of cross-gender females to maintain the fiction of their maleness. Whitehead suggests that women were barred from crossing over unless they were, or at least pretended to be, deficient physically.[23] However, despite some reports that cross-gender women in the Southwest had muscular builds, undeveloped secondary sexual characteristics, and sporadic or absent menstruation,[24] convincing physical evidence is noticeably lacking. In fact, the Mohave *hwame* kept a husband's taboos with regard to her menstruating or pregnant wife and ignored her own menses.[25] That such may have been the case in other tribes as well is borne out by the practice of the Ingalik cross-gender female. Among the Alaskan Ingalik, the *kashim* was the center of men's activities and the place for male-only sweat baths. The cross-gender female participated in the activities of the *kashim*, and the men were said not to perceive her true sex.[26] Cornelius Osgood suggests that she was able to hide her sex, but, as with the Mohave, the people probably ignored her physical sex in favor of her chosen role. Through this social fiction, then, cross-gender females dismissed the physiological functions of women and claimed an identity based on their performance of a social role.

Gender Equality

Women's ability to assume the cross-gender role arose from the particular conditions of kinship and gender in these tribes. The egalitarian relations of the sexes were predicated on the cooperation of autonomous individuals who had control of their productive activities. In these tribes women owned and distributed the articles they produced, and they had equal voice in matters affecting kin and community. Economic strategies depended on collective activity. Lineages or individuals had no formal authority; the whole group made decisions by consensus. People of both sexes could achieve positions of leadership through skill, wisdom, and spiritual power. Ultimately, neither women nor men had an inferior role but rather had power in those spheres of activity specific to their sex.[27]

Among these tribes, gender roles involved the performance of a particular set of duties. Most occupations necessary to the functioning of the group were defined as either male or female tasks. A typical division of labor allocated responsibilities for gathering, food preparation, child rearing, basket weaving, and making clothes to women, while men hunted, made weapons, and built canoes and houses. The allocation of separate tasks to each sex established a system of reciprocity that assured the interdependence of the sexes. Because neither set of tasks was valued more highly than the other, neither sex predominated.

Gender-assigned tasks overlapped considerably among these people. Many individuals engaged in activities that were also performed by the other sex without incurring disfavor. The small game and fish that Kaska and Klamath women hunted on a regular basis were an important contribution to the survival of the band. Some Klamath women made canoes, usually a man's task, and older men helped women with food preparation.[28] In the Colorado River area, both men and women collected tule pollen.[29] Engaging in such activities did not make a women masculine or a man feminine because, although distinct spheres of male and female production existed, a wide range of tasks was acceptable for both sexes. Because there was no need to maintain gender inequalities, notions of power and prestige did not circumscribe the roles. Without strict gender definitions, it was then possible for some Native American women to take up the male role permanently without threatening the gender system.

Another factor in creating the possibility of the cross-gender role for women was the nature of the kinship system. Kinship was not based on hierarchical relations between men and women; it was organized in the interest of both sexes. Each sex had something to gain by forming kin ties through

marriage,[30] because of the mutual assistance and economic security marital relations provided.[31] Marriage also created an alliance between two families, thereby broadening the network of kin on whom an individual could rely. Thus, marriage promoted security in a subsistence-level economy.

The marriage customs of these tribes reflected the egalitarian nature of their kinship system. Since status and property were unimportant, marriage arrangements did not involve any transfer of wealth or rank through the female. The small marriage gifts that were exchanged served as tokens of the woman's worth in the marriage relationship.[32] Furthermore, because of the unimportance of property or rank, individuals often had a series of marriages, rather than one permanent relationship; divorce was relatively easy and frequent for both women and men.[33] Marriages in these tribes became more permanent only when couples had children. Women were not forced to remain in a marriage, and either partner had the right to dissolve an unhappy or unproductive relationship.

This egalitarian kinship system had important ramifications for the cross-gender female. A daughter's marriage was not essential for maintenance of family rank; that is, a woman's family did not lose wealth if she abandoned her role as daughter. As a social male, she had marriage rights through which she could establish a household and contribute to the subsistence of the group. Additionally, because of the frequency of divorce, it was possible for a married cross-gender female to raise children. Evidence of cross-gender females caring for their wives' offspring is available only for the Mohave *hwame*. Women in other tribes, however, could also have brought children into a cross-gender marriage, since at least younger offspring typically went with the mother in a divorce.[34] A cross-gender woman might acquire children through marriage to a pregnant woman, or possibly through her wife's extramarital relationships with men. Cross-gender couples probably also adopted children, a practice common among heterosexual couples in many tribes.

Details from the Mohave help to illuminate the cross-gender parent–child relationship. The Mohave believed that the paternity of an unborn child changed if the pregnant woman had sex with another partner; thus, the cross-gender female claimed any child her wife might be carrying when they married. George Devereux states that such children retained the clan affiliation of the previous father.[35] But the clan structure of the Mohave was not strongly organized and possessed no formal authority or ceremonial functions.[36] The significant relationships were those developed through residence with kin. Thus, children raised in a cross-gender household established strong ties with those parents. The investment of parental care was reciprocated when these children became adults. In this way the cross-gender female remained a part of the network of kin through marriage.

Sexual Relations in the Cross-Gender Role

Sexual behavior was part of the relationship between cross-gender female and the women they married. Although the cross-gender female was a social male, Native Americans did not consider her sexual activity an imitation of heterosexual behavior. Her sexual behavior was recognized as lesbian – that is, as female homosexuality. The Mohave were aware of a range of sexual activities between the cross-gender female and her partner – activities that were possible only between two physiological females. Devereux recorded a Mohave term that referred specifically to the lesbian lovemaking of the *hwame* and her partner.[37] The Native American acceptance of lesbian behavior among cross-gender females did not depend on the presence of a male role-playing person; their acceptance

derived instead from their concept of sexuality.

Native American beliefs about sexuality are reflected in the marriage system. Theorists such as Gayle Rubin have implicated marriage as one of the mechanisms that enforce and define women's sexuality. According to Rubin, the division of labor "can...be seen as a taboo against sexual arrangements other than those containing at least one man and one woman, thereby enjoining heterosexual marriage."[38] Yet in certain Native American tribes other sexual behavior, both heterosexual and homosexual, was available and permissible within and outside of marriage. Homosexual behavior occurred in contexts within which neither individual was cross-gender nor were such individuals seen as expressing cross-gender behavior.[39] Premarital and extramarital sexual relations were also permissible.[40] Furthermore, through the cross-gender role, women could marry one another. Sexuality clearly was not restricted by the institution of marriage.

Native American ideology disassociated sexual behavior from concepts of male and female gender roles and was not concerned with the identity of the sexual partner. The status of the cross-gender female's partner is telling in this respect. She was always a traditional female; that is, two cross-gender females did not marry. Thus, a woman could follow the traditional female gender role, yet marry and make love with another woman without being stigmatized by such behavior. Even though she was the partner of a cross-gender female, she was not considered homosexual or cross-gender. If the relationship ended in divorce, heterosexual marriage was still an option for the ex-wife. The traditional female gender role did not restrict her choice of marital/sexual partners. Consequently, individuals possessed a gender identity, but not a corresponding sexual identity, and thus were allowed several sexual options. Sexuality itself was not embedded in Native American gender ideology.

Women on the Plains

The conditions that supported the develop-ment and continuation of the cross-gender role among certain western tribes were not replicated among the Plains tribes. Evi-dence of cross-gender females there is scant, while reports of male berdache are numer-ous. Whitehead suggests that the absence of cross-gender females resulted from the weakness of the cross-gender institution for women.[41] A more plausible explanation in-volves the particular historical conditions that differentiate the Plains tribes from the western tribes. Yet it is precisely these con-ditions that make accurate interpretation of women's roles and the female cross-gender role much more difficult for the Plains tribes.

The Plains Indian culture of nomadic buf-falo hunting and frequent warfare did not develop until the late eighteenth and early nineteenth centuries as tribes moved west in response to the expansion and development of colonial America. The new mode of life represented for many tribes a tremendous shift from an originally settled and horticul-tural or hunting and gathering lifestyle. With the introduction of the horse and gun, the growth of the fur trade, and pres-sure from westward-moving white settlers, tribes from the east and north were dis-placed onto the Plains in the late 1700s.[42] As the importance of hide trade with Euro-Americans increased in the early 1800s, it altered the mode of production among Plains tribes. Increased wealth and authority were accessible through trade and warfare. Individual males were able to achieve greater dominance while women's social and economic autonomy declined.[43] With the growing importance of hides for trade, men who were successful hunters required additional wives to handle the tanning. Their increasing loss of control in this pro-ductive sphere downgraded woman's status and tied her to marital demands. Recent work on the Plains tribes, however, indicates that this process was not consistent; women maintained a degree of autonomy and power not previously acknowledged.[44]

Early ethnographic descriptions of Plains Indian women were based on a Western gender ideology that was contradicted by actual female behavior. Although traditional Plains culture valued quiet, productive, non-promiscuous women, this was only one side of the coin. There was actually a variability in female roles that can only be attributed to women's continued autonomy. Beatrice Medicine provides an excellent discussion of the various roles open to women among the Blackfoot and Lakota. Such roles in-cluded the "manly-hearted woman," the "crazy woman" (who was sexually promis-cuous), the Sun Dance woman, and the chief woman or favorite wife.[45] According to Ruth Landes, Lakota women served in tribal government and were sometimes appointed marshalls to handle problems among women. Most Plains tribes had women war-riors who accompanied war parties for limited purposes on certain occasions, such as avenging the death of kin, and who re-ceived warrior honors for their deeds.[46] As Medicine states, "These varied role categor-ies . . . suggest that the idealized behavior of women was not as rigidly defined and followed as has been supposed."[47]

The presence of a variety of socially ap-proved roles also suggests that these were normative patterns of behavior for women that need not be construed as "contrary" to their gender role. Warrior women were not a counterpart of the male berdache, nor were they considered cross-gender.[48] Ethnograph-ers' attributions of masculinity to such be-havior seem to be a product of Western beliefs about the rigid dichotomization of gender roles and the nature of suitable pur-suits for women. That men simply accepted females as warriors and were not threatened by such behavior contradicts the notion that such women were even temporarily assum-ing the male role.[49] The men's acceptance was based on recognition of the women warriors' capabilities as women.

There were individual Plains women in the nineteenth century whose behavior throughout their lives exemplified a cross-gender role. They did not always cross-dress, but, like Woman Chief of the Crow, neither did they participate in female activities. They took wives to handle their households and were highly successful in hunting and raiding activities. They were also considered very powerful. Of these women, the Kutenai cross-gender woman always dressed in male attire and was renowned for her exploits as warrior and mediator and guide for white traders. Running Eagle of the Blackfoot lived as a warrior and married a young widow. Woman Chief became the head of her father's lodge when he died and achieved the third highest rank among the Crow. She took four wives.[50] Particularly since no records of earlier cross-gender women have been found, these few examples seem to constitute individual exceptions. What then was the status of the female cross-gender role among Plains tribes?

Part of the difficulty with answering this question stems from the nature of the data itself. Nineteenth-century observers rarely recorded information on Plains Indian women, "considering them too insignificant to merit special treatment."[51] These observers knew few women and only the more successful males. "Those who did become known were women who had acted as go-betweens for the whites and Indians,"[52] such as the Kutenai cross-gender female. Running Eagle and Woman Chief were also exceptional enough to be noticed by white traders. Except for the Kutenai woman, none of the women are identified as berdache in nineteenth-century reports, although all were cross-gender. Observers seem to have been unable to recognize the female cross-gender role. Indeed, no nineteenth-century reports mention cross-gender females among even the western tribes, al-

though later ethnographers found ample evidence of the role.

Ethnographers had no solid evidence of the female cross-gender role among Plains Indians. Several factors may help to explain this discrepancy. White contact with Plains tribes came earlier than with the western tribes and was more disruptive. The last cross-gender females seem to have disappeared among Plains tribes by the mid-nineteenth century, while in the Southwest this did not occur until the end of the century, much closer to the time when ethnographers began to collect data. Discrepancies also arise in informants' stories. The Kutenai denied the existence of cross-gender females among them, in contradiction with earlier evidence, and yet willingly claimed that such women lived among the Flathead and Blackfoot.[53] The Arapaho told Alfred Kroeber that the Lakota had female berdache, but there is no corroborating evidence from the Lakota themselves.[54] Informants were clearly reticent or unwilling to discuss cross-gender women. In her article on Native American lesbians, Paula Gunn Allen suggests that such information was suppressed by the elders of the tribes.[55] Most information on Plains Indian women was transmitted from elder tribesmen to white male ethnographers. But men were excluded from knowledge of much of women's behavior;[56] in this way much of the data on cross-gender females may have been lost.

The record of Plains cross-gender females remains limited. Certain social conditions may have contributed to the small number of women who assumed the role in the nineteenth century. During the 1800s the practice of taking additional wives increased with the men's need for female labor. This phenomenon may have limited women's choice of occupation. The pressures to marry may have barred women from a role that required success in male tasks only. The practice of sororal polygyny particularly would have put subtle pressures on families to assure that each daughter learned the traditional female role. Indeed, there were said to be no unmarried women among the Lakota.[57] Furthermore, given the constant state of warfare and loss of able-bodied men, the tribes were under pressure merely to survive. Such conditions in the 1800s discouraged women from abandoning their reproductive abilities through the cross-gender role. In fact, among the Lakota, women who insisted on leading men's lives were ostracized from the group and forced to wander by themselves.[58] Knowledge of the female cross-gender role may have persisted, but those few who actually lived out the role were exceptions in a changing environment.

The Demise of the Cross-Gender Role

By the late nineteenth century the female cross-gender role had all but disappeared among Native Americans. Its final demise was related to a change in the construction of sexuality and gender in these tribes. The dominant ideology of Western culture, with its belief in the inferior nature of the female role and its insistence on heterosexuality, began to replace traditional Native American gender systems.

Ideological pressures of white culture encouraged Native American peoples to reject the validity of the cross-gender role and to invoke notions of "proper" sexuality that supported men's possession of sexual rights to women. Communities expressed disapproval by berating the cross-gender female for not being a "real man" and not being properly equipped to satisfy her wife sexually. In effect, variations in sexual behavior that had previously been acceptable were now repudiated in favor of heterosexual practices. Furthermore, the identity of the sexual partner became an important aspect of sexual behavior.

The life of the last cross-gender female among the Mohave, Sahaykwisa, provides a clear example of this process. According

to Devereux, "Sahaykwisa...was born toward the middle of the last century and killed...at the age of 45. Sahaykwisa had at a certain time a very pretty wife. Other men desired the woman and tried to lure her away from the *hwame*." The men teased Sahaykwisa in a derogatory manner, suggesting that her lovemaking was unsatisfactory to her wife in comparison to that of a "real man." They ridiculed her wife and said, "Why do you want a transvestite for your husband who has no penis and pokes you with the finger?"[59] Such derision went beyond usual joking behavior until finally Sahaykwisa was raped by a man who was angered because his wife left him for Sahaykwisa. The community no longer validated the cross-gender role, and Sahaykwisa herself eventually abandoned it, only to be killed later as a witch. By accusing the cross-gender female of sexual inadequacy, men of the tribe claimed in effect that they had sole rights to women's sexuality, and that sexuality was appropriate only between men and women.

Conclusion

In attempting to fit the Native American cross-gender role into Western categories, anthropologists have disregarded the ways in which the institution represents native categories of behavior. Western interpretations dichotomize the gender roles for each sex, which results from erroneous assumptions about, first, the connection between biology and gender, and, second, the nature of gender roles. Callender and Kochems state, "The transformation of a berdache was not a complete shift from his or her *biological* gender to the opposite one, but rather an approximation of the latter in some of its social aspects."[60] They imply that anatomy circumscribed the berdache's ability to function in the gender role of the other sex. Whitehead finds the anatomical factor particularly telling for women, who were supposedly unable to succeed in the male role unless deficient physically as females.[61] These theorists, by claiming a mixed gender status for the berdache, confuse a social role with a physical identity that remained unchanged for the cross-gender individual.

Knowing the true sex of the berdache, Native Americans accepted them on the basis of their social attributes; physiological sex was not relevant to the gender role. The Mohave, for example, did not focus on the biological sex of the berdache. Nonberdache were said to "feel toward their possible transvestite mate as they would feel toward a true woman, [or] man."[62] In response to a newly initiated berdache, the Yuma "began to feel toward him as to a woman."[63] These tribes concurred in the social fiction of the cross-gender role despite the obvious physical differences, indicating the unimportance of biological sex to the gender role.[64]

Assumptions regarding the hierarchical nature of Native American gender relations have created serious problems in the analysis of the female cross-gender role. Whitehead claims that few females could have been cross-gender because she assumes the asymmetrical nature of gender relations.[65] In cultures with an egalitarian mode of production, however, gender does not create an imbalance between the sexes. In the western North American tribes discussed above, neither gender roles nor sexuality were associated with an ideology of male dominance. Women were not barred from the cross-gender role by rigid gender definitions; instead, they filled the role successfully. Although cross-gender roles are not limited to egalitarian societies, the historical conditions of nonegalitarian societies, in which increasing restrictions are placed on women's productive and reproductive activities, strongly discourage them from taking on the cross-gender role.

Anthropologists' classification of gender roles as dichotomous has served to obscure the nature of the Native American cross-gender role. For Whitehead, the male berdache is "less than a full man" but "more

than a mere woman,"[66] suggesting a mixed gender role combining elements of both the male and the female. Similarly, Callender and Kochems suggest that the berdache formed an intermediate gender status.[67] Native conceptualizations of gender, particularly in the egalitarian tribes, do not contain an invariable opposition of two roles. The Western ideology of feminine and masculine traits actually has little in common with these Native American gender systems, within which exist large areas of overlapping tasks.

The idea of a mixed gender role is particularly geared to the male berdache and assumes the existence of a limited traditional female role. Such a concept does not account for the wide range of behaviors possible for both the male and female gender roles. By contrast, the term "cross-gender" defines the role as a set of behaviors typifying the attributes of the other sex, but not limited to an exact duplication of either role. Attributes of the male berdache that are not typical of the female role – for example, certain ritual activities – do not indicate a mixed gender category. These activities are specialized tasks that arise from the spiritual power of the cross-gender individual.

The term "cross-gender," however, is not without its problems. Sue-Ellen Jacobs suggests that a person who from birth or early childhood fills this variant role may not be "crossing" a gender boundary. She prefers the term "third gender" because, as among the Tewa, the berdache role may not fit either a male or female gender category but is conceived instead as another gender.[68] Kay Martin and Barbara Voorheis also explore the possibility of more than two genders.[69] Certainly the last word has not been spoken about a role that has confounded researchers for at least one hundred years. But it is imperative to develop an analysis of variant gender roles based on the historical conditions that faced particular tribes since gender systems vary in different cultures and change as modes of production change.

NOTES

1 The term "berdache" is the more common term associated with the cross-gender role. It was originally applied by Europeans to Native American men who assumed the female role, and was derived from the Arabic *bardaj*, meaning a boy slave kept for sexual purposes. I prefer the term "cross-gender," first used by J. M. Carrier, particularly for the female role. See J. M. Carrier, "Homosexual Behavior in Cross-Cultural Perspective," in *Homosexual Behavior: A Modern Reappraisal*, ed. Judd Marmor (New York: Basic Books, 1980), pp. 100–22.

2 Sherry B. Ortner and Harriet Whitehead, eds., *Sexual Meanings: The Cultural Construction of Gender and Sexuality* (Cambridge: Cambridge University Press, 1981); Gayle Rubin, "The Traffic in Women: Notes on the 'Political Economy' of Sex," in *Toward an Anthropology of Women*, ed. Rayna R. Reiter (New York: Monthly Review Press, 1975), pp. 157–210.

3 Much feminist debate has focused on whether male dominance is universal, or whether societies with egalitarian relations exist. For a more comprehensive discussion of egalitarian societies, see Mina Davis Caulfield, "Equality, Sex and Mode of Production," in *Social Inequality: Comparative and Development Approaches*, ed. Gerald D. Berreman (New York: Academic Press, 1981), pp. 201–19; Mona Etienne and Eleanor Leacock, eds., *Women and Colonization: Anthropological Perspectives* (New York: J. F. Bergin, 1980); Eleanor Burke Leacock, *Myths of Male Dominance: Collected Articles on Women Cross-Culturally* (New York: Monthly Review Press, 1981); Karen Sacks, *Sisters and Wives: The Past and Future of Sexual Inequality* (Westport, CT: Greenwood Press, 1979); Rayna R. Reiter, ed., *Toward an Anthropology of Women* (New York: Monthly Review Press, 1975); and Eleanor Burke Leacock and Nancy O. Lurie, eds., *North American Indians in Historical Perspective* (New York: Random House, 1971).

4 Alfred L. Kroeber, "Psychosis or Social Sanction," *Character and Personality* 8, no. 3 (1940): 204–15, quote on p. 209.

5 Harriet Whitehead, "The Bow and the Burden Strap: A New Look at Institutionalized Homosexuality in Native North America," in Ortner and Whitehead, eds. (n. 2 above), pp. 80–115, quote on p. 86.

6 Charles Callender and Lee M. Kochems, "The North American Berdache," *Current Anthropology* 24, no. 4 (1983): 443–56.

7 These tribes by area are as follows: Subarctic – Ingalik, Kaska; Northwest – Bella Coola, Haisla, Lillooet, Nootka, Okanagon, Queets, Quinault; California/Oregon – Achomawi, Atsugewi, Klamath, Shasta, Wintu, Wiyot, Yokuts, Yuki; Southwest – Apache, Cocopa, Maricopa, Mohave, Navajo, Papago, Pima, Yuma; Great Basin – Ute, Southern Ute, Shoshoni, Southern Paiute, Northern Paiute; Plains – Blackfoot, Crow, Kutenai.

8 See S. C. Simms, "Crow Indian Hermaphrodites," *American Anthropologist* 5, no. 3 (1903): 580–1; Alfred L. Krocher, "The Arapaho," *American Museum of Natural History Bulletin* 18, no. 1 (1902): 1–150; Royal B. Hassrick, *The Sioux; Life and Customs of a Warrior Society* (Norman: University of Oklahoma Press, 1964); Ronald L. Olson, *The Quinault Indians* (Seattle: University of Washington Press, 1936); Ruth Murray Underhill, *Social Organization of the Papago Indians* (1939; reprint, New York: AMS Press, 1969).

9 George Devereux, "Institutionalized Homosexuality of the Mohave Indians," *Human Biology* 9, no. 4 (1937): 498–527.

10 Leslie Spier, *Yuman Tribes of the Gila River* (Chicago: University of Chicago Press, 1933).

11 Leslie Spier, *Klamath Ethnography*, University of California Publications in American Archaeology and Ethnology, vol. 30 (Berkeley: University of California Press, 1930).

12 E. W. Gifford, *The Cocopa*, University of California Publications in American Archaeology and Ethnology, vol. 31, no. 5 (Berkeley: University of California Press, 1933).

13 Devereux (n. 9 above), p. 503.

14 John J. Honigmann, *The Kaska Indians: An Ethnographic Reconstruction*, Yale University Publications in Anthropology, no. 51 (New Haven, CT: Yale University Press, 1954), p. 130.

15 Devereux (n. 9 above), pp. 508–9.

16 Gifford (n. 12 above).

17 Ibid, p. 294.

18 Honigmann (n. 14 above), p. 130.

19 Devereux (n. 9 above).

20 Spier, *Klamath Ethnography* (n. 11 above), p. 53.

21 Devereux (n. 9 above).

22 Ibid; Gifford (n. 12 above); Honigmann (n. 14 above).

23 Whitehead (n. 5 above), pp. 92–3.

24 C. Daryll Forde, *Ethnography of the Yuma Indians*, University of California Publications in American Archaeology and Ethnology, vol. 28, no. 4 (Berkeley: University of California Press, 1931), p. 157; Gifford (n. 12 above), p. 294; Devereux (n. 9 above), p. 510.

25 Devereux (n. 9 above), p. 515.

26 Cornelius Osgood, *Ingalik Social Culture*, Yale University Publications in Anthropology, no. 53 (New Haven, CT: Yale University Press, 1958).

27 Based on ethnographic data in Honigmann (n. 14 above); Gifford (n. 12 above); Leslie Spier, *Cultural Relations of the Gila and Colorado River Tribes*, Yale University Publications in Anthropology, no. 3 (New Haven, CT: Yale University Press, 1936), *Klamath Ethnography* (n. 11 above), and *Yuman Tribes* (n. 10 above); Theodore Stern, *The Klamath Tribe* (Seattle: University of Washington Press, 1966); Alfred L. Kroeber, *Mohave Indians: Report on Aboriginal Territory and Occupancy of the Mohave Tribe*, ed. David Horr (New York: Garland Publishing, 1974), and *Handbook of the Indians of California*, Bureau of American Ethnology Bulletin no. 78 (Washington, DC: Government Printing Office, 1925); William H. Kelly, *Cocopa Ethnography*, Anthropological Papers of the University of Arizona, no. 29 (Tucson: University of Arizona Press, 1977); Lorraine M. Sherer, *The Clan System of the Fort Mohave Indians* (Los Angeles: Historical Society of Southern California, 1965).

28 Julie Cruikshank, *Athapaskan Women: Lives and Legends* (Ottawa: National Museums of Canada, 1979); Spier, *Klamath Ethnography* (n. 11 above).

29 Gifford (n. 12 above).

30 The five tribes discussed here varied in forms of kinship, but this variation did not have a significant effect on the relations between the sexes. Lacking rank or wealth, kinship groups were not the focus of power or authority, hence whether a tribe was matrilineal or patrilineal was not as important as the overall relationship with kin on either side.

31 John J. Honigmann, *Culture and Ethos of Kaska Society*, Yale University Publications in Anthropology, no. 40 (New Haven, CT: Yale University Press, 1949), and *Kaska Indians* (n. 14 above).

32 Spier, *Klamath Ethnography* (n. 11 above); J. A. Teit, "Field Notes on the Tahltan and Kaska Indians: 1912–15," *Anthropologica* 3, no. 1 (1956): 39–171. Kroeber, *Handbook* (n. 27 above); Gifford (n. 12 above).

33 Kelly (n. 27 above); Spier, *Klamath Ethnography* (n. 11 above).

34 Kelly (n. 27 above).

35 Devereux (n. 9 above), p. 514.

36 Kelly (n. 27 above); Forde (n. 24 above).

37 Devereux (n. 9 above), pp. 514–15.

38 Rubin (n. 2 above), p. 178.

39 See Forde (n. 24 above), p. 157; Honigmann, *Kaska Indians* (n. 14 above), p. 127.

40 Spier, *Klamath Ethnography* (n. 11 above), and *Yuman Tribes* (n. 10 above); Kroeber, *Handbook* (n. 27 above).

41 Whitehead (n. 5 above), p. 86.

42 Gene Weltfish, "The Plains Indians: Their Continuity in History and Their Indian Identity," in Leacock and Lurie, eds. (n. 3 above).

43 Leacock and Lurie, eds. (n. 3 above); Alan Klein, "The Political-Economy of Gender: A 19th Century Plains Indian Case Study," in *The Hidden Half: Studies of Plains Indian Women*, ed. Patricia Albers and Beatrice Medicine (Washington, DC: University Press of America, 1983), pp. 143–73.

44 See Albers and Medicine, *The Hidden Half* (n. 43 above).

45 Beatrice Medicine, "Warrior Women – Sex Role Alternatives for Plains Indian Women," in Albers and Medicine, eds.(n. 43 above), pp. 267–80; see also Oscar Lewis, "Manly-Hearted Women among the North Piegan," *American Anthropologist* 43, no. 2 (1941): 173–87.

46 Ruth Landes, *The Mystic Lake Sioux* (Madison: University of Wisconsin Press, 1968).

47 Medicine (n. 45 above), p. 272.

48 Sue-Ellen Jacobs, "The Berdache," in *Cultural Diversity and Homosexuality*, ed.

Stephen Murray (New York: Irvington Press, in press); Medicine (n. 45 above), p. 269.

49 On male acceptance of women warriors, see Landes (n. 46 above).

50 Edwin Thompson Denig, *Of the Crow Nation*, ed. John C. Ewers, Smithsonian Institution, Bureau of American Ethnology, Bulletin no. 151, Anthropology Papers no. 33 (Washington, DC: Government Printing Office, 1953), and *Five Indian Tribes of the Upper Missouri*, ed. John C. Ewers (Norman: University of Oklahoma Press, 1961); Claude E. Schaeffer, "The Kutenai Female Berdache: Courier, Guide, Prophetess, and Warrior," *Ethnohistory* 12, no. 3 (1965): 193–236.

51 Patricia Albers, "Introduction: New Perspectives on Plains Indian Women," in Albers and Medicine, eds. (n. 43 above), pp. 1–26, quote on p. 3.

52 Katherine Weist, "Beasts of Burden and Menial Slaves: Nineteenth Century Observations of Northern Plains Indian Women," in Albers and Medicine, eds. (n. 43 above), pp. 29–52, quote on p. 39.

53 Harry H. Turney-High, *Ethnography of the Kutenai*, Memories of the American Anthropological Association, no. 56 (1941; reprint, New York: Kraus Reprint, 1969), and *The Flathead Indians of Montana*, Memoirs of the American Anthropological Association, no. 48 (1937; reprint, New York: Kraus Reprint, 1969).

54 Kroeber, "The Arapaho" (n. 8 above), p. 19.

55 Paula Gunn Allen, "Beloved Women: Lesbians in American Indian Cultures,"

Conditions: Seven 3, no. 1 (1981): 67–87.

56 Alice Kehoe, "The Shackles of Tradition," in Albers and Medicine, eds. (n. 43 above), pp. 53–73.

57 Hassrick (n. 8 above).

58 Jeannette Mirsky, "The Dakota," in *Cooperation and Competition among Primitive Peoples*, ed. Margaret Mead (Boston: Beacon Press, 1961), p. 417.

59 Devereux (n. 9 above), p. 523.

60 Callender and Kochems (n. 6 above), p. 453 (italics mine).

61 Whitehead (n. 5 above), p. 92.

62 Devereux (n. 9 above), p. 501.

63 Forde (n. 24 above), p. 157.

64 Data on the Navajo *nadle* are not included in this essay because the Navajo conception of the berdache was atypical. The *nadle* was considered a hermaphrodite by the Navajo – i.e., of both sexes physically – and therefore did not actually exemplify a cross-gender role. See W. W. Hill, "The Status of the Hermaphrodite and Transvestite in Navaho Culture," *American Anthropologist* 37, no. 2 (1935): 273–9.

65 Whitehead (n. 5 above), p. 86.

66 Ibid, p. 89.

67 Callender and Kochems (n. 6 above), p. 454.

68 Sue-Ellen Jacobs, personal communication, 1983, and "Comment on Callender and Kochems," *Current Anthropology* 24, no. 4 (1983): 459–60.

69 M. Kay Martin and Barbara Voorheis, *Female of the Species* (New York: Columbia University Press, 1975).

Part III

Sexuality in Childhood and Adolescence

Adults' beliefs and practices often have their origin in early childhood socialization. This is true of sexuality, too, even though we often try to protect children from exposure to sexual behavior, and discourage their natural curiosity about sex. As Thorne and Luria show, middle schools teach implicit rules for relationships between the sexes that set the stage for heterosexual relationships in adolescence. Many girls feel pressured into having sex around the time of puberty; Martin finds that they may "give in" to their boyfriends to keep their relationships with them, while many boys pursue sexual conquest to confirm their masculinity. These asymmetrical and unequal experiences show up even in deviant subcultures,

like the punks, although there are a few pockets of resistance, as Lauraine Leblanc describes. One consequence of gender inequality in adolescent sexual experience is the prevalent problem of teen motherhood in our society. Elaine Kaplan argues that lack of appropriate sex education in the schools, combined with dismal relationships with adults, makes some young women especially vulnerable to sexual manipulation by young men. Too many girls today find themselves alone and pregnant, without the social and emotional resources to raise their own children adequately. These articles all show the importance of rethinking society's approach to childhood and adolescent sexuality.

9 Sexuality and Gender in Children's Daily Worlds

Barrie Thorne and Zella Luria

The ambiguities of "sex" – a word used to refer to biological sex, to cultural gender, and also to sexuality – contain a series of complicated questions. Although our cultural understandings often merge these three domains, they can be separated analytically; their interrelationships lie at the core of the social organization of sex and gender.[1] In this essay we focus on the domains of gender and sexuality as they are organized and experienced among elementary school children, especially nine to eleven year-olds. This analysis helps illuminate age-based variations and transitions in the organization of sexuality and gender.

We use "gender" to refer to cultural and social phenomena – divisions of labor, activity, and identity which are associated with but not fully determined by biological sex. The core of sexuality, as we use it here, is desire and arousal. Desire and arousal are shaped by and associated with socially learned activities and meanings which Gagnon and Simon (1973) call "sexual scripts." Sexual scripts – defining who does what, with whom, when, how, and what it means – are related to the adult society's view of gender (Miller and Simon 1981).

In our culture, gender and sexuality are deeply interwined, especially for adults; "woman/man," and especially "femininity/masculinity" are categories loaded with heterosexual meanings. Erotic orientation and gender are not as closely linked in our culture's definitions of children. Although there is greater acknowledgment of childhood sexuality than in the past, we continue – often after quoting Freud to the contrary – to define children as innocent, vulnerable, and in need of protection from adult sexual knowledge and practice.[2]

Children are not, of course, asexual. They experience arousal, and they sometimes engage in practices (even some leading to orgasm) that adults call "sexual" (Kinsey et al. 1948, 1953). Some children learn and use sexual words at a relatively young age, and, as we will describe later, they draw on sexual meanings (although not necessarily adult understandings) in constructing their social worlds. But special taboos and tensions surround the feelings and language of sexuality in childhood. In our culture we limit the "fully sexual" (sexual acts tied to accepted adult meanings) to adolescence and adulthood. Among children any explicitly sexual activity, beyond ill-defined crushes, is treated as culturally deviant.

Nine to eleven year-old children are beginning the transition from the gender system of childhood to that of adolescence. They are largely defined (and define themselves) as children, but they are on the verge of sexual maturity, cultural adolescence, and a gender system organized around the institution of heterosexuality. Their experiences help illuminate complex and shifting relationships between sexuality and gender.

First we explore the segregated gender arrangements of middle childhood as contexts for learning adolescent and adult sexual scripts. We then turn from their separate worlds to relations *between* boys and girls, and examine how fourth and fifth grade children use sexual idioms to mark gender boundaries. Separate gender groups

and ritualized, asymmetric relations between girls and boys lay the groundwork
for the more overtly sexual scripts of adolescence.

Methods and Sources of Data

Our data are drawn from observations of
children in elementary school playgrounds,
classrooms, hallways, and lunchrooms. All
of the schools went up through sixth grade.
One of us (Thorne) was a participant-obser-
ver for eight months in a largely white,
working-class elementary school in California, a school with about 500 students (5
percent black, 20 percent Chicana/o, and
75 percent white). She also observed for
three months in a Michigan elementary
school with around 400, largely working-
class students (8 percent black, 12 percent
Chicana/o, and 80 percent white). Playground observations included all ages, but
emphasized fourth and fifth graders. The
other author (Luria) observed for one-and-
a-half academic years in a middle-class, suburban Massachusetts public school and in
an upper-middle-class private school in the
Boston area. Both schools had about 275
students – 17 percent black and 83 percent
white – in the fourth through sixth grades.[3]
A separate Massachusetts sample of 27
fourth and fifth graders was interviewed to
ascertain children's knowledge of what boys
and girls "should do" and know. We have
combined our data for this essay.

Throughout our fieldwork we tried to observe children in situations where they were
under less adult supervision and control and
hence more likely construct their own activities and social relations. Although we could
not pass as children, we did try to separate
ourselves from the adult authority systems
of the schools. We essentially tried to hang
out – watching, talking, and sometimes
playing with the children. We interacted
freely with the children and sometimes
elicited their understanding of ongoing situ-

ations. On a number of occasions, we each
observed significant breaking of school
rules, a backhanded compliment to our
trustworthiness, if not our invisibility.[4]

Elementary schools may not seem to be
the most fruitful contexts for gathering information about sexuality. Indeed, had we
observed the same children in more informal
and private settings, such as in neighborhoods or summer camps, we probably
would have observed more extensive sexual
talk and behavior (as did Fine, 1980, in an
ethnographic study of pre-adolescent boys
on Little League baseball teams).

On the other hand, children spend a great
deal of time in schools, and they often construct their own interactions within the structure of adult-controlled school days. The
presence of teachers and aides gave us many
opportunities to observe children guarding
their more secret lives from potential interference from adults, and to see children and
adults negotiating sexual meanings.[5] Furthermore, the dynamics of gender separation
and integration are especially vivid in densely
populated school settings.

The social categories of observers have no
simple bearing on the process of research,
but the fact that we are women may well
have affected what we saw and how we
interpreted it. Our gender enhanced access
to groups of girls, but the more public
nature of boy's groups made them generally
easier to observe. Age may mute the effects
of gender; just as very young boys may go
into women's bathrooms, so, by virtue of
age, adult women may cross ritual boundaries separating groups of boys from groups of
girls. We both found it easier to see and
articulate the social relations of boys than
those of girls, a skew also evident in the
literature. Having grown up as girls, we
may have had less detachment from their
interactions. In addition, until recently,
more research had been done on groups of
boys than on groups of girls, and categories
for description and analysis have come more
from male than female experience.

The Daily Separation of Girls and Boys

Gender segregation – the separation of girls and boys in friendships and casual encounters – is central to daily life in elementary schools. A series of snapshots taken in varied school settings would reveal extensive spatial separation between girls and boys. When they choose seats, select companions for work or play, or arrange themselves in line, elementary school children frequently cluster into same-sex groups. At lunchtime, boys and girls often sit separately and talk matter-of-factly about "girls' tables" and "boys' tables." Playgrounds have gendered spaces: boys control some areas and activities, such as large playing fields and basketball courts; and girls control smaller enclaves like jungle-gym areas and concrete spaces for hopscotch or jump-rope. Extensive gender segregation in everyday encounters and in friendships has been found in many other studies of elementary- and middle-school children (e.g., Best 1983; Eder and Hallinan 1978; Lockheed 1985). Gender segregation in elementary and middle schools has been found to account for more segregation than race (Schofield 1982).

Gender segregation is not total. Snapshots of school settings would also reveal some groups with a fairly even mix of boys and girls, especially in games like kickball, dodgeball, and handball, and in classroom and playground activities organized by adults. Some girls frequently play with boys, integrating their groups in a token way, and a few boys, especially in the lower grades, play with groups of girls.

The amount of gender segregation varies not only by situation, but also by school. For example, quantitative inventories in the Massachusetts schools indicated that in the private, upper-middle-class school, 65 percent of playground clusters were same-gender, compared with 80 percent in the matched, middle-class public school.[6] Social

class may help account for the difference, but so may school culture; the private school had initiated large group games, like one called "Ghost," which were not typed by gender. The extent of adult supervision also makes a difference. In general, there is more gender segregation when children are freer to construct their own activities.[7]

Gender arrangements in elementary schools have a "with-then-apart" structure (a term coined by Goffman 1977). In any playground, cafeteria, or classroom, there are mixed-gender as well as same-gender groups. Mixed-gender groups, and patterns of activity and solidarity which draw boys and girls together, need closer attention (see Thorne 1986). On the other hand, children so often separate themselves by gender – ritualizing boundaries between girls and boys, and talking about them as separate "teams" or "sides" – that they create bounded spaces and relationships in which somewhat different subcultures are sustained. In some respects, then, boys and girls occupy separate worlds.

Because of time spent and emotions invested in gender-differentiated worlds, girls and boys have somewhat different environments for learning. Gender-differentiated social relations and subcultures may teach distinctive patterns of talk (Maltz and Borker 1983) and forms of prosocial and antisocial behavior (Maccoby 1985). Our focus is on how the gender-specific contexts of middle and late childhood may help shape the sexual scripts – the social relations and meanings associated with desire – of adolescent boys and girls.

Interaction Among Boys

In daily patterns of talk and play, boys in all-male groups often build towards heightened and intense moments, moments one can describe in terms of group arousal with excited emotions. This especially happens when boys violate rules. In a Massachusetts fifth grade, four boys played a game called "Flak" which one of them had invented. The game took place on a $8\frac{1}{2}'' \times 11''$ piece of paper with drawings of spaceships with guns on each of the corners. The airspace in the middle of the paper was covered by short lines representing metal flak. The purpose of the game was to shoot down all opponents by using one's hand as a gun while making shooting noises. The danger was that one's shots could ricochet off the flak, destroying one's spaceship. The random straying of flak was such that there was no way – if the game was played honestly – to survive one's own shots. Boys playing the game evolved implicit (never stated) rules about cheating: cheating was permitted up to about one-fourth the distance to an opponent's corner, then the others could complain that flak would stop a player, but not before. At the instigation of the observer, the boys enthusiastically taught the game to the brightest girl in the class, who found the game "boring" and "crazy." The excitement the boys associated with the game was lost on her; she did not remark on the cheating.

Dirty words are a focus of rules, and rule breaking, in elementary schools. Both girls and boys know dirty words, but flaunting of the words and risking punishment for their use was more frequent in boys' than in girls' groups in all the schools we studied. In the middle-class Massachusetts public school, both male and female teachers punished ballplayers for frequent cries of "Shit" and "You fucked it up." But teachers were not present after lunch and before school, when most group-directed play took place. A female paraprofessional, who alone managed almost 150 children on the playground, never intervened to stop bad language in play; the male gym teacher who occasionally appeared on the field at after-lunch recess always did. Boys resumed dirty talk immediately after he passed them. Dirty talk is a stable part of the repertoire of boys' groups (also see Fine 1980). Such talk defines their groups as, at least in

part, outside the reach of the school's discipline.

Some of the dirty talk may be explicitly sexual, as it was in the Massachusetts public school when a group of five fifth-grade boys played a game called "Mad Lib" (also described in Luria 1983). The game consisted of a paragraph (in this case, a section of a textbook discussing the US Constitution) with key words deleted, to be filled in by the players. Making the paragraph absurd and violating rules to create excitement seemed to be the goal of the game. The boys clearly knew that their intentions were "dirty": they requested the field observer not to watch the game. Instead the observer negotiated a post-game interrogation on the rules of the game. The boys had completed the sentence, "The —— was ratified in —— in 1788," with "The *shit* was ratified in *Cuntville* in 1788."

The boys reacted with disbelief when the adult woman observer read the entire paragraph aloud, with no judgment, only requesting correction of pronunciation. The next day, in a gesture which connected rule violation to the interests of the male group, one of the boys asked the observer, "Hey lady, did ya watch the Celtics' game last night?" Sports, dirty words, and testing the limits are part of what boys teach boys how to do. The assumption seems to be: dirty words, sports interest and knowledge, and transgression of politeness are closely connected.

Rule transgression: comparing girls' and boys' groups

Rule transgression in *public* is exciting to boys in their groups. Boys' groups are attentive to potential consequences of transgression, but, compared with girls, groups of boys appear to be greater risk-takers. Adults tending and teaching children do not often undertake discipline of an entire boys' group; the adults might lose out and they cannot risk that. Girls are more likely to affirm the reasonableness of rules, and, when it occurs, rule-breaking by girls is smaller scale. This may be related to the smaller size of girls' groups and to adults' readiness to use rules on girls who seem to believe in them. It is dubious if an isolated pair of boys (a pair is the modal size of girls' groups) could get away with the rule-breaking that characterizes the larger male group. A boy may not have power, but a boys' *group* does. Teachers avoid disciplining whole groups of boys, partly for fear of seeming unfair. Boys rarely identify those who proposed direct transgressions and, when confronted, they claim (singly), "I didn't start it; why should I be punished?"

Boys are visibly excited when they break rules together – they are flushed as they play, they wipe their hands on their jeans, some of them look guilty. The Mad Lib game described above not only violates rules, it also evokes sexual meanings within an all-male group. Arousal is not purely individual; in this case, it is shared by the group. Farts and cunts – words used in the game – are part of a forbidden, undressed, sexual universe evoked in the presence of four other boys. The audience for the excitement is the gender-segregated peer group, where each boy increases the excitement by adding still a "worse" word. All of this takes place in a game ("rules") context, and hence with anonymity despite the close-up contact of the game.

While we never observed girls playing a Mad Lib game of this sort, some of our female students recall playing the game in grade school but giving it up after being caught by teachers, or out of fear of being caught. Both boys and girls may acquire knowledge of the game, but boys repeatedly perform it because their gender groups give support for transgression.

These instances all suggest that boys experience a shared, arousing context for transgression, with sustained gender group support for rule-breaking. Girls' groups may engage in rule-breaking, but the gender group's support for repeated public trans-

gression is far less certain. The smaller size of girls' gender groupings in comparison with those of boys, and girls' greater susceptibility to rules and social control by teachers, make girls' groups easier to control. Boys' larger groups give each transgressor a degree of anonymity. Anonymity – which means less probability of detection and punishment – enhances the contagious excitement of rule-breaking.

The higher rates of contagious excitement, transgression, and limit-testing in boys' groups mean that when they are excited, boys are often "playing" to male audiences. The public nature of such excitement forges bonds among boys. This kind of bonding is also evident when boys play team sports, and when they act aggressively toward marginal or isolated boys. Such aggression is both physical and verbal (taunts like "sissy," "fag," or "mental"). Sharing a target of aggression may be another source of arousal for groups of boys.[8]

The tie to sexuality in males

When Gagnon and Simon (1973) argued that there are gender-differentiated sexual scripts in adolescence, they implied what our observations suggest: the gender arrangements and subcultures of middle childhood prepare the way for the sexual scripts of adolescence. Fifth and sixth grade boys share pornography, in the form of soft-core magazines like *Playboy* and *Penthouse*, with great care to avoid confiscation. Like the Mad Lib games with their forbidden content, soft-core magazines are also shared in all-male contexts, providing explicit knowledge about what is considered sexually arousing and about attitudes and fantasies. Since pornography is typically forbidden for children in both schools and families, this secret sharing occurs in a context of rule-breaking.

While many theorists since Freud have stressed the importance of boys loosening ties and identification with females (as mother surrogates), few theorists have questioned why "communally aroused" males do not uniformly bond sexually to other males. If the male groups of fifth and sixth grade are the forerunners of the "frankly" heterosexual gender groups of the junior and high school years, what keeps these early groups from open homosexual expression? Scripting in same-gender peer groups may, in fact, be more about gender than about sexual orientation. Boys, who will later view themselves as having homosexual or heterosexual preferences, are learning patterns of masculinity. The answer may also lie in the teaching of homophobia.

By the fourth grade, children, especially boys, have begun to use homophobic labels – "fag," "faggot," "queer" – as terms of insult, especially for marginal boys. They draw upon sexual allusions (often not fully understood, except for their negative and contaminating import) to reaffirm male hierarchies and patterns of exclusion. As "fag" talk increases, relaxed and cuddling patterns of touch decrease among boys. Kindergarten and first-grade boys touch one another frequently and with ease, with arms around shoulders, hugs, and holding hands. By fifth grade, touch among boys becomes more constrained, gradually shifting to mock violence and the use of poking, shoving, and ritual gestures like "giving five" (flat hand slaps) to express bonding. The tough surface of boys' friendships is no longer like the gentle touching of girls in friendship.

"Fag talk," pornography, and the rules for segregation from girls create a separate, forbidden, and arousing area of life among boys. Group teasing for suspected crushes (which we discuss later) heightens the importance of the ambiguous opening toward the institutionalized heterosexuality of adolescence. The underside of this phenomenon is the beginning of homosexual relationships by some 11- and 12-year-old males and the rule-violating fantasy of early male masturbation (Bell et al. 1981; Kinsey et al. 1948). Fag talk helps keep homosexual experi-

ments quiet and heightens the import of the lessons of pornography and gender segregation. Homoeroticism and homophobia coexist, often in tension, in male peer groups of middle childhood, and in some later adolescent and adult male groups. Our hunch is that the high *arousal* of the peer group may provide much of the cuing for the homophobic control. For males, navigating the onset of masturbation and social sexuality is another example of handling rule violations. Miller and Simon (1981) point out that violating rules is felt to impart excitement and an almost moral fervor to early sexual events.

Interaction Among Girls

In contrast with the larger, hierarchical organization of groups of boys, fourth- and fifth-grade girls more often organize themselves in pairs of "best friends" linked in shifting coalitions. These pairs are not "marriages"; the pattern is more one of dyads moving into triads, since girls often participate in two or more pairs at one time. This may result in quite complex social networks. Girls often talk about who is friends with or "likes" whom; they continually negotiate the parameters of friendships.

For example, in the California school, Chris, a fifth-grade girl, frequently said that Kathryn was her "best friend." Kathryn didn't proclaim the friendship as often; she also played and talked a lot with Judy.[9] After watching Kathryn talk to Judy during a transition period in the classroom, Chris went over, took Kathryn aside, and said with an accusing tone, "You talk to Judy more than me." Kathryn responded defensively, "I talk to you as much as I talk to Judy."

In talking about their relationships with one another, girls use a language of "friends," "nice," and "mean." They talk about who is most and least "liked," which anticipates the concern about "popularity" found among junior high and high school girls (Eder 1985). Since relationships sometimes break off, girls hedge bets by structuring networks of potential friends. The activity of constructing and breaking dyads is often carried out through talk with third parties. Some of these processes are evident in a sequence recorded in a Massachusetts school:

> The fifth-grade girls, Flo and Pauline, spoke of themselves as "best friends," while Flo said she was "sort of friends" with Doris. When a lengthy illness kept Pauline out of school, Flo spent more time with Doris. One day Doris abruptly broke off her friendship with Flo and began criticizing her to other girls. Flo, who felt very badly, went around asking others in their network, "What did I do? Why is Doris being so mean? Why is she telling everyone not to play with me?"

On school playgrounds girls are less likely than boys to organize themselves into team sports. They more often engage in small-scale, turn-taking kinds of play. When they jump rope or play on the bars, they take turns performing and watching others perform in stylized movements which may involve considerable skill. Sometimes girls work out group choreographies, counting and jumping rope in unison, or swinging around the bars. In other synchronized body rituals, clusters of fifth- and sixth-grade girls practice cheerleading routines or dance steps. In interactions with one another, girls often use relaxed gestures of physical intimacy, moving bodies in harmony, coming close in space, and reciprocating cuddly touches.[10] We should add that girls also poke and grab, pin one another from behind, and use hand-slap rituals like "giving five," although less frequently than boys.

When the teacher of a combined fourth- and fifth-grade classroom in the California school pitted girls against boys for spelling and math contests, there were vivid gender group differences in the use of touch, space, and movement. During the contests the girls sat close together on desk tops, their arms and shoulders touching. Occasionally a gesture, such as a push or a lean way to one side, would move like a wave through their line. When one of them got a right answer, she would walk along the row of girls, "giving five" before returning to her place. The boys mostly stood along the other side of the classroom, leaning against desks; their bodies didn't touch except for "giving five" when one of them got a right answer.

In other gestures of intimacy, which one rarely sees among boys, girls stroke or comb their friends' hair. They notice and comment on one another's physical appearance such as haircuts or clothes. Best friends monitor one another's emotions. They share secrets and become mutually vulnerable through self-disclosure, with an implicit demand that the expression of one's inadequacy will induce the friend to disclose a related inadequacy. In contrast, disclosure of weakness among boys is far more likely to be exposed to others through joking or horsing around.

Implications for sexuality

Compared with boys, girls are more focused on constructing intimacy and talking about one-to-one relationships. Their smaller and more personal groups provide less protective anonymity than the larger groups of boys. Bonding through mutual self-disclosure, especially through disclosure of vulnerability, and breaking off friendships by "acting mean," teach the creation, sustaining, and ending of emotionally intimate relations. Girls' preoccupation with who is friends with whom, and their monitoring of cues of "nice" and "mean," liking and disliking, teach them strategies for forming and leaving personal relationships. In their interactions girls show knowledge of motivational rules for dyads and insight into both outer and inner realities of social relationships. Occasionally, girls indicate that they see boys as lacking such "obvious" knowledge.

Girls' greater interest in verbally sorting out relationships was evident during an incident in the Massachusetts public school. The fifth-grade boys often insulted John, a socially isolated boy who was not good at sports. On one such occasion during gym class, Bill, a high status boy, angrily yelled "creep" and "mental" when John fumbled the ball. The teacher stopped the game and asked the class to discuss the incident. Both boys and girls vigorously talked about "words that kill," with Bill saying he was sorry for what he said, that he had lost control in the excitement of the game. The girls kept asking, "How could anyone do that?" The boys kept returning to, "When you get excited, you do things you don't mean." Both girls and boys understood and verbalized the dilemma, but after the group discussion the boys dropped the topic. The girls continued to converse, with one repeatedly asking, "How could Bill be so stupid? Didn't he know how he'd make John feel?"

When talking with one another, girls use dirty words much less often than boys do. The shared arousal and bonding among boys which we think occurs around public rule-breaking has as its counterpart the far less frequent giggling sessions of girls, usually in groups larger than three. The giggling often centers on carefully guarded topics, sometimes, although not always, about boys.

The sexually related discourse of girls focuses less on dirty words than on themes of romance. In the Michigan school, first- and second-grade girls often jumped rope to rhymes about romance. A favorite was, "Down in the Valley Where the Green Grass Grows," a saga of heterosexual romance which, with the name of the jumper and a boy of her choice filled in, concludes: "...along came Jason, and kissed her on the cheek...first comes love, then comes marriage, then along comes Cindy with a baby carriage." In the Michigan and California schools, fourth- and fifth-grade girls talked privately about crushes and about which boys were "cute," as shown in the following

incident recorded in the lunchroom of the Michigan school:

> The girls and boys from one of the fourth-grade classes sat at separate tables. Three of the girls talked as they peered at a nearby table of fifth-grade boys. "Look behind you," one said. "Ooh," said the other two. "That boy's named Todd." "I know where my favorite guy is...there," another gestured with her head while her friends looked.

In the Massachusetts private school, fifth-grade girls plotted about how to get particular boy–girl pairs together.

As Gagnon and Simon (1973) have suggested, two strands of sexuality are differently emphasized among adolescent girls and boys. Girls emphasize and learn about the emotional and romantic before the explicitly sexual. The sequence for boys is the reverse; commitment to sexual acts precedes commitment to emotion-laden, intimate relationships and the rhetoric of romantic love. Dating and courtship, Gagnon and Simon suggest, are processes in which each sex teaches the other what each wants and expects. The exchange, as they point out, does not always go smoothly. Indeed, in heterosexual relationships among older adults, tension often persists between the scripts (and felt needs) of women and of men (Chodorow 1978; Rubin 1983).

Other patterns initially learned in the girls' groups of middle childhood later may be worked into more explicitly sexual scripts. In all the schools we studied, emphasis on appearance increased over the course of fifth grade, and symbols of cultural adolescence – lip gloss (kept hidden in desks and clandestinely passed from girl to girl), hairbrushes, and long-tailed combs – began to appear. However, the girls who first began to use these teen artifacts were not necessarily the ones who showed physical signs of puberty. In the California school, fourth- and fifth-grade girls talked about who was prettiest and confessed feelings of being ugly. Girls remark on their own and others' appearance long before they talk about issues of attractiveness to boys. The concern with appearance, and the pattern of performing and being watched, may be integrated into sexual expression later.

Children's Sexual Meanings and the Construction of Gender Arrangements

Girls and boys, who spend considerable time in gender-separate groups, learn different patterns of interaction which, we have argued, lay the groundwork for the sexual scripts of adolescence and adulthood. However, sexuality is not simply delayed until adolescence. Children engage in sexual practices – kissing, erotic forms of touch, masturbation, and sometimes intercourse (see Constantine and Martinson 1981; Finkelhor 1979). As school-based observers, we saw only a few overt sexual activities among children, mostly incidents of public, cross-gender kissing, surrounded by teasing, chasing, and laughter.

In elementary school life the overtly sexual is mostly a matter of words, labels, and charged rituals of play. In identifying this behavior as "sexual," we are cautious about imposing adult perspectives. When children say words like "fag" or "fuck," they rarely share adult meanings, as was apparent in their use of "fag" essentially as a synonym for "nerd" and as an epithet occasionally applied to girls as well as to boys.

Although their sexual knowledge is fragmentary and different from that of adults, children learn early on that certain words and gestures are forbidden and charged with special meaning. Adults and children jointly construct the domain considered to be "sexual." For example, both adults and children know and sometimes enforce taboos against the use of dirty words in school, as shown in an incident in the library of the California school:

"Miss Smith, Donny is being a bad boy, he's being nasty, he's looking up sex," a fourth-grade girl told the teacher as they stood near the card catalogue. "No I'm not, I'm looking up sunset," Donny said defensively.

Heterosexual teasing and the importance of third parties

The special loading of sexual words and gestures makes them useful for accomplishing non-sexual purposes. Sexual idioms provide a major resource which children draw upon as they construct and maintain gender segregation. Through the years of elementary school, children use with increasing frequency heterosexual idioms – claims that a particular girl or boy "likes," "has a crush on," or is "goin' with" someone from the other gender group. Unlike alternative, non-gendered terms for affiliation ("friends," "playmates"), heterosexual idioms imply that interaction between girls and boys has sexual overtones. Children rarely use sexual language to describe within-gender interaction. From an early age, the erotic is prescriptively heterosexual, and male (but, significantly, much less female) homophobic.

Children's language for heterosexual relationships consists of a very few, often repeated, and sticky words. In a context of teasing, the charge that a particular boy "likes" a particular girl (or vice versa) may be hurled like an insult. The difficulty children have in countering such accusations was evident in a conversation between the observer and a group of third-grade girls in the lunchroom of the Michigan school:

Susan asked me what I was doing, and I said I was observing the things children do and play. Nicole volunteered, "I like running, boys chase all the girls. See Tim over there? Judy chases him all around the school. She likes him." Judy, sitting across the table, quickly responded, "I hate him. I like him for a friend." "Tim loves Judy," Nicole said in a loud, sing-song voice.

Sexual and romantic teasing marks social hierarchies. The most popular children and the pariahs – the lowest status, excluded children – are most frequently mentioned as targets of "liking." Linking someone with a pariah suggests shared contamination and is an especially vicious tease.

When a girl or boy publicly says that she or he "likes" someone or has a boyfriend or girlfriend, that person defines the romantic situation and is less susceptible to teasing than those targeted by someone else. Crushes may be secretly revealed to friends, a mark of intimacy, especially among girls. The entrusted may then go public with the secret ("Wendy likes John"), which may be experienced as betrayal, but which also may be a way of testing the romantic waters. Such leaks, like those of government officials, can be denied or acted upon by the original source of information.

Third parties – witnesses and kibbitzers – are central to the structure of heterosexual teasing. The teasing constructs dyads (very few of them actively "couples"), but within the control of larger gender groups. Several of the white fifth graders in the Michigan and California schools and some of the black students in the Massachusetts schools occasionally went on dates, which were much discussed around the schools. Same-gender groups provide launching pads, staging grounds, and retreats for heterosexual couples, both real and imagined. Messengers and emissaries go between groups, indicating who likes whom and checking out romantic interest. By the time "couples" actually get together (if they do at all), the groups and their messengers have provided a network of constructed meanings, a kind of agenda for the pair. As we have argued, gender-divided peer groups sustain different meanings of the sexual. They also regulate heterosexual behavior by helping to define the emerging sexual scripts of adolescence (who "likes" whom, who might "go with" whom, what it means to be a couple).

In the California and Michigan schools, when children reported news from the play-ground to an adult observer, they defined two types of activities as especially newsworthy: physical fights (who fought with and beat up whom), and who "liked," had a crush on, or was "goin' with" whom. Like fights, purported romantic liaisons (e.g., "Frank likes Bonnie") are matters of public notice and of widespread rumor and teasing. The charge of "liking" or having a "girlfriend" or "boyfriend" may be constructed from very small clues – for example, that Frank sat down by or talked with Bonnie, or that he chose her as a partner in PE.

When a girl or boy consistently initiates talk or play with someone of the other gender group, she or he risks being teased. This risk is so severe that close friendships between boys and girls that are formed and maintained in other places like neighborhoods or church sometimes go underground during the school day.[11] Heterosexual meanings, which one might think would unite boys and girls, in fact may keep them apart. Children use heterosexual teasing to maintain and police boundaries between "the girls" and "the boys," defined as separate groups.

Heterosexually charged rituals

Boundaries between boys and girls are also emphasized and maintained by heterosexually charged rituals like cross-sex chasing.[12] Formal games of tag and informal episodes of chasing punctuate life on playgrounds. The informal episodes usually open with a provocation – taunts like "You can't get me!" or "Slobber monster!," bodily pokes, or the grabbing of possessions like a hat or scarf. The person who is provoked may ignore the taunt or poke, handle it verbally ("leave me alone!"), or respond by chasing. After a chasing sequence, which may end after a short run or a pummeling, the chaser and chased may switch roles.

Chasing has a gendered structure. When boys chase one another, they often end up wrestling or in mock fights. When girls chase girls, they less often wrestle one another to the ground. Unless organized as a formal game like "freeze tag," same-gender chasing goes unnamed and usually undiscussed. But children set apart cross-gender chasing with special names – "girls chase the boys"; "boys chase the girls"; "the chase"; "chasers"; "chase and kiss"; "kiss-chase"; "kissers and chasers"; "kiss or kill" – and with animated talk about the activity. The names vary by region and school, but inevitably contain both gender and sexual meanings.[13]

When boys and girls chase one another, they become, by definition, separate teams. Gender terms override individual identities, especially for the other team: "Help, a girl's chasin' me!"; "C'mon Sarah, let's get that boy"; "Tony, help save me from the girls." Individuals may call for help from, or offer help to, others of their gender. In acts of treason, they may also grab someone of their gender and turn them over to the opposing team, as when, in the Michigan school, Ryan grabbed Billy from behind, wrestled him to the ground, and then called, "Hey girls, get 'im."

Names like "chase and kiss" mark the sexual meanings of cross-gender chasing. The threat of kissing – most often girls threatening to kiss boys – is a ritualized form of provocation. Teachers and aides are often amused by this form of play among children in the lower grades; they are more perturbed by cross-gender chasing among fifth- and sixth-graders, perhaps because at those ages some girls "have their development" (breasts make sexual meanings seem more consequential), and because of the more elaborate patterns of touch and touch avoidance in chasing rituals among older children. The principal of one Michigan school forbade the sixth-graders from playing "pom-pom," a complicated chasing game, because it entailed "inappropriate touch."

Cross-gender chasing is sometimes structured around rituals of pollution, such as "cooties," where individuals or groups are treated as contaminating or carrying "germs." Children have rituals for transferring cooties (usually touching someone else and shouting "You've got cooties!"), for immunization (e.g., writing "CV" for "cootie vaccination" on their arms), and for eliminating cooties (e.g., saying "no gives" or using "cooties catchers" made of folded paper [described in Knapp and Knapp 1976]). Boys may transmit cooties, but cooties usually originate with girls. One version of cooties played in Michigan is called "girl stain"; the fourth-graders whom Karkau (1973) describes used the phrase "girl touch." Although cooties is framed as play, the import may be serious. Female pariahs – the ultimate school untouchables by virtue of gender and some added stigma such as being overweight or from a very poor family – are sometimes called "cootie queens" or "cootie girls." Conversely, we have never heard or read about "cootie kings" or "cootie boys."

In these cross-gender rituals girls are defined as sexual. Boys sometimes threaten to kiss girls, but it is girls' kisses and touch which are deemed especially contaminating. Girls more often use the threat of kissing to tease boys and to make them run away, as in this example recorded among fourth-graders on the playground of the California school:

> Smiling and laughing, Lisa and Jill pulled a fourth-grade boy along by his hands, while a group of girls sitting on the jungle-gym called out, "Kiss him, kiss him." Grabbing at his hair, Lisa said to Jill, "Wanna kiss Jonathan?" Jonathan got away, and the girls chased after him. "Jill's gonna kiss your hair," Lisa yelled.

The use of kisses as a threat is doubled-edged, since the power comes from the threat of pollution. A girl who frequently uses this threat may be stigmatized as a "kisser."

Gender-marked rituals of teasing, chasing, and pollution heighten the boundaries between boys and girls. They also convey assumptions which get worked into later sexual scripts: (1) that girls and boys are members of distinctive, opposing, and sometimes antagonistic groups: (2) that cross-gender contact is potentially sexual and contaminating, fraught with both pleasure and danger; and (3) that girls are more sexually defined (and polluting) than boys.

These meanings are not always evoked. Girls and boys sometimes interact in relaxed ways, and gender is not always salient in their encounters (see Thorne 1986). But sexual meanings, embedded in patterns of teasing and ritualized play, help maintain gender divisions; they enhance social distance, asymmetry, and antagonism between girls and boys. These patterns may persist in the sexual scripts of adolescence.

Conclusion

Social scientists have often viewed the heterosexual dating rituals of adolescence – when girls and boys "finally" get together – as the concluding stage after the separate, presumably non-sexual, boys' and girls' groups that are so prevalent in childhood. We urge a closer look at the organization of sexuality and of gender in middle and late childhood. The gender-divided social worlds of children are not totally asexual. And same-gender groups have continuing import in the more overtly sexual scripts of adolescence and adulthood.

From an early age "the sexual" is prescriptively heterosexual and male homophobic. Children draw on sexual meanings to maintain gender segregation – to make cross-gender interaction risky and to mark and ritualize boundaries between "the boys" and "the girls." In their separate gender groups, girls and boys learn somewhat different patterns of bonding – boys sharing the arousal of group rule-breaking; girls emphasizing the construction of intimacy, and themes of romance. Coming to adolescent sexual intimacy from different and asymmetric gender subcultures, girls and boys

bring somewhat different needs, capacities, and types of knowledge.

It is obvious that heterosexual acts require some form of cross-gender interaction. Among early adolescents, social support for such interaction comes from separate girls' and boys' groups that construct couples through talk and teasing long before dating is prevalent. Girls' and boys' groups do not measure with the same ruler; they promote different sexual meanings. An argument may be made that the audiences (those who share our measures) remain same-gender peer groups later as well as early in life. Perhaps our culture's concern with the question of the sex of the sexual partner has obscured how much our sexual life is tied to group gender arrangements. Gender segregation and its effects on the narrowing of the audiences to which we play are not limited to childhood. The social supports for gender segregation – in work and other institutions – are lifelong. Their effects extend into the organization of gender and of sexuality in later life.

Transitions not only involve continuity, but also disjuncture and loss. By the sixth and seventh grades, culturally defined heterosexual rituals (like "goin' with") have begun to replace the more relaxed and non-sexualized contact found between some girls and boys at earlier ages. Adult women who were "tomboys" often speak of adolescence as a painful time when they were pushed away from comfortable participation in boys' activities. Other adult women say they experienced entry into adolescent rituals of heterosexual dating as a time of loss, when intense, even erotic ties with other girls were altered and even suppressed (Rich 1980).

With the shift to adolescence, heterosexual encounters assume more importance. They may alter relations in same-gender groups. For example, Janet Schofield (1982) reports that for sixth- and seventh-grade children in a middle school, the popularity of girls with other girls was affected by their popularity with boys, while boys' status with other boys did not depend on their relations with girls.

As it is defined in this culture, entry into adolescence entails the assumption of sexuality as a core of identity. How, in the shift away from the less sexual definitions of gender in childhood, does sexuality become seen and experienced as an intrinsic "personal" characteristic? How are different sexualities constructed? Analysis of the somewhat separate systems of gender and sexuality, with attention to changes over the life course, may begin to provide answers to such questions.

NOTES

1   Physiological psychologists define "sex" as the structures and functions (dimorphisms) of biological *male*ness and *female*ness. They define "sexuality" as the social meanings that are attached to sex, i.e., masculinity, femininity, learned stimuli for sexual arousal. By these definitions, sexuality includes the *social* meanings that transform males and females to boys and girls, men and women – that is, "gender." Sexuality also includes the learning of the wide range of stimuli (virtually everything beyond direct genital touch) that produce sexual arousal (see Luria and Rose 1979). Depending on one's definitions, this essay deals with two aspects of what physiological psychologists call sexuality: gender *and* learned aspects of sexual arousal and sexual meanings, or what most sociologists call gender and sexuality (learned arousal/social meanings). Writing for a sociological audience, we – a sociologist and a psychologist – have chosen the latter language and conceptualization. Our usage is clarified in the body of the text.

2   In the Western world, this definition is made possible by the physical separation of the sexual life of adults from the everyday life of children, a privilege not extended to families who inhabit one room in much of the rest of the world.

3   In this essay, we have set out to trace general patterns in age-based relationships between sexuality and gender. We have not, except incidentally, explored possible variations by region, social class, and race or ethnicity. All

of these dimensions should be more fully addressed. For example, our data suggest that the transition to adolescent sexual scripts begins earlier in working-class than in middle-class or upper-middle-class schools. However, the transition began earlier in the Massachusetts, upper-middle-class private school than in the more middle-class public school. The relation of class, type of school, and age of transition to adolescent sexual scripts is obviously complex.

4   On the special challenges of fieldwork with children, see Fine and Glassner (1979) and Mandell (1985).

5   We will discuss the joint construction of "dirty words" later.

6   All playground clusters were counted, regardless of activity; such an inventory characterizes groups of children, rather than individuals. This may overrate the "quality" of cross-gender activity when, for example, a single girl integrates a soccer game, or when one boy chases a large group of girls (both types of groups, as well as those with more even gender ratios, were counted as mixed-gender).

7   In the private Massachusetts school, which had less gender segregation, children could stay indoors after lunch. Thus, they were more often under adult supervision than the public school children who, during the noontime recess, were all on the playground without adults organizing their activity.

8   For a related analysis of bonding among adult men, see Lyman (forthcoming).

9   All names are fictitious.

10 These patterns accord with other studies of gender differentiation in the use of space and touch; see Henley 1977. We noticed a pattern which distinguishes touch among children from patterns adults use to mark status. In adult hierarchies, subordinates tend to avoid initiating touch to dominate (Henley 1977). But, in a sort of courting gesture, subordinate children (both girls and boys) often initiate touch to more dominant or popular children of the same gender. Refusing these bids for acceptance or liking, the more popular sometimes shake away such touch; they also may verbally refuse physical contact ("Don't do that, it bothers me"). These gestures are powerful markers of social position.

11 This is especially a risk for lower status children. Those of top status run less risk in
crossing the gender divide.

12 See Thorne (1986) for more extended analysis of the marking and crossing of gender
boundaries among children.

13 This form of play is briefly analyzed in Best
(1983), Finnan (1982), and Sluckin (1981).

REFERENCES

Bell, Alan T., Martin S. Weinberg, and Sue K.
Hammsersmith 1981. *Sexual Preference: Its
Development in Men and Women*. Blooming-
ton: Indiana University Press.

Best, Raphaela 1983. *We've All Got Scars*. Bloomington: Indiana University Press.

Chodorow, Nancy 1978. *The Reproduction of
Mothering*. Berkeley: University of California
Press.

Constantine, Larry L. and Floyd M. Martinson
1981. *Children and Sex*. Boston: Little, Brown.

Eder, Donna 1985. "The cycle of popularity:
interpersonal relations among female adolescents." *Sociology of Education* 58: 154–65.

Eder, Donna and Maureen T. Hallinan 1978.
"Sex differences in children's friendships."
American Sociological Review 43: 237–50.

Fine, Gary Alan 1980. "The natural history of
preadolescent male friendship groups." Pp.
293–320 in Hugh C. Foot, Antony J. Chapman, and Jean R. Smith (eds.), *Friendship and
Social Relations in Children*. New York: Wiley.

Fine, Gary Alan and Barry Glassner 1979. "Participant observation with children: promise
and problems." *Urban Life* 8: 153–74.

Finkelhor, David 1979. *Sexually Victimized Children*. New York: Free Press.

Finnan, Christine R. 1982. "The ethnography of
children's spontaneous play." Pp. 358–80 in
George Spindler (ed.), *Doing the Ethnography
of Schooling*. New York: Holt, Rinehart &
Winston.

Gagnon, John H. and William Simon 1973.
Sexual Conduct. Chicago: Aldine.

Goffman, Erving 1977. "The arrangement
between the sexes." *Theory and Society* 4:
301–36.

Goodwin, Marjorie Harness 1980a. "Directive-
response speech sequences in girls' and boys'
task activities." Pp. 157–73 in Sally McCon-
nell-Ginet, Ruth Borker, and Nelly Furman

(eds.), *Women and Language in Literature
and Society*. New York: Praeger.

——1980b. "'He-said-she-said': formal cultural
procedures for the construction of a gossip
dispute activity." *American Ethnologist* 7:
674–95.

Henley, Nancy 1977. *Body Politics*. Englewood
Cliffs, NJ: Prentice-Hall.

Hughes, Linda A. 1983. "Beyond the Rules of the
Game: Girls' Gaming at a Friends' School."
Unpublished Ph.D. dissertation, University of
Pennsylvania Graduate School of Education.

——Forthcoming. "The study of children's
gaming." In Brian Sutton-Smith, Jay Mechling,
and Thomas Johnson (eds.), *A Handbook
of Children's Folklore*. Washington, DC:
Smithsonian.

Karkau, Kevin 1973. "Sexism in the fourth
grade." Pittsburgh: KNOW.

Kinsey, Alfred C., Wardell B. Pomeroy, and Clyde
E. Martin 1948. *Sexual Behavior in the Human
Male*. Philadelphia: Saunders.

Kinsey, Alfred C., Wardell B. Pomeroy, Clyde E.
Martin, and Paul H. Gebhard 1953. *Sexual
Behavior in the Human Female*. Philadelphia:
Saunders.

Knapp, Mary and Herbert Knapp 1976. *One
Potato, Two Potato*. New York: W. W. Norton.

Lever, Janet 1976. "Sex differences in the games
children play." *Social Problems* 23: 478–87.

Lockheed, Marlaine E. 1985. "Sex equity in classroom organization and climate." Pp. 189–217
in Susan S. Klein (ed.), *Handbook for Achieving Sex Equity Through Education*. Baltimore,
MD: Johns Hopkins University Press.

Luria, Zella 1983. "Sexual fantasy and pornography: two cases of girls brought up with pornography." *Archives of Sexual Behavior* 11:
395–404.

Luria, Zella and Mitchel D. Rose 1979. *The
Psychology of Human Sexuality*. New York:
Wiley.

Lyman, Peter. Forthcoming. "The fraternal bond
as a joking relationship." In Michael Kimmel
(ed.), *Changing Men*. Beverly Hills, CA: Sage.

Maccoby, Eleanor 1985. "Social groupings in
childhood: their relationship to prosocial and
antisocial behavior in boys and girls." Pp. 263–
84 in Dan Olweus, Jack Block, and Marian
Radke-Yarrow (eds.), *Development of Antisocial and Prosocial Behavior*. San Diego, CA:
Academic Press.

Maccoby, Eleanor and Carol Jacklin 1974. *The Psychology of Sex Differences*. Stanford, CA: Stanford University Press.

Maltz, Daniel N. and Ruth A. Borker 1983. "A cultural approach to male–female miscommunication." Pp. 195–216 in John J. Gumperz (ed.), *Language and Social Identity*. New York: Cambridge University Press.

Mandell, Nancy 1985. "The research role in observational fieldwork with preschool children." Paper presented at annual meetings of Eastern Sociological Association.

Miller, Patricia Y. and William Simon 1981. "The development of sexuality in adolescence." Pp. 383–407 in Joseph Adelson (ed.), *Handbook of Adolescent Psychology*. New York: Wiley.

Rich, Adrienne 1980. "Compulsory heterosexuality and lesbian existence." *Signs* 5: 631–60.

Rubin, Lillian 1983. *Intimate Strangers*. New York: Harper and Row.

Rubin, Zick 1973. *Liking and Loving*. New York: Holt.

Savin-Williams, Richard C. 1976. "An ethnological study of dominance formation and maintenance in a group of human adolescents." *Child Development* 47: 972–9.

Schofield, Janet 1982. *Black and White in School*. New York: Praeger.

Sluckin, Andy 1981. *Growing Up in the Playground*. London: Routledge & Kegan Paul.

Thorne, Barrie 1986. "Girls and boys together...but mostly apart: gender arrangements in elementary schools." Pp. 167–84 in Willard W. Hartup and Zick Rubin (eds.), *Relationships and Development*. Hillsdale, NJ: Lawrence Erlbaum.

Waldrop, Mary F. and Charles F. Halverson 1975. "Intensive and extensive peer behavior: longitudinal and cross-sectional analysis." *Child Development* 46: 16–19.

10 "I couldn't ever picture myself having sex…": Gender Differences in Sex and Sexual Subjectivity

Karin A. Martin

> I think there are very few girls I know who are having sex and actually enjoying it, most say it hurts especially the first time. The guys who are being promiscuous are actually enjoying it.
>
> *Middle-class 17-year-old girl*

Why do adolescents have sex? What kinds of internal and external factors influence their decisions to have sex? Is the experience of teenage sex different for boys and girls? These questions are left unanswered by much of the current research on teen sex. Chilman in describing teen sex research says that, "In general, many of the studies seem to be voyeuristic. Who does what, sexually, with whom, how, and when?"[1] She is right. Researchers have extensively studied the demographics of teenage sex[2] and sexual knowledge, attitudes, and behaviors.[3] Yet, there is little research about the experience of sex – if teens like it or not, how it makes them feel about themselves, if girls feel differently about it than boys do. "What sexuality means to adolescents, how it relates to other aspects of teenage life, and what strategies teens use to manage or incorporate it into their lives have not been studied in detail."[4] This chapter begins to fill this gap, again paying close attention to gender differences in agency and sexual subjectivity.

Throughout this chapter when I talk about "sex" I mean sexual intercourse because this is what teenagers mean when they talk about sex. There is a socially constructed line between all other forms of sexual petting and intercourse in teen cul-

ture. Intercourse is invested with more meaning and significance than any other act. I find that like puberty, first sexual experiences further solidify agency and sexual subjectivity in boys. Girls, however, feel less agentic and less sexually subjective after first sexual experiences.

In order to examine how teens further construct sexual subjectivity (or not), we need to understand why and how teens come to have sex, for the gender differences in the social and psychodynamic paths to first intercourse are telling. By paths to sex, I mean teens' interactions around, feelings about, expectations and knowledge about sex that cause teens to have sex. These include the meaning of dating or "going out" or having a boyfriend or girlfriend, expectations and experiences of sex, and the immediate social interaction between two teens, the "talk" or lack of it, that leads to sex.

Ideal Love…

Dating, "seeing each other" (dating) and "going out" (having a long-term monogamous relationship, the step after "seeing each other")[5] are all important cross-gender relationships that organize teen social life. For the most part, these relations mimic those of teens' images of adulthood. In them, most teens practice traditional gender roles and heterosexuality. This is true for both class groups and both genders. But these relationships do not only mimic adult heterosexuality, they also mimic children's play. Thorne and Luria observe that kids often play games that are "girls against the boys."[6] This oppositional gender strategy is carried into early stories of romantic relationship. Whenever boys complained about girlfriends or girls about unfaithful boyfriends, their stories took on this tone of the girls against the boys. For example, the boys whom I interviewed complained about their girlfriends, commitment, and monogamy.[7] They said things like 19-year-old Paul did: "I'm trying not to attach myself right now, until I go away to school. I don't want to deal with anyone in high school. I don't want to carry any baggage." Boys freely admitted that one was not supposed to admit to liking his girlfriend in teenage boy culture. I asked Scott, a working-class 18-year-old, "Do guys talk about their girlfriends?"

I don't ever talk to my guy friends about my girlfriend, except...well you never admit that you like her, never. You just say that she was a pain in the neck.

Girls, on the other hand, are immersed in romantic culture. They told stories of love...

Tell me about your boyfriend.
I love his personality. The way he treats me. The way he says he cares for me, it's really important to me. He's very outgoing. Umm, he's real funny, and he makes me laugh. Umm, he's, I think he's real nice lookin'. And he's not too tall. He's about 5′8″. So, he's just perfect. (Valerie)

...and sometimes of unfaithful boyfriends who betrayed them.

He's really stubborn, and he didn't care about anything, and he lied, he lied all the time. He wasn't loyal at all or anything like that. (Diana)

Psychoanalytic authors suggest that many girls and adult women take up a position of ideal love in relationship to their fathers in order to get vicarious access to subjectivity. Ideal love is submission to and adoration of an idealized other whom one would like to be like and from whom one wants confirmation and recognition. It is a form of identificatory love. Ideal love explains, according to Benjamin, why women's love often takes the form of the worship of a hero that a woman would actually like to be herself.[8]

At adolescence, many girls, in the process of growing up and away from their families, shift their ideal love from their fathers to male peers. The project of ideal love and the shift of ideal love from fathers to male peers is simultaneously a social and a psychodynamic one. By shifting their ideal love to male peers instead of fathers, girls can be recognized as participating in the adult world of heterosexual romance. Adolescents usually want to be recognized as grown up, independent, and able to do things. I argue that many girls, especially working-class girls, find ideal love to be the only route (although often an alienated one) to attaining agency and sexual subjectivity, and it has a particularly strong force in girls' heterosexual relationships at this age.

Teen culture emphasizes compulsory heterosexuality and facilitates girls' move to ideal love with male peers. There are very few lesbian or gay teen romance novels and thousands of heterosexual ones. Television shows that are geared to teens, like Beverly Hills 90210, and soap operas, a favourite pastime of many teens, rarely have gay characters and never have regular gay characters. However, heterosexuality and the adventures it poses almost entirely comprise the plots of such shows. There is little room for gay or lesbian identity or desire in most of this adolescent pop culture. This may be part of the reason why establishing a gay or lesbian identity as a teen is a difficult and relatively new phenomenon, as well as why many gay and lesbian teens also have had heterosexual experience.[9] This emphasis on compulsory heterosexuality shapes all girls' and boys' (although boys are less caught up in romantic culture) fantasies and realities.

In early adolescence, girls, especially white working-class girls, become absorbed in teen idols, teen romances, and pop rock ballads about love.[10] Then, as teens, many girls acquire boyfriends and construct narratives about their boyfriends that cast them in the light of ideal love. Stories of ideal love are not stories of passion and sexuality but are stories of romance and what sociologist Arlie Hochschild calls magnified moments. A magnified moment is "a moment of heightened importance to the individual. This can be an epiphany, a moment of intense glee, or unusual insight. Within cautionary stories, it can be a moment of unusual despair."[11] First dates, first looks, first meetings, as well as break ups, all are or contain magnified moments for girls in ideal love.

In narratives of ideal love girls often describe boys as heroes. They are "heroes of the high school" – athletes, military men, reggae singers, exceptional artists, boys who speak foreign languages, and older boys. Which boys are considered heroes depends on class. A smart boy is probably a "geek" at the working-class high school, but a potential hero and ideal love at the private, middle-class high school. Girls also sometimes compare boys to their fathers, providing the connection to early childhood rapprochement and first ideal love that Benjamin proposes.

The best way to understand what ideal love is, is to hear girls describe it to you. They get excited, interested. Their stories become detailed, and these details, however insignificant and minor they may be to the listener, are clearly important to the narrator. Their stories also get infused with romantic language and romantic words – flowers, fairy tale, letters, swept off my feet, magic, flirting, intense, beach, cute, beautiful, secrets. Descriptions of ideal love also clearly have a story to them. The narrator has put the events together to make a "fairy tale sort of story" for herself. I asked Jill to tell me about her boyfriend (a question that was always met with enthusiasm and to which I always got a long answer).

> It's a fairy tale sort of a story. He's in the Marine Corps, and he was over in the Middle East during the war. And there were names in the newspaper you could write to, and I wrote to a Sergeant, and he'd just gotten married and felt really awkward writing, so he gave the letter to my boyfriend, Alan. Alan and I wrote and when he came back to the States he sent me flowers and asked if he could meet me, and once he came up to meet me we've been together ever since. That's last year. He's stationed in the south. I just came back from visitin' him. It's really far. He's getting out the end of May; so we won't have to do that any more. Anyway, he's wonderful. He's a spitting image, like inside, how he acts, of my dad. My father always said, like teasing me when I was little, wait, you'll find someone exactly like me. And it's true. He's quiet. He only speaks his mind when asked. He's very secretive about his feelings. I've just started tapping into them myself. He'll do anything to help anyone out. Our relationship is going well. We communicate really good. He can mumble on about something for five minutes and someone else would be truly lost but I'd know exactly what he's talking about. We really trust each other, and I don't trust really easily and he doesn't either. He's had a bad past, and I have a bad past, so...

Kristen told a less complicated version of ideal love, and like Jill's military man, her ideal love is not an ordinary guy, but a reggae singer. He has special status. She told me about him at the beginning of our interview when I asked her what she daydreamed about.

> I always think about this guy I met this summer. I wicked fell in love, wicked bad. I didn't just love him, but I wicked fell-in-love. You know, swept me off my feet. I just think about his face, the way he used to sing to me. He was wicked awesome. He

used to like sing reggae to me. He was awesome. He was just one of a kind.

Even ex-boyfriends can be ideal loves. Stories of ex-ideal loves are similar to those of current ideal loves, except the ending to the story is different. Somewhere in the story there is usually a fatal flaw discovered or an unanticipated event, a magnified moment, that leads to the breakup. The tone of these stories shifts from romantic, to sad, to angry.

Tell me about him [your ex-boyfriend].
Well, he was intelligent. I mean, I don't look for intelligence as a primary factor anymore. I like going out with guys and I like being with them, but there are so many, in high school at least, either they are stupid or they act that way 'cause they think it's cool. But he was really intelligent. He, we can really talk. I mean, it wasn't just talk about like other people or like whatever, since we live so far away. We talked about like real things. We had like these really intense phone conversations until like one o'clock in the morning. I mean it was of course like difficult because in Europe [where they met], we did not do anything like romantic or kiss or anything at all, and then it was all like through the phone, and we started out, just like, kinda flirting. And then it just kind of got worse and worse and then it was just kind of like more and more and more intense you know. Everybody like almost saying what they mean, almost, almost, almost. And then one day, he just like wrote me this letter. "I think you're so beautiful inside and out, and I can't believe you know, that I didn't take advantage of the chance to get to know you better in Europe but...." You know, he ended the letter, like, "I think I love you." And I was like "OH MY GOD!" 'Cause I had been in love with him for like, I mean, well not like a long time, but for like three weeks. I really just knew. It was really wonderful. It was a great feeling, like a secure feeling. And that's one of the reasons that it really pissed me off that it didn't work out after a while. I was like "This is a big deal, this is

right you know. We're in love why isn't everything perfect?" I'm kinda like mad at him right now. I've called and I've written him letters but he just doesn't return any of it. And I had a lot of higher hopes for him at least, 'cause we were so close. *(Juliana)*

First meetings with ideal loves are often magnified moments. Danielle described one of the most magnified moments I heard in all my interviews. Her first meeting with her boyfriend was a magnified moment in itself, yet within this general story, there was literally one specific moment that she magnified – when she and the boy turned to each other and said the exact same thing at the same time. It was clear to me as the listener that this was the moment that cinched the story that they were "right" for each other because she prefaced the moment in her telling with a breathless, giggling "I have to tell you this."

How did you meet your boyfriend?
We met in August of last year. We met on the beach! It was real cute. Me and my friends were walking down the beach and three guys kept driving by in this car, and they're always like, "Hey, State College" 'cause I had this State College shirt on. And umm, they're like "Do you want a ride?" They looked nice. They weren't dirty or anything. So I'm like "Sure!" Well, I waited for my friends to decide. And we got in and we hung out at the beach. And like he chased after me 'cause they were trying to pull us in the water. It was sooo fun! I'll never forget it. And then like...I have to tell you this! He chased after me, and like he grabbed me and started swinging me around and I'm like "Aaaah!" and I got a big mouth. He's going "Promise you're not gonna scream. Promise you're not gonna scream if I let you go. Come on, shhh. They're gonna think I'm raping you or something." So he let me go and then we're walking back to where my friends are and then we both look at each other and go "You run too fast." And it was so cute! Then that night he called me at like twelve o'clock and we

talked 'til like five in the morning. And a couple of weeks later we started going out.

Over half of all the working-class girls in my sample told stories of ideal love as compared to one quarter of the middle-class girls. One reason for this is that working-class girls, who get little acknowledgment of their agency in other spheres, get recognition from others when they "accomplish" the task of acquiring a boyfriend. When I asked Linda, "What things make you feel good about yourself?" she replied, "When a guy calls me and asks me out on a date! Ahhh! That's the best. My mom can't believe I have so many dates." Esther, a working-class girl, said that she clearly got that message that boys, and especially a husband, were important accomplishments. They were things (among several others) that she and her mother fought about a lot.

> The most recent thing is I'm moving in with my boyfriend, and that's out of wedlock. She's a strict Catholic and that's a big thing, she wants me to get married ASAP, and she's bitching for more grandchildren, too. So she's really pushing that on me. We fight about my clothes, the way I act, how she doesn't like my way of reasoning or thinking. She thinks I'm too, I don't know, liberal, I guess maybe is the word. She thinks I'm just too outgoing for my own good. So she's always telling me about that, but the big thing is marriage right now.
> *So you don't want to get married.*
> No. No. I haven't even graduated from high school, and my big thing right now is just trying to start college.

Mothers, however, are not the only ones who think boyfriends are important for girls. Peers also see having a boyfriend as a sign of status and of accomplishment. Kendra claimed, "It's so important to have a boyfriend because it's really a sign ... to have something saying you're really attractive to someone is really important."

Another reason for this class difference in ideal love is middle-class girls remain in ideal love with their fathers well into adolescence, in contrast to working-class girls who switch their allegiance quite early. Middle-class girls' ideal love of their fathers not only facilitates their feelings of agency but delays their sexual involvement with boyfriends. For, as we will see below, girls often have sex in order not to lose their ideal love.

The propensity toward ideal love in these working-class teenage girls does offer them one source of agency. Because of ideal love, working-class girls are more likely to break through the "tyranny of nice and kind" that Brown and Gilligan describe. Several working-class girls made it clear that they were not subjected to Brown and Gilligan's "tyranny of nice and kind." This group of working-class girls often said that they "had to" speak their mind or that they were "loud." Usually they were mean and unkind when fighting about boys or defending their own reputations with boys. For example, Amanda, a savvy 15-year-old who talked at length about her boyfriends and the "guys" she met at the mall, described how she stuck up for herself in a fight with another girl who thought Amanda was stealing her boyfriend, which Amanda was.

> Like the other night she called me and I was just so mad. I was like, "I'm just fucking friends with him!" And I was yelling 'cause I have a big mouth and then she said something, something ... I can't remember but something "cunt" and then she was like, "I'm gonna nail you." And I was like, I'd kill her. She's so stupid, I could kill her. But like I wouldn't touch her unless she touched me first [points to her chest].

Thompson explains that there is a connection between this fighting and ideal love in working-class girls' lives.

> What girlfighters fight for, and those who fear girls fall back on, is dyadic intimacy: the one boy or man on whom they lay all

the chips of life. In the empathy of first love, they get this from the boys they will fight to keep forever. This is their great hope – the achievement that will make up for everything else: for being raised to serve men, for being their mothers' daughters.[12]

Thompson finds, as I do, that boyfriends are so important because a life organized around a man and mothering is many poor and working-class girls' only vision of the future.

But what about boys' roles in teenage love relationships? Boys do not usually reciprocate or lend support to girls' stories of ideal love. Take for example the boyfriend and girlfriend who told me how they met. The girl's story was full of the language of magnified moments and ideal love. The boy's story was very straightforward. He told me: "I think we met at the pool." She told me a much longer story. She said that they met at a party on Valentine's Day right after she had broken up with her last boyfriend. She had not wanted to go to the party, but her friends talked her into it. He had spent all night talking to her and teasing her, and then the next day he and his friends came in to where she worked. She was embarrassed because she charged him the wrong amount for something he bought, and she worried he would not like her anymore. She added at the end of her story that she had told him that he would never forget their anniversary, since it was Valentine's Day. Apparently, he had forgotten, or had not wanted to subscribe to such a romantic version of how they had met.

Boys rarely used the word love in discussing their feelings about their girlfriends or relationships. Love was something that they expressed to girls only reciprocally or out of awkwardness. Brent's story best exemplifies this phenomenon.

I didn't think anything was going to happen between us, but she was spending the night at my house, well, she stayed in my room, so I was just like on the bed, and she was on the floor and she was telling me about everything that was going on. And like I went down to hug her and everything, and she wouldn't let go and so I don't know how long we were hugging or anything, but we started kissing and it . . . God it was so strange and she told me that she loved me in the middle of it all, and (laughs) I knew a little bit more about what it meant than I did in sixth grade, what was I gonna say "Oh thanks?" So I told her I loved her too, but I knew I didn't really, umm, I mean . . .

Boys seem to be looking for a blend of friendship and sex in relationships with their girlfriends. They are not looking for romance or ideal love. Empirical research finds that men's friendships (and I suspect this is also true of teen boys' friendships) are based on doing things together rather than on talking or sharing emotions (as women's friendships are).[13] Talking, or having a "close" friend, is what some boys get and are looking for in relationships with their girlfriends. However, even boys who admit to wanting friendship, comment on the burden of commitment. Joe told me that he "went out with this girl for like a year, and I liked her a lot. We talked and went a lot of places together." Notice how brief his description of his girlfriend and their relationship is compared to girls' descriptions of their boyfriends. Since Joe did not seem very enthusiastic about his previous girlfriend I asked him, "Would you want to have a girlfriend now?" He replied, "Yeah, someone to talk to a lot. Like a good friend. Well, you also get too serious and get tied down a lot." I received this answer from many boys. They emphasized wanting a girlfriend, to have a friend, but not wanting too much commitment.

Would you want to have a girlfriend?
Yeah, well, I don't really have any real close friends, I have a lot of friends, but not really close, there's no one like close friend. The disadvantages would be that it's a lot of commitment, I think. *(Rick)*

Would you want to have a girlfriend?
It'd be someone to be with and talk to, but I feel that I wouldn't like, like, to feel that I have to devote a certain amount of time every night calling them. *(Eric)*

Given the short length of most teen relationships, boys' fears of and complaints about commitment seem unwarranted (or perhaps their fears of commitments are what cause such short relationships). I suspect that complaining about commitment and the amount of time one has to spend with a girlfriend has become part of establishing a sense of adult heterosexual masculinity. Finally, boys rarely express the feelings of romantic love that girls do. In particular, their stories have little of the romance, sadness, or melodrama that girls' stories have. There is little in boys' stories that suggest they are playing out a romantic narrative. Also, boys' stories, especially when they become stories of breaking up, often contain hostile feelings. I asked Paul why he started "going out" with his girlfriend.

I think I liked her innocence. At first it was great. We could laugh and everything, but then we started to fight. I was like "forget it."
Why did you break up?
Well, put it this way. She has a wicked attitude, like and I was stupid. I ended it and she changed her attitude. Fine. I thought I'd give her a second chance this year, turned out she had the attitude again so I said goodbye.
What kind of attitude did she have?
Well, "I can't change" or "This is me, I'm sorry I can't be nicer." It's like, no! She still has the attitude. She has a mouth that I'd like to stick a bar of soap in for two hours. So I don't want to deal with that.

This story is very different from those we hear from girls, even girls who have broken up with their boyfriends. Finally, we will see below that sex, too, is less tied to love (as the old story goes) for boys than for girls.

Expectations and Experiences of Sex...

Teenaged girls and boys have very different expectations and experiences of sex. Girls' expectations of sex range from romantic images portrayed by the media to fears that it will hurt, be painful, or scary, with the majority (well over half) falling in the latter category. There are no class differences or differences based on whether or not the girl had sex. I asked Tiffany about her first experience of sex, "Was it what you expected it to be like?" "No. Not at all. I expected the movie type thing." Erin had not yet had sex and thought,

I think that when you love somebody a real lot, I think that it's gonna be great, and umm, just like everything that's going on like with AIDS and pregnancy. It's scary. So once you're like using birth control and you check for AIDS and things like that, other STDs, and you're not worried at all, then it's just like the only thing you're gonna be thinking about is that other person, and it's gonna be good, but if you're distracted by all those other things, I think it's gonna take away from it.

Kristen had similar reservations:

I'm pretty scared 'cause of all the stories I've heard. And with STDs now I mean it's really scary. You can't be sure who he's been with. I mean they may say "I've only been with one other girl before and I was only with her once" or whatever and you don't know that. Umm, also, like doing the right thing. 'Cause you hear so many stories but like if it really comes down to it would I perform right or whatever? They say the first time hurts a lot, I don't know.

Other girls' expectations were even more negative. Amy, like many girls, said, "I thought it was gonna hurt really, really bad...." And Jill thought sex was "gross" when she was younger.

I thought it was disgusting! Until eighth grade. And I was appalled, and I thought it was the grossest thing. Umm, hearing friends talk about it, I did have friends who had sexual intercourse in the middle school, and they would tell everyone about it or whatever and I thought it was like disgusting!

Boys, on the other hand, had generally positive expectations about sex. They thought it would be pleasurable, and many said they looked forward to it or were curious about it. However, because boys are culturally supposed to think sex is good, it may have been more difficult for them to express negative expectations, although not impossible. Middle-class boys were able to express some of their anxieties about sex. They claimed a few more anxieties and were slightly less positive about their expectations than working-class boys, who were more invested in maintaining normative masculinity. Middle-class boys described expectations like Greg, a middle-class 16-year-old, and Dennis.

I expect it to be good. I hope it's good. I know guys who have done it and just really regretted it afterwards. (Greg)

I look forward to it. It's an experience I haven't had and I wonder what it's like, and I'll also be real nervous about how she feels and what it would be like and if I'd do it right, just basically that. (Dennis)

Dennis' admission that he worried whether or not he would "do it right" may be the most prevalent worry that boys have about sex. Laumann et al. found that young men (age 18–24) were most likely to have "anxiety about performance."[14]

Working-class boys, like Adam, Scott, and Rick, however, said they had few expectations about sex at all or only positive ones. They claimed respectively, "I'll just wait for the time to come. I'm not gonna worry about it"; "I thought it would be great. I couldn't wait to do it"; and "I think it'll be all right. I don't think it'll be scary or anything."

These expectations are in sharp contrast to girls'. No girl said that she looked forward to sex or that she expected it to be pleasurable.[15] Girls also have sex later than boys do, although girls more or less catch up in their late teens. In my sample about half of the girls (seventeen) and boys (ten) had had sex. However, according to Hayes, at age 15 only 5 percent of girls and 17 percent of boys have had sexual intercourse.[16] The percentage of both groups of teens who are sexually active increases as teens get older. By age 18 44 percent of girls and 64 percent of boys have had sexual intercourse. By age 20 most unmarried men and women are sexually active; over 80 percent of men and 70 percent of women have had sex once. (African-American teens and teens from lower socioeconomic class backgrounds have sex earlier than whites and those from higher socioeconomic class backgrounds.) This gender difference in age may be attributed to girls' more negative expectations of sex, as well as harsher proscriptions against sex for girls than boys. However, with such widely disparate expectations of sex, how do boys and girls decide to have sex, and why do teenage girls ever have sex given their negative expectations?

Although there is much research on which demographic factors may make teens more likely to have sex, there is little on how those decisions come about. There is no research that asks why boys have sex more than girls do and why they do so earlier. Teens do not add up their demographic variables to see if they should have sex. They have sex in the context of their lives and relationships. As Brooks-Gunn and Furstenberg (1989) note, "almost no information exists as to how teens initiate sexual activity."[17] From *their* perspective, how do teens decide to have sex?[18]

The Interactional Paths to Sex...

A girl's ideal love for a male peer *at adolescence* often adds a new dimension to ideal love – sex. However, this is not because the quality of girls' ideal love has changed or become more sexual, more passionate, or more desirous, but because male peers often insist on, provoke, or encourage girls to have sex. Several working-class girls said that the pattern in their high school was that many girls often had sex in their freshmen year because older boys saw them as easy targets, taught them how to party, and convinced them to have sex. The different paths that girls and boys take to having sex are generally that girls are pressured into sex, and boys do the pressuring. Both boys and girls see this as the pattern. Fourteen-year-old Adam said, "Well, I think the boys put a lot of pressure on the girls to do it." Girls acknowledge that boys pressure girls by using love. "Boys put so much pressure on you. It's just like TV – 'But I love you,' and girls just giving it up, and they shouldn't." Tiffany, beginning in the language of ideal love, said,

> It's nice to lie there in their warm, comforting arms, and if you have feelings for them it's so hard to look in their eyes and say no. I could only do it if I was really angry. I mean if he was forcing me I could, he'd be in for a fight, but if it was just like "Oh please, come on baby" no way could I say no.

Not all boys, especially younger boys, seem to realize that they are pressuring girls. The boys I spoke with assumed that girls, usually anonymous, generic girls – their girlfriends were the exception – wanted to have sex as much as they did. Boys told me, "Girls want to have sex, too. It's pretty much the same as boys." Or "I think they [girls] think the same thing about sex and wonder about sex and wanting to do it." However, a few middle-class boys (three)

acknowledged that sex, at least at first, was not as good for girls as for boys. For example, Rick, who is 15 and has not had sex, said, "It seems like for girls it would not be nearly as much fun, 'cause the first time is sort of nothing."

Older boys clearly do know that they are pressuring girls for sex. Anthropologist Peggy Reeve Sanday describes fraternity boys' common practice of "working a yes out." She recorded the following conversation between fraternity brothers:

> "Sometimes a woman has to resist your advances to show how sincere she is. And so, sometimes you've gotta help them along. You know she means no the first time, but the third time she could say no all night and you know she doesn't mean it"
>
> "Yeah, no always mean no at the moment, but there might be other ways of..."
>
> "Working a yes out?"
>
> "Yeah!"
>
> "Get her out on the dance floor, give her some drinks, talk to her for a while."
>
> "Agree to something, sign the papers..."
>
> "And give her some more drinks!"
>
> "Ply her with alcohol."[19]

The older boys I spoke with were not this explicit in indicating that they knew girls were sometimes reluctant. However, although both boys and girls often said that they "talked it over" with their partner before deciding to have sex, "talking it over" meant something different for boys and girls. Their descriptions of these "talks" and the tones of voices in which they spoke about them were quite different. Boys described things like middle-class 15-year-old, Craig did: "She was a little reluctant, but we just talked it over and decided it would be okay." Or like Scott did when I asked him, "How did you decide [to have sex]?" "It was easy after we talked it over," he replied.

Girls, however, were more reticent and much less likely to say it was easy when describing these conversations. For example, I asked the girls who had had sex the same question I asked Scott. "How did you decide to have sex?" Their answers were quite different from Scott's and most boys'. For example, Elaine, Diana, Kendra, and Jodi replied in typical ways.

It just happened really. I mean, I didn't want to 'cause I couldn't ever picture myself having sex, but umm, all my friends did, and umm, so it just happened and he was my first so...I thought it was right 'cause we were going out for two years before we did. *(Elaine)*

How did you decide to have sex?
I don't know. We like went out for three and a half months, and that's when we did it. We just talked about it and stuff that it was gonna hurt. And it did hurt! *(Diana)*

How did you make that decision [to have sex]?
I don't know. Umm, it seemed kind of natural, I don't know. I just thought about it and it just kind of happened. *(Kendra)*

Have you had sex?
Once. [*Said in a tiny, almost inaudible voice*].
How did you decide to have sex?
Well, it just sort of happened. I don't know.
How would you decide to do it again in the future?
I don't know. It would probably just come up again. *(Jodi)*

Girls express their feelings of missing agency with their repeated phrase "it just happened."[20]

Cook, Boxer, and Herdt find that lesbian teens report sexual sequencing that is first heterosexual then homosexual, while gay male teens report the reverse. The girls in their study also say that heterosexual sex was something that *happened to them*, while it was something the gay boys sought out. The authors propose that "the greater likelihood of sexual pressure and coercion

experienced by females from males predisposes girls to the heterosexual/homosexual sequence, not as a choice but as a consequence of growing up in a society where females encounter such experiences more than males."[21] I suggest that many lesbian teenagers and straight teenage girls have heterosexual sex for the same reasons – coercion.

Because the girls' answers to how they decided to have sex were often tinged with feelings of regret, shame, and hesitation, I became suspicious that many girls did not really *want* to have sex, and so I began asking boys and girls "Why do you think it is hard for some girls to say no if they really don't want to have sex?" Girls often answered this third person question in the first person or second person, moving the experience closer to themselves. Girls' answers, particularly working-class girls, reveal that their boyfriends often pressure them into sex. Notice the first- and second-person answers and the language of fear throughout girls' answers.

Because they'll be *scared* like, that the guy will just say forget it, and he'll just probably go off to another girl and ask them the same question. And he'll just go to a person that says yes and stay with them, and then he'll probably just do it and then leave. *(Ellen)*

'Cause you're afraid that they're gonna leave you. *(Amanda)*

'Cause they're afraid the boy won't like them anymore or something would happen, you know, he'd get mad. *(Stephanie)*

'Cause the boys break up with you or something like that. Or they say, "You don't love me." *(Valerie)*

Oh, it is. It is really hard [to say no]. Because some guys say "If you love me you would do it." And I mean you don't want to say no 'cause you're afraid that they're gonna break up with you if you do and you don't really want to say yes but you do anyways. I just . . . they do 'cause . . . *(sigh)*. *(Jodi)*

'Cause you don't want them to get mad at you. You don't want them to like . . . 'Cause I did that once and he kind of got pissed 'cause he said that he'd be hurting and stuff like that. But I just didn't want to and like he wasn't . . . he wasn't mad at me, but he was mad at that fact that he was gonna hurt. But I know a lot of guys, like I'll be hanging out with my friends and they'll go in the other room and the guy will come out pissed off 'cause they won't. *(Danielle)*

[It's hard to say no] 'Cause they don't want the guy to think that she's a sissy, or she's, she's nothing, or she's not gonna be popular, or no one will think she's pretty anymore. Just for self-esteem reasons I think. *(Linda)*

Finally, Samantha said straightforwardly that it is hard for some girls to say no to boys "'Cause they're afraid of them."

Working-class girls openly discussed this pressure *and* the fact they often felt compelled to give in to it. A few even revealed such coercive pressure without being asked. For example, one girl told me she had sex with her boyfriend the first time when they were playing Truth or Dare with friends, and she "had to" do the dare. She was not physically forced to have sex, but goaded into it by her boyfriend (and presumably other friends who were present). The middle-class girls were more often able to say no to sex. For example, 17-year-old Heather told me confidently,

That decision has definitely come up in the past two relationships I've had, because those people have been a lot older and umm, especially with Joey who was the last guy I went out with, umm. He sort of forced me to make that decision really early on, we had gone out for two weeks and all of sudden he was ready to have sex

and that was a natural progression for him and he assumed that I'd you know . . . I think that . . . to be in love with somebody probably comes once or twice or maybe three times in your life time and I don't believe my friends when they say they are in love with their boyfriends who they went out with for two weeks, umm, but I also don't know that you have to be *in* love with somebody, you know, to have sex with them. I think that if there's a potential for you to be in love with them and a really deep caring and definitely commitment and just feeling really comfortable with the person. Feeling like you could say anything to them, it's a pretty important prerequisite for having sex with them and I didn't feel like that with him after two weeks or after two months.

Similarly when I asked Kelly, "Why is it hard for some girls to say no to sex when they don't want to have sex?" she replied, "No problem! I mean, I really don't have any problem with that at all."

"Why do you think that others girls might?" I asked.

"I don't know, I just decided a long time ago that if this doesn't work out you know, there are a trillion other ones out there. So, I mean, I know, I know that there are . . . that I will find someone someday who is perfect. And until then I don't have to deal with any of these others." Middle-class girls are better able than working-class girls to refuse sex that they do not want for several reasons. As we have seen, they remain in ideal love with their fathers longer than working-class girls do and so are less likely to feel ideal love for a male peer. This makes it easier for them to say they do not want sex. It is as if the vicarious subjectivity that they receive via their relationships with their fathers is working for them. Others also have mothers who provide them with a subjectivity that helps them to feel like they can say no to sex they do not want (but even middle-class girls rarely want to say yes). Few mothers or fathers were able to provide their daughters with desire, and no girl expressed a confident, excited wish to have sex in the ways that some boys did. Also, Heather and Kelly were not only middle-class, but they were also in their late rather than early or middle teens, and being older seems to correlate with having a greater ability to refuse sex when one does not want it.

However, middle-class girls are not immune to giving in to their boyfriends' pressure to have sex. They are more reluctant to admit doing so than working-class girls are. They tell stories of pressure to have sex that disguise the pressure and the fact they gave in to it. Kendra, an opinionated middle-class girl, who prided herself on her self-confidence and assertiveness, reflected on her decision to have sex.

> How did I decide to? Umm, it just seemed kind of natural, I don't know. I mean I thought about it. It just seemed like it was right. I was fifteen.... He wanted to have sex with me and I had said no, I mean I didn't feel pressure and that's not why I said I would, but looking back I think it kind of took our relationship a step further and if I hadn't I don't know what we would have done. It would have been kind of stagnated I guess.

"The relationship will stagnate" is another version of "He'll break up with you if you say no." It is a story that can deny that a middle-class girl is really under pressure from boys and giving in to it. Middle-class girls are more invested in this disguise than working-class girls because they know from sex education and their knowledge of feminism that being "talked into it" is not the "right" reason for having sex. Regardless of how they discuss it, both middle- and working-class girls describe a variety of ways in which they are pressured or coerced into sex by their boyfriends. Such pressure clearly does not foster sexual subjectivity.

How does this gender dynamic of boys pressuring girls for sex and girls "giving in" get set up? I suggest that much of it is a result of the differing capacities for agency and sexual subjectivity that girls and boys

have constructed up until this point. Chilman suggests that there is a lack of a developmental perspective on teenage sex.[22] This is the case; the research on puberty and teen sex are two separate literatures. However, adolescents often become sexually active before they are completely "done" with puberty, and puberty is laden with meanings about sexual bodies. Puberty, as we saw, makes girls anxious about sex and their bodies and unsure of themselves and their abilities to act in the world. Puberty puts restrictions on girls' sexuality and self-confidence. Boys, on the other hand, come out of puberty feeling more grown up, more independent, and feeling generally positive about their bodies that are becoming more adult-like, and importantly, more masculine. When teens with these different capacities start dating each other, they have unequal abilities to negotiate for what they want; they have different wants; and the relationship means different things to them. Boys are more sure that they want sex, and as we have seen, they have higher expectations of sex. Girls, who are deeply invested in ideal love, are vague about when they will want sex and if they are "ready," especially since being ready rarely has anything to do with desire.

> I told him I'm not right now, that I'm not ready for it. And umm, when I'm ready I don't know if I'll still be with him, but I hope that he like understands that maybe we're not gonna have it for a while or ever. *(Erin)*

> *How would you decide to have sex?*
> You should be ready. I just want that.
> *How would you define being ready?*
> I don't know that's hard. Umm, if this guy is like the right one and you're not gonna regret it afterwards. Be thoughtful and have a good idea. *(Sondra)*

These feelings of unsureness make sense given girls' low expectations of sex. This psychodynamic disparity in agency and sexual subjectivity, laid upon the cultural inequalities between the genders, gives boys a greater capacity to push for what they want, and leaves girls less able to articulate what they want for themselves *and* less able to claim it forcefully (or to articulate what they don't want and forcefully refuse it). I do not suggest girls are without any agency or without any sexual subjectivity. Rather, within the interactions with her boyfriend, within the "We talked it over," a girl finds it particularly hard to hold her own aganst a boy's assuredness and convincing reasons. This is especially true when a girl finds herself in ideal love with this boy. It is important not to underestimate the role and power of ideal love in adolescent girls' lives. As much as sex is not about passion and lust for teen girls, it *is* about ideal love and fear of losing one's ideal love, if one refuses sex. As we have seen above, many girls make this connection, saying "He'll break up with you if you say no."

There are exceptions to this pattern. Some boys do not want to have sex (yet), and certainly did not pressure girls to. In my sample they tend to be younger, Catholic boys, or boys who wanted to be in love first (which correlates with being younger). Jim, a working-class boy, told me a story about fears of guilt and pregnancy.

> I'd just say no to have sex. Being Catholic that's basically the only opinion I hear. But...I don't know. I wouldn't really feel comfortable buying a condom anyways, and I wouldn't have sex without a condom 'cause I'd feel guilty, and I'd help out with a kid, and so I just wouldn't have sex at all.

Similarly, Brent, a middle-class boy, also was not in a hurry to have sex, not because of fear or guilt but because he felt he was too young and "not ready." He was one of the only boys who used the term "ready."

> I'm definitely not ready to have sex yet ...I'm not in control of my social life or academic life, and I'm not ready to start dealing with myself in that way. I'll be ready once I find somebody I love. I'm

not gonna do it before that because, because my friends some of them have already done it and they feel real shitty about it if they did it with some random person just to try it or something.

Other teens in my sample also had decided to postpone sex. Some rationally thought about the decision, about their feelings, about themselves and their partners and decided not to have sex. These teens were few. More often the teens who decided not to have sex as teens (at least not up until the point at which I interviewed them) did so because of "morals," religion, and AIDS. For these teens the decision was usually more abstract than for those who decided to have sex, because they usually were teens who did not have "serious" girlfriends or boyfriends.

Several girls and boys also said that either because of their religion or "morals" they wanted to wait. One 17-year-old middle-class boy and one 16-year-old working-class girl who had each decided they did not want to have sex, said it was because they did not want to "get AIDS." Meghan said,

> I'm gonna wait. Like with AIDS it really scares you. I wouldn't, I wouldn't do that. I'm gonna wait 'til, I don't believe in having sex before...a lot of people do it, you know what I mean...but now with everything, AIDS...

It is my impression that AIDS education has given teens who do not want to have sex, but do not want to be seen as "wimps" or "goody-goodies," an acceptable reason to decide against sex. It is more acceptable in teen culture to say one fears AIDS than to say one fears God, religion, parents, or pregnancy.

Experiences of Sex...

As we would expect, given such different paths to sex, boys and girls have very different experiences of sex. The girls who did have sex found that it lived up to their negative expectations. They often described the experience as painful, scary, disappointing, or confusing.

> There was a couple of times that I thought I had decided and I was like "Okay, okay!" and then "No, I can't! I can't!" He was like "Okay, okay." And it was like the third time that I had said that. I'm like "Okay." I was real scared. I was afraid it would hurt. I cried and it did hurt. *(Valerie)*

> I was fourteen. I was really nervous. I can remember shaking, and it wasn't the most intimate thing. The kid I was with was a virgin also, so we had no idea, or guidance or knowledge whatsoever about what we were doing. And we were downstairs on this couch and I was really shaking. My skirt was just pulled up and his pants down at his ankles. We just wung it. We were like "All right what the hell do we do?" It was like I can remember really brief. Not really intimate 'cause we were both scared out of our minds. I was shaking and I was just not feeling very sexual at that moment. It wasn't that great. I remember we just sat there side by side with our hands folded afterwards. That happened so what's next? It was mostly just silence for the rest of the night. *(Jill)*

> Actually I was kind of happy, well, I don't know how to explain it. In a way I felt really good because I had shared this with somebody, but it was the most painful experience of my life. *(Tiffany)*

> *Have you had sex with him?*
> Yeah. He was my first, and it hurt! Very much so. We went out for like three and a half months and that's when we did it.
> *How did you decide to have sex?*
> We just talked about it and stuff, that it was gonna hurt and stuff. 'Cause he was like my first in almost absolutely everything. And it did hurt! *(Danielle)*

As Thompson notes, it is ironic that "While girls hold their lovers responsible for virtually all the emotional pain they experience in relationships, they rarely blame them for sexual pain during first coitus. Instead they blame their own bodies."[23] Girls' experiences were not painful and scary because of some biological or natural necessity that first sex be bad for girls, but because girls often have sex when they do not physically or emotionally desire it, when they have little experiential knowledge about what sex will be like, how they will feel and how their bodies will feel. Girls' later and less frequent masturbation than boys contributes to their lack of subjective sexual body knowledge. Women who masturbate have better sex with their partners.[24] Finally, many girls move from kissing to intercourse in an extremely short period of time. Petting or "all the stuff that comes before" is often not a significant part of girls' sexual experiences. Jill said she was a tomboy and thought kissing was "gross" when she 13 but she had sex when she was 14. This leaves little time to learn about sexual pleasure. As Erin told me,

> I think it's basically that guys think that...like that sex, is like the way to get...is like what you should do, you should have sex even if you haven't done everything else, even if you're not like totally comfortable, I think that they think that it's just like something they have to do. And you know, girls just like want to take their time and take it slowly and go for everything, like that leads up to sex and things like that.

Tolman finds that two thirds of her sample of thirty girls said that they "experienced sexual desire."[25] However, Tolman did not interview boys, and it is unclear if the extent of these girls' desires would be equal to that of boys similarly sampled. Would what "counts" as desire be more narrowly defined if researchers listened to boys as well? Also, we must distinguish between sexual desire and sexual pleasure. Although teen girls may desire, few find sexual pleasure. Thompson found that only one fourth of her sample of 400 girls were "pleasure narrators." "The pleasure narrators describe taking sexual initiative; satisfying their own sexual curiosity; instigating petting and coital relations."[26] Lesbian teens were more likely to be pleasure narrators (when discussing sex with girls) than heterosexual teens were in her sample. However, even they are rare as most lesbians do not come out until their late teens or early twenties.[27]

I did not find as many pleasure narrators as Thompson did, perhaps because my sample of girls was not as broad. Kristen who had waited a "long time" (until she was 16) before having sex said that she was "just a bundle of joy" afterward because she was "so excited to call [her best friend] and just so psyched." A few girls, especially those who were older and middle class, said that sex was "better" or a "little better" after the first few times. Fullilove et al. also find that sex gets better for girls as they get older. The authors found that among poor black women, age was related to having more power in sexual communication, in being clear about what one wants, and in getting it.[28] In my study, Jill, an 18-year-old working-class girl, described her current sex life as pleasurable, although her sex at ages 14 and 15 was not. However, she focused her discussion on the relationship rather than on desire or physical pleasure.

> It's gotten a lot better! It's good. Ummm, I don't really know how to say this. Sex is like a bonus, you know. It's another way of bringing us closer, but it's not in any way the center point or the main point of the relationship. We just consider it something extra special in the relationship.

Cherri, a middle-class 19-year-old, now had orgasms (she was one of only three girls who said she did), and she too attributed it to the fact of "love." Cherri said, "As soon as I began to relax and trust, it happened. We have a really open communication kind of relationship, and that makes all the difference. We're really close." Finally,

Audrey, a middle-class 16-year-old, said that she was more physical than her boyfriend.

> I had a serious boyfriend. We went out for like four months. He was sweet and funny, and he thought I was pretty. But, I couldn't get him to talk to me. He was very quiet and closed off. He was also very clingy emotionally. It was sort of the opposite of the usual stereotype. He was more emotionally dependent and I was more physical.
> *What do you mean you were more physical?*
> I wanted to be touching and doing physical stuff more than he did and I wanted to go further sometimes.

Even these girls did not wholeheartedly embrace sexual experience and expressed a lot of ambivalence. For example, Audrey used an interesting strategy to resist having sex with her boyfriend. She decided that she and her boyfriend were going to have sex, and so wanting to be "responsible" she went to the doctor to get birth control pills. However, somewhere between starting the pills and sleeping with her boyfriend, she "cheated" on him. Cheating here means that she went out with another boy and kissed (and maybe petted), not that she had sex with him. Audrey then thought that since she had "cheated" on her boyfriend she must not be "ready" to have sex yet, and so decided not to. Kristen admitted to using the same strategy at one time as well. While strategies like "cheating" allow girls to assert control over their sexuality in an exciting way, they also express the ambivalence teenage girls, even girls who have "decided" to have sex, feel about sex.

Boys did not rave about their actual experiences of sex, but gave mild answers that claimed it was as they expected. They were much less negative and less ambivalent about their experiences than girls were, and they seemed less self-reflective. Scott said, "It was good. I was psyched to have done it." Craig only said, "I couldn't believe I saw a completely naked female body." Michael said with less confidence, "I felt okay. I kind of hoped I did okay. I didn't really know, you know, if she thought it was [okay]." These answers were typical of boys in general and boys of their class. Middle-class boys descriptions were slightly less confident and less positive.

Moffatt found in his research on sex among undergraduates that college men discussed sexual pleasure very little in their narrative descriptions of sex because "The male subtext on sexual pleasure was, in all probability, 'Of *course*, I enjoy sex. I'm a normal guy. It goes without saying!'"[29] This, I suspect, is why boys in my sample said little about pleasure specifically, but also did not tell stories of pain or disappointment as girls did. Discussion of boys' pleasure from sex arose only in the context of discussions about condoms. Both boys and girls claimed that often boys did not want to use condoms because as one middle-class boy claimed, "You can't feel anything." In discussing with Amy whether students would use condoms if they were made available in school, she said sympathizing with the boys, "I don't know if they would [use condoms]. 'Cause a lot of guys, I know don't like them. 'Cause they don't get enough satisfaction off them." While boys and some girls expressed concern about boys' lack of or lessened pleasure, there was little concern about girls' lack of pleasure. It was expected that girls would not like sex as much as boys, especially first sex.

Sex and Sexual Subjectivity...

What are the effects of first and early sexuality on teenage girls' and boys' selves? The sexual experiences that most boys have cause them to feel more subjective, agentic, and more like sexual subjects. The experience of girls "giving in" to boys solidifies boys' feelings of agency and sexual subjectivity. A boy now feels like he can will things

and make them happen. He can do, and do sexually.

Boys feel grown up and more masculine as a result of having sex. Sex has often been seen as the test of masculinity for men, as a "mainstay of identity."[30] Heterosexual sex also facilitates bonds between men. Teenage boys know that having sex makes them more masculine. In April of 1993 the media focused attention on a group of boys in suburban southern California who called themselves the "Spur Posse." (They were fans of the San Antonio Spurs.) These boys were in competition with each other to see who could have sex with the most girls. Each time they achieved orgasm with a different girl was a "point." These boys went on several television talk shows defending their competition and bragging about how many points they had. A 19-year-old was the highest scorer, with 66 points. Eight of these boys were arrested on various felony rape and sexual assault charges, but all were released except one boy who had allegedly had sex with a 10-year-old girl. Parents (especially fathers) met these stories with a "boys will be boys attitude." One father said, "Nothing my boy did was anything any red-blooded American boy wouldn't do at his age." One son said, "My dad used to brag to his friends. All the dads did. When we brought home girls they liked, they'd say cool, and tell their buddies....It's all the moms that are freaking out about this stuff. But that's probably that Freudian thing. You know, penis envy." However, one boy's mother said, "What can you do? It's a testosterone thing."[31] I use this extreme example to suggest that for teenage boys having sex brings status, and, in particular, masculine status, even in this distorted form.

The boys I interviewed did not describe anything like the "Spur Posse," perhaps because this story is extreme, or perhaps because boys tell different stories about sex to each other, to men, than they do to women. However, their discussions, especially working-class boys', did indicate that sex made them feel grown-up, masculine, and bonded with other men, and they did indicate that bragging and boasting about sex was part of teenage boy culture.

Many boys described what happens after sex to be talking about it or in some way conveying it to other boys. When I asked Scott if he told anyone after he had sex he said, "You don't really have to come out and tell your friends, they just sort of know. You kinda just give the impression." Similarly, Jack and Alex said after sex boys tell others they "did it," and Jack, in particular, says boys in fact "do it" to gain status from their friends.

> Boys do it so they can go tell their friends, "Yeah, Yeah!" You know. Although if it's your girlfriend you don't go tell your friends about it, but if it's like Sally off the Street then, yeah, you do. *(Jack)*

> 'Cause there are two things that guys talk about when they get together. Girls, sex, and sports. Those are the only things they have in common. Girls and sex are one. *(Alex)*

Some boys even "discussed" it with their fathers, thus making them truly feel grown up. Their fathers confirm the importance of sex and women to masculinity.

> Everybody talks about it. It's like . . . "Yeah, I did her, I did this!" Or let's see "I screwed her." We generally do talk about it a lot. It's our nature. My father says when you stop looking [at women] then it's time for the grave. *(Paul)*

Researchers have examined how parental attitudes and parent–child interactions affect teenagers' likelihood of having sex,[32] and interesting here is the finding that mothers' discussions of sex with sons and daughters lead to later intercourse but fathers' discussions with sons lead to earlier intercourse.[33]

For many boys, having sex may also relieve fears that they are not masculine enough, that they are a "faggot," a "wimp," a "sissy," a "baby," a "girl." No boy said this to me explicitly about himself, but many said sex was important for the masculinity of other boys. For example, Dennis, a middle-class 15-year-old, said, "I think for a lot of guys it looks macho and stuff to have, to be having sex." And recall Jack's comment which he made with swinging fists, that boys do it so they can tell their friends "Yeah! Yeah!" Having sex may be proof to oneself and others of masculinity. It is an accomplishment. Girls, like Jill, also described sex as an accomplishment for boys.

> If you're sitting around a table with guys, which happens, they're waiting around for some guy and he's late and his excuse is that he was getting "laid" or having sex, or whatever, it's okay. You know. If you're scoring with a girl or however they want to term it, they just look at it as an achievement or an accomplishment. That's not all of them, but you know, that's part of it. But for girls, most of us are "Oh, I'm in love, and stuff like that." Love and commitment are important for girls and for boys they look at it as an accomplishment.

Similarly, Jack told me that if he were to talk to his younger brother about sex he would tell him to use condoms and that the girl would "never stop calling him," but he would also "cheer him on a little." Thus, first and early experiences of sex lead boys to develop bonds with other men, masculinity, more agency and sexual subjectivity, and recognition for all these things from others.

By contrast, first and early experiences of sex generally lessen girls' feelings of subjectivity, agency, and sexual subjectivity. To restate: girls' first experiences of sex are usually negative. They say things like, "It was the most painful experience of my life." After sex girls often feel confused and unsure of themselves, their "decisions," their bodies, and sex. Many girls describe this confusion, which may take several forms, from fear of pregnancy, betrayal of friends and family, uncertainty about one's body. Kendra felt badly about herself for not having used contraception, and she was afraid she might be pregnant.

Did you use contraception the first time? (Breathes in deeply.) No. Which is really bad, and I knew it, and I was just like praying 'cause I, I mean I had sex ed. since I was in like third grade, and I knew that...it's not like I thought "Oh, your first time you can't get pregnant." But I was just like...and I thought I was pregnant, but then I got my period, but that was very stressful. I was like ready to go buy one of those pregnancy tests. Or I was like, Sherri, one of my good friends, she was like, "Okay, we're going to the pharmacy," and I was like "No, I don't want to go." But I wasn't [pregnant].[34]

Tiffany was in the midst of her confusion about sex when we talked. She felt betrayed by her body, her family, and her friends. Her tone as she talked at length about her experience of sex moved between solemn and frustrated.

We'd been going out a long time. And, we just felt that it was the right thing to do. We were gonna be responsible, definitely. And it was really a hard decision to make, because his parents are really Catholic, but they're not really much as Catholics – but like his mother, any girl that has a boyfriend, and she sleeps with him in her mind is a slut. And that's the way he's been brought up. He doesn't really agree with it. That made it really hard 'cause she was calling me a slut because I used a tampon. She found it in the garbage can and that made me so mad. I couldn't believe it. And that's so untrue and I don't know where she got that because you can still be a virgin and be using a tampon, and at that time I was. If she ever found out [that we were having sex now], I don't know what would really happen. We just made a decision because we felt that we love each other...I know I made the right decision. [But] it's really a hard test when you've got people saying well did you?

Especially my mother, she goes and takes me to Planned Parenthood and then she says "I feel like shit for taking you there." She can't deal with the fact that I'm on the pill. I mean she knows this guy and she thinks he's really nice and all, and it's just that she can't cope with it. It's not the way she was brought up. I can understand that, but it's also hard when you've got his side of the family and getting that view. I think the worst part was when I didn't get my period on time, that was a major scare for me. That really hurt. [Unlike many girls this girl used foam and condoms when she first had sex.] I don't know what's worse, knowing that you could be pregnant or knowing that you could have an infection. Because it makes you think, did I make the right decision having sex? There are so many problems that come with it. You know my parents didn't know when I first started having sex and then they found out and at first they were really nice about it because we all thought that I was pregnant at that time, and they were like "No one should have to go through this." And after that it was just like, it was weird, it was kind of like this permission, and everything makes you second guess yourself. And now, I just had a period, a really long, horrible period, now I've got this other one that's just not going away, and now I think I've got some type of infection. Nobody knows, except a couple friends, and my parents don't know and it kind of makes everything so much more complicated. I wake up tired. It makes me feel in a way like a slut. I know that I shared something with somebody that I loved, but now, I feel so disgusting. I think that's what kids need to be told – it's not just STDs and everything, but all these things that go along with it, the mental stress, my mom told me, and I didn't really believe her. I wouldn't not do it again. I would do it again. I don't feel bad about that, but I never knew. It just makes it so horrible, it takes away from the actual act of sex. I don't think it's sex that's so bad, it's everything else that's horrible. If anything that would stop me from doing it again because the mental worry is so hard and you know, before I had sex I was thinking this is the last time this person is gonna see me as a virgin. I was like, what I was doing in my mind was horrible. It was hard 'cause my parents aren't liberal people, and I wish that most kids would't have to go through that, and we wouldn't have to go sneaking around to some motel, we wouldn't have to lie about what you did that day. You wouldn't have to feel bad. All I want is for them to respect me. If I'm gonna feel good about myself I can't do it all on my own, and that's what I'm having trouble with right now.

Much of Tiffany's story reveals another longstanding complexity of sex for girls. If one has sex, does she become a "slut" or a "'ho'"? The double standard in sex is still firmly rooted in teenage culture. In fact, Ward and Taylor write of their research,

> Across six ethnic groups one observation was strikingly similar; all respondents introduced the universal theme of a double standard toward sexual behavior that is limiting and oppressive to females. In all groups, boys were generally allowed more freedom and were assumed to be more sexually active than girls.[35]

Girls, as well as boys in my sample, subscribe to this double standard, although many middle-class girls did note that it exists and is unfair. Erin critically told me,

> It's very different for boys, it's like "a good job" if they have sex with somebody and then they're rewarded and stuff and all the guys are just like "That's great!" You have sex, and you're a girl and it's like "Slut!" That's how it is and you know guys can like sleep around and stuff, even if it's dangerous, but girls – you do that and it's just like, it's not accepted. I think that's really warped since it takes two people to have sex. It's very different.

In general, however, girls and boys distinguish between "Sally off the Street" and a "girlfriend" or between "the real cross-your-legs type girls and your so-called sluts," and

there are no such distinctions made for boys. Although some girls are trying to create one by now referring to boys who treat girls badly and are only out for sex as "himbos," an alternative to bimbos. Many girls, like Tiffany, take the distinction of slut to heart and fear it. This is why ideal love is so important. If one has sex for love, she is not a slut, at least among these girls.

The meaning of slut, however, is highly variable and has changed somewhat in recent decades. Among the girls in my sample, simply having premarital sex was not enough to get labeled a slut, unless one was "too young" even in the eyes of peers to be having sex (consensus seemed to be that 12 or 13, pre-high school, was too young). Having multiple partners more often constitutes what one girl called "slut behavior." Similarly, Fullilove et al. (1990) in focus group discussions about sexuality with poor black women and teenage girls found that the definition of a "bad girl" was based on "sexual aggression; 'looseness,' that is giving sex in a casual manner without regard for who the partner was or requiring anything of the relationship; and 'tossing,' that is, giving sex in exchange for money or drugs."[36] Similarly, the girls whom I interviewed made distinctions between "regular" or "normal" girls and "girls who want it all the time," girls who "have it [sex] just to have it," and girls who "just do it to get in with the crowd, to be popular." Sociologist Ruth Horowitz in her study of urban Chicano youth found that girls who had sex before marriage were seen as "loose women," if they could not regain esteem by establishing themselves as mothers.[37] Regardless of its particular contextual meaning, the word slut holds a lot of power. Being called a slut or a ho – or feeling like one – is to feel degraded and dirty. Thus, this double standard adds to feelings of confusion after sex.

The feelings of confusion and uncertainty about sex span a wide range of time. Kendra and Tiffany describe these feelings in the weeks following sex. Elaine, on the other hand, felt confused and scared *immediately* after sex. I wondered if she had been more coerced than other girls or simply more willing to describe her feelings immediately following sex.

> I was kind of just like confused. I didn't know what to do. You know, I'd never had had it so, I just, I was...I went to the bathroom. I didn't know what to do, I didn't know, you know, I was really scared. I didn't know what, I didn't know what was supposed to happen or anything like that so.... Now that he left I wish that we never did.

Later when I asked Elaine what advice she would give to a younger girl who was trying to decide whether or not to have sex she replied adamantly, "Don't have it! I'd just tell them to wait until they're ready, you know. Don't rush into anything 'cause once you do, it's like, it's gone, you don't have anything." This feeling that one has nothing left after sex, is one that several girls expressed. They seemed to have felt they had lost some part of their selves. This expression also suggests how much girls see sex as boys taking something from them and not as a give-and-take or a two-way interaction that should be enjoyable for both people.

Thus, as Kendra's, Tiffany's and Elanie's stories demonstrate, after sex, a girl often does not know if sex is something she willed and made happen, if it was something she wanted or not. She feels unsure about her role in its occurrence. Gavey finds that some adult women have sex under similar conditions because it is easier than continuing to say no or because they sometimes fear being raped.[38] Teen girls certainly do not call what happened to them rape. In fact they often have a hard time defining the pressure they felt. As seen above, they were more willing to talk about it in the third person than in the first person. For a girl, acknowledging the coercive context in which she had sex admits to her lack of agency and makes her feel bad, whereas

claiming to have wanted sex denies her actual experience of coming to have sex and of the sex itself. On the other hand, saying she wanted to have sex might leave her labeled a slut. Thus, girls often reduced the story to "It just happened."

Narrative Work...

In order to manage such bad and conflicting feelings, girls tell stories, or do what I came to call narrative work, in order to try to make sense of their experiences of sex. Teenage girls use narrative work as a strategy for feeling better about confusing and disappointing sexual experiences. Part of what makes first sexual experiences so difficult is that girls must negotiate between several levels of scripts. Narrative work is shaped by cultural scripts or scenarios, interpersonal scripts, and intrapsychic scripts.[39] These scripts provide girls with stories of what sex is supposed to be like. On one hand, most cultural scripts claim that sex is good, magical, romantic. On the other hand, interpersonally, and collectively, teenage girls construct a multitude of scripts for first sex. These scripts claim that first sex hurts, that one should have sex if she is in love and should not if she is not, that sex is a way to keep a boyfriend. Narrative work also takes into account the teenage girls' own wishes and fantasies about sex. Finally, when in engaging in narrative work a teenage girl tells a story about what happened that takes into account all of these scripts *and* the experience of the event – sex. Because these scripts and the experience are so often in conflict with each other, it is a difficult task to negotiate between these. Narrative work is an attempt to reconcile these contradictory feelings and scripts about "deciding" to have sex. It is a method of balancing what happened, how things are "supposed" to happen (according to cultural and interpersonal scripts), and how one wants them to be. Narrative work also manages experience as well as emotion.[40]

The finding that teen girls do narrative work is significant in light of recent theorizing and research by Brown and Gilligan.[41] Brown and Gilligan argue that at adolescence girls' "real" or "authentic" knowledge about the world and about gender inequalities goes "underground." They claim that girls silence the truth of their experiences and forget what they know, in favor of a normative discourse. Girls are subjected to a "tyranny of nice and kind," according to Brown and Gilligan. This means that they tell positive, unconflictual stories about their experiences, painting themselves and others as "nice and kind."

My data suggests, instead, that while girls sometimes cast positive light on a bad experience, they generally have little problem recalling the negative "truth" of the experience. They are not silenced. They are able to hold in tension both the negative "truth" of the experience and a more positive version of the experience that allows them some agency and to tell a less conflict-ridden story. Brown and Gilligan also hear these conflicted stories,[42] but they see girls as always losing the battle for authenticity. This is because Brown and Gilligan are themselves deciding which narrative, of the many the girls are telling, is true. They do not tell the reader how they make these decisions, but they seem to think they know what the "real" feelings and "real" selves and "real" experiences of these girls are. I do not think we can make such distinctions.

In general, girls have to do much narrative work in order to feel okay about their sexual experiences. Working-class girls' experiences elicit more narrative work than middle-class girls'. Because middle-class girls have more subjective knowledge, more information about sex, and because they tend to be slightly older when they first have sex, their experiences of sex are not as negative as working-class girls' are and thus do not elicit narrative work as frequently.

In general, I suspect that audiences for these managed stories about sex were girls'

friends as well as themselves. As Thompson writes,

> Most teenage girls value friends a great deal. They are the essential audience for the talk about family, sex, and romance – the "you" in girls' most frequent phrase "you know," and the only therapists or counselors most girls have, their main line to comfort, advice, encouragement, and relief.[43]

Girls also used narrative work to convince themselves and me in the course of our interviews that they had not been coerced into sex, as this girl did.[44]

> We were going out for a while, and we just, we were downstairs, and I don't know. ...It's kinda like, he's kinda like, not a sexual person, but you know...all guys how they are. We just...I wasn't forced into it or anything. I wanted to, it was just I was worried...I don't mind. But like my mother was upstairs, and I was like "no, not here! My mother'll come down." You know, so it was kinda planned, not really but it was....It wasn't really what I expected, but it wasn't bad. It was like "that's what I've waited for?"

"I was worried," and "I don't mind," instead of "I wanted to," reveal that this girl was unsure about having sex. "All guys you know how they are," and "I was like 'No, not here!...'" suggest that she was pressured to have sex by her boyfriend. She also felt unsure about her experience – "It wasn't really what I expected" – and disappointed – "That's what I've waited for?" Yet not wanting to feel completely without agency or sexual subjectivity, she cannot bring herself to say outright that she was unsure and pressured to have sex. Instead she says, wanting me to understand, "You know, so it was kinda planned, not really but it was...."

Danielle struggled with similar confusing sexual experiences, and tells a similar contradictory story.

I regretted it kind of, kind of. We tried like five times and we couldn't 'cause it killed so bad. It was like Aaahhh! I love him, I'm glad I did it, but . . . No. I felt bad because I felt like I was a slut for some reason. I just felt real bad about it. But, well, it changed our relationship. It kind of broke the ice, but we had kind of already broke through it, you know. It just made us a lot closer. I don't know. I could tell it was different the day after, when we were together and stuff.

She vacillates between regret and gladness about having sex, between feeling like a slut and feeling like sex made them closer. The one thing she is clear about is that sex hurt. She weaves these feelings into a narrative that helps her to maintain some feelings of agency and sexual subjectivity. This narrative claims her experience of regret and pain, but also claims that she affected change by having sex (she made her relationship "closer") and that she made the right sexual decision (she was glad to have had sex because she loved him). These last two claims concur with both cultural and interpersonal scenarios.

Other girls, like Jodi and Valerie, managed their feelings the same way as the girl above vacillating between describing the negative and digging up something positive about their sexual experiences.

I was sore . . . I felt different. I can't explain the feeling, but I sort of felt different inside, you know. . . . Like, I didn't know if I wanted to go out with him anymore . . . I just felt weird.
Do you think that it changed anything in your relationship?
I think it brought us closer together. *(Jodi)*

It wasn't as bad as I thought it would be. I didn't really feel comfortable with it, but then, I got to feel a little better about it. It made us closer. *(Ellen)*

Finally, here is Kristen's story who said earlier in the interview that she would only have sex if she was "ready," "totally, totally, totally in love," and 16 years old. Her sister had told her if she adhered to these "morals" then she would have a good first sexual experience, and she would not get used. Here is what she said about first intercourse.

We started dating since I was in fifth grade, and we dated every single year and, umm, he always said "We're gonna have sex our freshmen year," but I didn't. This year when we started going out, we just . . . we've always had something going and umm, I like, if I was going out with someone else I'd always cheat on him with Jim (laughs). This year when we started going out, we went out for a while, and we like totally, totally, totally, we were like, we were in love, and we loved each other. And it was, like, I mean, I've gone out with so many guys, but like, you know, you just know. And umm, we went to a hotel room, and he asked me real sweetly [she says in a sweet voice and makes eyes] and you know then we had sex and it was awesome, like you just have to be totally ready. Like my friends said, "It's horrible, you're gonna cry, it's gonna kill you, you're not gonna enjoy yourself." I think it's just 'cause I waited so long and I was so ready, because it didn't hurt, well yeah, it did, but umm, it hurt but it wasn't horrible, I didn't cry. It was awesome.

"We went to a hotel room and he asked me real sweetly" provides evidence that she is having great sex because, as she said earlier in the interview, she and her peers believed that "you shouldn't go out with guys that don't treat you right." Then she shows that she was right to follow her "morals" adding, "You know, then, we had sex and it was awesome, like you just have to be totally ready." However, she describes the physical experience, "because it didn't hurt, well yeah, it did . . ." "It hurt, but it wasn't horrible, I didn't cry," holds together the whole story. It hurt but she did not cry like her friends did, therefore her experience was different from the experiences of her friends who did not wait and who had bad experiences. Her experience "was awesome." Kristen's definition of "awesome" sex is sex that does not hurt enough to make you cry. This story manages her many feelings and lets her balance the pain of sex, peer discourses, and the conviction that she had made the right decision by having sex when she was "ready," "in love" and 16 years old. It helps her to build many ambivalent feelings into a story that claims she has some sexual subjectivity, when she was not feeling entirely sexually subjective. Thus, narrative work is a strategy girls use to help maintain some sense of sexual subjectivity and agency in themselves after sex has left them feeling unsure of their ability to act with respect to their bodily, sexual selves.

In sum, first and early experiences of sex have different psychological outcomes (as well as material outcomes) for teenage boys and girls. Sexual experience for boys often results in them feeling grown up, masculine, bonded with other men, agentic, and sexually subjective. It is much more difficult for teenage girls to achieve such a positive outcome. Their first and early experiences of sex usually result in feeling confused, unsure of themselves and their bodies, and unclear about whether or not they did or can act agentically. Early experiences of sex, like puberty, make girls feel less sexually subjective and boys more.

NOTES

1 Chilman (1983) suggests that we need "somewhat open-ended, in-depth clinical studies that use both intensive interviews and appropriate tests that seek to understand more about the adolescent as a whole human being *who feels as well as thinks, values, and behaves*" (italics mine, p. 28). She goes on to say that with few exceptions "almost none of the research takes a developmental view of adolescent sexuality in the context of the feelings of teenagers about themselves, their families, and their society" (p. 30).
2 Brooks-Gunn and Furstenberg (1989), Furstenberg et al. (1987), Hayes (1987), Hofferth and Hayes (1987), Zelnick and Kantner (1980).
3 Padilla and Baird (1991), Wright et al. (1990).

4 Brooks-Gunn and Furstenberg (1989: 249).
5 These terms are probably specific to some subcultures of teenagers. The working-class teenagers used them more then the middle-class teenagers. Ruth Horowitz (1983) finds that urban Chicano youth in the midwest use these terms as well. Thorne's (1993) study (in Michigan and California) finds that children in early adolescence use the term "goin' with."
6 Thorne and Luria (1986).
7 Ward and Taylor (1994) also find white boys complain about their heterosexual relationships and give them very different meanings than girls do.
8 Benjamin (1988, 1986).
9 Raymond (1994), Cook, Boxer, and Herdt (1989).
10 Martin (1988).
11 Hochschild (1994).
12 Thompson (1994: 245).
13 Rubin (1985).
14 Laumann et al. (1994: 371).
15 Laumann et al. (1994) found that "only about 3 percent of women said that physical pleasure was their main reason for having first intercourse, compared to four times as many men who said this (12 percent)" (p. 329).
16 See Hayes (1987). However, I find these numbers for girls a bit low when comparing them to my sample in which, of girls who were an average age of about 16, half had sex. Many said they had sex at 14, 15, and 16 years old.
17 Brooks-Gunn and Furstenberg (1989: 256).
18 Thompson (1994, 1990) has investigated this question, but she has only interviewed girls, and so her claims about gender differences in this decision making are weak.
19 Sanday (1990: 113).
20 Laumann et al. (1994) found that about one-fourth of all women reported that they did not want to have sex the first time (p. 328).
21 Cook, Boxer, and Herdt (1989: 26).
22 Chilman (1983).
23 Thompson (1990: 345).
24 Hite (1976), Thompson (1990).
25 Tolman (1994).
26 Thompson (1990: 351).
27 Boys establish a sexual identity earlier, an average age of 15 (Anderson, 1990; Cook, Boxer, and Herdt 1989).

28 Fullilove et al. (1990).
29 Moffatt (1989, italics in original, p. 199).
30 Person (1980).
31 All quotes are from *Time* (April 5, 1993, p. 41).
32 See brief review by Treboux and Busch-Rossnagel (1991).
33 Fisher (1989).
34 There is much research on teen contraceptive use. Some general findings are: the older an adolescent is the more likely she/he is to use contraception and to use it correctly (Zelnick, Kantner, and Ford 1981). Low income, low educational aspirations, troubled relationships with parents, no sex education (although this is debated) are all thought to lead teens to have sex at an earlier age and to make them less likely to use contraception (Brooks-Gunn and Furstenberg 1989; Brooks-Gunn 1992). Girls know more about specific contraceptives than boys do, and girls' contraceptive knowledge has been studied more frequently (Brooks-Gunn and Furstenberg 1989).
35 Ward and Taylor (1994: 63).
36 Fullilove et al. (1990: 52–3).
37 See Horowitz (1983).
38 Gavey (1993).
39 Simon and Gagnon (1986).
40 See Hochschild (1983) for a theory of emotion management.
41 Brown and Gilligan (1992).
42 See pp. 120–1, for example, in Brown and Gilligan.
43 Thompson (1994: 228).
44 From preliminary interviews.

REFERENCES

Anderson, Dennis. (1990). Homosexuality in adolescence. *Atypical Adolescence and Sexuality*, Max Sugar, ed. New York: W. W. Norton.

Benjamin, Jessica. (1986). A desire of one's own: psychoanalytic feminism and intersubjective space. In *Feminist Studies/Critical Studies*, edited by Teresa de Lauretis. Bloomington: Indiana University Press.

——(1988). *The Bonds of Love*. New York: Pantheon Books.

Brooks-Gunn, Jeanne. (1992). The impact of puberty and sexual activity upon the health and education of adolescent girls and boys. In *Sex Equity and Sexuality in Education*, edited by Susan Shurberg Klein. Albany: State University of New York Press.

Brooks-Gunn, Jeanne and Frank F. Furstenberg. (1989). Adolescent sexual behavior. Special issue: children and their development: knowledge base, research agenda, and social policy application. *American Psychologist* 44: 249–57.

Brown, Lyn Mikel and Carol Gilligan. (1992). *Meeting at the Crossroads: Women's Psychology and Girls' Development*. Cambridge, MA: Harvard University Press.

Chilman, Catherine S. (1983). *Adolescent Sexuality in a Changing American Society*. Bethesda, MD: US Department of Health, Education, and Welfare.

Cook, Judith, Andrew Boxer, and Gilbert Herdt. (1989). First homosexual experiences reported by gay and lesbian youth in an urban community. Presented at the Annual Meetings of the American Sociology Association.

Fisher, Terri. (1989). An extension of the findings of Moore, Petersen, and Furstenberg (1986) regarding family sexual communication and adolescent sexual behavior. *Journal of Marriage and the Family* 51: 637–9.

Fullilove, Mindy Thompson, Robert E. Fullilove, Katherine Haynes, and Shirley Gross. (1990). Black women and aids prevention: a view toward understanding gender rules. *The Journal of Sex Research* 27: 1, 47–64.

Furstenberg, Frank F., S. Morgan, K. Moore, and J. Peterson. (1987). Race differences in the timing of adolescent intercourse. *American Sociological Review* 52: 511–18.

Gavey, Nicola. (1993). Technologies and effects of heterosexual coercion. In *Heterosexuality: A Feminism and Psychology Reader* edited by Sue Wilkinson and Celia Kitzinger. London: Sage Publications.

Hayes, C. D. (1987). *Risking the Future: Adolescent Sexuality, Pregnancy, and Childbearing, Volume II*. Washington, DC: National Academy of Science Press.

Hite, Shere. (1976). *The Hite Report: A Nationwide Study of Female Sexuality*. New York: Macmillan.

Hochschild, Arlie. (1983). *The Managed Heart*. Berkeley: University of California Press.

——(1994). The commercial spirit of intimate life and the abduction of feminism: signs from women's advice books. *Theory, Culture, and Society* 11: 2, 1–24.

Hoffereth, S. L. and C. D. Hayes. (1987). *Risking the Future: Adolescent Sexuality, Pregnancy, and Childbearing, Volume II.* Washington, DC: National Academy of Science Press.

Horowitz, Ruth. (1983). *Honor and the American Dream.* New Brunswick, NJ: Rutgers University Press.

Laumann, Edward O., John H. Gagnon, Robert T. Michael, and Stuart Michaels. (1994). *The Social Organization of Sexuality: Sexual Practices in the United States.* Chicago: University of Chicago Press.

Martin, Karin. (1988). Of romance and rock stars: teenage girls and the question of desire. Division Three Thesis, Hampshire College.

Moffatt, Michael. (1989). *Coming of Age in New Jersey: College and American Culture.* New Brunswick, NJ: Rutgers University Press.

Padilla, Amado and Traci Baird. (1991). Mexican-American adolescent sexuality and sexual knowledge: an exploratory study. *Hispanic Journal of Behavioral Sciences* 13: 95–104.

Person, Ethel. (1980). Sexuality as the mainstay of identity. *Signs* 5: 605–30.

Raymond, Diane. (1994). Homophobia, identity, and the meanings of desire: reflections on the cultural construction of gay and lesbian adolescent sexuality. In *Sexual Cultures and the Construction of Adolescent Identities*, edited by Janice Irvine. Philadelphia: Temple University Press.

Rubin, Lillian. (1985). *Just Friends.* New York: Harper and Row.

Sanday, Peggy Reeves. (1990). *Fraternity Gang Rape.* New York: New York University Press.

Simon, William and John Gagnon. (1986). Sexual scripts: permanence and change. *Archives of Sexual Behavior* 15: 2, 97–120.

Thompson, Sharon. (1990). Putting a big thing into a little hole: teenage girls' accounts of sexual initiation. *Journal of Sex Research* 27: 3, 341–61.

——(1994). What friends are for: on girls' misogyny and romantic fusion. In *Sexual Cultures and the Construction of Adolescent Identities*, edited by Janice Irvine. Philadelphia: Temple University Press.

Thorne, Barrie. (1993). *Gender Play.* New Brunswick, NJ: Rutgers University Press.

Thorne, Barrie and Zella Luria. (1986). Sexuality and gender in children's daily worlds. *Social Problems* 33: 176–90.

Tolman, Deborah. (1994). Daring to desire: culture and the bodies of adolescent girls. In *Sexual Cultures and the Construction of Adolescent Identities*, edited by Janice Irvine. Philadelphia: Temple University Press.

Treboux, Dominique and Nancy A. Busch-Rossnagel. (1991). Sexual behavior, sexual attitudes, and contraceptive use: age differences in adolescents. In *Encyclopedia of Adolescence Vols. 1 and 2*, edited by R. Lerner, A. Petersen, and J. Brooks-Gunn. New York: Garland.

Ward, Janie Victoria and Jill McLean Taylor. (1994). Sexuality education for immigrant and minority students: developing a culturally appropriate curriculum. In *Sexual Cultures and the Construction of Adolescent Identities*, edited by Janice Irvine. Philadelphia: Temple University Press.

Wright, David, Lori Peterson, and Howard Barnes. (1990). The relation of parental employment and contextual variables with sexual permissiveness and gender role attitudes of rural early adolescents. *Journal of Early Adolescence* 10: 382–98.

Zelnick, M. and J. F. Kantner. (1980). Sexuality, contraception, and pregnancy among metropolitan area teenagers: 1971–1979. *Family Planning Perspectives* 12: 230–7.

Zelnick, M., J. F. Kantner, and K. Ford. (1981). *Sex and Pregnancy in Adolescence.* Beverly Hills: Sage Publications.

11 "The punk guys will really overpower what the punk girls have to say": The Boys' Turf

Lauraine Leblanc

"So They Want Something": Sexual Pressure

Punk is a predominantly heterosexual subculture. Although there is sometimes room within punk for gay and lesbian self-expression, much of this has gradually been relegated to the spin-off queercore scene. Thus, the pressures of heterosexuality still dominate punk, as evinced by the seven bisexual girls I interviewed, all of whom were dating male punks. The numerical predominance of punk guys over punk girls may predispose bisexual punk girls toward selecting male lovers rather than seeking out female lovers among the few punk girls in the scene. However, given the amount of heterosexual pressure and banter within the subculture, as well as some punks' homophobic attitudes, many girls may have felt constrained into such choices. Thus, within the subculture, "compulsory heterosexuality" (Rich 1980) is as normative as in mainstream adolescent culture and romantic relationships develop among many of the same rituals of teenage courtship.

Thus, although punks may appear to be sexually deviant, their sexual relationships conform to many of the mainstream cultural standards governing adolescent relationships: male and female punks pair up, break up, and make up just like their nonpunk peers. Unlike the hippie subculture, which challenged monogamy with a "free love" ideology, punks rarely challenge the mainstream norms governing sex and romance. Beyond Johnny Rotten's purported characterization of sexual intercourse as "two minutes of squelching noises" and early punks' flirtation with homosexual and sadomasochistic self-expression, the punk subculture remains resolutely heterosexualist. The tragically dysfunctional relationship of Sid Vicious and Nancy Spungen often serves as somewhat of a model for punk relationships:

> Joanie: [Feminine punk girls are] going to end up with an asshole punk rock boyfriend that's like, "Fucking girl, blah, blah, blah." A beer-drinking punk rocker that likes his little teenage girls and kind of roughs them around and has petty arguments with them all the time ... That's like trendy punk rock relationships. "Like Sid and Nancy!"

Filmmaker Alex Cox (Cox and Wool 1986) immortalized this relationship in an eponymous film, summarizing its lesson as "love kills." As abusive as the Sid and Nancy relationship was, and as frightening as its example is as a model relationship, its role as a punk image underscores the heterosexuality of punk.

Fortunately, contrary to popular, subcultural, and parental expectations, within relationships male punks are usually no more rude nor violent than are nonpunk boyfriends (which is damning by faint praise):

> Andie: Actually, they are really good toward women ... other punks, punks are really, really sweet toward women. They have the most ... I think that they're even better than some of the men that they bring you flowers and stuff. They got, the punks

are like, "This is my little baby." They take care of you better than they take care of themselves. It's like they put you first all the time.

Sue: I've noticed that punk rock guys are the nicest boyfriends I've ever had in my life. They're not obligated to do anything. It's a pleasure-based society.... For the most part, they're going to actually be caring people. People have this misconception of punk guys just being ogres, but I've gone out with some really nice punk guys that were actually better than the other little boyfriends I've gone out with.

Sexual relationships between men and women within the subculture tend to conform to the monogamous style of mainstream heterosexual relations. Although punks may appear to be decadent and do have a propensity to wear bondage gear, many relationships replicate the standards of mainstream culture, with sadomasochistic practices being fairly uncommon. Heterosexual pairings among the punks, as among nonpunks, may lead to permanent commitments of cohabitation and marriage; a number of the girls I interviewed were engaged, married, or living with their boyfriends.

With this normative expectation of heterosexuality, retaining some traditional gender roles such as femininity and masculinity remains functional. This heterosexuality is further reinforced through interactions between male and female punks. Punk girls, as potential partners for the males, are expected to conform to mainstream standards of female heterosexuality, to present themselves as attractive and sexually available. These, in turn, are some of the central constitutive norms of femininity. Punk males, as are males in other youth subcultures, are instrumental in delineating the ways in which sexual expression occurs within the subculture.

Deirdre Wilson (1978) found that males in male-dominated delinquent subcultures played an important part in controlling

girls' sexuality by setting up paradoxical sets of expectations. They both attempted to engage girls in sexual activity and sanctioned girls who adopted a more liberal, instrumental, "masculine" view of sexual activity. Likewise, Mindy Stombler (1994) found that fraternity brothers both treated girls in their "little sister" organizations as sexual commodities, and yet also proffered negative sanctions to those girls deemed too promiscuous or "easy." As did males in these subcultures, punk guys also set up contradictory standards for the sexual behavior of punk girls.

Flirting or other sexual banter is a primary way in which punk males reinforce gender boundaries. Many punk girls reported that the males view them (or other girls) in a primarily sexual way:

LL: How do male punks treat you?
Denise: It's very much the same as always – it's like, depending on, usually the first, guys come up to me it's cause they're hitting on me, so they want something. Almost immediately, it's always the first thing out of my mouth, all the time, and it's "No, I'm engaged," and then after that we can kind of take it on to a different level. But it always starts out as, "I don't want to talk to you about what you believe I just want to get you in bed."

This banter could even extend to overt pressures for sex, culminating in attempted rape:

Justine: There's this one guy [at "punk park"] who could only speak English, and the only thing he could say [in French] is, "Veux-tu faire l'amour avec moi?" [Do you want to make love to me?] And he was harassing all the girls there. He was an asshole.... The guys that I thought were my friends, not even a year ago, nearly the last time I ran away, I thought he was my friend. I slept at his place and he wanted me to sleep with him. He said, "Hey, you have my hospitality. What are you going to give me for it?" He was getting violent. He wanted to make me, but I grabbed my shit and left.

Even when these interactions did not escalate to attempted rape, girls resented the ongoing sexual pressures which male punks applied:

> LL: *How do male punks treat you?*
> Basilisk: Either they all, they want to sleep with me, that's basically what it boils down to. And a lot of them want to sleep with me. It gets, it kind of gets annoying, because I don't want to sleep with a lot of them....That's what it goes like. You have, a majority of them, either they're nice to me, some of them are nice to me, they don't really bother me. And with some of them, they totally are like, they're all touchy-feely and oh, and if I don't sleep [with them], then they get pissed off at me if I don't sleep with them.

Although, as in Justine's and Basilisk's accounts, such sexual attention can become very annoying or threatening, some girls viewed this as harmless:

> Lola: We always mess, they always tease you around sexually, of course, but nothing bad. And they're all, they never make, really, advances and stuff, and they treat me like big brothers, really.

> Candace: I haven't had any problems with [punk guys]. But generally, they're hitting on you and it just depends who it is.

> Cora: It depends on the guy....There are guys here that will jump on any girl.... When I got here, not long ago, all the guys were all over me....They grab our boobs and we're always hugging, but it's just among friends.

For some punk girls, this sexual attention is what they first encounter with other punks:

> Clara: Here, as soon as they see a new girl, they spot her right away....Well, I started coming to the park last summer. At the start I was a little shy....Then, in the fall, there was a big rush, everyone wanted to go out with me one day. I was the new blood on the block.

Girls soon learned that sexual banter was an acceptable way for punk guys and girls to communicate, so the banter was not always one-sided:

> Clara: It seems to me that all the guys at the park are my friends. Shit. Like Ricky. Ricky, you talk to him, you kiss him, you grab his butt. He's a friend. They're almost all like that. Ricky, he's an exception... sex machine...

Most girls, although finding this somewhat bothersome, did not perceive such sexualized attention as threatening, merely annoying:

> Elle: Well, punk guys [here] really trip out on sex. I think that's really stupid. But besides that, it's okay. It doesn't bother me at all. It's fun.

The male punks who behaved flirtatiously or who engaged in sexual activity with punk girls played upon the sexual permissiveness of adolescent culture. However, male punks also set up contradictory expectations, proffering negative sanctions to girls who engaged in what they deemed to be promiscuity. As one girl reported, engaging in such sexual activity may then lead to a lessening of the type of "respect" that punk girls gain by behaving in male ways. Tori noted that this makes a difference in the ways the males treat girls:

> I think they treat me just a little bit different than they treat the other girls. Because, because I have been with that one person for so long....And I get, I get a lot of respect from the guys. I know I do. From, rather than when I was just...because there was...a point when I was younger that I did sell my ass when I was younger, like twelve or thirteen, down in New Orleans....Back then, I think maybe everybody thought I was a floozy or a hooker or whatever, which I was. I was, but I wasn't. I didn't sleep with everybody.

And now I just, nobody ever hears of me sleeping with anybody anymore and I get a lot of respect for that, I think.

Thus, sexual chastity, or at least monogamy, led to girls earning "respect" as well. However, as in other parts of teen culture, males were not held to so stringent a standard. Tori went on to discuss the ways in which more sexually active or promiscuous girls were treated:

> LL: *You said that the guys treat you differently than they treat other girls. Is that the difference?*
> Tori: I think so, yeah.
> LL: *They treat other girls like they're . . .*
> Tori: There's these three girls that are my best friends – I love them to death – they've been around with a couple of guys and so the guys kind of like – maybe not intentionally in a bad way, but it does come out in a bad way – talk about how that girl was or how that girl can be to you or something like that. And so that kind of sucks. And with me, they can't do that, because nobody out here has been with me. So, but I still love those girls to death and I still love the boys to death. I get along better with the boys than the girls, most of the time.

Whereas males who engage in sexual activity do not lose status (being "studs" or "players"), females who do, even within the punk subculture, become negatively labeled as "whores" or "sluts." Thus, although the males will initiate sexual activity, it is not the case that in engaging in sex girls can gain the male prerogative of promiscuity. Celia Cowie and Sue Lees (1981) argue that this maintains a gendered double standard with respect to sexual activity: girls who "do" are "slags," and girls who "don't" are "drags." In creating this distinction between the acceptability of sexual activity for males and for females, the males perpetuate a standard of behavior that reinforces gender distinctions within the punk subculture and highlights the relative inferiority of punk girls.

Conclusion

In all, punk males present and reward contradictory expectations of punk girls: they should be tough, like the guys, but they should also be pretty and sexually available. And yet, although they are expected to be sexual, they should not be overly promiscuous, for then they incur negative sanctions of being "sluts." Punk males also used these paradoxical expectations in order to create schisms between "types" of punk girls. Anna, who got "respect" from the males for her construction of an androgynous mode of self-presentation, reported that the punk males did distinguish between her "type" of punkness and that of other girls:

> Most of the time I was just treated like a pal or "tough girl" or, "She's cool, she's tough." That's usually how I got treated. There was always one or two of – they were more gothic, I guess, they were a little more feminine, they always wore the long black skirts and they'd have a little mohawk or the Robert Smith 'do – that they were always the heartthrobs that [the guys] liked. Because they were very, they'd never get into the pit, they'd stand on the side and stuff. And I just – I don't condemn anyone, if that's what they want to do – it's just always I get in and have fun, so I guess I got labeled more of a macho chick or whatever.

The male punks are certainly instrumental in establishing and maintaining boundaries between "tough girls" who are "respected" and other girls. As a result, the adoption of masculine characteristics becomes necessary for girls' creations of "respected" punk identities; paradoxically, however, the punk males expect and reinforce, to some extent, the girls' adoption of traditionally feminine characteristics. By expecting girls to be more masculine (rewarding this with "respect") and yet expecting them to be sexual partners who behave in traditionally feminine (read:

chaste) ways, male punks set up conflicting expectations:

> Jennie: They treat me like one of the guys. That sucks in a way, but I am.... Sometimes you want a little bit more, but that's not how they see me. That's what sucks....I wouldn't mind not being one of the guys. Because they expect you of all, they don't understand that, well, even though I wouldn't do this with you, I still have feelings and there's just sometimes you just need to talk to someone and they just don't understand it. "Well, what do you mean? You're one of the guys." You're just like, "No, you just don't understand."

Punk girls' constructions of forms of resistance often do not extend to their intimate contact with punk males. A measure of resistance, I have argued, requires three instances: a subjective account of oppression, an express desire to counter that oppression, and an action (broadly defined as word, thought, or deed) intended specifically to counter that oppression. The first category is satisfied: girls are not blind to the oppressiveness of punk's masculinity, and even equate it with that they encounter elsewhere: "I see sexism in day-to-day life all the fucking time, so it doesn't surprise me that it comes from punk males" (Hallie). Punk girls recognize and object to the complex role that the males in the subculture play in determining membership and status:

> Sue: A lot of the punk guys think, just like a lot of the skinhead guys think skinhead girls are just "Oi toys," because skinhead girls didn't have a big role in the skin scene. Whereas punk girls and guys – have you ever seen in *The Decline of Western Civilization*, or like UK...what was it? *Social Distortion on Tour* – all the punk guys are going, "Girls are icky," and the girls were wild. They eventually intertwined. They had to at some point. But, punk is a male-dominated scene. It's kind of "survival of the fittest" among the girls.

However, punk girls are divided in characterizing male punk "chivalry," abusiveness, or control as problematic. Some, like Lola, reported pleasure in the banter in which they engage with the males. Others, like Anna and Candace, were proud of their position as tough girls or objects of "respect." Even those girls who objected to the males' treatment did not report undertaking courses of action to resist that treatment, save ignoring it or avoiding the offensive male.

Given the characterization of punk as a subculture of resistance, and girls' constructions of punk identities as a core aspect of their own personal resistance, why do these girls continue to accept this type of treatment? The answer may lie in the constraints of the subcultural role that faces these girls. Punk girls recognize the male domination of the subculture, both numerically and normatively. Those girls who fail to recognize or reject the masculinity of punk, those whom Emily described as "the little girl punks that come out here, they're younger and stupid," who join for traditionally feminine reasons, such as wanting to meet men, do not participate long in the subculture; as Jennie stated: "[They] get kicked out [of the scene] because it's just like, 'No. That's not what it's all about.'" The girls who do achieve acceptance as punks are those who have achieved the acceptance of punk males by measuring up to the masculinist standards of the subculture. They are the "tough girls," the "macho chicks" who have commanded "respect." The girls who do "make it" in punk, in light of these masculinist norms, either self-select from a certain type or work to achieve it: "very assertive and aggressive girls" (Sue).

Punk girls thus accept, internalize, and project these norms, adopting many of these norms in their own assessments and expectations of other punk girls:

> Tori: It's harder to find a girl that can be as tough as a guy. Seriously – none, none of the male chauvinist crazy shit like that – a

girl should be able to drink as much as a guy and – [for] their body weight – be able to climb rocks and go hiking with them and camping with them and be able to sleep outside in the cold and not complain twenty-four hours a day. It's hard to find girls like that, but they are out there. We are out there.

Becoming or being a punk girl therefore requires not only that one reject mainstream notions of femininity, but that one encounter and prevail over the male domination of the punk scene itself:

> Sue: The punk guys will really overpower what the punk girls have to say. I think the punk girl thing is a very aggressive scene, and very assertive and aggressive girls tend to get into it. I don't know many really passive, timid little girls who are going to shave their heads and look like a freak, take harassment from everybody all the time, and then fight off the guys in the scene.

Punk girls, therefore, are likely to collude with, rather than resist the masculinism of punk. Only a few punk girls, like the Riot Grrrls, raise their voices in protest, stating, "We are tired of boy band after boy band, boy 'zine after boy 'zine, boy punk after boy punk after boy." Riot Grrrls, realizing that they will "never meet the hierarchical BOY standards of talented, or cool, or smart" argue that if they do meet them, "we will become tokens" (Riot Grrrl 1992). In challenging the masculinist standards of punk, Riot Grrrls have been marginalized, indeed, have formed their own subculture now quite distinct from punk. Punk girls who want to remain within the subculture restrict their resistance to the masculinism of punk to rhetorical, general comments rather than to confrontation of male punks:

> Sue: I think more girls should get into punk and tell these guys that are trying to shy them off just so it can be an elite punk men's thing to fuck off. And get involved,

who cares....It doesn't matter how attractive you are to the boy next door.

Sue thus placed the onus on changing the subculture on girls, rather than on the males' treatment of girls or in their definition and support of masculinist punk norms. In accommodating to the masculinist punk norms, the punk girls I interviewed did indeed become tokens, often isolated from other girls, both punk and mainstream. Few reported having girl friends, and thus their forms of resistance to the masculinity of punk would enjoy little support, and little chance of success.

In some ways, this has been the most difficult part of my analysis to present, because, unlike other chapters that celebrate punk girls' resistance, this one points out and condemns both male punks' behaviors in shaping punk norms and punk girls' collusion with these constraints. Many of the girls I interviewed, I suspect, would (and will) challenge this aspect of my analysis as misrepresenting the actualities of the punk subculture or as casting punk into a bad light. Throughout this project, I have sought to present, explore, and honor punk girls' accounts of their realities. In this one chapter, I challenge the validity of their subjectivities, of their accounts stating that they feel unfettered and unoppressed by their male peers. Punk girls do report experiences of oppression at the hands of males, but then fail to counter that oppression. Others, experiencing the same types of behaviors, merely ignore them or discount their effects. No form of resistance can be pure, untainted by stains of accommodation. It is in their dealings with male punks and with the masculinity of the subculture that punk girls' forms of resistance fail them, for the cost of resistance – expulsion from the subculture – may be too high. Those who do remain within the punk subculture instead use its resources to turn their forms of resistance outward to challenge both mainstream gender norms and their harassment by strangers.

REFERENCES

Cowie, Celia and Sue Lees. 1981. "Slags or Drags." *Feminist Review* 9: 17–31.

Cox, Alex and Abbe Wool. 1986. *Sid and Nancy*. Dir. Alex Cox; w. Alex Cox and Abbe Wool. Zenith Productions/Initial Pictures.

Rich, Adrienne. 1980. "Compulsory Heterosexuality and Lesbian Existence." *Signs* 5: 631–60.

Riot Grrrl. 1992. "What Is Riot Grrrl?" PO Box 11002, Washington, DC, 20008: Riot Grrrl.

Stombler, Mindy, 1994. "'Buddies' or 'Slutties': The Collective Sexual Reputation of Fraternity Little Sisters." *Gender and Society* 8: 293–323.

Wilson, Deirdre. 1978. "Sexual Codes and Conduct: A Study of Teenage Girls." In *Women, Sexuality, and Social Control*, ed. C. Smart and B. Smart, 65–73. London: Routledge and Kegan Paul.

12 Tough Times: Susan Carter

Elaine Bell Kaplan

I didn't know nothin' about nothin'.
Sixteen-year-old Marnie Martin

In the East Oakland neighborhood where 16-year-old Susan Carter lived with her two-month-old baby, her mother, and two sisters, there were no parks. Nor were there many supermarkets or movie theaters. Susan hung out with her friends at the East Oakland mall, a run-down shopping center peppered with fast-food stores, small clothing boutiques filled with trendy but inexpensive clothes, a Payless shoe store, and a popular video game arcade. Susan's family shared a small, neatly furnished two-bedroom apartment across the street from the mall. After the baby was born, Susan applied for AFDC, but her application was turned down when the welfare worker informed her that her mother's $1,100 monthly salary as a nursing assistant exceeded the maximum allowed families of four.

Tall and pretty, with large, almond-shaped eyes that flashed when she smiled, Susan was a curious mix of adolescent and adult. Sometimes she appeared to be much older than her years, almost worldly. The next moment, she was cute and giggly, an adolescent dressed in typical teenage gear: T-shirt and jeans. Often we talked as Susan pushed curly-haired Jarmella in her stroller as we walked around the neighborhood of tiny box-shaped single-family homes interrupted occasionally by three-story apartment buildings like Susan's.

I did not have to walk far down Susan's street to realize that few middle-class Black families lived in her neighborhood. Most middle-class families had retreated from these bleak surroundings to the Oakland hills or to upscale Piedmont. Their move out of this neighborhood was not un-usual. Most people who grow up in such inner-city surroundings want better schools, more space, a backyard, and less density. "If my son grows up to be a knuckle-head, it won't be because I didn't expose him to other possibilities," one writer observed after moving out of his inner-city neighborhood.[1]

The Black middle-class flight to suburbia left only three kinds of "success" stories to serve as role models for those like Susan who stayed behind: the flashy drug dealer, the sports figure, and the larger-than-life show business entertainer. Susan mostly saw the drug dealers cruising through the "hood" in BMWs with gold trim. Sports personalities, such as Michael Jordan and Larry Holmes, occasionally appeared at the Oakland Coliseum sports arena. After the events, and before they flew off to another city, dressed in beautiful and expensive jogging suits, they gave out autographs as part of promotional stunts.

Those people, being rich and famous, were special to Susan, and their lives did not register with her as the kind she could someday achieve. Susan's observations about her own life were textured by her mother's negative messages and her own observations of her friends' employment and unemployment potentials. Two close friends had recently applied for welfare. Almost all of Susan's school friends were in some kind of trouble; a few were selling drugs or were involved in gangs. She did not want to go that route, she insisted, but it was hard for this teenager to think of other paths to take when all she saw were three compelling, yet negative or unrealistic, models – the exaggerated success of drug dealers or sports or entertainment figures, compared with motherhood or work at McDonald's.

School Problems

Susan's story was hardly unique. Nor was the path that brought her to this place, the path she described as "coping with tough times." Susan told me about her school experiences one cool afternoon as we drove over to her high school, located in a predominantly Black school district noted for producing students with low test scores.[2] We parked in back of a square three-story brick building surrounded by a chainlink fence. On the other side of the fence, where a basketball lay between gum wrappers, dirty newspapers, and broken soda bottles, two boys were jumping up and down on a long wooden board.

Susan pointed to the darkened windows of her former classrooms: "I had English there, and Math in that one." School was "great" until the seventh grade, when Susan's classes became "boring and too easy," the teachers dull and uninspiring, and the work tedious. School was neither stimulating nor relevant. Most of the women she knew were working at low-level occupations or having children and, perhaps, getting married.

Susan did not get along with her teachers. Talking with her friends was easier than studying for classes. She began cutting classes to spend her days at the park with her friends talking about "this and that," and her school attendance "went downhill from there." "I wanted to go out with my friends," she told me. After a while most of her friends stopped coming to the park, but Susan stayed out of school anyway. Some days she fell asleep on the park bench. No matter how long and tedious the day was, she could not often bring herself to go back to school. By the end of the ninth grade, she was flunking most of her classes. "I didn't care." Her voice sounded convincing, but the "I don't care" attitude seemed like a front, hiding deep anxieties about herself and her ability to do well in school.[3]

Eventually Susan became passive and invisible when she was in the classroom. "I had to get out of school, just anything, to get out of school, something else besides school." She was bored. Susan did not consider transferring to another school. She began to believe she did not have the right attitude or motivation for school. Finally, two months after she learned she was pregnant, she dropped out of school – at the very age when school should have been a priority in her life.

Susan was similar to other Black Oakland students. According to an Oakland School District report, half of all Black students drop out of Oakland's schools. The dropout rates, always a problem, soared during the Reagan administration, when the school district suffered tremendous cutbacks. If children in Oakland's poor neighborhoods did manage to stay in school, one in five failed to complete basic courses in Math and English. Most of these children failed because their families did not have the economic and social resources to support adolescent children's academic performance.[4]

Bright, articulate, and yet bored, Susan did not blame the teachers or the school system. Why was school so difficult for her? Lacking her own explanation, she voiced the message of personal failure she had heard from those in authority: "It's all my fault." Everyone, including the school counselors, told her she was not working up to her potential. All she said in response was, "When I'm in class, it's like my mind stops working." She was convinced she should have worked harder. She brooded. "I must be lazy, because I'm not stupid. I can do the work."[5]

Several times Susan made the point that school was not for everyone. Anyway, she said a little defiantly, only a few of her classmates graduated from high school. To prove her point, she told me about 17-year-old Jean and 16-year-old Vicki, sisters who lived in an apartment upstairs. They had dropped out of school the previous year but seemed to be doing all right. Susan later admitted that Jean and Vicki were not finding work and were going to apply for welfare assistance. But Susan did not believe that a high school diploma was going to give her a better deal.[6]

Perhaps Susan and her teachers were right to blame Susan for a degree of her failure. But a number of studies show that teenage girls like Susan are taught to fail in school. In subtle and not so subtle ways, gender and race ideology operate in the class setting.

Michele Fine has explored the way gender ideology is reproduced in the high school experiences of 3,200 predominantly low-income Black students. The girls in her study tended to enroll in sex-typed vocational training courses, such as home economics, cosmetology, and secretarial programs, that teach skills for homemaking or jobs with low salaries and little life career advancement. Fine believes these girls accept this gender ideology because they do not have an alternative view of themselves.[7] They are often warned by their teachers, "You act like that, and you'll end up on welfare!" and encouraged to disparage the circumstances in which they live.

But Susan was missing out on more than just relevant school courses. In Susan's understanding of Jean's, Vicki's, or her own situation, it was not gender ideology that drove her out of school and made her seek refuge in the park or in intimate relationships. Susan lacked relationships with her teachers or other responsible adults in school, which would have enabled them and Susan to see beyond gender ideology and stereotypes about Black girls. Susan could not establish relationships with teachers and peers that would make school relevant. She only heard warnings from teachers that girls like her were prime candidates for poverty and welfare, so she could not see the importance of leaving the park bench.[8]

Susan spent most of her time avoiding school, partly because she was ignored, seemingly invisible in the classroom, and partly because the educational and cultural environment was so limited – there was no after-school program for Susan to attend since school funding was cut back. The cultural deprivation in Susan's school was appalling. What I saw at Susan's school confirmed Jonathan Kozol's insight that these schools are "extraordinarily unhappy places." Kozol, who has championed the rights of children for thirty years, writes, "[These schools] reminded me of 'garrisons' or 'outposts' in a foreign nation. The schools were marked frequently by signs that indicated DRUG-FREE ZONE. Their doors were guarded. Police sometimes patrolled the halls. The windows of the schools were often covered with steel grates." Kozol describes these Oakland schools as part of a "mainly nonwhite, poor and troubled system."[9]

These schools, plagued by violence, drugs, and gangs, reflect the drama in the world right outside the school door. "If you live to be thirty and not robbed, mugged, or drugged in this neighborhood, you're lucky," Susan grimly noted. Being surrounded by such an environment, school administrators focused on preserving law and order in their school yards, creating a prison atmosphere. Stern-faced school security guards stopped students to check their identification or room assignments.

School officials often blamed noisy and disruptive students for these school problems, but noise and chaos also seemed to be fostered by the teachers and administrators in the schools I observed. Authority figures barked orders over loudspeakers. At one school, where I had to sign in at the door after showing my identification to two burly guards, the principal and school staff interrupted class discussions, blasting their warnings over the loudspeaker: "If you are late, you must sign in at the first door; Mrs. Johnson's ten-thirty class will meet in room 234 for today only." At another school, a teenage mother informed me, a teacher kept a telephone on his desk, which rang frequently during the class hour.

The teachers and principal at one school I visited emphasized that students needed to learn "good" values. Some of the teachers interpreted those good values to mean gendered manners and attributes, which they passed off as graciousness and cleanliness. "Boys should remove their caps," a teacher informed me one day during my classroom visit, as she gave a teenager a demerit for wearing his cap in class. Another teacher told me she was impressed with the teen mothers, who "dress so neatly and brought their babies up so clean and neat." Yet a group of teen mothers bragged to me when I visited them at this same school that they received so little homework that they finished it during their forty-minute homeroom period.

The observation that the schools focus so much on teaching students "good" values and so little on teaching them how to put time and effort into their studies is striking not only because of the attitudes and values it discloses but also because it reveals the school environment in which Susan came to see only a few succeed. The path to success was too torturous for her to follow: "I couldn't read all that stuff in school, so I went to sleep." Her view was shared by other teen mothers. Education was not unimportant to these teen mothers. Most had been average to good students during their early school years. It was during adolescence that they began to drift away from school.[10] Although a few were still enthusiastic about education, most were like Susan, convinced by their own experiences and those of the people around them that education would not help them out of their situation. Susan's story, however, is much too complex to be explained by the lack of an adequate educational experience during adolescence or by the lack of opportunities. To understand why teenage Susan became a mother, we have to explore other factors as well.

Family Matters

When I asked Susan to talk about her personal life, she groaned. A sullen expression appeared on her moon-shaped face as she began to talk about her family. She was extremely angry at her mother. There had always been tension between them, and the hostility increased when Susan's mother realized she was expected to support her grandchild. Janet Carter, Susan's mother, had her own set of problems. Since he left, when Susan was young, Susan's father refused to pay child support and seldom visited the children. To make matters worse, Susan said, Janet Carter was experiencing problems at work. According to Susan, if her mother was not "bitchin'" about having to support her grandchild, she was grumbling "about her work and the long hours and the constant hassles with the patients and her supervisors."

Susan was sympathetic with her mother, who worked "like a dog," but she was also concerned because her mother's salary barely supported the family. Susan shook her head when I asked if her mother had other employment options. There was "nothing I can see"; most of the women she knew of her mother's age were on welfare, cleaned houses, or worked at McDonald's for $4.35 an hour. Susan's sympathy, however, only went so far. She believed her mother was not living up to her responsibility to love and support her daughter no matter what happened to her.

She blamed her mother for everything that had happened to her since her father had moved out. Until a few months before Susan became pregnant, her father occasionally visited the family or called his daughters to chat. Susan liked being with him. She recalled that when she stayed with him the summer she turned 13, he turned every occasion, like the nightly cookouts on the backyard grill, into a major event. That summer he found her a job typing letters and working on the computer at the local library. She was thrilled. On the next visit, everything changed:

> We just didn't get along at all. I just was going out and getting drunk and I'd come

home and I'd say everything to him. You know, all the things he did to my momma and all the things I hated him for when I was younger. 'Cause you know, he really hurt my momma a lot. I told him I hated him. I told him everything he deserved, and he didn't like me after that.

He did not like Susan's criticism one bit. He took her home and told her mother that he could not handle her. She could put Susan in a foster home for all he cared. She did not hear from him again until a year later, when she was eight months pregnant.

> He called and, ah, I mean my aunt got a hold of him. And I told him I was pregnant. He was pretty shocked. And the only thing he said was, "Well, I guess I really need to talk to you." And he said he was thinking about coming down in two weeks, down to the Bay area. And, ah, he told me he'd call me back later on that night. And he, ah (*nervous voice*), never did. I never heard from him after that. I really don't know what he thinks about me because he never did say. He really (*low voice*) didn't say.
>
> I think if my mother had stayed with my father and they would have talked to me and done a lot of things differently, I think I never would have gotten pregnant. I know I wouldn't have.
>
> *Why not?*
>
> I know my father, he would never had let me.... I would have been too scared to try anything with guys, just too scared. 'Cause my mother, I knew anything I did, I could do anything I wanted. She wouldn't care. And if she would care, she couldn't help. See, that's another reason I got pregnant.

She felt her father's strong authority as head of the house would have been enough to save her from getting pregnant. Because her father was absent from her life, she had no one to hold responsible for the way it was turning out. "She didn't support me enough," Susan wanted me to know. The absent men were merely shadowy figures in the background of this teenage mother's life. Joney, the baby's father, was no help either,

although he did promise Susan he would find a job and marry her as soon as he finished serving a two-year sentence for armed robbery.

Sexual Abuse: Uncle Freddy Dude

Susan was four years old when her uncle, who often baby-sat her, began sexually molesting her and his own three-year-old daughter. "He did it to me and my cousin Rachel." The molestation continued for four years:

> And that's one thing I'll never understand my mom. She knew that he did that to me. My whole family knows, and he still lives with my grandmother, and he's still in the family. She doesn't pay attention.... In fact, she doesn't even like me any more, because... I don't know...I guess she thinks...I hate it. And my mom still lets him come over here just to fix the car. I tell her, "Mom, I don't want him over here." And she says, "Well, Susan, he's got to fix my car." You know, her car comes first.
>
> *Did she say anything to him?*
>
> No, she never did. Never! And he came over here one time and we got into it. And he yelled at me. He can say anything he wants to me and she'll never stick up for me. Oh, that gets me so mad. I think, why would they do that? Why would they keep him in the family and stuff after what he did to me? If somebody did that to my daughter, I'd...I don't know what I'd do. I'd kill him.
>
> *Your daughter's here, and your uncle is still here. What are you going to do?*
>
> I would never let him around her. I don't even want him around me.... I'll take her away. I'll just leave.
>
> *Do you think that there may be a connection between the molestation by your uncle and your early pregnancy?*
>
> I don't know if that had anything to do with it. I know that after that I blocked it out. I know he was wrong. It just made me mad and I blocked it away. I just never wanted to think about it anymore. It didn't bother me after a while.

That is, she was not bothered until she began to have recurring dreams that stirred up her memories of the sexual abuse:

> You know the Freddy dude from the movie *Nightmare on Elm Street?* I had a bad nightmare about him. There was this same house that my uncle molested us in. And Freddy had us locked up there. When I woke up, I was crying. I was shaking. And I jumped in bed with my sister. This was not long ago. Before I got pregnant, I guess. I was suppose to see a psychologist. It was all blocked up and it had to come out sometime. Those feelings are still there.

Susan's story of early childhood sexual abuse reveals a complex issue that does not lend itself to simple explanations. Some evidence suggests a connection between premature and harmful sexual experiences and teenage pregnancy. A study of 445 Black teenage mothers reports that more than 60 percent of them were forced to have an unwanted sexual experience at some time in their lives; one-third were younger than twelve at the time of the first forced experience. More than one-quarter reported that they were harassed by family members.[11]

Although the study does not directly link sexual abuse and teenage pregnancy, it does suggest that sexual abuse may make young girls feel tremendously vulnerable and dependent. When girls like Susan Carter are sexually abused at an early age, they may learn to define themselves and others primarily in sexual terms. The teen mothers I talked with reported having ongoing nightmares, problems in school, and problems with intercourse, which are symptoms displayed by sexually abused victims.[12]

For a number of reasons, sexual abuse may be the most critical event in a girl's young life. As they move toward independence, adolescent girls seek security in some kind of attachment to others. They are handling crucial developmental issues, such as adult connections, physical maturation, and where to place their trust. Sexually abused teenage girls, who have found their love and trust betrayed, may have little emotional energy left to invest in other areas of their lives, such as doing well in school, and so may lose interest in them, especially if they can expect little extrinsic or intrinsic reward.

Is Susan's experience an exception in this study? I asked other teen mothers questions about sexual abuse. Some said, "Absolutely not!" A few were vague: something may have happened, but they could not remember the details. Only 26-year-old Tonya Banks, a stout and intense older teen mother, recalled being sexually abused by her uncle when she was eight years old.[13]

Many teen parent counselors at the Alternative Center, where I worked as a consultant, admitted hearing "a million stories" about sexual abuse. Some counselors believed these "stories" to be true; others were leery. Several believed that teen mothers had ulterior motives for their accusations: some may have been responding to the media's focus on sexual abuse, others looking for sympathetic attention.[14]

Jean Carroll, a teen parent program coordinator for the Oakland school district, raised her eyebrows when I asked whether she had data on sexual abuse. "Well, no. We don't really keep those kinds of reports." She did not know of any agencies with such records. She admitted, "We don't know how many cases, since the teen mothers may not tell us." According to this program coordinator, the staff of the parent programs could not keep records of these reports because it was committed to keeping the students' records confidential. It is ironic that this protective strategy allows a serious issue like sexual abuse to go unreported.[15]

Learning about Sexuality

Often during my visits with Susan, we would walk over to McDonald's to buy French fries, Susan's favorite food.[16] Several times a group of neighborhood teenage boys, lounging in front of the restaurant jostling with each other and slapping high fives, yelled, "I'm gonna git me some of that," when we walked past them. Susan would stare at the ground. One day a group of boys began jokingly to describe various sexual acts they wanted to perform on Susan. We made a hasty retreat. Susan was unnerved by the sexual harassment.

Michele Wallace describes the way men notice the physical development of a young girl such as Susan: "Some of the nice little old men who used to pat her on the head when she was a child begin to want to pat her on the ass when she is thirteen. The neighborhood pimps and hustlers begin to proposition her." Wallace contends that young girls (like Susan) are extremely vulnerable and are unprepared for the way men respond to their maturing bodies.[17]

Susan was typical of the other teenagers in this study in that she developed physical maturity early. The Black teenage participants of one study developed early signs of pubertal changes by age nine, with menarche coming at 12.5 years of age on the average. By the time they reached the age of 13 or 14, these girls found themselves confronting teenage boys' sexual advances earlier than White girls.[18]

While Black teenagers may physically mature earlier than other teenagers, all teenagers are maturing faster than the women of their mothers' generation. For instance, two generations ago teenage girls did not have to decide whether to have sex, take drugs, or drink until they were older. Today they make these choices in junior high school. A generation ago teenagers pursued hobbies and same-sex relationships. Now boys and girls often interact in peer groups. Girls today reach menarche, the time when they become capable of conception and sexual activity, as early as ten years old. The majority of the young women in my sample began menstruation between the ages of 11 and 13. During their mothers' generation the average girl started her menstrual cycle at age 13.[19]

Missing from Susan's talk about sexuality was a well-defined attitude about her sexuality or about abortion: "We just didn't worry about that stuff. We never thought about it – getting pregnant, really getting pregnant." The myth that they could not get pregnant during their first sexual intercourse was very popular among the te .a mothers.

The idea that teenagers do not understand their reproductive abilities may surprise some, but it is that very lack of knowledge – part of a general belief system holding that young girls do not need to know about their bodies – that rendered Susan and the other teen mothers largely ignorant about their sexuality: "I didn't really know nothin' about douching or about birth control."

Susan did not remember who told her about sex and sexuality, but she was sure it was not her mother: "My mother didn't tell me about menstruation until I had my period, and I almost died. Never! She didn't even wanna talk about it. My mother, she wouldn't talk to me to really let me know what this was." Most of the teenage mothers did not fully understand the menstrual cycle. Most did not acknowledge their first menstruation, although it signaled a major change in their lives. They did not make the connection between the start of menstruation and their ability to become pregnant.[20]

Nor did they discuss sexuality with their parents. Girls who did talk with their parents discussed dating and boyfriends but not sexual intercourse, morality, or birth control. Mostly, as Greer Litton Fox and others observe, teenage girls ask their mothers how to handle boyfriends on a date (prior to and not including sexual intercourse).[21] Despite the lack of communication about sexuality issues, the mothers of the teens kept close supervision of their daughters' menstruation cycles. Susan and many of the other teen mothers said their mothers questioned them consistently, recording their menstrual cycles on calendars every month. (Since these were self-reports, the teen mothers were able to keep the news of their missing monthly periods to themselves.)

Some of the teen mothers admitted they were curious about sex. Several tried to talk to their parents. Sixteen-year-old Marnie Martin recalled being a little frightened by her feelings and wanting to talk to her parents, but, "That was the problem! My parents didn't really talk to me about sex. They used to say that 'you couldn't really have sex.'" Marnie did find the courage to talk to her mother:

> I think I was 13 when I first started having sex. My best friend thought I was crazy, 'cause I went to my mother and said, "Well mom, I like this boy and I might be doing something with him and would you take me to get birth control?" And she said, "No, because once you start taking those pills you'll become sterile." See, I want kids. I love them and I want them. So it scared me. At the time the only thing I knew was condoms. I said no, I'm not going to mess with that. It wasn't as if she wasn't warned, because I came to her and asked. And my girlfriend said, "No, Marnie, that's a lie. I don't know why your mother said that."

Four teen mothers told me that their mothers fell back on what they had learned incorrectly from their own mothers. Tracy Alexander laughingly mimicked her mother's high-pitched voice: "You can get pregnant by kissing a boy." In a study on Black teenage mothers, Joyce Ladner has found that mothers pass on to their daughters the misinformation about sex and biological changes that their mothers had passed on to them. As Ellen Kisker notes, by using folk techniques and religious sanctions to limit information about sexuality, mothers not only misinform their daughters about sexuality but also impart their values. Marnie's mother did not approve of her daughter's desire to engage in sexual activity. But misinforming and scaring Marnie did not prevent her from becoming sexually active. Marnie's mother

did not comprehend the importance of sexuality for her daughter.[22]

The parents of many of these teen mothers believed that telling their daughters about birth control could be interpreted as permitting them to have sex. Several of the teen mothers' mothers admitted that they did not know what to say to their daughters or how to be open and frank about sexuality. When Marlee Conners, a shy woman in her late thirties, said she had told her 17-year-old daughter Jasmine about birth control, Jasmine claimed, "This is all in her mind. She don't tell me a thing." De Lesha Simons, a 17-year-old mother, recalled a similar story: "My mother said, 'I told you that.' I said, 'Ma, what you told me wasn't enough to fill a shoe.' I guess she thought she had told me." Susan's mother, Janet, did tell her, when Susan questioned her about sex, that she would learn more about it when she married.

Love at Fourteen

Susan met Joney Glover, a "cute" 17-year-old unemployed high school dropout, at a friend's party. He paid Susan a great deal of attention at the party, which she found very flattering. After that, they went everywhere together. Most of the teen mothers had similar stories – meeting the babies' fathers at parties or at school, where boys hung around the school yard. When an attractive girl crossed a boy's path, he gravitated to her very quickly, arranged for a meeting, and encouraged a friendship that became sexual in a short time. The "sexual hits" – the young men's pickup strategies – pervaded these teenage mothers' stories. When the girls reached the ages of 12 and 13, they found the boys at school talking to them, walking them home, and telling them how cute they looked in whatever they wore.

Elizah Anderson argues that unprotected teenagers such as Susan from mother-only households, or those who do not have a strong male presence in the household, may be attracted to young men eagerly selling themselves as ready for commitment. When I raised this point with Susan, she quickly assured me that Joney had not pressured her into sexual involvement. Joney was, after all, an ordinary boy in Susan's eyes. But according to Anderson ordinary boys may be acting within a social context that allows them to develop the kind of sexual harassment that writer Michele Wallace recalls. The social context within which Black boys' sexual skills are developed consists of poverty, poor educational facilities, high unemployment, fatalistic attitudes, and the need to "prove" oneself through early sexual experimentation. The boys' attitude toward these girls is also consistent with the patriarchal view of women as sexual objects.[23]

Susan did not know how racism and sexism might affect Black men like Joney. All she knew was that when she turned 13 her mother allowed her to stay out later than before. Her friends pressured her to drink, smoke pot, and have sex. "Everyone is doing it," they informed her. "So I had to go with the crowd, that's what it was." Joney began to pay attention to her: "He was coming to school all the time to meet me." She was "scared." She did not have the time to think through her feelings about sexuality, dating, or birth control: "When he asked me, I didn't know what to do. But I did it finally."[24]

Susan "did it," but sex did not have the erotic meaning usually associated with it: "It was disappointing. I regretted it afterward. I thought, God, is that all it is?" She laughed at the thought. I joined in the laughter because the other teen mothers had expressed similar feelings. Susan's question, "Is that all it is?" contradicted the common view that Black teenage girls have hot and shameless sex lives.

We adults often perceive the world of adolescents through our own steamy glasses. Sometimes, as Lillian Rubin so astutely notes, rather than wanting to have sexual relations, teenage girls may simply want to be kissed and caressed. According to Robert Cole and Geoffrey Stokes, teenagers differ from adults in their reasons for engaging in sexual activity: for teenagers like Susan (and perhaps Joney), sex may be a reprieve from "a life that can be, often enough, boring or demanding or puzzling."[25]

Cole and Stokes's observations made sense to me as I listened to Susan. In Susan's story I heard no words of hot desire or unbridled lust. Sex was a mechanical act, a way to release pent-up anxieties and tensions, as Cole and Stokes suggest, and perhaps an escape from her personal problems. This is not the view most have of teenage mothers' experiences. It would be easier to blame Susan, as so many others do, for letting this situation happen to her in the first place, but we must not overlook the environment in which Susan lives.

Elizah Anderson would not be surprised that Susan fell in love and became sexually involved with Joney. As Anderson notes, young Black women who face a bleak future, having only a limited education and few employment skills, may easily be captured by young men's whispered promises of "love forever."[26]

To add more complexity to Anderson's analysis, we have to understand that Susan did not think it was morally wrong to engage in sexual intercourse. Like many teenagers, Susan valued the spontaneity and romance of her relationship with Joney, which would have been compromised by planning for sex. Several teen mothers thought that having sex before marriage was a "sin" but admitted overcoming that belief when they fell in love, echoing Susan's comment: "For the first time, I was really in love. So we had sex."

Birth Control Knowledge

"Why didn't you use birth control?" I asked Susan. Despite Leon Dash's observation that the teenage mothers in his study were knowledgeable about contraception, Susan did not learn about birth control from her mother or anyone else. Several teen mothers I spoke with made the same claim as those in Dash's study, but in fact few knew about birth control or other issues regarding their sexuality. For example, none of the teen mothers could adequately discuss the man's role in reproduction. Only two were well informed about contraceptives.[27]

The use of contraceptives presents a dilemma to teenage girls. According to Kristen Luker, for the teenager to use contraceptives is an admission she is sexually active. If the teenage girl uses contraceptives, she loses all claim to spontaneity. If she buys contraceptives in the drugstore, she acknowledges in a fairly public place that she intends to have sex. Another part of the problem for teenagers is their ambivalence about norms governing their sexual behavior. Whose norms to follow – their peer group's or their parents'? How can they understand these norms, given that parents refuse to discuss them, other than to say, "You can't?"[28]

"Why didn't you take sex education classes in school?" I asked Susan. She wanted to take a course on sex education, she told me, but the school did not offer one. A few teen mothers said their schools did offer these classes, but they were not very helpful. Two teen mothers who attended their schools' sex education programs found them to be too clinical, the language too technical, the teacher too aloof, and the material too removed from their real experiences. In most cases these classes were held only one day during the semester. Marnie Martin was absent from school the day her class decided to discuss sex education material. By the time the next semester rolled around, she was pregnant and on welfare.

Why do so many teen mothers learn so little in sex education courses? The teen mothers were caught in the middle of the debate over what should be taught and

whether the family or the school is responsible for teaching sex education to children. On one side of this debate are fundamentalists and many others who argue that young girls do not need to know about their sexuality and that such education in fact promotes promiscuity. This view has been contradicted by several studies conducted by the Alan Guttmacher Institute finding that education programs increase knowledge but do not lead to promiscuous behavior.[29]

The media also bear responsibility for poor sex education. According to Millicent Philliber, whose study criticizes the media's portrayal of sex and sexual attractiveness, the media often depict adults being carried away by sexual passion, but they do not show that passion leads to coitus, or that coitus leads to pregnancy.[30]

Sex education courses may prevent some, but not many, teenage pregnancies. But it is imperative that teenagers like Susan Carter receive accurate information about their sexuality through such courses for another reason as well. As Susan's comments show, and as other teen mothers' descriptions of their early years will demonstrate throughout this book, these adolescent girls learned at an early age that they were sexual, but they did not learn about sexuality in a way that would give them a positive sense of being women. Mainly, they experienced the mainstream gender ideology operating through the men they met in the school yard and through the school that refused to give them adequate information about themselves as women. According to this ideology, for example, a girl's successful transition into adulthood depends in large part on her ability to attract boys: therefore sexual *naïveté* is advantageous since a knowledgeable girl may be labeled as being "too smart for her own good," and only "bad" girls develop strategies about sexual activity (or about any other area in their lives except for being married and having babies).

Dumbing Down Sex Education

Susan told me about an egg experiment conducted in a former class in lieu of a formal sex education course. As a lesson to deter teen pregnancies, each student was given an egg to care for. They had to give the eggs names and think of them as their newborn babies. The teachers believed that the students would learn about the difficulties of raising children if they had to carry the eggs everywhere and not break them. At the end of the week, the students were to write reports on the responsibility of caring for their "babies." Before the week was over, however, some of the braver students grew tired of the experiment and decided to end it. They took turns rolling their eggs down the corridor yelling, "Crack, baby, crack." The school abandoned the egg experiment after the cracked eggs left a yellow mess on the hallway floor.

Neither the sex education courses nor the egg experiment taught Susan or the other teen girls how to handle the daily sexual advances of the adolescent boys and young men. Access to important information about their sexuality was denied them. Whatever information they could glean was restricted to vague abstractions; the time allocated to its teaching was minimal. Such sex education was ineffective in preventing Susan's pregnancy, let alone addressing the severe social problems that underlie the phenomenon of teenage pregnancy.

Baby's Love

It was late in the evening. Susan and I were comfortable with each other, sitting on the small sofa in the living room, our feet curled up under us. This would be my last visit to Susan's home, and I wanted to ask a few remaining questions.

Why do you think you got pregnant?
Well, it wasn't planned.

Did he want you to have a baby before you got pregnant?
It was unexpected.
Did you want to have your baby?
Yeah.

I usually asked the teen mothers these questions several times, in different ways, throughout the course of our interviews. Often, I realized, they had not decided what they really thought about getting pregnant so young. It was usually during our final discussions that the teen mothers came to grips with their feelings about their pregnancies and about being teenage mothers. When I asked Susan again, she briefly paused before responding: "So... um, because it's...for a lot of reasons. I didn't want an abortion. I wanted my baby. I just thought...I guess I don't really know why (*high-pitched voice*) in some ways." This was the first time she admitted any feelings of confusion.

Susan and I continued our conversation:

Perhaps you want something from the baby that you didn't get growing up?

Susan answered quickly:

Oh, love. She makes me happy. It's fun watching her grow.
Did you miss out on something when you were growing up?
Oh yeah. My mother was too busy working and spending her time elsewhere to care very much about raising me.

Susan's comments tell us that she became pregnant in response to her feeling of alienation from her mother. The only way to handle that feeling was to give birth to a baby, thereby guaranteeing that she receive the love and security she needed. Those comments do not tell the whole story. She did not mention her own uncle's or father's role in this family drama. Nor did she mention how she felt taking classes she did not master. These important details were missing from her final comments, although they helped fill in the story of why 15-year-old Susan defied everyone's wish that she have an abortion and sought love and security in motherhood. She did talk about being proud of her relationship with Joney, the baby's father.

For the Love of Joney

Susan talked about Joney in glowing terms, calling him the "most supportive person in my life. He always gave me a lot of support." She informed me that Joney had "class": "He's not a lowlife. It's just that sometimes, his friends, they shoot up and they do crazy stuff." Joney had a history of doing "crazy stuff." She said in a low voice, "I kept telling him, you can't live like that 'cause it's going to catch up to you." It did catch up with him, and he was then serving time in a youth camp. But Susan was sure he would change. She felt confident that when he served his time, he would become the kind of man she wanted him to be. She expected he would find a job as a laborer on his release from the youth camp, because, as Susan put it, "He wants to make it so bad now, and settle down and marry me."

"Did he want the baby?" I wanted to know. Susan responded: "He came to me and said, 'Susan, don't carry my baby if you don't want to. 'Cause if you don't wanna keep it, just give it up for adoption. Whatever you do, that's okay.' He says a lot of things like that. He's so supportive." Susan and I read Joney's comments quite differently. Perhaps because he expressed his views in such negative terms, it struck me that in deciding to have this baby, Susan had taken on all the responsibility for the baby. I wondered what would happen to Susan and Jarmella if her relationship to Joney cooled. Would he hold her solely responsible for the baby's upbringing?

Susan settled back on the sofa. She began to talk quietly about Joney's other child: "He has a four-year-old son he doesn't know. He didn't care for the girl at all. Her

mom called him up and said, 'My daughter's in the hospital having your baby.' And she expected him to do everything for her after that, but he couldn't. He never got over that. He never paid any attention to her. He still doesn't. The kid looks just like him. But he still wonders if the baby's really his. The girl, she's a tramp." Susan believed Joney was right to ignore the girl and the baby. After all, she reasoned, "He doesn't know if the baby is his," although the baby looks just like Joney. Susan insisted with an air of smugness that because the girl was a tramp, she deserved the kind of treatment Joney gave her. She was also sure that Joney would not treat her the same way; she reminded me of how "supportive" he had always been to her.

In some ways Susan's story was about the normal transitional process girls go through during adolescence, when they are learning to handle a changing physiology and the beginning of sexuality identity. In other ways it was about societal pressures, the inadequacy of the sex education being taught to Susan at home and at school, and the freer expression of sexuality she saw in the media and from the boys who were beginning to relate to her in a sexual way. She had no strategies to handle these developmental and social issues.

Having been taught almost nothing about relationships with young men, Susan had no decision-making skill that might help her discern Joney's poor judgments about his other baby and his lifestyle. At this stage of Susan's life, she was doing what adolescents do: she was basing an attachment on what she saw as Joney's trust and sensitivity. She did not find love and security in her family. Susan's reliance on Joney's support became crucial after her family failed to comprehend the nature of her alienation from school. She began to look for support elsewhere after she was sexually abused for four years by her uncle, after her family failed to take her charges against her uncle seriously, and after she began to have disturbing dreams about that experience.

It was also hard for Susan to navigate the world outside her door. She had no strategy to handle the complexities of growing up in an urban environment ruined by drugs, delinquency, and unemployment.

It is in Susan's description of developmental issues and school and family problems that I have gained a deeper insight into the poverty of these teen mothers' relationships.

NOTES

1   David J. Dent, "The New Black Suburbs," *New York Times Magazine*, June 14, 1992, 22. Dent notes, "Middle-class blacks continue to follow their white counterparts to the suburbs." Between 1980 and 1990, the number of Blacks living in the suburbs increased by 34 percent. Also see Karen DeWitt, "Wave of Suburban Growth Is Being Fed by Minorities," *New York Times*, August 15, 1994, A1, A12.

2   "Oakland School District," broadcast on radio station KPFA, Berkeley, July 6, 1991.

3   See Goffman, *Stigma*.

4   "Oakland School District." For discussion of problems facing Black students see Sylvia T. Johnson, "Extra-School Factors in Achievement, Attainment, and Aspirations among Junior and Senior High School-Aged Black Youth" (paper prepared for the Committee on the Status of Black Americans, National Research Council, Washington, DC, 1987). Also see Roslyn A. Michelson and Stephen Samuel Smith, "Inner-City Social Dislocation and School Outcomes: A Structural Interpretation," in *Black Students*, ed. Gordon LaVern Berry and Joy Keiko Asamen (Newbury Park, CA: Sage Publications, 1989), 99–119; John Ogbu, *Minority Education and Caste* (New York: Academic Press, 1978). Ogbu reports that Black students find their culture in opposition to that of the school. See also Diane Scott-Jones, "Black Families and the Education of Black Children: Current Issues" (paper commissioned by the Committee on the Status of Black Americans, National Research Council, Washington, DC, 1987), 81; William G. Spady, "The Impact of School Resources on Students," in *Review of Research in Education*, vol. 1, ed. Fred N. Kerlinger (Ithaca, IL: F. E. Peacock, 1993), 102–34. On family

resources and academic performance, see Janice Hale-Benson, "The School Learning Environment and Academic Success," in Berry and Asamen, *Black Students*, p. 83. Also see Jacqueline Jordan Irvine, *Black Students and School Failure: Policies, Practices, and Prescription* (New York: Greenwood Press, 1990), 6.

5   Mark Snyder, "Self-Fulfilling Stereotypes," in *Racism and Sexism: An Integrated Study*, ed. Paula S. Rothenberg (New York: St. Martin's Press, 1988), 268. Snyder found that stigmatized people often believe the stereotypes about themselves. For similar ideas, see Michele Fine, "Sexuality, Schooling, and Adolescent Females: The Missing Discourse of Desire," *Harvard Educational Review* 58, no. 1 (February 1988): 64.

6   *National Center on Effective Secondary Schools Newsletter* (School of Education, University of Wisconsin–Madison) 4, no. 1 (spring 1989): 1. Also see William Lowes Boyd, "What Makes Ghetto Schools Work or Not Work?" (paper for conference "The Truly Disadvantaged," sponsored by the Social Science Research Council Committee for Research on the Urban Underclass and the Center for Urban Affairs and Policy Research, Northwestern University, Evanston, IL, October 19–21 1989), revised version (February 1990), 23; *National Center on Effective Secondary Schools Newsletter*, p. 4; Fine, "Adolescent Females"; Francis A. J. Ianni, *The Search for Structure: A Report on American Youth Today* (New York: Free Press, 1989), 143; R. C. Kessler and P. D. Cleary, "Social Class and Psychological Distress," *American Sociological Review* 45 (1980): 463–77. All of the authors argue that the life experiences of low-income Black teenagers bring about attitudes of distrust, fatalism, hostility, anti-intellectualism, apathy, hopelessness, and alienation.

7   Michele Fine, "Silencing in Public Schools," *Language Arts* 64 (1987): 157–74; "Adolescent Females," pp. 63–4. Fine writes, "expectations are often shaped unconsciously by the racist and sexist stereotypes that pervade our language" ("Adolescent Females," p. 64). Also see Paula S. Rothenberg, "The Prison of Race and Gender: Stereotypes, Ideology, Language, and Social Control," in Rothenberg, *Racism and Sexism*, p. 254.

8 See J. Brooks-Gunn and E. Reiter, "The Role of Pubertal Processes in the Early Adolescent Transition," in *The Developing Adolescent*, ed. S. Feldman and G. Elliot (Cambridge, MA: Harvard University Press, 1990), 24.

9 Kozol, *Savage Inequalities*, p. 221.

10 See Hale-Benson, "School Learning Environment."

11 Judith S. Musick, "The High-Stakes Challenge of Programs for Adolescent Mothers," in Edelman and Ladner, *Adolescence and Poverty*, pp. 111–37. According to Musick, childhood sexual victimization may leave a psychological residue of emotional discontinuity – a break between present and past, between thought and feeling, between actions and intentions – making the adolescent girl incline to both security-seeking behavior and security-threatening behavior.

12 Musick, "High-Stakes Challenge." Musick writes, "Teens told us their childhoods were filled with sexual abusive experiences that continued into early adolescence and beyond. Experiences were often coercive and sometimes aggressive, including rapes at knifepoint and boyfriends inviting their buddies to 'share' the frightened and confused victim." Also see John Briere, "The Long-term Clinical Correlates of Childhood Sexual Victimization" (paper presented at New York Academy of Science conference, New York, January 1987); Peter Blos, "The Child Analyst Looks at the Young Adolescent," in *Twelve to Sixteen: Early Adolescents*, ed. Jerome Kagan and Robert Coles (New York: W. W. Norton, 1972), 53.

13 See Brooks-Gunn and Reiter, "Role of Pubertal Processes," p. 24.

14 Private communication with Diane Russell, author of *The Secret Trauma: Incest in the Lives of Women* (New York: Basic Books, 1986). Russell was not surprised at the low number of reports of sexual abuse in my study. She suggests that statistics do not reveal the extent of the problem because many girls will not report sexual abuse. Also see Sharon Elise, "Teenage Mothers: A Sense of Self," in *African American Single Mothers: Understanding Their Lives and Families*, ed. Bette J. Dickerson (Thousand Oaks, CA: Sage Publications, 1995), 53–79. In Elise's study half of the 24 teenage mothers interviewed reported being sexually abused during early childhood. NBC's *Tom Brokaw Report* of July 8, 1992 finds that of 300 high school girls interviewed, one out of four said that she had experienced some form of sexual abuse. Also see Hilary M. Lips, *Women, Men and Power* (London: Mayfield Publishing, 1991), 122–3. Lips contends that our double standard about sexual expectations and morality means that rape victims experience as much social rejection as rapists. One reason for the different standard is the attempt to pressure people to adhere to social norms. I talked to Millicent Robinson, a guidance counselor at an Oakland school. Millicent's concern for students had gained her the respect of many of the school's teenage mothers. Concerned about the numerous incidents of sexual abuse informally reported to her by teen mothers, she sent a questionnaire about sexual abuse to all of the school's 260 students, 80 of whom were teenage mothers. Twenty percent of the 80 teen mothers and 15 percent of those who were not teen mothers reported that they had been sexually abused by a relative, usually a stepfather, during early childhood.

15 The way the counselors handled this problem is similar to the way rape cases are handled: victims are often not believed or are perceived to be the one responsible for the abuse.

16 The fact that eating at fast-food restaurants was a favorite activity for many of the teen mothers means nothing until you examine what it tells you about inner-city life. See, for example, Alix M. Freedman, "Habit Forming, Fast-Food Chains Play a Central Role in Diet of the Inner-City Poor," *New York Times*, December 19, 1990, 1, 4.

17 Michele Wallace, *Black Macho and the Myth of the Super Woman* (New York: Dial Press, 1978), 80. Adolescents may face serious problems if their physical development makes them appear to be more mature than they are. See Blos, "Child Analyst," p. 53.

18 Quida E. Westney, Reness R. Jenkins, June Dobbs Butts, and Irving Williams, "Dating and Sexual Patterns, Sexual Development and Behavior in Black Preadolescents," in *Young, Black and Male in America: An Endangered Species*, ed. Reginald Jones (Dover,

MA: Auburn House Publishing, 1988), 55–65.

19 Ibid; Maris A. Vinovskis, "An 'Epidemic' of Adolescent Pregnancy? Some Historical Considerations," *Journal of Family History* 6, no. 2 (summer, 1981): 205–30; P. Reichelt and H. Werley, "Contraception, Abortion, and Venereal Disease: Teenagers' Knowledge and the Effect of Education," *Family Planning Perspectives* 7 (1975): 83–8; Kagan and Coles, *Twelve to Sixteen.*

20 Perhaps one way to change the cultural attitude about the menstrual cycle would be to institute a ritual celebrating menstruation and budding sexuality. Such a ritual would honor adolescence as a special time in a young girl's life. We could use as an example the Bat Mitzva celebration held for Jewish girls when they reach the age of 13. Another useful example is the Nevada Washoe Indians' celebration of their girls' passage to adulthood. They hold a dance in the young girl's honor along with a month-long celebration in which the girl, the center of attention and affection, is praised for making the passage into adulthood. Susan Carter said that she simply wanted her mother to say, "Congratulations, you're growing up."

21 See Greer Litton Fox and Judith K. Inazu, "Patterns and Outcomes of Mother–Daughter Communication about Sexuality," *Journal of Social Issues* 36, no. 1 (1980): 113. Also see Musick, "High-Stakes Challenge," p. 130.

22 There may be several reasons for Tracy's mother's failure to inform her daughter about birth control. She herself may be confused and uninformed about sexuality. See Ellen Eliason Kisker, "Teenagers Talk about Sex, Pregnancy and Contraception," *Family Planning Perspectives* 17, no. 2 (March–April 1985): 89. Kisker's study on adolescents' sexual behavior finds that parents are not better informed than their children. Several of the adult mothers in this study admitted they did not feel comfortable discussing sexual matters with their children. Also see Fox and Inazu, "Patterns and Outcomes," p. 9. The authors reviewed literature on parent and child communication about sexuality. They found that mothers of adolescents will not share actual information about their own sexual behavior. Although 76 percent of the mothers in the study were using birth control, their children reported that their mothers did not use any form of birth control. The authors found that children never cite parents as the source of information about sexuality. Also see Deborah Anne Dawson, "The Effects of Sex Education on Adolescent Behavior," *Family Planning Perspectives* 18, no. 4 (July–August 1986): 45–50; Joyce Ladner and Ruby Morton Gourdine, "Intergenerational Teenage Motherhood: Some Preliminary Findings," *Sage* (fall 1984): 22–4. Also see Barbara Ann Sachs, "The Relationship of Cognitive Development to Interpersonal Problem Solving Abilities in Female Adolescents" (Ph.D. diss., University of California, Berkeley, 1981). Sachs makes several excellent suggestions for informing inner-city adolescents: offer them contraceptive information, offer information at differing cognitive levels, develop and test tools to screen levels of cognitive development so that adolescents can be placed in different groups for developmentally based teaching, and help those who have chosen contraception to plan step-by-step means to reach their goal of nonreproduction. I would suggest, however, that before we can give them control over their reproductive behavior, they need to feel there is a reason to control it. Also see Christine Galavotti, "Predictors of Risk-Taking, Preventive Behavior and Contraceptive Use among Inner-City Adolescents" (Ph.D. diss., University of California, Berkeley, 1987). Galavotti suggests that teenagers may not have a consistent view about control over health or pregnancy.

23 Elizah Anderson, "Sex Codes and Family Life among Poor Inner-City Youths," in *The Annals of the American Academy of Political and Social Science*, ed. William J. Wilson (Newbury Park, CA: Sage Publications, 1989), 59–78; Wallace, *Black Macho.*

24 See Sara McLanahan, "Family Structure and Stress: A Longitudinal Comparison of Two-Parent and Female-Headed Families," *Journal of Marriage and the Family* 9 (1983): 25. Also see G. Cvetknovitch and B. Grote, "Psychological Development and the Social Problem of Teenage Illegitimacy," in *Adolescent Pregnancy and Childbearing: Findings*

from Research, ed. C. Chilman (Washington, DC: US Department of Health and Human Services, 1980), 28; Robert Coles and Geoffrey Stokes, *Sex and the American Teenager* (New York: Harper & Row, 1985); M. L. Clark, "Friendships and Peer Relations of Black Adolescents," in *Black Adolescents*, ed. Reginald L. Jones (Berkeley: University of California Press, 1989), 174. Adolescents may be swayed to become sexually active by the belief that their friends are doing so.

25 Cole and Stokes, "Sex and the American Teenager." Cole and Stokes argue that other variables associated with socioeconomic status may also help explain the high rate of sexual activity among Black teenage males. For urban Black teenage males, poverty, poor educational facilities, high unemployment, fatalistic attitudes, and the need to "prove" oneself may play a significant role in early sexual experimentation. Private communication with Lillian Rubin, author of *Erotic Wars: What Happened to the Sexual Revolution?* (New York: Harper-Collins, 1990).

26 Anderson, "Sex Codes," pp. 59–78.

27 Dash, "Black Teenage Pregnancy," p. 9. Also see Judith Blake, *Comparative Youth Culture* (Boston: Routledge & Kegan Paul, 1985).

28 Kristen Luker, "Understanding the Risk-Taker," *The Family Planner* 30 (summer 1977): 1–2. Also see Kristen Luker, *Taking Chances: Abortion and the Decision Not to Contracept* (Berkeley: University of California Press, 1975); Judith Senderovitz and John M. Paxman, "Adolescent Fertility: Worldwide Concerns," *Population Bulletin* 40, no. 2 (April 1985): 22.

29 Alan Guttmacher Institute, *Fact Book on Teenage Pregnancy* (New York: Alan Guttmacher Institute, 1981). The Alan Guttmacher Institute reports that the general public supports sexuality education programs; however, the issue is controversial since opposition groups contend that information and education cause promiscuity.

30 See Susan Gustavus Philliber, "Socialization for Childbearing," *Journal of Social Issues* 36, no. 1 (1980): 230–45.

Part IV

Sexual Objectification

Sex sells. This has been a truism of capitalist marketing since the turn of the twentieth century, when images of scantily clad women were first used to advertise products. The trade in women's bodies takes many forms today, including pornography, prostitution, and sexualized service work. Scholars debate whether the effects of this sexual objectification are entirely negative for women. Patricia Hill Collins argues that popular culture often portrays black women as sexually promiscuous and degraded "Jezebels," with especially insidious consequences. This controlling image justifies black women's economic sexploitation, and enhances their vulnerability to rape. At the same time, myths of black male sexuality have contributed to the long history of violence against black men that often took the form of lynching. While the racist and sexist objectifica-tion of women in capitalism victimizes many women and men, some argue that women employed in sex work can engage in polit-ical struggle over the meaning of sexuality. People on this side of the debate argue that it is possible to find ways in the existing system of patriarchy to challenge male dom-ination. They believe that prostitution and pornography are possibly liberating for women, depending on the circumstances. Many of those writing in this perspective argue that women in sex work are like all women workers, and that they should have the same rights and privileges, like protec-tion from sexual harassment and discrimin-ation. Wendy Chapkis, Meika Loe, and Patti Giuffre and Christine Williams highlight the efforts of women in sexualized jobs to take control of the circumstances of their em-ployment.

13 The Sexual Politics of Black Womanhood

Patricia Hill Collins

Even I found it almost impossible to let her say what had happened to her as *she* perceived it...And why? Because once you strip away the lie that rape is pleasant, that children are not permanently damaged by sexual pain, that violence done to them is washed away by fear, silence, and time, you are left with the positive horror of the lives of thousands of children...who have been sexually abused and who have never been permitted their own language to tell about it.

Alice Walker 1988: 57

In *The Color Purple* Alice Walker creates the character of Celie, a Black adolescent girl who is sexually abused by her stepfather. By writing letters to God and forming supportive relationships with other Black women, Celie finds her own voice, and her voice enables her to transcend the fear and silence of her childhood. By creating Celie and giving her the language to tell of her sexual abuse, Walker adds Celie's voice to muted yet growing discussions of the sexual politics of Black womanhood in Black feminist thought. Black feminists have investigated how rape as a specific form of sexual violence is embedded in a system of interlocking race, gender, and class oppression (Davis 1978, 1981, 1989; Hall 1983). Reproductive rights issues such as access to information on sexuality and birth control, the struggles for abortion rights, and patterns of forced sterilization have also garnered attention (Davis 1981). Black lesbian feminists have vigorously challenged the basic assumptions and mechanisms of control underlying compulsory heterosexuality and have investigated homophobia's impact on African-American women (Clarke 1983; Shockley 1983; Smith 1983; Lorde 1984).

But when it comes to other important issues concerning the sexual politics of Black womanhood, like Alice Walker, Black feminists have found it almost impossible to say what has happened to Black women. In the flood of scholarly and popular writing about Black heterosexual relationships, analyses of domestic violence against African-American women – especially those that link this form of sexual violence to existing gender ideology concerning Black masculinity and Black femininity – remain rare. Theoretical work explaining patterns of Black women's inclusion in the burgeoning international pornography industry has been similarly neglected. Perhaps the most curious omission has been the virtual silence of the Black feminist community concerning the participation of far too many Black women in prostitution. Ironically, while the image of African-American women as prostitutes has been aggressively challenged, the reality of African-American women who work as prostitutes remains unexplored.

These patterns of inclusion and neglect in Black feminist thought merit investigation. Examining the links between sexuality and power in a system of interlocking race, gender, and class oppression should reveal how important controlling Black women's sexuality has been to the effective operation of domination overall. The words of Angela Davis, Audre Lorde, Barbara Smith, and Alice Walker provide a promising foundation for a comprehensive Black feminist analysis. But Black feminist analyses of sexual politics must go beyond chronicling how sexuality has been used to oppress. Equally important is the need to reconceptualize sexuality with an eye toward empowering African-American women.

A Working Definition of Sexual Politics

Sexual politics examines the links between sexuality and power. In defining sexuality it is important to distinguish among sexuality and the related terms, *sex* and *gender* (Vance 1984; Andersen 1988). Sex is a biological category attached to the body – humans are born female or male. In contrast, gender is socially constructed. The sex/gender system consists of marking the categories of biological sex with socially constructed gender meanings of masculinity and femininity. Just as sex/gender systems vary from relatively egalitarian systems to sex/gender hierarchies, ideologies of sexuality attached to particular sex/gender systems exhibit similar diversity. Sexuality is socially constructed through the sex/gender system on both the personal level of individual consciousness and interpersonal relationships and the social structural level of social institutions (Foucault 1980). This multilevel sex/gender system reflects the needs of a given historical moment such that social constructions of sexuality change in tandem with changing social conditions.

African-American women inhabit a sex/gender hierarchy in which inequalities of race and social class have been sexualized. Privileged groups define their alleged sexual practices as the mythical norm and label sexual practices and groups who diverge from this norm as deviant and threatening (Lorde 1984; Vance 1984). Maintaining the mythical norm of the financially independent, white middle-class family organized around a monogamous heterosexual couple requires stigmatizing African-American families as being deviant, and a primary source of this assumed deviancy stems from allegations about Black sexuality. This sex/gender hierarchy not only operates on the social structural level but is potentially replicated within each individual. Differences in sexuality thus take on more meaning than just benign sexual variation. Each individual becomes a powerful conduit for social relations of domination whereby individual anxieties, fears, and doubts about sexuality can be annexed by larger systems of oppression (Hoch 1979; Foucault 1980: 99).

According to Cheryl Clarke, African Americans have been profoundly affected by this sex/gender hierarchy:

> Like all Americans, black Americans live in a sexually repressive culture. And we have made all manner of compromise regarding our sexuality in order to live here. We have expended much energy trying to debunk the racist mythology which says our sexuality is depraved. Unfortunately, many of us have overcompensated and assimilated. . . . Like everyone else in America who is ambivalent in these respects, black folk have to live with the contradictions of this limited sexual system by repressing or closeting any other sexual/erotic urges, feelings, or desires. *(Clarke 1983: 199)*

Embedded in Clarke's statement is the theme of self-censorship inherent when a hierarchy of any kind invades interpersonal relationships among individuals and the actual consciousness of individuals themselves. Sexuality and power as domination become intertwined.

In her ground-breaking essay, "Uses of the Erotic: The Erotic as Power," Black feminist poet Audre Lorde explores this fundamental link between sexuality and power:

> There are many kinds of power, used and unused, acknowledged or otherwise. The erotic is a resource within each of us that lies in a deeply female and spiritual plane, firmly rooted in the power of our unexpressed or unrecognized feeling. In order to perpetuate itself, every oppression must corrupt or distort those various sources of power within the culture of the oppressed that can provide energy for change. For women, this has meant a suppression of the erotic as a considered source of power and information in our lives. *(Lorde 1984: 53)*

For Lorde, sexuality is a component of the larger construct of the erotic as a source of power in women. Lorde's notion is one of power as energy, as something people possess which must be annexed in order for larger systems of oppression to function.[1]

Sexuality becomes a domain of restriction and repression when this energy is tied to the larger system of race, class, and gender oppression. But Lorde's words also signal the potential for Black women's empowerment by showing sexuality and the erotic to be a domain of exploration, pleasure, and human agency. From a Black feminist standpoint sexuality encompasses the both/and nature of human existence, the potential for a sexuality that simultaneously oppresses and empowers.

One key issue for Black feminist thought is the need to examine the processes by which power as domination on the social structural level – namely, institutional structures of racism, sexism, and social class privilege – annexes this basic power of the erotic on the personal level – that is, the construct of power as energy, for its own ends.

Black Women and the Sex/gender Hierarchy

The social construction of Black women's sexuality is embedded in this larger, overarching sex/gender hierarchy designed to harness power as energy to the exigencies of power as race, gender, and social class domination. Pornography, prostitution, and rape as a specific tool of sexual violence have also been key to the sexual politics of Black womanhood. Together they form three essential and interrelated components of the sex/gender hierarchy framing Black women's sexuality.

Pornography and Black women's bodies

For centuries the black woman has served as the primary pornographic "outlet" for

white men in Europe and America. We need only think of the black women used as breeders, raped for the pleasure and profit of their owners. We need only think of the license the "master" of the slave women enjoyed. But, most telling of all, we need only study the old slave societies of the South to note the sadistic treatment – at the hands of white "gentlemen" – of "beautiful young quadroons and octoroons" who became increasingly (and were deliberately bred to become) indistinguishable from white women, and were the more highly prized as slave mistresses because of this. *(Walker 1981: 42)*

Alice Walker's description of the rape of enslaved African women for the "pleasure and profit of their owners" encapsulates several elements of contemporary pornography. First, Black women were used as sex objects for the pleasure of white men. This objectification of African-American women parallels the portrayal of women in pornography as sex objects whose sexuality is available for men (McNall 1983). Exploiting Black women as breeders objectified them as less than human because only animals can be bred against their will. In contemporary pornography women are objectified through being portrayed as pieces of meat, as sexual animals awaiting conquest. Second, African-American women were raped, a form of sexual violence. Violence is typically an implicit or explicit theme in pornography. Moreover, the rape of Black women linked sexuality and violence, another characteristic feature of pornography (Eisenstein 1983). Third, rape and other forms of sexual violence act to strip victims of their will to resist and make them passive and submissive to the will of the rapist. Female passivity, the fact that women have things done to them, is a theme repeated over and over in contemporary pornography (McNall 1983). Fourth, the profitability of Black women's sexual exploitation for white "gentlemen" parallels pornography's financially lucrative benefits for pornographers (Eisenstein 1983). Finally, the actual breeding of "quadroons and octoroons" not only reinforces the themes of Black women's passivity, objectification, and malleability to male control but reveals pornography's grounding in racism and sexism. The fates of both Black and white women were intertwined in this breeding process. The ideal African-American woman as a pornographic object was indistinguishable from white women and thus approximated the images of beauty, asexuality, and chastity forced on white women. But inside was a highly sexual whore, a "slave mistress" ready to cater to her owner's pleasure.[2]

Contemporary pornography consists of a series of icons or representations that focus the viewer's attention on the relationship between the portrayed individual and the general qualities ascribed to that class of individuals. Pornographic images are iconographic in that they represent realities in a manner determined by the historical position of the observers, their relationship to their own time, and to the history of the conventions which they employ (Gilman 1985). The treatment of Black women's bodies in nineteenth-century Europe and the United States may be the foundation upon which contemporary pornography as the representation of women's objectification, domination, and control is based. Icons about the sexuality of Black women's bodies emerged in these contexts. Moreover, as race/gender-specific representations, these icons have implications for the treatment of both African-American and white women in contemporary pornography.

I suggest that African-American women were not included in pornography as an afterthought but instead form a key pillar on which contemporary pornography itself rests. As Alice Walker points out, "the more ancient roots of modern pornography are to be found in the almost always pornographic treatment of black women who, from the moment they entered slavery...were subjected to rape as the 'logical' convergence of sex and violence. Conquest, in short" (Walker 1981: 42).

One key feature about the treatment of Black women in the nineteenth century was how their bodies were objects of display. In the antebellum American South white men did not have to look at pornographic pictures of women because they could become voyeurs of Black women on the auction block. A chilling example of this objectification of the Black female body is provided by the exhibition, in early nineteenth-century Europe, of Sarah Bartmann, the so-called Hottentot Venus. Her display formed one of the original icons for Black female sexuality. An African woman, Sarah Bartmann was often exhibited at fashionable parties in Paris, generally wearing little clothing, to provide entertainment. To her audience she represented deviant sexuality. At the time European audiences thought that Africans had deviant sexual practices and searched for physiological differences, such as enlarged penises and malformed female genitalia, as indications of this deviant sexuality. Sarah Bartmann's exhibition stimulated these racist and sexist beliefs. After her death in 1815, she was dissected. Her genitalia and buttocks remain on display in Paris (Gilman 1985).

Sander Gilman explains the impact that Sarah Bartmann's exhibition had on Victorian audiences:

> It is important to note that Sarah Bartmann was exhibited not to show her genitalia – but rather to present another anomaly which the European audience... found riveting. This was the steatopygia, or protruding buttocks, the other physical characteristic of the Hottentot female which captured the eye of early European travelers.... The figure of Sarah Bartmann was reduced to her sexual parts. The audience which had paid to see her buttocks and had fantasized about the uniqueness of her genitalia when she was alive could, after her death and dissection, examine both. *(ibid: 213)*

In this passage Gilman unwittingly describes how Bartmann was used as a pornographic object similar to how women are represented in contemporary pornography. She was reduced to her sexual parts, and these parts came to represent a dominant icon applied to Black women throughout the nineteenth century. Moreover, the fact that Sarah Bartmann was both African and a woman underscores the importance of gender in maintaining notions of racial purity. In this case Bartmann symbolized Blacks as a "race." Thus the creation of the icon applied to Black women demonstrates that notions of gender, race, and sexuality were linked in overarching structures of political domination and economic exploitation.

The process illustrated by the pornographic treatment of the bodies of enslaved African women and of women like Sarah Bartmann has developed into a full-scale industry encompassing all women objectified differently by racial/ethnic category. Contemporary portrayals of Black women in pornography represent the continuation of the historical treatment of their actual bodies. African-American women are usually depicted in a situation of bondage and slavery, typically in a submissive posture, and often with two white men. As Bell observes, "this setting reminds us of all the trappings of slavery: chains, whips, neck braces, wrist clasps" (Bell 1987: 59). White women and women of color have different pornographic images applied to them. The image of Black women in pornography is almost consistently one featuring them breaking from chains. The image of Asian women in pornography is almost consistently one of being tortured (ibid: 161).

The pornographic treatment of Black women's bodies challenges the prevailing feminist assumption that since pornography primarily affects white women, racism has been grafted onto pornography. African-American women's experiences suggest that Black women were not added into a preexisting pornography, but rather that pornography itself must be reconceptualized as an example of the interlocking nature of race, gender, and class oppression. At the heart of both racism and sexism are notions of biological determinism claiming that people of African descent and women possess immutable biological characteristics marking their inferiority to elite white men (Gould 1981; Fausto-Sterling 1989; Halpin 1989). In pornography these racist and sexist beliefs are sexualized. Moreover, for African-American women pornography has not been timeless and universal but was tied to Black women's experiences with the European colonization of African and with American slavery. Pornography emerged within a specific system of social class relationships.

This linking of views of the body, social constructions of race and gender, and conceptualizations of sexuality that inform Black women's treatment as pornographic objects promises to have significant implications for how we assess contemporary pornography. Moreover, examining how pornography has been central to the race, gender, and class oppression of African-American women offers new routes for understanding the dynamics of power as domination.

Investigating racial patterns in pornography offers one route for such an analysis. Black women have often claimed that images of white women's sexuality were intertwined with the controlling image of the sexually denigrated Black woman: "In the United States, the fear and fascination of female sexuality was projected onto black women; the passionless lady arose in symbiosis with the primitively sexual slave" (Hall 1983: 333). Comparable linkages exist in pornography (Gardner 1980). Alice Walker provides a fictional account of a Black man's growing awareness of the different ways that African-American and white women are objectified in pornography: "What he has refused to see – because to see it would reveal yet another area in which he is unable to protect or defend black women – is that where white women are depicted in pornography as 'objects,' black women are depicted as animals. Where white women are depicted as human bodies if not beings, black women are depicted as shit" (Walker 1981: 52).

Walker's distinction between "objects" and "animals" is crucial in untangling gender, race, and class dynamics in pornography. Within the mind/body, culture/nature, male/female oppositional dichotomies in Western social thought, objects occupy an uncertain interim position. As objects white women become creations of culture – in this case, the mind of white men – using the materials of nature – in this case, uncontrolled female sexuality. In contrast, as animals Black women receive no such redeeming dose of culture and remain open to the type of exploitation visited on nature overall. Race becomes the distinguishing feature in determining the type of objectification women will encounter. Whiteness as symbolic of both civilization and culture is used to separate objects from animals.

The alleged superiority of men to women is not the only hierarchical relationship that has been linked to the putative superiority of the mind to the body. Certain "races" of people have been defined as being more bodylike, more animallike, and less godlike than others (Spelman 1982: 52). Race and gender oppression may both revolve around the same axis of disdain for the body; both portray the sexuality of subordinate groups as animalistic and therefore deviant. Biological notions of race and gender prevalent in the early nineteenth century which fostered the animalistic icon of Black female sexuality were joined by the appearance of a racist biology incorporating the concept of degeneracy (Foucault 1980). Africans and women were both perceived as embodied entities, and Blacks were seen as degenerate. Fear of and disdain for the body thus formed a key element in both sexist and racist thinking (Spelman 1982).

While the sexual and racial dimensions of being treated like an animal are important, the economic foundation underlying this treatment is critical. Animals can be economically exploited, worked, sold, killed, and consumed. As "mules," African-American women become susceptible to such treatment. The political economy of pornography also merits careful attention. Pornography is pivotal in mediating contradictions in changing societies (McNall 1983). It is no accident that racist biology, religious justifications for slavery and women's subordination, and other explanations for nineteenth-century racism and sexism arose during a period of profound political and economic change. Symbolic means of domination become particularly important in mediating contradictions in changing political economies. The exhibition of Sarah Bartmann and Black women on the auction block were not benign intellectual exercises – these practices defended real material and political interests. Current transformations in international capitalism require similar ideological justifications. Where does pornography fit in these current transformations? This question awaits a comprehensive Afrocentric feminist analysis.

Publicly exhibiting Black women may have been central to objectifying Black women as animals and to creating the icon of Black women as animals. Yi-Fu Tuan (1984) offers an innovative argument about similarities in efforts to control nature – especially plant life – the domestication of animals, and the domination of certain groups of humans. Tuan suggests that displaying humans alongside animals implies that such humans are more like monkeys and bears than they are like "normal" people. This same juxtaposition leads spectators to view the captive animals in a special way. Animals acquire definitions of being like humans, only more openly carnal and sexual, an aspect of animals that forms a major source of attraction for visitors to modern zoos. In discussing the popularity of monkeys in zoos, Tuan notes: "some visitors are especially attracted by the easy sexual behavior of the monkeys. Voyeurism is forbidden except when applied to subhumans" (ibid: 82). Tuan's analysis suggests that the public display of Sarah Bartmann and of the countless enslaved African women on the auction blocks of the antebellum American South – especially in proximity to animals – fostered their image as animalistic.

This linking of Black women and animals is evident in nineteenth-century scientific literature. The equation of women, Blacks, and animals is revealed in the following description of an African woman published in an 1878 anthropology text:

> She had a way of pouting her lips exactly like what we have observed in the orang-utan. Her movements had something abrupt and fantastical about them, reminding one of those of the ape. Her ear was like that of many apes.... These are animal characters. I have never seen a human head more like an ape than that of this woman. *(Halpin 1989: 287)*

In a climate such as this, it is not surprising that one prominent European physician even stated that Black women's "animallike sexual appetite went so far as to lead black women to copulate with apes" (Gilman 1985: 212).

The treatment of all women in contemporary pornography has strong ties to the portrayal of Black women as animals. In pornography women become nonpeople and are often represented as the sum of their fragmented body parts. Scott McNall observes:

> This fragmentation of women relates to the predominance of rear-entry position photographs.... All of these kinds of photographs reduce the woman to her reproductive system, and, furthermore, make her open, willing, and available – not in control.... The other thing rear-entry position photographs tell us about women is that they are animals. They are animals because they are the same as dogs – bitches in heat who can't control themselves. *(McNall 1983: 197–8)*

This linking of animals and white women within pornography becomes feasible when grounded in the earlier denigration of Black women as animals.

Developing a comprehensive analysis of the race, gender, and class dynamics of pornography offers possibilities for change. Those Black feminist intellectuals investigating sexual politics imply that the situation is much more complicated than that advanced by some prominent white feminists (see, for example, Dworkin 1981) in which "men oppress women" because they are men. Such approaches implicitly assume biologically deterministic views of sex, gender, and sexuality and offer few possibilities for change. In contrast, Afrocentric feminist analyses routinely provide for human agency and its corresponding empowerment and for the responsiveness of social structures to human action. In the short story "Coming Apart," Alice Walker describes one Black man's growing realization that his enjoyment of pornography, whether of white women as "objects" or Black women as "animals," degraded him:

> He begins to feel sick. For he realizes that he has bought some of the advertisements about women, black and white. And further, inevitably, he has bought the advertisements about himself. In pornography the black man is portrayed as being capable of fucking anything...even a piece of shit. He is defined solely by the size, readiness and unselectivity of his cock. *(Walker 1981: 52)*

Walker conceptualizes pornography as a race/gender system that entraps everyone. But by exploring an African-American *man's* struggle for a self-defined standpoint on pornography, Walker suggests that a changed consciousness is essential to social change. If a Black man can understand how pornography affects him, then other groups enmeshed in the same system are equally capable of similar shifts in consciousness and action.

Prostitution and the commodification of sexuality

In *To Be Young, Gifted and Black* Lorraine Hansberry creates three characters: a young domestic worker, a chic professional, middle-aged woman, and a mother in her thirties. Each speaks a variant of the following:

> In these streets out there, any little white boy from Long Island or Westchester sees me and leans out of his car and yells – "Hey there, *hot chocolate*! Say there, Jezebel! Hey you – 'Hundred Dollar Misunderstanding'! YOU! Bet you know where there's a good time tonight . . . " Follow me sometimes and see if I lie. I can be coming from eight hours on an assembly line or fourteen hours in Mrs. Halsey's kitchen. I can be all filled up that day with three hundred years of rage so that my eyes are flashing and my flesh is trembling – and the white boys in the streets, they look at me and think of sex. They look at me and that's *all* they think. . . . Baby, you could be Jesus in drag – but if you're brown they're sure you're selling! *(Hansberry 1969: 98)*

Like the characters in Hansberry's fiction, all Black women are affected by the widespread controlling image that African-American women are sexually promiscuous, potential prostitutes. The pervasiveness of this image is vividly recounted in Black activist lawyer Pauli Murray's description of an incident she experienced while defending two women from Spanish Harlem who had been arrested as prostitutes: "The first witness, a white man from New Jersey, testified on the details of the sexual transaction and his payment of money. When asked to identify the woman with whom he had engaged in sexual intercourse, he unhesitatingly pointed directly at me, seated beside my two clients at the defense table!" (Murray 1987: 274). Murray's clients were still convicted.

The creation of Jezebel, the image of the sexually denigrated Black woman, has been vital in sustaining a system of interlocking race, gender, and class oppression. Exploring how the image of the African-American woman as prostitute has been used by each system of oppression illustrates how sexuality links the three systems. But Black women's treatment also demonstrates how manipulating sexuality has been essential to the political economy of domination within each system and across all three.

Yi-Fu Tuan (1984) suggests that power as domination involves reducing humans to animate nature in order to exploit them economically or to treat them condescendingly as pets. Domination may be either cruel and exploitative with no affection or may be exploitative yet coexist with affection. The former produces the victim – in this case, the Black woman as "mule" whose labor has been exploited. In contrast, the combination of dominance and affection produces the pet, the individual who is subordinate but whose survival depends on the whims of the more powerful. The "beautiful young quadroons and octoroons" described by Alice Walker were bred to be pets – enslaved Black mistresses whose existence required that they retain the affection of their owners. The treatment afforded these women illustrates a process that affects all African-American women: their portrayal as actual or potential victims and pets of elite white males.[3]

African-American women simultaneously embody the coexistence of the victim and the pet, with survival often linked to the ability to be appropriately subordinate as victims or pets. Black women's experiences as unpaid and paid workers demonstrate the harsh lives victims are forced to lead. While the life of the victim is difficult, pets experience a distinctive form of exploitation. Zora Neale Hurston's 1943 essay, "The 'Pet' Negro System," speaks contemptuously of this ostensibly benign situation that combines domination with affection. Written in a Black oratorical style, Hurston notes, "Brother and Sisters, I take my text this morning from the Book of Dixie. . . . Now it says here, 'And every white man shall be allowed to pet himself a Negro. Yea, he shall take a black man unto himself to pet and cherish, and this same Negro shall be perfect in his sight'" (Walker 1979: 156). Pets are treated as exceptions and live with the constant threat that they will no longer be "perfect in his sight," that their owners will tire of them and relegate them to the unenviable role of victim.

Prostitution represents the fusion of exploitation for an economic purpose – namely, the commodification of Black women's sexuality – with the demeaning treatment afforded pets. Sex becomes commodified not merely in the sense that it can be purchased – the dimension of economic exploitation – but also in the sense that one is dealing with a totally alienated being who is separated from and who does not control her body: the dimension of power as domination (McNall 1983). Commodified sex can then be appropriated by the powerful. When the "white boys from Long Island" look at Black women and *all* they think about is sex, they believe that they can appropriate Black women's bodies. When they yell "Bet you know where there's a good time tonight," they expect commodified sex with Black women as "animals" to be better than sex with white women as "objects." Both pornography and prostitution commodify sexuality and imply to the "white boys" that all African-American women can be bought.

Prostitution under European and American capitalism thus exists within a complex web of political and economic relationships whereby sexuality is conceptualized along intersecting axes of race and gender. Gilman's (1985) analysis of the exhibition of Sarah Bartmann as the "Hottentot Venus" suggests another intriguing connection between race, gender, and sexuality in nineteenth-century Europe – the linking of the icon of the Black woman with the icon of the white prostitute. While the Hottentot woman stood for the essence of Africans as a race, the white prostitute symbolized the sexualized woman. The prostitute represented the embodiment of sexuality and all that European society associated with it: disease as well as passion. As Gilman points out, "it is this uncleanliness, this disease, which forms the final link between two images of women, the black and the prostitute. Just as the genitalia of the Hottentot were perceived as parallel to the diseased genitalia of the prostitute, so too the power of the idea of corruption links both images" (ibid: 237). These connections between the icons of Black women and white prostitutes demonstrate how race, gender, and the social class structure of the European political economy interlock.

In the American antebellum South both of these images were fused in the forced prostitution of enslaved African women. The prostitution of Black women allowed white women to be the opposite; Black "whores" make white "virgins" possible. This race/gender nexus fostered a situation whereby white men could then differentiate between the sexualized woman-as-body who is dominated and "screwed" and the asexual woman-as-pure-spirit who is idealized and brought home to mother (Hoch 1979: 70). The sexually denigrated woman, whether she was made a victim through her rape or a pet through her seduction, could be used as the yardstick against which the cult of true womanhood was measured. Moreover, this entire situation was profitable.

Rape and sexual violence

Force was important in creating African-American women's centrality to American images of the sexualized woman and in shaping their experiences with both pornography and prostitution. Black women did not willingly submit to their exhibition on southern auction blocks – they were forced to do so. Enslaved African women could not choose whether to work – they were beaten and often killed if they refused. Black domestics who resisted the sexual advances of their employers often found themselves looking for work where none was to be found. Both the reality and the threat of violence have acted as a form of social control for African-American women.

Rape has been one fundamental tool of sexual violence directed against African-American women. Challenging the pervasiveness of Black women's rape and sexual extortion by white men has long formed a prominent theme in Black women's writings. Autobiographies such as Maya Angelou's *I Know Why the Caged Bird Sings* (1970) and Harriet Jacobs's "The Perils of a Slave Woman's Life" (1860/1987) from *Incidents in the Life of a Slave Girl* record examples of actual and threatened sexual assault. The effects of rape on African-American women is a prominent theme in Black women's fiction. Gayl Jones's *Corregidora* (1975) and Rosa Guy's *A Measure of Time* (1983) both explore interracial rape of Black women. Toni Morrison's *The Bluest Eye* (1970), Alice Walker's *The Color Purple* (1982), and Gloria Naylor's *The Women of Brewster Place* (1980) all examine rape within African-American families and communities. Elizabeth Clark-Lewis's (1985) study of domestic workers found that mothers, aunts, and community othermothers warned young Black women about the threat of rape. One respondent in Clark-Lewis's study, an 87-year-old North Carolina Black domestic worker, remembers, "nobody was sent out before you was told to be careful of the white man or his sons" (ibid: 15).

Rape and other acts of overt violence that Black women have experienced, such as physical assault during slavery, domestic abuse, incest, and sexual extortion, accompany Black women's subordination in a system of race, class, and gender oppression. These violent acts are the visible dimensions of a more generalized, routinized system of oppression. Violence against Black women tends to be legitimated and therefore condoned while the same acts visited on other groups may remain nonlegitimated and nonexcusable. Certain forms of violence may garner the backing and control of the state

while others remain uncontrolled (Edwards 1987). Specific acts of sexual violence visited on African-American women reflect a broader process by which violence is socially constructed in a race- and gender-specific manner. Thus Black women, Black men, and white women experience distinctive forms of sexual violence. As Angela Davis points out, "it would be a mistake to regard the institutionalized pattern of rape during slavery as an expression of white men's sexual urges.... Rape was a weapon of domination, a weapon of repression, whose covert goal was to extinguish slave women's will to resist, and in the process, to demoralize their men" (Davis 1981: 23).

Angela Davis's work (1978, 1981, 1989) illustrates this effort to conceptualize sexual violence against African-American women as part of a system of interlocking race, gender, and class oppression. Davis suggests that sexual violence has been central to the economic and political subordination of African-Americans overall. But while Black men and women were both victims of sexual violence, the specific forms they encountered were gender specific.

Depicting African-American men as sexually charged beasts who desired white women created the myth of the Black rapist.[4] Lynching emerged as the specific form of sexual violence visited on Black men, with the myth of the Black rapist as its ideological justification. The significance of this myth is that it "has been methodically conjured up when recurrent waves of violence and terror against the black community required a convincing explanation" (Davis 1978: 25). Black women experienced a parallel form of race- and gender-specific sexual violence. Treating African-American women as pornographic objects and portraying them as sexualized animals, as prostitutes, created the controlling image of Jezebel. Rape became the specific act of sexual violence forced on Black women, with the myth of the Black prostitute as its ideological justification.

Lynching and rape, two race/gender-specific forms of sexual violence, merged with their ideological justifications of the rapist and prostitute in order to provide an effective system of social control over African-Americans. Davis asserts that the controlling image of Black men as rapists has always "strengthened its inseparable companion: the image of the black woman as chronically promiscuous. And with good reason, for once the notion is accepted that black men harbor irresistible, animal-like sexual urges, the entire race is invested with bestiality" (ibid: 27). A race of "animals" can be treated as such – as victims or pets. "The mythical rapist implies the mythical whore – and a race of rapists and whores deserves punishment and nothing more" (ibid: 28).

Some suggestive generalizations exist concerning the connection between the social constructions of the rapist and the prostitute and the tenets of racist biology. Tuan (1984) notes that humans practice certain biological procedures on plants and animals to ensure their suitability as pets. For animals the goal of domestication is manageability and control, a state that can be accomplished through selective breeding or, for some male animals, by castration. A similar process may have affected the historical treatment of African-Americans. Since dominant groups have generally refrained from trying to breed humans in the same way that they breed animals, the pervasiveness of rape and lynching suggests that these practices may have contributed to mechanisms of population control. While not widespread, in some slave settings selective breeding and, if that failed, rape were used to produce slaves of a certain genetic heritage. In an 1858 slave narrative, James Roberts recounts the plantation of Maryland planter Calvin Smith, a man who kept 50–60 "head of women" for reproductive purposes. Only whites were permitted access to these women in order to ensure that 20–25 racially mixed children were born annually. Roberts also tells of a second planter who competed with Smith in breeding mulattos, a group that at that time brought higher prices, the "same as men strive to raise the most stock of any kind, cows, sheep, horses, etc." (Weisbord 1975: 27). For Black men, lynching was frequently accompanied by castration. Again, the parallels to techniques used to domesticate animals, or at least serve as a warning to those Black men who remained alive, is striking.

Black women continue to deal with this legacy of the sexual violence visited on African-Americans generally and with our history as collective rape victims. One effect lies in the treatment of rape victims. Such women are twice victimized, first by the actual rape, in this case the collective rape under slavery. But they are victimized again by family members, community residents, and social institutions such as criminal justice systems which somehow believe that rape victims are responsible for their own victimization. Even though current statistics indicate that Black women are more likely to be victimized than white women, Black women are less likely to report their rapes, less likely to have their cases come to trial, less likely to have their trials result in convictions, and, most disturbing, less likely to seek counseling and other support services. Existing evidence suggests that African-American women are aware of their lack of protection and that they resist rapists more than other groups (Bart and O'Brien 1985).

Another significant effect of this legacy of sexual violence concerns Black women's absence from antirape movements. Angela Davis argues, "if black women are conspicuously absent from the ranks of the antirape movement today, it is, in large part, their way of protesting the movement's posture of indifference toward the frame-up rape charge as an incitement to racist aggression" (Davis 1978: 25). But this absence fosters Black women's silence concerning a troubling issue: the fact that most Black women are raped by Black men. While the historical legacy of the triad of pornography, prostitution, and the institutionalized rape of Black women may have created the larger social context within which all African-Americans reside, the unfortunate current reality is that many Black men have internalized the controlling images of the sex/gender hierarchy and condone either Black women's rape by other Black men or their own behavior as rapists. Far too many African-American women live with the untenable position of putting up with abusive Black men in defense of an elusive Black unity.

The historical legacy of Black women's treatment in pornography, prostitution, and rape forms the institutional backdrop for a range of interpersonal relationships that Black women currently have with Black men, whites, and one another. Without principled coalitions with other groups, African-American women may not be able to effect lasting change on the social structural level of social institutions. But the first step to forming such coalitions is examining exactly how these institutions harness power as energy for their own use by invading both relationships among individuals and individual consciousness itself. Thus understanding the contemporary dynamics of the sexual politics of Black womanhood in order to empower African-American women requires investigating how social structural factors infuse the private domain of Black women's relationships.

NOTES

1   French philosopher Michel Foucault makes a similar point: "I believe that the political significance of the problem of sex is due to the fact that sex is located at the point of intersection of the discipline of the body and the control of the population" (Foucault 1980: 125). The erotic is something felt, a power that is embodied. Controlling sexuality harnesses that power for the needs of larger, hierarchical systems by controlling the body and hence the population.
2   Offering a similar argument about the relationship between race and masculinity, Paul Hoch (1979) suggests that the ideal white

man is a hero who upholds honor. But inside lurks a "Black beast" of violence and sexuality, traits that the white hero deflects onto men of color.
3   Any group can be made into pets. Consider Tuan's (1984) discussion of the role that young Black boys played as exotic ornaments for wealthy white women in the 1500s to the early 1800s in England. Unlike other male servants, the boys were the favorite attendants of noble ladies and gained entry into their mistresses' drawing rooms, bedchambers, and theater boxes. Boys were often given fancy collars with padlocks to wear. "As they did with their pet dogs and monkeys, the ladies grew genuinely fond of their black boys" (ibid: 142).
4   See Hoch's (1979) discussion of the roots of the white hero, black beast myth in Eurocentric thought. Hoch contends that white masculinity is based on the interracial competition for women. To become a "man," the white, godlike hero must prove himself victorious over the dark "beast" and win possession of the "white goddess." Through numerous examples Hoch suggests that this explanatory myth underlies Western myth, poetry, and literature. One example describing how Black men were depicted during the witch hunts is revealing. Hoch notes, "the Devil was often depicted as a lascivious black male with cloven hoofs, a tail, and a huge penis capable of supermasculine exertion – an archetypal leering 'black beast from below'" (ibid: 44).

REFERENCES

Andersen, Margaret. 1988. *Thinking about Women: Sociological Perspectives on Sex and Gender*, 2nd edn. New York: Macmillan.

Angelou, Maya. 1969. *I Know Why the Caged Bird Sings*. New York: Bantam.

Bart, Pauline B. and Patricia H. O'Brien. 1985. "Ethnicity and Rape Avoidance: Jews, White Catholics and Blacks." In *Stopping Rape: Successful Survival Strategies*, edited by Pauline B. Bart and Patricia H. O'Brien, 70–92. New York: Pergamon Press.

Bell, Laurie, ed. 1987. *Good Girls/Bad Girls: Feminists and Sex Trade Workers Face to Face*. Toronto: Seal Press.

Clarke, Cheryl. 1983. "The Failure to Transform: Homophobia in the Black Community." In

Home Girls: A Black Feminist Anthology, edited by Barbara Smith, 197–208. New York: Kitchen Table Press.

Clark-Lewis, Elizabeth. 1985. *"This Work Had a' End": The Transition from Live-In to Day Work*. Southern Women: The Intersection of Race, Class and Gender. Working Paper 2. Memphis, TN: Center for Research on Women, Memphis State University.

Davis, Angela Y. 1978. "Rape, Racism and the Capitalist Setting." *Black Scholar* 9 (7): 24–30.

—— 1981. *Women, Race and Class*. New York: Random House.

—— 1989. *Women, Culture, and Politics*. New York: Random House.

Dworkin, Andrea. 1981. *Pornography: Men Possessing Women*. New York: Perigee.

Edwards, Ann. 1987. "Male Violence in Feminist Theory: An Analysis of the Changing Conceptions of Sex/Gender Violence and Male Dominance." In *Women, Violence and Social Control*, edited by Jalna Hanmer and Mary Maynard, 13–29. Atlantic Highlands, NJ: Humanities Press.

Eisenstein, Hester. 1983. *Contemporary Feminist Thought*. Boston: G. K. Hall.

Fausto-Sterling, Anne. 1989. "Life in the XY Corral." *Women's Studies International Forum* 12 (3): 319–31.

Foucault, Michel. 1980. *Power/Knowledge: Selected Interviews and Other Writings 1972–1977*, edited by Colin Gordon. New York: Pantheon.

Gardner, Tracey A. 1980. "Racism and Pornography in the Women's Movement." In *Take Back the Night: Women on Pornography*, edited by Laura Lederer, 105–14. New York: William Morrow.

Gilman, Sander L. 1985. "Black Bodies, White Bodies: Toward an Iconography of Female Sexuality in Late Nineteenth-Century Art, Medicine, and Literature." *Critical Inquiry* 12 (1): 205–43.

Gould, Stephen Jay. 1981. *The Mismeasure of Man*. New York: W. W. Norton.

Guy, Rosa. 1983. *A Measure of Time*. New York: Bantam.

Hall, Jacqueline Dowd. 1983. "The Mind that Burns in Each Body: Women, Rape, and Racial Violence." In *Powers of Desire: The Politics of Sexuality*, edited by Ann Snitow, Christine Stansell, and Sharon Thompson, 329–49. New York: Monthly Review Press.

Halpin, Zuleyma Tang. 1989. "Scientific Objectivity and the Concept of 'The Other.'" *Women's Studies International Forum* 12 (3): 285–94.

Hansberry, Lorraine. 1959. *A Raisin in the Sun*. New York: Signet.

—— 1969. *To Be Young, Gifted and Black*. New York: Signet.

Hoch, Paul. 1979. *White Hero Black Beast: Racism, Sexism and the Mask of Masculinity*. London: Pluto Press.

Hurston, Zora Neale. [1937] 1969. *Their Eyes Were Watching God*. Greenwich, CT: Fawcett.

Jacobs, Harriet. [1860] 1987. "The Perils of a Slave Woman's Life." In *Invented Lives: Narratives of Black Women 1860–1960*, edited by Mary Helen Washington, 16–67. Garden City, NY: Anchor.

Jones, Gayl. 1975. *Corregidora*. New York: Bantam.

—— 1976. *Eva's Man*. Boston: Beacon.

Lorde, Audre. 1982. *Zami, A New Spelling of My Name*. Trumansberg, NY: The Crossing Press.

—— 1984 *Sister Outsider*. Trumansberg. NY: The Crossing Press.

McNall, Scott G. 1983. "Pornography: The Structure of Domination and the Mode of Reproduction." In *Current Perspectives in Social Theory, Volume 4*, edited by Scott McNall, 181–203. Greenwich, CT: JAI Press.

Morrison, Toni. 1970. *The Bluest Eye*. New York: Pocket Books.

Murray, Pauli, 1987. *Song in a Weary Throat: An American Pilgrimage*. New York: Harper & Row.

Naylor, Gloria, 1980. *The Women of Brewster Place*. New York: Penguin.

—— 1988. *Mama Day*. New York: Vintage.

Shockley, Ann Allen. 1974. *Loving Her*. Tallahassee, FL: Naiad Press.

—— 1983. "The Black Lesbian in American Literature: An Overview." In *Home Girls: A Black Feminist Anthology*, edited by Barbara Smith, 83–93. New York: Kitchen Table Press.

Smith, Barbara, 1983. "Introduction." In *Home Girls: A Black Feminist Anthology*, edited by Barbara Smith, xix–lvi. New York: Kitchen Table Press.

Spelman, Elizabeth V. 1982. "Theories of Race and Gender: The Erasure of Black Women." *Quest* 5 (4): 36–62.

Tuan, Yi-Fu. 1984. *Dominance and Affection: The Making of Pets*. New Haven, CT: Yale University Press.

Vance, Carole S. 1984. "Pleasure and Danger: Toward a Politics of Sexuality." In *Pleasure and Danger: Exploring Female Sexuality*, edited by Carole S. Vance, 1–27. Boston: Routledge & Kegan Paul.

Walker, Alice. ed. 1979. *I Love Myself When I Am Laughing. And Then Again When I Am Looking Mean and Impressive: A Zora Neale Hurston Reader*. Old Westbury, NY: Feminist Press.

—— 1981. "Coming Apart." In *You Can't Keep a Good Woman Down*, 41–53. New York: Harcourt Brace Jovanovich.

—— 1982. *The Color Purple*. New York: Washington Square Press.

—— 1988. *Living by the Word*. New York: Harcourt Brace Jovanovich.

Weisbord, Robert G. 1975. *Genocide?: Birth Control and the Black American*. Westport, CT: Greenwood Press.

14 The Meaning of Sex

Wendy Chapkis

The sexualization of the female body historically has been a concern for women's rights activists. According to feminist historian Sheila Jeffreys, many prominent suffragists at the turn of the century believed that the "sexualization of women led to her being considered fit for no other career than that of sexual object and affected the opportunities of all women for education, work, and general self-development."[1] As a result, they often endorsed purity campaigns which aimed "to free women from the 'degradation of her temple to solely animal uses,' so that she might take a full part in all the areas of life previously arrogated to man."[2] Women's identification with sex was understood, then, to be an important obstacle in the recognition of women as civil subjects rather than simply sexual objects.

Other early women's rights activists challenged this understanding of sex as primarily an expression of women's oppression, arguing instead that sex could and should be an arena of expanded freedom for women. *Freewoman* magazine, for example, founded in 1911 by a former suffragist activist, Dora Marsden, did not shy away from discussions of marriage reform, extramarital and nonmonogamous sex, and (male) homosexuality. From the perspective of the "freewoman," "spinsters" advocating male sexual restraint and purified sexual practices were not only politically misguided but personally repressed. As one correspondent to the *Freewoman* declared:

> it will be an unspeakable catastrophe if our richly complex Feminist movement with its possibilities of power and joy, falls under the domination of sexually deficient and disappointed women...[3]

Similarly acrimonious disputes over the role of sexuality in women's liberation and oppression have dominated debate among women in "second-wave" feminism of the late twentieth century. By the 1980s these disputes had escalated into feminist "sex wars." One effect of organizing conversations around sex as a "war" of positions was the need to define neatly dichotomous and hostile camps. Typically positioned on the one side are "Radical Feminists," portrayed as unrelentingly hostile to sex, which is seen as the source of women's oppression. On the other side, are "Sex Radical" feminists, who are portrayed in equally oversimplified terms as unvaryingly positive toward sex, which is understood as no more than a source of pleasure and power in women's lives.

The reality is far more complex. Feminist thinking on the subject of sex defies simple division into two coherent positions. Not only have many feminists argued in favor of a third camp[4] beyond the two polarized ones, but important differences of perspective exist within the two identified camps. Within so-called Radical Feminism, for instance, there exist at least two distinctive visions of sex. One of these perspectives selectively embraces some limited number of sexual practices as long as they are mutual and loving in their expression, while the other opposes all practices of sexuality because they are understood to be, invariably, expressions of male dominance over women. Similarly, within so-called Sex Radical feminism, distinctions can be made between those who understand sex to be inherently benign; those who see sex as potentially oppressive but only for those women who "choose" to embrace an identity as "victim"; those who view sex as neither inherently empowering nor oppressive but a contested terrain in which women must organize and demand their rights; and those who understand sex to be a cultural practice open to subversive performance and resignification. Within these debates over the meaning and function of sex, practices of prostitution serve as a central trope. The prostitute thus comes to function as both the most literal of sexual slaves and as the most subversive of sexual agents within a sexist social order.

Radical Feminism

Sociologist Steven Seidman argues that within American culture there exist two opposing perspectives on sexuality: "sexual romanticism" and "libertarianism." While libertarians, according to Seidman, believe sex to be benign whether as an expression of love or of pleasure, romanticists firmly tie sex to affection, intimacy, and love:

> Sex, say romanticists, is a way to express intimate feelings; it always implicates the core inner aspects of the self. It should never be approached casually or with an eye to mere erotic pleasure.... It should be gentle, caring, nurturing, respectful and entail reciprocal obligations.[5]

Within Seidman's system of classification, all feminists who oppose prostitution and pornography are relegated to the category of sexual romanticist. But, as Radical Feminist Karen Davis argues, "there are lots of good reasons to dislike objectified sex that do not reduce to a morality of love."[6] While some Radical Feminists do attack prostitution and pornography as corrupting practices undermining a natural foundation of "positive" sex, or eros, based on love, other anti-prostitution feminists see commercial sex as only the most demystified form of sex, which is, by definition, oppressive to women. While the former position might be called a kind of pro-"positive" sex feminism, the latter is outspokenly anti-sex.

Pro-"positive" sex feminism

For those feminists engaged in the recuperative project of attempting to uncover an eros free of the distortions of patriarchy, prostitution and pornography represent a useful foil. They serve as the antithesis of "positive" sexuality. Gloria Steinem, for example, defines the erotic as a "mutually pleasurable sexual expression...rooted in eros or passionate love, and thus in the idea of positive choice, free will, the yearning for a particular person." This she distinguishes from the "pornographic" which

> begins with a root meaning "prostitution"...thus letting us know that the subject is not mutual love, or love at all, but domination and violence against women. ...It ends with a root meaning "writing about"...which puts still more distance between subject and object, and replaces a spontaneous yearning for closeness with objectification and a voyeur.[7]

From this perspective, then, sex can be divided between its "positive" expression in passionate love and its violent articulation in pornographic objectification.

In the hyperbolic terms of feminist writer Jean Bethke Elshtain,

> does not anonymous lovemaking, free from constraints, mimic rather than challenge the anonymous killing of war?...[We must] rethink whether the sexual liberation standard was from its inception the generalization of a norm of adolescent male sexuality writ large onto the wider social fabric.[8]

As Elshtain's comments suggest, for feminist sexual romanticists, certain sexual practices are not only understood to be inherently bad, but also, and not coincidentally, gendered male. Robin Morgan, for instance, argues against a "male sexual style" which emphasizes "genital sexuality, objectification, promiscuity, emotional noninvolvement" in favor of a female-centered sexuality, which would place a "greater trust in love, sensuality, humor, tenderness, commitment."[9] Similarly, Dutch feminist Ariane Amsberg argues:

> It seems to me that prostitution is something that only men could have invented. Women need more of an emotional connection when they are sexually active.... For most people, or at least for most women, sex is absolutely about intimacy and a safe, loving relationship.[10]

When love, relationship, and mutual pleasure are the only appropriate context for sex, cash and contract cannot substitute as evidence of reciprocity. Kathleen Barry thus argues that positive sex "must be earned through trust and sharing. It follows then that sex cannot be purchased."[11] From this perspective, the practice of prostitution is not really sex at all, but an abuse of sex. This misrepresentation sold as sex through prostitution and pornography endangers the possibility of real, positive sexual experience. Commercial sexual culture is seen to be as contaminating as a virus. Kathleen Barry states:

> Pornography no longer describes only the sexual activities between prostitutes and their customers. Sexual liberation has brought into the home many of the bizarre sexual activities that men have demanded with prostitutes. Pornography depicts not just what one can do with a whore but with one's lover, one's wife, and even one's daughter. Through pornography, time-honored distinctions of society are now blurring and the gap is quickly closing between love and violence, madonnas and whores.[12]

Prostitution, then, is seen to be increasingly the model for private sexuality even when there is no formal exchange of money for sex:

> Public sexuality is institutionalized through the massive production and distribution of pornography and through the industrialization of prostitution which has the effect of reducing sex to an object and reducing women to sex [which] objectifies sex into a thing to be gotten, had or taken, disengages sex from its human experience, its dimensionality and places it in a marketing condition *whether in fact it is marketed or not*.... Public sexual exploitation increasingly is becoming the model for private sexual behavior.[13]

Commercial sex, therefore, can be held responsible for both literal and symbolic violence against women. In order to protect women and to preserve the possibility of positive sexual experience, prostitution and pornography must not only be abolished, but their contaminating effect on sexual fantasy and practice must be actively challenged.

This has led some pro-"positive" sex feminists to advocate a politics of cultural cleansing. At "The Sexual Liberals and the Attack on Feminism Conference,"[14] organized in 1987 by Radical Feminists, participants discussed whether it was possible to reclaim any aspect of sex for use by women:

> Ultimately, [British author Sheila] Jeffreys believes that it is possible for lesbians to come up with a vision of egalitarian sexuality, one that doesn't have *all the residue* of heteropatriarchal society. She is doubtful, however, whether heterosexual relations can ever be *cleansed* to the point of equality.[15]

> ...Jeffreys was asked to elaborate on her earlier admission that she has had disturbing fantasies or has been aroused by pornographic material. In response, she commented on her efforts to *purge herself* of undesirable fantasies. She said she has given up fantasizing altogether; she took some time off from sex in order to try something *completely different*.... She suggested that giving up fantasies was a strategy to *cleanse the movement* of S/M.[16]

> ...The answer, according to [feminist sex therapist] Stock is to develop our own model.... We should continue to question

sexuality in order to *detoxify* ourselves from this culture.[17]

For pro-"positive" sex feminists, then, sexuality may be able to be reclaimed from the patriarchy, but not in forms easily recognizable to us as sex. Because prostitution and pornography have already infiltrated our imaginations, women's fantasies and sexual activities must be cleansed of their residue. Pro-"positive" sex feminists advocate the abolition of practices of prostitution both in order to prevent further contamination of the erotic by the pornographic, and to free women from the burdens of sexual objectification by men. The objectification of women through the commodification of sex is understood to reinforce what Carole Pateman calls "male sex-right":

> when women's bodies are on sale as commodities in the capitalist market, the terms of the original [sexual] contract cannot be forgotten; the law of male sex-right is publicly affirmed, and men gain public acknowledgement as women's sexual masters – that is what is wrong with prostitution.[18]

Nancy Fraser, in a sympathetic critique of Pateman's argument, notes, however, that it is marriage and not prostitution that "establishes a long-term, hierarchical status relation whose terms are predetermined and unalterable, and whose roles are assigned according to sex." While a notion of male sex-right may well underlie the patriarchal meaning of sexual difference defining femininity as "subjection," the commodified version of that relationship through prostitution may offer a (limited) challenge to notions of boundless male dominance. The client or employer does not acquire unlimited command over the worker (except significantly, in cases of outright slavery). Thus, Fraser suggests, it is misleading to assimilate "commodification to command" because "even as the wage contract establishes workers as subject to the boss's command in the employment sphere, it simultaneously constitutes that sphere as a limited sphere."[19]

Anti-sex feminism

If, from the vantage point of romanticist feminism, a form of positive sexuality can be recovered through purification and selective abolition (of prostitution and pornography), from the perspective of other Radical Feminists, sex itself must be abolished. From the perspective of anti-sex feminists, there is nothing sexual to recover or reclaim because the very meaning of sex is male domination. Prostitution and pornography only reveal this message most clearly. Catharine MacKinnon, for example, argues that

> sexuality itself is a social construct, gendered to the ground. Male dominance here is not an artificial overlay upon an underlying inalterable substratum of uncorrupted essential sexual being.[20]

For this reason, MacKinnon dismisses romanticist feminism as liberal:

> The critical yet formally liberal view of Susan Griffin [*Pornography and Silence: Culture's Revenge Against Nature*, 1981] conceptualizes eroticism as natural and healthy but corrupted and confused by the "pornographic mind." Pornography distorts Eros, which preexists and persists, despite male culture's pornographic "revenge" upon it. Eros is, unaccountably, still there.[21]

Because sex is understood not to be "contaminated" but rather constituted by male domination, these feminists argue that the practice itself must be abandoned. Karen Davis argues that

> being "anti-sex" is not being against sexuality *per se*, merely against everything that has been organized as sex, everything one has been able to experience as sex within the constraints of our culture.[22]

One of the most explicit statements of this position has been articulated by the Southern

Women's Writing Collective, who organized under the title "Women Against Sex." WAS advocates a strategy of "sex resistance":

> All sex acts subordinate women... all actions that are part of the practice of sexuality partake of the practice's political function or goal.... Thus all sex acts (and their depictions) mean the same thing, though some mean it more than others.[23]

Apparently, while sex always means male dominance, some forms of sexual practice – such as prostitution, s/m, or heterosexual penetration – are more clearly expressive of that dynamic than others (lesbian "vanilla" sex within the bonds of loving relationship, for example). Still, even the most apparently benign kinds of sex are still sex, and hence still an enactment of male supremacy.

From this perspective, it is not enough to reject some of the more apparently abusive sexual practices, it is also necessary to recognize that the language and symbolism of those acts are the building blocks for even that which women perceive to be their most authentic sexual selves. According to WAS, feminist sex resistance must involve resisting "patriarchy's attempt to make its work of subordinating women easier by 'consensually' constructing her desire in its own oppressive image."[24] Female desire must be recreated entirely outside the practices and symbols of contemporary culture. What desire would look like divorced from sex cannot be known:

> Any act which did not subordinate women would literally not be a sex act, but would be "something else."... The practice that could make this happen does not exist. In our feminist future, an act outwardly identical to a sex act might be informed by an entirely different practice. It might stand in a different relationship to conceptual and empirical male force. But the feminist future is where we want to go/be after the defeat of male supremacy – and that is to say, after dismantling the practice of sexuality.[25]

Sex, therefore, cannot be a tool for dismantling male supremacy because it is created by and for it, and is thus inextricably implicated in it. Sex, from this perspective, is "in" us but not "of" us. It is not ours to do with as we would, it does us. The only possible strategic response is opposition to sex:

> There is no way out on the inside of the practice of sexuality except out.... The function of this practice permits no true metamorphoses.[26]

Similarly, Andrea Dworkin insists that sex resists resignification:

> Experience is chosen for us, then imposed on us, especially in intercourse, *and so is its meaning*... We have no freedom and no extravagance in the questions we can ask or the interpretations we can make.... Our bodies speak their language. Our minds think in it. The men are inside us through and through.[27]

Within the anti-sex framework, woman is constituted as and through sex. Thus, not only is sex synonymous with male supremacy and female objectification, but woman is synonymous with whore. Andrea Dworkin states:

> The metaphysics of male sexual domination is that all women are whores. This basic truth transcends all lesser truths in the male system.

In the anti-sex invocation of "whore" (much like that of the romanticists), the prostitute is divorced from the notion of sex *worker* who negotiates a literal exchange of sex for money and is reduced to the position of sex *object* (that is, woman-as-sex, not women-does-sex). "Whore," like "woman," becomes a passive condition rather than a place of active engagement within the social and cultural order. Thus, Catharine MacKinnon insists "men say all women are whores. We say men have the power to make this our fundamental condition."[28] Similarly, Kathleen Barry warns that "women exist as objects and as such will be taken if they don't give themselves."[29]

Women exist only as passive bodies because men have the power to make it so. Within anti-sex and romanticist feminist rhetoric, the prostitute becomes the symbol of women's abject powerlessness under conditions of male objectification and domination; they are simply objects in a marketplace.

> That is what prostitution is about: it is about bodies being exchanged on a market.... So what you have is a lot of bodies in Manila, a lot of bodies in Thailand, a lot of bodies in Saigon that have been used for prostitution. Now what do you do with them [after the US troops withdraw from the region and no longer support the sex trade]? You don't send them home to mother. Prostitution doesn't work that way.[30]

Kathleen Barry thus explains the development of sex tourism in areas that once served as "rest and recreation" centers for American soldiers as strictly the result of traffickers' ingenuity. Women's need for continued employment plays no part; they are only "bodies that have been used for prostitution," soiled and thus no longer suitable to be sent home to mother.[31] Such language joins forces with the power it seeks to challenge. The dialectics of struggle disappear entirely into an apparently seamless system of male supremacy.[32] Male power is constantly reaffirmed even as it is denounced. In this way, anti-sex and romanticist feminist rhetoric tends to reproduce the very ideology it intends to destablize.

By constantly reiterating that women are whores, and that whores are no more than objects, such feminists blind themselves to the fact that prostitutes, no less than any other worker, and no less than any other woman, engage in acts of negotiation, resistance, and subversion that belie their designation as passive objects. Anti-sex feminism,

like pro-"positive" sex feminism, cannot accommodate this reality. Indeed, reality is understood to be identical to the image of it men would wish to impose. MacKinnon states:

> Gender is sexual. Pornography constitutes the meaning of that sexuality. Men treat women as who they see women as being. Pornography constructs who that is. *Men's power over women means that the way men see women defines who women can be.*[33]

Because the positions "inside" culture are defined as fixed, to act defiantly from within the sexual order by making subversive use of that culture is understood to be impossible. The only "radical" feminist act is one of opposition and resistance. The cultural order must be refused.

Sex Radical Feminism and the Meaning of Sex

Contemporary feminist sexual politics encompass positions beyond those of purification and resistance. Some feminists reject the distinction between "positive" and "perverted" sexuality and simultaneously insist on active engagement within the sexual order rather than the abolition of it. Steven Seidman categorizes these alternative positions as sexual "libertarianism." According to Seidman, while sexual romanticists assume that "certain sexual acts carry an intrinsic moral meaning," libertarians "frame sex as having multiple meanings... and [see it as] legitimate in multiple social settings."[34] Because libertarians resist the idea that sexual meaning is fixed, individuals (rather than the community) must determine whether an act is right or wrong for him or her. A libertarian notion of "consent" thus replaces a romanticist notion of "responsibility" as the ultimate measure of the ethics of any sexual activity. Seidman insists that this has the effect of individualizing the meaning of sex to the point where social structures such as gender inequality necessarily disappear from the account.[35]

Just as Seidman's category of sexual romanticism is too narrow to account for the divergent perspectives within Radical Feminism, so too is his designation "libertarian" inadequate to describe the diversity of positions within feminist Sex Radicalism. Among feminists broadly defined as Sex Radicals, a distinction can be drawn between those most closely aligned with the extreme individualism of libertarian ethics and politics, and those who explicitly situate sex (and the individuals enacting it) within structures of power and privilege.

Sexual libertarianism

Sexual libertarianism offers a reversal of the image of sex presented in anti-sex feminism. Both insist that sex, as represented in prostitution and pornography, must be read as reality, and both conclude that the encoded message is one of power. Where these groups diverge is on the question of who holds that power. One of the most prominent voices of the libertarian perspective is Camille Paglia, whose uncompromising pronouncements on sex make her a fair match for such anti-sex feminists as Andrea Dworkin and Catharine MacKinnon. According to Paglia,

> What you see in pornography and prostitution is the reality of sex. It is not a patriarchal distortion. It is the ultimate physical reality. So a feminist who claims to understand sexuality but cannot deal with pornography or topless clubs is no expert. She is a censor. She is a prude.[36]

While Dworkin and MacKinnon read messages of male power and female subjection in commercial sexual culture, Paglia sees the reverse:

> Men are run ragged by female sexuality all their lives. From the beginning of his life to the end, no man ever fully commands any woman. It's an illusion.... That's what the strip clubs are about: not woman as victim, not woman as slave, but woman as goddess.[37]

Paglia insists that women's association with sex should be seen as her source of greatest power, not as the root of her oppression and abuse. Paglia thus intends not only to complicate the notion of women's sexual victimization by men, but to reverse it. It is men who are "run ragged" and feel powerless in the presence of women's sexuality:

> The feminist line is, strippers and topless dancers are degraded, subordinated, and enslaved; they are victims, turned into objects by the display of their anatomy. But women are far from being victims – women *rule*; they are in total control.... The feminist analysis of prostitution says that men are using money as power over women. I'd say, yes, that's all that men *have*. The money is a confession of weakness. They have to buy women's attention. It's not a sign of power; it's a sign of weakness.[38]

If women rule sexually and enjoy total control in their encounters with men, then those who claim to be victims of male sexual violence have only themselves to blame. In this way, sexual power is removed from any social or political context and instead becomes an attribute available to any individual alert enough to claim it.[39] Author bell hooks criticizes this libertarian feminist position for "embracing outmoded sexist visions of female sexual agency and pleasure." Such a politics, she argues, lacks imagination as it conceives of "sexual agency only by inverting the patriarchal standpoint and claiming it as their [women's] own."[40]

hooks is not alone among contemporary feminists in rejecting both the radical individualism of libertarianism as well as the ubiquitous female sexual victimization of Radical Feminism. Many Sex Radical feminists explicitly situate sex within a culture of male domination; sex is understood to be constructed by this culture without being fully determined by it. Carole Vance, for example, suggests that

> to focus only on pleasure and gratification ignores the patriarchal structure in which women act, yet to speak only of sexual violence and oppression ignores women's experience with sexual agency and choice and unwittingly increases the sexual terror and despair in which women live.[41]

Unlike libertarians, feminist Sex Radicals do not fully substitute an ethic of consent for one of responsibility. Social and political context beyond the individual continue to figure prominently in their interpretation and assessment of sex. For example, during her tenure as editor of the lesbian sex magazine *On Our Backs*, Marcy Sheiner objected to photos in another erotic publication, *Future Sex*, on the grounds that they were both racist and sexist. Sheiner challenged these images of sex tourism for glossing over a context of unequal power and privilege:

> I'm the first to admit that these images and ideas generate sexual excitement in many people, even those who are ethically opposed to them. But is arousal potential the sole criteria for what goes into a sex magazine? ... [This question] has plagued me since I penned and sold my first pornographic story several years ago. So while I champion freedom of expression, and continue to create sexual materials, I can't kid myself into believing there are black and white answers to the ethical questions raised during the course of my work.[42]

A similar tension was revealed in 1991 when Bobby Lilly, a leader of a mixed-gender anti-censorship organization in California, CAL-ACT, reported on the struggles of sex workers and Sex Radical feminists to gain a voice within the largest American feminist organization, the National Organization for Women. A male reader returned the issue with the words "what irrelevant garbage" scrawled across the top. He also circled the words "Equal Rights Amendment" and "patriarchal" in the article, commenting that "this has nothing to do with the fight against censorship." Lilly, who "didn't know whether to laugh, cry, or spit," replied that as a feminist and a Sex Radical, her anti-censorship politics could never be gender-blind.[43] Sex Radical feminists and libertarians may both embrace a politics of sexual "free speech," but they diverge on the issue of whether an erotic ethic needs to extend beyond the formal question of consent.

Sexual subversion

Unlike sexual libertarians, feminist Sex Radicals generally accept romanticist and anti-sex feminists' analyses of sex as deeply implicated in structures of inequality. But what distinguishes the Sex Radical perspective is the notion that sex is a terrain of struggle, not a fixed field of gender and power positions. Jana Sawicki explains:

> Neither wholly a source of domination nor of resistance, sexuality is also neither outside power nor wholly circumscribed by it. Instead, it is itself an arena of struggle. There are no inherently liberatory or repressive sexual practices, for any practice is cooptable and any is capable of becoming a source of resistance.[44]

Sex Radical feminists thus share with romanticist and anti-sex feminists a sense of outrage at the existing sexual order, but reject a politics of purification or abolition in favor of one of subversion from within sexual practice. This offers a vision of political struggle not predicated on a cleansing of culture or on a move outside of culture.

From this perspective, acts of apparent complicity may also be acts of subversive resistance. Just as a colonized people may make use of the language of the colonizer in transgressive ways, women are understood to be able to subversively resignify sexual language and practices through using them in unintended ways. Pat Califia, for example, argues that lesbians can liberate a sexual vocabulary for their own use by seizing words previously used against them:

> Words that have been used in anti-sex, anti-lesbian ways can be coopted. By using these terms with pride, lesbians can liberate them and change their meaning. The word "dyke" has already been transformed this way.[45]

Daphne Marlatt has described this subversive relationship to the symbolic order in terms of being "an inhabitant of language, not master, nor even mistress... inside language she leaps for joy, shoving out the walls of taboo and propriety."[46] Such attempts to redefine and reinhabit the sexual order are in part a response to the impossibility of moving to a place outside of culture to create entirely anew. Teresa de Lauretis argues that

> paradoxically, the only way to position oneself outside of that discourse is to displace oneself within it – to refuse the question as formulated, or to answer deviously (though in its words), even to quote (but against the grain).[47]

In addition to the impossibility of moving to a place outside of culture, some feminists argue that a politics predicated on an abolition of the sexual order rather than engagement with it leaves women further impoverished. Betsy Warland, for example, acknowledges the shortcomings of sexual speech in describing women's experiences and desires, but urges women nonetheless to refuse to abandon it:

> the language itself does not reflect women's sensual experience. For most of us, however, it is our native tongue. The only language we have... so when we abandon words, it isn't a simple matter of leaving them behind but rather a turning

over of our power to those who keep them: speechlessness the consequence.[48]

Ntozake Shange wrestles with a similar concern in her decision to make use of sexual speech in her writing:

> One part of the exploitation of people of color – especially women – has been to rob us of any inner life, to rob us of our own sexuality and sensuality.... I hesitate to strip us of a concrete and vital language for sexual activities and desires and fantasies, because I don't think we can afford to lose too much more.[49]

But feminists like Shange who regard sexual language as a crucial resource for women are far from reverent in their uses of it:

> I'm taking words that men have used to make us dirty. I'm taking them to make us able to use them any way we choose... I can get myself in a big bind and never be able to write anything that is honest if I can't somehow uproot words or images that have been malignant and make them constructive for me.[50]

Pat Califia further argues that the meaning of sexual practice no less than sexual language is dependent on the context in which it is employed:

> No erotic act has an intrinsic meaning. A particular sexual activity may symbolize one thing in the majority culture, another thing to members of a sexual subculture.... The context within which an erotic act occurs can also alter its meaning.[51]

It is precisely this commitment to locating sex within a cultural and political context that distinguishes feminist Sex Radicals such as Califia from libertarians such as Paglia. While Paglia would generalize the apparent control a performer has over a client in a strip club to assert that all women "are in total control" of sexual interactions with men, Califia would read the interaction and its meaning as context dependent.

Even in subcultural enactments of sex, dominant culture always remains important. Anne McClintock notes that within the "control frame of cash and fantasy" of commercial s/m, for example, men can "surrender" power to women while still maintaining control outside of that limited frame:

> In the private security of fantasy, men can indulge secretly and guiltily their knowledge of women's power, while enclosing female power in a fantasy land that lies far beyond the cities and towns of genuine feminist change.[52]

McClintock concludes that within the "magic circle" of subcultural sex, "social and personal contradictions can be deployed or negotiated, but need not be finally resolved, for the sources and ends of these paradoxes lie beyond the individual."[53] As sociologist Robert Connell concludes, a true "democracy of pleasure" requires an equalization of resources among and between men and women.[54]

While sexual libertarianism can ignore what lies beyond the individual, feminism cannot. Women are still disproportionately poor, overworked, and underpaid; women are still the deliberate targets of male sexual violence; women's bodies are still heavily regulated by state policies criminalizing subcultural sexual practices and restricting access to birth control and abortion; and women are still stigmatized and punished for sexual activity beyond the confines of monogamous heterosexual marriage. These realities codetermine women's experience of sex.

The key difference, then, between Sex Radical feminists and Radical Feminists does not rest on whether attention should be paid to the structures of gender inequality in which sex is constructed, enacted, and represented. Rather, the two perspectives differ in their assessments of whether the meaning and function of sex are fully determined by that sexist social order. While Radical Feminists insist that the sexual (mis)representations of patriarchy create "reality" because of the absolute power of men to make them function as such, feminist Sex Radicals understand sex to be a cultural tactic which can be used both to destabilize male power as well as to reinforce it. In much the same way, Michel de Certeau argues that culture

> articulates conflicts and alternately legitimizes, displaces, or controls the superior force. It develops in an atmosphere of tensions, and often of violence [and] the tactics of consumption, the ingenious ways in which the weak make use of the strong, thus lend a political dimension to everyday practices.[55]

Practices of prostitution, like other forms of commodification and consumption, can be read in more complex ways than simply as a confirmation of male domination. They may also be seen as sites of ingenious resistance and cultural subversion. For this reason, Sex Radical feminists insist that the position of the prostitute cannot be reduced to one of a passive object used in a male sexual practice, but instead can be understood as a place of agency where the sex worker makes active use of the existing sexual order. Indeed, the Whore is often invoked by feminist Sex Radicals as a symbol of women's sexual autonomy and, as such, as a potential threat to patriarchal control over women's sexuality. Rebecca Kaplan suggests:

> Women are usually called whores for being openly or highly sexual. Men who yell at women will often call them a "whore" and a "dyke" in the same breath. How is it that a woman can be simultaneously accused of having too much sex with men (whore) and too little sex with men (dyke)? This should make us realize that both of these terms condemn women's sexual autonomy. Whores and dykes are a threat to heteropatriarchy because both set their own rules

for sex – rules which deny men the right to unlimited access to women's sexuality. Of course, prostitution can be critiqued like any other capitalist venture, but in a world in which a woman's body is so devalued, telling a man that he has to pay for access to it can be a radical act of self-determination.

Pat Califia concurs:

> The slut is, in Dworkin's parlance, male property – a victim of male violence – a woman who accepts male definition of her sexuality. Instead, I believe that she is someone men hate because she is potentially beyond their control. . . . A whore does not sell her body. She sells her time. So she has time that is not for sale, that belongs to no one but herself. Domesticated women don't dare put a price on their time.[56]

The slut, the dyke, and the whore are thus embraced by Sex Radicals as a potent symbolic challenge to confining notions of proper womanhood and conventional sexuality. Because Sex Radicals, like libertarians, embrace a vision of sex freed of the constraints of love, commitment, and convention, prostitution and pornography are understood to be useful to enhance sexual exploration and diversity. While Kathleen Barry and other pro-"positive" sex feminists condemn prostitution for introducing "bizarre" pornographic practices into private sexual behavior, Pat Califia celebrates commercial sex for very similar reasons:

> If you don't know that there's a whole group of people who engage in a particular sexual behavior, it makes it much more difficult to imagine yourself ever being able to do it. And porn is one of the commonest ways that people discover there are other folks out there who like to do cunnilingus, anal sex, gay sex, get tied up, have threesomes . . .[57]

Similarly, Lisa Duggan, Nan Hunter, and Carole Vance argue that

pornography carries many messages other than woman-hating: it advocates sexual adventure, sex outside of marriage, anonymous sex, group sex, voyeuristic sex, illegal sex, public sex. . . . Women's experience of pornography is not as universally victimizing as the [MacKinnon/Dworkin anti-pornography] ordinance would have it.[58]

Of course, Sex Radicals' invocation of prostitution and pornography as tools of liberation forged by undomesticated outlaw whores is as much of a rhetorical trope as the Radical Feminists' depiction of commercial sex as realm of oppression populated by sexual slaves and exploited objects. Ira Levine, who has long worked in the adult film industry, reports, for example, that "outlaw" is not an identity all sex workers embrace:

> It's amazing how in so many ways, many people in the porn industry have the same rather conventional values as people in any other industry. Do not assume that this is a bunch of wild bohemian personalities. We have our share of them, but we have an awful lot of people who struggle to lead conventional lives in spite of what they're doing. I think a lot of those people are missing out on the one real advantage of this job: the freedom of being a leper. After you've already done something loathsome to the majority of the population, you have a certain amount of latitude. I think it's a shame that these people feel an obligation to prove to everyone that they're really just perfectly normal people.

Similarly, Carol Queen, a California sex worker and writer, notes that, far from being sexually enlightened, many prostitutes share the sexual prejudices of dominant culture:

> Unlike many women working in the sex trades, I actually have a background in sex education. I want to think well of the erotic desires of the people who come to me. I don't think of clients as kinky or

perverted. I like it that they can come to me and say "I would like you to put your hand in my butt" or "I would like you to piss on me." One of the things that I know I am providing is a sexual safe space for people who haven't had that before. And I'm probably more safe for them than most prostitutes because I honour their desire. One piece of the puzzle of how to improve sex work is that sex workers could be trained in human sexuality, and other people could be assisted in developing both their own sex awareness and their communication skills.[59]

The reality of commercial sex (and the experiences of those performing erotic labor) is far more varied than either Radical or Sex Radical feminist rhetoric can express. Prostitution functions as an effective trope in these competing discourses of female sexuality, but the use of the sex worker as a symbol has also served to obscure the real complexity of her life.

NOTES

1   Jeffreys (1985), p. 47.
2   Ibid, p. 32.
3   Ibid, p. 97.
4   See, for example, Ferguson (1984) and Sawicki (1988).
5   Seidman (1992), p. 187.
6   Davis (1990), p. 35.
7   Steinem (1978), p. 54.
8   Elshtain (1988), pp. 53–5.
9   Morgan (1977), p. 181. Several critics have called this "femininism": "The femininist view of sex is ... women have sex as an expression of intimacy, but orgasm is seen as a male goal": Rubin (1982), p. 215.
10 Interview with Ariane Amsberg, 1994, Amsterdam.
11 Barry (1979), p. 270.
12 Ibid, p. 205.
13 Barry, plenary address at the Nordic Prostitution Conference, Helsinki, Finland, May, 1995. Emphasis mine. Barry opened her remarks with a strongly worded denunciation of conference organizers' decision to include a condom in conference packets: "The packet of material I received this morn-

ing [had] a condom in it which I assume is either part of the approach to normalization of prostitution or is it indeed a suggestion to those of us who have received it that we should be using it that way? I find this not at all cute or funny, I find it not at all educational or productive. I find it insulting."
14 For a conference report, see Kulp and Mudd (1987), pp. 6–7.
15 Ibid, p. 6, Emphasis mine.
16 Ibid, p. 7. Emphasis mine.
17 Ibid. Emphasis mine.
18 Pateman (1988), p. 208.
19 Fraser (1993), pp. 174, 176.
20 MacKinnon (1987), p. 149.
21 Ibid, p. 148.
22 Davis (1990), p. 26.
23 Southern Women's Writers' Collective (1987), p. 3.
24 Ibid.
25 Ibid, p. 4.
26 Ibid.
27 Dworkin (1987), pp. 134–5. Emphasis mine.
28 MacKinnon (1987), p. 59.
29 Barry (1979), p. 218.
30 Barry (1992).
31 Ibid.
32 MacKinnon notes that "Marxism teaches that exploitation and degradation somehow produce resistance and revolution. It's been hard to say why. What I've learned from women's experience with sexuality is that exploitation and degradation produce grateful complicity in exchange for survival." MacKinnon (1987), p. 61.
33 Ibid, p. 148.
34 Seidman (1992), pp. 187–8.
35 Ibid.
36 Wells (1994), p. 132.
37 Ibid.
38 Ibid, p. 58.
39 Other writers challenging so-called "victim feminism" include American feminists Katie Roiphe (1993) and Naomi Wolf (1993). In her version of "power feminism," Roiphe, for instance, scrutinizes rape and other crimes of male violence against women for evidence of women's own complicity. A similar strategy is at work in current attempts to redefine racism as a question of individual failure; see D'Souza (1995).
40 hooks (1994), p. 80.
41 Vance (1984), p. 1.

42 Sheiner (1994), p. 4. It is interesting to note that the author of the offending piece defends his work in a reply to Sheiner by arguing that she misinterpreted his intent: "I was trying to convey exactly the sense of revulsion at the use of Third World women [in sex tourism]. I agree completely with those who deplore it, and always have. The sexual image in this piece was intended to be grotesque."

43 Lilly (1991), pp. 1–3.
44 Sawicki (1988), p. 185.
45 Califia (1980), p. 27.
46 Marlatt (1991), p. 260.
47 de Lauretis (1984), p. 5.
48 Warland (1991), p. 263.
49 Shange (1994), p. 34.
50 Ibid, pp. 38–9.
51 Califia (1980), p. 107.
52 McClintock (1993), p. 102.
53 Ibid, p. 113.
54 Connell (1995).
55 Taussig (1987), p. 16.
56 Califia (1988), p. 20.
57 Ibid, p. 22.
58 Duggan et al. (1985), p. 145.
59 Interview with Carol Queen, 1992, San Francisco, CA.

REFERENCES

Barry, Kathleen. 1979. *Female Sexual Slavery*. New York: Avon Books.
——1992. "Trafficking in Women: Serving Masculine Systems." Speech given at the National Organization for Women conference, Chicago.
Califia, Pat. 1980. *Sapphistry: The Book of Lesbian Sexuality*. Tallahassee: Naiad Press.
——1988. *Macho Sluts*. Boston: Alyson Publications.
Connell, Robert. 1995. "Democracies of Pleasure: thoughts on the goals of radical sexual politics." In *Social Postmodernism*, edited by Steven Seidman and Linda Nicholson. Cambridge: Cambridge University Press.
Davis, Karen. 1990. "I Love Myself When I am Laughing: A New Paradigm for Sex." Paper presented at the Queer Theory Conference, University of California at Santa Cruz, February 1990.
De Lauretis, Teresa. 1984. *Alice Doesn't*. Bloomington: Indiana University Press.
D'Souza, Dinesh. 1995. *The End of Racism*. New York: Free Press.

Duggan, Lisa, Nan Hunter, and Carole Vance. 1985. "False Promises." In *Women Against Censorship*, edited by Varda Burstyn. Vancouver: Douglas and McIntyre.
Dworkin, Andrea. 1987. *Intercourse*. New York: Free Press.
——1988. *Letters From a War Zone*. New York: E. P. Dutton.
Elshtain, Jean Bethke. 1988. "Why We Need Limits." In *Utne Reader* September/October, pp. 53–5.
Ferguson, Ann. 1984. "Sex War." *Signs* 10: 1, pp. 106–12.
Fraser, Nancy. 1993. "Beyond the Master/Subject Model." *Social Text* 37: 174, 176.
hooks, bell. 1994. *Outlaw Culture*. New York: Routledge.
Jeffreys, Sheila. 1985. *The Spinster and Her Enemies: Feminism and Sexuality, 1880–1930*. London: Pandora.
Kulp, Denise and Karen Mudd. 1987. "The Sexual Liberals and the Attack on Feminism." *Off Our Backs* 17 (5).
Lilly, Bobby. 1991. "Musings on the Patriarchy and Other Thoughts." In *CAL-PEP News* 5: 10, June 12, pp. 1–2.
McClintock, Anne. 1993. "Maid to Order." *Social Text* 37: 103–4.
MacKinnon, Catharine. 1987. *Feminism Unmodified: Discourses on Life and Law*. Cambridge, MA: Harvard University Press.
Marlatt, Daphne. 1991. "Musing with Mothertongue." In *Intimate Wilderness*, edited by Judith Barrington. Portland, OR: Eighth Mountain Press.
Morgan, Robin. 1977. *Going Too Far*. New York: Random House.
Pateman, Carole. 1988. *The Sexual Contract*. Stanford, CA: Stanford University Press.
Roiphe, Katie. 1993. *The Morning After*. Boston: Little, Brown.
Rubin, Gayle. 1982. "The Leather Menace." In *Coming to Power*. Samois, Boston: Alyson Publications.
Sawicki, Jana. 1988. "Identity Politics and Sexual Freedom." In *Feminism and Foucault*, edited by Irene Diamond and Lee Quinby. Boston: Northeastern Press.
Seidman, Steven. 1992. *Embattled Eros*. New York: Routledge.
Shange, Ntozake. 1994. "Where Do We Stand On Pornography: Roundtable Discussion." *Ms. Magazine* 4: 4, January/February, p. 34.

Sheiner, Marcy. 1994. Letter to the Editor. *Future Sex* 2, p. 4.

Southern Women's Writers' Collective. 1987. "Sex Resistance in Heterosexual Arrangements." Photocopied pamphlet.

Steinem, Gloria. 1978. "Erotica and Pornography: A Clear and Present Difference." *Ms. Magazine*, November, p. 54.

Taussig, Michael. 1987. "History as Commodity." *Food and Foodways*, vol. 2; Harvard Academic Publishers.

Vance, Carole S., ed. 1984. *Pleasure and Danger: Exploring Female Sexuality*. Boston: Routledge.

Warland, Betsy. 1991. "Untying the Tongue." In *Intimate Wilderness*, edited by Judith Barrington. Portland, OR: Eighth Mountain Press.

Wells, Melanie. 1994. "Woman as Goddess: Camille Paglia Tours Strip Clubs." *Penthouse* October, p. 132.

Wolf, Naomi. 1993. *Fire With Fire*. New York: Random House.

15 Working for Men: At the Intersection of Power, Gender, and Sexuality

Meika Loe

This essay is an investigation into power, gender, and sexuality in the workplace. This research is based on six months of participant observation and interviews at a restaurant I will call "Bazooms."[1] Bazooms is an establishment that has been described both as "a family restaurant" and as "a titillating sports bar."[2] The name of this restaurant, according to the menu, is a euphemism for "what brings a gleam into men's eyes everywhere besides beer and chicken wings and an occasional winning football team." Breasts, then, form the concept behind the name.

The purpose of this article is to examine the dynamics of power, gender, and sexuality as they operate in the Bazooms workplace. This is a setting in which gender roles, sexuality, and job-based power dynamics are all being constructed and reconstructed through customer, management, and waitress interactions. The first half of the article describes how power, gender, and sexuality shape, and are concurrently shaped by, Bazooms's management and customers. The second half deals specifically with how Bazooms waitresses attempt to reshape these dynamics and to find strategies for managing the meaning and operation of gender, power, and sexuality. By using Bazooms waitresses as examples, I hope to show that women are not merely "objectified victims" of sexualized workplaces, but are also active architects of gender, power, and sexuality in such settings.

The Bazooms Workplace Environment

Bazooms is the fastest-growing restaurant chain in the nation. Each "store" that a franchise owner buys is refurbished before opening in order to look "homey" and welcoming. Christmas lights line the windows year-round, a jukebox plays continuously, pictures of Bazooms girls and famous people cover the wood-paneled walls, Bazooms merchandise hangs from the ceilings, and wooden tables and stools are dispersed around the floor. Every Bazooms is organized physically so that from any table one can watch "America's cheerleaders" (as they call the waitresses) "do their thing," slinging orders into the kitchen on an overhead cable while standing on a pedestal, hula-hooping, hokey-pokeying (dancing in a circle), and so forth. Bazooms waitresses wear "tantalizing" outfits that expose a sexual slogan on the back and display the name of the establishment on the front (the O's look like breasts).

When I applied for a job at Bazooms in the winter of 1994, the first thing I was told was "The 'Bazooms girl' is what this restaurant revolves around; she is a food server, bartender, hostess, table busser, promo girl, and more." At the job interview I was shown a picture of a busty blonde in a tight top and short shorts leaning seductively over a plateful of buffalo wings and was asked if I would be comfortable wearing the Bazooms uniform. Then I was told that the managers try to make the job "fun," by supplying the "girls" with "toys" like hula hoops to play with in between orders. Finally, I was asked to sign Bazooms's official sexual harassment policy form, which explicitly states: "In a work atmosphere based upon sex appeal, joking and innuendo are commonplace."

Sixty "lucky" women were chosen to be "Bazooms girls" out of about 800 applications. Most of the "new hires" were local college students, ranging in age from 18 to 28 years, and as I found out later, more than several were mothers. The hiring process was extremely competitive owing to the fact that Bazooms hired minors and inexperienced waitresses. Also, everyone had been told that working at Bazooms could be quite lucrative. The general "Bazooms girl type" seemed to be white, thin, with blonde or brown hair, although there were several black, Chicana, and Asian American women in the bunch.[3] We all went through full-time training together (which included appearance training, menu workshops, song learning, alcohol and food service licensing, and reviewing the employee manual), and eventually were placed in a new location opened in Southern California.

Women work at Bazooms for a variety of reasons. No one in management ever asked me why I was applying, and I never told them, but the fact is that I applied for a position as a Bazooms girl because I wanted to know more about how the women who worked there experienced and responded to a highly sexualized workplace. I worked there for six months, during which I "became the phenomenon" (Mehan and Wood 1975).[4]

During my six months of participant observation and interviews with coworkers, I explained that I was interviewing people in my place of work as part of a class research project.[5] I made no attempt to construct a random sample of Bazooms girls to interview; rather I interviewed those whom I felt closest to, and worked regularly with, and who I thought would feel comfortable responding honestly to my questions. The waitresses I interviewed for the most part were very committed to their jobs. Some were upset with their conditions of employment, and their voices may stand out for the reader. But I should emphasize that others, whose voices may not attract notice, expressed general contentment with the job.

In the pages that follow I will present their views and my observations about the ways in which power, gender, and sexuality are constructed and negotiated in the sexualized workplace of a Bazooms restaurant.

Job-Based Power

Formal power

Gender and power at Bazooms are reflected in its management structure. In this restaurant, four men manage more than 100 employees working various shifts: 60 Bazooms girls and 40 kitchen guys. In addition, both the franchise owners and the founders are all male. This is not rare. According to Catharine MacKinnon (1980), countless studies have shown that "women are overwhelmingly in positions that other people manage, supervise, or administer. Even in 'women's jobs' the managers are men" (p. 60). As in most workplace environments, formal authority and power are concentrated in management positions at Bazooms. In everything from scheduling to paychecks, floor assignments, and breaks, managers have the last word. In this way, Bazooms girls are placed in a subordinate position. This is not an unusual finding. MacKinnon contends that as "low-prestige" workers, women are often placed in positions of dependence upon men for economic security, hiring, retention, and advancement.

In these dependent situations, a woman's job is literally on the line all the time. One waitress whom I interviewed described management procedures for getting a worker fired at a Colorado Bazooms as follows:

> All of a sudden, we would have menu tests and we were told that if we missed too many we would be fired. Now, I know I missed about twenty. These girls they wanted to fire missed less than that, I'm sure. They were fired right away because they missed some... but they didn't say a thing to me. Or, if they really wanted to get rid of certain people, they would put up

one schedule, then put a different copy up with different hours (the "real" one) after the girls left. The girls wouldn't know, so they were fired for not showing up to their shifts. *(Jeni)*

Disciplinary action based upon "company rules" is one of management's most common exertions of power. Before every shift, managers hold "jump start" which, in theory, is supposed to motivate the workers to "get out there and have fun." Instead it becomes an ideal time for management to assert authority. Each waitress is quickly checked for uniform cleanliness, "natural" yet "styled" hair, make-up, and so forth. Then the group is counseled on "proper" Bazooms girl behavior and attitude. Sometimes "pop quizzes" are given to each woman, with questions about proper Bazooms girl service and responsibilities. At other times, lectures are given reiterating rules that have been ignored or broken earlier in the week. The practice of "jump start," at the beginning of each shift, operates in a way that makes power relations explicit. Lori was simply told at jump start in front of fifteen others: "That necklace doesn't work," leaving her feeling hurt, confused, and uncomfortable.[6] Contrary to its name, jump start usually does little to build morale. At another jump start, Janine was told to take her hair down:

> I felt like I was going to cry. I spent all of this time and effort putting it into a French twist, all pretty and styled and they tell me to take it down. The rest of the night I felt so self-conscious, I did a really bad job on the floor.

In short, male management's right to exercise veto power over each worker's appearance, attitude, and so forth reflects gendered power relations at Bazooms.

Informal power

Besides having the ultimate say in formal matters such as scheduling, hiring, and firing, male managers sustain dominance at Bazooms in other, more subtle, ways. Eleanor LaPointe (1992: 382) identifies a number of "interactional techniques" often used by men to sustain dominance and maintain the inferior status of women. At Bazooms such power was exercised by the use of derogatory terms of address, disciplinary actions, direct orders, threats, general avoidance of waitresses' concerns, cynicism, and even humiliation. For instance, the fact that female employees between the ages of 18 and 30 are called girls by Bazooms managers and customers alike is an example of such an "interactional technique" used to sustain dominance. Everyone knows that the managers (all men in their twenties and thirties) are not to be called boys (neither are the "kitchen guys" to be called boys). Yet, by seeing and addressing the "low-status" employees as girls (based upon the "Bazooms girl" concept), one can retain dominance as a manager or customer (since waitresses are referred to by all as Bazooms girls) and maintain the subordinate status of female employees. Humiliating comments during the work shift about personal appearance (such as those that Lori and Janine received) from managers is another example of an interactional technique causing Bazooms girls to feel that they aren't respected or that they are treated poorly. In the words of one (Trina), "[The management] has no respect for any of us waitresses. No respect."

Gender

It has already been established that Bazooms is a "gendered workplace," where, according to MacKinnon (1980), women "tend to be employed in occupations that are considered 'for women,' to be men's subordinates on the job and to be paid less than men both on the average and for the same work." Thus, women work "as women" (ibid: 59). In 1980, 64 percent of working women were employed in "women's jobs," that is, "jobs noted for their sex-typing in workplace settings characterized by sex segregation" (Reskin and Hartmann 1986: 23). The notion of "women's work" is based upon the gendered division of labor, in which women occupy roles that are seen as "natural." Besides taking on "female" tasks, in the sex-typed workplace it is commonly known that a woman at work must "act like a woman." This may mean embodying "traditionally female" behaviour and roles, besides dressing or behaving "feminine."[7] Women's work, to Paules (1991), involves "job tasks which center around traditionally female duties: serving, waiting, smiling, flattering; and emphasize putatively female qualities: patience, sociability, submissiveness" (ibid: 170).

Behavior rules

Management codes and guidelines shape gendered identities in work environments. At Bazooms, women work as "girls." According to one Bazooms manager, "What differentiates us from every other restaurant in the marketplace are the Bazooms girls. That's the reason that there's a Bazooms concept, that's the reason that we're successful." The employee handbook describes why only women are hired to be food servers at Bazooms:

> Since its inception, Bazooms' business success has been based upon the "Bazooms girl." The Bazooms girl motif and ambiance is the essence of the unique and profitable business theme developed by Bazooms which now benefits all of us. Bazooms is in the entertainment industry where authenticity is an essential qualification. As such, we consider the exclusive hiring of wholesome, attractive females as entertainers/servers to be a bona fide occupational qualification.

The following are Bazooms girl guidelines selected from the employee handbook:

- Wholesome-looking, All American cheerleading types (the kind you would be proud to take home to mother). Prom-like appearance.
- Hair should always be styled. The girls are always "on stage" and should be camera-ready at all times.
- Make-up needs to be worn. It should not be excessive, and at the same time it needs to highlight her natural features.
- Always smiling, extremely friendly and courteous.
- Always should appear to be having a great time.
- Extremely attentive to all customers.

Simultaneously she is "the girl next door," the "cheerleader," the "actress" (always camera-ready), the "good daughter" (attentive, subservient), the "prom queen," and the shining, happy personality. One waitress said matter-of-factly, "It's like they [managers] have an ideal image in their heads of us" (Katy). With all of these demands placed upon her, the Bazooms girl is constantly in the process of learning how to adapt to the company's expectations, and acting out her gender (according to men's rules).

Appearance rules

It is clear from these guidelines that the "Bazooms girl" role embodies what are seen as traditionally "feminine" (in this case, many "girlish") qualities. One way gender is symbolized is through uniform style, which, according to LaPointe (1992: 382), "incorporates a gendered meaning into the work."[8] The uniforms, short shorts, and choice of tight tank top, crop, or tight T-shirt, may be part of the popular "beach theme," which Bazooms likes to accentuate, but it carries gendered meaning as well. Few men, if any, work in what is considered a "neighborhood restaurant" wearing a size too small dolphin shorts and a shirt showing off his midriff and chest.[9] But for a woman this is "beach wear," revealing her truly feminine characteristics.

Barbara Reskin and Patricia Roos (1987) argue that the "sexual division of labor is grounded in stereotypes of innate sex differences in traits and abilities, and maintained by gender-role socialization and various social control mechanisms" (ibid: 9). The Bazooms girl role and image is based upon ideas about femaleness, as we have seen. Ideas of "femininity" are implicit and explicit in her role: slimness, smiles, curvaceousness, youthfulness, "highlighted" features, and natural charm. The director of training at Bazooms advised new hires to "look like you are going on a date. You were chosen because you all are pretty. But I say makeup makes everyone look better. Push-up bras make everyone look better. And we all want to look our best." These "feminine ideals" not only define "the perfect" Bazooms girl, but are used by management to constantly reify femininity in the workplace through the dissemination of "rules" and the use of discipline to uphold these rules. In this way, through interaction, not only power relations but gender roles are constantly being defined and redefined in the workplace.

Emotional labor

The gendered workplace demands more than manipulation of behavior and appearance. Arlie Hochschild's (1979) ethnography of flight attendants introduces another type of labor that is common in female-dominated occupations, which she dubs "emotional labor." Emotional labor requires one to *induce or suppress feeling* in order to sustain an outward countenance that produces the desired state of mind in others (Hochschild 1983: 7). Thus, emotion workers must always "display" an image that is determined by management, and "over time 'display' comes to assume a certain relation to feeling" (ibid: 90). Hochschild found that emotion workers, over time, may become estranged from their true feelings, which are ignored, disguised,

or created in order to achieve a desired image.[10]

Hochschild's notion of "display" and manipulation of feeling can be found at Bazooms, especially among the female employees. According to management, the Bazooms girl, when on the floor, is expected to "perform as if [she] is on stage." This means embodying a specific image, sustaining an outward countenance, and behaving in specific ways. One manager with whom I spoke put it this way:

> Well, after working eight years I can pretty much tell who will be perfect for the job and who won't [*By looking at them?*] Well, by talking with them and seeing what type of personality they have. You know, they must be performers as Bazooms girls. Nobody can be bubbly that long, but when you're working you *put on an act.* (Tony)

As Greta Paules (1991: 160) put it, "By furnishing the waitress with a script, a costume, and a backdrop of a servant, the restaurant is encouraging her to become absorbed in her role – to engage in deep acting."

The list of "Bazooms girl guidelines" distributed to all new hires outlines that part of the job script that entails "always smiling" and "appear[ing] to have a great time." What is implied here is the emotional labor that the Bazooms girl must engage in, in suppressing frustration, bad feelings, frowns, and fatigue and instead conveying a corporate image that is separate from how she really feels.[11] Disguising and creating emotion is all "part of the job." And just as one's labor and one's image become commodified, so does one's "emotional labor." A writer for a major newspaper said simply, "[Bazooms] is about tanned, perpetually smiling servers (they're called [Bazooms] girls)." Thus, the Bazooms girl, her appearance, her behavior, and her ability to "sustain an outward countenance" are at the core of the Bazooms concept.

The corporate image that Bazooms projects of happy, sexy, eager-to-serve workers is what sells. What became clear to me on one of my first days on the job was that emotional labor is demanded not only by management, but by customers as well. For instance, one afternoon I approached a table full of marines without a smile or a "Can I help you?" look on my face. Their first words to me were, "You look pissed." I felt I had to make excuses for what I realized was poor emotion management on my part.

Deference is a large portion of emotion work, according to Hochschild. "Ritualized deference is always involved when one is in a subordinate position" (Reskin and Roos 1987: 8). Clearly, in the service industry, employees (the majority women) are expected to have been trained in "niceness" from an early age (girls are made of sugar and spice and everything nice). So "working as women" (or girls) naturally assumes that "a friendly and courteous manner" will be incorporated into the job. During training at Bazooms new hires were instructed to "kill them [rude customers] with kindness and class." In other words, suppress any desire to yell or lecture rude customers, and instead, defer to the old maxim "the customer always is right," and treat them only with kindness. In this case, emotion work entails being at the service of others to the point of devaluing oneself and one's own emotions. Because of their subordination and vulnerable positioning, women become easy targets of verbal abuse, and of others' (managers', customers', even colleagues') displaced feelings. When kindness is not effective enough in handling rude customers, Bazooms asks their waitresses to defer to the management. "Problems" are then handled by the men, who must also manage their emotions, but they are more allowed to wield anger, since they have been socialized to express "negative" emotions from an early age (Hochschild 1983: 163).

In a gendered workplace one cannot ignore the gender roles that employees are expected to enact. At Bazooms, sex-typed behavior, appearance, and emotion management are all part of the Bazooms girl concept. This concept is commodified and sold, producing pressures from management (who see the Bazooms girl as the secret to their success) and customers (who come expecting happy and smiling, sexy "girls") on waitresses to perfectly embody the Bazooms girl image.

The Sexualized Workplace

It is beyond my – my mental capacity to understand how anyone could walk into a [Bazooms] restaurant and apply for a job and look at the sign and look at the – the concept and look at the uniform and not understand that female sex appeal is an essential ingredient in the concept. (Mr. McNeil, manager of Bazooms, Minnesota)

At the turn of the century Emma Goldman suggested: "Nowhere is woman treated according to the merit of her work but rather as a sex. . . . She must assert herself as a personality, not as a sex commodity" (Goldman 1970: 7, 12). Close to a century later, Catharine MacKinnon related a similar point in her book *Sexual Harassment of Working Women*: "Most women perform the jobs they do because of their gender, with the element of sexuality pervasively explicit." According to Goldman, MacKinnon, and other feminist theorists, women not only work "as women" but as *sexualized* women.

Bazooms makes no secret about sexuality as a part of its key to success. The employee manual states in its sexual harassment policy that employees should be aware that they are employed in an establishment "based upon female sex appeal." As Mr. McNeil pointed out, everything right down to the waitresses' uniforms and the name of the restaurant connotes sex appeal. The slang term *bazooms* is usually used in the context of male desire and breast fetishism; it is a term that treats one part of the female body as an object of sexual desire. Tanya, director of training for Bazooms, answered a new hire's question about the term *bazooms* in this way:

> So what if [Bazooms] means "tits." That doesn't offend me. It's all in fun... just six guys in Florida trying to be goofy. They used to want us to hide the fact that it means breasts. But now we figure, Why be ashamed of it? You girls should never be ashamed of where you work. And if anyone asks you what it means, you just say, "Whatever you want it to mean."

Why is female sex appeal such a great marketing success? Probably because it appeals to male fantasy. Customers (roughly 85 percent male at my workplace) buy into the commodified Bazooms girl, which they hear about everywhere. Since "no publicity is bad publicity" to Bazooms, Bazooms girls have been highlighted in popular magazines such as *Playboy*. In a leading national business magazine, Bazooms is described as a place with "food, folks, and fun, and a little bit of sex appeal." In fact, according to this magazine, the idea for Bazooms came from a Florida football player/contractor in 1983 who wanted "a mildly profitable excuse for swilling beer and ogling blondes." Thus, Bazooms is premised on women's bodies, and their presence in male fantasies. This premise can be seen and heard constantly in the restaurant. Pages from the Bazooms girl calendar (similar to the *Sports Illustrated Swimsuit Calendar* but with "actual Bazooms girls" wearing Bazooms merchandise and bikinis) are posted in the men's bathroom. The kitchen workers in the back have been heard playing the song "Five steps to sucking dick." Women in "tantalizing" outfits that display a sexual slogan on the back and the name of the establishment on the front are everywhere one looks, fulfilling Bazooms girl responsibilities (such as hula-hooping, serving, posing for pictures, signing T-shirts with the phrase "Bazooms and Hugs," etc.)

Barbara Gutek (1985: 17) found that there were "three *traditionally female roles* [emphasis added] that women may choose or be forced to adopt in the workplace: pet, mother, and sex object." All of these feminized roles are at work at Bazooms. The Bazooms waitress is cherished as the Bazooms girl, who flirts, smiles, and teases the male customer. In this way she is the pet. She is nurturing, almost mothering in her service (pouring catsup, keeping drink glasses full, shucking oysters, etc.) and in her "natural" wholesomeness ("the kind of girl you would want to take home to mother"). Finally, she is the one in the very small outfit, showing off her body both in routine waitressing tasks and in tasks designed for this purpose, such as hula-hooping (this is considered part of her job), standing on a pedestal, reaching up high (which lifts up her shirt) to sling orders down an overhead cable into the kitchen, and singing "YOU check us out! YOU check us out! UGGH" (known as "the grunt song"): She is sex object. The Bazooms girl "acts out" the virgin *and* the whore dichotomy for men.

Comments that customers made to me reflect the "titillating" nature of Bazooms, and the expectations they have about what the waitresses symbolize. One man said he didn't want to embarrass himself, but he thought that I was "too wholesome" to work at Bazooms. Answering my question about why he didn't think I fit in, he whispered to me, "You are not slutty enough." Another male customer called me over to remark, "I've been watching you all night and I think you have to be the most innocent-looking girl here. This means that you must have a wild side and I like that." Both of these comments encapsulate this male fantasy of the virgin/whore. I was obviously too much "virgin" for both of them, but the second man made up for this by fantasizing that I had a "wild side" (the "whore" was simply latent or hidden away).

Further comments and behaviors reflected the sexualized expectations of customers. I asked one man who looked interested in buying a shirt, "Can I show you something?" pointing to the merchandise counter. The customer responded, "I'll tell you what I want to see..." and tossed a dollar my way. Another customer commented to me, "I will leave here dreaming about either the food or the women. I think it will be the women." In these limited exchanges with customers, it is clear that male fantasy is an explicit part of the Bazooms experience.

It is in this sexually charged workplace catering to male fantasy that "masculine culture" emerges. A major newspaper describes Bazooms as "a lot of men's idea of big fun." With women (Bazooms girls) "acting out" feminine roles (pet, mother, sex object), men (customers) perform as well. At Bazooms, customers perform masculinity rituals, often in groups. One might encounter groups of male customers engaging in a number of masculine "acts." These generally include flirting with waitresses and vying for their attention, joking about body parts and other publicly taboo subjects, challenging each other in the area of alcohol consumption, setting each other up with waitresses, making requests for hula-hooping, and so on. For example, comments such as "You give good head" can be heard among groups of males when a waitress is pouring beer. One man asked, "Why don't you wear the low-cut tank top?" while another said, "My friend wants to meet that girl over there. Can you get her to come over?"

In their study of Brady's Bar, an establishment in many ways similar to Bazooms, James P. Spradley and Brenda J. Mann (1975) discuss the ways in which waitresses are involved in the masculinity rituals of customers. Spradley and Mann found that "Brady's Bar is primarily a place where males can come to play out exaggerated masculine roles, acting out their fantasies of sexual prowess, and reaffirming their own male identities" (ibid: 131). In such a masculine-identified place, the role of the waitress takes on an objectified nature, as

the woman is necessary in order for the man to "highlight the virtues of strength, toughness, assertiveness, and dominance over females," in such a "male ceremonial" setting. "As she enters the give and take of social encounter, the female waitress and the customer alike will find their presence important for men, as audience, as sexual object, as marginal participant" (ibid: 133).

Socialized through interaction with customers, Bazooms girls learn to "manage feeling" in order to keep the customers as happy as possible. "The masculinity rituals [in the bar] would not be effective without the cooperation of the waitress. She has learned to respond demurely to taunts, invitations, and physical invasions of her personal space.... The cultural expectations are clear: she should remain dependent and passive" (Spradley and Mann 1975: 133). In this way, gendered sexual identities, expectations, and roles are shaped through customer interaction. As the "audience, marginal participant, and sex object," the Bazooms girl is there to "enhance" masculine culture (add to the eroticism by playing out visual and interactive elements of male fantasy) and at the same time, enjoy the attention she gets as "the object" (ibid).

The fact that Bazooms is male-identified is well illustrated by the feelings of intimidation experienced by female customers. The most common question asked by a female customer upon entering the restaurant is "Am I the only woman in here?" Although there are between six and fourteen Bazooms girls within the restaurant at any given time, the "men's club" atmosphere is quite obvious. One evening a group of adults came to celebrate a woman's birthday. When asked to stand and dance with salt and pepper shakers in her hands (as Bazooms makes all people celebrating their birthdays do), this woman would not stand up, obviously for reasons of embarrassment and intimidation. At 9:00 p.m. this woman got "boos" from certain corners of the restaurant because she would not take part in this Bazooms ritual. This one example reveals how intimidating such a male-oriented place can be. Although it describes itself as a "family restaurant," it is directed at single males (unaccompanied by women).

Sexual harassment and "sex joking"

Frances Donovan worked in Chicago restaurants around 1919 to expose the life of a waitress. Although she sided with men and blamed women for the sexual activity that took place where she worked, she did admit that "even in the restaurants where the relations between the patrons and the waitresses were not actively sexual, there was the constant stimulation of dirty jokes and unclean conversation" (Segrave 1994: 131). Seventy-five years later, in her study of sex in the workplace, Gutek (1985: 144) found that of a random national sample of 827 "traditionally employed women . . . 75 percent said that sexual jokes and comments were common in their places of work."

Similarly, Spradley and Mann (1975) found joking to be a powerful force in the work environment they studied. The "joking relationship" was essential to establishing the "masculine atmosphere" of Brady's Bar, "centering on insults made in jest, direct references to sexual behavior, comments about anatomical features with sexual meanings, and to related topics normally taboo for conversations between men and women" (ibid: 95).

I observed numerous examples of this sort of sexual harassment/"sex joking" at Bazooms. Comments made by customers such as "You give good head," or "Your lips would be so nice to kiss," or "I wish I were in the shower with all of you," are not common at Bazooms, but they also are not taboo. I was warned by one Bazooms girl when I went to apply for the job: "You do have to put up with a lot of shit."

A national business magazine reports that "appropriate activities among [Bazooms] customers include winking, leering, nudging and smirking." According to Bazooms girl Sheri, there's something about the Bazooms

environment that permits behaviors one wouldn't find at another restaurant. "What makes it different is that Bazooms customers are a little more open because of the atmosphere. They [customers] are a lot more forward – instead of waiting a couple of times to establish themselves as regulars until they attempt to ask you something." Trina also pointed out other ways in which Bazooms customers are anything but subtle in the Bazooms environment:"

> It's really rare to be harassed at other places. But the kissing noises, referring to your body parts in any way, "hey-babying" and wiggin out [at Bazooms] . . . it's not worth my pride. Looks I don't consider sexual harassment because you can look all you want but once someone says something that offends you, that is pushing it. (Trina)

What a sexually permissive environment allows for is room for degrading comments, sexist behaviors, and "insults made in jest." As a consequence, women working at Bazooms reported feelings of hurt, embarrassment, and humiliation. As one stated:

> This guy, [the manager's] friend, we were joking around and he was rude in an obnoxious way. I tapped him on the shoulder . . . and he goes, "Don't you touch me!" I just jumped back, my mouth dropped, and I felt humiliated 'cuz he said it so loudly. My eyes started to water and I stayed away the rest of the night. Later he apologized and said he was just joking but come on, I've seen how he treats me. At Bazooms, sometimes you just get treated like meat. (Trina)

Kanja also felt embarrassed and upset about behavior that occurred at Bazooms.

> The worst experience was when this rock station was in the restaurant and they were asking me and another Bazooms girl about which actresses had real or fake boobs. The last question was whether I had real or fake boobs. I just sat there silent, I was

so upset. And then they started asking bra sizes at one of the tables. That just makes me so mad. *(Kanja)*

In restaurants subtle yet pervasive forms of sex joking and sexual harassment are used as social distancing techniques that reinforce a waitress's vulnerable position and maintain her inferiority (LaPointe 1992: 388; MacKinnon 1980: 60). The joking relationship is asymmetrical; so, while women may "marginally participate," they must be careful not to say things that would appear coarse or crude. Thus, insults operate mostly one-way, initiated and followed up on by men (Spradley and Mann 1975: 97).

Some Bazooms girls mentioned that they wished they knew how to "manage" better when it came to uncomfortable comments, sex joking, and innuendo. Here Katy expresses this notion of not letting the male customers and their comments bother her:

> It's weird, a little frightening at [Bazooms]. You go in there wearing a little outfit and they are just staring like that. You have to learn how to deal with people more sexually than just talking to them. It's something you need to learn, like how to talk without blushing – without letting them get to me. I want to be like "HEY!" Now I just get so embarrassed and walk away. They say stuff, sometimes they'll comment on your boobs or your butt or they'll say, "Oh yeah..." It's all flattery but sometimes it can be disgusting. *(Katy)*

Part of the job responsibilities of the Bazooms girl is to be able to "put up with shit." In Katy's case, she realizes that she has to learn a lot in terms of dealing with customers' sexual comments (being the "conversational cheerleader") and not letting herself be bothered by them. Hochschild's emotion management takes the form of "sex-joking or harassment management" in this case. While Bazooms's management espouses an open-door policy for all workers, Bazooms girl Jeni describes management's ideal Bazooms girl:

What they want is the ones who can deal with people and shit and don't complain. They don't want you there if you are going to stick up for yourself.

Gutek found that women working in female-dominated occupations (i.e., "traditionally female jobs") are less likely to report and view sexual harassment as a problem, because it is "part of the job" (Gutek 1985: 136). The idea that sexual harassment is part of the job at Bazooms came up constantly in subtle ways during my interviews. The fact that these women expected to have to learn to deal with sex joking and sexist behaviors from customers or managers is a commentary on what women are willing to put up with in the nineties workplace. For instance, after responding "no" to my question "Have you had any rude customers here?" Christiana thought for a while and then said, "Well, this guy did grab my butt." Did that anger her? "Well, I don't like it but I've kind of had to get used to it. I mean, if you want good tips you have to." Bazooms's sexual harassment policy states specifically: "Sexual harassment does not refer to occasional compliments of a socially acceptable nature. It does not refer to mutually acceptable joking or teasing. It refers to behavior which is unwelcome, that is personally offensive, that debilitates morale, and that, therefore, interferes with work effectiveness" (Bazooms Employee Handbook).

The part that managers play in the "elimination" of sexual harassment at Bazooms has been criticized severely in sexual discrimination and harassment lawsuits in at least three states. A leading law journal charged recently that Bazooms's managers are breaking their own sexual harassment policies, and "promoting misogyny and inflicting it on their own employees and inviting the public to come in and inflict it on the employees." Ex-Bazooms girls point to one of Bazooms's most popular merchandise items – the Bazooms girl calendar – as an example of corporate misogyny. The calendar contains jokes referring to the stupidity of Bazooms girls, with the months out of order "because the Bazooms girls put it together." Media accounts say that managers defend these degrading comments as "humor, like Polish jokes." Degrading signs are posted at some Bazooms restaurants like the one in South Carolina where your receipt reads: "Caution: Blondes thinking."

Agency

What is missing so far in this analysis is women's responses to these dynamics. There is no question that by following workplace rules of dress and demeanor, Bazooms girls were participants in the interplay of power, gender, and sexuality in the Bazooms workplace. Some waitresses dressed and behaved in ways that emphasized their sexuality and encouraged male patrons' attention – strategies that were seen to result in bigger tips. The financial bottom line no doubt underlay most Bazooms girls' calculations about the trade-off between sometimes demeaning dress and behavior expectations and the wages and tips they could expect to receive. There were limits, however, to how much unwelcome attention or harassment the waitresses would tolerate. When these limits were reached, Bazooms girls resisted and manipulated their gendered and sexualized workplace role in a variety of ways.

In *Weapons of the Weak* James Scott (1985) catalogues the various strategies used by the relatively powerless to resist authority. Subordinates resist and subvert authority by using a variety of backstage and up-front behaviors, such as confusion or denseness, slowness or foot-dragging, pilfering, performing shabby work, tampering, and lampooning, as well as sarcastic mimicry, or work evasion. Bazooms waitresses both actively and passively resist and manipulate the gendered and sexualized roles that are expected of them. LaPointe (1992) discusses specific informal strategies

that waitresses use in negotiating their boundaries and dealing with domination in the workplace. These may include refusing to acknowledge verbal or gestural advances, using teamwork to gain status, warning others about "offensive individuals," and defining abuse as part of the job (ibid: 391).

At Bazooms waitresses work within and against the constraints imposed by these factors in at least three ways: (1) They attempt to undermine or otherwise challenge the power structure, (2) they manipulate gender to preserve self-image, and (3) they both coopt and counteract sexualized identities.

Undermining and challenging the power structure

At Bazooms, formal power can be undermined by informal means. Challenges to the established power structure at Bazooms mainly take the form of gossip. Waitresses often expressed negative sentiments and shared complaints about management's constant exercise of authority.[12] During any given shift, one may overhear comments made by waitresses such as, "They always pick out the bad instead of rewarding or encouraging us on the good stuff" (Lori), or "You know we aren't respected at all" (Trina), or "I've never been in a restaurant where the workers are so badly treated" (Kelly), or "They are on a total power trip. Especially since they are in control of a lot of girls, and because they are men, they are taking that authority a bit too far" (Teri). Thus, by coming together and sharing grievances, gossip can be a form of resistance.

In some cases at Bazooms, waitresses have been known to challenge managers directly on their policies. One waitress, after being denied a break for eight hours, let one of the managers know how she was feeling. "I was so mad I was pretty much crying and he said 'Get in the office. What's wrong with you?' I said, 'You know, you have no respect for any of us waitresses.' He said, 'You know, I should just send you home for good.' Then

I shut up" (Trina). This was a clear use of the interactional technique of threatening a waitress with the loss of her job to sustain the established power structure at Bazooms (classical management dominance and waitress subordination). In Trina's case, a boundary was set by management that could not be crossed unless she was willing to sacrifice her job. She "vented" backstage, by saying to me:

> If it comes down to it and [the manager] tries to get me fired, I will fight it. I've never been late, I'm a hard worker, and I bust my ass. I'm professional and I'm always dressed when I walk in. I'll take them. There are plenty of girls who will back me up on how the management treats us.

Another waitress became defensive and upset when she was told that her hair wasn't styled enough. In talking back, this waitress challenged authority and used informal power to get her way. (The manager on that particular day decided it was not worth arguing about and let her keep her hair the way it was.) In both of these cases, established power boundaries were consciously tested by management and waitress alike.

It is clear that even after indirect and direct challenges to the established power hierarchy by waitresses, management retains its ultimate power over workers. Direct challenges to authority generally are squelched, as reflected in Teri's statement, "You can't talk back or you will get fired or written up. It's a power play." Bazooms wouldn't be Bazooms without the established power hierarchy (males on top). Nonetheless it is important to note that the women who work at Bazooms do not simply accept these power relations. They struggle to create solidarity and actively resist the passivity management wants from them.

Gender-based strategies

Just as waitresses attempt to resist the power structure at Bazooms, they also resist and manipulate gender roles to fit their needs. As one would expect, not all of the women hired at Bazooms were comfortable with the Bazooms girl role they were supposed to embody on the job. Much of the controversy about taking a job at Bazooms centers around the uniforms. About half of my interviewees described initial nervousness and insecurity about the uniforms. But at the time of most of the interviews (two to three months after the interviewees had started work), these thoughts had changed.

> At first it was hard wearing the uniform. But after a couple of weeks I got used to it, since everyone else is wearing one and it's the same as wearing sweats. What is wrong is that I've heard managers tell girls at this store to get smaller shorts. They didn't let me have a medium shirt, and they said my Colorado Bazooms shirt was too big and I couldn't wear it. That is wrong. (Kelly)

> The only thing I hate about the Bazooms uniform is that they tie the knots [on the back of the tank top] so tight that I can't breathe. And the nylons, they are always running and I have to buy new ones. They tried to get me to wear XX small shorts and I minded that. They made me try it on and I'm, like, "I'm not wearing this!" But the Xsmall isn't bad. (Sheri)

> The first time I saw the outfits I was nervous. I was, like, "I don't want to walk around in that!" Now, after I have seen them for so long, they are nothing. Except when people wear them too small with their butts hanging out. I can't stand that; it looks terrible. (Teri)

Each waitress went through a socializing process that often began with feeling nervous, even opposing the uniform. Waitresses then went through a period of adjustment based upon the fact that each wore the same thing as her coworkers did. Thus, as the definition of *normal* was revised, the nervous comments and complaints tended to subside. Yet, not everyone wears the same thing in the same ways. As their comments suggest, waitresses make choices about what to wear, and how to wear their outfits. The women made these choices based upon how comfortable they felt with the Bazooms girl image and their calculations about the financial utility of various style choices. Choices about whether to show cleavage, to wear a T-shirt (seen as more conservative by not highlighting the breasts) or a tank, to hike up the shorts, and so forth are also examples of negotiating the Bazooms girl's sexualized image. In other words, through manipulation of uniforms, these women manipulated the Bazooms girl concept to fit their own self-images and goals.

At least one waitress found that the uniform worked to her advantage in some ways:

> At another restaurant, they'd always get mad at me for spilling beer on the ground when I pour it. But you can get away with it at Bazooms because you are wearing this cute little outfit. It has to do with your image – you're a girl and you're wearing a skimpy little outfit. So of course they are going to be nice to you. *(Sandra)*

One Bazooms girl in Minnesota is an example of someone who did not get used to the uniform. She filed a lawsuit against Bazooms for sexual discrimination, among other things, and according to a major network news broadcast, "she is still waitressing to pay for college, but now she wears long pants and a long-sleeved shirt." Rejecting the concept altogether is an important form of resistance. Undoubtedly, many waitresses have quit because they are uncomfortable with the Bazooms girl concept and its associated behaviors.

But dress codes aren't the only thing that waitresses actively negotiate. Along with the dress codes come other pressures associated with "femaleness," especially in terms of appearance. Several waitresses stated that appearance-based insecurities often became obsessions:

> A lot of the girls are obsessed with the way they look. I know with our society looks are so important. I care about how I look. And there's not one girl in there who isn't really pretty. But I walk in there and people are talking about losing weight and stuff. It's too much based upon looks. I tell them "I can tell you how to lose fat, and I can do it if I want, but I like eating what I eat." *(Trina)*

> Places like Bazooms can mess you up if you don't know who you are. It's all glamour. I walked in there knowing who I am: a responsible, reliable person who loves herself, Jesus, my kids, my husband, and I don't need to look in the mirror twenty-four hours a day, seven days a week to look at my hair. *(Katy)*

By being aware of pressures to be thin and pretty, and counseling their coworkers on resisting these pressures, Trina and Katy were actively redefining gender ideals in the workplace.

Counteracting and coopting sexual identities

Women who dress to get attention, to show off their bodies, to look or feel "sexy" in our society, often end up getting labeled "whore," or "slut," and may be seen as "asking for it." Many of the Bazooms waitresses were concerned that their provocative outfits would force them into one of these sexualized roles. In response to a sexual slogan printed on the back of every T-shirt and tank, one Bazooms girl stated, "My hair covers the slogan, and we're not those kind of girls anyway." Nonetheless, Bazooms girls are associated with "those kind of girls," that is, sex workers or prostitutes working in a sexually charged environment where sex appeal is part of the product commodified and sold in the marketplace to men. The girls I worked with became aware of these associations early on, and they spent much time sharing and reacting to these negative associations. One waitress was in the bathroom and overheard two customers comment to each other: "You'd better use the seat covers." "We don't know who these girls have been with." This she shared with the other waitresses, one of whom commented:

> "[Professional football players] come in here and think they are 'the ones,' that we'll do anything for them." According to one waitress, "One football player said, 'I'm just gonna make my rounds in this restaurant and get to all of them.' Well, [we] are not that stupid. Some may jump at the chance but [we] don't like being put down like that." *(Kelly)*

Some of the women who work at Bazooms attempt to counteract these negative associations. One Bazooms girl remarked, "We need to educate men. Just because you are wearing this uniform doesn't mean that you are asking for anything, doesn't mean that you want anything more than a job." Several Bazooms girls made a point of telling customers that they were college students, or mothers, waitressing in order to save up money for education or family expenses. In this way the "girls" challenge the Bazooms girl (ditzy, sexual pawn) image most customers have and try to make the role more personal and respectable by sharing their own stories.

Some of the women, on the other hand, do not resist the negative associations but use them to achieve their own ends. In coopting the "bad girl" role, some hope to appeal to customers by using sex appeal to their advantage, hoping to get bigger tips (or more attention) this way. To Katy, "learning to deal with people more sexually" is to be able to control the situation in order to avoid embarrassment. Although it is harder to get people to admit to using the sexualized image for their own ends, once in a while stories fly among customers and waitresses about "what some [Bazooms] girls will do for money." Playing up the sexualized Bazooms girl role can be a serious money-making strategy.

> I've seen girls hula-hoop and get money thrown at them. Then they lean over and give the cleavage shot to the men. And at the downtown store the girls do things with pitchers of beer to make it look like a wet T-shirt contest. These things just do not work for me at all. *(Karon)*

> I don't get real into it and flirty. Some [of the girls] are flirty and that's part of their personality. But I'm not sure of the kind of treatment they get. I'm nice and I give them good service without anything else. *(Sheri)*

> It's not like I work there for the attention but I don't mind it at all. *(Lori)*

There appears to be a split among these women: those who try to resist the Bazooms girl role, downplaying the sexualized, flirty image, and those who coopt it, embellishing it as their own. One employee rejects the company's expectation; another turns it to her own ends. While all of the waitresses knew of women who have coopted this sexualized role, the attached stigma means that few will admit to doing it themselves. Lori came the closest, saying she didn't mind the attention.

Negotiation of sexuality and sexual harassment

There are times when the Bazooms game goes too far. What may be fun and games to one woman may be sexual harassment to another. Responses to crudeness or to offensive comments or actions by customers take many different forms at Bazooms. Katy says that when customers deal "sexually" with her, "I just get so embarrassed and walk away. But if they said something that offended me, I'd just go to the managers. I wouldn't even hesitate." Trina concurs, saying, "We don't have to put up with jack. I won't take [offensive remarks]. It's not worth my pride. I give customers the gnarliest looks." Kristy's response to offensive remarks is different: "I usually just laugh and walk away." As illustrated in these differing instances, women are responding in varied ways to the sexualized nature of the job, and to offensiveness from customers.

Women are themselves often deeply ambivalent about the limits of acceptable sexual innuendo and behavior from male customers. For instance, Lee, a Bazooms girl, was teaching a man how to dance to the birthday song with salt and pepper shakers in his hands. He asked if he could shake the salt and pepper shakers, gesturing towards her breasts. She slapped him on the arm (somewhat playfully), reprimanding him with "How old are you, twelve?" Then during the song she danced with him and gave him a hug afterwards. It looked as if Lee expressed her anger at a customer's crudeness (by slapping him), and then, realizing that she hadn't managed her emotions, became very flirty and nice, trying to make up for her slip. When I asked her later for her reaction, she said the incident had been bothering her all day. It seemed as though Lee reacted out of gut instinct, and then tried to correct this for any number of reasons (personal embarrassment, management censure, saving face in front of managers and customers, or concern for the tip). In retrospect, since the incident obviously had been upsetting for her, she may have questioned whether masking her true feelings was the right thing to do.

Harassment is taken for granted as part of the job at Bazooms. By defining abuse as part of the job, waitresses can continue to work without necessarily internalizing or accepting the daily hassles and degradations as aspects of their self-definitions or sense of self-worth (LaPointe 1992: 391). In other words, if women enter into a waitressing job expecting crude remarks, degrading uniforms, and unnecessary management-based power plays, they may prepare themselves for the worst by setting personal boundaries, with conditions attached.

The waitress (Christine) who had her "butt grabbed" made a decision to deal with the harassment in a way that she thought would bring a higher tip. And it did. Another waitress, Twayla, made a decision to react quite differently in a similar circumstance. "I turned right around and told him, 'You will not do these things to me.'" These two women weighed personal priorities and dealt with similar sexual behavior in different ways. Christine decided to allow a man to cross a particular boundary – but for a price, turning the incident to her advantage. Twayla made clear her boundary would not be crossed.

These examples point to the fact that women are not just victims in instances of harassment. They may indeed be at a disadvantage, but a victims-only perspective views women one-dimensionally. To see the other dimensions, one must view them as agents (economically, sexually, and otherwise), actively setting boundaries, negotiating circumstances, reacting, and in many cases resisting. Of course there is a point when informal forms of resistance may not be enough. LaPointe (1992: 383) suggests that the high turnover rates in the restaurant industry (and other service industries) may be a reaction to unwanted sexual harassment. In some cases negotiating room may be so narrow that quitting is a woman's only defense.

It is clear that Bazooms is a place where men use women for attention, to play up fantasies of sexual prowess, to affirm and reaffirm masculinity, to assert power, and to have a good time. Can we also say that, at the same time, women are using men for some of the same things? There is a reason why so many women make the decision to work at Bazooms. According to Kelly, "Bazooms can be really fun for a while. The girls eat it up too, just as much as the guys."

Just as males enact and affirm their masculinity at Bazooms, women (Bazooms girls) act out certain feminine roles and affirm a particular kind of femininity. Working at Bazooms can be "a huge self-esteem boost" (Lori), because Bazooms girls are getting what some consider to be positive attention in the form of flirting, flattery, and daily affirmation that they are indeed sexy, desirable women. Not only do Bazooms girls get attention and affirmations, but they are making commission as well. These aspects of the job may matter more to some than to others. My fellow waitresses who were single moms tended to be more interested in the tips; others may have been more concerned with affirmation and self-esteem.

For others, self-esteem is more undermined than affirmed by the sexualization of the workplace, and the tips are not worth the price. "Bazooms is kind of degrading sometimes," says Trina. "[Customers] refer to us as if we are stupid. It's hard to explain, the way they talk...they are talking down to us." Of course, contempt sometimes goes the other way. Trina goes on to add that the waitresses don't respect the customers either. "I think the waitresses kind of look down on the men. Because all of them – it's like they are dirty old men."

Conclusion

Bazooms is a good deal more than a "family" restaurant or a place where men can "swill beer and ogle blondes." It is a theater in which dramas of power, gender, and sexuality are played out. Within this drama, women play an explicitly subordinate role. As MacKinnon, LaPointe, Reskin and Roos, and Hochschild point out, their behaviors are severely constrained by the realities of employment in the service sector. Women are hired to put on a specific performance, and at Bazooms they are constrained by the formal script that Bazooms encourages its employees to follow. Furthermore, women are limited greatly by the assumptions men make about the appropriate and desirable place for women, especially in a sexually charged atmosphere. In the Bazooms environment, it is easy to classify these women as objects.

Yet women are also actively shaping their own experiences at Bazooms. The constraints on their actions are severe, but within them women struggle to retain their self-esteem, exercise power, and affirm the identities they value. Paules quotes Scott when she states, "What may be accomplished within this symbolic straitjacket is nonetheless something of a testament to human persistence and inventiveness" (Paules 1991: 164).

Bazooms girls are not helpless performers. They are women struggling to find ways to alter their roles, rewrite the script, and refashion the nature of the drama. The constraints mean that their options are relatively few, and while some of what they manage to accomplish is readily apparent, such as drawing the line in situations of sexual harassment, a good deal of their agency manifests itself in subtle ways. A different hairdo, a refusal to wear the uniform in a way the managers would like, an attempt to bring personal histories into the job to educate customers, a quietly voiced contempt for customers and managers – these become vehicles of assertion, ways of maintaining some semblance of control in an environment that supports only one role: the objects of male fantasy. Women sometimes also turn the play to their own advantage, finding opportunities to increase tips, support their kids, and even find some affirmation of self-worth.

In sum, the waitress is not a passive casualty of the hardships of her work. Within the structure of the job, she has developed an arsenal of often subtle but undeniably effective tactics to moderate the exploitive elements of her occupation and secure attention to her own needs (Paules 1991: 171). Few people passively watch their lives go by. The notion of agency suggests that workers in all fields, regardless of their formal options, actively take at least some control of their own destinies. In the voices of Trina, Katy, Christiana, and others we can hear women responding to their circumstances and asserting themselves as agents within the Bazooms drama.

NOTES

1   For reasons of confidentiality, all names used in this essay have been changed. Identifying traits (of this establishment) have been removed and identifying references are not included. This essay was cleared through the University of California Human Subjects Committee as a student project.

2   Bazooms's management likes to characterize their establishment as catering to families, probably in order to counter the sexy, bachelor-pad reputation that the local media assign to the establishment.

3   Interestingly, only about half of the chosen group would be considered "busty" by society's standards.

4   This falls under the category of opportunistic research or "auto-ethnography," in which the researcher becomes a participant in the setting so as not to alter the flow of interaction unnaturally, as well as to immerse oneself and grasp the depth of the subjectively lived experience (Denzin and Lincoln 1994).

5   I am aware that covert research has come under significant attack from social scientists. The issue seems to be that of disguise: misrepresentation of self in order to enter a new or forbidden domain, and deliberate misrepresentation of the character of research one is engaged in (Denzin and Lincoln 1994). These issues do not apply to my project, since I did not disguise myself in any way in order to get "in" at Bazooms. The management did not ask why I was applying and I therefore did not volunteer the information. Furthermore, I was up front with my subjects about "doing a school project," upon interviewing them. Finally, with names and identities changed throughout, I cannot see this report inflicting harm in any way. All quotes (from waitresses) are based upon recorded interviews.

6   Greta Paules (1991) notes that "the common interdiction in service dress codes against conspicuous jewelry may serve the same purpose as medieval decrees forbidding low-ranking employees to wear gold. In each case those of subordinate status are prohibited from assuming symbols of wealth or status that might obscure their position and blur class lines" (p. 134).

7   Statistics from the US Department of Labor, Bureau of Labor Statistics, 1984, show that the service industry was made up of 60 percent female workers (Reskin and Hartmann 1986: 22).

8   LaPointe (1992) argues that requiring employees to wear degrading uniforms emphasizes their "low status" and distinguishes them from their superiors.

9   Recent news coverage did report that, based upon a four-year investigation, Bazooms is being charged $22 million by the Equal Employment Opportunity Commission for sex discrimination in hiring. Yet, amid recent controversy over the EEOC's decision, Bazooms Company took out full-page ads in major national newspapers to insist that men do not belong as servers at Bazooms. Each ad featured a picture of a brawny man ludicrously dressed in a Bazooms girl uniform.

10   It must be mentioned that, like women, males are also often required to do "emotional labor" in the workplace. Nonetheless, as Hochschild points out, females hold the majority of responsibility for emotion work. According to Hochschild:

> With the growth of large organizations calling for skills in personal relations, the womanly art of status enhancement and the emotion work that it requires has been made more public, more systematized, more standardized. It is performed by mostly middle-class women in largely public-contact jobs. Jobs involving emotional labor comprise over a third of all jobs. But they form only a quarter of all jobs that men do, and over half of all the jobs that women do. *(Hochschild 1983: 171)*

11   This information parallels what Hochschild found in her study on flight attendants. Hochschild found that to them, a smile is not separate from the self, but an extension of the self, which represents the corporate "image" that a flight attendant must embody, and the "feelings" that must be "managed" in order to achieve this image. "To show that

the enjoyment takes effort is to do the job poorly. Similarly, part of the job is to disguise fatigue and irritation. . . . Otherwise the labor would show in an unseemly way, and the product – passenger contentment – would be damaged" (Hochschild 1983: 8). This example shows that outward emotion work, such as sustaining smiles, involves inner emotion work (disguising fatigue, anger, etc.) to achieve this image.

12 It is important to add that some of the waitresses believe "management is just doing their job," and don't complain.

REFERENCES

Denzin, N. K. and Y. S. Lincoln. 1994. *Handbook of Qualitative Research.* Thousand Oaks, CA: Sage.

Goldman, Emma. 1970. *The Traffic in Women.* Ojai, CA: Times Change Press.

Gutek, Barbara. 1985. *Sex and the Workplace.* San Francisco: Jossey-Bass.

Hochschild Arlie. 1979. "Emotion Work, Feeling Rules, and Social Structure." *American Journal of Sociology* 85 (3): 551–72.

—— 1983. *The Managed Heart.* Berkeley: University of California Press.

LaPointe, Eleanor. 1992. "Relationships with Waitresses: Gendered Social Distance in Restaurant Hierarchies." *Qualitative Sociology* 15 (4): 377–93.

MacKinnon, Catharine. 1980. "Women's Work," and "Sexual Harassment Cases." Pp. 59–66 and 111–13 in *Sexuality in Organizations,* edited by D. A. Neugarten and J. M. Shafritz. Oak Park, IL: Moore Publishing.

Mehan, H. and H. Wood. 1975. *The Reality of Ethnographic Methodology.* New York: Wiley.

Paules, Greta, 1991. *Dishing It Out: Power and Resistance Among Waitresses in a New Jersey Restaurant.* Philadelphia: Temple University Press.

Reskin, B. F. and H. Hartmann. 1986. *Women's Work; Men's Work: Sex Segregation on the Job.* Washington, DC: National Academy Press.

Reskin, B. F. and P. A. Roos. 1987. "Status Hierarchies and Sex Segregation." Pp. 3–22 in *Ingredients for Women's Employment Policy.* New York: State University of New York Press.

Scott, James. 1985. *Weapons of the Weak: Everyday Forms of Peasant Resistance.* Ithaca, NY: Yale University Press.

Segrave, Kerry. 1994. *The Sexual Harassment of Women in the Workplace, 1600 to 1993.* London: McFarland.

Spradley, James P. and Brenda J. Mann. 1975. *The Cocktail Waitress, Woman's Work in a Man's World.* New York: Wiley.

Wagner, Ellen J. 1992. *Sexual Harassment in the Workplace.* Bellvue, WA: Creative Solutions.

Whyte, W. F. 1948. *Human Relations in the Restaurant Industry.* New York: Arno.

16 Boundary Lines: Labeling Sexual Harassment in Restaurants

Patti A. Giuffre and Christine L. Williams

Sexual harassment occurs when submission to or rejection of sexual advances is a term of employment, is used as a basis for making employment decisions, or if the advances create a hostile or offensive work environment (Konrad and Gutek 1986). Sexual harassment can cover a range of behaviors, from leering to rape (Ellis, Barak, and Pinto 1991; Pryor 1987; Reilly et al. 1992; Schneider 1982). Researchers estimate that as many as 70 percent of employed women have experienced behaviors that may legally constitute sexual harassment (MacKinnon 1979; Powell 1986); however, a far lower percentage of women claim to have experienced sexual harassment. Paludi and Barickman (1991) write that "the great majority of women who are abused by behavior that fits legal definitions of sexual harassment – and who are traumatized by the experience – do not label what has happened to them 'sexual harassment'" (ibid: 68).

Why do most women fail to label their experiences as sexual harassment? Part of the problem is that many still do not recognize that sexual harassment is an actionable offense. Sexual harassment was first described in 1976 (MacKinnon 1979), but it was not until 1986 that the US Supreme Court included sexual harassment in the category of gender discrimination, thereby making it illegal (Paludi and Barickman 1991); consequently, women may not yet identify their experiences as sexual harassment because a substantial degree of awareness about its illegality has yet to be developed.

Many victims of sexual harassment may also be reluctant to come forward with complaints, fearing that they will not be believed, or that their charges will not be taken seriously (Jensen and Gutek 1982). As the Anita Hill–Clarence Thomas hearings demonstrated, women who are victims of sexual harassment often become the accused when they bring charges against their assailant.

There is another issue at stake in explaining the gap between experiencing and labeling behaviors "sexual harassment": many men and women experience some sexual behaviors in the workplace as pleasurable. Research on sexual harassment suggests that men are more likely than women to enjoy sexual interactions at work (Gutek 1985; Konrad and Gutek 1986; Reilly et al. 1992), but even some women experience sexual overtures at work as pleasurable (Pringle 1988). This attitude may be especially strong in organizations that use and exploit the bodies and sexuality of the workers (Cockburn 1991). Workers in many jobs are hired on the basis of their attractiveness and solicitousness – including not only sex industry workers, but also service sector workers such as receptionists, airline attendants, and servers in trendy restaurants. According to Cockburn (1991) this sexual exploitation is not completely forced: many people find this dimension of their jobs appealing and reinforcing to their own sense of identity and pleasure; consequently, some men and women resist efforts to expunge all sexuality from their places of work.

This is not to claim that all sexual behavior in the workplace is acceptable, even to some people. The point is that it is difficult to label behavior as sexual harassment because it forces people to draw a line between illicit and "legitimate" forms of sexuality at work – a process fraught with ambiguity. Whether a particular interaction is identified as harassment will depend on the intention of the harasser and the interpretation of the interchange by the victim, and both of these perspectives will be highly influenced by workplace culture and the social context of the specific event.

This article examines how one group of employees – restaurant workers – distinguishes between sexual harassment and other forms of sexual interaction in the workplace. We conducted an in-depth interview study of waitpeople and found that complex double standards are often used in labeling behavior as sexual harassment: identical behaviors are labeled sexual harassment in some contexts and not others. Many respondents claimed that they *enjoyed* sexual interactions involving co-workers of the same race/ethnicity, sexual orientation, and class/status backgrounds. Those who were offended by such interactions nevertheless dismissed them as natural or inevitable parts of restaurant culture.[1] When the same behavior occurred in contexts that upset these hegemonic heterosexual norms – in particular, when the episode involved interactions between gay and heterosexual men, or men and women of different racial/ethnic backgrounds – people seemed willing to apply the label sexual harassment.

We argue that identifying behaviors that occur only in counterhegemonic contexts as sexual harassment can potentially obscure and legitimate more insidious forms of domination and exploitation. As Pringle (1988: 95) points out, "Men control women through direct use of power, but also through definitions of pleasure – which is less likely to provoke resistance." Most women, she writes, actively seek out what

Rich (1980) termed "compulsory heterosexuality" and find pleasure in it. The fact that men and women may enjoy certain sexual interactions in the workplace does not mean they take place outside of oppressive social relationships, nor does it imply that these routine interactions have no negative consequences for women. We argue that the practice of labeling as "sexual harassment" only those behaviors that challenge the dominant definition of acceptable sexual activity maintains and supports men's institutionalized right of sexual access and power over women.

Methods

The occupation of waiting tables was selected to study the social definition of sexual harassment because many restaurants have a blatantly sexualized workplace culture (Cobble 1991; Paules 1991). According to a report published in a magazine that caters to restaurant owners, "Restaurants ...are about as informal a workplace as there is, so much so as to actually encourage – or at the very least tolerate – sexual banter" (Anders 1993: 48). Unremitting sexual banter and innuendo, as well as physical jostling, create an environment of "compulsory jocularity" in many restaurants (Pringle 1988: 93). Sexual attractiveness and flirtation are often institutionalized parts of a waitperson's job description; consequently, individual employees are often forced to draw the line for themselves to distinguish legitimate and illegitimate expressions of sexuality, making this occupation an excellent context for examining how people determine what constitutes sexual harassment. In contrast, many more sexual behaviors may be labeled sexual harassment in less highly sexualized work environments.[2]

Eighteen in-depth interviews were conducted with male and female wait staff who work in restaurants in Austin, Texas. Respondents were selected from restaurants that employ equal proportions of men and women on their wait staffs. Overall, restaurant work is highly sex segregated: women make up about 82 percent of all waitpeople (US Department of Labor 1989), and it is common for restaurants to be staffed only by either waitresses or waiters, with men predominating in the higher-priced restaurants (Cobble 1991; Hall 1993; Paules 1991). We decided to focus only on waitpeople who work in mixed-sex groups for two reasons. First, focusing on waitpeople working on integrated staffs enables us to examine sexual harassment between co-workers who occupy the same position in an organizational hierarchy. Co-worker sexual harassment is perhaps the most common form of sexual harassment (Pryor 1987; Schneider 1982), yet most case studies of sexual harassment have examined either unequal hierarchical relationships (e.g., boss–secretary harassment) or harassment in highly skewed gender groupings (e.g., women who work in nontraditional occupations) (Benson and Thomson 1982; Carothers and Crull 1984; Gruber and Bjorn 1982). This study is designed to investigate sexual harassment in unequal hierarchical relationships, as well as harassment between organizationally equal co-workers.

Second, equal proportions of men and women in an occupation implies a high degree of male–female interaction (Gutek 1985). Waitpeople are in constant contact with each other, help each other when the restaurant is busy, and informally socialize during slack periods. In contrast, men and women have much more limited interactions in highly sex-segregated restaurants and indeed, in most work environments. The high degree of interaction among the wait staff provides ample opportunity for sexual harassment between men and women to occur and, concomitantly, less opportunity for same-sex sexual harassment to occur.

The sample was generated using "snowball" techniques and by going to area restaurants and asking waitpeople to volunteer for the study. The sample includes eight men

and ten women. Four respondents are Latina/o, two African American, and twelve white. Four respondents are gay or lesbian; one is bisexual; thirteen are heterosexual. (The gay men and lesbians in the sample are all "out" at their respective restaurants.) Fourteen respondents are single; three are married; one is divorced. Respondents' ages range from 22 to 37.

Interviews lasted approximately one hour, and they were tape-recorded and transcribed for this analysis. All interviews were conducted by the first author, who has over eight years' experience waiting tables. Respondents were asked about their experiences working in restaurants; relationships with managers, customers, and other co-workers; and their personal experiences of sexual harassment. Because interviews were conducted in the fall of 1991, when the issue was prominent in the media because of the Hill–Thomas hearings, most respondents had thought a lot about this topic.

Findings

Respondents agreed that sexual banter is very common in the restaurant: staff members talk and joke about sex constantly. With only one exception, respondents described their restaurants as highly sexualized. This means that 17 of the 18 respondents said that sexual joking, touching, and fondling were common, everyday occurrences in their restaurants. For example, when asked if he and other waitpeople ever joke about sex, one waiter replied, "about 90 percent of [the jokes] are about sex." According to a waitress, "at work . . . [we're] used to patting and touching and hugging." Another waiter said, "I do not go through a shift without someone . . . pinching my nipples or poking me in the butt or grabbing my crotch. . . . It's just what we do at work."

These informal behaviors are tantamount to "doing heterosexuality," a process analogous to "doing gender" (West and

Zimmerman 1987).[3] By engaging in these public flirtations and open discussions of sex, men and women reproduce the dominant cultural norms of heterosexuality and lend an air of legitimacy – if not inevitability – to heterosexual relationships. In other words, heterosexuality is normalized and naturalized through its ritualistic public display. Indeed, although most respondents described their workplaces as highly sexualized, several dismissed the constant sexual innuendo and behaviors as "just joking," and nothing to get upset about. Several respondents claimed that this is simply "the way it is in the restaurant business," or "just the way men are."

With only one exception, the men and women interviewed maintained that they enjoyed this aspect of their work. Heterosexuality may be normative, and in these contexts, even compulsory, yet many men and women find pleasure in its expression. Many women – as well as men – actively reproduce hegemonic sexuality and apparently enjoy its ritual expression; however, in a few instances, sexual conduct was labeled as sexual harassment. Seven women and three men said they had experienced sexual harassment in restaurant work. Of these, two women and one man described two different experiences of sexual harassment, and two women described three experiences.

We analyzed these 17 accounts of sexual harassment to find out what, if anything, these experiences shared in common. With the exception of two episodes (discussed later), the experiences that were labeled "sexual harassment" were not distinguished by any specific words or behaviors, nor were they distinguished by their degree of severity. Identical behaviors were considered acceptable if they were perpetrated by some people, but considered offensive if perpetrated by others. In other words, sexual behavior in the workplace was interpreted differently depending on the context of the interaction. In general, respondents labeled their experiences sexual harassment only if

the offending behavior occurred in one of three social contexts: (1) if perpetrated by someone in a more powerful position, such as a manager; (2) if perpetrated by someone of a different race/ethnicity; or (3) if perpetrated by someone of a different sexual orientation.

Our findings do not imply that sexual harassment did not occur outside of these three contexts. Instead, they simply indicate that our respondents *labeled* behavior as "sexual harassment" when it occurred in these particular social contexts. We will discuss each of these contexts and speculate on the reasons why they were singled out by our respondents.

Powerful position

In the restaurant, managers and owners are the highest in the hierarchy of workers. Generally, they are the only ones who can hire or fire waitpeople. Three of the women and one of the men interviewed said they had been sexually harassed by their restaurants' managers or owners. In addition, several others who did not personally experience harassment said they had witnessed managers or owners sexually harassing other waitpeople. This finding is consistent with other research indicating people are more likely to think that sexual harassment has occurred when the perpetrator is in a more powerful position (e.g., Ellis' Barak, and Pinto 1991).

Carla describes being sexually harassed by her manager:

> One evening, [my manager] grabbed my body, not in a private place, just grabbed my body, period. He gave me like a bear hug from behind a total of four times in one night. By the end of the night I was livid. I was trying to avoid him. Then when he'd do it, I'd just ignore the conversation or the joke or whatever and walk away.

She claimed that her co-workers often give each other massages and joke about sex, but she did not label any of their behaviors sexual harassment. In fact, all four individuals who experienced sexual harassment from their managers described very similar types of behavior from their co-workers, which they did not define as sexual harassment. For example, Cathy said that she and the other waitpeople talk and joke about sex constantly: "Everybody stands around and talks about sex a lot.... Isn't that weird? You know, it's something about working in restaurants and, yeah, so we'll all sit around and talk about sex." She said that talking with her co-workers about sex does not constitute sexual harassment because it is "only joking." She does, however, view her male manager as a sexual harasser:

> My employer is very sexist. I would call that sexual harassment. Very much of a male chauvinist pig. He kind of started [saying] stuff like, "You can't really wear those shorts because they're not flattering to your figure.... But I like the way you wear those jeans. They look real good. They're tight." It's like, you know [I want to say to him], "You're the owner, you're in power. That's evident. You know, you need to find a better way to tell me these things." We've gotten to a point now where we'll joke around now, but it's never ever sexual, ever. I won't allow that with him.

Cathy acknowledges that her manager may legitimately dictate her appearance at work, but only if he does so in professional – and not personal – terms. She wants him "to find a better way to tell me these things," implying that he is not completely out-of-line in suggesting that she wear tight pants. He "crosses the line" when he personalizes his directive, by saying to Cathy "*I like* the way you wear those jeans." This is offensive to Cathy because it is framed as the manager's personal prerogative, not the institutional requirements of the job.

Ann described a similar experience of sexual harassment from a restaurant owner:

> Yeah, there's been a couple of times when a manager has made me feel real uncomfortable and I just removed myself from the situation.... Like if there's something I really want him to hear or something I think is really important there's no touching. Like, "Don't touch me while I'm talking to you." You know, because I take that as very patronizing. I actually blew up at one of the owners once because I was having a rough day and he came up behind me and he was rubbing my back, like up and down my back and saying, you know, "Oh, is Ann having a bad day?" or something like that and I shook him off of me and I said, "You do not need to touch me to talk to me."

Ann distinguishes between legitimate and illegitimate touching: if the issue being discussed is "really important" – that is, involving her job status – she insists there be no touching. In these specific situations, a back rub is interpreted as patronizing and offensive because the manager is using his powerful position for his *personal* sexual enjoyment.

One of the men in the sample, Frank, also experienced sexual harassment from a manager:

> I was in the bathroom and [the manager] came up next to me and my tennis shoes were spray-painted silver so he knew it was me in there and he said something about, "Oh, what do you have in your hand there?" I was on the other side of a wall and he said, "Mind if I hold it for a while?" or something like that, you know. I just pretended like I didn't hear it.

Frank also described various sexual behaviors among the waitstaff, including fondling, "joking about bodily functions," and "making bikinis out of tortillas." He said, "I mean, it's like, what we do at work.... There's no holds barred. I don't find it offensive. I'm used to it by now. I'm guilty of it myself." Evidently, he defines sexual behaviors as "sexual harassment" only when perpetrated by someone in a position of power over him.[4]

Two of the women in the sample also described sexual harassment from customers. We place these experiences in the category of "powerful position" because customers do have limited economic power over the waitperson insofar as they control the tip (Crull 1987). Cathy said that male customers often ask her to "sit on my lap" and provide them with other sexual favors. Brenda, a lesbian, described a similar experience of sexual harassment from women customers:

> One time I had this table of lesbians and they were being real vulgar towards me. Real sexual. This woman kind of tripped me as I was walking by and said, "Hurry back." I mean, gay people can tell when other people are gay. I felt harassed.

In these examples of harassment by customers, the line is drawn using a similar logic as in the examples of harassment by managers. These customers acted as though the waitresses were providing table service to satisfy the customers' private desires, instead of working to fulfill their job descriptions. In other words, the customers' demands were couched in personal – and not professional – terms, making the waitresses feel sexually harassed.

It is not difficult to understand why waitpeople singled out sexual behaviors from managers, owners, and customers as sexual harassment. Subjection to sexual advances by someone with economic power comes closest to the quid pro quo form of sexual harassment, wherein employees are given the option to either "put out or get out." Studies have found that this type of sexual harassment is viewed as the most threatening and unambiguous sort (Ellis, Barak, and Pinto 1991; Fitzgerald 1990; Gruber and Bjorn 1982).

But even in this context lines are drawn between legitimate and illegitimate sexual behavior in the workplace. As Cathy's comments make clear, some people accept the employers' prerogative to exploit the workers' sexuality, by dictating appropriate "sexy" dress, for example. Like airline attendants, waitresses are expected to be friendly, helpful, and sexually available to the male customers (Cobble 1991). Because this expectation is embedded in restaurant culture, it becomes difficult for workers to separate sexual harassment from the more or less accepted forms of sexual exploitation that are routine features of their jobs. Consequently, some women are reluctant to label blatantly offensive behaviors as sexual harassment. For example, Maxine, who claims that she has never experienced sexual harassment, said that customers often "talk dirty" to her:

> I remember one day, about four or five years ago when I was working as a cocktail waitress, this guy asked me for a "Slow Comfortable Screw" [the name of a drink]. I didn't know what it was. I didn't know if he was making a move or something. I just looked at him. He said, "You know what it is, right?" I said, "I bet the bartender knows!" (laughs).... There's another one, "Sex on the Beach." And there's another one called a "Screaming Orgasm." Do you believe that?

Maxine is subject to a sexualized work environment that she finds offensive; hence her experience could fit the legal definition of sexual harassment. But because sexy drink names are an institutionalized part of restaurant culture, Maxine neither complains about it nor labels it sexual harassment: once it becomes clear that a "Slow Comfortable Screw" is a legitimate and recognized restaurant demand, she accepts it (albeit reluctantly) as part of her job description. In other words, the fact that the offensive behavior is institutionalized seems to make it beyond reproach in her eyes. This finding is consistent with others' findings that those who work in highly sexualized environments may be less likely to label offensive behavior "sexual harassment" (Gutek 1985; Konrad and Gutek 1986).

Only in specific contexts do workers appear to define offensive words and acts of a sexual nature as sexual harassment – even when initiated by someone in a more powerful position. The interviews suggest that workers use this label to describe their experiences only when their bosses or their customers couch their requests for sexual attentions in explicitly personal terms. This way of defining sexual harassment may obscure and legitimize more institutionalized – and hence more insidious – forms of sexual exploitation at work.

Race/ethnicity

The restaurants in our sample, like most restaurants in the United States, have racially segregated staffs (Howe 1977). In the restaurants where our respondents are employed, men of color are concentrated in two positions: the kitchen cooks and bus personnel (formerly called busboys). Five of the white women in the sample reported experiencing sexual harassment from Latino men who worked in these positions. For example, when asked if she had ever experienced sexual harassment, Beth said:

> Yes, but it was not with the people ... it was not, you know, the people that I work with in the front of the house. It was with the kitchen. There are boundaries or lines that I draw with the people I work with. In the kitchen, the lines are quite different. Plus, it's a Mexican staff. It's a very different attitude. They tend to want to touch you more and, at times, I can put up with a little bit of it but ... because I will give them a hard time too but I won't touch them. I won't touch their butt or anything like that.
> [Interviewer: So sometimes they cross the line?]
> It's only happened to me a couple of times. One guy, like, patted me on the butt and I went off. I lost my shit. I went off on him. I said, "No. Bad. Wrong. I can't speak Spanish to you but, you know, this is it." I told the kitchen manager who is a guy

and he's not ... the head kitchen manager is not Hispanic. ... I've had to do that over the years only a couple of times with those guys.

Beth reported that the waitpeople joke about sex and touch each other constantly, but she does not consider their behavior sexual harassment. Like many of the other men and women in the sample, Beth said she feels comfortable engaging in this sexual banter and play with the other waitpeople (who were predominantly white), but not with the Mexican men in the kitchen.

Part of the reason for singling out the behaviors of the cooks as sexual harassment may involve status differences between waitpeople and cooks. Studies have suggested that people may label behaviors as sexual harassment when they are perpetrated by people in lower-status organizational positions (Grauerholz 1989; McKinney 1990); however, it is difficult to generalize about the relative status of cooks and waitpeople because of the varied and often complex organizational hierarchies of restaurants (Paules 1991: 107–10). If the cook is a chef, as in higher-priced restaurants, he or she may actually have more status than waitpeople, and indeed may have the formal power to hire and fire the waitstaff. In the restaurants where our respondents worked, the kitchen cooks did not wield this sort of formal control, but they could exert some informal power over the waitstaff by slowing down food orders or making the orders look and/or taste bad. Because bad food can decrease the waitperson's tip, the cooks can thereby control the waitperson's income; hence servers are forced to negotiate and to some extent placate the wishes and desires of cooks to perform their jobs. The willingness of several respondents to label the cooks' behavior as sexual harassment may reflect their perception that the cooks' informal demands had become unreasonable. In such cases, subjection to the offensive behaviors is a term of employment, which is quid pro quo sexual harassment. As mentioned previously, this type of sexual harassment is the most likely to be so labeled and identified.

Because each recounted case of sexual harassment occurring between individuals of different occupational statuses involved a minority man sexually harassing a white woman, the racial context seems equally important. For example, Ann also said that she and the other waiters and waitresses joke about sex and touch each other "on the butt" all the time, and when asked if she had ever experienced sexual harassment, she said,

> I had some problems at [a previous restaurant] but it was a communication problem. A lot of the guys in the kitchen did not speak English. They would see the waiters hugging on us, kissing us and pinching our rears and stuff. They would try to do it and I couldn't tell them, "No. You don't understand this. It's like we do it because we have a mutual understanding but I'm not comfortable with you doing it." So that was really hard and a lot of times what I'd have to do is just sucker punch them in the chest and just use a lot of cuss words and they knew that I was serious. And there again, I felt real weird about that because they're just doing what they see go on everyday.

Kate, Carla, and Brenda described very similar racial double standards. Kate complained about a Mexican busser who constantly touched her:

> This is not somebody that I talk to on a friendly basis. We don't sit there and laugh and joke and stuff. So, when he touches me, all I know is he is just touching me and there is no context about it. With other people, if they said something or they touched me, it would be funny or... we have a relationship. This person and I and all the other people do not. So that is sexual harassment.

And according to Brenda:

> The kitchen can be kind of sexist. They really make me angry. They're not as bad as they used to be because they got warned. They're mostly Mexican, not even Mexican American. Most of them, they're just starting to learn English.
>
> [Interviewer: What do they do to you?]
>
> Well, I speak Spanish, so I know. They're not as sexual to me because I think they know I don't like it. Some of the other girls will come through and they will touch them like here [points to the lower part of her waist]. ... I've had some pretty bad arguments with the kitchen.
>
> [Interviewer: Would you call that sexual harassment?]
>
> Yes. I think some of the girls just don't know better to say something. I think it happens a lot with the kitchen guys. Like sometimes, they will take a relleno in their hands like it's a penis. Sick!

Each of these women identified the sexual advances of the minority men in their restaurants as sexual harassment, but not the identical behaviors of their white male co-workers; moreover, they all recognize that they draw boundary lines differently for Anglo men and Mexican men: each of them willingly participates in "doing heterosexuality" only in racially homogamous contexts. These women called the behavior of the Mexican cooks "sexual harassment" in part because they did not "have a relationship" with these men, nor was it conceivable to them that they *could* have a relationship with them, given cultural and language barriers – and, probably, racist attitudes as well. The white men, on the other hand, can "hug, kiss, and pinch rears" of the white women because they have a "mutual understanding" – implying reciprocity and the possibility of intimacy.

The importance of this perception of relationship potential in the assessment of sexual harassment is especially clear in the cases of the two married women in the sample, Diana and Maxine. Both of these women said that they had never experienced sexual harassment. Diana, who works in a family-owned and operated restaurant, claimed that her restaurant is not a sexualized work environment. Although people occasionally make *double entendre* jokes relating to sex, according to Diana, "there's no contact whatsoever like someone pinching your butt or something." She said that she has never experienced sexual harassment:

> Everybody here knows I'm married so they're not going to get fresh with me because they know that it's not going to go anywhere, you know so...and vice versa. You know, we know the guys' wives. They come in here to eat. It's respect all the way. I don't think they could handle it if they saw us going around hugging them. You know what I mean? It's not right.

Similarly, Maxine, who is Colombian, said she avoids the problem of sexual harassment in her workplace because she is married:

> The cooks don't offend me because they know I speak Spanish and they know how to talk with me because I set my boundaries and they know that....I just don't joke with them more than I should. They all know that I'm married, first of all, so that's a no-no for all of them. My brother used to be a manager in that restaurant so he probably took care of everything. I never had any problems anyway in any other jobs because, like I said, I set my boundaries. I don't let them get too close to me.
>
> [Interviewer: You mean physically?]
>
> Not physically only. Just talking. If they want to talk about, "Do you go dancing? Where do you go dancing?" Like I just change the subject because it's none of their business and I don't really care to talk about that with them...not because I consider them to be on the lower levels than me or something but just because if you start talking with them that way then you are just giving them hope or something. I think that's true for most of the guys here, not just talking about the cooks....I do get offended and they know that so sometimes they apologize.

Both Maxine and Diana said that they are protected from sexual harassment because they are married. In effect, they use their marital status to negotiate their interactions with their co-workers and to ward off unwanted sexual advances. Furthermore, because they do not view their co-workers as potential relationship "interests," they conscientiously refuse to participate in any sexual banter in the restaurant.

The fact that both women speak Spanish fluently may mean that they can communicate their boundaries unambiguously to those who only speak Spanish (unlike the female respondents in the sample who only speak English). For these two women, sexual harassment from co-workers is not an issue. Diana, who is Latina, talks about "respect all around" in her restaurant; Maxine claims the cooks (who are Mexican) aren't the ones who offend her. Their comments seem to reflect more mutual respect and humanity toward their Latino co-workers than the comments of the white waitresses. On the other hand, at least from Maxine's vantage point, racial harassment is a bigger problem in her workplace than is sexual harassment. When asked if she ever felt excluded from any groups at work, she said:

> Yeah, sometimes. How can I explain this? Sometimes, I mean, I don't know if they do it on purpose or they don't but they joke around you about being Spanish....Sometimes it hurts. Like they say, "What are you doing here? Why don't you go back home?"

Racial harassment – like sexual harassment – is a means used by a dominant group to maintain its dominance over a subordinated group. Maxine feels that, because she is married, she is protected from sexual harassment (although, as we have seen, she is subject to a sexualized workplace that is offensive to her); however, she does experience racial harassment where she works, and she feels vulnerable to this because she is one of very few nonwhites working at her restaurant.

One of the waiters in the sample claimed that he had experienced sexual harassment from female co-workers, and race may have also been a factor in this situation. When Rick (who is African American) was asked if he had ever been sexually harassed, he recounted his experiences with some white waitresses:

> Yes. There are a couple of girls there, wait-people, who will pinch my rear.
> [Interviewer: Do you find it offensive?]
> No (laughs) because I'm male.... But it is a form of sexual harassment.
> [Interviewer: Do you ever tell them to stop?]
> If I'm really busy, if I'm in the weeds, and they want to touch me, I'll get mad. I'll tell them to stop. There's a certain time and place for everything.

Rick is reluctant about labeling this interaction "sexual harassment" because "it doesn't bother me unless I'm, like, busy or something like that." In those cases where he is busy, he feels that his female co-workers are subverting his work by pinching him. Because of the race difference, he may experience their behaviors as an expression of racial dominance, which probably influences his willingness to label the behavior as sexual harassment.

In sum, the interviews suggest that the perception and labeling of interactions as "sexual harassment" may be influenced by the racial context of the interaction. If the victim perceives the harasser as expressing a potentially reciprocal relationship interest, they may be less likely to label their experience sexual harassment. In cases where the harasser and victim have a different race/ethnicity and class background, the possibility of a relationship may be precluded because of racism, making these cases more likely to be labeled "sexual harassment."

This finding suggests that the practices associated with "doing heterosexuality" are profoundly racist. The white women in the sample showed a great reluctance to label unwanted sexual behavior sexual harassment when it was perpetrated by a potential (or real) relationship interest – that is, a white male co-worker. In contrast, minority men are socially constructed as potential harassers of white women: any expression of sexual interest may be more readily perceived as nonreciprocal and unwanted. The assumption of racial homogamy in heterosexual relationships thus may protect white men from charges of sexual harassment of white women. This would help to explain why so many white women in the sample labeled behaviors perpetrated by Mexican men as sexual harassment, but not the identical behaviors perpetrated by white men.

Sexual orientation

There has been very little research on sexual harassment that addresses the sexual orientation of the harasser and victim (exceptions include Reilly et al. 1992; Schneider 1982, 1984). Surveys of sexual harassment typically include questions about marital status but not about sexual orientation (e.g., Fain and Anderton 1987; Gruber and Bjorn 1982; Powell 1986). In this study, sexual orientation was an important part of heterosexual men's perceptions of sexual harassment. Of the four episodes of sexual harassment reported by the men in the study, three involved openly gay men sexually harassing straight men. One case involved a male manager harassing a male waiter (Frank's experience, described earlier). The other two cases involved co-workers. Jake said that he had been sexually harassed by a waiter:

> Someone has come on to me that I didn't want to come on to me.... He was another waiter [male]. It was laughs and jokes the whole way until things got a little too much and it was like, "Hey, this is how it is. Back off. Keep your hands off my ass." ... Once it reached the point where I felt kind of threatened and bothered by it.

Rick described being sexually harassed by a gay baker in his restaurant:

> There was a baker that we had who was really, really gay.... He was very straight-forward and blunt. He would tell you, in detail, his sexual experiences and tell you that he wanted to do them with you.... I knew he was kidding but he was serious. I mean, if he had a chance he would do these things.

In each of these cases, the men expressed some confusion about the intentions of their harassers – "I knew he was kidding but he was serious." Their inability to read the intentions of the gay men provoked them to label these episodes sexual harassment. Each man did not perceive the sexual interchange as reciprocal, nor did he view the harasser as a potential relationship interest. Interestingly, however, all three of the men who described harassment from gay men claimed that sexual banter and play with other *straight* men did not trouble them. Jake, for example, said that "when men get together, they talk sex," regardless of whether there are women around. He acceded, "people find me offensive, as a matter of fact," because he gets "pretty raunchy" talking and joking about sex. Only when this talk was initiated by a gay man did Jake label it as sexual harassment.

Johnson (1988) argues that talking and joking about sex is a common means of establishing intimacy among heterosexual men and maintaining a masculine identity. Homosexuality is perceived as a direct challenge and threat to the achievement of masculinity and consequently, "the male homosexual is derided by other males because he is not a real man, and in male logic if one is not a real man, one is a woman" (ibid: 124). In Johnson's view, this dynamic not only sustains masculine identity, it also shores up male dominance over women; thus, for some straight men, talking about sex with other straight men is a form of reasserting masculinity and male domin-

ance, whereas talking about sex with gay men threatens the very basis for their masculine privilege. For this reason they may interpret the sex talk and conduct of gay men as a form of sexual harassment.

In certain restaurants gay men may in fact intentionally hassle straight men as an explicit strategy to undermine their privileged position in society. For example, Trent (who is openly gay) realizes that heterosexual men are uncomfortable with his sexuality, and he intentionally draws attention to his sexuality in order to bother them:

> [Interviewer: Homosexuality gets on whose nerves?]
> The straight people's nerves.... I know also that we consciously push it just because, we know, "Okay. We know this is hard for you to get used to but tough luck. I've had my whole life trying to live in this straight world and if you don't like this, tough shit." I don't mean like we're shitty to them on purpose but it's like, "I've had to worry about being accepted by straight people all my life. The shoe's on the other foot now. If you don't like it, sorry."
> [Interviewer: Do you get along well with most of the waitpeople?]
> I think I get along with straight women. I get along with gay men. I get along with gay women usually. If there's ever going to be a problem between me and somebody it will be between me and a straight man.

Trent's efforts to "push" his sexuality could easily be experienced as sexual harassment by straight men who have limited experience negotiating unwanted sexual advances. The three men who reported being sexually harassed by gay men seemed genuinely confused about the intentions of their harassers, and threatened by the possibility that they would actually be subjected to and harmed by unwanted sexual advances. But it is important to point out that Trent works in a restaurant owned by lesbians, which empowers him to confront his straight male co-workers. Not all restaurants provide the sort of atmosphere that makes this type of engagement possible; indeed, some restaurants have policies explicitly banning the hiring of gays and lesbians. Clearly, not all gay men would be able to push their sexuality without suffering severe retaliation (e.g., loss of job, physical attacks).

In contrast to the reports of the straight men in this study, none of the women interviewed reported sexual harassment from their gay or lesbian co-workers. Although Maxine was worried when she found out that one of her co-workers was lesbian, she claims that this fact no longer troubles her:

> Six months ago I found out that there was a lesbian girl working there. It kind of freaked me out for a while. I was kind of aware of everything that she did towards me. I was conscious if she walked by me and accidently brushed up against me. She's cool. She doesn't bother me. She never touches my butt or anything like that. The gay guys do that to the [straight] guys but they know they're just kidding around. The [straight] guys do that to the [straight] girls, but they don't care. They know that they're not supposed to do that with me. If they do it, I stop and look at them and they apologize and they don't do it anymore. So they stay out of my way because I'm a meanie *(laughs)*.

Some heterosexual women claimed they feel *more* comfortable working with gay men and lesbians. For example, Kate prefers working with gay men rather than heterosexual men or women. She claims that she often jokes about sex with her gay co-workers, yet she does not view them as potential harassers. Instead, she feels that her working conditions are more comfortable and more fun because she works with gay men. Similarly, Cathy prefers working with gay men over straight men because "gay men are a lot like women in that they're very sensitive to other people's space." Cathy also works with lesbians, and she claims that she has never felt sexually harassed by them.

The gays and lesbians in the study did not report any sexual harassment from their gay and lesbian co-workers. Laura, who is bisexual, said she preferred to work with gays and lesbians instead of heterosexuals because they are "more relaxed" about sex. Brenda said she feels comfortable working around all of her male and female colleagues – regardless of their sexual orientation:

> The guys I work with [don't threaten me]. We always run by each other and pat each other on the butt. It's no big deal. Like with my girlfriend [who works at the same restaurant], all the cocktailers and hostesses love us. They don't care that we're gay. We're not a threat. We all kind of flirt but it's not sexual. A lesbian is not going to sexually harass another woman unless they're pretty gross anyway. It has nothing to do with their sexuality; it has to do with the person. You can't generalize and say that gays and lesbians are the best to work with or anything because it depends on the person.

Brenda enjoys flirtatious interactions with both men and women at her restaurant, but distinguishes these behaviors from sexual harassment. Likewise, Lynn, who is a lesbian, enjoys the relaxed sexual atmosphere at her workplace. When asked if she ever joked about sex in her workplace, she said:

> Yes! (laughs) All the time! All the time – everybody has something that they want to talk about on sex and it's got to be funny. We have gays. We have lesbians. We have straights. We have people who are real Christian-oriented. But we all jump in there and we all talk about it. It gets real funny at times. . . . I've patted a few butts . . . and I've been patted back by men, and by the women, too! (laughs).

Don and Trent, who are both gay, also said that they had never been sexually harassed in their restaurants, even though both described their restaurants as highly sexualized.

In sum, our interviews suggest that sexual orientation is an important factor in understanding each individual's experience of sexual harassment and his or her willingness to label interactions as sexual harassment. In particular, straight men may perceive gay men as potential harassers. Three of our straight male respondents claimed to enjoy the sexual banter that commonly occurs among straight men, and between heterosexual men and women, but singled out the sexual advances of gay men as sexual harassment. Their contacts with gay men may be the only context where they feel vulnerable to unwanted sexual encounters. Their sense of not being in control of the situation may make them more willing to label these episodes sexual harassment.

Our findings about sexual orientation are less suggestive regarding women. None of the women (straight, lesbian, or bisexual) reported sexual harassment from other female co-workers or from gay men. In fact, all but one of the women's reported cases of sexual harassment involved a heterosexual man. One of the two lesbians in the sample (Brenda) did experience sexual harassment from a group of lesbian customers (described earlier), but she claimed that sexual orientation is *not* key to her defining the situation as harassment. Other studies have shown that lesbian and bisexual women are routinely subjected to sexual harassment in the workplace (Schneider 1982, 1984); however, more research is needed to elaborate the social contexts and the specific definitions of harassment among lesbians.

The exceptions

Two cases of sexual harassment were related by respondents that do not fit in the categories we have thus far described. These were the only incidents of sexual harassment reported between co-workers of the same race: in both cases, the sexual harasser is a white man, and the victim, a white woman. Laura – who is bisexual – was sexually harassed at a previous restaurant by a cook:

This guy was just constantly badgering me about going out with him. He like grabbed me and took me in the walk-in one time. It was a real big deal. He got fired over it too....I was in the back doing something and he said, "I need to talk to you," and I said, "We have nothing to talk about." He like took me and threw me against the wall in the back....I ran out and told the manager, "Oh my God. He just hit me," and he saw the expression on my face. The manager went back there...and then he got fired.

This episode of sexual harassment involved violence, unlike the other reported cases. The threat of violence was also present in the other exception, a case described by Carla. When asked if she had ever been sexually harassed, she said,

I experienced two men, in wait jobs, that were vulgar or offensive and one was a cook and I think he was a rapist. He had the kind of attitude where he would rape a woman. I mean, that's the kind of attitude he had. He would say totally, totally inappropriate [sexual] things.

These were the only two recounted episodes of sexual harassment between "equal" co-workers that involved white men and women, and both involved violence or the threat of violence.[5]

Schneider (1982, 1991) found the greatest degree of consensus about labeling behavior sexual harassment when that behavior involves violence. A victim of sexual harassment may be more likely to be believed when there is evidence of assault (a situation that is analogous to acquaintance rape). The assumption of reciprocity among homogamous couples may protect assailants with similar characteristics to their victims (e.g., class background, sexual orientation, race/ethnicity, age) – *unless* there is clear evidence of physical abuse. Defining only those incidents that involve violence as sexual harassment obscures – and perhaps even legitimizes – the more common occurrences that do not involve violence, making it all the more diffi-cult to eradicate sexual harassment from the workplace.

Discussion and Conclusion

We have argued that sexual harassment is hard to identify, and thus difficult to eradicate from the workplace, in part because our hegemonic definition of sexuality defines certain contexts of sexual interaction as legitimate. The interviews with waitpeople in Austin, Texas, indicate that how people currently identify sexual harassment singles out only a narrow range of interactions, thus disguising and ignoring a good deal of sexual domination and exploitation that take place at work.

Most of the respondents in this study work in highly sexualized atmospheres where sexual banter and touching frequently occur. There are institutionalized policies and practices in the workplace that encourage – or at the very least tolerate – a continual display and performance of heterosexuality. Many people apparently accept this ritual display as being a normal or natural feature of their work; some even enjoy this behavior. In the in-depth interviews respondents labeled such experiences as sexual harassment in only three contexts: when perpetrated by someone who took advantage of their powerful position for personal sexual gain; when the perpetrator was of a different race/ethnicity than the victim – typically a minority man harassing a white woman; and when the perpetrator was of a different sexual orientation than the victim – typically a gay man harassing a straight man. In only two cases did respondents label experiences involving co-workers of the same race and sexual orientation as sexual harassment – and both episodes involved violence or the threat of violence.

These findings are based on a very small sample in a unique working environment, and hence it is not clear whether they are generalizable to other work settings. In less sexualized working environments, individuals may be more likely to label all offensive sexual advances as sexual harassment, whereas in more highly sexualized environments (such as topless clubs or striptease bars), fewer sexual advances may be labeled sexual harassment. Our findings do suggest that researchers should pay closer attention to the interaction context of sexual harassment, taking into account not only gender but also the race, occupational status, and sexual orientation of the assailant and the victim.

Of course, it should not matter who is perpetrating the sexually harassing behavior: sexual harassment should not be tolerated under any circumstances. But if members of oppressed groups (racial/ethnic minority men and gay men) are selectively charged with sexual harassment, whereas members of the most privileged groups are exonerated and excused (except in cases where institutionalized power or violence are used), then the patriarchal order is left intact. This is very similar to the problem of rape prosecution: minority men are the most likely assailants to be arrested and prosecuted, particularly when they attack white women (LaFree 1989). Straight white men who sexually assault women (in the context of marriage, dating, or even work) may escape prosecution because of hegemonic definitions of "acceptable" or "legitimate" sexual expression. Likewise, as we have witnessed in the current debate on gays in the military, straight men's fears of sexual harassment justify the exclusion of gay men and lesbians, whereas sexual harassment perpetrated by straight men against both straight and lesbian women is tolerated and even endorsed by the military establishment, as in the Tailhook investigation (Britton and Williams, forthcoming). By singling out these contexts for the label "sexual harassment," only marginalized men will be prosecuted, and the existing power structure that guarantees privileged men's sexual access to women will remain intact.

Sexual interactions involving men and women of the same race and sexual orientation have a hegemonic status in our society, making sexual harassment difficult to identify and eradicate. Our interviews suggest that many men and women are active participants in the sexualized culture of the workplace, even though ample evidence indicates that women who work in these environments suffer negative repercussions to their careers because of it (Jaschik and Fretz 1991; Paludi and Barickman 1991; Reilly et al. 1992; Schneider 1982). This is how cultural hegemony works – by getting under our skins and defining what is and is not pleasurable to us, despite our material or emotional interests.

Our findings raise difficult issues about women's complicity with oppressive sexual relationships. Some women obviously experience pleasure and enjoyment from public forms of sexual engagement with men; clearly, many would resist any attempt to eradicate all sexuality from work – an impossible goal at any rate. Yet, it is also clear that the sexual "pleasure" many women seek out and enjoy at work is structured by patriarchal, racist, and heterosexist norms. Heterosexual, racially homogamous relationships are privileged in our society: they are institutionalized in organizational policies and job descriptions, embedded in ritualistic workplace practices, and accepted as legitimate, normal, or inevitable elements of workplace culture. This study suggests that only those sexual interactions that violate these policies, practices, and beliefs are resisted and condemned with the label "sexual harassment."

We have argued that this dominant social construction of pleasure protects the most privileged groups in society from charges of sexual harassment and may be used to oppress and exclude the least powerful groups. Currently, people seem to consider the gender, race, status, and sexual orientation of the assailant when deciding to label behaviors as sexual harassment. Unless we acknowledge the complex double standards people use in "drawing the line," then sexual domination and exploitation will undoubtedly remain the normative experience of women in the workforce.

NOTES

1 It could be the case that those who find this behavior extremely offensive are likely to leave restaurant work. In other words, the sample is clearly biased in that it includes only those who are currently employed in a restaurant and presumably feel more comfortable with the level of sexualized behavior than those who have left restaurant work.

2 It is difficult, if not impossible, to specify which occupations are less highly sexualized than waiting tables. Most occupations probably are sexualized in one way or another; however, specific workplaces may be more or less sexualized in terms of institutionalized job descriptions and employee tolerance of sexual banter. For example, Pringle (1988) describes some offices as coolly professional – with minimal sexual joking and play – whereas others are characterized by "compulsory jocularity." Likewise, some restaurants may deemphasize sexual flirtation between waitpeople and customers, and restrain informal interactions among the staff (one respondent in our sample worked at such a restaurant).

3 We thank Margaret Andersen for drawing our attention to this fruitful analogy.

4 It is also probably significant that this episode of harassment involved a gay man and a heterosexual man. This context of sexual harassment is discussed later in this essay.

5 It is true that both cases involved cooks sexually harassing waitresses. We could have placed these cases in the "powerful position" category, but did not because in these particular instances the cooks did not possess institutionalized power over the waitpeople. In other words, in these particular cases the cook and waitress had equal organizational status in the restaurant.

REFERENCES

Anders, K. T. 1993. Bad sex: Who's harassing whom in restaurants? *Restaurant Business*, January 20, pp. 46–54.

Benson, Donna J. and Gregg E. Thomson. 1982. Sexual harassment on a university campus: The confluence of authority relations, sexual interest and gender stratification. *Social Problems* 29: 236–51.

Britton, Dana M. and Christine L. Williams. Forthcoming. Don't ask, don't tell, don't pursue: Military policy and the construction of heterosexual masculinity. *Journal of Homosexuality.*

Carothers, Suzanne C. and Peggy Crull. 1984. Contrasting sexual harassment in female- and male-dominated occupations. In *My troubles are going to have trouble with me: Everyday trials and triumphs of women workers*, edited by K. B. Sacks and D. Remy. New Brunswick, NJ: Rutgers University Press.

Cobble, Dorothy Sue. 1991. *Dishing it out: Waitresses and their unions in the twentieth century.* Urbana: University of Illinois Press.

Cockburn, Cynthia. 1991. *In the way of women.* Ithaca, NY: I.L.R. Press.

Crull, Peggy. 1987. Searching for the causes of sexual harassment: An examination of two prototypes. In *Hidden aspects of women's work*, edited by Christine Bose, Roslyn Feldberg, and Natalie Sokoloff. New York: Praeger.

Ellis, Shmuel, Azy Barak, and Adaya Pinto. 1991. Moderating effects of personal cognitions on experienced and perceived sexual harassment of women at the workplace. *Journal of Applied Social Psychology* 21: 1320–37.

Fain, Terri C. and Douglas L. Anderton. 1987. Sexual harassment: Organizational context and diffuse status. *Sex Roles* 17: 291–311.

Fitzgerald, Louise F. 1990. Sexual harassment: The definition and measurement of a construct. In *Ivory power: Sexual harassment on campus*, edited by Michele M. Paludi. Albany: State University of New York Press.

Grauerholz, Elizabeth. 1989. Sexual harassment of women professors by students: Exploring the dynamics of power, authority, and gender in a university setting. *Sex Roles* 21: 789–801.

Gruber, James E. and Lars Bjorn. 1982. Blue-collar blues: The sexual harassment of women auto workers. *Work and Occupations* 9: 271–98.

Gutek, Barbara A. 1985. *Sex and the workplace.* San Francisco: Jossey-Bass.

Hall, Elaine J. 1993. Waitering/waitressing: Engendering the work of table servers. *Gender & Society* 7: 329–46.

Howe, Louise Kapp. 1977. *Pink collar workers: Inside the world of women's work.* New York: Avon.

Jaschik, Mollie L. and Bruce R. Fretz. 1991. Women's perceptions and labeling of sexual harassment. *Sex Roles* 25: 19–23.

Jensen, Inger W. and Barbara A. Gutek. 1982. Attributions and assignment of responsibility in sexual harassment. *Journal of Social Issues* 38: 122–36.

Johnson, Miriam. 1988. *Strong mothers, weak wives.* Berkeley: University of California Press.

Konrad, Alison M. and Barbara A. Gutek. 1986. Impact of work experiences on attitudes toward sexual harassment. *Administrative Science Quarterly* 31: 422–38.

LaFree, Gary D. 1989. *Rape and criminal justice: The social construction of sexual assault.* Belmont, CA: Wadsworth.

McKinney, Kathleen, 1990. Sexual harassment of university faculty by colleagues and students. *Sex Roles* 23: 421–38.

MacKinnon, Catherine A. 1979. *Sexual harassment of working women: A case of sex discrimination.* New Haven, CT: Yale University Press.

Paludi, Michele and Richard B. Barickman. 1991. *Academic and workplace sexual harassment.* Albany: State University of New York Press.

Paules, Greta Foff. 1991. *Dishing it out: Power and resistance among waitresses in a New Jersey restaurant.* Philadelphia: Temple University Press.

Powell, Gary N. 1986. Effects of sex role identity and sex on definitions of sexual harassment. *Sex Roles* 14: 9–19.

Pringle, Rosemary. 1988. *Secretaries talk: Sexuality, power and work.* London: Verso.

Pryor, John B. 1987. Sexual harassment proclivities in men. *Sex Roles* 17: 269–90.

Reilly, Mary Ellen, Bernice Lott, Donna Caldwell, and Luisa DeLuca. 1992. Tolerance for sexual harassment related to self-reported sexual victimization. *Gender & Society* 6: 122–38.

Rich, Adrienne. 1980. Compulsory heterosexuality and lesbian existence. *Signs* 5: 631–60.

Schneider, Beth E. 1982. Consciousness about sexual harassment among heterosexual and lesbian women workers. *Journal of Social Issues* 38: 75–98.

—— 1984. The office affair: Myth and reality for heterosexual and lesbian women workers. *Sociological Perspectives* 27: 443–64.

—— 1991. Put up and shut up: Workplace sexual assaults. *Gender & Society* 5: 533–48.

US Department of Labor, Bureau of Labor Statistics. 1989, January. *Employment and earnings*. Washington, DC: Government Printing Office.

West, Candace and Don H. Zimmerman. 1987. Doing gender. *Gender & Society* 1: 125–51.

Part V

Sexuality and Religion

Religion is a very important institution in our society for shaping attitudes and behaviors regarding sexuality. Almost every organized religion specifies the appropriate forms of sexual relationship. In Part V we include articles on Evangelical and Pentecostal Christianity, Orthodox Judaism, and Islam. For the most part, religious affiliation is associated with traditional attitudes about sexuality, gender, and the family. That is, the more closely affiliated one is with one's religion, the more likely one is to subscribe to traditional values: sex only in marriage; husband and wife have traditional gender roles; the purpose of sex is intimacy and ultimately procreation. But the beliefs and practices of religious people are more varied and complex than this suggests. John Bartkowski shows there is disagreement even within the leadership of Christian organizations about how men and women ought to behave. He examines the Promise Keepers and shows that men bring very different values and sensibilities about sex to this essentially conservative movement. Although many mainstream religious organizations object strongly to any sexual expression outside of heterosexual marriage, studies suggest that the same proportion of gays and lesbians consider themselves religious as do heterosexuals. Some gays and lesbians, wishing to avoid persecution by mainline religion, have formed their own churches, such as the Metropolitan Community Church. Although religion is associated with sexual conservatism, it is one of the few venues in our society where people discuss the importance of sexuality in their lives and for society, making it both a conservative and a creative force.

17 Breaking Walls, Raising Fences: Masculinity, Intimacy, and Accountability among the Promise Keepers

John P. Bartkowski

Godly Masculinities: Competing Definitions of Christian Manhood among Leading Promise Keepers

How do leading spokesmen for the Promise Keepers define masculinity and articulate their vision of godly manhood? A detailed analysis of advice manuals written by two very different Promise Keeper authors lays bare the competing discourses[1] of masculinity advanced by leaders of this evangelical men's movement.

Essentialist appeals to gender difference: The Promise Keeper discourse of instrumentalist masculinity

Many leading Promise Keepers advance a highly instrumentalist vision of masculinity (Bartkowski 1999a). Among the most enthusiastic purveyors of instrumentalist masculinity is Edwin Louis Cole, a popular Promise Keeper author and speaker cited (albeit briefly) in Messner's (1997) volume. Cole's *Maximized Manhood: A Guide to Family Survival* (1982) is in its eighteenth printing and boasts 800,000 copies in print. The instrumentalist brand of masculinity invoked by the likes of Cole is predicated on the notion of innate, categorical, and largely immutable gender difference (i.e., radical essentialism) (Bartkowski 1997a, 1997b, 2001, forthcoming). According to purveyors of this radical essentialist discourse, manhood is characterized by aggression, strength, and rationality – qualities that are counterposed to "feminine" responsiveness, sensitivity, and emotionalism. Masculinity is also thought to be manifested through men's long-range vision and achievement-mindedness, again as juxtaposed to women's apparent penchant for nurturance and intuitive grasp of life's "fine-print."

Cole places a premium on this putative chasm of gender difference: "It is possible to get spirituality from women, but strength always comes from men. A church, a family, a nation is only as strong as its men. Men you are accountable. There is no sleek escape chute. God requires manhood of all men" (Cole 1982: 72). In contrast to masculine strength, Cole claims that intimacy is what "every woman craves" (ibid: 78–9, 82). Indeed, masculine assertiveness and feminine emotionalism would seem to be endemic to virtually all aspects of male–female relationships: "even women who are promiscuous feel a measure of guilt in having sexual relations without any love. So, prior to submitting to a man's love-making, they ask the age-old question, 'Do you love me?'" (ibid: 82).

Such categorical claims are advanced to marshal support for Cole's vision of gendered social roles, particularly in the domestic realm. Cole defends a patriarchal family structure in which the husband is the undisputed "priest" or "head" of the household (ibid: 82, 102, ch. 10). Married women are even believed to desire male leadership within the home (ibid: 77). And how could it be otherwise? Cole (ibid: 66, 68, 108, 109) argues that two of the essential characteristics of manhood are courage and decisiveness, which together provide men with an escape from sappy sentimentalism: "Courage has always been a requirement of leadership.... God has planned for someone to take charge. Men – it is you" (ibid: 107, 111). "*The Kingdom of God is based on truth, not human sentiment*. Decisions must be made the same way. Decision-making is one of the marks of a man. Every man I know that is a success is decisive" (ibid: 66, emphasis in original).

Underlying this radical essentialism is a belief in the divinely ordained propriety of heterosexuality, as well as an intolerance for the "sin" of homosexuality and "gender blending." Cole (ibid: 34) characterizes the end times as a point when "the 'problem person' plunges into a Christless eternity... and homosexual 'problems' will be no more." He concludes that the "perversion" of homosexuality will be eradicated in this lifetime only if males "begin to tackle sin like men" (ibid), and he expresses his deep displeasure with the contemporary "feminized" man: "I like real men. . . . I don't like the pussyfooting pipsqueaks who tippy toe through the tulips. . . . I like men to be men" (ibid: 35).

If such apocalyptic rhetoric fails to arouse his male readership to their God-ordained calling as "decisive leaders," Cole points to the person that he considers to be the paragon of toughness – Jesus Christ. Not unlike early twentieth-century evangelists who advocated "muscular Christianity" and painted Jesus as a "man's man" (DeBerg 1990; Kimmel 1996), Cole reminds his readers that Jesus's "arms gripped that scourge of cords and drove the money-changers out of the temple. . . . Jesus was a fearless leader, defeating Satan, casting out demons, commanding nature, rebuking hypocrites. . . . God wants to reproduce this manhood in all men. . . . Since to be like Jesus – Christlike – requires a certain ruthlessness, manhood does also" (Cole 1982: 62–3).

Evangelizing the men's liberation movement: The Promise Keeper discourse of expressive masculinity

In contrast to the discourse of instrumentalist masculinity outlined above, a competing vision of godly manhood emerges from other leading Promise Keepers. Gary Oliver's *Real Men Have Feelings Too* (1993), one of many manuals sold through the Promise Keepers organization and endorsed by PK founder Bill McCartney, clearly articulates the contours of this expressive masculinity. In stark contrast to the discourse of instrumentalist masculinity advanced by the likes of Cole, Oliver (1993: 23–32) argues that traits commonly associated with being male (e.g., bravery, strength, stoicism, an insatiable sex drive, a preoccupation with achievement) are *not* really "masculine" at all. In addition, he contends that characteristics typically associated with being a woman (e.g., gentleness, compassion, tenderness, meekness, sensitivity) are *not* really the property of an essential "feminine" temperament (ibid: 19–20). Rather, Oliver contends that traits often linked with womanliness are actually "human" traits clearly exemplified by Jesus Christ. He therefore laments that "sin has so damaged and distorted our culture that what God designed to characterize healthy people now characterizes only women. That's tragic!" (ibid: 20; see also 61–2, 65–6).

Oliver's manual has a very different agenda than that which guides Cole's treatise. Rather than have men "maximize their (instrumentalist) manhood," Oliver (ibid: 19) argues for a more sensitized masculinity – one in which men can learn "how to be human, how to feel, how to love, how to be better husbands, fathers, and friends." Indeed, Oliver is quite critical of radical views of gender difference, claiming that such "myths of masculinity" have "produced a generation of men who define themselves by the negative. Whatever women are, whatever strengths or attributes they have, whatever characteristics they possess, positive or negative, men aren't. And if women are emotional, then real men aren't. And any attempt to say they could be or should be is [mistakenly seen as] an attempt to 'feminize' men" (ibid: 37).

Therefore, throughout his advice manual, Oliver encourages men to explore, trust, and express their emotions rather than place the "mind over emotions"; to recognize that the free expression of emotions is supported by a careful reading of the Bible; and to acknowledge the physical, psychological, and relational benefits of this emotionally expressive masculinity (ibid: 46–9, 68, 70–2). Especially noteworthy is Oliver's (ibid: ch. 12) treatment of conflict resolution. In contrast to instrumentalist defenses of a patriarchal family, Promise Keeper purveyors of expressive manhood articulate various levels of support for marital egalitarianism through direct or implicit references to "mutual submission" (see Bartkowski 1997a, 1997b, 1999b, 2001, forthcoming). To make his case for marital egalitarianism, Oliver's treatment of effective conflict resolution mixes popular psychological rhetoric, men's liberationism, and biblical references. Using a married couple as an example of this process, Oliver (ibid: 230) outlines five different "conflict styles" that couples may employ; assesses each conflict style with regard to meeting one's "personal needs" and the couple's "relationship needs"; and then provides seven steps to follow so that couples may achieve "resolution" – the conflict style that he recommends above all others – which entails "discuss[ing] and decid[ing] on a mutually acceptable solution." So, whereas Cole is dismayed by men's relinquishing of family leadership, Oliver laments that men are often reluctant to find a mutually acceptable solution to family problems. Oliver (ibid: 230–1) even recommends that spouses flip a coin to move them through a decision-making impasse rather than rely on a patriarchal authority-in-reserve. If a husband and wife are locked in a stalemate, concludes Oliver, "it's better to try something that might work than something that is a proven failure" (ibid: 231).

Remaking Godly Manhood: Identity Negotiation and Gender Practice in PK Accountability Groups

How, then, do these competing discourses of masculinity impact the social relationships and subjective identities of Promise Keeper members? The remainder of this study examines the idioculture (Fine 1987) of PK accountability groups, and illuminates the types of social interaction facilitated by these encounters. Fine (ibid: 125) conceptualizes an idioculture as a "system of knowledge, beliefs, behaviors, and customs shared by members of an interacting group to which members can refer and that serve as the basis of further interaction." An idioculture, as I use the term, is a *dynamic* amalgam of localized beliefs and practices that, taken together, stand in *uneasy tension* and require *continual negotiation*. So, rather than suggesting that accountability groups practice a wholesale acceptance of either instrumentalist or expressive manhood, I demonstrate that these all-male small groups produce a melange masculinity that selectively combines key elements from the competing gender discourses outlined above.

One key feature of the Promise Keepers organization is its emphasis on the formation of grassroots "accountability groups" among its rank-and-file members. Not unlike twelve-step programs and consciousness-raising groups that have proliferated in the last several decades, PK accountability groups are intended to complement, channel, and sustain the collective effervescence experienced by many men who attend the Promise Keeper stadium conferences. Accountability groups aim to assist PK members in "putting into practice" the Seven Promises to which they are exposed during PK stadium conferences. Accountability groups, as the name implies, also provide for the mutual monitoring of PK members' ongoing "walk with the Lord" through intimate peer exchanges.

Based on fieldwork conducted over a three-year period, I attended the meetings of several different accountability groups – ranging in size from about five to fifteen men – as well as weekly all-male lunchtime gatherings frequented by many local members of PK. Men's experiences in accountability groups also figured prominently in many of the nineteen in-depth interviews I conducted (primarily during the summer of 1998), as well as countless informal conversations I have had with local members of PK during the course of my fieldwork. Nearly all of the men that I interviewed actively participated in accountability groups, and virtually all interviewees had attended at least one stadium conference. As part of my fieldwork, I also attended a PK stadium conference in San Antonio during the summer of 1999.

Why do many PK men attend accountability groups? Although specific motivations vary, virtually all of these accountability group attendees agree that the spiritual "high" produced by the stadium rallies would ultimately fade without the emotional openness and close peer monitoring provided in these small-group forums. One respondent, Jeff, describes accountability groups as "a must.... Without that kind of small group activity, that sharing to get involved in, [stadium conference attendance]...will just be a mountain-top experience and you'll fall back into whatever pattern you've been in for your whole life – because that's what you know."

These accountability groups are consequently believed to be critical to cultivating the godly manhood that is championed by Promise Keeper luminaries and members alike. Men in PK regularly portray accountability groups as the site in which the "real work" of promise-keeping is actively facilitated.

Breaking Down the Walls with Expressive Masculinity: Equality and Intimacy in Accountability Groups

In many respects, the idioculture of PK accountability groups subverts instrumentalist gender ideals that lionize "toughness" in men and valorize social hierarchy. Among the more striking aspects of these gatherings is the positioning of PK men's bodies in space. Accountability groups typically consist of some sort of circular space – often chairs arranged tightly together in an enclosed circle – regardless of the number of men attending the group. When men arrive during the course of these meetings, the circle of attendees is typically expanded to envelop the new arrivals. The geography of these gatherings is designed to assist men in achieving two key goals embraced by Promise Keeper accountability groups and the organization at large: the recognition of equality among all men, and the fostering of intense intimacy with one's PK compatriots.

Equality, communitas, and accountability

The circular inscription of space within these accountability groups symbolizes an ideal of equality and a striving for genuine *communitas* (Turner and Turner 1978) among PK attendees. Consistent with the PK emphasis on "breaking down the walls" that often divide men one from another, several of these groups consist of members who differ in age (teens to retirees), ethnicity (Anglo, African American, Hispanic), and social class (e.g., college professors seated next to auto mechanics who were themselves adjacent to unemployed men). Similarly, these groups aim to build bridges across different Christian (though mostly Protestant) denominations – e.g., Methodist, Baptist, Assembly of God.

The geography of the accountability group places men with these diverse backgrounds and life experiences face-to-face. Each man in the circle is flanked on either side by his fellows, and this close-quarters arrangement stimulates conversational exchanges that often flow freely and openly from one participant to another. The inscription of space in PK accountability groups, then, aims to level the pernicious social hierarchies that pit men against one another in various social arenas (secular and religious) "outside" of the circle.

Steve, a prominent local leader of PK in Texas, commonly raises the issue of "breaking down walls" with men in accountability groups, training seminars for local members, and even words of encouragement distributed quite regularly to many PK members via his e-mail listserve. Through these various forums, Steve urges local Promise Keepers to bridge the chasms that so often divide believers of different stripes. One of Steve's e-mailed messages underscores this very point. Steve begins by citing Philippians 1: 3–6, in which Paul reminds his fellow first-century Christians of their "partnership in the gospel." Steve uses this biblical reference to tell many of his PK brothers that they, too, are united as *partners in the gospel....* God has a wonderful plan for each of His children – no matter what stage we are in.... We may be serving in different capacities, different ministries, or different churches, but *we're all on the same team*" (emphasis added). Yet another message delivered from Steve to many of his compatriots challenges more privileged brothers to reach out beyond their insular social circles to men of "different income levels, different education levels, different talent levels, different spiritual levels.... We each have a message to share and we're encouraged to share that message with *all*, so that some might be saved" (emphasis in the original).

The appeal of this egalitarian rhetoric and the democratized structure of accountability groups resonates with longstanding evangelical Protestant themes of equality among all Christians ("the priesthood of all believers";

"all have sinned and fallen short of the glory of God") (Bartkowski 1998, 2001; Juster 1994). In most recent memory, such themes have been raised by biblical feminists and equality-minded evangelicals who criticize the authoritarian sensibilities of other leading conservative Protestants (Bartkowski 1997b). Although many Promise Keepers would probably not see themselves as heirs to the egalitarian legacy of evangelical feminism, the very structure of PK accountability groups and much PK rhetoric has clearly been informed by biblical feminist critiques waged against "unChristian" forms of domination and exclusion.

Tempering equality in accountability groups

The democratic rhetoric and the egalitarian use of space in PK accountability groups outlined above nevertheless stands in tension with several hierarchical and exclusionary facets of these groups' idioculture. First, although accountability groups are predicated on an ethic of equality among men, the exclusion of women from these gatherings is indeed noteworthy. Can genuine *communitas* ever be fully achieved in a space reserved solely for men? Although there appears to be no clear-cut answer to this question (see below), Messner (1997: xiv) suggests that the very notion of a "men's movement" – i.e., an organization that excludes women by design – can preclude gender egalitarianism by setting up women as an "other" against which men define themselves.

Second, the nascent egalitarianism manifested in these local PK groups is tempered by men's frequent references to male family leadership. In casting men as "leaders" of their families, many members of PK eschew a thorough-going domestic egalitarianism and thereby reject the secularism and "radical" feminism such commitments would seem to imply. Interestingly, however, the men with whom I interacted invariably chose their words quite carefully on this score. Many of the men invoke the neo-patriarchal language of a husband's "servant-leadership" – as opposed to the less qualified (and somewhat dated) notion of "husband-headship." "Servant-leadership" – a term that rhetorically conceives of a kinder, gentler patriarchy – has recently been adopted by leading evangelicals, including many PK speakers and authors (Bartkowski 1997a, 1997b, 2001). Moreover, my respondents' references to male family leadership (or, again, "servant-leadership") are in many cases flanked by nods toward "mutual submission" – a term initially coined by biblical feminists in the late 1960s. The use of such contradictory language by my subjects again underscores the uneasy tension between patriarchal convictions and egalitarian sensibilities manifested in the Promise Keepers and, more broadly, within late twentieth-century evangelicalism.

Finally, the leadership structures – both formal and informal – that often emerge within these accountability groups exist in tension with the egalitarian ethos of such meetings. Leadership within accountability groups can be based on formal organizational ties with the Promise Keepers (e.g., Point Men, Ambassadors), length of tenure as a born-again Christian or Promise Keeper, age, and other stratification mechanisms. The actual implementation of leadership within these groups may entail calling the accountability meeting, initiating the discussion (sometimes by way of introducing a "theme" for that meeting), and charting the temporal trajectory of the meeting (i.e., the transition from fellowshipping to thematic discussions to prayer time). Yet, for reasons explicated above, heavy-handed leadership in these gatherings would be hard-pressed to enlist the support of accountability group attendees – once again underscoring the democratic values that permeate these gatherings.

In the end, accountability groups provide for many of the men a sense of equality with their fellows even as they serve to reify particular types of social hierarchies. Indeed, it is only in preserving a sense of social order – God's order – that the men become liberated to explore the unfamiliar terrain of equality, social leveling, and solidarity during these encounters. The very structure of accountability groups and the exchanges that occur there consequently envelop a set of antinomies – equality and difference, leveling and hierarchy, expressivism and instrumentalism – that stand in productive tension for many of the PK men who frequent these gatherings.

Embracing liminality: intimacy and accountability

A much more daunting task faced by Promise Keepers who frequent accountability groups concerns the interpersonal negotiation of intimacy among these godly men. Apart from fostering a sense of equality among local members of PK, the enclosed accountability circles described above have immediate practical ramifications for the men who attend these gatherings – namely, the facilitation of emotional sensitivity for one's compatriots along with extreme (inter)personal vulnerability. The circular geography of accountability groups is designed to distinguish the secure confines designated for emotional "brotherly" exchanges on the one hand from the public arena of instrumentalist masculinity on the other.

How successful are these accountability groups in providing a liminal milieu (Turner and Turner 1978) for local members of PK? Does this circular space actually foster the intense brotherly intimacy sought by these attendees? My observational and interview data suggest that emotionally expressive masculinity within accountability groups is in abundant supply. Many of the men that I interviewed and observed remarked that it is within the context of these private, enclosed gatherings that they can "be themselves" or can "become transparent" to their "brothers." When I first sat in on accountability groups and other small-group PK gatherings, I was unprepared for the blatantly confessional character of these encounters. In such forums, men talk openly about a range of otherwise highly private topics that they would be hard pressed to lay bare in the "outside world": various problems with the law; assorted sexual "improprieties"; as well as thorny interpersonal dilemmas with their wives, children, colleagues, and friends. One interview respondent even recounted how, at a recent accountability group meeting, otherwise "strong men" ended up weeping profusely and rolling on the floor in anguish after learning that the vast majority of them had been sexually abused as children.

During both accountability meetings and in interviews men often commented on their relief in sharing such burdens with their brothers via these small-group gatherings. Indeed, the sharing of these men's innermost struggles with a select group of equally vulnerable compatriots provided many attendees with a powerful emotional discharge ("cathexis," in the Freudian sense) that had often been absent from their other peer relationships. A 20-year-old first-timer to one accountability group was moved nearly to tears by conveying a series of misadventures in his recent past which had included, among other confessed transgressions, a conviction on felony charges and jail time. He explained how, after having been abandoned by a girlfriend with whom he had fathered a child, he faced the challenge of raising his young daughter on his own. As this young Latino man completed his "confession" and vowed to continue his turnaround, his initially somber tone visibly gave way to giddy relief. On the heels of his cathartic discharge, this newcomer reflexively called attention to the overwhelming sense of relief produced by exposing his checkered past to other men who would still, he hoped, accept him as a "brother in Christ." Recognizing their young brother's vulnerability, several of the older men took the opportunity to reaffirm this bold

newcomer and reciprocated his transparency by proceeding to share their own life's struggles with other men in the circle. Through such exchanges, accountability groups directly subvert traditional notions of instrumentalist masculinity which decry "sissified" men and lionize "manly toughness."

Raising Fences with Instrumentalist Masculinity: Dividing Practices and the Management of Homosocial Intimacy

Despite the positive affect that is produced through the intimate bonds described above, the emotional openness that characterizes PK accountability groups also requires many of their attendees to engage in the management of homosocial intimacy. It is important to keep in mind that PK fits the sociological definition of a homosocial organization because it fosters "social preferences for one's own gender [that do] not necessarily imply erotic attraction" (Britton 1990: 423). In this way, homosociality (i.e., social encounters formally designated as all-male or all-female) may facilitate intense social bonds (e.g., intimate, emotional exchange) without the emergence of erotic or sexual attraction.

Nevertheless, homosocial intimacy requires "management" within the PK context for several reasons. First, homosocial intimacy is a direct product of intense, on-the-fly emotional exchanges, such as those noted above, that often occur within PK accountability groups. Because PK members' man-to-man relationships are predicated on (stereotypically) "feminine"/expressive qualities such as vulnerability, intimacy, and intense emotionalism, they risk calling attention to the utter contingency and malleability of gender. Although liminal experiences can be terribly liberating, such social encounters may simultaneously invite a widespread sense of disorientation if they are not "tempered" by mechanisms of social control (cf., Juster 1994).

Second, the challenges associated with homosocial intimacy among PK men also stem from more durable structural and historical forces long confronted by male evangelicals. Historians have highlighted the longstanding feminization of evangelical Protestantism in American culture (e.g., Juster 1994), and social researchers have charted the many (only partly successful) attempts of religious conservatives to masculinize this "religion of the heart" (e.g., DeBerg 1990; Bartkowski 1997b, 1998). In short, then, Promise Keeper men are "at risk" of being doubly feminized – first by their expressive interactional practices with their brothers (which, as noted above, often violate instrumentalist definitions of masculinity), and then by their evangelical convictions (which carry a decidedly gendered historical residue).

How, then, do the Promise Keepers seek to promote intimate relations among its members without thoroughly undermining a traditionalist sex–gender matrix or reinforcing the historical conflation of evangelicalism and femininity? My research findings highlight three strategies through which the Promise Keepers manage homosocial intimacy. Following Foucault (1977), I describe these strategic responses to homosocial intimacy broadly as "dividing practices" that are deployed organizationally and (inter)subjectively by many Promise Keepers. Drawing on the logic and, at times, the actual form of instrumental masculinity, these dividing practices use the play of difference – actually, *differánce* (Derrida 1974) – to define godly masculinity in juxtaposition to a strategically chosen "other" (male homosexuality, erotic intimacy, and femininity).

Godly, not gay

First, some elites among the PK leadership use a key dividing practice – an overtly *anti-gay ideological stance* – to tame the potentially subversive character of homosocial intimacy among its members. PK has produced an official position paper condemning homosexuality, and Ed Cole (whose rhetoric was analyzed above) is not the only Promise Keeper leader to express his disdain for the "sin" of homosexuality. Bill McCartney, the founder of PK, actively campaigned against gay rights when Colorado's Amendment 2 stimulated political controversy across the nation.

The articulation of overtly anti-gay rhetoric by Bill McCartney and Ed Cole is not a novel phenomenon among religious conservatives. Many leading evangelicals have advanced similar critiques now for several decades. However, the vocal heterosexism emanating from some (though not all) leading PKs is unique inasmuch as it represents a strategic and "functional" dividing practice for this group's all-male membership. Flanked by this anti-gay ideology and the naturalization of heterosexuality, the radical gender innovations of PK – from stadium rallies of tear-filled men to the extreme intimacy promoted in accountability groups – are bounded and therefore made "safe." Within accountability groups, the *gender identities* of PK members can therefore be dissected, critiqued, and even subverted while their (hetero)*sexual identities* remain intact and unquestioned throughout these encounters. In this way, PK disrupts the gendered dimension of "tough," unemotional instrumentalist masculinity while making strategic "use" (cf., Fine 1987: 132–3) of this discourse's critical appraisal of homosexuality.

Brothers! Desexualizing homosocial intimacy

Apart from this *writ large* organizational tactic, there is a second dividing practice that is used to negotiate homosocial intimacy among many Promise Keepers members: *the desexualization of men's homosocial bonds*. In an effort to disentangle intimacy from sexuality – and, more specifically, homosociality from homosexuality – many PK members characterize their strong emotional attachments to one another under the rubric of familial bonds. It is no accident that PK men – leaders and members alike – often refer to one another as "brothers." In a telling (though by no means universal) commentary, one member of PK remarked that perhaps the most redeeming aspect of the Promise Keepers is that the members "love each other – but in the right way, like brothers." By using familial terminology to refer to their PK "brothers," many Promise Keepers imply that "brotherly love" – like actual sibling relationships – can be intensely emotional without being "tainted" by sexual desire.

Nevertheless, mere rhetorical references to "brotherly love" do not thoroughly manage the bonds of homosocial intimacy for all Promise Keepers alike. PK members are not literally family, and the vast majority of them do not share actual biological ties. Consequently, men's bodies sometimes become implicated in the desexualization of this brotherly love. The bodily negotiation of homosocial intimacy is evidenced quite clearly in the experiences of one member of PK, Abel. Abel, a born-again Latino who was reared largely by his Catholic mother, openly acknowledges his own effeminate demeanor and its impact on his relationships with some of his PK brothers. Abel attributes his "high, squeaky voice," his obvious lisp, and his distinctively "feminine way of walking" to his mother's overriding influence on him as a youngster. Alongside these effeminate qualities, Abel has a penchant for rejecting his PK brothers' handshakes in favor of hugs. Abel's proclivity for tactile affection sometimes produces discomfort for the PK members who happen to be on the receiving end of his warm displays of brotherly love. In such cases, the persistent Abel says that he can usually win over his uncomfortable compatriots, essentially convincing them that there is nothing unmanly in openly displaying his affection for his "brothers."

Interestingly, as Abel uses the word "brother" during our conversation, he often flexes one of his arms while clenching his fist. In striking this restrained pseudo-bodybuilding pose during our conversation, Abel uses his otherwise "feminine" body to contrast for himself – and for his PK compatriots, I suspect – the "strength" and "power" of brotherly love with more suspect forms of male-to-male contact. Abel's body serves as a site for the reproduction of instrumentalist masculinity (literally, muscular Christianity) because his expressive social practices and feminine demeanor risk subverting this traditionalist discourse of manhood altogether.

Essential masculinity as not-femininity: scripture, sports, and sex

A final dividing practice sometimes employed to negotiate homosocial bonds of intimacy among the Promise Keepers entails the *reification of essential masculinity* – often as juxtaposed to perceived feminine predispositions (e.g., nurturance, sensitivity). First, many PK leaders and members commonly cite biblical passages thought to confer God's injunctions for "strong" all-male fellowships. A favorite passage, from the Book of Proverbs, reads: "As iron sharpens iron, one man sharpens another." As many Promise Keepers interpret this passage, the "iron" masculinity of one man is needed to sharpen the "iron" masculinity of another – anything "softer" or "weaker" than this durable metal/masculinity will simply be incapable of molding members into the men God intends them to be.

Sports is a second medium through which essentialist depictions of godly manhood are constructed and maintained among the Promise Keepers. Sports heroes are prominently featured in PK pastoral media, including the Promise Keepers' own *Man of his word* New Testament that is provided free-of-charge to men who "accept Christ" and sign a PK "decision card" affirming their spiritual commitment at stadium conferences. The PK *Man of his word* New Testament features glossy spreads on a range of (literally) muscular Christians – from professional football players Reggie White, Anthony Munoz, and Mike Singletary to Olympic wrestler Dan Russell. Such depictions of the muscular and athletic male body masculinize spirituality and dovetail neatly with the venue in which PK conferences are held – namely, sports stadiums.

Many of my subjects commented extensively about their experiences at PK stadium conferences – which are perhaps best described as part religious retreat, part sports event, and part rock concert (this last attribute courtesy of performances by PK's own *Maranatha Promise Band* and, at PK-San Antonio '99, a Christian rock group called *The Katinas*). Clearly, some of the most moving aspects of these conferences are linked to the men's reinscription of the sports stadium space with a highly sensitized masculinity that includes singing, weeping, and embracing – affective, physical forms of contact that are somewhat reminiscent of the post-touchdown pile-on of male athletes evidenced during professional football games in the US. At any rate, the stadium confines would seem to "structure" (literally and figuratively) the practice of masculinity in these venues. Men can transform and express themselves within the safe confines of this highly masculinized arena by spiritualizing sports rituals – e.g., pushing the physical limits of their voices (and their ears) by cheering as loudly as possible for Jesus, collectively performing "the wave" for Christ, or chanting loudly back and forth, "We love Jesus, yes we do! We love Jesus, how 'bout you?"

Moreover, among some men, the essence of manhood is reaffirmed through a dividing practice which sexually juxtaposes perceptions of the "masculine body" against those of its "feminine" counterpart. Jeff's narrative of tribulation-turned-emancipation illuminates how gender difference can serve as an important resource in PK identity negotiation and sexual struggle. Through Jeff's involvement in PK and men's fellowships, he has been able to overcome what he calls an "incredibly shaming" problem with masturbation – a sexual practice he characterizes as an "intimacy killer." It was at Jeff's first PK conference that he decided to share this thrity-year struggle with his brothers during a small-group prayer session. The men in the group were largely unprepared for Jeff's tearful admission about his struggle with masturbation. Jeff describes the other men's collective reaction as "jaw-open." However, he "found out later [that] they had the same difficulty [with masturbation]. It just simply hit too close to home" for his shocked brothers.

Jeff gained a sense of relief in sharing this dilemma with his brothers, but was disappointed that no one in that prayer session ever held him "accountable" by inquiring about his autoeroticism after that time. Undeterred, Jeff forged ahead with his involvement in PK. Ultimately, he was able to quit masturbating with the help of an accountability partner he met at a men's retreat. As Jeff recounts: "I had tried on my own [to quit masturbating] and thought, 'I can beat this. I can beat this.'" But, on his own, Jeff could not resolve his problem. The turning point for Jeff occurred "when [he] finally got to the point where [he] gave it over to the Lord, and found again it was the accountability part." Jeff now firmly believes in the transformative power of brotherly accountability: "Believe me, this is something that you don't want anybody asking you about. You can imagine. You don't want somebody calling you up [to ask you if you have been masturbating that week]. And when they do, you certainly don't want to have to say: 'Man, I just, you know, I've fallen again. I just can't do anything about it.'" Thus, the panoptic gaze of brotherly surveillance provided Jeff with an avenue for resolving his longstanding private trouble. Yet, this avenue toward resolution was long, winding, and fraught with obstacles requiring Jeff's careful navigation.

On the advice that Jeff had received at his first PK conference, he had initially gone home to confess this problem to his wife. "They had told us, not specifically about [masturbation], but if you have got these [sexual] things going on – if you've been unfaithful or any of this stuff – the number one thing you have got to do is go home and tell your wife. Go home and tell her now – which I thought was bold. And I thought it was incredible." I asked Jeff to recount his wife's reaction.

> Oh boy. She didn't [pause]. It was almost like [the men's] reaction [at the initial PK prayer session]. She had no idea. She was stunned. Again, that was one of those things that made me aware of how important Promise Keepers is. Because, she really isn't built for that....
> INT: So a group of guys could hold you accountable in a way your wife could not?
> She could, but I think there are certain issues [pause].... My friend terms it [this way]: "They are not built for that type of warfare." [My wife] didn't understand. She loved the intimacy aspect of it, the fact that I was opening up to her. But it's not something I could repeatedly ask her about or have her ask me about.
> INT: Because she doesn't struggle with that issue, you're saying?
> Exactly. She doesn't understand.

Every element in Jeff's masturbation narrative makes sense to him when viewed through the lens of essential gender difference. Men's distinctive penchant for masturbation is marshaled to explain: (1) Jeff's own longstanding problem with autoeroticism (as a man, he struggles with masturbation); (2) his prayer group brothers' "jaw-open" reaction to his admission (as men, they too struggle with masturbation); (3) his wife's stunned response to his confession (as a woman, she does not struggle with such profound autoerotic impulses); and (4) his eventual triumph in this "spiritual war" through brotherly accountability (with the help of God and a diligent brother,

men can overcome such sexual improprieties as masturbation). This "male problem" and the spiritual warfare it entails would seem to require a "male solution" such as the Promise Keepers. Women are simply "not built for that type of spiritual warfare." For PK men who struggle with these and other "men's issues," the theme of essential gender difference gives meaning to their collective tribulation and provides them with hope for ultimate reconciliation – i.e., as Promise Keepers, they will be held accountable for their actions by other godly men. Again, "as iron sharpens iron, one man sharpens another."

Nevertheless, this essentialist dividing practice employed by some of the PK rank-and-file is bounded by caveats designed to quiet charges of sexism, and typically steers clear of the unqualified radical essentialism touted by the likes of Ed Cole. Why are PK men who make references to gender difference typically much more guarded in articulating their views about the essence of masculinity? In short, notions of intractable gender difference simply do not square with these men's intimate encounters with their PK brothers. Here again, Jeff's portrayal of categorical – yet malleable – gender difference is consistent with personal transformations that PK has wrought for him. He says that men have a "tendency" for "carrying" private hurts "by themselves.... Women have a much easier time [expressing their hurts]. And again, I hate to keep using those generic terms, but [women] are relational by nature. They can talk about things a lot more freely than we do. *But that's changing. And I think Promise Keepers is one of the main reasons that is happening*" (emphasis added).

NOTE

1 The discourses of masculinity outlined here are not exhaustive of Promise Keepers' definitions of godly masculinity. Other Promise Keeper authors (e.g., Crabb 1991; Smalley 1988; Wagner 1994; see Bartkowski 1997a,

1997b, 2001, forthcoming) advance some innovative reconstructions of these competing discursive regimes.

REFERENCES

Bartkowski, J. P. 1997a. Debating patriarchy: Discursive disputes over spousal authority among evangelical family commentators. *Journal for the Scientific Study of Religion* 36: 393–410.

—— 1997b. Gender reinvented, gender reproduced: The discourse and negotiation of spousal relations within contemporary evangelicalism. Ph.D. dissertation: University of Texas.

—— 1998. Changing of the gods: The gender and family discourse of American evangelicalism in historical perspective. *The History of the Family* 3: 97–117.

—— 1999a. Gender, power, and godly masculinities. In *Standing on the promises: The Promise Keepers*, edited by D. Claussen, chapter 3 (in press). Cleveland, OH: Pilgrim Press.

—— 1999b. One step forward, one step back: "Progressive traditionalism" and the negotiation of domestic labor in evangelical families. *Gender Issues* 17: 40–64.

—— 2001. *Remaking the Godly Marriage: Gender Negotiation in Evangelical Families*. New Brunswick, NJ: Rutgers University Press.

—— forthcoming. *The Promise Keepers: Servants, Soldiers amd Godly Men*. New Brunswick, NJ: Rutgers University Press.

Britton, D. 1990. Homophobia and homosociality: An analysis of boundary maintenance. *The Sociological Quarterly* 31: 423–39.

Cole, E. L. 1982. *Maximized manhood: A guide to family survival*. Springdale, PA: Whitaker House.

Crabb, L. 1991. *Men and women: Enjoying the difference*. Grand Rapids, MI: Zondervan.

DeBerg, B. A. 1990. *Ungodly women: Gender and the first wave of American fundamentalism*. Minneapolis, MN: Fortress Press.

Derrida, J. 1974. *Of grammatology*. Baltimore, MD: Johns Hopkins University Press.

Fine, G. A. 1987. *With the boys: Little league baseball and preadolescent culture*. Chicago, IL: University of Chicago Press.

Foucault, M. 1977. *Discipline and punish: The birth of the prison*. New York: Vintage.

Juster, S. 1994. *Disorderly women: Sexual politics and evangelicalism in revolutionary New England*. Ithaca, NY: Cornell University Press.

Kimmel, M. S. 1996. *Manhood in America: A cultural history*. New York: Free Press.

Messner, M. A. 1997. *Politics of masculinities: Men in movements*. Thousand Oaks, CA: Sage.

Oliver, G. J. 1993. *Real men have feelings too*. Chicago, IL: Moody Press.

Smalley, G. 1988. *If only he knew: Understanding your wife*. Grand Rapids, MI: Zondervan.

Turner, V. and E. L. B. Turner. 1978. *Image and pilgrimage in Christian culture: Anthropological perspectives*. New York: Columbia University Press.

Wagner, E. G. (with D. Gruen). 1994. *Strategies for a successful marriage: A study guide for men*. Colorado Springs, CO: Promise Keepers/NavPress.

18 Sex-Segregated Living: Celebrating the Female

Debra Renee Kaufman

The Laws of Niddah: Menstrual Impurity and Sexual Prohibition

In Jewish law the menstruant woman has a defined status: she is a *niddah* (excluded person). The laws which define this status are complex. They rest on the foundation of two different contexts: the laws surrounding purity and impurity and those surrounding sexual prohibitions. The niddah appears in Leviticus in two contexts: laws intent on excluding an impure person or object from entering the Temple (Biale 1984: 147), together with other forms of defilement, impurity, and death (Leviticus 11: 24 – 15:33)[1] and laws regulating forbidden sexual relations (Leviticus 18 and 20). Adler (1976) writes that the cycle of *tumah* (impurity) and *tabarah* (purity) is the way in which the Jew acts out her or his death and resurrection:

> *Tumah* is the result of our confrontation with the face of our own mortality. It is the going down into darkness. *Taharah* is the result of our reaffirmation of our own immortality. It is the reentry into light. *Tumah* is evil or frightening only when there is no further life. Otherwise, *tumah* is simply part of the human cycle. To be *tameh* [ritually impure] is not wrong or bad, often it is necessary and sometimes it is mandatory. *(Adler 1976: 64)*

In the ancient religious worldview, she reasons, tumah was not perceived as causing physical consequences, nor was it viewed as dangerous in any way. Since some of the basic human functions and behaviors cause tumah, every member of society regularly underwent the cycle from tumah to taharah

(an accepted component of the human condition). Biale underscores Adler's point when she notes that there is no particular gravity attached to impurity, let alone indication that it is considered an offense or sin. Again, the state of impurity in and of itself is not a transgression; it meant only that an individual could not enter or partake of food in the Temple precincts in Jerusalem until purified. In Leviticus 15, writes Biale, impurity is an objective, if not undesirable, state which one should seek to avoid and remove by following proper ritual (Biale 1984: 154). Similarly, Biale argues, in Leviticus 15, intercourse with a niddah causes a state of impurity, but "there is no hint that it is considered a sin" (ibid: 155).[2]

To counteract the state of impurity (the length of time one remained impure varied according to type of tumah contracted),[3] immersion in a ritual bath (mikveh),[4] a natural gathering of freely flowing water or its equivalent, was necessary. Symbolically, the contact with death could then be reversed and a person returned to a state of ritual purity. Adler describes the mikveh as a "primal sea from which all life comes, the womb of the world, the amniotic tide in which the unborn child is rocked" (Adler 1976: 68). To be reborn, she writes, "one must reenter this womb and drown in living water" (ibid). In this way, she notes, we confront and experience our own death and resurrection.[5] It is a renewal, a recreation, a regeneration of the life forces. In the ancient cultic world, the tangible communal reward was access to the sanctuary (Greenberg 1981)....

It is clear that the laws concerning a woman in niddah could be viewed in oppositional ways. Using Washbourn's "demonic" and "graceful" categories, Ginsburg elaborates:

> The graceful is that which integrates a woman's physiology into a wider social and symbolic framework. The demonic reduces female identity to its biological aspects. In the initial context of purification rites for the temple [sic], the Jewish laws concerning the nidda reflect a graceful development that includes women in sexual sanctions applied to all members of the community. In the second Levitical reference, the menstruant woman is selected out from the rest of the community as offensive in terms of her reproductive physiology. These two interpretive options have been differentially stressed as women's social roles have changed according to historical and material circumstances. (Ginsburg 1981: 4)

Feminists have pointed to the insidious dimensions of the belief in menstrual impurity and that such beliefs continue to exist in a more diluted form in our contemporary culture (Douglas 1966). The rituals concerning the menstruating woman can be interpreted as either "graceful" or "demonic," to use Washbourn's terms. How do these contemporary ba'alot teshuvah experience niddah and mikveh?

Practicing Family Purity Laws

According to talmudic law, separation between husband and wife should be maintained for at least twelve days, five for the actual period of flow and seven additional days during which no bleeding is visible (called "clean" or "white" days). On the evening of her seventh "white" day, or any day thereafter upon her choosing, a woman goes to the mikveh.

On that day she handles no sticky substances that might adhere to her skin. Before the ritual immersion she removes all foreign things from her body, such as wigs, jewelry, Bandaids, nail polish, and makeup. She cuts her nails, takes an ordinary bath, washes and combs her hair, and brushes her teeth. In fact, food is prohibited after her bath and before her immersion in the mikveh.[6] Usually a woman makes an appointment with the attendant to use the mikveh after sunset. Once in the ritual pool, with her legs slightly apart, arms outstretched and fingers spread, she immerses herself completely until every strand of hair is covered. This act performed in the presence of an attendant, is repeated twice after she recites a prayer blessing the act of immersion.

When asked about the family purity laws, these newly Orthodox women almost unanimously used the "graceful" rather than the "demonic" to characterize their experiences and feelings about niddah and mikveh. Most eschewed the understanding of themselves as "unclean" and referred to the counting of the postmenstrual days as the "white," not "clean" days. "During niddah," explained one particularly articulate woman, who, although a ba'alat teshuvah, had come so far in her own studies that she taught seminars on the laws of niddah, "the woman falls between categories of life and death." She noted that she often calls upon nonlegal but traditional sources of explanation to frame discussions of niddah and mikveh. "For instance, when it is questioned why women and not men are still subject to impurity rituals, I look to traditional explanations. . . . [Y]ou can find one that suggests that women are closer to God because of their ability to create life and that they are therefore subject to purity rituals . . . still another views the woman's body as a 'holy' temple.[7] I like to think of a woman's cycle as part of all the sacred time rhythms in Judaism – the Shabbat, holidays. . . ."

The following quotations underscore how important and meaningful the laws of niddah are to these women: "Even before I became religious and was living with my boyfriend (now my husband), we began to practice the laws of niddah. I thought it the most wonderful thing, it made good sense."

A Ph.D. in psychology who lived with her then lover, now husband,[8] in Jerusalem noted that the laws of niddah most fully interested her when she was introduced to orthodox Jewish law, while occasionally attending a ba'al teshuvah institute in Israel:

I had counseled many young people about sexual practices when I lived in the United States. When I first read about taharat hamishpacha they made absolutely good sense to me...psychologically speaking, that is. I leaned over in bed and shared with Daniel [a fictitious name] what I was reading. We made a commitment to try this practice for at least one month. We got separate beds. I went to the mikveh and when next we made love it was wonderful. I smile now, really not because I am embarrassed, but because of how much I have grown since then. You see, then it seemed like a lark; it made good psychological sense to me. Now it has so much more meaning....I practice niddah with other women and we share in a sacred ritual that connects us to our past and with our children and their children.

But not all introductions to sexual orthodoxy are so sanguine. Another woman recalls her first introduction to the laws of niddah:

I was terrified of water and immersion. I knew I could not be an Orthodox mother and wife if I was not able to use the mikveh. I went for counseling and it did not help. My boyfriend [now husband] said that we should marry anyway and that this would somehow be resolved. We loved each other and would live like sister and brother if necessary until I could overcome my fear. I tried going to the mikveh several times before we were married. The first time I went to the mikveh, the attendant talked with me for several hours; I could not immerse myself. After several tries over the first few months, I finally decided to try it slowly, very slowly. As I went under for the first time I concentrated

on how this one act linked me to generations of other women....I lost my fear completely. I truly felt renewed, like a new woman capable of anything I really set my mind to. I'll also say that my friends were especially supportive in this...we all had a big party at my house afterward.

Almost all women noted the positive functions of the family purity laws. Most frequently cited were claims of increased sexual interest and pleasure within the marriage. Although newly married women were more likely to complain about sexual separation, those married over longer periods of time and with more children found the laws quite positive over the adult life cycle. One woman notes:

When we were first married I found it hard to consider sexual separation as a positive thing. In fact, during my menstrual cycle I felt I wanted to be held and loved more than at other times of the month. But I must admit over the years it truly serves as a renewal...it is really like being a bride again...well, almost.

Even among the newly married, many claimed that forced separation heightened desire.

Others referred to the autonomy and control they experienced when practicing the laws of niddah. Invoking Virginia Woolf, one woman noted, "It allows me a bed of my own." Others referred to the increased time for themselves: "I can curl up with a good book during niddah and not feel in the least bit guilty." Other women emphasized the increased time for themselves, and still others spoke of a kind of control over their sexuality. "I can say no with no pretense of a headache if I wish," claimed one newly married woman. Other women suggested that the family purity laws provide a sexual rhythm to marriage for both partners.

Because these women have to attend intimately to their bodies to engage in sexual activity according to religious law, many speak of an increased awareness of their bodies they had never known before, evident in the following response:

> At this time of the month I am acutely aware of myself, everything is heightened because I am paying attention to what is happening inside of me. Over the years it is building a cycle for me; it's a rhythm that is related to me and my body alone.

While most of the women seem to enjoy the rejuvenation and spiritual uplifting of going to the mikveh, not all were uniformly happy about the length of time they were separated from their husbands during the month. Indeed, if anything, it was length of time, not the practice of the laws, about which women complained. However, even their complaints were expressed in positive terms. A good number of women suggested that the practices surrounding the period of niddah force them and their husbands to learn new forms of communication and, perhaps more important, to use those newly found skills.[9] "Most men don't know how to talk things out," claims one woman, "but since approximately one-half of my year is spent in niddah, I have found that we are forced to talk about things more and that he has learned to show his love in ways more important than just physical contact."

From the earliest literature on marital satisfaction (Bernard 1971) to the more recent (Schwartz and Blumstein 1983), it is clear that communication (sexual and otherwise) is a major problem for middle-class women. Specific data on the frequency of sexual intercourse and sexual satisfaction and experimentation were not forthcoming. Modesty rules inhibit truly open discourse about such details. However, when discussing the marital purity laws, almost all women made some references to the laws of onah. They told me that women are entitled to an active and satisfying sexuality in marriage.[10] Perhaps because they are ba'alot teshuvah and not frum from birth, as they often categorize other Orthodox women, these women may have been more forthcoming than other Orthodox women about their sexuality. "Do you know that a husband cannot abstain from sex without regard to his wife's feelings and needs?" noted one woman. "Onah," suggested one ba'alat teshuvah who had studied in a yeshiva in Israel, "concern a woman's sexual pleasure, not her procreative functions." One woman noted that even in "ancient times a woman could seek a divorce if her husband did not properly support her or sexually satisfy her." "Do you know," claimed one woman, "according to halakhah, my husband is commanded to kiss *every* part of my body?"[11]

In Jewish orthodoxy, men are commanded to marry, to procreate, and to perform their conjugal duties at regular times.[12] The main obligations for women are to observe the laws associated with a menstruant woman. They are not commanded to marry and they are explicitly exempted from the duty of procreation. As Biale writes: "Other than the general obligation not to consistently and unreasonably refuse sexual relations with the husband, women do not really have 'sexual obligations' in marriage" (Biale 1984: 122). On the other hand, men are specifically instructed to please and satisfy their wives.[13]

Feldman (1974) notes that a man can deny himself, but not his wife, pleasure.[14] Moreover, he says, a man cannot force his attentions on his wife, but must be attentive to her needs and cues for sexual intercourse. Since the legislation around onah is concerned with a woman's sexual pleasure, not her procreative needs, husbands' obligations to satisfy their wives sexually are detailed in the Talmud and the Code.

While I do not believe that all of these women are sexually satisfied, in control of their sexuality, or personally happy with marriage, it is quite clear that they believe that the laws of niddah and mikveh function positively for women within marriage. Frequently women would state, "My husband cannot take me for granted" or, as one woman put it, "My husband's sexual desire is not the only consideration." One woman who had been married to another man before her current marriage bluntly acknowledged that her heterosexual life prior to this marriage was a disaster:

> To put it crudely, my former husband's main interest in life was in his pockets and what's between them. Money and sex. We communicated about nothing and had a lot of sex. After a while I found that he was having affairs with at least two other women. By then I didn't care, I just wanted out of the marriage and I didn't want my children growing up with him as their father.... Even before I remarried, I knew that a marriage in the Orthodox community was one in which I could have faith. I mean that literally. Every aspect would be a part of something larger than just us... something spiritual and holy.

These twentieth-century women use female-linked religious symbols as a way of limiting and controlling males.[15] Like those in the social purity movement of the nineteenth century, who deplored the sexual double standard and wished not to extend men's sexual privileges to women, the ba'alot teshuvah speak of niddah and mikveh as a way of sexually constraining *both* men and women. Therefore, modesty and the family purity laws are double-edged. Although they serve as a means of social control, particularly of women, they are also a means of obtaining control – by restraining oneself and others.[16]

However, the experiences these women describe are more than responses to controlling males or accommodation techniques. While they do believe that the laws encourage men to respect them as sexual beings, increase their own self-respect (particularly toward their bodies), and heighten sexual desire, there seems to be more than that. The symbolic framework emerging from their language, imagery, and experiences moves beyond the self and the dyad to the community at large. Indeed the pride with which one leader of her community took in

taking me on a tour of the newly completed mikveh was unmistakable. The women had raised the money in their own sisterhood and helped the architect with the design. The more affluent the community, the more commodious and luxurious the mikveh. One mikveh I visited was constructed all in redwood with a sauna and an elaborate dressing room. Blow-dryers and vanity tables were also available. One community boasts the only solar-heated mikveh in the country.

Without the mikveh the community of believers that calls itself Orthodox could not be reproduced. Therefore, the immersion in the mikveh is more than personal sanctity. It also represents the sanctity of the community. The mikveh, although legally required for women only, has deep symbolic and communal meaning. It is used as the final step in conversion to Judaism. A groom sometimes uses the mikveh before his wedding, some Jews purify themselves before the Sabbath or holy days, and it may be used by men and women whenever they want to renew or establish a deeper commitment to Judaism. No woman doubted the importance of the mikveh to the community. As one woman put it: "There is no doubt about it... if a choice has to be made, a community has to build a mikveh before it can build a shul or even acquire a Sefer Torah."

But it is to yet another larger community that mikveh unites these women. "I feel connected to history and to other women," says one ba'alat teshuvah who has practiced the laws of niddah since her marriage twelve years before. Feeling a sense of history, one woman mused: "The Jews at Masada used the mikveh." "Each time I use the mikveh I feel I come back to the center of Judaism and to my own core," a woman married fifteen years proclaimed. What became clear after several years of interviewing was that for these women the core of Judaism emanates from activities and obligations shared with other women even, and perhaps most ironically, when speaking of the religious ritual surrounding their hetero-sexuality.

A heightened air of sensuousness and in-timacy surrounds the practices of niddah and mikveh. These rituals create a world in which women, not men, are the central actors despite the heterosexual goals. "I have been to the mikveh all over the world," stated one ba'alat teshuvah, "and there is a sense of togetherness. There are unspoken codes among women . . . no one ever counts or questions another woman's use of the mikveh." Indeed there is some-thing private, almost secretive, and emphat-ically intimate about the ways in which the women describe their experiences. "I feel closer to all women who share in the prac-tice of mikveh," claimed one woman. "We share all kinds of unspoken secrets with one another. After all we celebrate our bodies, our sexuality, our regenerative powers in the same way. . . . "

After immersion in the mikveh, women and men are allowed to resume sexual inter-course. Forgetting that completion of the mikveh ritual is often a prelude to sexual activity, I once almost overstayed my wel-come at one respondent's home. I had accompanied one woman to the mikveh, where we met others from the same commu-nity, including the woman with whom I had the next interview. My next interviewee and I spoke for a while at the mikveh and then I accompanied her to her home to continue the interview. As we concluded the interview, she smiled at me and said that although she was enjoying the conver-sation she really did not want to make it a long night. She then hesitated, and I, be-latedly picking up her cue, left soon there-after.

Nothing attests to the social construction of sexuality and the true meaning of the erotic better than how these women describe the religious rituals which heighten their sexuality. Many find erotic fantasies in the social act of "cleansing the body" for purity purposes. A woman married three years states:

All the connotations of being a bride again are brought back. It is even more than the anticipation of making love but the whole secret sharing of it with other women, a friend I may meet at the mikveh or the friend who might take care of the baby when I go, that makes it all more, I don't know, sort of sexy.

By maintaining and preserving appear-ances of chastity and not talking directly about their sexuality, the ba'alot teshuvah seem to stimulate and deepen their sense of sexuality.[17] Although head-coverings and hemlines may vary from community to com-munity and from woman to woman, all women abide in some way by the code of modesty in dress, conversation, personal habits, and in public displays of affection with men. Prior to their entrance into the Orthodox community, most would have found tzniut an alien concept; or as one woman put it, "'Victorian' – you know, 'prudish.'" Eschewing prudish and Victor-ian reasons for abiding by these modesty customs, one woman compared them to the values of a sexually liberated society. The same ba'alat teshuvah who taught sem-inars on the family purity laws notes: "I find that those things we consider so intim-ate – like a kiss or a hug – meaningless if you give them to everyone. It's easy to 'turn on' in this community, hard to do so out there."

The practices of niddah and mikveh cele-brate the woman, body and soul. The ritual both constrains and extends. For the ba'alot teshuvah, the family purity laws represent the purity rites surrounding the entrance to the Second Temple. Renewal and regener-ation of life forces are themes that run throughout these women's commentaries. The themes of sexual and sacred are con-comitant for them. Immersion in the mikveh nullifies their state of impurity and gives rise for them to another cycle of sexuality and generativity.

Wechsler argues that the ritual cycle of niddah and mikveh help women recover the deep, spiritual meaning that accompanies their recurring cycles. She writes:

> The women who can enter this ritual and participate in such a fullness of meaning may experience an affinity and a powerful reconciliation with the source of all that is. This is, at a deep level, the dynamic of atonement.[18] Rather than being outside the sacred circle, this dynamic oscillation places her firmly within it. (Wechsler 1981: 24)

Women's separateness, apartness, and even otherness are microcosmically emblematic of the Orthodox community itself – a community separate, apart, and "other" from the larger "gentile" society.[19] As noted earlier, one ba'alat teshuvah suggested that women represent the values attached to the "community as a whole." Menstrual impurity for these ba'alot teshuvah is experienced as part of the symbolism of death and rebirth through the cycles of their own bodies. For most, their recurring impurity is connected to holiness. Jewish marriage, and consequently, conjugal relations are seen as "holy" – the "sanctuary here on earth" – as many women voiced it. These women's association with the purity cycle becomes for them a symbolic claim upon the community at large.

Faye Ginsburg provides one of the few empirical examples of the practices of the laws of niddah and the use of mikveh. Reporting on her data from two upwardly mobile Syrian Jewish communities, she demonstrates how the rituals transform the most explicitly private and individual of relationships into matters of public concern and even collective pressure (Ginsburg 1981: 9):

> In the most delicate and seemingly individual of social arenas, these rituals give Syrian Jewish women authority and collective strength in shaping male sexuality. Using a potent symbolic vocabulary, women are actively creating a situation in which their biological and social experience of being female is integrated grace-

fully and powerfully into communal life. (ibid: 18)

For Ginsburg, these rituals allow women to maintain social power, moral authority, and control over the sexuality of men. The laws, she notes, provide a symbolic barrier that women impose not only on themselves and their daughters, but, more important, on men.

Although many of the ba'alot teshuvah under study appreciate or at least allude to the ways in which the laws surrounding sexuality protect women, there is evidence that this is not the only appeal of the laws of family purity. The many remarks about heightened sexuality and a better sense of their own bodies bespeaks more than simple control or restraint over men within marriage. Eschewing an open and uninhibited approach to sexuality, these ba'alot teshuvah refer to the sensuous, emotional, and evocative features of sexuality. Many believe they are reconnecting sexuality to something more sensuous and spiritual than what they experienced prior to their return to orthodoxy. The experience and meaning of sexuality supersedes, for them, the dyad alone. These ba'alot teshuvah connect their most private experiences to a wider social and communal setting where sexuality is socially defined, not individually developed. For many of these women, sexuality and mothering are communal acts, more extensive than self-experience, thereby linking women beyond themselves, or the dyad, to the larger religious community.

NOTES

1   In the ancient religious worldview governed by categories of pure and impure, defilements and impurities were generally associated with the loss of any of the life-giving juices which nurture body tissue. The laws of purity and impurity include other instances of contamination besides the case of the niddah. For instance, contact with a corpse, leprosy, seminal discharges, or contact with certain insects could place an individual in a state of impurity.

Adler (1976) explains that the menstrual blood, which inside the womb was a potential nutrient, is a token of dying when shed.

2 Biale (1984) recognizes the striking contradiction between Leviticus 15 and Leviticus 18 and 20. In the latter, intercourse with a *niddah* is an offensive sexual transgression (ibid: 155). Biale also notes that in two late books in the Bible, Ezekiel and Ezra, the term *niddah* appears as a metaphor for moral impurity and debasement (ibid: 154).

3 Biale (1984) notes that a woman who has given birth is also considered a *niddah*. The period of her impurity depends on the sex of her child (Leviticus 12: 1–8). If it is a son, the woman waits an additional thirty-three days after the first seven days of her *niddah*. If it is a daughter, the time of impurity is doubled. In keeping with her general interpretation that impurity is not a punitive condition and that the birth of a daughter is not more disappointing than that of a son, she conjectures that "underlying this legislation is the sense that the birth of a female who will one day herself menstruate and give birth, is seen as 'doubly bloody' and doubly impure" (ibid: 152).

4 Since the destruction of the Second Temple, women's recurring impurity is the only one which is explicitly recognized as such and which still requires a subsequent ritual of purification. The legal obligation for ritual immersion is confined to brides just before their weddings and to married women. Converts also immerse themselves as a sign of rebirth into the tradition. Also, new pots and dishes often are immersed in the *mikveh* before use, since all parts of daily life are to be sanctified.

5 In her insightful paper on ritual purity and Jewish women Wechsler (1981) contends that the relationship between sanctity and defilement is a "dialectical one" (p. 16). Blood, and particularly menstrual blood, she writes, is intimately bound with life and death. She explains: "[C]hildbirth is the culmination of the mystery of life, and menstruation bespeaks of life in death (and vice versa).... [W]omen's sexuality is thereby linked, ineluctably, to death as well as to life. It points to the fullness of life – birth, sexuality, death – and to its passage" (ibid: 12). She suggests that the purity laws of the early stages of Semitic culture reflect this duality. For a broader overview, see especially Mary Douglas (1966).

6 Ginsburg (1981) and Greenberg (1981) note that the removal of foreign substances and bathing before the woman goes to the *mikveh* make clear that the ritual is not an act of hygiene, but rather one of spiritual cleanliness.

7 Wechsler develops this idea when she writes: "Jewish marriage is the 'new' Holy Tabernacle. As a woman's status of pure or impure regulates conjugal relations – a symbol for access to the sanctuary – it is still a valid category" (Wechsler 1981: 18).

8 Most *ba'alot teshuvah* marry other *ba'alei teshuvah*. That is, had they been practicing orthodoxy, they most likely would not have been openly living together.

9 While all the women in this sample practiced the laws of *niddah* not all adhered scrupulously to the practice of *negiah*. In this practice, couples will not hand things directly to one another nor will they have any physical contact during the wife's menses. Only one-quarter of the women who fell under the modern Orthodox rubric kept *negiah*, while almost half of those who fell under the strictly Orthodox category (and virtually all of those within the Hasidic category) practiced *negiah*. There are mixed balakhic interpretations for this practice, some stressing purity or impurity, others the fear of sexual arousal. (For a more complete discussion see Greenberg 1981: 116.) Bunim (1986) finds similar distinctions in the practice of the family purity laws in her study of Orthodox women. Among the women she studied, all the members of the Kollel adhere strictly to the laws. Agudah and Young Israel women were less fastidious about their observance. One woman in Bunim's study did not practice *niddah* and two did not practice *mikveh* regularly (all were Modern Orthodox). In my study all the women observed *niddah* and *mikveh*, although the non-Hasidic women were less fastidious than the Hasidic women.

10 Ehrenreich, Hess, and Jacobs (1986) report something similar among New Right women, who, claim the authors, believe that they should get something for their sexual efforts, rather than simply submitting or sacrificing themselves to their husbands.

11   Although most of the statements made by
the women tend to have some legal and/or
traditional basis in Judaism, this was the
hardest for me to trace. Both Biale (1984)
and Feldman (1974) suggest that female
sexual pleasure is an important part of the
Jewish sexual ethic. Biale suggests that the
correct Hebrew reading of the biblical legislation that a man is to "cheer his wife" is the
key to understanding that a man must put
his wife's pleasure and satisfaction before his
own when he makes love to her (Biale 1984:
135). She also notes that there are no laws
prohibiting a wide range of sexual expression in Jewish orthodoxy (ibid: 138).

12   Biale believes that, according to Orthodox
interpretation, male sexuality is seen as a
greater threat than women's to familial and
social structure. Therefore, she claims, it
must be restrained through controls of marriage, procreative duties, and men's numerous responsibilities toward their wives. She
also notes that there are powerful taboos
against male homosexuality and masturbation (Biale 1984: 122).

13   Biale (1984) and Feldman (1974) cite
sources where men are given very specific
instructions on how to please their wives.
Biale (1984) notes that there is a tension in
the literature regarding views about foreplay, talking during sex in order to increase
arousal, and prolonging the sexual act (see
especially ch. 5). Women's sexual needs are
anchored in law to ensure their fulfillment,
writes Biale.

14   The basis of the sexual ethic comes from
differing views of female and male sexuality.
Although women's passion is considered to
be as great as men's, writes Biale (1984: 122),
they are considered temperamentally unable
to initiate sex. This is considered to be the
second part of the "curse of Eve." From the
passage "Yet your desire shall be for your
husband, and he shall rule over you" (Gen-
esis 3: 16) comes the interpretation that the
woman is unable to act to fulfill her sexual
desire and that all overt sexual initiative will
come from the male, not the female.

15   The focus on female sexuality (although
with radically different conclusions) is of
key importance to both *ba'alot teshuvah*
and some woman-centered feminists. Catharine MacKinnon is quoted as saying "Sexu-

ality is to feminism what work is to
Marxism: that which is most one's own, yet
most taken away." Some feminists gain control over their bodies and sexuality by
following separatist policies; many of the
ba'alot teshuvah do so by appealing to
Orthodox Jewish laws.

16   However, *control* is a relative term. For instance, Hasidic women depend upon their
rebbes and recognized Torah authorities in
their communities for answers to questions
about Jewish law. Irrespective of the Orthodox orientation, all Torah authorities are
men. Non-Hasidic women are less likely to
ask questions of such men and more likely to
seek answers on their own. In this way, they
entertain a wider range of interpretations for
their questions. Despite Hasidic women's
greater dependence upon Torah authorities,
many of them made it clear that one learns
to ask the question according to the answer
one wishes to receive (which means, of
course, knowledge of the laws and possible
interpretations). For instance, when women
are coming out of *niddah* and dubious about
a "clean" or "unclean" stain, they are expected to have a *pesek* (Torah authority)
decide. One Hasidic woman looked me
straight in the eye and said, "Do you really
think I'd send my underwear to a *rav* to look
at under the light?" It appears that as *ba'alot
teshuvah* become more secure in their orthodoxy, questions to be decided by rabbinic
authority are fewer. Of the four women
who acknowledged having asked for
halakhic information about sexual matters,
three confided that this had to do with fertility problems. One woman was trying to
change her *niddah* cycle to match more
closely her own period of ovulation. It is
interesting that none of the women in this
study were loath to obtain medical assistance for fertility problems. My discussions
with rabbis and lay leaders made it clear that
these kinds of questions are handled on a
case-by-case basis.

17   In *Sex and Destiny* Germaine Greer (1984)
argues that chastity has a double virtue in
that it endows sexual activity with added
importance by limiting its enjoyment to
special persons and special times.

18   There are several ways in which the *ba'alot
teshuvah* interpret their status as returnees

or those atoning. While there is some distrust of *ba'alei teshuvah* among those who are "born" Orthodox, the theological status of a returnee is unambivalent. The *ba'alot teshuvah*, while perhaps unsure in their practices of orthodoxy, are quite clear that they are in a special state of holiness since they have chosen to become Orthodox. All Jews, according to orthodoxy, are presumably "returning" or "atoning" from birth.

19   See also Baskin (1985), who notes that all three of the commandments specifically directed at women have to do with separation. She writes: "[A]ll three can symbolize the chasm between the sacred and the profane, the holy and the secular, the realm of men who obey commandments and that of women who suffer disabilities, and ultimately between the realms of life and death themselves" (ibid: 8).

REFERENCES

Adler, R. 1976. "Tumah and Taharah: Ends and Beginnings." Pp. 63–71 in E. Koltrun (ed.), *The Jewish Woman: New Perspectives*. New York: Schocken.

Baskin, J. 1985. "The Separation of Women in Rabbinic Judaism." Pp. 3–18 in Y. Y. Haddad and E. B. Findly (eds.), *Women, Religion and Social Change*. Albany, NY: State University of New York Press.

Biale, R. 1984. *Women and Jewish Law*. New York: Schocken.

Bunim, S. 1986. "Religious and Secular Factors of Role Strain in Orthodox Jewish Mothers." Ph.D. dissertation, Wurzweiler School of Social Work, Yeshiva University.

Douglas, M. 1966. *Purity and Danger: An Analysis of Concepts of Pollution and Taboo*. London: Routledge and Kegan Paul.

Ehrenreich, B., E. Hess, and G. Jacobs 1986. *Remaking Love*. Garden City, NY: Doubleday/Anchor.

Feldman, D. 1974. *Marital Relations, Birth Control and Abortion in Jewish Law*. New York: Schocken.

Giddens, A. 1984. *The Constitution of Society: An Outline of the Theory of Structuration*. Berkeley: University of California Press.

Ginsburg, F. 1981. "Power, Purity and Pollution: The Revival of Menstrual Rituals in a Jewish Community." Unpublished manuscript, City University of New York.

Greenberg, B. 1981. *On Women and Judaism: A View from Tradition*. Philadelphia: Jewish Publication Society of America.

Greer, G. 1984. *Sex and Destiny*. New York: Harper & Row.

Sennett, R. 1974. *The Fall of Public Man*. New York: Random House.

Wechsler, M. 1981. "Ritual, Purity and Jewish Women." Unpublished paper, Harvard University.

19 The Metropolitan Community Churches and the Gay Agenda: The Power of Pentecostalism and Essentialism

R. Stephen Warner

Entrepreneurial and Pastoral Beginnings

In October 1968, eight months before Stonewall, when the patrons of a gay bar in New York rose in protest of a vice squad raid, Troy Perry did something equally audacious in Los Angeles. He met 12 people in his living room in the first worship service of a homosexual-affirming religious group which he called the "Metropolitan Community Church." He deliberately chose the form of the American religious congregation to bring a gospel of God-given homosexuality to the gay community. In 1990, the denomination he founded and still heads, the Universal Fellowship of Metropolitan Community Churches, claimed some 12,576 communicant members in 195 congregations in the United States (Bedell 1993: 253), and nearly 100 congregations in 15 other countries worldwide.

Already in 1970, Perry was the top vote-getter in balloting for the Conference Committee of the North American Conference of Homophile Organizations (Duberman 1993: 312). By the early 1980s, according to Altman's survey of homosexual rights movements, the Metropolitan Community Churches were "perhaps the closest there is to a grassroots national organization" for gay rights.

> The network provided by [gay] religious groups, in particular the MCC,... are the largest organized sector of the gay community, and like other religious groups they can draw on strong reserves of commitment and dedication.... [I]n many places the church is the only form of the gay movement that exists. *(Altman 1982: 123)*

The Metropolitan Community Church has put the issue of rights for sexual minorities permanently on the agenda of the mainline churches (and in such forums as *Christian Century*) and has fought numerous public battles for gay rights, in particular the successful campaign against the 1978 Briggs initiative in California (Dart 1991).

The background of the MCC could hardly have seemed less auspicious, however. In 1963 Troy Perry was a 23-year-old high school dropout with a wife and two children who had been preaching for nearly ten years in Georgia, Florida, Alabama, Illinois, and California, when he decided once and for all that he was homosexual. He confessed his orientation to his superior in the pentecostal Church of God of Prophecy in Santa Ana, California, and was immediately defrocked. His wife left for home in Alabama with the boys (whom he did not see again for 19 years), and he left the parsonage in order to learn how to be a gay man in southern California.

For five years Perry kept mostly away from church, moving between his mother's home in suburban Los Angeles, gay bars and coffee shops in West Hollywood, a sales job with Sears, Roebuck, and a two-year hitch in the Army, until a crisis precipitated the reconciliation of his early Christian and latter-day homosexual selves. In despair over the breakup of what he calls his first intense love affair, he attempted suicide by slashing his wrists, but in a hospital emergency room he felt God's love in the voice of a friendly stranger. He confessed in his heart that he had made an idol of his erstwhile lover, putting that man in the rightful place of God. With this act of repentance, Perry recalls, "I knew that I had passed the major crisis of my life. . . . I knew that God cared about me and that He was with me, all the way – wherever that would lead me" (Perry 1972: 111; for another version of this memoir, see Perry and Swicegood 1990: 30).

Shortly thereafter, still in the glow of his own epiphany, Perry tried unsuccessfully to bring God's comfort to another former lover, called Carlos, who had been arrested in a vice raid on a gay bar. Carlos knew that his carefully closeted life had been ruined, and he laughed in derision when Perry told him that God loved him nonetheless. Perry was moved:

> I felt the weight of his disaster upon me. I had made my way back to God enough, and I was still Pentecostal enough that I knew I could talk to God. So I knelt down and said, "All right, God, if it's Your will, if You want to see a church started as an outreach into our community, You just let me know when." And that still small voice in the mind's ear just let me know – now!
> *(Perry 1972: 8)*

With that, Perry placed an ad with his own picture in the new gay paper in Los Angeles, the *Advocate*, and he spread the word in his favorite bar, The Patch. The ad said that the Metropolitan Community Church, himself preaching, was holding religious services every Sunday at a Huntington Park address (which happened to be Perry's own home). The first Sunday after the ad appeared, October 6, 1968, there were 12 people to greet

Perry as he walked into his specially decorated living room carrying a Bible and wearing a borrowed ecclesiastical robe. Most of them were friends like his housemate Willie Smith, and only three were strangers attracted by the ad. The next week, there were 13 people in the congregation. Then 15. But the fourth Sunday, only eight people came, and Perry thanked God for preparing him in advance for disappointment with a sermon on the topic, "Despise Not the Day of Small Things." The week after, however, there were more than 20, and the congregation reached 300 within a year, meeting by then in the theater building where Willie Smith worked as projectionist.

Within four years Perry's MCC congregation numbered some 800 members and became a force to be reckoned with among Los Angeles churches. In the spring of 1969 Perry went on a salary of $150 per week and was able to quit his outside job to become a full-time pastor (Enroth and Jamison 1974: 36; Swicegood 1974: 219–20). For Perry, the success of the church "meant, among other blessings, a steady income and hot meals on the dining room table" (Perry and Swicegood 1990: 48). Thus did Perry reconcile his early ministerial vocation with his gay life.

In so doing, he trod ironically familiar ground. Alongside George Whitefield in the eighteenth century, Charles Grandison Finney in the nineteenth, and his older contemporary Oral Roberts, Perry was a religious entrepreneur (Warner 1993: 1051, 1057, 1081). As Perry recalls it, "The only way I knew to begin a church was the way I had been taught in the South, and I still do not know any other – that is, to tell people openly who you are and where they can find you" (Perry and Swicegood 1990: 37).

To be successful, Perry's strategy required that there be a cultural market for his ideas, and his life as a gay man between 1963 and 1968 had introduced him to it. A distinctive gay male urban subculture had developed in the years after World War II in the United States, and Los Angeles was one of the cities

– San Francisco, San Diego, Houston, Chicago, Miami, and New York were others – to which gay men migrated in search of its bars and tea rooms. In the culturally open atmosphere of the 1960s, gay newspapers began to appear (Adam 1987a; D'Emilio 1983; Epstein 1987; FitzGerald 1986; Godfrey 1988). So the word about Troy Perry's new church got around town quickly.

Indeed, Perry's own relatively untroubled state of mind owed much to that subculture. *The Homosexual in America*, by the pseudonymous Donald Webster Cory (1951), which Perry found in a bookstore's gay magazine section early in the 1960s, convinced him that he belonged to the category of homosexuals and precipitated his initial decision to give up his family and his church. He had been able to come out from his closet with relative ease because in Los Angeles he could readily find gay meeting places, like Pagola's and The Patch, and models of openness like Willie Smith. Convinced as a boy by Christian preachers that God loved him, he was convinced as an adult by a gay network that his homosexuality was not to be borne alone. Troy Perry thus built his church on the grounds of both a Christian heritage and a nascent homosexual community.

Many of the MCC's first communicants had deep-seated but long-frustrated religious yearnings. As part of a study of homosexual identity, sociologist Barry Dank surveyed the Los Angeles membership two years after the founding and discovered that more than half of those responding had previously been members of the clergy or had seriously considered a ministerial career (Dank 1973: 84–6, 243). One of Perry's first recruits was the Revd. Richard Ploen, a minister and college teacher with a solid Presbyterian background, who helped Perry with the church's evolving doctrine and liturgy. Another recruit was "Papa" John Hose, a former minister, who organized the first MCC satellite church in San Diego. It seemed that there were many gay men eager to hear the gospel of God's unconditional love, and some of them wanted to go to work for the new church (Enroth and Jamison 1974: p. 65; Perry 1972: 129, 135, 192; Dart 1969).

Perry's first MCC sermon told the story of Job, a good man upon whom devastation had been visited but who stubbornly defied the patronizing assurances of his peers that he must have done something to incur the wrath of God. Job stood by his righteousness and faith – "I know that my Redeemer liveth" (Job 19: 25) – and was ultimately vindicated by a vision of God Himself. Everyone in the room was moved to tears by Perry's evangelical message, and he was inspired to begin his second Sunday service with the pentecostal refrain that has since become his trademark: "If you love the Lord this morning, would you say 'amen!'"

As his congregation grew over the months, so did his confidence. "Here before his congregation stood a showman out of the same mold as the pulpit greats of the past such as Aimee Semple McPherson and Billy Sunday. Energy flowed from Troy Perry and ignited his entire congregation." Those are the words of Perry's ghostwriter, Charles Lucas, three years after the founding, but Dennis Altman, radical theoretician of the gay movement and no partisan of religion, concurs, calling Perry "perhaps the most charismatic leader yet produced by the American gay movement" (Altman 1982: 27; Lucas 1972: 230). Perry also had a sense of humor. Early in the MCC years, Laud Humphreys suggested to Perry that he was the Martin Luther King of the gay movement, but Perry countered that Martin Luther *Queen* would be more like it (Humphreys 1972: 151). On the sole occasion I have heard him preach (in June 1988), Perry radiated vitality and cheer and never seemed to pause for breath. At the door after the service, he gave parishioners a powerful embrace and the visitor a piercing gaze. Although I recognized then what I later read freely acknowledged in his two autobiographies – that he is not a scholar, an intellectual, or even an eloquent speaker – I did not wonder that people were willing to follow him (see also Glaser 1988: 38–9; Dank 1973: 25; Swicegood 1974; Tobin and Wicker 1972: 229; cf. Perry 1972; Perry and Swicegood 1990).

Perry's teaching developed from the revelation that one can be both gay and Christian. Theologically, Perry would say, God comes first. With his pentecostal background and off-and-on Bible college training, Perry is at home with the language and symbols of conservative Protestantism. He thinks of God in personal and supernatural, New Testament terms. He always insists that the MCC is first of all a Christian church, a church universal enough to reach out to all God's children. From the outset, some of his strongest supporters, including his mother, have been members of the straight world. In that sense, the MCC resists being called "the gay church."

Yet Perry also teaches that in the life of the individual, sexual orientation comes first. He rather fancifully claims a sensual memory of the joining of sperm and ovum in his own conception as a homosexual, and he knows as a matter of faith that homosexuality is "preordained" (Perry 1972: 10; see also Perry and Swicegood 1990: 235). Indeed, if there is one article of faith which unites Christian gay men today it is that their sexual orientation is indelible. It is something over which they can and ought to have no control. For Troy Perry, the combination of that conviction with the evangelical image of a benevolent and powerful God produces a surpassing affirmation of gay identity. So it is that the first and most significant gay church should be theologically conservative, not liberal. "For the MCC member the conversion experience takes the form: Jesus loves *all* men; He loves even gay people; ergo gay is good" (Bauer 1976: 125; see also Sullivan 1994).

But Perry had ideological work to do with the Bible. At the coffee hour following the first MCC service, he had been unprepared for the plea of one young gay man, torn between the good news of Perry's message

and dread from his own fundamentalist background, that he contend with God's word on homosexuality as found in scripture. Perry asked for two weeks' study time. More consequential for the fundamentalists he had to address than the widespread but shallow use of the Sodom story as a rebuke to sexual perversity (many scholars think the sin of Sodom was lack of hospitality to strangers) were the outright condemnation of homosexual acts in the Mosaic Law (e.g., Leviticus 20: 13) and the "due penalty" of God pronounced by the Apostle Paul upon men inflamed with lust for one another (Romans 1: 27) (Swicegood 1974: 143ff.).

Perry brought determination to his task along with knowledge gained in several courses of formal Bible study. Most important for his hermeneutic efforts, his love of the Lord antedated his knowledge of the Bible. In early adolescence, he had come under the influence of his Aunt Bea, pastor of a pentecostal assembly in rural Georgia, who spoke before her congregation the prophecy that Troy was called to be a preacher. It was in Aunt Bea's church that, barely out of childhood, Perry gave his first four-minute sermon. For Troy Perry, religion had always been a matter of love, not law.

His solution to the apologetic problem was twofold. He first assimilated the Levitical prohibition of homosexual relations to the Old Testament law from which Jesus freed the faithful: rules and regulations concerning diet, dress, slave-holding, and myriad other matters (see also Sullivan 1994: 52). He then elevated above Paul's evident homophobia three other lessons from the New Testament: Jesus's message of love, the silence of the gospels themselves on the subject of homosexuality, and Jesus's own personal life as an unmarried peripatetic who kept company with 12 men. A good deal more Bible work has been done in the 20 years since Perry's initial problem-driven study (e.g., Arthur 1982), and positive models for same-sex relationships have been found in the stories of Ruth and Naomi, David and Jonathan, and Jesus and the disciple John. But the outlines of Perry's first solution stand today in the teaching of the MCC and other gay religious groups. Gay Christians like Troy Perry have not forgotten the evangelical tradition; they have found in its pentecostal variant a vision of grace with which to subdue a judgment of law.

On the basis of his army service, Perry had a model of a heterogeneous but same-sex organization recruiting without regard to race, color, or creed, and he expected a religiously heterogeneous – albeit homosexual – assembly to appear in response to his advertisements. So he determined in advance to be pragmatically eclectic on the matter of ritual forms. For the first service, he took the advice and borrowed the robe of a minister friend who insisted that the modest circumstances of Perry's living room had to be set off by the dignity of clerical attire. Perry now wears a white cassock and black stole for services and a clerical collar and black shirt for his daily routine. Another friend advised Perry that Hollywood sophisticates would expect wine for communion, not the evangelical's grape juice, and that a weekly communion called for a sermon of no more than 20 minutes. MCC services now offer a choice of juice or wine.

Two other liturgical features developed to become characteristic of the MCC. Perry's one-time roommate, Willie Smith, who was raised a Seventh Day Adventist, inaugurated the "Singspiration," a pre-service hymnfest, during the first year, and many congregations now celebrate it. Even more entrenched in the MCC is an extended, emotionally and physically touching communion, where individual congregants or (more often) couples are enveloped in a lengthy embrace by the server, who whispers a personalized prayer into their ears (for a description, see Riley 1991: 18–22).

Thus, MCC services have come to feel like an eclectic mix of Catholic, Episcopal, and Lutheran liturgical forms with the preaching style, gospel hymns, and democratic prayer circle of twentieth-century charismatic fellowships. In his survey of pioneering MCC members, Dank found that those originally Roman Catholic were a plurality among the respondents, about a quarter, while those of Baptist background accounted for 14 percent (Dank 1973: 35–7; see also Enroth and Jamison 1974), proportions close to the makeup of the general religious population (Roof and McKinney 1987). The liturgical mix evidently worked, and a great variety of observers over the years have found the MCC service "a powerful statement of unity" (Gorman 1980: 70–2), "impressive and moving" (Coleman 1971: 117), and "the most grateful celebration of Christ I had ever attended" (Mollenkott 1979; see also Enroth and Jamison 1974: 31–4; Lyles 1983; Swicegood 1974: 186; Glaser 1988: 38–9).

Yet the MCC is not for everyone, what with systematically varying religious tastes. One group in Atlanta was inspired by Troy Perry's vision but put off by high church elements in the local MCC service, and they formed their own, more traditionally evangelical, congregation in 1977 (Thumma 1987: 123–5). On the other end of the spectrum, Laud Humphreys – gay man, ordained Episcopal priest, and sociology professor – told me that he could not stomach even the faint echo of biblical fundamentalism in Perry's preaching (interview with Laud Humphreys, Los Angeles, June 29, 1988). The MCC has, in other words, a denominational culture.

Like conventional religious organizations, MCCs are social as well as religious centers. This is an observation made by those friendly as well as those hostile to the enterprise. Dank, an admirer of Perry's work, said of the MCC in 1970 that

the church has members who vary in religiosity from fundamentalist Protestant to agnostic and atheist. Two of the most active members, and the most socially committed, have been an agnostic and a Jew. Socially one can find the homosexually "married couple" seeking friends, to the persons who come to church to find "one-night stands" *(Dank 1973: 33–4)*

Bauer reports, on the basis of participant observation in the Denver parish of the MCC, that the congregation welcomed the cruiser. "The attitude is that 'They are here, as opposed to a gay bar, and are listening to the word of God'" (Bauer 1976: 121). Evangelical critics Enroth and Jamison (1974) have a less charitable view of the same phenomenon.

The upshot is that Perry and his early followers had the audacity to claim for homosexuals the social space given over to subcultural groups through American churches. The claim was not automatically honored. Soon after the founding, the church was visited by a contingent from the police vice squad seemingly bent on entrapment (Perry 1972: 137–8; Dank 1973: 29), and the congregation's early rental agreement with the Huntington Park Women's Club was abrogated when the club found out what kind of "church" their tenants were. The Los Angeles church was burned in 1973 and other MCC churches – in San Francisco, Nashville, New Orleans, and Atlanta – have been the target of arsonists over the years (Perry and Swicegood 1990: 71–2, 76). Yet, "church" has legitimating and mobilizing power in our society, and the MCC has taken advantage of it. Humphreys (1972: 152) observed:

> There are several advantages to such gay religious organizations. Due to the nation's tradition of religious freedom, gay churches enjoy some protection from legal and social stigma. This form of stigma redemption enables gays to deduct contributions to their cause from income taxes, as well as to profit from the tax-exempt status of their parsonages and meeting places. They can sponsor dances with little likelihood of police interference and provide an umbrella for a wide range of social, publishing, and service activities.

A church was the ideal vehicle to address the twin needs of people like Carlos, Perry's friend under arrest: to stop persecution of gays by straight society and to heal gays' internal wounds. The solidarity provided by congregational religious life was the key to both ends.

Evangelical Theology and Essentialist Anthropology

The ideology of the homophile movement was contested during the first years of the MCC, and gay Christians made a fateful contribution to the debate. Just when liberationists proclaimed the end of fixed sexual categories, Troy Perry preached that homosexuality was innate. Until recently, the former position was received wisdom among intellectuals, but the latter has become the party line within the gay community itself.

Perry drew on lessons from the reformist stage of the movement for black civil rights (see Bloom 1987: 120–54). Gays, in this view, were a persecuted minority, but their first step to emancipation was to overcome their own fear. Only then could they stand together, face their oppressors, and demand the rights due to all persons. This much Perry learned from reading *The Homosexual in America* (Cory 1951).

> When I finished the book I knew without the shadow of a doubt that I was a homosexual; I was gay. And there was just nothing for me to be afraid of any longer. This was it. I could honestly look at myself in the mirror, and say to myself, "You know something, you're a homosexual." And it didn't upset me. *(Perry 1972: 78)*

Perry's 1972 autobiography opens with these words (ibid: 3):

> One thing is sure. We homosexuals must all learn to rid ourselves of the sense of shame that we have been conditioned to

accept from the heterosexual world. Such shame is no longer acceptable to any of us. How could we go on being ashamed of something that God created? Yes, God created homosexuals and homosexuality. It exists throughout history, and all over the world.

Coming out together would banish fear and conquer shame, which

comes, I think, through a sense of being alone. I'm sure that all homosexuals feel alone – often desperately alone – for long stretches of time. I know I did. And, being alone, being lonely, gives anyone a sense of solitary isolation. That is what has made us vulnerable to the oppressive nature of the heterosexual world.

In effect, Perry set out to build a positive identity on the basis of a given, previously devalued, category, "homosexuality." It was an audacious strategy, similar to Foucault's "reverse affirmation," wherein a stigmatized group rallies around the label applied to them and asserts their pride in that identity (Epstein 1987: 17–18, citing Foucault 1980: 101). Yet it was crucial to Perry's achievement that the basis of identity, "homosexuality," was a gift of God, not an arbitrary social imposition.

At the same time that Perry was drawing hundreds of recruits to his church, a more thoroughgoing assault on prejudice closer to Foucault's ideal was underway from people who wanted to overturn socially imposed gender categories themselves. At Catholic University in Washington, DC, in 1970, a polite conference on religion and homosexuality heard an impolite proclamation from the DC Gay Liberation Front that began, "We demand that you stop examining our homosexuality and become homosexual yourselves" (Rueda 1982: 325). Stemming more from the cultural politics of the late 1960s than from the militant reformism of the early 1960s, radical gay liberation proposed to free all people from the dichotomized social shackles of homosexual versus hetero-

sexual roles and masculine versus feminine identities. Drawing on the theories of Herbert Marcuse (that sexual repression is the foundation of social oppression) and the empirical findings of Alfred Kinsey and his associates (that there is a continuum rather than a dichotomy of heterosexual to homosexual experience), liberationists sought to unleash the bisexual and androgynous potential in everyone. *Homosexual: Oppression and Liberation* (Altman 1973) is usually cited as a theoretical manifesto of this phase of the movement.

By now there is an immense academic literature on these matters, and the poles represented by Perry and Altman reflect positions now known as "essentialism" and "constructionism." The issues are complex, and they include debates on the etiology of same-sex attraction (see Ruse 1988; Gagnon 1987; Bell, Weinberg, and Hammersmith 1981; Whitam and Mathy 1986; Burr 1993). But the prior question is whether it makes sense to speak of homosexuality as a thing at all, as a state or condition which does or does not characterize the sexuality of a given individual, or whether homosexuality is not better understood as a concept that has been contingently applied to label (and stigmatize) a part of the infinite and plastic range of human behavior (Boswell 1982–3). Such a simple matter as the indefinite article ("I am a homosexual" versus "I am homosexual") signals a philosophic gulf. The former idea, homosexuality as an essence, is the older and more conventional modern view, both in common sense language and in social scientific and medical literature until the 1960s. The latter, homosexuality as a construct, is newer, postmodern, and more intellectually daring.

For our purposes, it is remarkable that, after an initial flirtation with the constructionist position around 1969–72, the gay community in the United States hewed to the essentialist alternative. At first, there was no consensus on the etiological question, what "causes homosexuality," and in fact many gay men evinced some hostility to the very question. But they did agree on the reality of homosexuality. The shoe fit, and they wore it (FitzGerald 1986: 57–8; Epstein 1987: 11–12; Adam 1987b: 747; Risman and Schwartz 1988: 129; Fierstein 1988: 52).

The arguments for essentialism are many. Historian John Boswell studies the continuity of gay culture, which would disappear if the category were arbitrarily and externally imposed. Philosopher Michael Ruse adjudicates etiological theories, which would be nonsense if there were not something to explain. Sociologist Frederick Whitam wants to secure civil rights for homosexuals, and he believes that society is willing in principle to recognize rights for ascriptively defined groups, who are not responsible for their condition. "If the categories 'homosexual/heterosexual' and 'gay/straight' are the inventions of particular societies rather than real aspects of the human psyche, there is no gay history" (Boswell 1982–3: 93; see also Ruse 1988; Whitam and Mathy 1986; Grahn 1984).

The counterarguments are also many. For some, essentialism raises the specter of genocide, an ideology convenient for those who would as soon do away with homosexuals altogether. The innate homosexuality theory also justifies a policy of neglect with respect to AIDS as an essentially "gay disease" that straight society need not worry about. Essentialism divides gays from those who, by reason of their social stigma, are natural political allies. Essentialism reifies gender categories which disadvantage women in general and thereby tends to divide gay men from lesbians and feminists (Van Gelder 1991). Essentialism violates what many sociologists believe to be true about human personality (see Epstein 1987; Richardson 1983–4; Thumma 1987).

But constructionists have, from the grassroots gay point of view, some unsavory allies themselves. They include therapists who trade on "curing" homosexuality, and cultural conservatives who maintain the childhood seduction theory in order to deny school teaching jobs to gays. Above all,

there are the religious conservatives who insist that homosexuality is a "choice" subject to moral condemnation. Evangelical theologian Carl Henry, for example, says, "What the gay world needs is redemption, not reinforcement" (cited approvingly in Enroth and Jamison 1974: 133; see also Pattison and Pattison 1980; Dallas 1992; for surveys of the issues as they bear on religion see Thumma 1987; Hewitt 1983).

To these threats, homophile Christians respond with endless variations on the essentialist theme. Troy Perry:

> I caught the brass ring. And, I'm sure that homosexuality was in my genes, and in my soul, from the very beginning. *(Perry 1972: 10)*

Chris Glaser, rejected candidate for ordination in the Presbyterian church:

> Homosexuality is not a philosophy. It's what God made me. *(Glaser 1989)*

Virginia Ramey Mollenkott, Plymouth Brethren scholar:

> One of the things I did was sit in front of a mirror, look myself in the eye, and say over and over again, "Virginia, you're a lesbian. God knew you were a lesbian from the foundation of the world, and God loved you, just as you are." *(Mollenkott 1986)*

"Thomas," member of a gay evangelical church in Atlanta, quoting a translation of Psalm 100, verse 3:

> It is He that hath made us and not we ourselves. *(Cited in Thumma 1987: 133)*

Malcolm Boyd, Episcopal priest:

> Gays have a "natural God-given sexual orientation" since they are "human beings created in God's image." "In time I offered thanks to God for the gift of being gay." *(Boyd 1986: 74, 76, 2)*

John McNeill, ex-Jesuit:

> God so created humans that they develop with a great variety of both gender identities and sexual-object choices.... Always and everywhere a certain percentage of men and women develop as homosexuals or lesbians. They should be considered as part of God's creative plan. Their sexual orientation has no necessary connection with sin, sickness, or failure; rather, it is a gift from God to be accepted and lived out with gratitude. God does not despise anything that God has created. *(McNeill 1987: 243)*

Andrew Sullivan, Roman Catholic layman and editor of *The New Republic*:

> Like faith, one's sexuality is not simply a choice; it informs whole ways of being.... And like faith, it points toward something other and more powerful than the self. *(Sullivan 1994: 47)*

Revd. Elder Nancy Wilson, MCC clergywoman since 1972:

> The first time Wilson went into a lesbian bar it was as if she had spent all her life to that point in Wonderland and had now walked through the looking glass back into the real world. It was a place where she could be all of who she was. "These are my people," she thought, and she used the Greek word, *ethne*, to express this. Through them, she felt linked to other of her people in every culture and in every epoch. *(Interview with Nancy Wilson, 1989)*

John Shelby Spong, Episcopal Bishop of Newark, New Jersey:

> Research consistently seems to support the assertion that sexual orientation is not a matter of choice; that it is not related to any environmental influence; that it is not the result of an overbearing mother or absent father or a seductive sexual encounter. *(Spong 1988: 71–2)*

Thomas Hanks, reviewing Greenberg (1988) in the UFMCC newsletter:

> If homosexuality is a social construct then conceivably a homosexual public school teacher might seduce a student and socially "construct/recruit" a homosexual out of an innocent heterosexual adolescent. *(Hanks 1990)*

Mary Borhek, whose son is gay, formerly a member of an independent pentecostal church, now an Episcopalian:

> I would point out that no one *chooses* his or her sexual orientation; it is a "given" with which each person has to learn to live. *(Borhek 1982: 462)*

A group of parents of lesbians and gays, associated with Dignity:

> We "lean toward a biological cause" in part so as to put "an end to the blame game." *(Griffin, Wirth, and Wirth 1986: 29–30)*

The power of gay Christian essentialism is that it (1) invokes a powerful and benevolent God to proclaim the issue of homosexuality to be beyond human control, thereby concentrating the energy of gays themselves on changing their circumstances; (2) frees parents from doubt; (3) denies that homosexuality is in any way contagious; (4) expresses solidarity with grassroots gay culture; and (5) demands, as a matter of simple justice, inclusion of gays as simply another tile in the American mosaic. The strategy is pluralist, not revolutionary, since gays are presented to be the same as the rest of Americans by virtue of being trivially different: "We go to bed with members of our own sex" (D'Emilio 1983; Altman 1982: 123).

It seems likely that grassroots essentialism stands behind what Randy Shilts called "the marked lack of hysteria among most Americans" toward the AIDS epidemic and what critic Susan Sontag conceded were "checks on the impulse to stigmatize people with the disease," even as it may have detracted from the urgency with which the medical crisis was addressed. Increased incidence of "gay bashing" cannot be denied, but neither can the political victories homophiles have won in most legislative referenda and the increased civil tolerance shown in public opinion polls in the 1980s (Shilts 1987: 353, 284, 519, 570; Sontag 1988: 97–9). If gay people are *essentially* different, the mass of society can feel the safer behind their symbolic boundary (see Douglas 1966). At the same time, essentialism seems to promote reconciliation with parents, since they are freed from self-recriminations and from anger over their children's willful rejection of their values. Outspoken parents, as represented in the nationwide organization Parents and Friends of Lesbians and Gays (PFLAG), pull essentialism in a pluralist rather than separatist direction (Griffin, Wirth, and Wirth 1986).

Always a pluralist reform movement rather than a radical reconstruction movement, the MCC was a repository of traditionalism available to gays gravitating toward moral conservatism in sexual relationships as knowledge of AIDS spread in the late 1980s and romance, dating, coupling, and family values came in style in the gay male community (FitzGerald 1986: 119; Risman and Schwartz 1988: 142; Fierstein 1988: 48). From the beginning the MCC has celebrated "holy unions" for committed couples who have lived together half a year and wish to proclaim public vows. In the same spirit, Nancy Wilson, current pastor of the MCC Mother Church and elected UFMCC Elder, refuses to concede "family values" to the straight world: "I am a daughter, a sister, an aunt and a niece; a spouse in a committed relationship for ten years; a godmother; and a pastor to a local congregation (and to a worldwide MCC family)" (Wilson 1987: 845).

Above all, MCC congregations provide a setting for emotionally supportive interaction. The touching that has always characterized MCC services – the hand-to-hand prayer circle, the communion embrace – has acquired new sacramental meaning in the era of AIDS for those deemed untouchable elsewhere. The implicit trust inherent to a group known to each other first of all by their common stigma is deepened in testimony and prayer sessions by the disclosure of symptoms and test results. The heavy burden of giving care to the sick is borne more readily by those who know they are not alone and fear that they may need care next (see Cherry and Mitulski 1988; Riley 1991).

The theological wellspring of the MCC is the spirituality of Troy Perry, a life-long pentecostal, who has prophesied in tongues from the MCC pulpit and gone into the desert to seek God's guidance (Perry and Swicegood 1990: 161, 307). Unlike many theological liberals and feminist theologians, Perry adheres to a concept of God as a personal and majestic transcendent being with the power to create homosexuals as well as heterosexuals and to demand that he, Perry, defy convention and establish a church for those of God's children left out by those who misunderstand this. Perry is empowered by that experience of God, and he founded the MCC on it. According to its bylaws, the UFMCC explicitly "moves in the mainstream of Christianity" and is officially committed to the historic creeds' affirmations of the trinity, the authority of scriptures, and salvation by faith (UFMCC 1991). Perry has struggled to defend the MCC's theological and liturgical conservatism against assaults from what he calls "unitarian and less evangelical" pastors in the denomination, and he seems genuinely convinced that "all would be well" for the MCC only so long as "our church continued to follow Jesus" (Perry and Swicegood 1990: 307).

Toward the Future?

To mention Perry's "struggle" is to acknowledge that the MCC's ideology is not solely conservative. Beginning in 1972, under the prodding of its articulate women clergy, the

UFMCC committed itself officially to gender equality and adopted inclusive language first for the officers specified in its bylaws and later for use in worship. The 1976 General Conference adopted "Once to Every Soul [instead of 'Man'] and Nation" as its theme hymn, and in 1981 the General Conference adopted inclusive language as denominational policy. Now, by local congregational option, the Lord's Prayer may be addressed to "Our Creator" or "Our Sustainer" and the Gloria Patri has become "glory be to our maker" (Enroth and Jamison 1974: 82–4; Birchard 1977; UFMCC 1991; author's field notes). These innovations were seen by Perry in evangelistic terms: "I came to the decision that... whatever language will reach the largest number of people is the language Metropolitan Community Church will use" (Perry and Swicegood 1990: 308; cf. Iannaccone and Miles 1990).

At first, lesbians, whose population numbers perhaps one-third to one-half as many as gay men in the United States, were severely underrepresented in MCC congregations. Near the end of the first decade of the church's existence, a lesbian critic could say that the "MCC has made progress toward grooming a number of women pastors of real competence, but in general Lesbians are few and far between and those who are attracted are not usually women who would identify themselves as Lesbian-feminists" (Krody 1977: 151). Some of the early women clergy identified more with older lesbian categories like "butch" than with newer feminist sensibilities. But in recent years lesbians, including feminists, are becoming more prominent in the MCC, partly through the efforts of those very competent pastors Krody refers to, and partly because of the toll wrought by AIDS on the numbers of male MCC members and clergy. Reportedly, women now number 40 percent of MCC clergy and 30 percent of members (Eastman interview 1989).

Inclusive language represents the MCC's collective attempt to bridge a gap that plagues homophile organizations even more than straight ones, the fact that the "gay-and-lesbian" conjunction is a product of social construction and movement politics, but not of folk culture, let alone any essential reality. Since the development of homosexual cultures after World War II, gay men and lesbians have had separate spaces – their own bars – and very different manners. In ideology, lesbian feminists uphold values of cooperation and equality in contrast to masculine values of dominance. Lesbians are more likely than gay men to have no religious affiliation or to identify with a "personal spirituality" or other non-Christian religion. Women in the MCC are more likely than men to describe themselves as theologically liberal. Lesbians are far more likely to be monogamous than gay men. Pornography is more important for gay men than for lesbians, and increasingly so as a means of safe sex in the world of AIDS. A lesbian is more likely to identify as such when she is already in love with another woman or because of a belief in women's solidarity, a gay man because of generalized attraction for persons of the same sex. Furthermore, women coming to lesbianism since Stonewall are likely to have done so within the context of supportive political groups and therefore do not have the problem with guilt and self-hatred that many gay men do. Constructionist theory is therefore closer to lesbian than gay male experience. (This paragraph based on Adam 1987a; Altman 1982: 45–47; Cherry 1992; Esterberg 1990; Faderman 1984; FitzGerald 1986: 35, 56–7; Herek 1985; McKirnan and Peterson 1987; Neitz 1988; Reback 1988; Risman and Schwartz 1988; Ruse 1988: 9–10; and author's field notes).

Take "Goddess" language, for example. Perry does not approve of it, and he so expressed himself in a pastoral letter to the UFMCC membership in 1989. Yet the pastor of "SisterSpirit," a hybrid pagan-MCC congregation in Oregon, does use Goddess language, and for several years in the 1980s "De Colores," a multiethnic feminist group at UFMCC headquarters, experimented with God-languages. There was something of a showdown on the issue at the General Conference of 1989, held in Minneapolis, when Nancy Wilson and five other women visited Perry in his suite to protest his pastoral letter. Herself deeply ambivalent about Goddess language, Wilson led the group in solidarity with those for whom it is empowering. According to Wilson, Perry backed down a bit from the position taken in his letter and said that his letter was just an expression of his "opinion." "When you say something, people listen," Wilson recalls telling him. "So please be more careful if it's just an opinion" (Wilson interview, 1989).

The MCC today is increasingly gender integrated as a denomination, but there tends to be intercongregational gender differentiation. For example, the Mother Church, Perry's own first MCC pulpit, is now majority lesbian under its second woman pastor (Wilson interview and author's field notes). Not all lesbians have the same religious needs and not all are theologically liberal; Dusty Pruitt, former Naval officer and later pastor of MCC Long Beach, prefers the original pentecostally inspired MCC spirituality to goddess worship (interview with Dusty Pruitt, Princeton, New Jersey, October 2, 1993). Nonetheless, in some congregations feminist lesbians are bringing New Age spirituality, goddess worship, and universalism into the originally pentecostal and trinitarian MCC mix. The unsettled relationship and ideological differences between gays and lesbians is without doubt the main internal source of change in the UFMCC today.

REFERENCES

Adam, B. D. 1987a. *The Rise of a Gay and Lesbian Movement*. Boston: Twayne Publishers.
——1987b. "Review of Whitam and Mathy 1986." *Contemporary Sociology* 16 (September): 747–8.

Altman, D. 1973. *Homosexual: Oppression and Liberation*. New York: Avon Books.
——1982. *The Homosexualization of America, The Americanization of the Homosexual*. New York: St. Martin's Press.
Arthur, L. R. 1982. *Homosexuality and the Conservative Christian*. Los Angeles: Samaritan Theological Institute.
Bartlet, D. L. 1977. "A Biblical Perspective on Homosexuality." *Foundations: A Baptist Journal of History and Theology* 20 (April–June): 133–47.
Bauer, P. F. 1976. "The Homosexual Subculture at Worship: A Participant Observation Study." *Pastoral Psychology* 25 (winter): 115–27.
Bedell, K. 1993. *Yearbook of American and Canadian Churches, 1993*. Nashville, TN: Abingdon, for the National Council of Churches.
Bell, A. P., M. S. Weinberg, and S. K. Hammersmith. 1981. *Sexual Preference: Its Development in Men and Women*. Bloomington: Indiana University Press.
Birchard, R. 1977. "Metropolitan Community Church: Its Development and Significance." *Foundations: A Baptist Journal of History and Theology* 20 (April–June): 127–32.
Bloom, J. M. 1987. *Class, Race, and the Civil Rights Movement*. Bloomington: Indiana University Press.
Borhek, M. V. 1982. "Can the NCC Accept a Gay Denomination?" *Christian Century* 99 (April 14): 461–2.
Boswell, J. 1980. *Christianity, Social Tolerance, and Homosexuality: Gay People in Western Europe from the Beginning of the Christian Era to the Fourteenth Century*. Chicago: University of Chicago Press.
——1982–3. "Revolutions, Universals and Sexual Categories." *Salmagundi* 58/59 (fall/winter): 89–113.
Boyd, M. 1984. *Take Off the Masks*. Philadelphia: New Society.
——1986. *Gay Priest: An Inner Journey*. New York: St. Martin's Press.
Burr, C. 1993. "Homosexuality and Biology." *Atlantic Monthly* 271 (March): 47–65.
Carrington, C. 1990. "Respectability: The Inclusion of Gay Men and Lesbians in the Congregational Life of Liberal Protestantism." Paper presented at annual meeting of the Society for the Scientific Study of Religion, Virginia Beach, VA.

Cherry, K. 1991. "UFMCC Has Ecumenical Impact." *Keeping in Touch* (UFMCC newsletter) July.

——1992. "Survey Reveals UFMCC Women's Needs." *Keeping in Touch* (UFMCC newsletter) March.

Cherry, K. and J. Mitulski. 1988. "We Are the Church Alive, the Church with AIDS." *Christian Century* 105 (January 27): 85–8.

Cleath, R. 1970. "The Homosexual Church." *Christianity Today* 14 (September 11): 48–50.

Coleman, G. D. 1987. "The Vatican Statement on Homosexuality." *Theological Studies* 48: 727–34.

Coleman, J. A. 1971. "The Churches and the Homosexual." *America* 124 (February 6): 113–17.

Cooper, A. 1989–90. "No Longer Invisible: Gay and Lesbian Jews Build a Movement." *Journal of Homosexuality* 18 (3–4): 83–94.

Cory, D. W. (pseudonym for E. Sagarin). 1951. *The Homosexual in America: A Subjective Approach*. New York: Greenberg.

Dallas, J. 1992. "Born Gay?" *Christianity Today* 36 (June 22): 20–3.

Dank, B. M. 1973. *The Development of a Homosexual Identity: Antecedents and Consequents*. Dissertation, Department of Sociology, University of Wisconsin.

Dart, J. 1969. "A Church for Homosexuals." *Los Angeles Times* (December 8): B1, B5.

——1991. "Church for Gays Alters Mainline Religions' Views." *Los Angeles Times* (June 7): A1, A36–7.

D'Emilio, J. 1983. *Sexual Politics, Sexual Communities: The Making of a Homosexual Minority in the United States, 1940–1970*. Chicago: University of Chicago Press.

Douglas, M. 1966. *Purity and Danger: An Analysis of the Concepts of Pollution and Taboo*. London: Routledge and Kegan Paul.

Duberman, M. 1993. *Stonewall*. New York: Dutton.

Enroth, R. E. and G. E. Jamison. 1974. *The Gay Church*. Grand Rapids, MI: Eerdmans.

Epstein, S. 1987. "Gay Politics, Ethnic Identity: The Limits of Social Constructionism." *Socialist Review* 17 (May–August): 9–54.

Esterberg, K. G. 1990. "Salience and Solidarity: Identity, Correctness, and Conformity in a Lesbian Community." Paper presented at annual meeting of the American Sociological Association, Washington, DC.

Faderman, L. 1984. "The 'New Gay' Lesbians." *Journal of Homosexuality* 10 (winter): 85–95.

Fierstein, H. 1988. Playboy Interview; conducted by H. Stein. *Playboy* 35 (August): 43–57.

FitzGerald, F. 1986. *Cities on a Hill: A Journey Through Contemporary American Cultures*. New York: Simon and Schuster.

Foucault, M. 1980. *The History of Sexuality*, vol. 1: *An Introduction*. New York: Vintage.

Gagnon, J. 1987. Review of Whitam and Mathy 1986. *American Journal of Sociology* 93 (November): 742–4.

Glaser, C. 1988. *Uncommon Calling: A Gay Man's Struggle to Serve the Church*. San Francisco: Harper and Row.

——1989. "Gays, Lesbians, and the Church." Talk given at Nassau Presbyterian Church, Princeton, NJ, March 12.

Godfrey, B. J. 1988. *Neighborhoods in Transition: The Making of San Francisco's Ethnic and Nonconformist Communities*. Berkeley and Los Angeles: University of California Press.

Gorman, E. M. 1980. *A New Light on Zion: A Study of Three Homosexual Religious Congregations in Urban America*. Unpublished Ph.D. dissertation, Department of Anthropology, University of Chicago.

Grahn, J. 1984. *Another Mother Tongue: Gay Words, Gay Worlds*. Boston: Beacon Press.

Greenberg, D. F. 1988. *The Construction of Homosexuality*. Chicago: University of Chicago Press.

Griffin, C. W., M. J. Wirth, and A. G. Wirth. 1986. *Beyond Acceptance: Parents of Lesbians and Gays Talk About Their Experiences*. Englewood Cliffs, NJ: Prentice-Hall.

Hanks, T. 1990. Review of Greenberg 1988. *Keeping in Touch* (May): 3–4.

Herek, G. M. 1985. "On Doing, Being, and Not Being: Prejudice and the Social Construction of Homosexuality." *Journal of Homosexuality* 12 (fall): 135–51.

Hewitt, T. F. 1983. *The American Church's Reaction to the Homophile Movement, 1948–1978*. Dissertation, Department of Religion, Duke University, Durham, NC.

Humphreys, L. 1972. *Out of the Closets: The Sociology of Homosexual Liberation*. Englewood Cliffs, NJ: Prentice-Hall.

Iannaccone, L. R. and C. A. Miles. 1990. "Dealing With Social Change: The Mormon

Church's Response to Change in Women's Roles." *Social Forces* 68 (June): 1231–50.

Krody, N. 1977. "An Open Lesbian Looks at the Church." *Foundations: A Baptist Journal of History and Theology* 20 (April–June): 148–62.

Lucas, C. 1972. "Postscript." Pp. 229–32 in *The Lord Is My Shepherd and He Knows I'm Gay: The Autobiography of the Rev. Troy D. Perry as told to Charles Lucas.* Los Angeles: Nash Publishing.

Lyles, J. C. 1982. "What's Good for the NCC." *Christian Century* 99 (December 1): 1222–3.

——1983. "The Unity They Seek." *Christian Century* 100 (June 1): 539–40.

McKirnan, D. and P. L. Peterson. n.d. [1987.] *General Findings From the Social Issues Survey: Population Characteristics, Substance Abuse and AIDS Risk Among Homosexuals.* Unpublished report, Department of Psychology, University of Illinois at Chicago.

McNeill, J. J. 1987. "Homosexuality: Challenging the Church to Grow." *Christian Century* 104 (March 11): 242–6.

Mollenkott, V. R. 1979. "Joyful Worship in the Midst of Danger." *Christian Century* 96 (September 26): 910.

——1986. "Gay/Lesbian Gifts to the Church." *Windy City Times,* November 13: 12.

Neitz, M. J. 1988. "Sacramental Sex in Modern Witchcraft Groups." Paper presented at annual meeting of the Midwest Sociological Society, Minneapolis, MN.

Pattison, E. M. and M. L. Pattison. 1980. "'Ex-Gays': Religiously Mediated Change in Homosexuals." *American Journal of Psychiatry* 137 (December): 1553–62.

Perry, T. D. 1972. *The Lord Is My Shepherd and He Knows I'm Gay: The Autobiography of the Rev. Troy D. Perry as told to Charles Lucas.* Los Angeles: Nash Publishing.

Perry, T. D. and T. L. P. Swicegood. 1990. *Don't Be Afraid Anymore: The Story of Reverend Troy Perry and the Metropolitan Community Churches.* New York: St. Martin's Press.

Pruitt, D. 1993. "Power and Powerlessness: The Appeal of Charismatic Christianity to the Gay and Lesbian Community." Paper presented to the ISAE Consultation on Pentecostal Currents in the American Church, Princeton, NJ.

Reback, C. 1988. "Lesbian Virgins: A Study of Redefining Identities." Paper presented at annual meetings of the American Sociological Association, Atlanta, GA.

Richardson, D. 1983–4. "The Dilemma of Essentiality in Homosexual Theory." *Journal of Homosexuality* 9 (winter–spring): 79–90.

Riley, C. T. 1991. "'Our God Too': Family Formation and Normalization in the Metropolitan Community Church of Pittsburgh." Paper presented at annual meeting of the Society for the Scientific Study of Religion, Pittsburgh.

Risman, B. 1988. "Review of Whitam and Mathy 1986." *Social Forces* 67 (December): 553–4.

Risman, B. and P. Schwartz. 1988. "Sociological Research on Male and Female Homosexuality." *Annual Review of Sociology* 14: 125–47.

Roof, W. C. and W. McKinney. 1987. *American Mainline Religion.* New Brunswick, NJ: Rutgers University Press.

Rueda, E. 1982. *The Homosexual Network: Private Lives and Public Policy.* Greenwich, CT: Devin Adair.

Ruse, M. 1988. *Homosexuality: A Philosophical Inquiry.* Oxford: Blackwell Publishers.

Shilts, R. 1987. *And the Band Played On: Politics, People, and the AIDS Epidemic.* New York: St. Martin's Press.

Sontag, S. 1988. "AIDS and Its Metaphors." *The New York Review of Books* 35 (October 27): 89–99.

Spong, J. S. 1988. *Living in Sin? A Bishop Rethinks Human Sexuality.* San Francisco: Harper and Row.

Sullivan, A. 1994. "Alone Again, Naturally: The Catholic Church and the Homosexual." *The New Republic* 211 (November 28): 47–55.

Swicegood, T. 1974. *Our God Too.* New York: Pyramid Books.

Thumma, S. 1987. *Straightening Identities: Evangelical Approaches to Homosexuality.* Unpublished master of divinity thesis, Candler School of Theology, Atlanta, GA.

Tobin, K. and R. Wicker. 1972. *The Gay Crusaders.* New York: Paperback Library.

UFMCC 1991. *Universal Fellowship of Metropolitan Community Churches By-Laws: Revised at General Conference XV.* Los Angeles: UFMCC.

Van Gelder, L. 1991. "The 'Born That Way' Trap." *MS* (May/June): 86–7.

Warner, R. S. 1993. "Work In Progress Toward a New Paradigm for the Sociological Study of Religion in the United States." *American Journal of Sociology* 98 (March): 1044–93.

—— 1994. "The Place of the Congregation in the American Religious Configuration." Pp. 54–99 in *American Congregations*, vol. 2, *New Perspectives in the Study of Congregations*, edited by J. Lewis and J. Wind. Chicago: University of Chicago Press.

Warren, C. A. B. 1974. *Identity and Community in the Gay World*. New York: Wiley-Interscience.

Whitam, F. L. and R. M. Mathy. 1986. *Male Homosexuality in Four Societies: Brazil, Gua-temala, the Philippines, and the United States*. New York: Praeger.

Wilson, N. L. 1987. "A Gay Witness to Pope John Paul II." *Christian Century* 104 (October 7): 845–6.

Windy City Times: Chicago's Gay and Lesbian Newsweekly. 1985–91.

Wuthnow, R. 1988. *The Restructuring of American Religion: Society and Faith Since World War II*. Princeton, NJ: Princeton University Press.

20 The Muslim Concept of Active Female Sexuality

Fatima Mernissi

The Function of Instincts

The Christian concept of the individual as tragically torn between two poles – good and evil, flesh and spirit, instinct and reason – is very different from the Muslim concept. Islam has a more sophisticated theory of the instincts, more akin to the Freudian concept of the libido. It views the raw instincts as energy. The energy of instincts is pure in the sense that it has no connotation of good or bad. The question of good and bad arises only when the social destiny of men is considered. The individual cannot survive except within a social order. Any social order has a set of laws. The set of laws decides which uses of the instincts are good or bad. It is the use made of the instincts, not the instincts themselves, that is beneficial or harmful to the social order. Therefore, in the Muslim order it is not necessary for the individual to eradicate his instincts or to control them for the sake of control itself, but he must use them according to the demands of religious law.

> When Muhammad forbids or censures certain human activities, or urges their omission, he does not want them to be neglected altogether, nor does he want them to be completely eradicated, or the powers from which they result to remain altogether unused. He wants those powers to be employed as much as possible for the right aims. Every intention should thus eventually become the right one and the direction of all human activities one and the same.[1]

Aggression and sexual desire, for example, if harnessed in the right direction, serve the purposes of the Muslim order; if suppressed or used wrongly, they can destroy that very order:

> Muhammad did not censure wrathfulness with the intention of eradicating it as a human quality. If the power of wrathfulness were no longer to exist in man, he would lose the ability to help the truth to become victorious. There would no longer be holy war or glorification of the word of God. Muhammad censured the wrathfulness that is in the service of Satan and reprehensible purposes, but the wrathfulness that is one in God and in the service of God deserves praise.[2]
>
> ... Likewise when he censures the desires, he does not want them to be abolished altogether, for a complete abolition of concupiscence in a person would make him defective and inferior. He wants the desire to be used for permissible purposes to serve the public interests, so that man becomes an active servant of God who willingly obeys the divine commands.[3]

Imam Ghazali (1050–1111) in his book *The Revivification of Religious Sciences*[4] gives a detailed description of how Islam integrated the sexual instinct in the social order and placed it at the service of God. He starts by stressing the antagonism between sexual desire and the social order: "If the desire of the flesh dominates the individual and is not controlled by the fear of God, it leads men to commit destructive acts."[5] But used according to God's will, the desire of the flesh serves God's and the individual's interests in both worlds, enhances life on earth and in heaven. Part of God's design on earth is to ensure the perpetuity of the human race, and sexual desires serve this purpose:

Sexual desire was created solely as a means to entice men to deliver the seed and to put the woman in a situation where she can cultivate it, bringing the two together softly in order to obtain progeny, as the hunter obtains his game, and this through copulation.[6]

He created two sexes, each equipped with a specific anatomic configuration which allows them to complement each other in the realization of God's design.

God the Almighty created the spouses, he created the man with his penis, his testicles and his seed in his kidneys [kidneys were believed to be the semen-producing gland]. He created for it veins and channels in the testicles. He gave the woman a uterus, the receptable and depository of the seed. He burdened men and women with the weight of sexual desire. All these facts and organs manifest in an eloquent language the will of their creator, and address to every individual endowed with intelligence an unequivocal message about the intention of His design. Moreover, Almighty God did clearly manifest His will through his messenger (benediction and salvation upon him) who made the divine intention known when he said "Marry and multiply". How then can man not understand that God showed explicitly His intention and revealed the secret of His creation? Therefore, the man who refuses to marry fails to plant the seed, destroys it and reduces to waste the instrument created by God for this purpose.[7]

Serving God's design on earth, sexual desire also serves his design in heaven.

Sexual desire as a manifestation of God's wisdom has, independently of its manifest function, another function: when the individual yields to it and satisfies it, he experiences a delight which would be without match if it were lasting. It is a foretaste of the delights secured for men in Paradise, because to make a promise to men of delights they have not tasted before would be ineffective.... This earthly delight, imper-

fect because limited in time, is a powerful motivation to incite men to try and attain the perfect delight, the eternal delight and therefore urges men to adore God so as to reach heaven. Therefore the desire to reach the heavenly delight is so powerful that it helps men to persevere in pious activities in order to be admitted to heaven.[8]

Because of the dual nature of sexual desire (earthly and heavenly) and because of its tactical importance in God's strategy, its regulation had to be divine as well. In accordance with God's interests, the regulation of the sexual instinct was one of the key devices in Muhammad's implementation on earth of a new social order in then-pagan Arabia.

Female Sexuality: Active or Passive?

According to George Murdock, societies fall into two groups with respect to the manner in which they regulate the sexual instinct. One group enforces respect of sexual rules by a "strong internalization of sexual prohibitions during the socialization process", the other enforces that respect by "external precautionary safeguards such as avoidance rules", because these societies fail to internalize sexual prohibitions in their members.[9] According to Murdock, Western society belongs to the first group while societies where veiling exists belong to the second.

Our own society clearly belongs to the former category, so thoroughly do we instil our sex mores in the consciences of individuals that we feel quite safe in trusting our internalized sanctions.... We accord women a maximum of personal freedom, knowing that the internalized ethics of premarital chastity and postmarital fidelity will ordinarily suffice to prevent abuse of their liberty through fornication or adultery whenever a favourable opportunity presents itself. Societies of the other type... attempt to preserve premarital chastity by secluding their unmarried girls or providing them with duennas or other such external devices as veiling, seclusion in harems or constant surveillance.[10]

However, I think that the difference between these two kinds of societies resides not so much in their mechanisms of internalization as in their concept of female sexuality. In societies in which seclusion and surveillance of women prevail, the implicit concept of female sexuality is active; in societies in which there are no such methods of surveillance and coercion of women's behaviour, the concept of female sexuality is passive.

In his attempt to grasp the logic of the seclusion and veiling of women and the basis of sexual segregation, the Muslim feminist Qasim Amin came to the conclusion that women are better able to control their sexual impulses than men and that consequently sexual segregation is a device to protect men, not women.[11]

He started by asking who fears what in such societies. Observing that women do not appreciate seclusion very much and conform to it only because they are compelled to, he concluded that what is feared is *fitna*: disorder or chaos. (*Fitna* also means a beautiful woman – the connotation of a *femme fatale* who makes men lose their self-control. In the way Qasim Amin used it *fitna* could be translated as chaos provoked by sexual disorder and initiated by women.) He then asked who is protected by seclusion.

If what men fear is that women might succumb to their masculine attraction, why did they not institute veils for themselves? Did men think that their ability to fight temptation was weaker than women's? Are men considered less able than women to control themselves and resist their sexual impulse? ... Preventing women from showing themselves unveiled expresses men's fear of losing control over their minds, falling prey to *fitna* whenever they are confronted with a non-veiled woman. The implications of such an insti-

tution lead us to think that women are believed to be better equipped in this respect than men.[12]

Amin stopped his inquiry here and, probably thinking that his findings were absurd, concluded jokingly that if men are the weaker sex, they are the ones who need protection and therefore the ones who should veil themselves.

Why does Islam fear *fitna*? Why does Islam fear the power of female sexual attraction over men? Does Islam assume that the male cannot cope sexually with an uncontrolled female? Does Islam assume that women's sexual capacity is greater than men's?

Muslim society is characterized by a contradiction between what can be called "an explicit theory" and "an implicit theory" of female sexuality, and therefore a double theory of sexual dynamics. The explicit theory is the prevailing contemporary belief that men are aggressive in their interaction with women, and women are passive. The implicit theory, driven far further into the Muslim unconscious, is epitomized in Imam Ghazali's classical work.[13] He sees civilization as struggling to contain women's destructive, all-absorbing power. Women must be controlled to prevent men from being distracted from their social and religious duties. Society can survive only by creating institutions that foster male dominance through sexual segregation and polygamy for believers.

The explicit theory, with its antagonistic, machismo vision of relations between the sexes is epitomized by Abbas Mahmud al-Aqqad.[14] In *Women in the Koran* Aqqad attempted to describe male–female dynamics as they appear through the Holy Book. Aqqad opened his book with the quotation from the Koran establishing the fact of male supremacy ("the men are superior to them by a degree") and hastily concludes that "the message of the Koran, which makes men superior to women is the manifest message of human history, the history of

Adam's descendants before and after civilization."[15]

What Aqqad finds in the Koran and in human civilization is a complementarity between the sexes based on their antagonistic natures. The characteristic of the male is the will to power, the will to conquer. The characteristic of the female is a negative will to power. All her energies are vested in seeking to be conquered, in wanting to be overpowered and subjugated. Therefore, "She can only expose herself and wait while the man wants and seeks."[16]

Although Aqqad has neither the depth nor the brilliant systematic deductive approach of Freud, his ideas on the male–female dynamic are very similar to Freud's emphasis on the "law of the jungle" aspect of sexuality. The complementarity of the sexes, according to Aqqad, resides in their antagonistic wills and desires and aspirations.

> Males in all kinds of animals are given the power – embodied in their biological structure – to compel females to yield to the demands of the instinct (that is, sex).... There is no situation where that power to compel is given to women over men.[17]

Like Freud, Aqqad endows women with a hearty appetite for suffering. Women enjoy surrender.[18] More than that, for Aqqad women experience pleasure and happiness only in their subjugation, their defeat by males. The ability to experience pleasure in suffering and subjugation is the kernel of femininity, which is masochistic by its very nature. "The woman's submission to the man's conquest is one of the strongest sources of women's pleasure."[19] The machismo theory casts the man as the hunter and the woman as his prey. This vision is widely shared and deeply ingrained in both men's and women's vision of themselves.

The implicit theory of female sexuality, as seen in Imam Ghazali's interpretation of the Koran, casts the woman as the hunter and the man as the passive victim. The two theories have one component in common, the woman's *qaid* power ("the power to deceive and defeat men, not by force, but by cunning and intrigue"). But while Aqqad tries to link the female's *qaid* power to her weak constitution, the symbol of her divinely decreed inferiority, Imam Ghazali sees her power as the most destructive element in the Muslim social order, in which the feminine is regarded as synonymous with the satanic.

The whole Muslim organization of social interaction and spacial configuration can be understood in terms of women's *qaid* power. The social order then appears as an attempt to subjugate her power and neutralize its disruptive effects. The opposition between the implicit and the explicit theories in Muslim society would appear clearly if I could contrast Aqqad and Imam Ghazali. But whereas the implicit theory is brilliantly articulated in Imam Ghazali's systematic work on the institution of marriage in Islam, the explicit theory has an unfortunate advocate in Aqqad, whose work is an amateurish mixture of history, religion and his own brand of biology and anthropology. I shall therefore contrast Imam Ghazali's conception of sexual dynamics not with Aqqad's but with that of another theoretician, one who is not a Muslim but who has the advantage of possessing a machismo theory that is systematic in the elaboration of its premises – Sigmund Freud.

Imam Ghazali vs. Freud: Active vs. Passive

In contrasting Freud and Imam Ghazali we are faced with a methodological obstacle, or rather what seems to be one. When Imam Ghazali was writing the chapter on marriage in his book *The Revivification of Religious Sciences*, in the eleventh century, he was endeavouring to reveal the true Muslim belief on the subject. But Freud was endeavouring to build a scientific theory, with all that the word "scientific" implies of objectivity and universality. Freud did not think that he was elaborating a European theory of female sexuality; he thought he was elaborating a universal explanation of the human female. But this methodological obstacle is easily overcome if we are "conscious of the historicity of culture".[20] We can view Freud's theory as a "historically defined" product of his culture. Linton noted that anthropological data has shown that it is culture that determines the perception of biological differences and not the other way around.

> All societies prescribe different attitudes and activities to men and to women. Most of them try to rationalize these prescriptions in terms of the physiological differences between the sexes or their different roles in reproduction. However, a comparative study of the statuses ascribed to women and men in different cultures seems to show that while such factors may have served as a starting point for the development of a division, the actual prescriptions are almost entirely determined by culture. Even the psychological characteristics ascribed to men and to women in different societies vary so much that they can have little physiological basis.[21]

A social scientist works in a biographically determined situation in which he finds himself "in a physical and socio-cultural environment as defined by him, within which he has his position, not merely his position in terms of physical space and outer time or of his status and role within the social system but also his moral and ideological position."[22] We can therefore consider Freud's theory of sexuality in general, and of female sexuality in particular, as a reflection of his society's beliefs and not as a scientific (objective and ahistorical) theory. In comparing Freud and Imam Ghazali's theories we will be comparing the two different cultures' different conceptions of sexuality, one based on a model in which the female is passive, the other on one in which the female is active. The purpose of the comparison is to highlight the particular character of the Muslim theory of male-female dynamics, and not to compare the condition of women in the Judeo-Christian West and the Muslim East.

The novelty of Freud's contribution to Western contemporary culture was his acknowledgement of sex (sublimated, of course) as the source of civilization itself. The rehabilitation of sex as the foundation of civilized creativity led him to the reexamination of sex differences. This reassessment of the differences and of the consequent contributions of the sexes to the social order yielded the concept of female sexuality in Freudian theory.

In analysing the differences between the sexes, Freud was struck by a peculiar phenomenon – bisexuality – which is rather confusing to anyone trying to assess sex differences rather than similarities:

> Science next tells you something that runs counter to your expectations and is probably calculated to confuse your feelings. It draws your attention to the fact that portions of the male sexual apparatus also appear in women's bodies, though in an atrophied state, and vice-versa in the alternative case. It regards their occurrence as indications of bisexuality as though an individual is not a man or a woman but always both – merely a certain amount more one than the other.[23]

The deduction one expects from bisexuality is that anatomy cannot be accepted as the basis for sex differences. Freud made this deduction:

> You will then be asked to make yourself familiar with the idea that the proportion in which masculine and feminine are mixed in an individual is subject to quite considerable fluctuations. Since, however, apart from the very rarest cases, only one kind of sexual product, ova or semen, is nevertheless present in one person, you are bound then to have doubts as to the

decisive significance of those elements and must conclude that what constitutes masculinity or femininity is an unknown characteristic which anatomy cannot lay hold of.[24]

Where then did Freud get the basis for his polarization of human sexuality into a masculine and a feminine sexuality, if he affirms that anatomy cannot be the basis of such a difference? He explains this in a footnote, apparently considering it a secondary point:

> It is necessary to make clear that the conceptions "masculine" and "feminine", whose content seems so unequivocal to the ordinary meaning, belong to the most confused terms in science and can be cut up into at least three paths. One uses masculinity and femininity at times in the sense of activity and passivity, again in the biological sense and then also in the sociological sense. The first of these three meanings is the essential one and the only one utilizable in psychoanalysis.[25]

The polarization of human sexuality into two kinds, feminine and masculine, and their equation with passivity and activity in Freudian theory helps us to understand Imam Ghazali's theory, which is characterized precisely by the absence of such a polarization. It conceives of both male and female sexuality partaking of and belonging to the same kind of sexuality.

For Freud, the sex cells' functioning is symbolic of the male–female relation during intercourse. He views it as an antagonistic encounter between aggression and submission.

> The male sex cell is actively mobile and searches out the female and the latter, the ovum, is immobile and waits passively....This behaviour of the elementary sexual organism is indeed a model for the conduct of sexual individuals during intercourse. The male pursues the female for the purpose of sex union, seizes hold of her and penetrates into her.[26]

For Imam Ghazali, both the male and female have an identical cell. The word sperm (*ma'*, "water drop") is used for the female as well as for the male cell. Imam Ghazali referred to the anatomic differences between the sexes when clarifying Islam's position on coitus interruptus (*'azl*), a traditional method of birth control practised in pre-Islamic times. In trying to establish the Prophet's position on *'azl*, Imam Ghazali presented the Muslim theory of procreation and the sexes' contribution to it and respective roles in it.

> The child is not created from the man's sperm alone, but from the union of a sperm from the male with a sperm from the female...and in any case the sperm of the female is a determinant factor in the process of coagulation.[27]

The puzzling question is not why Imam Ghazali failed to see the difference between the male and female cells, but why Freud, who was more than knowledgeable about biological facts, saw the ovum as a passive cell whose contribution to procreation was minor compared to the sperm's. In spite of their technical advancement, European theories clung for centuries to the idea that the sperm was the only determining factor in the procreation process; babies were prefabricated in the sperm[28] and the uterus was just a cozy place where they developed.

Imam Ghazali's emphasis on the identity between male and female sexuality appears clearly in his granting the female the most uncontested expression of phallic sexuality, ejaculation. This reduces the differences between the sexes to a simple difference of pattern of ejaculation, the female's being much slower than the male's.

> The difference in the pattern of ejaculation between the sexes is a source of hostility whenever the man reaches his ejaculation before the woman.... The woman's ejaculation is a much slower process and during that process her sexual desire grows stronger and to withdraw from her before

she reaches her pleasure is harmful to her.[29]

Here we are very far from the bedroom scenes of Aqqad and Freud, which resemble battlefields more than shelters of pleasure. For Imam Ghazali there is neither aggressor nor victim, just two people cooperating to give each other pleasure.

The recognition of female sexuality as active is an explosive acknowledgement for the social order with far-reaching implications for its structure as a whole. But to deny that male and female sexuality are identical is also an explosive and decisive choice. For example, Freud recognizes that the clitoris is an evident phallic appendage and that the female is consequently more bisexual than the male.

> There can be no doubt that the bisexual disposition which we maintain to be char- acteristic of human beings manifests itself much more plainly in the female than in the male. The latter has only one principal sexual zone – only one sexual organ – whereas the former has two: the vagina, the true female organ, and the clitoris, which is analogous to the male organ.[30]

Instead of elaborating a theory which in- tegrates and elaborates the richness of both sexes' particularities, however, Freud elabor- ates a theory of female sexuality based on reduction: the castration of the phallic fea- tures of the female. A female child, bisexual in infancy, develops into a mature female only if she succeeds in renouncing the clit- oris, the phallic appendage: "The elimin- ation of the clitorial sexuality is a necessary precondition for the development of femi- ninity."[31] The pubertal development process brings atrophy to the female body while it enhances the phallic potential of the male's, thus creating a wide discrepancy in the sexual potential of humans, depending on their sex:

> Puberty, which brings to the boy a great advance of libido, distinguishes itself in the

girl by a new wave of repression which especially concerns the clitoral sexuality. It is a part of the male sexual life that sinks into repression. The reinforcement of the inhibitions produced in the woman by the repression of puberty causes a stimulus in the libido of the man and forces it to increase its capacity; with the height of the libido, there is a rise in the overesti- mation of the sexual, which can be present in its full force only when the woman re- fuses and denies her sexuality.[32]

The female child becomes a woman when her clitoris "acts like a chip of pinewood which is utilized to set fire to the harder wood."[33] Freud adds that this process takes some time, during which the "young wife remains anesthetic".[34] This anesthesia may become permanent if the clitoris refuses to relinquish its excitability. The Freudian woman, faced with her phallic partner, is therefore predisposed to frigidity.

> The sexual frigidity of women, the fre- quency of which appears to confirm this disregard (the disregard of nature for the female function) is a phenomenon that is still insufficiently understood. Sometimes it is psychogenic and in that case accessible to influence; but in other cases it suggests the hypothesis of its being constitutionally determined and even of being a contribu- tory anatomical factor.[35]

By contrast with the passive, frigid Freud- ian female, the sexual demands of Imam Ghazali's female appear truly overwhelming, and the necessity for the male to satisfy them becomes a compelling social duty: "The virtue of the woman is a man's duty. And the man should increase or decrease sexual intercourse with the woman ac- cording to her needs so as to secure her virtue."[36] The Ghazalian theory directly links the security of the social order to that of the woman's virtue, and thus to the satis- faction of her sexual needs. Social order is secured when the woman limits herself to her husband and does not create *fitna*, or chaos, by enticing other men to illicit intercourse. Imam Ghazali's awe of the overpowering sexual demands of the active female appears when he admits how difficult it is for a man to satisfy a woman.

> If the prerequisite amount of sexual intercourse needed by the woman in order to guarantee her virtue is not assessed with precision, it is because such an assessment is difficult to make and difficult to satisfy.[37]

He cautiously ventures that the man should have intercourse with the woman as often as he can, once every four nights if he has four wives. He suggests this as a limit, otherwise the woman's sexual needs might not be met.

> It is just for the husband to have sexual intercourse with his wife every four nights if he has four wives. It is possible for him to extend the limit to this extreme. Indeed, he should increase or decrease sexual intercourse according to her own needs.[38]

Freud's and Ghazali's stands on foreplay are directly influenced by their visions of female sexuality. For Freud, the emphasis should be on the coital act, which is primarily "the union of the genitals",[39] and he deemphasizes foreplay as lying between normal (genital) union and perversion, which consists "...in either an anatomical transgression of the bodily regions destined for sexual union or a lingering at the intermediary relations to the sexual object which should normally be rapidly passed on the way to definite sexual union".[40]

In contrast, Imam Ghazali recommends foreplay, primarily in the interest of the woman, as a duty for the believer. Since the woman's pleasure necessitates a lingering at the intermediary stages, the believer should strive to subordinate his own pleasure, which is served mainly by the genital union.

> The Prophet said, "No one among you should throw himself on his wife like beasts do. There should be, prior to coitus, a messenger between you and her." People

asked him, "What sort of messenger?" The Prophet answered, "Kisses and words."[41]

The Prophet indicated that one of the weaknesses in a man's character would be that

> he will approach his concubine-slave or his wife and that he will have intercourse with her without having prior to that been caressing, been tender with her in words and gestures and laid down beside her for a while, so that he does not harm her, by using her for his own satisfaction, without letting her get her satisfaction from him.[42]

The Fear of Female Sexuality

The perception of female aggression is directly influenced by the theory of women's sexuality. For Freud the female's aggression, in accordance with her sexual passivity, is turned inward. She is masochistic.

> The suppression of woman's aggressiveness which is prescribed for them constitutionally and imposed on them socially favours the development of powerful masochistic impulses, which succeed, as we know, in binding erotically the destructive trends which have been diverted inwards. Thus masochism, as people say, is truly feminine. But if, as happens so often, you meet with masochism in men, what is left for you but to say that these men exhibit very plainly feminine traits.[43]

The absence of active sexuality moulds the woman into a masochistic passive being. It is therefore no surprise that in the actively sexual Muslim female aggressiveness is seen as turned outward. The nature of her aggression is precisely sexual. The Muslim woman is endowed with a fatal attraction which erodes the male's will to resist her and reduces him to a passive acquiescent role. He has no choice; he can only give in to her attraction, whence her identification with *fitna*, chaos, and with the anti-divine and anti-social forces of the universe.

The Prophet saw a woman. He hurried to his house and had intercourse with his wife Zaynab, then left the house and said, "When the woman comes towards you, it is Satan who is approaching you. When one of you sees a woman and he feels attracted to her, he should hurry to his wife. With her, it would be the same as with the other one."[44]

Commenting on this quotation, Imam Muslim, an established voice of Muslim tradition, reports that the Prophet was referring to the

fascination, to the irresistible attraction to women God instilled in man's soul, and he was referring to the pleasure man experiences when he looks at the woman, and the pleasure he experiences with anything related to her. She resembles Satan in his irresistible power over the individual.[45]

This attraction is a natural link between the sexes. Whenever a man is faced with a woman, *fitna* might occur: "When a man and a woman are isolated in the presence of each other, Satan is bound to be their third companion."[46]

The most potentially dangerous woman is one who has experienced sexual intercourse. It is the married woman who will have more difficulties in bearing sexual frustration. The married woman whose husband is absent is a particular threat to men: "Do not go to the women whose husbands are absent. Because Satan will get in your bodies as blood rushes through your flesh."[47]

In Moroccan folk culture this threat is epitomized by the belief in Aisha Kandisha, a repugnant female demon. She is repugnant precisely because she is libidinous. She has pendulous breasts and lips and her favourite pastime is to assault men in the streets and in dark places, to induce them to have sexual intercourse with her, and ultimately to penetrate their bodies and stay with them for ever.[48] They are then said to be inhabited. The fear of Aisha Kandisha is more than ever present in Morocco's daily life. Fear of the castrating female is a legacy of tradition and is seen in many forms in popular beliefs and practices and in both religious and mundane literature, particularly novels.

Moroccan folk culture is permeated with a negative attitude towards femininity. Loving a woman is popularly described as a form of mental illness, a self-destructive state of mind. A Moroccan proverb says

Love is a complicated matter
If it does not drive you crazy, it kills you.[49]

The best example of this distrust of women is the sixteenth-century poet Sidi Abderahman al-Majdoub. His rhymes are so popular that they have become proverbs.

Women are fleeting wooden vessels
Whose passengers are doomed to destruction.

Or:

Don't trust them [women], so you would not be betrayed
Don't believe in their promises, so you would not be deceived
To be able to swim, fish need water
Women are the only creatures who can swim without it.[50]

And finally:

Women's intrigues are mighty
To protect myself I run endlessly
Women are belted with serpents
And bejewelled with scorpions.[51]

The Muslim order faces two threats: the infidel without and the woman within.

The Prophet said, "After my disappearance there will be no greater source of chaos and disorder for my nation than women."[52]

The irony is that Muslim and European theories come to the same conclusion:

women are destructive to the social order – for Imam Ghazali because they are active, for Freud because they are not.

Different social orders have integrated the tensions between religion and sexuality in different ways. In the Western Christian experience sexuality itself was attacked, degraded as animality and condemned as anti-civilization. The individual was split into two antithetical selves: the spirit and the flesh, the ego and the id. The triumph of civilization implied the triumph of soul over flesh, of ego over id, of the controlled over the uncontrolled, of spirit over sex.

Islam took a substantially different path. What is attacked and debased is not sexuality but women, as the embodiment of destruction, the symbol of disorder. The woman is *fitna*, the epitome of the uncontrollable, a living representative of the dangers of sexuality and its rampant disruptive potential. We have seen that Muslim theory considers raw instinct as energy which is likely to be used constructively for the benefit of Allah and His society if people live according to His laws. Sexuality *per se* is not a danger. On the contrary, it has three positive, vital functions. It allows the believers to perpetuate themselves on earth, an indispensable condition if the social order is to exist at all. It serves as a "foretaste of the delights secured for men in Paradise",[53] thus encouraging men to strive for paradise and to obey Allah's rule on earth. Finally, sexual satisfaction is necessary to intellectual effort.

The Muslim theory of sublimation is entirely different from the Western Christian tradition as represented by Freudian psychoanalytic theory. Freud viewed civilization as a war against sexuality.[54] Civilization is sexual energy "turned aside from its sexual goal and diverted towards other ends, no longer sexual and socially more valuable".[55] The Muslim theory views civilization as the outcome of satisfied sexual energy. Work is the result not of sexual frustration but of a contented and harmoniously lived sexuality.

The soul is usually reluctant to carry out its duty because duty [work] is against its nature. If one puts pressures on the soul in order to make it do what it loathes, the soul rebels. But if the soul is allowed to relax for some moments by the means of some pleasures, it fortifies itself and becomes after that alert and ready for work again. And in the woman's company, this relaxation drives out sadness and pacifies the heart. It is advisable for pious souls to divert themselves by means which are religiously lawful.[56]

According to Ghazali, the most precious gift God gave humans is reason. Its best use is the search for knowledge. To know the human environment, to know the earth and galaxies, is to know God. Knowledge (science) is the best form of prayer for a Muslim believer. But to be able to devote his energies to knowledge, man has to reduce the tensions within and without his body, avoid being distracted by external elements, and avoid indulging in earthly pleasures. Women are a dangerous distraction that must be used for the specific purpose of providing the Muslim nation with offspring and quenching the tensions of the sexual instinct. But in no way should women be an object of emotional investment or the focus of attention, which should be devoted to Allah alone in the form of knowledge-seeking, meditation, and prayer.

Ghazali's conception of the individual's task on earth is illuminating in that it reveals that the Muslim message, in spite of its beauty, considers humanity to be constituted by males only. Women are considered not only outside of humanity but a threat to it as well. Muslim wariness of heterosexual involvement is embodied in sexual segregation and its corollaries: arranged marriage, the important role of the mother in the son's life, and the fragility of the marital bond (as revealed by the institutions of repudiation and polygamy). The entire Muslim social structure can be seen as an attack on, and a defence against, the disruptive power of female sexuality.

NOTES

1   Ibn Khaldun, *The Muqaddimah, An Introduction to History*, translated by Franz Rosenthal, Princeton, NJ, 1969, pp. 160–1.
2   Ibid., p. 161.
3   Ibid.
4   Abu Hamid al-Ghazali, *Ihya Ulum al-Din*, Cairo, n.d.
5   Ibid., p. 28.
6   Ibid., p. 25.
7   Ibid.
8   Ibid., p. 27.
9   George Peter Murdock, *Social Structure*, New York, 1965, p. 273.
10 Ibid.
11 Qasim Amin, *The Liberation of Women*, Cairo, 1928, p. 64.
12 Ibid., p. 65.
13 Al-Ghazali, *The Revivification of Religious Sciences*, vol. II, chapter on marriage; and Mizan al-'Amal, *Criteria for Action*, Cairo, 1964.
14 Abbas Mahmud al-Aqqad, *Women in the Koran*, Cairo, n.d.
15 Ibid., p. 7; the verse he refers to is verse 228 of sura 2, which is striking by its inconsistency. The whole verse reads as follows:

> And they [women] have rights similar to those [of men] over them in kindness, and men are a degree above them.

I am tempted to interpret the first part of the sentence as a simple stylistic device to bring out the hierarchical content of the second part.
16 Ibid., p. 24.
17 Ibid., p. 25. The biological assumption behind Aqqad's sweeping generalizations is obviously fallacious.
18 Ibid., p. 18.
19 Ibid., p. 26.
20 A. Schultz, "The Problem of Social Reality", *Collected Papers*, vol. 1, the Hague, n.d., p. 101.
21 Ralph Linton, *The Study of Man*, London, 1936, p. 116.
22 Schultz, *Collected Papers*, p. 9.
23 Sigmund Freud, *New Introductory Lectures on Psychoanalysis*, College Edition, New York, 1965, p. 114.
24 Ibid.
25 Sigmund Freud, *Three Contributions to the Theory of Sex*, 2nd edn, New York, 1909, p. 77.
26 Freud, *New Introductory Lectures*, p. 114.
27 Al-Ghazali, *Revivification of Religious Sciences*, p. 51.
28 Una Stannard, "Adam's Rib or the Woman Within", *Transaction*, November–December 1970, vol. 8, special issue on American Women, pp. 24–36.
29 Al-Ghazali, *Revivification*, p. 50. Not only is the woman granted ejaculation, she is also granted the capacity to have nocturnal ejaculation and "sees what the man sees in sleep". (Ibn Saad, *Kitab al-Tabaqat al-Kubra*, Beirut, 1958, vol. 8, "On Women", p. 858.)
30 Sigmund Freud, *Sexuality and the Psychology of Love*, New York, 1963, pp. 196–7.
31 Ibid., p. 190.
32 Freud, *Three Contributions*, p. 78.
33 Ibid.
34 Ibid.
35 Freud, *New Introductory Lectures*, p. 132.
36 Al-Ghazali, *Revivification*, p. 50.
37 Ibid.
38 Ibid.
39 Freud, *Three Contributions*, p. 14.
40 Ibid., p. 15.
41 Al-Ghazali, *Revivification*, p. 50.
42 Ibid.
43 Freud, *New Introductory Lectures*, p. 116.
44 Abu Issa al-Tarmidi, *Sunan al-Tarmidi*, Medina, n.d., vol. II, p. 413, B: 9, H: 1167.
45 Abu al-Hasan Muslim, *al-Jami' al-Sahih*, Beirut, n.d., vol. III, Book of Marriage, p. 130.
46 Al-Tarmidi, *Sunan al-Tarmidi*, p. 419, B: 16, H: 1181. See also al-Bukhari, *Kitab al-Jami' al-Sahih*, Leyden, Holland, 1868, vol. III, K: 67, B: 11.
47 Al-Tarmidi, *Sunan al-Tarmidi*, p. 419, B: 17, H: 1172.
48 Edward Westermark, *The Belief in Spirits in Morocco*, Abo, Finland, 1920.
49 Edward Westermark, *Wit and Wisdom in Morocco: A Study of Native Proverbs*, London, 1926, p. 330.
50 Sidi Abderahman al-Majdoub, *Les Quatrains du Mejdoub le Sarcastique, Poète Maghrébin du XVIième Siècle*, collected and translated by J. Scelles-Millie and B. Khelifa, Paris, 1966, p. 161.

51 Ibid., p. 160.
52 Abu Abdallah Muhammad Ibn Ismail al-Bukhari, *Kitab al-Jami' al-Sahih*, Leyden, Holland, 1868, p. 419, K: 67, B: 18.
53 Al-Ghazali, *Revivification*, p. 28.

54 Sigmund Freud, *Civilization and Its Discontents*, New York 1962.
55 Sigmund Freud, *A General Introduction to Psychoanalysis*, New York 1952, p. 27.
56 Al-Ghazali, *Revivification*, p. 32.

Part VI

Leisure and Recreation

How a society organizes leisure and recreation can tell us a great deal about sexual norms and their consequences. What we do for "fun" often bolsters, but occasionally transgresses, the rules governing the more serious parts of our lives. For example, although heterosexuality is the hegemonic norm in Western society, the mass media contain a variety of messages about sexuality that often resist that dominant ideal. Television talk shows are a prime example of this, as sexual nonconformists are often the featured guests. Yet despite the pervasive and growing number of alternative lifestyles represented in the mass media, Joshua Gamson and Meenakshi Durham show that consumers are still encouraged to embrace rather narrow versions of acceptable sexuality. Sports is another social institution that shapes sexual practices and desires. Like the other social institutions we have examined, it contains implicit and explicit messages about appropriate and inappropriate sexual expression. Although sports are not really "about" sex, like the other institutions we have looked at, they participate in socializing men and women into gender roles, and endorse hegemonic heterosexuality. Finally, the serious business of sex tourism is explored. Julia Davidson and Jacqueline Taylor remind us that one society's "fun" can result in another's economic and social exploitation.

21 Publicity Traps: Television Talk Shows and Lesbian, Gay, Bisexual, and Transgender Visibility

Joshua Gamson

Tolerance is the result not of enlightenment, but of boredom.
Quentin Crisp (1997: 204)

On American television over the last year, one could watch a handsome doctor apologize to his boyfriend for hitting him (*Melrose Place*), a black gay city government professional placing bets with his female coworker on the sexual preferences of a cute male focus group participant (*Spin City*), and two chiseled soap-opera hunks discussing their upcoming cohabitation as a straight relative awkwardly offers his blessing (*All My Children*). Nothing out of the ordinary or stereotypical in the villains-or-victims sense; just good-looking, professional gay men who could be your next door neighbors. There are still some problems (none of the making out that the straight *Melrose* characters get to do all the time, always the bridesmaid and never the bride), but the 1990s have witnessed a storm of "happen to be gay" television, culminating in the much-hyped coming-out of *Ellen's* central character and star.

By the conventions of much gay and lesbian media studies and advocacy, this is a dream come true. After all, since taking off with Vito Russo's ground-breaking *The Celluloid Closet* (1987), studies of the portrayals of gay men and lesbians in film and television have soundly demonstrated how homosexual lives have been subject to systematic exclusion and stereotyping as victims and villains; how "aspects of gay and lesbian identity, sexuality, and commu-

nity that are not compatible or that too directly challenge the heterosexual regime are excluded" from mainstream television (Fejes and Petrich 1993: 412; see also Gross 1989); how television has produced "stereotypical conceptualizations of AIDS that vilify gays and legitimate homophobia" (Netzhammer and Shamp 1994: 104); how even "positive" portrayals of lesbians "serve as mechanisms to perpetuate hetero/sexism" (Hantzis and Lehr 1994: 118; see also Moritz 1994). Now, having made the move from occasional soupy movie-of-the-week issue to soap and sitcom regulars, lesbians and gay men look more or less like everybody else on sitcoms and soaps: clean, with really good apartments. Their homosexuality is more or less incidental, not much more than a spicy character flip. This would seem to be progress.

The desire to be publicly recognized is especially powerful for marginalized groups, whose cultural visibility is often so minimal, or distant enough from the way people live their lives to render them unrecognizable even to themselves. The positive effects of visibility are quite plain: "Cultural visibility can prepare the ground for gay civil rights protection", as Rosemary Hennessy sums it up, and "affirmative images of lesbians and gays in the mainstream media...can be empowering for those of us who have lived most of our lives with no validation at all from the dominant culture" (Hennessy 1994–5: 31–2). The desire to be recognized, affirmed, validated, and to lay the cultural groundwork for political change, in fact, are so strong they have tended to inhibit careful analysis of the dynamics of becoming visible. At a time when a major sitcom character and the lesbian playing her have come out amidst a coterie of gay and lesbian supporting characters, when a drag queen has her own talk show on VH-1, when big movie stars no longer see gay roles as career poison, and when one soap opera has had a transsexual storyline and another a gay talk-show-murder storyline, it is no longer enough to think in terms of invisibility and stereotyping. Cultural visibility, especially when it is taking place through commerce, is not a direct route to liberation; in fact, it can easily lead elsewhere.

Talk shows, which have been making nonconforming sex and gender lives public for a good two decades, are a great place to turn for complication. The dramatic new visibility in commercial television fiction, and the slower changes in commercial popular nonfiction media (Alwood 1996) is only the spread of the logic and imagery of TV talk shows, which long ago incorporated lesbians, gay men, transgenders, and bisexuals into their daily dramas. What makes them interesting spots, moreover, is not only the high visibility of gay, lesbian, bisexual, and transgender people, but the (at least partial) *agency* of those people within the genre. Until very recently, lesbians and gay men had little input into our own representation. Almost without exception, the literature on homosexuality and the media has therefore treated the process of representation as a one-sided one. Larry Gross captures this approach very well:

> Representation in the mediated "reality" of our mass culture is in itself power; certainly it is the case that nonrepresentation maintains the powerless status of groups that do not possess significant material or political power bases. Those who are the bottom of the various hierarchies will be kept in their place in part through their relative invisibility; this is a form of symbolic annihilation. When groups or perspectives do attain visibility, the manner of that representation will itself reflect the biases and interests of those elites who define the public agenda. And those elites are mostly white, mostly middle-aged, mostly male, mostly middle- and upper-middle class, and (at least in public) entirely heterosexual. *(Gross 1994: 143)*

On talk shows, however, bisexuals, lesbians, transgendered people, and gay men are actively invited to participate, to "play themselves" rather than be portrayed by others, to refute stereotypes rather than simply watch them on the screen. Talk shows mess up our thinking about the difficulties and delights of becoming visible – and, in a more general sense, about the political benefits and dilemmas of cultural representation. And as the dust settles, they can clear our thinking up.

Beginning with a brief introduction to the recent class-cultural history of US daytime television talk, I want to point towards three related political difficulties that talk show visibility brings to the fore and exacerbates. First, drawing from interviews with talk show producers and guests, I suggest that the shows build on and make heavier a class division in gay, lesbian, bisexual, and transgender political organizing – a division tied to the political tension between the pursuit of either a queer difference or an acceptable sameness. Talk show producers, in part as a response to the organized control activities of activists, have turned to those with little connection to middle-class gay, transgender, bisexual, or lesbian organizing, with little interest or experience in the politics of representation, giving themselves freer reign as producers and infuriating many middle-class activists. The longstanding invisibility (both outside and within gay and lesbian communities) of gay, lesbian, bisexual, and transgender people of color, and of those from lower economic statuses, is cracked open by the talk shows; yet at the same time the shows, with their selection of nasty, rowdy, exhibitionist, not-great-to-look-at poor and working-class guests, encourage those interested in social acceptability to disown the visibility of some of their own. A predicament already present in the politics of sexual social change is brought to a head: as we make ourselves visible, do those among us with less status get to speak just as anyone else (increasing the risk of further stigma as the price for democratic diversity) or do the more acceptable get the upper hand (reproducing class and racial hierarchies as the price for gaining legitimacy)? Any path to visibility must face this question.

Second, drawing from content analysis of talk show transcripts and videos, I argue that the production of rowdy outrageousness draws out and intensifies animosities between the populations (gay men, lesbians, bisexuals, transgendered people) making up the larger movement. Tolerance of visible gayness, put simply, is bought largely through the further stigmatization of bisexuality and gender nonconformity. Talk shows are surely too money-oriented, capricious, and thin to do much deliberate ideological service, but both their loose liberal-therapeutic dogmas and their everyday pursuits – even, and perhaps especially, when they are fixated solely on the "personal" – lead them nonetheless to sharpen political lines of division.

Finally, drawing from focus group interviews with heterosexual talk show viewers, I argue that gay, lesbian, bisexual, and transgender visibility triggers deeper battles over the meaning and ownership of public space. Heterosexual liberal viewers tend to see talk shows as damaging, exploitative contributors to the ongoing victimization of sex and gender deviants. Sympathy for the "exploited," however, is often tempered by a sometimes subtle, sometimes brash animosity towards "trash" – those people who will display themselves outrageously, the bad, low-class queers. Thus, right up next to "leave them alone" is "leave me alone": get out of my face, stop flaunting it. Conservative talk show viewers tend to take this pos-

ition to the extreme, understanding talk shows as part of a pro-gay publicity apparatus, one of many ways in which queer life is "shoved down their throats."

Talk shows on sex and gender nonconformity are experienced, then, largely as funny pieces in the midst of serious culture wars; primarily through the class divisions to which they are beholden, they encourage viewers to separate "bad" gays from "good" ones, and to link the appearances of sexual nonconformists to inappropriate uses of public space. The various political battles that talk shows elicit, profit from, and amplify, all take a part in a more general war: over the lines between public and private and over who benefits from changing or conserving current public–private divisions. Talk shows open up these cultural battles not so much through the particular discussions they facilitate, not through anything specific that gets said, but through their simple encouragement of publicly visible sex and gender nonconformity. Symbolic political battles over sex and gender norms energize a bigger whirlwind, and are then sucked right into it. Through talk shows, class and sex and publicity and gender provocatively mix, offering more general lessons about the dilemmas of publicity.

Class, Queerness, and Public Visibility

Talk shows, in a general sense, stretch back to earlier public traditions emerging from different, and sometimes opposed, class cultures, and they still operate with the awkward tension between sensation and conversation growing from these roots. Propriety, of course, is not a middle-class property and working-class and underclass people certainly do not own irreverence and emotion, but the talk show genre is fashioned from particular cultural pieces historically associated with different classes: relatively sober, deliberative, "polite" middle-class forms of participating in and presenting public culture embodied in literary circles and the lyceum, for instance, and irreverent, wild, predominantly lower-class public leisures such as the carnival, the cabaret, the tabloid, and the nineteenth-century theater (see Gamson 1998, ch. 2; Munson 1994; Shattuc 1997).

For their first twenty years, beginning with *Donahue* in the early 1970s, television talk shows were heavily weighted towards the middle-class, people-sitting-around-talking-about-issues model. But with the quick suc-cess of *Ricki Lake* in the mid-1990s – which targeted a younger, more mixed-race audi-ence through the programming of rowdy, conflict-filled, interpersonal subjects and a studio audience made up primarily of young audiences – the balance tipped. *Ricki* and her imitators demonstrated the success of a com-bination of class voyeurism and class em-powerment, inviting guests who were much less likely than *Donahue*'s or *Oprah*'s to be highly educated, organizationally affiliated, and middle class, and audiences who were also more likely to be young, urban, work-ing- or poverty-class people of color. Guests were less commonly recruited, moreover, through organizations, and more commonly through toll-free numbers flashed on the screen: the guests nominated themselves for TV appearances (see Gamson 1998; Grind-staff 1997; Tuchman 1974).

Having discovered the profitable appeal of younger, less educated, more boisterous guests, talk shows have come to feature calm, educated, older guests less and less; they simultaneously appropriate, exagger-ate, and give expression to the straightfor-ward, not-afraid-of-conflict emotionalism of some poverty-class and working-class cultures, providing imagery of gays, les-bians, transgenders, and bisexuals from all kinds of racial, cultural, and class back-grounds. At the same time, using the low-risk strategy of class voyeurism, many shows select guests from the bottom of the social barrel. Nearly anyone can feel superior watching people whose speech, dress, bodies, relationships, and accents mark them as "trash."

Especially as the "outrageous" shows took off, and the class (and age) profile of the genre started to shift, middle-class activist guests found themselves and their political agendas edged out. The gay, lesbian, bisex-ual, and transgendered people who have slowly replaced them – often flamboyant, unaffiliated, untrained in political agendas, and of lower educational, economic, and social status – threaten the mainstreaming agenda of many in the gay movement. They can be loud-mouthed, foul-mouthed, freak-ish, radical, obnoxious, stereotypical, ir-rational, emotional: that is, great talk show guests. They emphasize, deliberately and not, a queer *difference* from the mainstream, and not a terribly appealing one, since on these talk shows it is conflated with "lower class," which is equated with various sorts of ugliness, which do not make the best case for tolerance, acceptance, freedom, and rights.

This dynamic brings to a head class div-isions within gay, lesbian, bisexual, and transgender life. Legitimacy, in talk show land as elsewhere, is associated with sym-bols of social class (educated speech, calm manner, clean dress); uneducated speech, rambunctious manner, and showy dress sig-nify a dismissible lower status. If talk shows are now filled with "trashy" people (many of them people of color), and also with queers, sexual difference is easily conflated with class and racial inferiority; if "classy" white gay people have no monopoly on the conversation, sexual difference can no longer be legitimized by an association with higher educational, racial and class status. Those seeking mainstream legitimacy therefore avoid the stigma of rowdy, poor and working-class, mixed-color shows, aligning with the polite, middle-class, pre-dominantly white strand of talk shows. Tele-vision talk show visibility thus amplifies the class divisions of the populations on which the shows greedily feed.

Many middle-class activist guests, who had earlier had a virtual monopoly on the non-heterosexual talk show guest list, are trying to move towards the demonstration that gay people (or cross-dressers, or bisexuals, or transsexuals) are regular, civilized, unthreatening, reasonable, conforming folks – for good reason, since media images elsewhere have tipped so heavily in the other direction. Craig Dean, for instance, went on *Donahue* twice – the second time on a show that included a gay wedding:

> We were going up there to talk. And talk about issues, you know, and I knew the show was a freak show to begin with because of what they were doing. Not only was it a gay black couple, but it was a short black man – it was a freak show. And they wanted us to come on to lend legitimacy to what they were doing. They wanted to use us, you know, and I felt for the good of the gay rights movement, that we needed to be there to present something a little more palatable to the American public.... These guys came up, vrooom, they got married. There was no humanization – and people reacted like, "You faggots, look at this shit you're putting in our face." As opposed to "We love each other and we're going to express our commitment to each other." Yeah, there's a really big difference, so I'm pissed at what happened. *(Priest 1995: 117)*

Gay writer Eric Marcus intentionally dresses up as "sort of the boy next door, well-educated, well-groomed, polite, would never get angry at anyone, wouldn't hurt anyone, not a threat at all." By comparison to right-wing discredited psychologist Paul Cameron ("he's sitting there talking about fecal matter and all the semen that we ingest, and I'm sitting next to him in a blue shirt, nice crisp tie, my hair's combed properly, I'm very polite"), and even to activist-writer Michelangelo Signorile ("he came across as a nut case"), he looks "sane" and "normal." But increasingly, Marcus promotes his books and his "best possible case for gay people" in an environment in which the polite, well-educated, well-groomed image is an anomaly. While they still help

sell his books, the talk shows have started to run counter to Marcus's political agenda. Marcus offers the example of a gay kid at the *Sally* show wearing a midriff t-shirt, elbow length gloves, pearls, a top hat, and makeup.

> If I were in charge, I would say, "Stay home." I think of those television talk shows as propaganda that can be used in a very productive way. Someone like that doesn't help further my political agenda. He's on there, I'm on there, so people do get to see that gay people come from all walks of life, but in that moment of the show he created quite an uproar, and the argumentativeness of the show increased because of this kid with the elbow length gloves and makeup. So the argument is lost because of what he looks like.

And so two political impulses battle it out through these appearances. We must behave appropriately in public, says one, and work through our ugly stuff in private, in a doctor's office maybe, the way classy people do. Shrink, shmink, says the other, let's go on TV. We are sick of being told what to do and where we can do it, and we're going to take our scary, inappropriate selves as public as we can go.

Ironically, it is in part because of the successes and increased savvy of movement activists in the talk show arena that many middle-class organizers now find themselves on the defensive. For one thing, from the point of view of talk shows, they have pretty much had their time. For another, they have trained themselves in the basics of using-the-talk-show-for-our-own-purposes, and their haggling and negotiating and caution makes them sometimes more trouble than they're worth. It is much easier simply to turn to guests with little agenda other than a few minutes of TV fame and an out-of-town trip. "I wish there was a pool of nice gay folks they called on to do these sorts of things," says Marcus, "but these shows thrive on combativeness, on arguments.

They don't want reasonable guests, except as so-called experts."

The fact that not-nice, unreasonable people who get crazy are many shows' guests of choice has led some mainstream organizations to simply refuse to assist shows altogether. For the Renaissance Education Association, an organization which provides "education and support to the transgender community and the general public," talk shows had been an important tool for both visibility and outreach throughout the 1980s and early 1990s. By the time I spoke with members in 1996, they had decided to impose a moratorium on talk show appearances by their members, inspired partly by a moratorium call by the Executive Director of the Sexuality Information and Education Council of the US (SIECUS) (Hafner 1995: 6, 16). Transsexual radio host Cheryl-Ann Costa describes similar talk about talk shows in her own circles.

> Springer had a person who had a sex change, and they dragged his family on there. His two sons saying, "We ain't going to talk to him anymore." And his little 11-year-old daughter stands up in the audience, says, "I don't want to ever see him again." And Springer stands up with his last 5 minute little comment and says, "If you're thinking about having one of these things and you brought kids into the world, why don't you just keep your pants on until they're grown up and out of the house and then do what you're going to do." That was an outright attack on our community and we are desperately trying to dry up his supply of transgenders. They'll still find people. They're going to have to find an awful lot of rogue people, though, people that aren't connected, because anybody who's connected with anything, we're going to basically say, "This show is quarantined." We're going to shut him down as far as transsexuals are concerned.

Opting out, of course, is no guarantee of change. "You get people in our own community who are willing to say anything the producers want them to say in order to create that controversy," says a member of the Manhattan Gender Network, a transgender organization. "The problem is, those of us who don't want to have our brains picked on national television, we leave that to those people who will do whatever is necessary, who look to get on every talk show that they possibly can."

Talk shows, Marcus notes, "show us in all of our awful diversity": swearing Hispanic homosexuals, tongue-kissing mountain boys, borough broads, dysfunctional Ozark lesbians, guys in pearls and makeup, rogue transsexuals in giant pink hair, gay kids without media training. But many middle-class activists see little advantage to this diversity, which would only seem to increase the stigma they are trying to remove in the pursuit of civil rights. This is primarily a pragmatic position (we cannot afford these images right now), but one also often tinged with animosity (these people don't know how to behave in public), and the confidence that comes from having long felt entitled to call the shots (these people don't get it). Mainstreaming activists are rightly concerned that talk shows provide a distorted image of gay life – but then again, the image, although more socially acceptable, was no less distorted when it was only white, middle-class, gay movement movers and shakers. Lurking underneath the concern, encouraged by the class dynamics of TV talk, are hints of class, racial, and regional superiority. When gay was just *us*, things were going so well, people seem to want to say. Why did they have to go and give *those* people the microphone?

Talk shows certainly did not *create* the division between moderates with an eye towards assimilation, who want to demonstrate middle-class legitimacy and similarity to heterosexuals, and in-your-face radicals, who use the difference from heterosexuals to create space for themselves. This is a long-standing strategic dispute in sex and gender politics, as it is in most social movements. For a good long time, picking up extra steam in the last decade, civil-rights strategists favoring integration into the "normal" have met with resistance from others favoring a transgressive, confrontational "queer" politics which pushes at the boundaries of normality (D'Emilio 1983; Gamson 1995; Seidman 1996; Vaid 1995; Warner 1993). Of course, it takes a somewhat different form here, since most of the anti-assimilation imagery comes not from organized radical activists, but from unaffiliated individuals seizing the opportunity for televisual confirmation of their social significance. Talk shows, though, take the line between "fringe" and "center" – a divider that, in my own eyes and the eyes of many others, is neither necessary nor productive for political organizing by sex and gender dissidents – and dig away at it, deepening it into an almost-unbridgeable chasm. (This comes not just from the strategies of outrageousness-selling shows, but also from those like *Oprah*, which create a "respectable" environment in which people from the wrong side of the tracks are excluded.) The structure of the talk show world intensifies the tension over who rightfully represents "gayness," making it nearly impossible for legitimacy-seeking activists *not* to close ranks, disrespecting and disowning their own.

This is no deliberate divide-and-conquer on the part of talk show producers. The opening up of the center–fringe, or sameness–difference, fault line is a result of the way producers make their money, and of the ambivalence built into the talk show genre (high/low class, polite/rude, rational/emotional). An array of "fringe" characters make it to talk TV because of how they play on screen, and because they are easy to recruit and easier to manipulate; they say and do things in public that others are not always willing to say and do. In a genre shot through with class-cultural divisions, in a place where authentic class-cultural expression is indistinguishable from its exaggerated display, where "trash" is a synonym for "lower class," working-class guests

(and, through that weird American confusion of race and class, often guests of color as well) are placed directly against the comfortable calm of the middle-class mainstream; bisexual, gay, lesbian, and transgender guests who are not middle class are quite easily placed in the same trash basket. It is not too surprising that many middle-class activists and viewers, informed by a sense that political gains are at stake, are not too excited about joining them there.

Normality and Public Visibility

The talk show world rips open existing class divisions within transgender, bisexual, lesbian, and gay politics, but not only these: it also rips away at the tenuous alliance among these nonconforming populations, primarily by rewarding some populations with "acceptability" at the expense of others. Many mainstream gay activist guests and viewers express the worry not only that images of dysfunctional, angry and uneducated parts will be taken to represent the whole, but that disproportionate representation of "abnormal" parts will make it harder for all of us to become "normal." The freaks – especially the gender freaks – are giving us all a bad name.

Again, this is a pre-existing tension, and the attempt to ally all sorts of sex and gender dissidents under one flag – drag queens, passing transsexuals, guppies, lipstick lesbians, dykes, cross-dressers, queer kids, monogamous and non-monogamous bisexuals, and so on – is relatively new, complex and extremely hard-going (Vaid 1995). Bisexuals and transgendered people, most notably, have waged difficult battles for recognition and inclusion in organizations and celebrations, and centrist gay men and lesbians argue, with some realpolitikal evidence on their side, that some battles (the Employment Non-Discrimination Act, for instance) are not currently winnable with bisexuals and transgenders on the list of claimants. The talk show world reinforces these divisions not only by using transgendered people as display objects and bisexuals as symbols of promiscuity, but also by offering homosexuals a tempting option: distance yourself from bisexuals and transgendered people, keep your sex and gender practices conservative, and you will be rewarded with acceptance.

Take, for instance, the common "love triangle" structure into which many shows on bisexuality are structured. On a 1992 *Jane Whitney* show on bisexuality, while a white, bearded bisexual guest named Cole is attacking the myth of bisexuality as simultaneous relationships ("I don't have to be in a relationship with both a man and a woman"), a label appears under his image. "Cole," it reads, "Intimate with both men and women." The show, like many others on bisexuality, is structured as a series of triangles: Cole is involved with Hector (who doesn't appear) and with Laura (Latina, bisexual) who is involved with Marcia (African American, lesbian); Jill is involved with both Woody and Rebecca, who has a long-term lover. ("No," says Whitney introducing them, "they're not involved with Laura. They're another bisexual triangle.") Not surprisingly, despite a variety of attempts by panelists to disaggregate bisexuality and non-monogamy, and to distinguish committed, honest non-monogamy from sex-crazed disloyalty, commitment and sexual monogamy become the focus of audience questions and attacks. "How do you decide," asks a young white guy with long, rock-star hair, "flip a coin?" to laughter and applause. "They're changing their preferences every day like they're changing their shirts," says an older white man, and soon a young blond man asks, "Why do you have to have sex with all of them?" to which a tie-wearing, buzz-cut man adds, "As a gay man, I think you're doing a disservice, you should be pursuing the one person and not all this free love." "Don't you believe in commitment?" a series of people ask in a variety of ways. Given the show's Marcia and Laura and Cole and Hector set-up, the answers, all

of them well articulated, get lost in the applause for monogamy (Unitel Video 1992).

What is also lost, though, is any concern with the "abnormality" of same-sex relationships, in place of an attack on non-monogamous relationships (equated on the show with bisexual ones). Sexual loyalty, whoever its subjects, is what's really being protected here. In fact, audience members and the host express sympathies and concern for the gay boyfriends and lesbian girlfriends of bisexuals, whose partners "can't commit" (as when *Jane Whitney*'s Marcia, for example, the sole lesbian on the panel, is encouraged to stop putting up with being a "third wheel"). In these very common "triangle" shows, where bisexuality functions primarily as a stand-in for promiscuity and is therefore denigrated, monogamous sexuality gets the high ground, taking monogamous *homosexuality* along for the ride. In this cultural set-up, from the point of view of gay men or lesbians on the verge of mainstream acceptance and political gains, allying with bisexuals is indeed a risky proposition.

The appearance of cross-dressing on gay-themed shows, which can often lead to the denigration of homosexuality, is a flashy mirror of this process. The early 1990s series of shows on conventionally feminine lesbians, for instance, used the term "lipstick lesbians" as something of a mind-blower and stereotype-breaker, as Maury Povich's introduction, spiked with the straight-porn image of girly-girls going at it, captures: "They are beautiful, they're sexy, glamorous, and successful, so one would assume that they have more men than they can handle. But it's not the men they want. Instead, these stunning beauties prefer other women" (cut to video of women's bodies putting on lingerie and lipstick and nail polish). "What about the women who are butch and proud of it?" (cut to shots of Dykes on Bikes and other butch lesbians in a pride march).

There is much talk here about debunking stereotypes, many questions about how one can be simultaneously lesbian and conventionally feminine, a gratuitous male guest named Tommy who thinks he can "turn a lesbian straight," and much manly-man ribbing. (Maury to four young guys in the front row: "You're not interested anymore, right?" Guy: "No, we've been interested from the start." Maury: "Well, you know, hot blood has no conscience, guys.") But it is the presence of *Village Voice* writer Donna Minkowitz, a broad-faced, short-haired, witty and somewhat wired woman, that galvanizes the audience. Wearing a red blazer and men's pants and shoes, Minkowitz talks with an impish smile about being attracted to "women in military uniforms, women in LL Bean jackets, women who look like they mean business." Over the course of the show, Minkowitz is pelted with insults. Her violation, it seems, is not being lesbian, but being unconventionally female. Povich asks Tommy, the apparent expert on heterosexual male desire, whether he thinks the two femme women on the panel are attractive (yes), and then if he thinks Donna is attractive (no). Big applause. Several times, the camera pans Donna from toe to head, as if to punctuate the point. Minkowitz explains herself well ("I'm not trying to embody a man, excuse me, I'm trying to embody a butch lesbian, which is something I love, I'm not trying to be a man, I'm trying to be Donna Minkowitz, in all my glory"), but there is not much of a reception for her argument that "sex roles are crazy, they're just a fiction." Instead, she is told she's "a frustrated male, you look like you want to be a man and were born a woman, unfortunate, I guess," and "you like to wear men's clothes, you like to wear a jockstrap?" While her lesbianism is generally unproblematic, or at least goes uncondemned, her gender nonconformity is penalized with vigor (Paramount Pictures 1992). Indeed, a lesbian who is unmarked, unbutch, who obeys the norms of gender conformity, looks exciting, pretty, and normal by comparison. A public alliance between lesbians who "pass" ("stunning beauties") and those

who do not ("frustrated males") is rendered more difficult to make; same-sex desire itself comes to seem unremarkable, but only if the coalition of women who "look like women" (hetero and homo) is favored over that of women who love women.

Even a 1992 *Donahue* show, in many ways a typical bigot-bashing political debate about an anti-gay referendum in Concord, California, manages to set "good," gender-conforming gays against "bad" gays in drag. Pastor Lloyd Mashore and his colleague square off against a young activist named Ken Stanley and another pastor; the anti-gay activists argue about special rights, the homosexual agenda, family values, picnics and Little League ball games, while the pro-gay activists talk about equal rights, pride, and love; Phil asks, as always, "What do you want to do with these gay people?" The audience takes this side and that one. But what tips the discussion is the presence of Gil Block, in his persona as Sadie, one of the Sisters of Perpetual Indulgence.

Gil as Sadie is dressed in full red, white, and blue drag, with red gloves, a big white wig, one dramatic eye with white stars over blue shadow and the other with red stripes over white shadow. Political theater, he claims, but once a male caller attacks Sadie, the audience lets loose a barrage of hostility. "Oh, get off the stage," another caller says to audience applause, "you're up there on the platform dressed like an idiot, and you expect to be taken seriously." ("Something should be done with them," she continues, "All they seem to do is cause problems. If we all got together and talked about it, maybe we could figure out what could be done with them. I really think they should all go back in the closet and make life peaceful again.") The two gay activists fighting discrimination are fine, says an audience member shortly thereafter, but Gil, who "is making a mockery of what they're trying to do, is just stupid." Gil tries to talk about being a patriotic American, but it doesn't really work. "I don't understand," says a young white man with a Philadelphia accent, "how dressing up like an oversized Captain America is going to help the gay cause." Laughter, applause. ("I think they should keep it to themselves," adds a young Southern white woman with hoop earrings. "I don't make a big point that I'm heterosexual.") A male caller finishes him off: "I'm 26 years old, I'm a gay white male, and I'm embarrassed by the man on the end there," he says. "People think I come home from work and put on a dress and swing from the chandeliers because of people like him" (Multimedia Entertainment 1992). The young man captures the political division talk shows amplify and reinforce: between chandelier-swinging, cross-dressing flamboyants and suit-wearing, privacy-loving passers. The political affinities between them – their shared lack of civil rights protections, for example – are overshowed by the colorful, provocative lines of gender convention so favored by talk shows.

Thus we reach one of the talk show's true political scandals. The scandal isn't so much that talk shows ambush people, or cynically use people's intimate lives to make a buck, or any of that utterly unsurprising and ugly activity. Nor is it even the fact of their drawing of lines that irks; after all, line-drawing is one of the things that culture is always about. The scandal is the *kinds* of lines they emphasize, setting apart potentially powerful sets of political and cultural partners, helping to cut the threads tying working-class lesbian to transsexual to drag queen to gay professional to butch lesbian to bisexual to rural gay kid. That's not of course something they do alone, but they are central to the process, partly because they help it along in such unintentional ways, such entertaining ways, and partly because they mix it, to great effect, with pleas for tolerance, enlightenment, and love. Those alliances are critical because we are engaged in a strange, complicated conflict, which talk shows embody but by no means exhaust: a fight over public space.

Sexual Nonconformity and the Public–Private Divide

"You know what? Nobody has any business in the bedrooms of any nation or in the closets. If you want to be gay, just be gay, like just be gay and shut up about it." *Donahue* audience member (*Multimedia Entertainment 1995a*)

"I'm sick to death of the entertainment industry cramming homosexuality down our throats. It's disgusting and I'm fed up with it." *Donahue* caller (*Multimedia Entertainment, 1992*)

"No one's suggesting that you shouldn't be gay," host Jerry Springer tells an 18-year-old gay man in men's pants and sweater, painted nails and high heels, blatantly misrepresenting the sentiments of many in his audience. "If you're gay, you're gay, period. But why is it necessary to just let everybody know all the time?" Having recruited gay male guests on the basis of their effeminacy and cross-dressing – many of whom are treated to hoots and hollers from a ridiculing audience – Springer wonders aloud at the end of his show about "why gays so often seem to flaunt their sexuality, almost an exaggeration of their effeminateness". He understands it, he tells his viewers, since if you put yourself in the position of having your "sexuality constantly repressed or kept in the closet," you would see that "most of us would go crazy." Many gays, he says, are understandably angry, and unwilling to take it any more. "And they're coming out with a vengeance," he says, "suddenly a militancy polite society has never witnessed before" (Multimedia Entertainment 1995b).

In the midst of the obvious hypocrisy and the moldy, ignorant equation of male homosexuality and effeminacy, Springer accidentally makes an excellent point: "polite society" is annoyed. His show scripts a backlash against gay visibility (and transgender and bisexual visibility, to a lesser degree) that is quite commonplace, exposing and participating in a culture war that is partly his own creation. "The homosexuals wouldn't have any problem at all if they would just keep it to themselves, and stop trying to act like they're special cause they're gay," says a caller to the *Donahue* show with Reverend Mashore facing off against Sister Sadie, as the camera catches smiling, applauding faces. "Why is there such a need to come out of the closet?" an audience member asks on another *Donahue*, this one on gay cops (Multimedia Entertainment 1994). Indeed, the talk show structural emphasis on separating "appropriate" gay people (middle-class professionals, especially those who pass as heterosexual) from "inappropriate" (lower- and poverty-class people, especially those who do not pass) is powered by an overlapping tension that talk shows manifest: between their push, in alliance with gay people and others, to make "private" matters public, and the various people interested in keeping certain things, such as homosexuality, away from public view. For many in "polite society," it seems, public declarations of lesbian, gay, transgender, or bisexual identity are inherently inappropriate, impolite, and nobody's business.

"I really don't have anything against your sexuality," a man tells John and Jerry, who had just kissed each other hello on a "gay and gorgeous" *Jenny Jones* show, for instance. "But the intimacy, the things that men and women that I think should be doing, stroking your hair – I see you guys holding hands and kissing. I'm sorry, but it really, it disgusts me" (Jenny Jones Show 1995). Why do you have to flaunt it? audience members ask in various ways on TV talk shows. Why do you have to have parades, and why do you have to go on television announcing it to everybody? Talk shows, as prime purveyors of public visibility of sex and gender nonconformity, are terrific foci for the anxieties and hostilities that a queer presence evokes.

Daytime talk television, in fact, by publicizing the "private," widens yet another fault line in gay and lesbian politics. "Privacy" is already quite a vexed, complex political issue in sexual politics. On the one hand, lesbian and gay political and social life in the past quarter of a century has been built on making sexual identities public, arguing that ours is a political and social status; since everyone is implicated in oppressing us, in part by keeping us invisible and spreading lies about us, it is everybody's business that we are gay. What we do out of bed, not what we do in bed, is what is most relevant about us. Coming out in public, especially through major public institutions such as schools, the workplace, and communications media, is a way of asserting the public relevance of what others deem private – that is, demonstrating and demonstrating against a second-class, stigmatized social status. (The more recent bisexual and transgender movements have followed this same model.) Talk shows, as we have amply seen, are approached by activists in this light.

At the same time, guided by the logic of constitutional claims-making, gay and lesbian activists have long put forward an argument that retains traditional divisions between private and public, in order to pursue protection under the individual "right to privacy" (Mohr 1988). The only difference between homo and hetero, they have said, is what we do in bed, and what we do in bed is nobody's business, and especially not the business of the government. Thus comments such as this one, from a 30-year-old Latina secretary, in the midst of a discussion of talk shows with a bunch of women: "I feel like it's none of my business. Whatever you do in your bedroom is no concern of mine, just like what I do in my bedroom is none of your business." This is about sex, sex belongs in private, and personal privacy is protected from public intrusion. (The political right, tellingly, has used the basic elements of this argument to great effect, arguing that homosexuality is indeed private, sexual behavior, and that sexual behavior is not the basis for either minority status or rights.) While the legal argument for privacy is certainly not incompatible with public visibility, talk shows seem to run against the rhetorical gist of privacy claims. Many heterosexual talk show participants and viewers seize hold of this conflict: you keep saying how your sexuality is none of my business, yet here you are again on television chatting and yelling and kissing and getting married and making fools of yourselves. If you want privacy, then keep it private.

Talk shows invite this perspective on themselves, largely because they seem to be the sorts of places where, to many viewers, all kinds of people are doing and saying things that are nobody else's business. Television itself, as Joshua Meyrowitz (1985 chapter 6) has pointed out, messes with the public–private lines: it is a "public" space brought into the "privacy" of home. Daytime talk shows, given that they profit from the discussion of taboo subjects, are hotbeds of impropriety and the discussion of impropriety, more or less by definition; these public living rooms, moreover, sit noticeably in your own private one. The discussion and display of atypical sexualities and genders is often filtered through an ambivalence about just who is doing what now in public – and, more fundamentally, just to whom public space belongs. The first clue to this dynamic comes from the common "where do they find these people?" disdain expressed by all kinds of talk show viewers. Many of the viewers with whom I had discussions, even though they often watch the less genteel fare, take offense at the unseemliness of it all, disparaging guests who bring private talk out of the house, airing their dirty laundry in front of God and everybody when they should be down in their own basement washing it. "I can't believe they would air all this stuff on the air, I mean in front of a general public, so to speak," says Barbara, a 56-year-old non-working African-American woman in one of my heterosexual discussion groups. "It's so sleazy," Joni, a white woman a few years older,

agrees. "Who needs to put that garbage in your head?" Every discussion includes this kind of statement (more often from older participants than younger). "I think it's getting a little, um, past risqué to the point of really just obnoxious and distasteful," says Ed, a 54-year-old African-American human resources director in another group, for instance. "Distasteful. Distasteful," he repeats. "It's just very distasteful for people to get on national TV and just tell all of their business".

The divider between inappropriate and appropriate public talk is, moreover, as viewers' conversations capture, a marker of social status; the aversion of middle-class viewers for "sensationalistic," "exploitative" programming expresses an aversion for the déclassé. "It's like middle class and lower class," Judi, a 32-year-old homemaker, explains simply, as discussion turns to the comparison of *Oprah*'s audience with *Richard Bey*'s. Joni responds by explaining why she prefers *Oprah*:

> On one show she did, she said, "Aren't these a very clean audience?" Because they all looked dressed, they all looked like nice, middle-class people. They didn't look trashy. Everybody looked so nice and clean. And it's true, she gets a better class of people. And if I have to watch something, I'd rather watch that. *Oprah* has an average American that knows that they don't spit in public, and they don't do certain things in public, and that's how they conduct themselves. Whether it's false or not, it's civilized. That's what we do in America.

It is not just spitting in public that we don't do. We don't *display our sexual selves in public*. Judith, a 55-year-old white teacher in another group, makes the connection between class, privacy, and sexuality quite explicit.

> I wouldn't watch all this garbage. Who's sleeping with who, what's going on with this couple because they were two women

living together, or whatever. I can't better myself, I can't get more class to me, and I think class is very important. I think a lot of people have lost it. And this is all just – people are entitled to their private lives. It should be private. And anything that's put on display is just garbage. There's nothing wrong with having sexual topics on television. To put it on display is what's wrong. When it's private, you work with it, but when you put it on television live, it becomes dirt. If you're going to open it up, have a psychologist there, make it a very proper thing.

The public display of "private life," especially sexuality, is not something classy people do. It is improper. Watching it, one becomes dirtier, less classy. In the eyes of many middle-class talk show watchers, sexual impropriety is really just the most important and obvious version of unsavory uses of public space. It is not so much the *gayness* that is bothersome, it's the *publicness*.

So, for many viewers, an ambivalence about homosexuality maps quite effortlessly onto an ambivalence about the making-public of sexual status, which itself maps onto a more generalized resistance to changes in what they see as their own public territory: a queer presence easily becomes another example of people behaving improperly. Even though very few talk show discussions of homosexuality are discussions of sexual practice, they are easily and commonly swept into the category of "inappropriate." As viewers invariably point out, for one thing, talk shows in recent years have tipped the balance towards sensationalized, exploitative treatments of sex and gender differences, going for the "sleazy," the "circus," the "extreme," and so on – so that homosexuality, bisexuality, and gender-crossing appear largely in the pile marked "distasteful." Moreover, homosexuality and bisexuality are more often than not, even when they are not framed as purely sexual on a show, placed by viewers in the category of "sexual." While viewers often emphasize

"tasteful" presentations of sex and gender nonconformists (a focus on individual experience, a respectful conversation), it is nonetheless a short step from the general grouchiness about what are seen as gauche, low-class uses of the public space of television to a specific animosity towards the public visibility of gay people. Talk shows make it especially easy for same-sex desire to slide quickly into the category of things that are not the business of polite, civilized, clean, nice people to hear about. They offer occasions for middle-class social anxieties about changes in public space to come into sharper focus, by attaching to the unruly class cultures and unusual sexual beings who seem to populate the public space of talk shows.

For liberal viewers, this tends to be expressed as a concern for the damage done to decent gay folks by "fringe" gay guests, for instance, who might be taken to represent the whole. The problem with those talk show guests, they say, is that they do not know how to keep it quiet. But listen a bit more closely, and you begin to hear how the charge that people "flaunting it" on talk shows blends smoothly into a general resistance to gayness in public space. Judi, a 32-year-old white homemaker, has this to say, for instance:

> My girlfriend's sister is gay, and they're living their lives the way they want to. On TV, they're doing it for the gimmick, they want the attention, whereas my friends aren't like that at all. They don't flaunt it around. If they love each other, that's their problem. They don't sit there and advertise it all the time.

Rosanne, a 47-year-old white bookkeeper in another group, has a different starting point, but comes back to a similar punchline:

> I don't particularly even like to walk down the street and see a guy and a girl making out, so seeing two guys kiss or two girls kiss, it annoys me just as much to see a guy

and a girl carrying on in the middle of the street. I think if everybody believes in what they want to believe in, and don't try to make a big issue out of it, like, "Oh, you have to let me do this because I'm a lesbian," or "You have to let me do this because I'm a gay," everybody just staying on their own road, whether it's a road of what some people call normal and some people call abnormal.

When she continues later, it becomes clear where talk show impropriety fits into Roseanne's picture: keep anything but talking behind closed doors:

> Let's educate some people, let people become aware of what's going on, and try to do it in a subtle way that doesn't make everything seem like smut. And if they're doing it behind their private doors, that's their business. If they come out sitting next to each other and talking and everything else, that's fine. If they start lovey-dovey, to me, I don't think it's appropriate for anyone to act that way. Whatever you do in your own home, and everything else, that's fine.

For Bobby, a 24-year-old African-American interior decorator, it is not just "lovey-dovey" behavior that is the problem, but any public announcement of homosexuality:

> My understanding on a lot of gay shows is, like gay people have to force their sexuality on you. They want to let you know that they're gay so bad. They have to let you know. I don't have to let a person know that I'm a heterosexual male. I mean, I don't force it on people. We already have rights for men and rights for women. I don't see why it has to be gay rights and all that type of stuff. Why do they have to let people know that they're gay and this is what we do? I don't see why. I get annoyed with it, by them always forcing on you, and they have to be so flamboyant and so gay and so out there. Just keep it to yourself.

Ask liberal talk show watchers what they think about shows on gay people, and this is often what comes out of them, right alongside "live and let live": don't flaunt it, keep it to yourself, stay off my road.

Viewers with conservative views on homosexuality, who often tend to be more tuned in to the political aspects of homosexuality, demonstrate this connection most clearly: they tend to see talk shows as part of a damaging intrusion by the wrong people into public space. Vincent, a 63-year-old telephone company manager and the most vehement conservative on gay issues in a group of male conservatives, is very upfront about this. Over the course of the discussion, he argues against same-sex marriage ("if they do it for the homosexuals to get married, they're going to have to do the same damn thing for the Man–Boy Love Association"), the Supreme Court ("talking about how you can't restrict even porno on the internet"), gay protests at the St Patrick's Day Parade ("the homosexuals were promoting their lifestyle"), and a *New Yorker* cover of two male sailors kissing. "Why can't it be 'don't ask, don't tell?'" he asks. "They don't want to be satisfied with that today. It's not hatred against them, believe me when I say I have a feeling for them and what they're going through, but damn it, don't tell, keep it in the closet." Talk shows, for him and the other men in that discussion group ("it's sort of like social engineering," says Dave, a 45-year-old engineer), fit into a more general assault by gay people into what they see as their own public space. "Homosexuals are here to stay," Vincent says. "The talk shows only bring them to the forefront. They are here to stay, just like the pornographic shows, where you can go buy tapes and so forth and so on." In another hint of the way middle-class politeness plays into a condemnation of gay publicness, he offers the example of a homosexual glee club, whose members were "professional people, they're not running around the streets or anything like that."

The talk shows gave me the wrong picture of these people. I think if they want to promote themselves, they should have something like this choir I saw. They weren't hurting anybody, and they were pretty damn good singers. Have your own lifestyle. Have your own lifestyle. Have your own clubs, your own choirs. Don't stick your nose into St Patrick's Day Parade. Don't stick your nose here and there. In many instances it's in your face, and I don't think it should be that way. These people should have their own lifestyle. Don't ask, don't tell.

Unless you are singing, that is, please keep quiet, or at least keep it away from us. Stick to your own road.

A group of conservative women, talking about how topics become passé after a while, winds up quite close to Vincent's perspective. "It's like, if that's what they want to do, if that's how you want to live, live that way," says Lynn, a 34-year-old white saleswoman. "But it would have been better if they'd stayed in the closet and no one knew. Now it's like, we have to have these rights, gays have to have these rights." *They're pushing*, says Peggy, a 59-year-old non-working woman. "They're pushing too far," Lynn agrees, invoking the privacy argument. "It's not anybody else's business. If you want to be gay, you know, stay in your house with your partner and do what you have to do. But to have to like parade down the street and show everybody, I don't like that." *I don't either*, Peggy says. *They're flaunting it*. For these women, the visibility of sexual nonconformity on talk shows is continuous with a more general invasion of public space, a sort of tasteless greediness, by gays and lesbians, who parade down streets and now parade on television right into our homes.

The sense that talk shows are part of an invasion, that when they involve gay people they must be battled rather than watched, can be extraordinarily intense. In the midst of a long, heated argument in a male discussion group, Jim ("Rush Limbaugh is my main man"), a 55-year-old retired police officer, puts it as clearly as it can be put.

> I'm not anti-gay, I just don't want the gays invading my space. I tolerate them, but I don't want them coming in my face. I think the gays and lesbians, it was better when they were in the closet. Now they come out, and they're trying to force their views on us. More and more every day. Lesbians and gays, fine, they want to do their thing, fine, but don't get in my space. Because I have my beliefs, and I don't want them messing with my family, because my family's the way I raised my family. I'm a churchgoer, I'm a father, and I don't want to see this happen to my children, or my grandchildren. And I want them to stay where they are, and don't impose their views on everybody else. *I don't want my space invaded, very simply, and I'll fight to keep my space from being invaded. I don't want them in my house, period.* They're right in your face, all the time, and the shows don't help. The shows don't help. They have the people right out there, and they're flaunting it. The talk shows make it look like, oh, it's great, it's better than what you might have. I've always tolerated their lifestyle, I just don't want them to put it in my face, that's all, and when they do it on TV, they're putting it in your face.

Exploitation and propriety are of no concern here, but the elements left are shared with more liberal, gay-sympathetic viewers: *keep out of my face, keep out of my space*.

When sex and gender statuses become politicized – when the personal becomes political – as the feminist movement has dramatically demonstrated, they often meet with this kind of backlash. This makes good sense, since what under the old rules had seemed like a natural privilege (man public, woman domestic; heterosexual public, homosexual secret) is now claimed to be an exertion of power. The political battle becomes, in part, a battle over ownership of public space. Both talk shows and gay, lesbian, bisexual, and transgender movements (along with the feminist movement) have been aggressively moving previously private issues into the public sphere; television has, moreover, taken the newly public back into the privacy of home. That move, and all the anxieties about changes in the public sphere that congeal around it, make talk shows politically relevant despite the hollow twaddle of which they are so often composed.

Privacy and sexual supremacy, daytime talk and the previously private, talk shows and sex and gender movements – these relationships are undeniably tight. For those with an interest in protecting traditional divisions between public and private, TV talk shows featuring lesbians, gays, bisexuals, and transgenders thus look and feel like a double whammy. The shows want to make public space something entirely different, by giving it to people who have never before made much successful claim on it. Liberal heterosexual viewers worry about exploitation and propriety, beneath which seems to lurk a sense that they are losing control of public space; conservative viewers bring that anxiety to its extreme, watching those shows, when they can stand to, as though they are holding their fists in front of their faces, ready to fend off the onslaught. While lesbian and gay, bisexual, and transgender activists are waging their struggles for visibility, these viewers are waging their own battle with the television set. They are blocking their throats from the talk shows' fast and furious force-feeding of sex and gender deviance. They are wishing these people would just shut up, not quite understanding why they need to flaunt it in other people's faces, why they have to use television to stick queer noses where they don't belong.

Conclusion: Visibility and Collective Identity

All told, talk shows make "good publicity" and "positive images" and "affirmation" hard concepts to hold. They offer a visibility

that diversifies even as it amplifies internal class conflicts, that empowers even as it makes public alliances between various sub-populations more difficult, that carves out important new public spaces even as it plays up an association between public queerness and the decay of public decorum. Talk shows suggest that visibility cannot be strategized as either positive or negative, but must be seen as a series of political negotiations.

For instance, a glance at the emphasis on outrageousness that many talk shows have come to promote – the source of much complaining about negative imagery of lesbian, gay, transgender, and bisexual people – makes it hard to hold onto the notion that talk show selection of "the fringes" is necessarily and always a bad thing. This kind of exoticizing imagery certainly makes social acceptability harder to gain by over-emphasizing difference, often presented as frightening, pathological, pathetic, or silly; it is annoying and painful for pretty much everybody involved. But at the same time it can push out a space: an emphasis on difference, especially on a scary kind of difference, can keep those watching at a distance. Like the in-your-face radicalism of some recent "queer" organizing, a freaky otherness is useful, for some purposes. When people push away from you, or think of you as harmless and dismissible, they tend to leave you alone, and sometimes being left alone is exactly what is needed for independent political and cultural organizing. As one queer writer put it in the early 1990s, "If I tell them I am queer, they give me room. Politically, I can think of little better. I do not want to be one of them. They only need to give me room" (Chee 1991: 15). The same might be said of the talk shows' money-driven interest in the more provocative edges of lesbian, bisexual, transgender, and gay populations: while they Other us, they also give us *room*. Of course, this is also exactly the problem many people have with them, since at least the appearance of normality seems necessary to winning political *rights*. It's a tension built into talk show visibility, and into the emergence of other marginalized people into commercial media recognition. As Jane Schacter (1997: 728) points out, what's "positive" or "negative" depends "in large part upon what underlying theory of equality has been adopted – one that prizes assimilation or transformation, sameness or difference." The same imagery that is damaging for some kinds of political work (assimilation into the mainstream) is effective for other kinds (the autonomous carving-out of political space). Both kinds of work are necessary. Talk shows, simply through their pursuit of ratings, inadvertently amplify a political dilemma inherent in becoming visible, in which both exaggerating and playing down our collective eccentricity is vital.

Indeed, the same risk-averse logic of television that has led to the sensationalizing of sexual and gender nonconformity (the weirder it is, the less the risk of people changing channels) has made the sensations repeat and repeat (it worked before, or it works for others, so let's keep doing it). The shocking gets less and less preposterous as it is repeated; the selection of a population's stigmatized extremes may hem in the population as a whole, but the habitual selection of extremes may simply deaden the stigma. "It is not the simple statement of facts that ushers in freedom," Quentin Crisp (1997: 204) has suggested. "It is the constant repetition of them that has this liberating effect." Over time, the talk shows have managed to do for their audiences what no one else has: to make televised homosexuality, and even transsexualism and bisexuality, nearly dull. The "fringes," as they show up on TV every week, become run of the mill; they become like a desperate Madonna, whose simulated sex and outside-the-clothing lingerie drew yawns after not too long. Critics of talk shows here have a point: talk shows, through their continual exhibition of the most colorful side-show figures, "define deviance down." From the perspective of those resisting a political and cultural system that labels them deviant, this is a good thing: the edges of normality push ever outward. Tolerance, Crisp informs us, is boredom's offspring. Where exactly is the "positive" in all of this, and where the "negative"?

The difficulty goes much deeper than any talk show will ever go. Talk shows accentuate not only the tension between legitimacy-buying and diversity-promoting visibility but also central dilemmas of collective identity. A sense of collective identification – that this is us, that we are each other – is personally and politically critical: it is an anchor, offering the comforts and resources of family and, at least in this political system, a foundation from which to organize and wage political battles. Identity requires stable, recognizable social categories. It requires difference, knowing where you end and where others begin. It thus makes good sense to do as gay and lesbian movements, modeling themselves on civil rights movements, have done: to build a quasi-ethnicity, with its own political and cultural institutions, festivals, and neighborhoods. Underwriting this strategy, moreover, is typically the notion that gays and lesbians share the same sort of essential self, one with same-sex desires (D'Emilio 1983; Epstein 1987; Seidman 1993). All of this solidifies the social categories of "gay" and "lesbian," clarifying who "we" are and are not, even as it also stabilizes the categories of "heterosexual man" and "heterosexual woman."

At the same time, though, it is exactly through the fixed, dichotomous categorization into apparently distinct species of gay and straight (and male and female) that anti-gay, anti-bisexual, and anti-transgender oppression is perpetuated. Even as the categories that mark us as different are necessary for claiming rights and benefits, making them unworkable provides its own protections; if there is no sure way to distinguish gay from straight, for instance, the basis for anti-gay legislation is arguably weakened. From this angle, *muddying* the categories rather than shoring them up, pointing out their instability and fluidity along with their social roots, is the key to liberation. The political advantages of scrambling the code are always also in competition with those of keeping it clear, not only for people who want to retain their status on a sexual hierarchy, but also for people resisting that hierarchy, who need a coherent sense of collective identity, a cohesive foundation from which to fight, for instance, for rights as gay people.

This tension between a politic that treats the homo–hetero divide as a given and goes about the business of equalizing the sides, and a politic that seeks to *attack the divide itself*, always present in contemporary gay and lesbian politics, has come to the fore most recently with the controversial emergence of "queer" movements in politics and academia. Queer theory and politics, as Michael Warner puts it, protests "not just the normal behavior of the social but the *idea* of normal behavior" (Warner 1993: xxvii). Especially with the vocal challenge from transgendered and bisexual people – who do not so easily fit into the gay–straight and man–woman binary worldview – the question of the unity, stability, viability, and political utility of sexual identities has been called into question. The queer politics of "carnival, transgression, and parody," with its "anti-assimilationist" and "decentering" politics, has been met with heavy resistance from those rightly seeing it as a threat to civil rights strategies (Stein and Plummer 1996: 134; see also Epstein 1996; Gamson 1995). The problem, of course, is that both the category-strippers and the category-defenders are right: fixed identity categories are both the basis for oppression and the basis for political power.

Talk shows create much of their sex-and-gender fare, especially when transgender and bisexual people are involved, on exactly this tension. Talk shows, even though they reinstate them, mess up those reassuring dichotomies. On talk shows, the categories stretch and contract, stretch and contract.

Much talk show visibility, for one thing, is "queer," in the meaning of the term favored by academics, spotlighting "a proliferation of sexualities (bisexual, transvestite, pre- and post-op transsexual, to name a few) and the compounding of outcast positions along racial, ethnic, and class, as well as sexual lines – none of which is acknowledged by the neat binary division between hetero- and homosexual" (Hennessy 1994–5: 34). The disruptions are fleeting, as audiences work hard to put the categories back together, but they are disturbances nonetheless.

For lesbian, gay, bisexual, and transgender collectives, in particular, these moments of diverse visibility are a crisis: both an opportunity to challenge the *cultural* logic of homo–hetero distinction, and a threat to the sense that "we" make the kind of sense we need, *politically*, to make. Talk shows, with their peculiar interest in the out-there and the in-between, bring out this queer dilemma. The ubiquity of people who do not quite fit the simple categories advances an important cultural agenda, by reminding viewers that the "neat binary division between hetero- and homosexual" is not as neat as all that, tarnishing the certainty of clear, natural differences between sexualities and genders. Even with all the attempts to defuse the identity threats housed by these sorts of disruptions, the sense that "normal" and "natural" are distinguishable from their opposites unravels in bits and pieces. Media visibility, talk shows tell us, is riddled with this difficulty – and the more diverse and democratic it gets, the more the dilemma comes alive.

The conditions of visibility, of course, are not of our own making. The tight rope on which bisexuals, transgenders, gays, and lesbians balance as we emerge into visibility gets especially tangled in a time and place where the "public" into which we walk is a space in turmoil. Talk shows, which make their money primarily by publicizing personal issues, only make this anxiety easier to see. Sex and gender nonconformists participate in, and detonate, an anxiety about the shifting boundaries between public and private – much as they have taken a place in other "moral panics," such as the 1950s equation of homosexuality and communism, where pervasive fears and anxieties attach to sexual "deviants" (see D'Emilio 1983; Rubin 1993; Weeks 1981). The very televised presence of gay, lesbian, bisexual, and transgendered people makes public space, to many people, appear to be crawling with indecency. In an environment where public and private have blurred into new forms, gay, lesbian, bisexual, and transgender visibility comes to symbolize a breakdown in the meaning of publicness.

The charge of public indecency is, moreover, a call to get out: this is *my* space, it says, and you do not belong here. Becoming media-visible, especially if your social identity is rooted in a status previously understood to belong to the realm of "private" life, calls the question on who owns public space. The issue of what can and cannot be spoken about and seen in public, which the televised collective coming out of the past twenty years evokes, is really the issue of who is and is not considered a legitimate member of "the public." This ongoing cultural war over public space and public participation is what makes talk shows – even when they are devoid of anything remotely political – socially relevant, and turns them into such zany, vibrant, coarse scenes. In part, they exist to isolate the socially challenging in a discredited space, offering the heady opportunity to be lords and ladies of a vapid kingdom, while the real powerhouses command the rest of the empire. In part, they exist to provide a concrete locale at which the question of just what public space can look like, and under just whose jurisdiction it falls, is kept alive for everybody to look at and toss around. Entering media space means joining this fight, and the other ones attached to it, with these questions and predicaments scribbled on your hand.

REFERENCES

Abt, Vicki and Seesholtz, Mel (1994) "The Shameless World of Phil, Sally and Oprah: Television Talk Shows and the Deconstructing of Society," *Journal of Popular Culture* 195–215.

Alwood, Edward (1996) *Straight News: Gays, Lesbians, and the News Media.* New York: Columbia University Press.

Calhoun, Craig, ed. (1992) *Habermas and the Public Sphere.* Cambridge, MA: MIT Press.

Carpignano, Paolo, Andersen, Robin, Aronowitz, Stanley, and DiFazio, William (1990) "Chatter in the Age of Electronic Reproduction: Talk Television and the 'Public Mind,'" *Social Text* 25: 33–55.

Chee, Alexander (1991) "A Queer Nationalism," *Out/Look* 11: 15.

Chidley, Joe (1996) "Taking In the Trash," *McClean's* (19 Feb.): 50–3.

Clark, Danae (1993) "Commodity Lesbianism" in Henry Abelove, Michele Aina Barale, and David Halperin (eds.) *The Lesbian and Gay Studies Reader,* pp. 186–201. New York: Routledge.

Crisp, Quentin (1997) [1968] *The Naked Civil Servant.* New York: Penguin.

D'Emilio, John (1983) *Sexual Politics, Sexual Communities: The Making of a Homosexual Minority in the United States.* Chicago, IL: University of Chicago Press.

Empower America (1995) "Press Conference," Washington, DC: Federal Document Clearing House, October 26.

Epstein, Steven (1987) "Gay Politics, Ethnic Identity: The Limits of Social Constructionism," *Socialist Review* 17 (3–4): 9–54.

——(1996) "A Queer Encounter: Sociology and the Study of Sexuality," in Steven Seidman (ed.) *Queer Theory/Sociology,* pp. 145–67. Cambridge, MA: Blackwell Publishers.

Fejes, Fred and Petrich, Kevin (1993) "Invisibility, Homophobia and Heterosexism: Lesbians, Gays and the Media," *Critical Studies in Mass Communication* (December): 396–422.

Gabler, Neal (1995) "Audience Stays Superior to the Exploitalk Shows," *Los Angeles Times* (March 19): M1.

Gamson, Joshua (1995) "Must Identity Movements Self-Destruct? A Queer Dilemma," *Social Problems* 42 (3): 390–407.

330 JOSHUA GAMSON

——(1998) *Freaks Talk Back: Tabloid Talk Shows and Sexual Nonconformity*. Chicago, IL: University of Chicago Press.

Grindstaff, Laura (1997) "Producing Trash, Class, and the Money Shot: A Behind the Scenes Account of Daytime TV Talkshows," in James Lull and Stephen Hinerman (eds.) *Media Scandals*. London: Polity Press.

Gross, Larry (1989) "Out of the Mainstream: Sexual Minorities and the Mass Media," in Ellen Seiter (ed.) *Remote Control: Television, Audiences, and Cultural Power*, pp. 130–49. New York: Routledge.

——(1994) "What Is Wrong with this Picture? Lesbian Women and Gay Men on Television," in R. Jeffrey Ringer (ed.) *Queer Words, Queer Images: Communication and the Construction of Homosexuality*, pp. 143–56. New York: New York University Press.

Habermas, Jürgen (1991) *The Structural Transformation of the Public Sphere*. Cambridge: MIT Press.

Hafner, Debra W. (1995) "Talk Show Chaos," *Renaissance News & Views* (September): 6, 16.

Hantzis, Darlene M. and Lehr, Valerie (1994) "Whose Desire? Lesbian (Non) Sexuality and Television's Perpetuation of Hetero/Sexism," in R. Jeffrey Ringer (ed.) *Queer Words, Queer Images: Communication and the Construction of Homosexuality*, pp. 107–21. New York: New York University Press.

Heaton, Jeanne Albronda and Wilson, Nona Leigh (1995) *Tuning in Trouble: Talk TV's Destructive Impact on Mental Health*. San Francisco, CA: Jossey-Bass.

Hennessy, Rosemary (1994–5) "Queer Visibility in Commodity Culture," *Cultural Critique* (winter): 31–75.

Jenny Jones Show (1995) "Jenny Jones" (*Gorgeous and Gay!* March 21).

Kirk, Marshall and Madsen, Hunter (1989) *After the Ball: How America Will Conquer Its Fear & Hatred of Gays in the 90s*. New York: Plume.

Kurtz, Howard (1996) *Hot Air: All Talk, All the Time*. New York: Times Books.

Livingstone, Sonia and Lunt, Peter (1994) *Talk on Television: Audience Participation and Public Debate*. London: Routledge.

Meyrowitz, Joshua (1985) *No Sense of Place: The Impact of Electronic Media on Social Behavior*. New York: Oxford University Press.

Mohr, Richard (1988) *Gays/Justice: A Study of Ethics, Society, and Law*. New York: Columbia University Press.

Moritz, Marguerite J. (1994) "Old Strategies for New Texts: How American Television is Creating and Treating Lesbian Characters," in R. Jeffrey Ringer (ed.) *Queer Words, Queer Images: Communication and the Construction of Homosexuality*, pp. 122–42. New York: New York University Press.

Multimedia Entertainment (1992) "Donahue" (*Concord Anti-Gay Referendum*, February 13).

Multimedia Entertainment (1994) "Donahue" (*Gay Cops*, June 9).

Multimedia Entertainment (1995a) "Donahue" (*What, They're Gay? Lipstick Lesbians and Gorgeous Gay Guys*, September 12).

Multimedia Entertainment (1995b) "The Jerry Springer Show" (*Please Act Straight!* October 23).

Munson, Wayne (1994) *All Talk: The Talkshow in Media Culture*. Philadelphia, PA: Temple University Press.

Netzhammer, Emile C. and Shamp, Scott A. (1994) "Guilt by Association: Homosexuality and AIDS on Prime-Time Television," in R. Jeffrey Ringer (ed.) *Queer Words, Queer Images: Communication and the Construction of Homosexuality*, pp. 98–106. New York: New York University Press.

Paramount Pictures (1992) "Maury Povich" (*Lipstick Lesbians*, May 29).

Priest, Patricia J. (1995) *Public Intimacies: Talk Show Participants and Tell-All TV*. Cresskill, NJ: Hampton Press.

Rose, Brian G. (1985) "The Talk Show," in Brian G. Rose (ed.) *TV Genres: A Handbook and Reference Guide*. Westport, CT: Greenwood Press.

Rubin, Gayle (1993) [1984] "Thinking Sex: Notes for a Radical Theory of the Politics of Sexuality," in Henry Abelove, Michele Aina Barale, and David Halperin (eds.) *The Lesbian and Gay Studies Reader*, pp. 3–44. New York: Routledge.

Russo, Vito (1987) *The Celluloid Closet: Homosexuality in the Movies*, 2nd edn. New York: Harper & Row.

Schacter, Jane S. (1997) "Skepticism, Culture and the Gay Civil Rights Debate in Post-Civil-Rights Era," *Harvard Law Review* 110 (January): 684–731.

Seidman, Steven (1993) "Identity Politics in a 'Postmodern' Gay Culture: Some Historical and Conceptual Notes," in Michael Warner (ed.) *Fear of a Queer Planet*. Minneapolis: University of Minnesota Press.

—— (ed.) (1996) *Queer Theory/Sociology*. Cambridge, MA: Blackwell Publishers.

Shattuc, Jane (1997) *The Talking Cure: TV Talk Shows and Women*. New York: Routledge.

Stein, Arlene and Plummer, Ken (1996) "'I Can't Even Think Straight': 'Queer' Theory and the Missing Sexual Revolution in Sociology," in Steven Seidman (ed.) *Queer Theory/Sociology*, pp. 129–44. Cambridge, MA: Blackwell Publishers.

Tuchman, Gaye (1974) "Assembling a Network Talk Show," in Gaye Tuchman (ed.) *The TV Establishment: Programming for Power and Profit*, pp. 119–35. Englewood Cliffs, NJ: Prentice-Hall.

Unitel Video (1992) "Jane Whitney" (*Bisexuality*, December 17).

Vaid, Urvashi (1995) *Virtual Equality: The Mainstreaming of Gay and Lesbian Liberation*. New York: Anchor Books.

Warner, Michael, ed. (1993) *Fear of a Queer Planet*. Minneapolis: University of Minnesota Press.

Weeks, Jeffrey (1981) *Sex, Politics, and Society: The Regulation of Sexuality Since 1800*. New York: Longman.

Weintraub, Jeffrey (1996) "The Theory and Politics of the Public/Private Distinction," in Jeffrey Weintraub and Krishan Kumar (eds.) *Public and Private in Thought and Practice: Perspectives on a Grand Dichotomy*, pp. 1–42. Chicago, IL: University of Chicago Press.

Weintraub, Jeffrey and Kumar, Krishan, eds. (1996) *Public and Private in Thought and Practice: Perspectives on a Grand Dichotomy*. Chicago, IL: University of Chicago Press.

22 Girls, Media, and the Negotiation of Sexuality: A Study of Race, Class, and Gender in Adolescent Peer Groups

Meenakshi Gigi Durham

Adolescence for girls in the United States has been characterized as "a troubled crossing,"[1] a period marked by severe psychological and emotional stresses. Recent research indicates that the passage out of childhood for many girls means that they experience a loss of self-esteem and self-determination as cultural norms of femininity and sexuality are imposed upon them.[2]

Much attention has been paid over the last decade or more to the role of the mass media in this cultural socialization of girls:[3] clearly, the media are crucial symbolic vehicles for the construction of meaning in girls' everyday lives. The existing data paint a disturbing portrait of adolescent girls as well as of the mass media: on the whole, girls appear to be vulnerable targets of detrimental media images of femininity. In general, the literature indicates that media representations of femininity are restrictive, unrealistic, focused on physical beauty of a type that is virtually unattainable as well as questionable in terms of its characteristics, and filled with internal contradictions. At the same time, the audience analysis that has been undertaken with adolescent girls reveals that they struggle with these media representations but are ultimately ill-equipped to critically analyze or effectively resist them.

These studies are linked to the considerable body of research documenting adolescent girls' difficulties with respect to issues such as waning self-esteem,[4] academic troubles,[5] negative body image,[6] conflicts surrounding sexuality,[7] and other issues related to girls' development. Although the majority of these studies were conducted with upper-middle-class White girls, some of them take into account the impact of race, ethnicity, and class on girls' experiences of adolescence. These findings indicate that – contrary to popular belief – girls of color and girls from lower socioeconomic backgrounds are very hard hit by adolescence and have fewer available resources for help with problems like eating disorders, pregnancies, or depression.[8]

Bearing these issues and their implications for girls in mind, this study seeks to broaden and deepen our understanding of the role of the mass media in girls' socialization, with a particular emphasis on the context in which this socialization takes place. New theories of child development contend that socialization is context-specific and that the peer groups of childhood and adolescence are responsible for the transmission of cultural norms as well as the modification of children's personality characteristics.[9] However, most of the research done to date on adolescence and mass media does not take into account the peer group dynamics involved in media use, nor the race and class factors that might influence these processes.

The key question in this study, then, is how peer group activity and social context affect adolescent girls' interactions with mass media, especially in terms of their dealings with issues of gender and sexuality. This study consisted of a long-term participant observation of middle-school girls combined with in-depth interviews with the girls and their teachers. A significant aspect of the study is that the girls were from sharply varying race and class backgrounds, and these factors were crucial components of the analysis.

Literature Review

Roberts has observed that in the United States, our understanding of media influences on adolescents revolves around two themes: "that 'objectionable' media messages teach objectionable beliefs and behaviors, and that young people are particularly susceptible to such messages."[10] In an overview of some thirty years of scholarship on the mass media and youth, Strasburger notes that the main research question posed in these studies was what direct effects the media – especially television – have had on adolescents.[11] While most of this research is principally concerned with the relationship between violent media content and aggressive audience behaviors, the topic of sex has been a focus of rising interest as increased rates of teen pregnancy, teenage abortions, AIDS, and other sexually transmitted diseases have generated major public health and policy discussions.

It is incontestable that adolescents rely heavily on the mass media for learning about sex. Surveys consistently indicate that the media rank just behind peers and parents as a source of information about sex and sexuality.[12] One survey found that teenagers who watched more TV with sexual content were also more likely to have begun sexual intercourse.[13] This relationship held regardless of perceived peer encouragement to engage in sex and across race and gender groups. It appears that teenagers also tend to selectively *choose* diets of highly sexualized media. Greenberg et al. found that the prime-time TV shows viewed

most often by ninth and tenth graders contained just under three sexual references per hour, and that the movies they favored contained even more frequent and explicit sexual references.[14] Similarly, analyses of print media read by teenaged girls demonstrate a heavy emphasis on sex and sexuality.[15]

Yet how this consumption of sexualized media content plays out in terms of adolescents' lived experiences is still not well understood. We know little about the influence of the mass media in boys' constructions of gender and sexuality,[16] and still less about girls. This latter is particularly troubling in light of recent speculation that girls' internalization of sexual mores is negative and problematic, leading to low self-esteem and sometimes self-destructive behaviors.[17] McRobbie suggests that ethnographic work – and specifically participant observation – is the only way to get at an understanding of "the social conditions and experiences which play a role in constituting [younger people's] subjectivities and identities."[18] Some work of this kind has been undertaken in England with regard to media and adolescents,[19] but in the United States this type of work is still rare. In one of the few ethnographic investigations of this nature, Brown, White, and Nikopoulou found that adolescent girls' responses to sexual content in media changed with their physical and emotional development, moving from disinterest to fascination or "intrigue" to resistance.[20] This study shed considerable light on girls' use of media to shape their own perceptions of sex and relationships, but it was limited in its scope – partly because only White middle-class girls from college-educated families were interviewed, and partly because they were studied in the private and secluded spaces of their bedrooms and diaries rather than in the peer environments where their ideas would be lived out.

Similarly, Duke and Kreshel's more recent in-depth interviews with teenage girls about magazines and body image represents, as they write, "a first step toward privileging the words of girls,"[21] yet it too relies on the voices of mainly White, middle-class girls who were interviewed individually. Individual interviews can offer an understanding of the interiorized, personal processes with which girls engage mass media, but again they cannot address how these processes are lived out via interpersonal interactions.

This study, then, seeks to break away from the conventional approaches to the study of teenage girls and media by stressing the significance of the peer group context and by foregrounding the fluid interplay of racial, ethnic, and class identifications within those groups.

Method

Background of the study

In order to gain a deep understanding of the social processes at work in adolescent girls' peer groups, a participant observation was conducted over a five-month period at two middle schools in a midsize city in the southwestern United States. The schools were very dissimilar. The first school, which I will call East Middle School,[22] was located on the "nonwhite" side of the racially segregated metropolis. The segregation is not, of course, officially codified; rather, the informal color line is the interstate highway that runs through the center of town. All areas to the east of the highway are tacitly designated as the African American and Latino[23] sections. The west side is the White side. The west side is also more affluent, more developed, supposedly safer, and more desirable in terms of real-estate values. The second school, West Middle School, was located on the west side of the city, in a different school district from East Middle School.

East Middle School was situated within the city limits, in an impoverished residential neighborhood that was very close to the interstate highway. Heavily trafficked streets bounded all sides of the schoolyard. The school building was a concrete block;

inside, there was little natural light. "Bilingual education" – i.e., classes for children whose dominant language is Spanish – was conducted in makeshift "portables" at the back of the school building. East Middle School had a total student enrollment of 1,164, of which the majority were African American (60 percent, or 704 students). The next largest student ethnic group comprised Latino students (26 percent, or 298 students). Thirteen percent (157) of the students were Anglo/White. A majority of the students (76.5 percent) were categorized by the school district as "economically disadvantaged."

By contrast, West Middle School was located many miles outside of the city in a picturesque hilly area. It, too, was in a residential neighborhood, but the houses were half-million-dollar properties with landscaped yards. The school was on its own street. From the schoolyard, the vista was one of rolling hills and open sky. The West school building was also made of concrete, but there were large windows that let in plenty of sunlight. The lunch cafeteria had a bay window that looked onto an atrium. The surroundings were peaceful and quiet.

West Middle School had a total student enrollment of 804. Of these, 732 students (91 percent) were Anglo/White. The minority population was minuscule: 27 students (3 percent) were Latino; 6 students (.07 percent) were African American; and 36 students (4 percent) were Asian/Pacific Islander. Only 2.5 percent of the West Middle School students were classified as "economically disadvantaged" by the school district.

Fieldwork was carried out over five months, from January through May of 1997, during which time the researcher visited the schools as often as possible and for as great a length of time as possible. This was usually a period of three or four hours, two or three times a week. Frequently, the researcher was able to spend the entire day at a school. At each school, the researcher gained access to an eighth-grade classroom, with the cooperation of the teachers. Observations began in an honors social studies class at East Middle School, and a class for gifted and talented students at West Middle School, but as the researcher got to know the students, their activities in other classes, during breaks, and in the lunch cafeteria were also observed. At lunchtime, the friendship groups from the classrooms expanded to include girls and boys from other grades and classes.

Peer groups at both schools were largely gender-segregated, although boys often spent time with groups that were centrally composed of girls (girls, on the other hand, did not attach themselves to male peer groups). At East Middle School some peer groups were segregated by race, while others were mixed-race. One clear division was between the recent Spanish-speaking immigrants (the "Mexicanos," as they were called) and other students, particularly the second- and third-generation Latino students who openly reviled the Mexicanos, calling them "wetbacks" and worse. At West Middle School racial segregation was not an issue because of the minimal number of nonwhite students.

While many peer groups existed at both schools, the researcher became closely involved with just a few, and the findings discussed here are based on observations and interviews with the members of these few. The group names came from the girls themselves – terms like "preps" and "gangstas" were used by the students to identify various peer groupings. At East Middle School, the groups studied were:

1   The "preps." These girls were academic achievers, involved in school activities like student government and cheerleading, and relatively affluent in comparison to the rest of the students. They were known as the popular crowd. The group was fairly large, but its core members were Ariana (14, biracial – Latino and African American), Brittany (14, Anglo), Lourdes (14, Latina), Nona (15, African

American), Marta (15, biracial – Latino and Native American), Rosa (14, Latina), and Rachel (14, African American). Girls who frequently associated with this group also included Mariah (14, African American), Mariana (14, Latina), Mercedes (15, Latina), and Janina (13, Latina).

2   The "gangstas." These girls were affiliated with the juvenile gangs of East Middle School and were considered to be at risk of academic and social failure by school authorities. Many of them were academic underachievers, and they tended not to be involved in school-sanctioned extracurricular activities. These girls were not economically advantaged, and many of them came from very troubled family backgrounds, with drug-addicted parents, histories of domestic violence, etc. The girls in this group included Nydia (15, Latina), Maria (15, Latina), Vanessa (14, Latina), Amy (14, Latina), and sometimes Mariana and Mercedes, who floated between the prep group and the gangsta group.

At West Middle School, two peer groups were studied:

1   The "preps." These girls were academic achievers, also involved in extracurricular activities like sports and cheerleading. They were considered to be "popular." They came from wealthy families and were trendsetters with regard to fashion, music, and the like, among the other students. The three girls who were central to this group were Jenny (14), Tara (14), and Sydney (14). All three were of Anglo/European ethnicity. The boys who were associated with them were athletes and the "skater" crowd.

2   The "regular girls." These girls were academic achievers but were not considered to be "popular," although they had many friends and were well-regarded by most of the other students. All of them were of

Anglo/European ethnicity; one, Judith, was Jewish. The girls in this group were Audrey (14), Emma (15), Jonquil (14), Judith (14), Bobbi (14), and Lila (15). Judith and Bobbi were best friends.

Analysis

While references to mass media abounded in the peer group conversations observed at both schools, it is important to note at the outset that none of the groups made any use of the *news* media in their day-to-day peer interactions. Discussions of politics and current events did not arise during the five months of observations; rather, popular culture was the common currency among the girls, and the media with the greatest communicatory utility were television, consumer magazines, and movies. These observations corroborate recent findings of declining use of the news media by young people.[24]

Media references cropped up much more frequently in the conversations of the students at West Middle School than at East. Students at East Middle School did use the mass media, but in their peer group discussions they were much more likely to talk about their community and church activities, their friends and relatives, and the incidents in their daily lives – for instance, the *quince-anera* celebrations which many of the Latina girls were planning. At West Middle School, by contrast, media references were almost constant: talk of movies, TV shows, and pop music featured in every conversation.

At both schools, mass media were in evidence. For example, most of the girls at both schools subscribed to *YM* and *Seventeen* magazines and carried them in their backpacks. Girls at both schools watched TV shows like *The X Files*, *Friends*, *Seinfeld*, *Daria*, *Sabrina the Teenage Witch*, and *Buffy the Vampire Slayer*. Girls at West Middle School were more likely to have seen current movies than the girls at East; they were also more involved with pop music.

The pervasiveness of popular culture at both schools was tied very closely to the single most important theme that emerged from the data: the dominance of the sociocultural norm of heterosexuality in the girls' lives. While this was addressed and negotiated in different ways depending on various contextual factors, compulsory heterosexuality functioned as the core ideology underpinning the girls' interpersonal and intragroup transactions, although it was seldom explicitly acknowledged. What was striking was that this norm of heterosexuality was central to the social worlds of girls at both schools, and it guided the girls' behaviors and beliefs regardless of their racial, ethnic, and class differences, although it manifested itself in different ways based on these cultural variances.

The girls' efforts to understand and adapt to perceived social norms of heterosexuality played out principally through their ongoing constructions of femininity. The use of the mass media was woven into those constructions and served in various ways to cement the girls' identities within their peer groups as well as to secure their relationships to the broader social world. Themes of heterosexuality criss-crossed the girls' conversations and actions in multiple ways, but certain practices occurred frequently and repeatedly enough to constitute clearly discernible modalities of mass mediated heterosexual expression. These are described and analyzed in detail, below, under the thematic headings of (1) the discipline of the body, (2) brides and mothers, (3) homophobia and sexual confusion, and (4) iconic femininity.

The discipline of the body: cosmetics, clothes, and diets

Bartky points out that "femininity is an artifice" and that women engage in "disciplinary practices that produce a body which in gesture and appearance is recognizably feminine."[25] My observations of the schoolgirls at East and West Middle Schools indicate that these disciplinary practices are acquired fairly early in life and are essential to the maintenance of adolescent girls' peer group configurations. At both schools, peer relationships hinged on these techniques for molding the female body in group-sanctioned ways.

Cosmetics and grooming. At East Middle School, the application of cosmetics was a common group occurrence and one that sometimes transpired with the aid of magazines like *YM*, *Seventeen*, and *Glamour*. This happened most often among the "gangsta" girls, and it usually occurred in the classroom when students were given unstructured work time. On several occasions I observed them braiding and styling each others' hair, painting each others' fingernails, and applying makeup. During the yearbook class one afternoon, for example, when some students were writing stories or working on layouts, a group of the "gangsta" girls drifted together; one pulled out a makeup bag and began to apply cosmetics to another, while several gathered around to watch and comment. Most of the girls in this gathering belonged to the same friendship group, with a few outsiders joining them. Other girls who belonged to different peer groups kept away from them; one commented that the classroom wasn't a beauty salon.

Mariana, the 14-year-old Latina girl who was doing the make-over, went about it with great concentration, first applying lip-liner, then lipstick, then powder foundation, then eyeshadows of various colors, and finally mascara to her friend Mercedes' face. The girls were quiet and rapt while this was going on, watching the process in almost reverent silence, but after it was over they began to talk.

LAURA: That looks good. That looks cute.
MARIANA: I saw in *YM* that if you put white eyeshadow on like that, it makes your eyes look bigger.
MERCEDES (OPENING HER EYES WIDE):   Does it work?

MARIANA: I don't know. Yeah. A little bit, maybe.
NYDIA: Her hair is pretty. My hair is so ugly.
LAURA: Your hair is pretty.
NYDIA: Naw, it's all dry and damaged. *(Much discussion about their hair...)*
NYDIA: I like long hair. I want long hair. What shampoo do you use?
MERCEDES: Pantene Pro-V.
MARIANA: I use Wella conditioner.
MERCEDES: My hair is all dry and I have split ends.

Nydia pulled a *Seventeen* magazine out of her backpack and flipped though it until she found an ad for Suave conditioner. "I need this," she said. "It's mois...tur...izing," she read from the ad, stumbling over the pronunciation. "'To replenish moisture in dry or damaged hair.' That's me."

This episode serves as an exemplar of the girls' preoccupation with the tools and techniques required to achieve physical beauty, and their use of mass media for guidance in the acquisition of those commodities. At East Middle School the girls who were more knowledgeable about beautification were also more "popular," which is to say that they were the central figures in their peer groups.

Clothes. Further, at East Middle School, peer groups were defined in part by their costuming. Conversations with the girls confirmed this: the main groups of girls were the "gangstas," students who were gang-identified; the "gangsta wannabes," who dressed and acted like gang affiliates, but who were not included in gang activities; the "preps," who were the honor students and the cheerleaders; and the "dorks," the social outcastes. The dorks, according to Ariana, a member of the prep group, "didn't know how to dress." The Latina girls in the "gangsta" group had thin plucked eyebrows, wore dark lipstick and heavy eye makeup, and had chemically lightened their hair color. The girls in the prep group wore minimal makeup, but they plucked their eyebrows and sometimes experimented with hairstyles within a very conservative range of options (ponytails or sometimes curled hair). Their clothes usually reflected current trends in shopping-mall fashions. The "dorks" wore bluejeans and tee-shirts and tended not to draw attention to themselves via their costuming.

At West Middle School the groups, or "cliques" as they were called by the students, were also marked by their appearance and costuming. As Judith, a 14-year-old Jewish girl, explained,

> Some of the cliques have um like certain styles. Like the most popular people are kind of like preps, and they wear like The Gap and J. Crew, and then the other groups that kind of get stuff like that are, the skater group who are like grunge influenced...and then um, like there's this one group of girls that are like really into Contempo clothes, and they wear that a lot.

Her friend Bobbi added: "The people at the prep tables wear Nike, and Nike, and Nike, and Nike...then there are the Kickers. You know, like cowboy wear. Like, they wear cowboy boots." Judith: "We don't like that style."

Consumer fashion thus was the principal means by which group identity was demarcated, although pop music was also used in the same way. Fashion traits seemed to be derived from advertising; music was related to clothing, and these connections were made from MTV as well as peer references. The skaters listened to hard rock and heavy metal music; the preps made much of knowing which bands were currently "hot" on the charts. The Kickers listened to country music.

Despite these identifiers, many students were emphatic about not conforming to group norms. In individual conversations, they were clear about the characterizing features of the different cliques, and they all identified themselves as iconoclasts and nonconformists even when they belonged to cliques:

JUDITH: My style is kind of different from everyone else's. I don't really think too much about what I wear as long as I like it.

BOBBI: If I feel comfortable, if I like what I'm wearing...I'm not out to please anybody else.

LILA: If I find something I like, then I wear it, but if everybody starts painting their nails silver or something then you'd have to stop.

JENNY: I try to be my own person. I just buy clothes that I like and that are comfortable.

TARA: I don't conform to fashion trends or whatever.

JENNY (TO TARA):   For fashion, you copy me.

In an interesting paradox, the West Middle School girls were quick to point out and criticize each others' compliance with mediated and peer standards for dress and appearance, but they denied their own participation in that system. Their peer group conversations, however, belied an intense interest in fashion and the fashion media, e.g.:

BOBBI: "E" is the best. I watch that all the time. I love that.

JUDITH: It's fun looking at the pretty clothes but I, sometimes I'll be like, I wouldn't want to wear that.

BOBBI: Yeah, I'd never want to wear that on the street. If you were on the street and I was like that I'd be like (makes horrified face).

BOTH: No!

J: I don't know who buys those clothes.

B: They can't be like happy or anything, they'll always be like, got to get 'em off.

J: And then I really like Joan Rivers trashing them, I love that, it's so good, like after the Academy Awards, like the Oscars or the

Grammys or the Golden Globes she always has these fashion shows.

B: Have you seen the clothes that *she* wears?

J: Yeah, I know.

B: My goodness! I would not wear those! Like that pink thing, she had this ruffly thing.... She was like, we're going to see who's wearing the ugly dresses, and I was like, you!

J: Yeah, I mean, she is pretty good, sometimes she has like really bad taste, like some of the things that I think are like really ugly on people she's like, oh that's beautiful beautiful, and I don't really agree sometimes. But I also just like looking and seeing what the stars are wearing.

B: Yeah, me too.

Diet and Weight. At East Middle School the girls were extremely critical of those who showed no interest in conforming to media-driven standards of fashion and beauty, and they were also very open about their own interest in those standards.

This was particularly striking during a conversation about food and dieting that occurred at the lunch table among the "popular" girls at East. One of the girls, Ariana, had brought to the table a newspaper article about teenagers' eating habits, which the girls all looked at. The article described teenage girls' poor eating habits, stating that teen girls are "more likely to skip meals, avoid milk, eat away from home, and fret about their weight."

BRITTANY: It's true, this is how we eat. Milk has calcium, doesn't it? I don't drink milk.

RACHEL: I only drink milk on cereal.

BRITTANY: I only drink water and tea.

ROSA: I drink everything except water and milk.

BRITTANY: I'm addicted to tea.

MARTA: I'm addicted to Dr. Pepper.

BRITTANY: I used to starve myself.

ARIANA: I did, too. It's easy after the first day. The first day is hard. But after that it's easy, you don't notice it.

MARTA: We don't eat real food, we'd get food poisoning.

They were eager to reify the connections between themselves and the girls described in the article, and it was important to them to find points of similarity between themselves and the news article's mediated construction of "teenage girls," however negative that construction might be.

Despite this, these girls did not usually discuss their bodies or their weight to any significant degree in their peer group conversations; nor did the girls in the "gangsta" group. At West Middle School, however, there was more open talk about body norms and more criticism of girls whose bodies did not conform to the ideal.

BOBBI: There is a girl who will wear like really really tight pants and like stripes with flowers or something, things that don't go together at all.

JUDITH: Who?

BOBBI: Kathy Smith. [*author's note: name changed to protect privacy*]

JUDITH: That's a fashion faux pas right there. Not to say any names or anything, but she wears like tank tops with really thin straps but she doesn't really have the body for it...

BOBBI: It isn't her fault!

JUDITH: It isn't her fault or anything but I think she wears the wrong kind of stripes, I think there's certain kinds of stripes that like reveal certain things...and then she wore the opposite kind that reveal certain things....She just looks all wrong. She does not have the right body for those kind of clothes.

The girls at West school were sensitized to issues of body image and eating disorders, and these topics cropped up frequently in their conversations. Eating disorders were a serious problem at this school; teachers informed me that a student had recently died of anorexia nervosa. Yet, interestingly, the girls' discussions hovered around *resistance* to dysfunctional images of body; they used discourse around these issues to find solidarity in critiquing problematic concepts of body.

AUDREY: Like anorexia and all that stuff, I don't understand that. It's just so stupid, I don't get it. How can you not eat?
JONQUIL: I couldn't ever be bulimic and keep throwing up.
EMMA: And there are some people at school, these girls, they'll eat like a carrot, 'cause they're afraid the guys will see them eating. I hate that.
AUDREY: At lunch, I eat like so much, I eat like three pieces of pizza every day. I don't care what guys think. People have to eat. That's just natural...
JONQUIL: Biology.
AUDREY: Yeah. And people, they're afraid they'll think they're pigs or something if they eat too much. So they'll like go to the bathroom and eat. Some people eat lunch in the bathroom.
EMMA: It's   so   sad.   You   know Laurel....She kind of copies things off magazines and TV and things... she's into like being perfect and skinny and not eating.
AUDREY: But you have to eat! I feel like saying, eat something!

Conversations with one of the teachers revealed that Jonquil in fact had had some problems with eating disorders; how many of the others had suffered from them was not ascertainable, but the issue was clearly on their minds. Here, the peer group served as a means of consolidating ideas about rejecting and resisting damaging ideals for female bodies. Individually, their engagement with their bodies may have been different, more self-critical and less defiant,[26] but the group context appeared to moderate those tendencies in more progressive directions. The conversation reflected the paradoxical nature of eating disorders and the

culture of thinness in US society:[27] while the girls understood eating disorders as pathological and abnormal, they would not admit their own involvement with these problems even as they subscribed in their daily lives to mediated norms of slenderness and beauty. As Siebecker notes:

[Eating] disorders have been regarded as bizarre psychological phenomena that affect a minority of emotionally disturbed women. The problem has thus been isolated from the experiences of other women and marginalized into a psychological category. This has in effect thrown up a smokescreen between the clinically diagnosed eating disorder sufferer and the rest of women in society: If the smokescreen came down, what women would see is that, while we do not all actually have eating disorders, we are not so different from those sufferers.[28]

The girls' conversation kept the smokescreen up, distancing the girls with obvious eating problems from the sociocultural norms of thinness and beauty that pervaded the group members' everyday lives.

Brides and mothers. Flipping through magazines in the classroom, Nydia and Maria pause at an advertisement featuring a bride in a formal white wedding dress. They examine the photograph for several minutes.

NYDIA: Oh, that's a pretty dress.
MARIA: She looks so beautiful.
NYDIA: I want to have a long dress like that. I want a big veil and flowers.

At East Middle School mediated images of brides and motherhood were of vital interest to the girls. Again and again, they discussed TV and celebrity weddings with admiration and obsessive attention to detail.

ARIANA: You know what I did? I saw this wedding on TV, and the guys all wore Wranglers and tuxedo shirts... and then the bridesmaids were late, and the bride got wet and her hair got all messed up...

MARTA: What are you talking about?

ARIANA: A wedding where these guys wore Wrangler jeans and tuxedo shirts and jackets...

BRITTANY: That's how you're gonna get married.

MARTA: She's gonna have horses at the reception. (*Giggles.*)

ROSA: I want a formal wedding. Ariana, what color were the bridesmaids' dresses?

ARIANA: Pink, a really gross pink. I'm having pastel colors for my wedding.

BRITTANY: Did any of you watch the Waltons reunion?

Rosa: I did!

MARTA: I watched "The Brady Girls Get Married." Marcia and Jan were going to have a double wedding, but they kept fighting about what kind of wedding to have...

BRITTANY: What kind did they want?

MARTA: I don't know, one wanted to go all formal, and the other one wanted something modern, I think. One ended up wearing a short gown, I think they call them tea-length? The other one was long.

ROSA: I want a long gown. And lots of bridesmaids. Big weddings are nice.

ARIANA: Weddings should be special. It's your day, your special day.

On another occasion, when the girls were working in the computer lab on the Internet, a group of them found Madonna's home page and zeroed in instantly on photographs of her with her baby. They were especially delighted with one image of her when she was pregnant, exclaiming aloud about how "sweet" and "adorable" it was.

This valorization of marriage and maternity appeared to be in line with the trends in their lives. Teenage pregnancy is a significant problem at East Middle School – it is the main reason that girls drop out of that school. During the five months of this observation, on four different occasions, former seventh- and eighth-graders returned for campus visits with their babies in their arms. Their appearances were not greeted with any derision or gossip from their erst-

while classmates; rather, they were feted and embraced, the babies were cooed over, and the girls spoke with some longing of the day when they too would be mothers.

Culturally, teenage pregnancy was a norm among this student population. Many of the 14- and 15-year-old girls disclosed that their mothers were in their late twenties and early thirties. Some of the girls seemed to experience some conflict about the pressure toward maternity and their knowledge of other possibilities; they talked sometimes about the issue of abortion and whether it was sinful or not. The African-American girls tended to be more in favor of abortion as an option. The Latina girls were more opposed to it, for religious reasons.

Two of the "gangsta" girls had one extended conversation about their plans for the future; both intended to go to college and were clear and emphatic about not wanting to get pregnant before then.

MARIA: I am not getting married until I'm older. Like, 60. And I'm not having no babies.

NYDIA: I don't want a baby messin' up my life. I'm going to wait till after I go to college.

Maria became pregnant at the end of that academic year and dropped out of school.

By contrast, teenage pregnancy was invisible at West Middle School, and marriage and maternity were never mentioned in the girls' peer group conversations over the five months of this observation. The subjects did not seem to be relevant to the white, upper-middle-class girls' lives at all.

Homophobia and sexual confusion. On April 30, 1997, the TV show *Ellen* aired its notorious "coming-out" episode, in which the main character declared herself a lesbian. The show precipitated a discussion of homosexuality among the girls in the "prep" group at East Middle School; this conversation reiterated the refrain of homophobia that was a constant current in the students' lives at both East and West Middle Schools.

While overt discrimination based on race was rare at both schools, homophobia was an openly declared prejudice in the peer groups that were studied. Words like "fag" and "queer" were used casually as epithets; gossip about students' sexual orientations were a way of marking the social outcasts. At East Middle School the "coming-out" episode of *Ellen* served as a catalyst for a brief, impassioned exchange about the iniquity of homosexuality.

ROSA: I don't think she should have done that. It's just wrong to go on TV and put that in front of everybody.
ARIANA: She should just keep it to herself.
BRITTANY: I think it's a sin and it shouldn't be on TV.

At the time, there was also a festival in town that the local hippies had celebrated for about twenty-five years. Marta asked me if I had ever been to it and whether "funny people" were there.

I asked her what she meant by "funny people" and she said, "You know. Like *Ellen*." She said she was afraid of those people.

None of the girls in the peer group expressed opinions that differed from these, but later that day, Nona was looking through a *People* magazine in class and came across a photograph of Ellen DeGeneres. At that point she paused and said thoughtfully to her teacher, who was sitting nearby, "It's kind of good that they showed that on TV because it lets people who are gay know that people's lives are like that."

Her comment was unusual in a milieu where gay-bashing was considered high sport. At West Middle School homophobia was similarly open and aggressive. One student, Jenny – one of the most popular girls in the eighth grade – had a notebook covered with pictures cut out of magazines. The right side of the notebook displayed pictures of celebrity figures she disliked, and the left side was adorned with photos

of people she admired. Prominent on the right side of the notebook was the band Luscious Jackson, and Jenny had written "Sucks! Dikes, too!" (*sic*) across their image.

The "regular girls" were very aware of the rhetoric of compulsory heterosexuality in teen magazines and talked about it with some anger. As Audrey put it, "They make it seem like if you don't have a boyfriend, you're just nothing, which is really... I don't think it's true." Later, she added, "All of the articles are so superficial, they make you think like you have to be pretty to have friends or you have to have a boyfriend to be cool... and that's kind of stupid..." Interestingly, in phrasing this resistance, she acknowledged her own susceptibility to the rhetoric. In other conversations these girls expressed aversion to the concept of homosexuality and distress at the idea of other students identifying themselves as gay or lesbian.

One of these girls, Lila, was very reflective about the homophobia that was rampant in the school, and she talked about this during a more directed discussion with me and a male friend of hers, James. Lila was clearly struggling with her sexuality and was conflicted about how to cope with her peer environment.

LILA: A lot of people at this school think that like I'm only into everything because I want attention. But it's really not that way. One of my friends and I, in order to help me dump my boyfriend, we pretended to be lesbians. You know? (*To James*) Remember?
JAMES: Oh, yeah, yeah, yeah.
LILA: So that went on for about a week, and then we were like, oh it's just a joke, we were just trying to get rid of my boyfriend, you know, and people at school are still keeping it up.... There was this guy who like came up to me last week and said, "Why don't you leave our school so that we can get the scum out of here? Why don't you go to another school and stop polluting ours?" Some guy punched me six times and threw me on the ground.

ME: Hmm.

LILA: Although, I didn't really care, because you know, "Oh, no! He called me a dyke! I'm going to die!" and he's really mad at me because I didn't react. I mean, he calls me a lesbian and then walks away. I'm like, "Oh, no! I'm gonna die!"

Lila was derisive of the boy's bigotry, yet she was careful to couch her experience in terms of having "pretended" to be a lesbian. Students were open in their rejection of homosexuality and their need to position themselves in the heterosexual mainstream. In order to bolster this positioning, they chose role models whom they considered to epitomize femininity in terms of the heterosexual ideal.

Iconic femininity. At both schools, the girls made frequent references to media figures who served as emblems or icons of ideal femininity. At East Middle School these included Whitney Houston, Toni Braxton, Brandy, and Selena. The latter was a somewhat controversial figure, however. The movie about Selena's life had recently appeared in theaters, and most of the girls had seen it. Lourdes, a member of the "prep" group, said the two role models in her life were "my mom and Selena": "My mom because she gave everything in her life to make sure I have what I have. And Selena because she was beautiful and strong."

However, Selena did not fare as well under the scrutiny of the "gangsta" girls:

NYDIA: My mama wanted me to get a shirt like she had. But I didn't want to wear it. I didn't want to look like her. She ugly, with her big fake lips and her fake hair."
(Other girls laugh.)
VANESSA: I heard she had a fake booty.
NYDIA: Yeah. My cousin told me there was this show, and when she turned around she had to grab her butt 'cause it was falling off.... But in the movie they got that other girl who looks like her. You know how they say people can come back from the dead?

Well, I think she came back from the dead with a different name. But it's her.

(Parenthetically, it should be observed that the students at East Middle School were sometimes confused about media in terms of chronology, life, and death. Many of the students were convinced that the rapper Tupac Shakur had not died because a film in which he appeared was released after the reports of his death. To them, this indicated that his death was faked, and that he was alive because the film was playing and he was in it.)

The East Middle School girls were critical and mocking of many white celebrities, especially the stars of television shows aimed at teenage girls. "I just don't like it that she changes her clothes and she does her hair and her makeup all perfect even though she's fighting monsters," Rosa said of *Buffy the Vampire Slayer.* But they took nonwhite singers and actresses more seriously and were vocal in their admiration of them.

At West Middle School the girls admired Claire Danes, Tyra Banks, Neve Campbell, and, above all, Drew Barrymore. Several of the popular girls cited her as their "hero":

JENNY: She's really pretty, she's an actress. I want to be an actress when I grow up.
TARA: I really like Drew Barrymore. She ditched her mother when she was 15. She's real independent.

They seemed unaware of Barrymore's declared bisexuality, and it can only be speculated how a knowledge of it might have altered their admiration of her or challenged their biases.

The "regular girls" tended to be more critical of the models who appeared in teen magazines and the rhetoric accompanying their images, but they did admire certain film and television actresses, including Melissa Joan Hart and Claire Danes.

All of the women who were chosen by the girls as role models or heroines exemplified media and sociocultural ideals of beauty; and they were admired by the girls specifically for their beauty, although other characteristics were sometimes mentioned as reasons for revering them. But none of the girls professed to admire women who had not been identified in the mass media as being physically beautiful according to dominant standards.

Conclusions

The girls' overall use of the mass media to reconstruct ideals of heterosexuality with regard to physical appearance, the goals of marriage and maternity, and active homophobia reveal a fairly direct appropriation of the dominant ideology of femininity. Race and class factors impacted the ways in which the parameters of ideal femininity were defined; but in general, the peer context was one in which emergent gender identity was consolidated via constant reference to acceptable sociocultural standards of femininity and sexuality.

This conformity was not seamless; pockets of resistance occurred in peer group discussions, but when they did, their functioning was paradoxical. In the West Middle School girls' dialogue about eating disorders, or the "gangsta" girls' rejection of the prospect of early motherhood, the privileged voices in the discussion shut out some of the participants in such a way that their personal struggles with these issues could not be recognized. Jonquil's history of eating disorders, Maria's sexual activity that culminated in pregnancy a few months later, Lila's sexual ambiguity could not be given full voice. Thus, the peer group served to achieve ideological closure in terms of how issues of gender and power could be addressed.

This functioning adds a new dimension to the studies that have looked at girls' individual responses to media texts. Duke and Kreshel found that girls "were not as uniformly vulnerable to media messages concerning the feminine ideal as was expected."[29] Frazer found girls to be aware of the distinctions between magazine portrayals and real life, although she did point out that the conventions and "registers" of discourse constrained what the girls said.[30] Numerous theorists have posited a fluid and mobile relationship between mass media and the receiver; especially in the cultural studies literature, it is supposed that readers are able to reappropriate the meanings of messages according to their various life circumstances.[31] It does appear that girls *on their own* may be somewhat more able to critically examine and deconstruct media messages than in the peer group context. Therefore, the role of the adolescent peer group is a complex one: the group dynamic serves to mask and neutralize individual experiences of social and cultural processes. The group is a microcosm for the creation of social structure via the renegotiation of dominant and oppositional ideological positions.

In the peer groups in this study, surface levels of resistance cloaked some of the participants' more private and interiorized struggles with dominant codes of femininity. The group discourse provided a text that could be analyzed, but the research cited earlier in this essay, as well as information gathered by this researcher from sources outside of the peer groups, point to the existence of subtexts that tended to be suppressed by the group process. Some evidence of this kind of suppression was provided by the West Middle School girls' insistence that they were individuals when their outward behaviors indicated complete capitulation to the norms of the group. Another mark of such masking was the conspicuous absence of teen pregnancy in the peer discourse at West Middle School; it was a taboo topic in peer discussion, so if a girl at West had undergone a pregnancy, her experience would be completely invalidated by the group's tacit doctrine of denial.

Similarly, eating disorders were not openly discussed at East Middle School, yet the girls' casual references to starving themselves in one conversation indicated that body image issues were of more concern than was openly evidenced. Thompson points out that eating disorders among Latina and African-American women tend to be severe because they are not taken seriously or diagnosed quickly.[32] The girls at East Middle School were uncritical and unreflexive about the norm of thinness to which they subscribed.

Thus, this research indicates that while race and class were differentiators of girls' socialization and concomitant media use, the differences highlighted the ways in which their different cultures functioned to uphold different aspects of dominant ideologies of femininity.

Watkins suggests that minority youth in particular have generated cultural practices of resistance that have grown out of their social marginalization.[33] Such resistance was not obviously manifested among the girls at East and West Middle Schools, yet the potential for resistance was an ever-present subcurrent. At West Middle School, for example, the peer group discourse among the "regular girls" was more resistant than that of the "preps." Because peer acceptance is of paramount importance in girls' culture,[34] a real subversion of dominant norms *could* certainly happen in a peer group where that was part of the group identity. It is possible that the peer group's social standing with respect to other groups would influence the degree of resistance expressed in the group. A larger study in which more, and more diverse, peer groups were observed would be needed to further investigate these phenomena.

It could be argued that the girls' observed tendency to accept dominant norms of femininity was related to the fact that most of the subjects were honors students – academic achievers who conformed to social expectations in every aspect of their lives. Yet an adherence to codes of what might be called "hegemonic femininity" was also evident in the behaviors of the "gangsta"

group from East Middle School, who were considered to be at risk of dropping out, delinquency, and other "antisocial" behaviors. In fact, they demonstrated even more interest in costuming, makeup, beautification, and maternity than did the more "prosocial" peer groupings. It can be tentatively concluded from these data, then, that the peer group generally serves to consolidate dominant constructions of gender and sexuality.

However, race and class factors appear to intercede in the process of meaning-making, within as well as around the peer group context. The predominantly white, upper-middle-class students at West Middle School were primary targets of advertising-driven media, and they concomitantly paid significantly more attention to the mass media than did students at East Middle School. Nonetheless, media were used to shore up systems of belief held by students at both schools.

Hermes has observed that "media use and interpretation exist by grace of unruly and unpredictable, but in retrospect understandable and interesting choices and activities of readers."[35] Among the girls in this study, a key strategy for blending into the peer group involved participating in activities that marked the limits of acceptable femininity; however, these were deployed within their racial, cultural, and class environments. Deviance from normative sexuality was a means of identifying the social outcast; conformity was a way of bonding with the group, and mass media were used as instruments in the bonding process.

These findings have multiple implications. First, they establish the centrality of mass media in adolescent society and underscore the links between socialization into dominant norms of sexuality and consumer culture. The teenagers in this study were hyperaware of the need to use the media to find their foothold in the group. Their uses of the media were more than discursive: consumption of the necessary products that openly established their acceptance and understanding of sexual norms was a necessary part of peer interaction. Thus socialization into femininity was linked to the multimillion dollar fashion, beauty, and diet industries that thrive on women consumers. As McCracken has pointed out, "the material object that advertising tries to sell is never sufficient in itself: it must be validated, often only in fantasy, by additional meanings."[36] The peer group is the context in which these additional meanings are given authority.

Second, perhaps more important, it makes clear that the peer group must be taken into account in the contemplation of interventions or counteractions against the mediated norms that play into girls' gendered behaviors. Such interventions tend to be "top-down," devised and administered by adults; yet the significance of the peer group in girls' social lives indicates that the most effective resistant practices would germinate and take root within the peer group. In this study, the peer group was shown to be a training ground where girls learned to use the mass media to acquire the skills of ideal femininity, but it was also a place where rejection of these norms could sometimes be voiced. This study points to a relationship between peer attitudes toward mediated constructions of female beauty, body type, motherhood, and homosexuality, and teenage girls' real-life experiences of eating disorders, teenage pregnancy, depression related to sexual orientation, and problems with self-esteem. All of these issues engage questions of power, gender, race, and class.

While girls individually have some sense of the social environment that operates to regulate their expressions of gender and sexuality, and while they may try on an individual level to resist damaging normative constructions of femininity, the peer group dynamic tends to mitigate against such resistance. Effective interventions for girls must work within the peer context to try to encourage more nuanced and less univocal conceptualizations of normative femininity. Beyond this, the peer group's relationship to broader levels of society must be taken into account. Interventions such as media literacy efforts will not be effective unless they are sensitive to issues of race, class, and culture; a recognition of institutionalized networks of power that constrain and limit girls' autonomy is necessary before strategies for resistance and emancipation can be devised.

NOTES

1 Lyn Mikel Brown and Carol Gilligan, *Meeting at the Crossroads: Women's Psychology and Girls' Development* (New York: Ballantine Books, 1992).

2 Peggy Orenstein, *Schoolgirls: Young Women, Self-Esteem, and the Confidence Gap* (New York: Doubleday, 1994); Mary Pipher, *Reviving Ophelia: Saving the Selves of Adolescent Girls* (New York: Ballantine, 1994); Lori Stern, "Disavowing the Self in Female Adolescence," in *Women, Girls and Psychotherapy: Reframing Resistance*, ed. Carol Gilligan, Annie G. Rogers, and Deborah L. Tolman (New York: Haworth Press, 1991), 105–17.

3 Margaret Duffy and Micheal Gotcher, "Crucial Advice on How to Get the Guy: The Rhetorical Vision of Power and Seduction in the Teen Magazine *YM*," *Journal of Communication Inquiry* 21 (spring 1996): 32–48; Lisa Duke and Peggy J. Kreshel, "Negotiating Femininity: Girls in Early Adolescence Read Teen Magazines," *Journal of Communication Inquiry* 22 (January 1998): 48–71; Meenakshi Gigi Durham, "Dilemmas of Desire: Representations of Adolescent Sexuality in Two Teen Magazines," *Youth and Society* 29 (March 1998): 369–89; Ellen McCracken, *Decoding Women's Magazines: From Mademoiselle to Ms.* (New York: St. Martin's Press, 1993); Angela McRobbie, "Jackie: An Ideology of Adolescent Femininity," in *Mass Communication Review Yearbook* vol. 4, ed. Ellen Wartella, D. Charles Whitney, and Sven Windahl (Beverly Hills, CA: Sage, 1983), 251–71; Angela McRobbie, "Shut Up and Dance: Youth Culture and Changing Modes of Femininity," in *Postmodernism and Popular Culture*, ed. Angela McRobbie (London: Routledge, 1994), 155–76; Kate Pierce, "A Feminist Theoretical Perspective on the Socialization of Teenage Girls through

Seventeen Magazine," *Sex Roles* 23 (1990): 491–500; Kate Pierce, "Socialization of Teenage Girls through Teen-Magazine Fiction: The Making of a New Woman or an Old Lady?" *Sex Roles* 29 (1993): 59–68.

4 Brown and Gilligan, *Meeting at the Crossroads*; Pipher, *Reviving Ophelia*.

5 Orenstein, *Schoolgirls*; American Association of University Women Educational Foundation, *How Schools Shortchange Girls* (Washington, DC: American Association of University Women, 1992).

6 Susan Bordo, *Unbearable Weight: Feminism, Western Culture, and the Body* (Berkeley: University of California Press, 1993); Naomi Wolf, *The Beauty Myth: How Images of Beauty Are Used Against Women* (New York: Anchor, 1991).

7 Sue Lees, *Sugar and Spice: Sexuality and Adolescent Girls* (Harmondsworth, England: Penguin, 1993); Naomi Wolf, *Promiscuities* (New York: Random House, 1997).

8 Jill McLean Taylor, Carol Gilligan, and Amy M. Sullivan, *Between Voice and Silence: Women and Girls, Race and Relationship* (Cambridge, MA: Harvard University Press, 1995); Becky W. Thompson, *A Hunger So Wide and Deep: American Women Speak on Eating Problems* (Minneapolis: University of Minnesota Press, 1994).

9 Judith Rich Harris, "Where Is the Child's Environment? A Group Socialization Theory of Development," *Psychological Review* 102 (1995): 458–89.

10 Donald F. Roberts, "Adolescents and the Mass Media: From 'Leave It to Beaver' to 'Beverly Hills 90210,'" *Teachers College Record* 94 (spring 1993): 629.

11 Victor C. Strasburger, *Adolescents and the Media: Medical and Psychological Impact* (Thousand Oaks, CA: Sage, 1995).

12 Hershel D. Thornburg, "Adolescent Sources of Information on Sex," *Journal of School Health* 51 (April 1981): 274–7; David Pearl, Lorraine Bouthilet, and Joyce Lazar, eds., *Television and Behavior: Ten Years of Scientific Progress and Implications for the Eighties* (Rockville, MD: National Institute of Mental Health, 1982); Louis Harris and Associates, *Attitudes about Television, Sex, and Contraception Advertising* (New York: Planned Parenthood Association of America, 1987).

13 Jane D. Brown and Susan F. Newcomer, "Television Viewing and Adolescents' Sexual Behavior," *Journal of Homosexuality* 21 (January/February 1991): 77–92.

14 Bradley S. Greenberg, Cynthia Stanley, Michelle Siemicki, Carrie Heeter, Anne Soderman, and Renato Linsangan, "Sex Content on Soaps and Prime-Time Television Series Most Viewed by Adolescents," in *Media, Sex, and the Adolescent*, ed. Bradley S. Greenberg, Jane D. Brown, and Nancy Buerkel-Rothfuss (Cresskill, NJ: Hampton Press, 1993), 29–44; Bradley S. Greenberg, Michelle Siemicki, Sandra Dorfman, Carrie Heeter, Cynthia Stanley, Anne Soderman, and Renato Linsangan, "Sex Content in R-Rated Films Viewed by Adolescents," in *Media, Sex, and the Adolescent*, ed. Greenberg, Brown, and Buerkel-Rothfuss, 45–58.

15 Duffy and Gotcher, "Crucial Advice on How to Get the Guy"; Durham, "Dilemmas of Desire"; McCracken, *Decoding Women's Magazines*.

16 Melissa A. Milkie, "Social World Approach to Cultural Studies: Mass Media and Gender in the Adolescent Peer Group," *Journal of Contemporary Ethnography* 23 (October 1994): 354–80; James L. Peterson, Kristin A. Moore, and Frank F. Furstenberg, "Television Viewing and Early Initiation of Sexual Intercourse: Is There A Link?" *Journal of Homosexuality* 21 (January/February 1991): 93–118.

17 Carole R. Beal, *Boys and Girls: The Development of Gender Roles* (New York: McGraw-Hill, 1994); Orenstein, *Schoolgirls*; Pipher, *Reviving Ophelia*.

18 Angela McRobbie, "Different, Youthful Subjectivities: Toward A Cultural Sociology of Youth," in *Postmodernism and Popular Culture*, ed. Angela McRobbie (London: Routledge, 1994), 193.

19 For example, Elizabeth Frazer, "Teenage Girls Reading Jackie," *Media Culture and Society* 9 (October 1987): 407–25.

20 Jane D. Brown, Anne Barton White, and Lia Nikopoulou, "Disinterest, Intrigue, Resistance: Early Adolescent Girls' Use of Sexual Media Content," in *Media, Sex, and the Adolescent*, ed. Greenberg, Brown, and Buerkel-Rothfuss, 177–95.

21 Duke and Kreshel, "Negotiating Femininity," 55.

22 The names of all schools, students, social workers, teachers, and places have been changed so as to preserve anonymity and confidentiality.

23 The word "Latino" was used to describe the ethnicity of a group of students who were mainly US-born Mexican Americans; the group also included students of Puerto Rican, Cuban, and other Central and South American origin. Some of these students were mixed-race and self-identified in ways other than according to the school's classification system. In this essay the corollary term "Mexicanos" is used to designate first-generation Mexican immigrants to the United States. This term was used by the schoolchildren at East Middle School to distinguish second- and third-generation students from new immigrants.

24 Kevin G. Barnhurst and Ellen Wartella, "Newspapers and Citizenship: Young Adults' Subjective Experience of Newspapers," *Critical Studies in Mass Communication* 8 (June 1991): 195–209; Kevin G. Barnhurst and Ellen Wartella, "Young Citizens, American TV Newscasts, and the Collective Memory," *Critical Studies in Mass Communication* 15 (September 1998): 279–305; Leo Bogart, *Commercial Culture: The Media System and the Public Interest* (New York: Oxford University Press, 1995).

25 Sandra Lee Bartky, "Foucault, Femininity, and the Modernization of Patriarchal Power," in *Feminism and Foucault: Reflections on Resistance*, ed. Irene Diamond and Lee Quinby (Boston: Northeastern University Press, 1988), 64.

26 See Duke and Kreshel, "Negotiating Femininity."

27 Bordo, *Unbearable Weight*.

28 July Siebecker, "Women's Oppression and the Obsession with Thinness," in *Women: Images and Realities*, ed. Amy Kesselman, Lily D. McNair, and Nancy Schniedewind (Mountainview, CA: Mayfield, 1995), 107.

29 Duke and Kreshel, "Negotiating Femininity."

30 Frazer, "Teenage Girls Reading Jackie."

31 Ien Ang, *Watching "Dallas": Soap Opera and the Melodramatic Imagination* (London: Methuen, 1985); John Fiske, "British Cultural Studies and Television," in *Channels of Discourse, Reassembled*, ed. Robert C. Allen (Chapel Hill: University of North Carolina Press, 1992), 284–326; Stuart Hall, "Encoding/Decoding," in *Culture, Media, Language: Working Papers in Cultural Studies, 1972–79*, ed. Stuart Hall, Dorothy Hobson, Andrew Lowe, and Paul Willis (London: Hutchinson, 1980), 128–38; David Morley, *The Nationwide Audience: Structure and Decoding* (London: Hutchinson, 1980).

32 Thompson, *A Hunger So Wide and Deep*.

33 S. Craig Watkins, *Representing: Hip-Hop Culture and the Production of Black Cinema* (Chicago: University of Chicago Press, 1998).

34 Griffiths, *Adolescent Girls and Their Friends*; Brown and Gilligan, *Meeting at the Crossroads*; Evans and Eder, "No Exit."

35 Joke Hermes, *Reading Women's Magazines: An Analysis of Everyday Media Use* (Cambridge, England: Polity Press), 25.

36 McCracken, *Decoding Women's Magazines*, 67.

23 Becoming 100 Percent Straight

Michael A. Messner

Many years ago I read some psychological studies that argued that even for self-identified heterosexuals it is a natural part of their development to have gone through "bisexual" or even "homosexual" stages of life. When I read this, it seemed theoretically reasonable, but did not ring true in my experience. I have always been, I told myself, 100 percent heterosexual! The group process of analyzing my own autobiographical stories challenged the concept I had developed of myself, and also shed light on the way in which the institutional context of sport provided a context for the development of my definition of myself as "100 percent straight." Here is one of the stories.

When I was in the ninth grade I played on a "D" basketball team, set up especially for the smallest of high school boys. Indeed, though I was pudgy with baby fat, I was a short 5'2", still prepubescent with no facial hair and a high voice that I artificially tried to lower. The first day of practice I was immediately attracted to a boy I'll call Timmy, because he looked like the boy who played in the *Lassie* TV show. Timmy was short, with a high voice, like me. And like me, he had no facial hair yet. Unlike me, he was very skinny. I liked Timmy right away, and soon we were together a lot. I noticed things about him that I didn't notice about other boys: he said some words a certain way, and it gave me pleasure to try to talk like him. I remember liking the way the light hit his boyish, nearly hairless body. I thought about him when we weren't together. He was in the school band, and at the football games I'd squint to see where he was in the mass of uniforms. In short, though I wasn't conscious of it at the time, I was infatuated with Timmy – I had a crush on him. Later that basketball season, I decided – for no reason that I could really articulate then – that I hated Timmy. I aggressively rejected him, began to make fun of him around other boys. He was, we all agreed, a geek. He was a faggot.

Three years later Timmy and I were both on the varsity basketball team, but had hardly spoken a word to each other since we were freshmen. Both of us now had lower voices, had grown to around 6 feet tall, and we both shaved, at least a bit. But Timmy was a skinny, somewhat stigmatized reserve on the team, while I was the team captain and starting point guard. But I wasn't so happy or secure about this. I'd always dreamed of dominating games, of being the hero. Halfway through my senior season, however, it became clear that I was not a star, and I figured I knew why. I was not aggressive enough.

I had always liked the beauty of the fast break, the perfectly executed pick and roll play between two players, and especially the long 20-foot shot that touched nothing but the bottom of the net. But I hated and feared the sometimes brutal contact under the basket. In fact, I stayed away from the rough fights for rebounds and was mostly a perimeter player, relying on my long shots or my passes to more aggressive teammates under the basket. But now it became apparent to me that time was running out in my quest for greatness: I needed to change my game, and fast. I decided one day before practice that I was gonna get aggressive. While practicing one of our standard plays, I passed the ball to a teammate, and then ran to the spot at which I was to set a pick on a defender. I knew that one could sometimes get away with setting a face-up screen on a player, and then as he makes contact with you, roll your back to him and plant your elbow hard in his stomach. The beauty of this move is that your own body "roll" makes the elbow look like an accident. So I decided to try this move. I approached the defensive player, Timmy, rolled, and planted my elbow deeply into his solar plexus. Air exploded audibly from Timmy's mouth, and he crumbled to the floor momentarily.

Play went on as though nothing had happened, but I felt bad about it. Rather than making me feel better, it made me feel guilty and weak. I had to admit to myself why I'd chosen Timmy as the target against whom to test out my new aggression. He was the skinniest and weakest player on the team.

At the time, I hardly thought about these incidents, other than to try to brush them off as incidents that made me feel extremely uncomfortable. Years later I can now interrogate this as a sexual story, and as a gender story unfolding within the context of the heterosexualized and masculinized institution of sport. Examining my story in light of research conducted by Alfred Kinsey a half-century ago, I can recognize in myself what Kinsey saw as a very common fluidity and changeability of sexual desire over the life-course. Put simply, Kinsey found that large numbers of adult "heterosexual" men had previously, as adolescents and young adults, experienced sexual desire for males. A surprisingly large number of these men had experienced sexual contact to the point of orgasm with other males during adolescence or early adulthood. Similarly, my story invited me to consider what is commonly called the "Freudian theory of bisexuality." Sigmund Freud shocked the post-Victorian world by suggesting that all people go through a stage, early in life, when they are attracted to people of the same sex.[1] Adult experiences, Freud argued, eventually led most people to shift their sexual desire to what he called an appropriate "love object" – a person of the opposite sex. I also considered my experience in light of what lesbian feminist author Adrienne Rich called the institution of compulsory heterosexuality. Perhaps the extremely high levels of homophobia that are often endemic in

boys' and men's organized sports led me to deny and repress my own homoerotic desire through a direct and overt rejection of Timmy, through homophobic banter with male peers, and the resultant stigmatization of the feminized Timmy. Eventually I considered my experience in the light of what radical theorist Herbert Marcuse called the sublimation of homoerotic desire into an aggressive, violent act as serving to construct a clear line of demarcation between self and other. Sublimation, according to Marcuse, involves the driving underground, into the unconsious, of sexual desires that might appear dangerous due to their socially stigmatized status. But sublimation involves more than simple repression into the unconscious. It involves a transformation of sexual desire into something else – often into aggressive and violent acting out toward others. These acts clarify the boundaries between oneself and others and therefore lessen any anxieties that might be attached to the repressed homoerotic desire.

Importantly, in our analysis of my story, the memory group went beyond simply discussing the events in psychological terms. The story did perhaps suggest some deep psychological processes at work, but it also revealed the importance of social context – in this case, the context of the athletic team. In short, my rejection of Timmy and the joining with teammates to stigmatize him in ninth grade stands as an example of what sociologist R. W. Connell calls a moment of engagement with hegemonic masculinity, where I actively took up the male group's task of constructing heterosexual/masculine identities in the context of sport. The elbow in Timmy's gut three years later can be seen as a punctuation mark that occurred precisely because of my fears that I might be failing in this goal.

It is helpful, I think, to compare my story with gay and lesbian "coming out" stories in sport. Though we have a few lesbian and bisexual coming out stories among women athletes, there are very few from gay males. Tom Waddell, who as a closeted gay man finished sixth in the decathlon in the 1968 Olympics, later came out and started the Gay Games, an athletic and cultural festival that draws tens of thousands of people every four years. When I interviewed Tom Waddell over a decade ago about his sexual identity and athletic career, he made it quite clear that for many years sports was his closet:

> When I was a kid, I was tall for my age, and was very thin and very strong. And I was usually faster than most other people. But I discovered rather early that I liked gymnastics and I liked dance. I was very interested in being a ballet dancer...[but] something became obvious to me right away – that male ballet dancers were effeminate, that they were what most people would call faggots. And I thought I just couldn't handle that...I was totally closeted and very concerned about being male. This was the fifties, a terrible time to live, and everything was stacked against me. Anyway, I realized that I had to do something to protect my image of myself as a male – because at that time homosexuals were thought of primarily as men who wanted to be women. And so I threw myself into athletics – I played football, gymnastics, track and field...I was a jock – that's how I was viewed, and I was comfortable with that.

Tom Waddell was fully conscious of entering sports and constructing a masculine/heterosexual athletic identity precisely because he feared being revealed as gay. It was clear to him, in the context of the 1950s, that being known as gay would undercut his claims to the status of manhood. Thus, though he described the athletic closet as "hot and stifling," he remained there until several years after his athletic retirement. He even knowingly played along with locker room discussions about sex and women as part of his "cover."

> I wanted to be viewed as male, otherwise I would be a dancer today. I wanted the male, macho image of an athlete. So I

was protected by a very hard shell. I was clearly aware of what I was doing...I often felt compelled to go along with a lot of locker room garbage because I wanted that image – and I know a lot of others who did too.

Like my story, Waddell's points to the importance of the athletic institution as a context in which peers mutually construct and reconstruct narrow definitions of masculinity. Heterosexuality is considered to be a rock-solid foundation of this concept of masculinity. But unlike my story, Waddell's may invoke a dramaturgical analysis.[2] He seemed to be consciously "acting" to control and regulate others' perceptions of him by constructing a public "front stage" persona that differed radically from what he believed to be his "true" inner self. My story, in contrast, suggests a deeper, less consciously strategic repression of my homoerotic attraction. Most likely, I was aware on some level of the dangers of such feelings, and was escaping the risks, disgrace, and rejection that would likely result from being different. For Waddell, the decision to construct his identity largely within sport was to step into a fiercely heterosexual/masculine closet that would hide what he saw as his "true" identity. In contrast, I was not so much stepping into a "closet" that would hide my identity; rather, I was stepping out into an entire world of heterosexual privilege. My story also suggests how a threat to the promised privileges of hegemonic masculinity – my failure as an athlete – might trigger a momentary sexual panic that can lay bare the constructedness, indeed, the instability of the heterosexual/masculine identity.

In either case, Waddell's or mine, we can see how, as young male athletes, heterosexuality and masculinity was not something we "were," but something we were doing. It is significant, I think, that although each of us was "doing heterosexuality," neither of us was actually "having sex" with women (though one of us desperately wanted to). This underscores a point made by some recent theorists that heterosexuality should not be thought of simply as sexual acts between women and men. Rather, heterosexuality is a constructed identity, a performance, and an institution that is not necessarily linked to sexual acts. Though for one of us it was more conscious than for the other, we were both "doing heterosexuality" as an ongoing practice through which we sought to do two things:

- avoid stigma, embarrassment, ostracism, or perhaps worse if we were even suspected of being gay;
- link ourselves into systems of power, status, and privilege that appear to be the birth-right of "real men" (i.e., males who are able to compete successfully with other males in sport, work, and sexual relations with women).

In other words, each of us actively scripted our own sexual and gender performances, but these scripts were constructed within the constraints of a socially organized (institutionalized) system of power and pleasure.

Questions for Future Research

As I prepared to tell this sexual story publicly to my colleagues at the sport studies conference, I felt extremely nervous. Part of the nervousness was due to the fact that I knew some of them would object to my claim that telling personal stories can be a source of sociological insights. But a larger part of the reason for my nervousness was due to the fact that I was revealing something very personal about my sexuality in such a public way. Most of us are not accustomed to doing this, especially in the context of a professional conference. But I had learned long ago, especially from feminist women scholars, and from gay and lesbian scholars, that biography is linked to history. Part of "normal" academic discourse has been to hide "the personal" (including the

fact that the researchers are themselves people with values, feelings, and, yes, biases) behind a carefully constructed facade of "objectivity." Rather than trying to hide or be ashamed of one's subjective experience of the world, I was challenging myself to draw on my experience of the world as a resource. Not that I should trust my experience as the final word on "reality." White, heterosexual males like me have made the mistake for centuries of calling their own experience "objectivity," and then punishing anyone who does not share their worldview by casting them as "deviant." Instead, I hope to use my experience as an example of how those of us who are in dominant sexual/racial/gender/class categories can get a new perspective on the "constructedness" of our identities by juxtaposing our subjective experiences against the recently emerging worldviews of gay men and lesbians, women, and people of color.

Finally, I want to stress that in juxtaposition neither my own nor Tom Waddell's story sheds much light on the question of why some individuals "become gay" while others "become" heterosexual or bisexual. Instead, I should like to suggest that this is a dead-end question, and that there are far more important and interesting questions to be asked:

- How has heterosexuality, as an institution and as an enforced group practice, constrained and limited all of us – gay, straight, and bi?
- How has the institution of sport been an especially salient institution for the social construction of heterosexual masculinity?
- Why is it that when men play sports they are almost always automatically granted masculine status, and thus assumed to be heterosexual, while when women play sports, questions are raised about their "femininity" and sexual orientation?

These kinds of questions aim us toward an analysis of the workings of power within institutions – including the ways that these workings of power shape and constrain our identities and relationships – and point us toward imagining alternative social arrangements that are less constraining for everyone.

NOTES

1   The fluidity and changeability of sexual desire over the life-course is now more obvious in evidence from prison and military populations, and single-sex boarding schools. The theory of bisexuality is evident, for example, in childhood crushes on same-sex primary schoolteachers.
2   Dramaturgical analysis, associated with Erving Goffman, uses the theater and performance to develop an analogy with everyday life.

REFERENCES

Haug, Frigga (1987) *Female Sexualization: A Collective Work of Memory*, London: Verso.

Lenskyj, Helen (1986) *Out of Bounds: Women, Sport and Sexuality*, Toronto: Women's Press.

——(1997) "No fear? Lesbians in sport and physical education," *Women in Sport and Physical Activity Journal* 6 (2): 7–22.

Messner, Michael A. (1992) *Power at Play: Sports and the Problem of Masculinity*, Boston: Beacon Press.

——(1994) "Gay athletes and the Gay Games: in interview with Tom Waddell," in M. A. Messner and D. F. Sabo (eds.) *Sex, Violence and Power in Sports: Rethinking Masculinity*, Freedom, CA: The Crossing Press, pp. 113–19.

Pronger, Brian (1990) *The Arena of Masculinity: Sports, Homosexuality, and the Meaning of Sex*, New York: St. Martin's Press.

24 Fantasy Islands: Exploring the Demand for Sex Tourism

Julia O'Connell Davidson and Jacqueline Sanchez Taylor

In a useful review of prostitution cross-culturally and historically, Laurie Shrage observes that "one thing that stands out but stands unexplained is that a large percentage of sex customers seek (or sought) sex workers whose racial, national, or class identities are (or were) different from their own" (Shrage 1994: 142). She goes on to suggest that the demand for African, Asian, and Latin American prostitutes by white Western men may "be explained in part by culturally produced racial fantasies regarding the sexuality of these women" and that these fantasies may be related to "socially formed perceptions regarding the sexual and moral purity of white women" (ibid: 48–50). Kempadoo also draws attention to the "over-representation of women of different nationalities and ethnicities, and the hierarchies of race and color within the [international sex] trade" and observes, "That sex industries today depend upon the eroticization of the ethnic and cultural Other suggests we are witnessing a contemporary form of exoticism which sustains postcolonial and post-cold war relations of power and dominance" (Kempadoo 1995: 75–6).

This chapter represents an attempt to build on such insights. Drawing on our research with both male and female Western heterosexual sex tourists in the Caribbean,[1] it argues that their sexual taste for "Others" reflects not so much a wish to engage in any specific sexual practice as a desire for an extraordinarily high degree of control over the management of self and others as sexual, racialized, and engendered beings. This desire, and the Western sex tourist's power

to satiate it, can only be explained through reference to power relations and popular discourses that are simultaneously gendered, racialized, and economic.

White Western Men's Sex Tourism

Empirical research on sex tourism to Southeast Asia has fairly consistently produced a portrait of Western male heterosexual sex tourists as men whose desire for the Other is the flip side of dissatisfaction with white Western women, including white Western prostitute women. Lee, for example, explores the demand for sex tourism as a quest for racially fantasized male power, arguing that this is at least in part a backlash against the women's movement in the West: "With an increasingly active global feminist movement, male-controlled sexuality (or female passivity) appears to be an increasingly scarce resource. The travel advertisements are quite explicit about what is for sale: docility and submission" (Lee 1991: 90; see also Jeffreys 1997). Western sex tourists' fantasies of "docile" and "willing" Asian women are accompanied, as Kruhse-Mount Burton (1995: 196) notes, by "a desexualization of white women...who are deemed to be spoiled, grasping and, above all, unwilling or inferior sexual partners." These characteristics are also attributed to white prostitute women. The sex tourists interviewed by Seabrook (1997: 3) compared Thai prostitutes "very favorably with the more mechanistic and functional behavior of most Western sex workers." Kruhse-Mount Burton states that where many

Australian participants in sex holidays criticized prostitutes in Australia "for being emotionally and sexually cold and for making little effort to please, or to disguise the commercial nature of the interaction," they stressed "the warmth, affection, femininity, youth and beauty of Asian prostitutes, combined with an aptitude for disguising the mercenary aspect of the arrangement" (Kruhse-Mount Burton 1995: 193–4).

Our own interview work suggests that Western male heterosexual sex tourists to the Caribbean typically share these attitudes and beliefs – a finding that is unsurprising given that many have also been prostitute users in Southeast Asia, either as tourists or as members of the armed forces. They often believe that Western women enjoy excessive powers in relation to men. The following extract from an interview with an American sex tourist and an American expatriate in the Dominican Republic in 1998 illustrates just how bitter such men can be about Western women's (perceived) encroachment on men's territory and traditional authority:

EXPATRIATE: I pay $1,100 child support a month [to his American ex-wife] ... 17 percent of your gross income for one child she gets, 25 percent for two, 33 percent for three. I've no idea what happens to men who have four kids.... Women's lib in America in the United States has killed marriage in America for any man who has brains....I wouldn't even marry a rich woman....[In the Dominican Republic] they're raised different. Women's lib hasn't hit here....

SEX TOURIST: In the States, [women] hire folks with cameras....They go to bed with cameras. If they wake up with a bruise, they take a picture of it. Call it abuse. Possible abuse.

EXPATRIATE: In the United States, if you grab your wife like that, and you yell at her, put a little black blue mark, just a little one, she'll ...

SEX TOURIST: When you've got a goddamn female announcing the NBA basketball game.... These females go into the men's locker rooms, but the males cannot go into the ladies' locker rooms. Most of these girls are dykes anyways.

Our interview work with sex tourists who are or have been domestic prostitute users also lends support to the view that their sex tourism is a means of accessing the gendered power that they feel they lack in the West:

They're not like prostitutes....They stay with you all day....They rub in the sun tan oil, bring us the towel, she even washes your feet. What English tart would do that?...The problem is getting rid of them. Once you've bought them, they stick to you. They even fight with each other over you. It's wicked. *(English sex tourist in the Dominican Republic)*

[Prostitution in Europe and North America is] all businesslike. It's by the hour, like a taxi service, like they've got the meter running....There's no feeling. If I wanted to fuck a rubber doll, I could buy one and inflate it....A prostitute in Europe will never kiss you. In Canada, it's ridiculous. You know, if you go with a prostitute and you don't pay her, you know what? They call it rape. You can be in court on a rape charge. *(Canadian sex tourist in Cuba)*

There is a sense in which Western men's sex tourism can be said "to constitute...a collective behavior oriented toward the restoration of the 'generalized belief' of what it is to be male" (Kruhse-Mount Burton 1995: 201). These are people who, by and large, equate true masculinity with unbridled sexuality over women more generally. Men like this experience the fact that some (though certainly not all) Western women are in a position to take legal action against men who physically abuse them as an infringement of rightful male authority. The fact that many (though again certainly not all) Western prostitutes are in a position to impose their own boundaries on the degree of physical intimacy implied by the prostitution contract (for example by refusing to kiss clients on the mouth or to engage in unprotected penetrative and/or oral sex) and are also in a position to turn down clients' requests to spend the night or a few days with them is likewise experienced as a threat to, or denial of, traditional male identity.

Though we recognize that sex tourism provides Western men with opportunities "to reaffirm, if only temporarily, the idealized version of masculine identity and mode of being," and that in this sense sex tourism provides men with opportunities to manage and control both themselves and others as engendered beings, we want to argue that there is more to the demand for sex tourism than this (ibid: 202). In the remainder of this chapter we therefore interrogate sex tourists' attitudes toward prostitute use, sexuality, gender, and "race" more closely, and further complicate matters by considering white Western women's and black Western men and women's sex tourism to the Caribbean.

Western Sexuality and Prostitute Use

Hartsock observes that there is "a surprising degree of consensus that hostility and domination, as opposed to intimacy and physical pleasure" are central to the social and historical construction of sexuality in the West (Hartsock 1985: 157). Writers in the psychoanalytic tradition suggest that the kind of hostility that is threaded through Western sexual expression reflects an infantile rage and wish for revenge against the separateness of those upon whom we depend. It is, as Stoller puts it, "a state in which one wishes to harm an object," and the harm wished upon objects of sexual desire expresses a craving to strip them of their autonomy, control and separateness – that is, to dehumanize them, since a dehumanized sexual object does not have the power to reject, humiliate or control (Stoller 1986: 4).

The "love object" can be divested of autonomy and objectified in any number of ways, but clearly the prostitute woman, who is in most cultures imagined and socially constructed as an "unnatural" sexual and social Other (a status which is often enshrined in law), provides a conveniently ready-dehumanized sexual object for the client. The commercial nature of the prostitute–client exchange further promises to strip all mutuality and dependency from sexual relations. Because all obligations are discharged through the simple act of payment, there can be no real intimacy and so no terrifying specter of rejection or engulfment by another human being. In theory, then, prostitute use offers a very neat vehicle for the expression of sexual hostility and the attainment of control over self and others as sexual beings. Yet for many prostitute users, there is a fly in the ointment:

> Prostitute women may be socially constructed as Others and *fantasized* as nothing more than objectified sexuality, but in reality, of course, they are human beings. It is only if the prostitute is imagined as stripped of everything bar her sexuality that she can be *completely* controlled by the client's money/powers. But if she were dehumanized to this extent, she would cease to exist as a person.... Most clients appear to pursue a contradiction, namely to control as an object that which cannot be objectified. (*O'Connell Davidson 1998: 161*)

This contradiction is at the root of the complaints clients sometimes voice about Western prostitutes (Graaf et al. 1992; Plumridge and Chetwynd 1997). It is not always enough to buy access to touch and sexually use objectified body parts. Many clients want the prostitute to be a "lover" who makes no claims, a "whore" who has sex for pleasure not money, in short, a person (subject) who can be treated as an object. This reflects, perhaps, deeper inconsistencies in the discourses which surround prostitution and sexuality. The prostitute woman is viewed as acting in a way wholly inconsistent with her gender identity. Her perceived sexual agency degenders her (a woman who takes an impersonal, active, and instrumental approach to sex is not a "real" woman) and dishonors her (she trades in something which is constitutive of her personhood and cannot honorably be sold). The prostitute-using man, by contrast, behaves "in a fashion consistent with the attributes associated with his gender (he is active and sexually predatory, impersonal, and instrumental), and his sexual transgression is thus a minor infraction, since it does not compromise his gender identity" (O'Connell Davidson 1998: 127). A paradox thus emerges:

> The more that men's prostitute use is justified and socially sanctioned through reference to the fiction of biologically determined gender roles and sexuality, the greater the contradiction implicit in prostitution. In order to satisfy their "natural" urges, men must make use of "unnatural" women. *(ibid: 128)*

All of this helps to explain the fact that, even though their sexual interests may be powerfully shaped by a cultural emphasis on hostility and domination, prostitute use holds absolutely no appeal for many Western men.[2] Fantasies of unbridled sexual access to willingly objectified women are not necessarily fantasies of access to prostitute women. Meanwhile, those who do use prostitutes in the West imagine and manage their own prostitute use in a variety of different ways (see O'Connell Davidson 1998). At one extreme are men who are actually quite satisfied with brief and anonymous sexual use of women and teenagers whom they imagine as utterly debased and objectified "dirty whores." (For them, the idea of using a prostitute is erotic in and of itself.) At the other extreme are those who regularly visit the same prostitute woman and construct a fiction of romance or friendship around their use of her, a fiction which helps them to imagine themselves as seen, chosen,

and desired, even as they pay for sex as a commodity. Between these two poles are men who indulge in a range of (often very inventive) practices and fantasies designed to create the illusion of balance between sexual hostility and sexual mutuality that they personally find sexually exciting. How does this relate to the demand for sex tourism?

Let us begin by noting that not all Western male sex tourists subjectively perceive their own sexual practices abroad as a form of prostitute use. This reflects the fact that even within any one country affected by sex tourism, prostitution is not a homogeneous phenomenon in terms of its social organization. In some countries sex tourism has involved the maintenance and development of existing large-scale, highly commoditized sex industries serving foreign military personnel (Truong 1990; Sturdevant and Stoltzfus 1992; Hall 1994). But it has also emerged in locations where no such sex industry existed, for instance, the Gambia, Cuba, and Brazil (Morris-Jarra 1996; Sanchez Taylor 1997; Perio and Thierry 1996). Moreover, even in countries like Thailand and the Philippines, where tourist-related prostitution has been grafted onto an existing, formally organized brothel sector serving military demand, tourist development has *also* been associated with the emergence of an informal prostitution sector (in which prostitutes solicit in hotels, discos, bars, beaches, parks, or streets, often entering into fairly protracted and diffuse transactions with clients).

This in itself gives prostitution in sex tourist resorts a rather different character to that of prostitution in red-light districts in affluent, Western countries. The sense of difference is enhanced by the fact that, in many places, informally arranged prostitution spills over into apparently noncommercial encounters within which tourists who do not self-identify as prostitute users can draw local/migrant persons who do not self-identify as prostitutes into profoundly unequal and exploitative sexual relationships. It also means that sex tourism presents a diverse array of opportunities for sexual gratification, not all of which involve straightforward cash for sex exchanges in brothels or go-go clubs or on the streets, and so provides the sex tourist with a veritable "pic 'n' mix" of ways in which to manage himself as a sexual and engendered being. He can indulge in overt forms of sexual hostility (such as selecting a numbered brothel prostitute from those on display in a bar or brothel for "short time" or buying a cheap, speedy sexual service from one of many street prostitutes), or he can indulge in fantasies of mutuality, picking up a woman/teenager in an ordinary tourist disco, wining and dining and generally simulating romance with her for a day or two and completely denying the commercial basis of the sexual interaction. Or, and many sex tourists do exactly this, he can combine both approaches.

Now it could be argued that, given the fact that Western men are socialized into a view of male sexuality as a powerful, biologically based need for sexual "outlets," the existence of multiple, cheap, and varied sexual opportunities is, in itself, enough to attract large numbers of men to a given holiday resort. However, it is important to recognize the numerous other forms of highly sexualized tourism that could satisfy a wish to indulge in various sexual fantasies and also a desire for control over the self as a sexual and engendered being. Sex tourists could, for example, choose to take part in organized holidays designed to facilitate sexual and romantic encounters between tourists (such as Club 18–30 and other singles holidays), or they could choose to take all-inclusive holidays to resorts such as Hedonism or destinations renowned for promiscuous tourist–tourist sex, such as Ibiza or Cap d'Azur. These latter offer just as many opportunities for anonymous and impersonal sex in a party atmosphere as well as for intense but ultimately brief and noncommitted sexual romances. What they do not offer is the control that comes from paying for sex or the opportunity to indulge

in racialized sexual fantasies, which helps to explain why sex tourists reject them in favor of sexual experience in what they term "Third World" countries. This brings us to questions about the relationship between the construction of "Otherness" and sex tourism.

"Otherness" and Western Men's Sex Tourism

For obvious reasons, sex tourists spend their time in resorts and *barrios* where tourist-related prostitution is widespread. Thus they constantly encounter what appear to them as hedonistic scenes – local "girls" and young men dancing "sensuously," draping themselves over and being fondled by Western tourists, drinking and joking with each other, and so on. Instead of seeing the relationship between these scenes and their own presence in the resort, sex tourists tend to interpret all this as empirical vindication of Western assumptions of "non-Western peoples living in idyllic pleasure, splendid innocence or Paradise-like conditions – as purely sensual, natural, simple and uncorrupted beings" (Kempadoo 1995: 76). Western sex tourists (and this is true of black as well as white informants) say that sex is more "natural" in Third World countries, that prostitution is not really prostitution but a "way of life," that "They" are "at it" all of the time.

This explains how men who are not and would not dream of becoming prostitute users back home can happily practice sex tourism (the "girls" are not really like prostitutes and so they themselves are not really like clients, the prostitution contract is not like the Western prostitution contract and so does not really count as prostitution). It also explains the paranoid obsession with being cheated exhibited by some sex tourists, who comment on their belief that women in certain sex tourist resorts or particular brothels or bars are "getting too commercial" and advise each other how to avoid being "duped" and "exploited" by a "real professional," where to find "brand new girls," and so on (see O'Connell Davidson 1995; Bishop and Robinson 1998).

It also points to the complex interrelations between discourses of gender, "race," and sexuality. To begin with, the supposed naturalness of prostitution in the Third World actually reassures the Western male sex tourist of his racial or cultural superiority. Thus we find that sex tourists continue a traditional Western discourse of travel which rests on the imagined opposition between the "civilized" West and the "barbarous" Other (Grewal 1996: 136; Kempadoo 1996: 76; see also Brace and O'Connell Davidson 1996). In "civilized" countries only "bad" women become prostitutes (they refuse the constraints civilization places upon "good" women in favor of earning "easy money"), but in the Third World (a corrupt and lawless place where people exist in a state of nature), "nice girls" may be driven to prostitution in order to survive ("they have to do it because they've all got kids" or "they're doing it for their families"). In the West, "nice girls" are protected and supported by their menfolk, but in the Third World, "uncivilized" Other men allow (or even demand that) their womenfolk enter prostitution. In interviews, Western male sex tourists contrast their own generosity, humanity, and chivalry against the "failings" of local men, who are imagined as feckless, faithless, wife-beaters, and pimps. Even as prostitute users, Other men are fantasized as inferior moral beings who cheat and mistreat the "girls."

In this we see that sex tourism is not only about sustaining a male identity. For white men it is also about sustaining a *white* identity. Thus, sex tourism can also be understood as a collective behavior oriented toward the restoration of a generalized belief about what it is to be white: to be truly white is to be served, revered, and envied by Others. For the black American male sex tourists we have interviewed, sex tourism appears to affirm a sense of Western-ness and so of inclusion in a privileged

world. Take, for example, the following three statements from a 45-year-old black American sex tourist. He is a New York bus driver and ex-vice cop, a paid-up member of an American-owned sex tourist club, Travel & the Single Male, and he has used prostitutes in Thailand, Brazil, Costa Rica, and the Dominican Republic:

> There's two sides to the countries that I go to. There's the tourist side and then there's the real people, and I make a habit of going to the real people, I see how the real people live, and when I see something like that...I tend to look at the little bit I've got at home and I appreciate it....

> I've always been proud to be an American....I always tip in US dollars when I arrive. I always keep dollars and pesos, because people tend to think differently about pesos and dollars....

> They always say at hotels they don't want you to bring the girls in; believe me, that's crap, because you know what I do? Reach in my pocket and I go anywhere I want.

Meanwhile, sexualized racisms help the sex tourist to attain a sense of control over himself and Others as engendered and racialized sexual beings. Here it is important to recognize the subtle (or not so subtle) variations of racism employed by white Western men. The sex tourists we have interviewed in the Caribbean are not a homogeneous group in terms of their "race" politics, and this reflects differences of national identity, age, socioeconomic background, and racialized identity. One clearly identifiable subgroup is comprised of white North American men aged forty and above, who, though perhaps not actually affiliated with the Klan, espouse a white supremacist worldview and consider black people their biological, social, and cultural inferiors. They use the word "nigger" and consider any challenge to their "right" to use this term as "political correctness." As one sex tourist complained, in the States "You can't use the N word, nigger. Always when I was raised up, the only thing was the F word, you can't use the F word. Now you can't say cunt, you can't say nigger."

For men like this, black women are imagined as the embodiment of all that is low and debased, they are "inherently degraded, and thus the appropriate partners for degrading sex" (Shrage 1994: 158). As unambiguous whores by virtue of their racialized identity, they may be briefly and anonymously used, but they are not sought out for longer term or quasi-romantic commercial sexual relationships. Thus, the sex tourist quoted above told us that when he and his cronies (all regular sex tourists to the Dominican Republic) see another American sex tourist "hanging round" with a local girl or woman who has the phenotypical characteristics they associate with Africanness, they call out to him, "How many bananas did it take to get her down out of the tree?" and generally deride him for transgressing a racialized sexual boundary which should not, in their view, be openly crossed.

The Dominican females that men like this want sexual access to are light skinned and straight haired (this is also true in Cuba and in the Latin American countries where we have undertaken fieldwork). They are not classified as "niggers" by these white racists, but instead as "LBFMs" or "Little Brown Fucking Machines," a catch-all category encompassing any female Other not deemed to be either white or "African." The militaristic and imperialist associations of this term (coined by American GIs stationed in South east Asia) simultaneously make it all the more offensive and hostile and all the more appealing to this type of sex tourist, many of whom have served in the armed forces (a disturbing number of whom have also been or currently are police officers in the United States) and the rest of whom are "wanna-be vets" – men who never made it to Vietnam to live out their racialized–sexualized fantasies of masculine glory.

Shrage and Kruhse-Mount Burton's comments on the relationship between fantasies of hypersexual Others and myths about white women's sexual purity are also relevant to understanding this kind of sex tourist's worldview. An extract from an article posted on an Internet site written by and for sex tourists entitled "Why No White Women?" is revealing:

> Q: Is it because white women demand more (in terms of performance) from their men during Sex? and white men cannot deliver?
> A: In my case, it's just that my dick is not long enough to reach them up on the pedestal they like to stand on.

If whiteness is imagined as dominance, and woman is imagined as subordination, then "white woman" becomes something of a contradiction. As Young notes, "For white men, white women are both self and other: they have a floating status. They can reinforce a sense of self through common racial identity or threaten and disturb that sense through their sexual Otherness" (Young 1996: 52). White supremacists have to place white women on a pedestal (iconize them as racially, morally, and sexually pure), since whiteness and civilization are synonymous and "civilization" is constructed as the rejection of base animalism. But keeping them on their pedestal requires men to constantly deny what they imagine to be their own needs and nature and thus white women become the object of profound resentment.

Not all Western male sex tourists to the Caribbean buy into this kind of overt, denigrating racism. In fact, many of them are far more strongly influenced by what might be termed "exoticizing" racisms. Younger white Europeans and North Americans, for example, have been exposed to such racisms through the Western film, music, and fashion industries, which retain the old-school racist emphasis on blackness as physicality but repackage and commoditize this "animalism" so that black men and women become the ultimate icons of sporting prowess, "untamed" rebelliousness, "raw" musical talent, sexual power and so on (see hooks 1992, 1994; Young 1996). As a consequence, many young (and some not so young) white Westerners view blackness as a marker of something both "cool" and "hot."

In their own countries, however, their encounters with real live black people are not only few and far between, but also generally something of a disappointment to them. As one British sex tourist to Cuba told us, black people in Britain are "very stand-offish.... They stick to their own, and it's a shame, because it makes divisions." What a delight it is for men like this to holiday in the Caribbean, then, where poverty combined with the exigencies of tourist development ensure that they are constantly faced by smiling, welcoming black folk. The small black boy who wants to shine their shoes; the old black woman who cleans their hotel room; the cool, young, dreadlocked black man on the beach who is working as a promoter for some restaurant or bar; the fit, young black woman soliciting in the tourist disco – all want to "befriend" the white tourist. Finally, interviews with black American male sex tourists suggest that they too sexualize and exoticize the women they sexually exploit in the Third World ("Latin women are hot," "Latin girls love sex").

Both the sexualized racism that underpins the category LBFM and the exoticizing sexualized racism espoused by other sex tourists help to construct the Other prostitute as the embodiment of a contradiction, that is, as a "whore" who does it for pleasure as much as for money, an object with a subjectivity completely attuned to their own, in short, the embodiment of a masturbatory fantasy. Time and again Western sex tourists have assured us that the local girls really are "hot for it," that Third World prostitutes enjoy their work and that their highest ambition is to be the object of a Western man's desire. Their belief that Third World prostitutes are genuinely economically desperate rather than making a free choice to prostitute for "easy money"

is clearly inconsistent with their belief that Third World prostitutes are actually acting on the basis of mutual sexual desire, but it is a contradiction that appears to resolve (at least temporarily) an anxiety they have about the relationship between sex, gender, sexuality, and "race."

The vast majority of the sex tourists we have interviewed believe that gender attributes, including sexual behavior, are determined by biological sex. They say that it is natural for women to be passive and sexually receptive as well as to be homemakers, child rearers, dependent upon and subservient toward men, which is why white Western women (prostitute and nonprostitute alike) often appear to them as unsexed. Thus the sex tourist quoted at the beginning of this chapter could only explain women's presence on traditional male terrain by imagining them as sexually "unnatural" ("Most of these girls are dykes anyways"). White women's relative economic, social, and political power as well as their very whiteness makes it hard for Western male sex tourists to eroticize them as nothing more than sexual beings. Racism/ethnocentrism can collapse such tensions. If black or Latin women are naturally physical, wild, hot, and sexually powerful, there need be no anxiety about enjoying them as pure sex. Equally, racism settles the anxieties some men have about the almost "manly" sexual power and agency attributed to white prostitutes. A Little Brown Fucking Machine is not unsexed by prostituting, she is "just doing what comes naturally." Since the Other woman is a "natural" prostitute, her prostitution does not make her any the less a "natural woman." All these points are also relevant to understanding the phenomenon of female sex tourism.

"Otherness" and Female Sex Tourism

Western women's sexual behavior abroad (both historically and contemporaneously) is often viewed in a rather different light compared to that of their male counterparts, and it is without doubt true that Western women who travel to Third World destinations in search of sex differ from many of the Western male sex tourists discussed above in terms of their attitudes toward prostitution and sexuality. Few of them are prostitute users back home, and few of them would choose to visit brothels while abroad or to pay street prostitutes for a quick "hand job" or any other sexual service (although it should be noted that some women do behave in these ways). But one of the author's (Sanchez Taylor) ongoing interview and survey research with female sex tourists in Jamaica and the Dominican Republic suggests that there are also similarities between the sexual behavior of Western women and men in sex tourist resorts.

The Caribbean has long been a destination that offers tourist women opportunities for sexual experience, and large numbers of women from the United States, Canada, Britain, and Germany as well as smaller numbers of women from other European countries and from Japan (i.e., the same countries that send male sex tourists) engage in sexual relationships with local men while on holiday there (Karch and Dann 1981; Pruitt and LaFont 1995; Chevannes 1993). Preliminary analysis of data from Sanchez Taylor's survey of a sample of 104 single Western female tourists in Negril, Sosúa, and Boca Chica shows that almost 40 percent had entered into some form of sexual relationship with a local man.[3] The survey data further suggest that these were not chance encounters but rather that the sexually active female tourists visit the islands in order to pursue one or more sexual relationships. Only 9 percent of sexually active women were on their first trip; the rest had made numerous trips to the islands, and over 20 percent of female sex tourists reported having had two or more different local sexual partners in the course of a two- to three-week stay. Furthermore female sex tourists, as much as male sex tourists, view their sexual experiences as integral to their holiday – "When in Jamaica you have

to experience everything that's on offer," one black American woman explained, while a white woman working as a tour representative for a US package operator said: "I tell my single women: come down here to love them, fuck them, and leave them, and you'll have a great time here. Don't look to get married. Don't call them."

Like male sex tourists, these women differ in terms of their age, nationality, social class, and racialized identity, including among their ranks young "spice girl" teenagers and students as well as grandmothers in their sixties, working-class as well as middle-class professionals, or self-employed women. They also differ in terms of the type of sexual encounters they pursue and the way in which they interpret these encounters. Some are eager to find a man as soon as they get off the plane and enter into multiple, brief, and instrumental relationships; others want to be romanced and sweet-talked by one or perhaps two men during their holiday. Around 40 percent described their relationships with local men as "purely physical" and 40 percent described them as "holiday romances." Twenty percent said that they had found "true love." Almost all the sexually active women surveyed stated that they had "helped their partner(s) out financially" by buying them meals, drinks, gifts, or by giving cash, and yet none of them perceived these relationships as commercial sexual transactions. Asked whether they had ever been approached by a gigolo/prostitute during their stay in Jamaica, 90 percent of them replied in the negative. The data collected in the Dominican Republic revealed similar patterns of denial.

The informal nature of the sexual transactions in these resorts blurs the boundaries of what constitutes prostitution for Western women just as it does for Western men, allowing them to believe that the meals, cash, and gifts they provide for their sexual partners do not represent a form of payment for services rendered but rather an expression of their own munificence. It is only when women repeatedly enter into a series of extremely brief sexual encounters that they begin to acknowledge that, as one put it, "It's all about money." Even this does not lead them to view themselves as prostitute users, however, and again it is notions of difference and Otherness that play a key role in protecting the sex tourist from the knowledge that they are paying for the sexual attentions they receive. As Others, local men are viewed as beings possessed of a powerful and indiscriminate sexuality that they cannot control, and this explains their eagerness for sex with tourist women, regardless of their age, size, or physical appearance. Again, the Other is not *selling* sex, just "doing what comes naturally."

As yet, the number of black female sex tourists in Sanchez Taylor's survey and interview sample is too small to base any generalizations upon,[4] but so far their attitudes are remarkably consistent with those voiced by the central character in Terry Macmillan's 1996 novel *How Stella Got Her Groove Back*, in which a black American woman finds "love and romance" with a Jamaican boy almost half her age and with certainly less than half her economic means.[5] Stella views her own behavior in a quite different light from that of white male sex tourists – she disparages an older white male tourist as "a dirty old man who probably has to pay for all the pussy he gets" (Macmillan 1996: 83). It is also interesting to note the ways in which Macmillan "Otherizes" local men: the Jamaican boy smells "primitive"; he is "exotic and goes with the Island"; he is "Mr Expresso in shorts" (ibid: 142, 154). Like white female sex tourists interviewed in the course of research, Macmillan further explains the young Jamaican man's disinterest in Jamaican women and so his sexual interest in an older American woman by Otherizing local women through the use of derogatory stereotypes. Thus, Jamaican women are assumed to be rapacious, materialistic, and sexually instrumental – they only want a man who owns a big car and house and

money – and so Jamaican men long for women who do not demand these things (i.e., American women who already possess them).

Like their male counterparts, Western female sex tourists employ fantasies of Otherness not just to legitimate obtaining sexual access to the kind of young, fit, handsome bodies that would otherwise be denied to them and to obtain affirmation of their own sexual desirability (because the fact is that some female sex tourists are themselves young and fit looking and would be easily able to secure sexual access to equally appealing male bodies at home), but also to obtain a sense of power and control over themselves and others as engendered, sexual beings and to affirm their own privilege as Westerners. Thus they continually stress their belief that people in the Caribbean "are different from Westerners." Sexual life is one of the primary arenas in which this supposed difference is manifest. More than half of the female sex tourists surveyed in Jamaica stated that Jamaicans are more relaxed about teenage sex, casual sex, and prostitution than Westerners. In response to open-ended questions, they observed that "Jamaican men are more up front about sex," that "Jamaicans are uninhibited about sex," that "Jamaicans are naturally promiscuous," and that "sex is more natural to Jamaicans." In interviews, female sex tourists also reproduced the notion of an opposition between the "civilized" West and the "primitive" Third World. One Scots grandmother in her early forties described the Dominican Republic as follows: "It's just like Britain before its industrial phase, it's just behind Britain, just exactly the same. Kids used to get beat up to go up chimneys, here they get beaten up to go polish shoes. There's no difference."

Western female sex tourists' racisms, like those of male sex tourists, are also many-layered and nuanced by differences in terms of nationality, age, and racialized identity. There are older white American female sex tourists whose beliefs about "race" and attitudes toward interracial sex are based upon an ideology that is overtly white supremacist. The black male represents for them the essence of an animalistic sexuality that both fascinates and repels. While in their own country they would not want to openly enter a sexual relationship with a black man, in a holiday resort like Negril they can transgress the racialized and gendered codes that normally govern their sexual behavior, while maintaining their honor and reputation back home. As one Jamaican gigolo commented:

> While they are here they feel free. Free to do what they never do at home. No one looking at them. Get a Black guy who are unavailable at home. No one judge them. Get the man to make they feel good then they go home clean and pure.

This observation, and all the sexual hostility it implies, is born out by the following extract from an interview with a 45-year-old white American woman from Chicago, a regular sex tourist to Negril:

> [Jamaican men] are all liars and cheats. ... [American women come to Negril because] they get what they don't get back home. A girl who no one looks twice at back home, she gets hit on all the time here, all these guys are paying her attention, telling her she's beautiful, and they really want her.... They're obsessed with their dicks. That's all they think of, just pussy and money and nothing else.... In Chicago, this could never happen. It's like a secret, like a fantasy and then you go home.

When asked whether she would ever take a black boyfriend home and introduce him to her friends and family, she was emphatic that she would not – "No, no, never. It's not like that. This is something else, you know, it's time out. Like a fantasy." This is more than simply a fantasy about having multiple anonymous sexual encounters without getting caught and disgraced. It is

also a highly racialized fantasy about power and vengeance. Women like the sex tourist quoted above are looking for black men with good bodies, firm and muscle-clad sex machines that they can control, and this element of control should not be overlooked. It is also important to female sex tourists who reject white supremacist ideologies, and there are many of these, including white liberals and young white women who value Blackness as a "cool" commodity in the same way that many young white men do, and black American and black British female sex tourists.

These latter groups do not wish to indulge in the overtly hostile racialized sexual fantasy described by the woman quoted above, but they do want to live out other fantasies, whether they be "educating and helping the noble savage," or being the focus of "cool" black men's adoring gaze, or being the central character of a Terry Macmillan novel.[6] No matter what specific fantasy they pursue, female sex tourists use their economic power to initiate and terminate sexual relations with local men at whim, and within those relationships, they use their economic and racialized power to control these men in ways in which they could never command a Western man. These are unaccustomed powers, and even the female sex tourists who buy into exoticizing rather than hostile and denigrating racisms appear to enjoy them as such.

For white women, these powers are very clearly linked to their own whiteness as well as to their status and economic power as tourist women. Thus they contrast their own experience against that of local women (remarking on the fact that they are respected and protected and not treated like local women) *and* against their experience back home (commenting on how safe they feel in the Caribbean walking alone at night and entering bars and discos by themselves, observing that local men are far more attentive and chivalrous than Western men). Take, for example, the comments of "Judy," a white American expatriate in the

Dominican Republic, a woman in her late fifties and rather overweight:

> When you go to a disco, [white] men eye up a woman for her body, whatever. Dominicans don't care because they love women, they love women. It's not that they're indifferent or anything. They are very romantic, they will never be rude with you, while a white man will say something rude to you, while Dominican men are not like that at all. A white man will say to me, like, "slut" to me and I have been with a lot of Dominican men and they would never say anything like that to you. They are more respectful. Light cigarettes, open doors, they are more gentlemen. Where white men don't do that. So if you have been a neglected woman in civilization, when you come down here, of course, when you come down here they are going to wipe you off your feet.

The Dominican Republic presents women like Judy with a stage upon which to simultaneously affirm their femininity through their ability to command men and exact revenge on white men by engaging sexually with the competition, i.e., the black male. For the first time she is in a position to call the shots. Where back home white female sex tourists' racialized privilege is often obscured by their lack of gender power and economic disadvantage in relation to white men, in sex tourist resorts it is recognized as a source of personal power and power over others. Meanwhile, their beliefs about gender and sexuality prevent them from seeing themselves as sexually exploitative. Popular discourses about gender present women as naturally sexually passive and receptive, and men as naturally indiscriminate and sexually voracious. According to this essentialist model of gender and sexuality, women can never sexually exploit men in the same way that men exploit women because penetrative heterosexual intercourse requires the woman to submit to the male – she is "used" by him. No matter how great the asymmetry between female tourist and local male in terms of their age or economic, social, and racialized power, it is still assumed that the male derives benefits from sex above and beyond the purely pecuniary and so is not being exploited in the same way that a prostitute woman is exploited by a male client. This is especially the case when the man so used is socially constructed as a racialized, ethnic, or cultural Other and assumed to have an uncontrollable desire to have sex with as many women as he possibly can.

Conclusion

The demand for sex tourism is inextricably linked to discourses that naturalize and celebrate inequalities structured along lines of class, gender, and race/Otherness; in other words, discourses that reflect and help to reproduce a profoundly hierarchical model of human sociality. Although sex tourists are a heterogeneous group in terms of their background characteristics and specific sexual interests, they share a common willingness to embrace this hierarchical model and a common pleasure in the fact that their Third World tourism allows them either to affirm their dominant position within a hierarchy of gendered, racialized, and economic power or to adjust their own position upward in that hierarchy. In the Third World, neocolonial relations of power equip Western sex tourists with an extremely high level of control over themselves and others as sexual beings and, as a result, with the power to realize the fantasy of their choosing. They can experience sexual intimacy without risking rejection; they can evade the social meanings that attach to their own age and body type; they can transgress social rules governing sexual life without consequence for their own social standing; they can reduce other human beings to nothing more than the living embodiments of masturbatory fantasies.

In short, sex tourists can experience in real life a world very similar to that offered in fantasy to pornography users: "Sexuality and sexual activity are portrayed in pornography as profoundly distanced from the activities of daily life. The action in pornography takes place in what Griffin has termed 'pornotopia,' a world outside real time and space" (Hartsock 1985: 175). To sex tourists, the resorts they visit are fantasy islands, variously peopled by Little Brown Fucking Machines, "cool" black women who love to party, "primitive smelling" black studs who only think of "pussy and money," respectful Latin gentlemen who love women. All the sex tourist has to do to attain access to this fantasy world is to reach into his or her pocket, for it is there that the sex tourist, like other individuals in capitalist societies, carries "his social power as also his connection with society" (Marx 1973: 94). That the Western sex tourist's pocket can contain sufficient power to transform others into Others, mere players on a pornographic stage, is a testament to the enormity of the imbalance of economic, social, and political power between rich and poor nations. That so many Westerners *wish* to use their power in this way is a measure of the bleakness of the prevailing model of human nature and the human sociality that their societies offer them.

NOTES

1   In 1995 we were commissioned by ECPAT (End Child Prostitution in Asian Tourism) to undertake research on the identity, attitudes, and motivations of clients of child prostitutes. This involved ethnographic fieldwork in tourist areas in South Africa, India, Costa Rica, Venezuela, Cuba, and the Dominican Republic. We are currently working on an Economic and Social Research Council–funded project (Award no. R 000 23 7625) which builds on this research through a focus on prostitution and the informal tourist economy in Jamaica and the Dominican Republic. Taking these projects together, we have interviewed some 250 sex tourists and sexpatriates and over 150 people involved in tourist-related prostitution (women, children, and men working as prostitutes, pimps, procurers, brothel keepers, etc.).

2   The fact that not all men are prostitute users is something that is often forgotten in radical feminist analyses of prostitution which, as Hart has noted, encourage us to view "either all men as prostitutes' clients or prostitutes' clients as somehow standing for/being symbolic of men in general" (Hart 1994: 53).

3   Because the survey aims to support exploration and theory development in a previously underresearched field, purposive (nonprobability) sampling methods were employed (Arber 1993: 72). Sanchez Taylor obtained a sample by approaching all single female tourists in selected locations (a particular stretch of beach, or a given bar or restaurant) and asking them to complete questionnaires.

4   Four out of eighteen single black British and American female tourists surveyed had entered into sexual relationships with local men. Sanchez Taylor also interviewed four more black female sex tourists.

5   In Negril, gigolos often refer to black American female sex tourists as "Stellas," after this fictional character.

6   Macmillan hints at the transgressive elements of a black Western female sex tourist's excitement – Stella's desire for the "primitive"-smelling younger man makes her feel "kind of slutty," but she likes the feeling.

REFERENCES

Arber, Sarah. "Designing Samples." *Researching Social Life*, ed. Nigel Gilbert, 68–92. London: Sage, 1993.

Bishop, Ryan and Lillian S. Robinson. *Night Market: Sexual Cultures and the Thai Economic Miracle*. New York: Routledge, 1998.

Brace, Laura and Julia O'Connell Davidson. "Desperate Debtors and Counterfeit Love: The Hobbesian World of the Sex Tourist." *Contemporary Politics* 2.3 (1996): 55–78.

Chevannes, Barry. "Sexual Behaviour of Jamaicans: A Literature Review." *Social and Economic Studies* 42.1 (1993).

Graaf, Ron de, Ine Vanwesenbeek, Gertjan van Zessen, Straver Visser, and Jan Visser. "Prostitution and the Spread of HIV." *Safe Sex in Prostitution in The Netherlands*, 2–24. Amsterdam: Mr A. de Graaf Institute, 1992.

Grewal, Inderpal. *Home and Harem: Nation, Gender, Empire and the Cultures of Travel.* London: Leicester University Press, 1996.

Hall, C. Michael. "Gender and Economic Interests in Tourism Prostitution: The Nature, Development and Implications of Sex Tourism in South-East Asia." *Tourism: A Gender Perspective,* ed. Vivien Kinnaird and D. Hall. London: Routledge, 1994.

Hart, Angie. "Missing Masculinity? Prostitutes' Clients in Alicante, Spain." *Dislocating Masculinity: Comparative Ethnographies,* ed. Andrea Cornwall and Nancy Lindisfarne, 48–65. London: Routledge, 1994.

Hartsock, Nancy. *Money, Sex, and Power.* Boston: Northeastern University Press, 1985.

hooks, bell. *Black Looks: Race and Representation.* London: Turnaround; Boston: South End Press, 1992.

—— *Outlaw Culture: Resisting Representations.* London: Routledge, 1994.

Jeffreys, Sheila. *The Idea of Prostitution.* Melbourne: Spinifex, 1997.

Karch, Cecilia A. and G. H. S. Dann. "Close Encounters of the Third Kind." *Human Relations* 34 (1981): 249–68.

Kempadoo, Kamala. "Prostitution, Marginality, and Empowerment: Caribbean Women in the Sex Trade." *Beyond Law* 5.14 (1994): 69–84.

—— "Regulating Prostitution in the Dutch Caribbean." Paper presented at the 20th annual conference of the Caribbean Studies Association, Curaçao, Netherlands Antilles, May 1995.

—— "Dominicanas en Curaçao: Mitos y Realidades." *Género y Sociedad* 4.1 (May–August 1996): 102–30.

Kruhse-Mount Burton, Suzy. "Sex Tourism and Traditional Australian Male Identity." *International Tourism: Identity and Change,* ed. Marie-Françoise Lanfant, John Allcock, and Edward Bruner, 192–204. London: Sage, 1995.

Lee, Wendy. "Prostitution and Tourism in South-East Asia." *Working Women: International Perspectives on Labour and Gender Ideology,* ed. N. Redclift and M. Thea Sinclair, 79–103. London: Routledge, 1991.

Macmillan, Terry. *How Stella Got Her Groove Back.* New York: Penguin, 1996.

Marx, Karl. *Grundrisse.* Harmondsworth, England: Penguin, 1973.

Morris-Jarra, Monica. "No Such Thing as a Cheap Holiday." *Tourism in Focus* 26 (autumn 1996): 6–7.

O'Connell Davidson, Julia. *Prostitution, Power and Freedom.* Cambridge: Polity Press, 1998.

Perio, Gaelle and Dominique Thierry. *Tourisme Sexuel au Bresil et en Colombie.* Rapport D'Enquete. TOURCOING, 1996.

Plumridge, Elizabeth and Jane Chetwynd. "Discourses of Emotionality in Commercial Sex." *Feminism & Psychology* 7.2 (1997): 165–81.

Pruitt, Deborah and Suzanne LaFont. "For Love and Money: Romance Tourism in Jamaica." *Annals of Tourism Research* 22.2 (1995): 422–40.

Sanchez Taylor, Jacqueline. "Marking the Margins: Research in the Informal Economy in Cuba and the Dominican Republic." Discussion Paper No. S97/1, Department of Sociology, University of Leicester, 1997.

Seabrook, Jeremy. *Travels in the Skin Trade: Tourism and the Sex Industry.* London: Pluto Press, 1997.

Shrage, Laurie. *Moral Dilemmas of Feminism.* London: Routledge, 1994.

Stoller, Robert. *Perversion: The Erotic Form of Hatred.* London: Karnac, 1986.

Sturdevant, Saundra and Brenda Stolzfus. *Let the Good Times Roll: Prostitution and the U.S. Military in Asia.* New York: The New Press, 1992.

Truong, Than Dam. *Sex, Money and Morality: The Political Economy of Prostitution and Tourism in South East Asia.* London: Zed Books, 1990.

Young, Lola. *Fear of the Dark: "Race," Gender and Sexuality in the Cinema.* London: Routledge, 1996.

Part VII

Sexual Politics and Social Change

Some would argue that sexuality is on the front line of politics. On matters of abortion, teen pregnancy, gay marriage, and other issues, this certainly seems to be the case. Social attitudes have changed radically during the past century, but social norms continue to restrict our sexual choices, according to a recent national study of American sexual attitudes and practices (Michael, Gagnon, Laumann and Kolata). At the same time, we live in an increasingly mobile and globalizing world, in which Euro-American sexual cultures collide with different ethnic/immigrant groups, creating new forms of family and sexuality (Cantú); gay/lesbian cultures challenge the "naturalness" of heterosexual dominance (Stacey); and women, publicly and privately, contest male power (Schneider and Jenness). Yet individuals remain divided on the matter of whether sexual liberalization is a good thing or not, as contemporary resistance to lesbian/gay marriage and women's sexual freedom suggests. Clearly, we live in a highly sexualized society and also a profoundly sex-negative one.

25 Sex and Society

Robert T. Michael, John H. Gagnon, Edward O. Laumann, and Gina Kolata

In private and in public, within our families and among our friends, most of us are living the sexual lives that society has urged upon us. Social networks match up couples, sexual preferences are learned or mimicked within networks, social forces push Americans toward marriage and so richly reward wedded couples that marriage turns out to be the best way to have regular sex and the best way to have a happy sex life.

But there is more to social forces than social networks, social scripts, and a widespread conviction that marriage is the ultimate goal for nearly everyone. There also are social attitudes and beliefs, the very beliefs that show up in many of the contradictory messages that we all hear about the power and the pleasure – and the shame – of sexuality.

These attitudes and beliefs underlie some of the bitter social debates of our day. Should there be limits on a woman's right to an abortion? Should sex education be taught in schools? Should we treat homosexuality as just another lifestyle or should we consider it a sin or abnormality?

One way to look at the roots of these arguments is to ask whether there is any relationship between sexual behavior and deep-seated feelings about sexual morality. And if there is a relationship between behavior and beliefs, who is likely to hold which attitudes? Are highly educated people more likely to be libertarians? Do religious people have fewer sexual partners? Do people who view sex as a form of recreation do different things in bed than people who say their sexual behavior is guided by their religious beliefs?

In a broader sense, looking for such a relationship tests our entire thesis that sexual behavior is a social behavior, determined, shaped, and molded by society like other more visible behaviors – religious practices or recreational habits, for example. If sexual behavior were a completely independent force, not subject to conscious thoughts but controlled instead by hormones, or whipped up by drives, then it should matter little what a person's attitudes are.

We asked our respondents about their attitudes and beliefs about sexual behavior, and, separately, we asked them what appealed to them sexually and what they did. This enabled us to put the pieces together. We found that there is a strong, robust link between attitudes and sexual behavior, and that it suggests why so many social issues related to sex are so contentious. Not only do people's underlying attitudes about questions of sexual morality predict what sort of sex they have in the privacy of their bedrooms, but they even predict how often people *think* about sex.

From the different attitudes and, correspondingly, different behavior of men and women, of older and younger people, and of people of different religions, we can suggest why it is that there is a war between the sexes, why it is that many women complain that men will not commit themselves to marriage, and why it is that many older people are dismayed by the sexual practices of the young.

To learn about attitudes and beliefs, we asked several questions about opinions regarding sexual behavior and other related topics, nine of which we discuss below. For example, we asked respondents to tell us how they felt about premarital sex. Was it always wrong, almost always wrong, sometimes wrong, or not wrong at all? We asked about sex between people of the same gender. Was it always, almost always, sometimes, or never wrong? We asked respondents if their religious beliefs guided their behavior. Then, with the replies to nine such questions in hand, we used a method called cluster analysis to divide the population into groups according to their opinions about those nine issues. Although people in each group varied, overall they had a general set of similar beliefs about key issues.

Cluster analysis is a frequently used tool of social scientists who often need to find patterns in masses of data and are not aided by strong theory in their quest. In our case, we did not know ahead of time how people would sort themselves out by their answers to these questions and we knew, at the outset, that there were a large number of possible combinations of answers to our nine questions. Since each person answered all nine questions about his or her attitudes and beliefs, and since we are focusing here on whether the respondents agreed or disagreed with each statement, there are a total of 2^9 or 512 ways to answer the set of nine questions. But, we reasoned, if there are logical or belief-driven patterns to the answers, there should be certain clusters of replies among all these possibilities. A man, for example, who says his religious convictions guide his views toward sexuality might also say that sex outside of marriage is always wrong, that teenage sex is always wrong, that extramarital sex is always wrong, and that abortions should be prohibited.

Cluster analysis underlies many studies in which people are categorized according to their replies to an array of questions rather than a single one. For example, a cluster analysis looking for voting patterns might group people according to their replies to such questions as: Should capital punishment

be abolished? Should all companies be required to practice affirmative action? Should handguns be outlawed? Should women have the right to an abortion for any reason? Should states provide vouchers for parents who choose to send their children to private schools? People in each group would have similar answers to the questions. While one question characterizes a person's political views, and while each person in a cluster will not give exactly the same answers as every other person in the cluster, the pattern of their replies could be a good indication of their political leanings.

In this particular analysis we divided the respondents into three broad categories on the basis of their attitudes. First is the *traditional* category, which includes about one-third of our sample. These people say that their religious beliefs always guide their sexual behavior. In addition, they say that homosexuality is always wrong, that there should be restrictions on legal abortions, that premarital sex, teenage sex, and extramarital sex are wrong.

Second is what we call the *relational* category, whose members believe that sex should be part of a loving relationship, but that it need not always be reserved for marriage. These people, who make up nearly half of our sample, disagree with the statement that premarital sex is always wrong, for example. Most, however, say that marital infidelity is always wrong and that they would not have sex with someone they did not love. The third group is the *recreational* category, who constitute a little more than a quarter of the sample. Their defining feature is their view that sex need not have anything to do with love. In addition, most of those in this third group oppose laws to prohibit the sale of pornography to adults.

Within each of these categories, however, people varied in their attitudes, and so we subdivided the categories to further characterize our respondents. A man would be part of the relational group, for example, if he thinks extramarital sex is always wrong and that he would not have sex with anyone unless he loved her. But he might also say that same-gender sex is always wrong. A woman who is in a different group in that category might agree with him about extramarital sex and sex with a partner she loved, but disagree about same-gender sex being wrong.

Table 25.1 shows how the groups are categorized, according to people's replies to the nine questions on attitudes.

The columns show the percentages of our population who agree with the statements in the column on the extreme left. We divided the traditional category into "conservative" and "pro-choice" groups essentially according to their opinions on abortion. Although people in this category nearly all believe that premarital sex among teenagers, same-gender sex, and extramarital sex are always wrong, they split on whether a woman should be able to have an abortion.

The relational category breaks down into three groups, which we have labeled as religious, conventional, and contemporary religious. Those in the religious group said that religious beliefs shape their sexual behavior and tended to say that they oppose sex between people of the same gender and they oppose abortions. The conventional group is more tolerant than the religious group toward teenage sex, pornography, and abortion and is far less likely to say they are influenced by religious beliefs. But most think that same-gender sex and extramarital sex are always wrong. The contemporary religious group is much more tolerant of homosexuality but people in this group say that they are guided by their religious beliefs.

In the recreational category, there are two groups. One, which we call pro-life, consists of people who oppose both homosexuality and abortion for any reason but who are more accepting of teenage sex, extramarital sex, and pornography. The second group is the libertarian group. They have the most accepting position on all the items. None of this libertarian group considers religion as a guide to their sexual behavior.

Just dividing the respondents into these groupings on the basis of their opinions, however, tells only part of the story. We also want to know how the groups differ by social characteristics. Men and women gravitate to different groups, as seen in table 25.2. So do older and younger people and so do blacks and whites. The distribution of people into groups reveals why the formation of social policy regarding sexual issues is so contentious and so complex.

The top rows of table 25.2 tells us that women are more likely to have the opinions we labeled "traditional" and are much less likely to have the views we called "recreational." By age, we see that the older men and women are disproportionately "traditional" and much less likely to hold the "recreational" views.

With distributions like this, it is no wonder that the battle between the sexes rages. Lance Morrow, a columnist for *Time* magazine, bemoaned men's fate. Women, he complained, have a particularly pejorative view of hapless men, thinking and saying something like "Men-are-animals-I-don't-care-if-they're-not-doing-anything-at-the-moment-they're-thinking-about-it-and-they-will-when-they-have-a-chance." Some women, on the other hand, have sniped that men are not so blameless, pointing out that many men still leer at women when they walk down the street, and some men act like they have to be dragged kicking and screaming into marriage, behaving as if marriage is a ball and chain.

The distribution of men and women in the attitude clusters tells us, at least, that many more women than men are looking for love and consider marriage to be a prerequisite for sex. When women bitterly complain that the men they meet are not interested in long-term commitments, their laments have a ring of truth. Many more men than women are looking for sexual play and pleasure, with marriage or even love not necessarily a part of it. After all, men in the recreational category may be unlikely to feel that linking sex with marriage is high on their list of

Table 25.1 Description of seven normative orientations toward sexuality

	Traditional			Relational		Recreational		Total sample
	Conservative	Pro-choice	Religious	Conventional	Contemporary religious	Pro-life	Libertarian	
1 Premarital sex is always wrong	100.0[a]	23.6	0.0	0.4	0.8	6.5	0.0	19.7
2 Premarital sex among teenagers is always wrong	99.5	90.3	78.6	29.1	33.6	65.7	19.7	60.8
3 Extramarital sex is always wrong	98.2	91.0	92.1	94.2	52.1	59.3	32.0	76.7
4 Same-gender sex is always wrong	96.4	94.4	81.9	65.4	6.4	85.9	9.0	64.8
5 There should be laws against the sale of pornography to adults	70.6	47.2	53.1	12.2	11.7	14.9	6.4	33.6
6 I would not have sex with someone unless I was in love with them	87.5	66.0	98.0	83.8	65.3	10.1	19.5	65.7
7 My religious beliefs have guided my sexual behavior	91.3	72.9	74.7	8.7	100.0	25.0	0.0	52.3
8 A woman should be able to obtain a legal abortion if she was raped	56.3	98.6	82.3	99.1	99.3	84.3	99.8	88.0
9 A woman should be able to obtain a legal abortion if she wants it for any reason	0.5	100.0	0.0	87.4	84.9	9.3	88.6	52.4
N = 2,843	15.4%	15.2%	19.1%	15.9%	9.3%	8.7%	16.4%	100.0%

[a] Indicates the percentage of persons in the "Conservative Traditional" cluster who believe that premarital sex is always wrong. Oversample was excluded from analysis, as were respondents who had missing values for one or more items. Clusters were derived by minimizing the squared Euclidean distance between members within each cluster. All items were dichotomized before clustering, column percentages.

Table 25.2 Distribution of normative orientations within demographic groups

Social characteristics	Normative orientation		
	Traditional	Relational	Recreational
GENDER			
Men	26.9%	40.1%	33.0%
Women	33.7	47.6	18.7
AGE			
Men			
18–24	17.4	46.9	35.7
25–29	21.0	46.2	32.9
30–39	26.2	38.6	35.2
40–49	31.2	38.2	30.5
50–59	40.1	31.3	28.6
Women			
18–24	23.0	51.8	25.3
25–29	27.5	54.6	17.9
30–39	34.6	46.6	18.8
40–49	34.5	44.9	20.6
50–59	47.0	43.4	9.6
MARITAL/RESIDENTIAL STATUS			
Men			
Noncohabiting	18.4	39.7	42.0
Cohabiting	8.6	48.4	43.0
Married	36.4	39.0	24.5
Women			
Noncohabiting	31.9	46.8	21.3
Cohabiting	23.9	50.4	25.6
Married	36.2	48.1	15.8
EDUCATION			
Men			
Less than high school	31.6	39.5	28.8
High school graduate or equivalent	28.3	40.9	30.8
Any college	25.0	39.8	35.2
Women			
Less than high school	36.6	47.6	15.9
High school graduate or equivalent	38.3	46.0	15.7
Any college	30.4	48.7	20.9
RELIGION			
Men			
None	11.7	39.1	49.2
Mainline Protestant	24.2	43.8	32.0
Conservative Protestant	44.5	30.1	25.3
Catholic	17.8	49.6	32.6
Women			
None	10.4	44.4	45.2
Mainline Protestant	30.9	51.4	17.7
Conservative Protestant	50.5	38.4	11.2
Catholic	22.2	58.0	19.8

Table 25.2 *Cont.*

Social characteristics	Normative orientation		
	Traditional	Relational	Recreational
RACE/ETHNICITY			
Men			
White	26.1	41.6	32.3
Black	32.4	25.4	42.3
Hispanic	25.3	45.1	29.7
Women			
White	30.5	48.3	21.2
Black	45.3	45.8	8.9
Hispanic	40.7	43.2	16.1

Percentages in rows total 100 percent.

priorities. When men note that their girlfriends are always trying to lure them into making a commitment to exclusivity or that their relationships seem to end with an ultimatum – marry me or get out – there is a good reason for it.

The conflicting goals of men and women – and particularly young men and young women – are played out in the lines the men may use when they meet women. And at no time is this more true than in adolescence and young adulthood, the very time that men are most likely to be part of all-male groups who have recreational attitudes toward sex.

Elijah Anderson, a sociologist at the University of Pennsylvania, tells how black teenagers in an inner-city neighborhood take on these roles: "The lore of the streets says there is a contest going on between the boy and girl before they even meet. To the young man, the woman becomes, in the most profound sense, a sexual object. Her body and mind are the object of a sexual game, to be won for his personal aggrandizement." And to win a young woman, Anderson says, the young man devises a rap, "whose object is to inspire sexual interest."[1]

The young women, on the other hand, want "a boyfriend, a fiancé, a husband, and the fairy-tale prospect of living happily ever after with one's children in a good house in a nice neighborhood," Anderson says. So the young man, trying to have sex with a woman, "shows her the side of himself that he knows she wants to see, that represents what she wants in a man." He may take the young woman to church, visit her family, help her with chores. But after the young man has sex with the young woman, he often leaves her for a new conquest.

The teenage woman "may know she is being played but given the effectiveness of his rap, his presentation of self, his looks, his age, his wit, his dancing ability, and his general popularity, infatuation often rules," Anderson notes.

Put differently, we see in this typical script the competitive marketplace for sexual partners. The young man is emphasizing those of his attributes that he thinks will attract the young woman. He engages in negotiations and interchanges designed, with all his strategic skills, to persuade her that a friendship that includes sex will be to her liking. She, similarly, emphasizes her attributes that she thinks might attract the most appealing guy. She carefully calibrates her encouragement and insists on behavior that wraps sex into the bundle of activities that she desires.

Whether the outcome is a single sex episode or a more steady dating relationship or even a longer-term sexual partnership, each of these young people offers and withholds, explores and considers, and reaches agreement about the sex. The strategic behavior by each, designed to attract the partner and achieve the objective that each seeks, embeds the individual's endeavor in a social context that typically involves competition.

The table also shows us that the married men and women are least likely to hold the recreational view of sexuality, while the not-married men are far more likely to hold that set of views. The cohabiting men and women, on the other hand, are least likely to hold the traditional views of sexuality. Of course, these unmarried men and women are also likely to be younger than those who are married, so the pattern by marital status partly just mirrors the pattern we noted above that older (and married) people hold more traditional views while the younger (unmarried) people are more likely to be in the recreational category. This contributes to the battle of the generations. Older people, often the parents of teenagers or of people in their twenties, tend to have a very different view of the purpose of sex.

The age distribution also suggests the possibility that people change their attitudes over the years (though our data cannot confirm this), moving from times, in their youth, when they thought love need have nothing to do with sex to times, when they grow older, when loving relationships become more central to sexuality. People seem to move along the spectrum from libertarian toward conservative as they age. This could be one reason why 58 percent of our respondents who said premarital sex is always wrong also told us that they themselves had had sex before they were married. And it could explain why 26 percent of our respondents who told us that teenage sex is always wrong also said that they had had sex when they were teenagers. These differences by age might, on the other hand, reflect lifelong held differences of opinion of those born in the 1930s, the 1940s, and so

on, but we speculate that these opinions change with age.

When we look at the relationship between race, religion, and education and attitudes about sex, we can see why people tend to feel more comfortable when they choose partners like themselves. The table shows, for example, that few who are not religious are part of the traditional category, but 48 percent of conservative Protestants are traditionalists. People with no religion are most likely to be part of the recreational category – nearly half are found here.

Our findings also show that the clichéd strife between black men and black women may, in fact, reflect fundamentally different attitudes about sex. Black women are more likely than white or Hispanic women to be traditionalists and are noticeably less likely than other women to be in the recreational category – fewer than 10 percent of black women have recreational views toward sex. But black men are noticeably more likely than other men to be in the recreational group – more than 40 percent have recreational views.

The pattern seen in table 25.2 by education level is not dramatic, but it is quite systematic. Those with less than a high school level of education are more likely to hold traditional views about sexuality and less likely to hold recreational views; those with college education are just the opposite: they are more likely to hold the recreational views and least likely to hold the traditional views.

We did not have strong expectations or theories about how people's views of sexuality might be related to their social characteristics. But our findings seem to confirm the notion that people's beliefs about sexual morality are part of a much broader social and religious outlook that helps define who they are. Their orientations are reinforced by their friends and family and others in their social networks.

The next question is whether what people believe about sexual behavior is linked to what they actually do sexually. It is one

Table 25.3   Selected sexual behaviors within normative groups

Panel A: Men

	Normative orientation		
Sexual behaviors	Traditional	Relational	Recreational
PARTNERS LAST YEAR: NONCOHABITING			
None	40.6%	22.4%	12.8%
One	30.2	41.0	27.9
Two or more	29.2	36.6	59.4
PARTNERS LAST YEAR: MARRIED			
Zero or one	97.0	96.0	84.9
Two or more	3.0	4.0	15.1
LAST YEAR SEX FREQUENCY			
None	12.5	8.8	8.4
Three times a month or less	31.4	34.2	35.9
Once a week or more	56.1	57.1	55.7
THINK ABOUT SEX			
Twice a month or less	13.4	14.1	7.1
Twice a week or less	40.8	35.3	27.0
Daily or more	45.8	50.6	65.9
MASTURBATE			
Never	50.2	35.5	25.6
Three times a month or less	32.1	38.5	39.4
Once a week or more	17.7	26.0	35.0
HAD ORAL SEX (ACTIVE OR PASSIVE) WITH PRIMARY PARTNER IN LAST YEAR			
Yes	56.4	78.2	80.7
HAD ANAL SEX DURING LIFETIME			
Yes	18.7	23.1	32.3
EVER HAD SAME-GENDER PARTNER SINCE AGE 18			
Yes	2.6	4.5	7.8

Panel B: Women

	Normative orientation		
Sexual behaviors	Traditional	Relational	Recreational
PARTNERS LAST YEAR: NONCOHABITING			
None	46.7	25.2	14.6
One	39.1	52.6	36.6
Two or more	14.1	22.2	48.8
PARTNERS LAST YEAR: MARRIED			
Zero or one	98.0	98.5	92.5
Two or more	2.0	1.5	7.5
LAST YEAR SEX FREQUENCY			
None	18.5	10.8	8.0
Three times a month or less	31.5	34.0	39.6

Once a week or more	50.0	55.1	52.4
THINK ABOUT SEX			
Twice a month or less	45.0	36.8	30.1
Twice a week or less	40.6	44.0	39.0
Daily or more	14.3	19.2	30.8
MASTURBATE			
Never	69.0	56.6	37.5
Three times a month or less	26.0	35.4	50.2
Once a week or more	5.0	8.1	12.3
HAD ORAL SEX (ACTIVE OR PASSIVE) WITH PRIMARY PARTNER IN LAST YEAR			
Yes	55.9	73.9	83.6
HAD ANAL SEX DURING LIFETIME			
Yes	13.2	19.5	37.5
EVER HAD SAME-GENDER PARTNER SINCE AGE 18			
Yes	0.8	3.0	8.6

Percentages in columns total 100 percent within the categories; the "no" percentages are omitted in the last three.

thing to have a certain set of attitudes, but it is another thing to have those attitudes determine your most private acts, wishes, and thoughts. Yet that is what we find, as seen in table 25.3. Membership in a particular attitudinal group is closely associated with what their sexual practices are. It is even correlated with how often people think about sex and how often they have sex.

The top portion of both panels of table 25.3 shows the number of sex partners in the past year for the men and women who are not living with a partner. We see there that those who have traditional views about sexuality mostly have zero or one partner and only a relatively small percentage had two or more sex partners in the past year: about 30 percent of the men and about 14 percent of the women have that many. But of those who held recreational views of sexuality, about 60 percent of the men and nearly 50 percent of the women had two or more sex partners in the past year. Their attitudes and opinions, as characterized by the three categories of traditional, relational, and recreational, do in fact distinguish these unmarried and noncohabiting respondents quite effectively in terms of their number of sex partners in the past year.

To be sure, there are a few of those with a traditionalist view who have several sex partners, and a few of those with a recreationalist's view who have no sex partner or one partner, but in the main, the views they held are very consistent with the number of partners they had in the past year.

The same is true of those who are married, as seen in the second set of rows in table 25.3. For the men who were traditionalists or relationalists, only 3 or 4 percent had more than one sex partner in the past year, but as many as 15 percent of those who were recreationalists had more than one. The same pattern is seen for the married women where only 1 or 2 percent of the traditionalists and relationalists had more than one partner but more than 7 percent of the recreationalists had more than one. The tremendous influence of marital status on the number of sex partners is seen here, with a vast majority of the married men and women having zero or one sex partner in the past year, and the unmarried much more likely to have several, but within both marital statuses the influence of these opinions shines through.

In contrast, people's views about sex had little bearing on how often they had sex. Roughly half of those in each of the three categories report having sex once a week or more. Although somewhat fewer recreationalists said they did not have sex at all last year, the difference between them and those in other groups was not very great. We suspect it reflects the fact that people in the recreational group are more likely to be young and may not have yet found a sexual partner, however much they may want to.

Whether they are actually having sex or not, people who are recreationalists are much more likely than traditionalists to think about sex every day and are much more likely to masturbate. Those in the recreational group are twice as likely as those in the traditionalist group to report that they masturbated once a week or more.

Oral and anal sex and sex with someone of the same gender follow the same patterns, as is seen in the bottom three rows of table 25.3. Recreationalists are more likely than traditionalists to have had oral sex in the last year with their partner. They also are more likely to have had anal sex. And they are more likely to have had same-gender sex. In fact, as we move along the scale from traditionalist to recreationalist, the frequency of oral sex, anal sex, and same-gender sex increases.

Overall, people's sexual opinions and their behavior mesh quite closely. We cannot tell whether the opinions prompted the behavior or whether the behavior prompted the opinions, or both, but the relationship is clear.

From these findings on attitudes, beliefs, and sexual behavior along with our findings on sexual networks and choices of sexual partners, we can start to see why America has such heated social policy debates about sexual issues such as abortion, public nudity, gay rights, and pornography.

As table 25.2 showed, opinions and social characteristics seem to go hand in hand. The young have one set of opinions about sexuality while older adults have another; conservative Protestants have one set of views while those without religious affiliations have another; the less educated tend to have different views than the well educated. Table 25.3 showed that people's attitudes are reflected in their behavior, so different groups really do act differently.

People tend to choose sexual partners who are just like themselves in education, religion, and race or ethnicity. Now we see that we have probably paired off with someone who has many of our own opinions about sexuality. That is, in fact, probably a key reason why we choose partners from our own social group. Of course, opinions also may shift and become more similar as the partnership continues, but when that happens, it only makes the partnership stronger. It can be very difficult to maintain a sexual relationship with someone who strongly disagrees with you about such matters as whether abortion or extramarital sex is always wrong or whether religious beliefs always guide sexual behavior.

Our friends and families, the members of our social networks, also tend to be like us in social characteristics, and so they are likely to share many of our opinions about sexual behavior. Consequently, when we have discussions with our friends we tend to be speaking to people who are like us and who agree with us about sex. So we tend to get reinforcement for our views. That is probably one of the main reasons why our opinions are so internally consistent and so well reflected in our sexual behavior.

But all this reinforcement and consistency makes it very threatening to change our views, to become convinced by an outside argument or to change an opinion about one aspect of sexual behavior, such as whether extramarital sex is always wrong, without changing any other opinions. Our opinions, behavior, and social networks all tend to encourage us to hold to those views that help tie all these opinions, beliefs, and behavior together. And when we see these sets of behaviors as woven together by our religious beliefs and our ethical principles, we are, quite understandably, reluctant to give ground. So the national debates on so many of these sexual issues become heated and all sides become entrenched. No wonder we are a nation that is deeply conflicted about sexual matters and that the disputes seem to go on forever, with no compromises in sight.

And with this we have traveled full circle, going from an investigation of what people do and who they are to who they are and what they do and what they believe about sex. We began our study by asking whether sexual behavior could be studied in the same way as other social behaviors and, if so, whether it followed any social rules. We asked whether the privateness of sexual behavior and the powerful myths put it in a class apart from other social behaviors or whether, when we drew back the curtain and looked at what really happens, sexual behavior would turn out to be not so mysterious after all.

In every instance, our data have shown that social forces are powerful and persistent in determining sexual behavior. We have found that our society constrains us, nudging us toward partners who are like ourselves. But, at the same time, it frees us, putting us together with people who have the same sorts of general understandings about sex that we do and so easing our way into sexual intimacies and revelations. We also found that although America may not be as sexy a place as it is often portrayed, most people are satisfied with the sexual lives they have chosen or that were imposed upon them.

America is not the golden land of eroticism where everybody who is young and beautiful has a hot sex life. Nor is it a land where vast hordes of miserable people, kicked out of the sexual banquet, lick their wounds in silence and resentment. Instead, it is a nation that uses social forces to encourage sexual norms and whose sexual behavior is, in large measure, socially determined. It is a nation of people who are for the most part content, or at least not highly dissatisfied, with the sexual lots they have drawn.

And, for those who feel the status quo is far from ideal, we have found that the costs of breaching the social pressures may be high, and the rewards of going along may be great. But by seeing where and how the pressures are brought to bear, we can break away from the myths and magical thinking that have captured us in the past. With unclouded eyes, we can ask whether we really want changes in sexual behavior and, if so, what the benefits and costs of these changes might be.

NOTE

1   Elijah Anderson, *Streetwise: Race, Class, and Change in an Urban Community* (Chicago: University of Chicago Press, 1990).

26 A Place Called Home: A Queer Political Economy: Mexican Immigrant Men's Family Experiences

Lionel Cantú

Introduction

Driving the Interstate 5 Freeway near San Diego and the San Onofre border checkpoint there are large yellow signs graphically depicting a fleeing family (father leading, mother, and child – legs flailing behind). The almost surreal signs are meant to warn motorists of the danger of "illegal" immigrant families trying to cross the busy lanes. This image reveals not only the extreme risks that many immigrants are willing to take to get to the United States but also the way in which we imagine these immigrants. While most motorists probably do not think of a sexual message when they see the warning sign, it's there for us to see; if we only really look. The sign is symbolic at multiple levels: a nuclear family unit, heteronormative in definition, a threat to the racial social order by virtue of its reproductive potential. The sign is also symbolic of the current state of international migration studies: sexuality is an implicit part of migration that has been overlooked – ignored.

In this chapter I examine some of the ways in which sexuality, understood as a dimension of power, has shaped the lives, intimate relationships, and migratory processes of Mexican men who immigrate to the US. More specifically, I utilize ethnographic data to examine how traditional family relations and alternative support systems such as "chosen families" (Weston 1991) influence migration among Mexican immigrant men who have sex with men (MSMs). The men whom I interviewed and

introduce in this essay had a variety of sexual identities both prior to and after migration. An important part of my research, therefore, is to examine from a queer materialist perspective dimensions which shape the social relations of families of origin and families of choice, and thus the intimate context by which identity itself is shaped. I argue for a theoretical move towards a *queer political economy* in order to understand the dynamics which shape "the sexuality of migration" and the fluidity of identities in a global context.

Border Crossers: Family, Migration, Identity

The immigrant men who I interviewed for my research ranged in age from their early twenties to early forties and lived in the greater Los Angeles area. I met these men during my dissertation research fieldwork from 1997 through December of 1999 by making initial contacts through organizations, fliers, and friends and then using a snowball sampling technique to meet others. While each of these men's stories were in their own way unique, there were also similarities that became more evident as my research progressed.

Most of the men came from the Pacific states of Mexico and approximately two-thirds came from the state of Jalisco. About half described their communities of origin as small cities or towns, with only a couple describing their origins as rural; but migration to larger cities (such as Guadalajara or border cities like Tijuana) prior to migrating to the United States was also a common experience. All the men included here were 16 years old or older when they immigrated. Most came from lower-middle-class Mexican backgrounds and had at least a high-school education. Like many of their straight counterparts, many were undocumented. Only two of the men who I met were not working at the time of their interview; one man was unable to work due to health reasons related to AIDS/HIV, the other was looking for work. Several of the men were actually holding down more than one job; one full-time and one part-time. The average income of the men was $20–25,000. English fluency ranged among the men relative to their time in the United States, but none was completely fluent in English. Due in part to this, the men interviewed reported daily lives that were for the most part Spanish speaking. In addition, nearly all estimated that more than 75 percent of their social circles were Latino.

In the following pages I will introduce six of the twenty men whom I formally interviewed. I selected these particular interviews as representative of the range of experiences related to me. However, the interview excerpts included below should not be considered representative of all Mexican immigrant men who have sex with men (MSMs) to the United States – the diversity of experiences is far greater than can be captured here. The men I have included identified as either bisexual or homosexual (gay) at the time of the interviews. In addition, I do not include the voice of transgendered Mexican immigrants, although some of the men do have experience with cross-dressing. Yet the voices represented here do reveal the complexity of the sexuality of migration and the importance of including sexuality in our analysis. I will first provide a general description of these men and then discuss their experiences as they relate to family, migration, and sexual identity.

- *Lalo* is a 33-year-old immigrant from Guadalajara, Jalisco. The fifth of nine children, Lalo comes from what he describes as a "very poor" class background. He migrated to the United States in 1983 and is a legal resident who currently lives in Fountain Valley.

- *Armando* is a 32-year-old Mexican national born in the state of Jalisco where he spent eight years in a seminary studying to be a priest. He is the oldest of eight children (four boys and four girls). He moved to the United States in 1995 and is an undocumented immigrant. He currently lives in Santa Ana but lived in Los Angeles with his brother when we met.

- *Gabriel* is a 23-year-old undocumented immigrant who has lived in the Orange County area for the past five years where he works as a Medical Assistant. The fourth of six children, Gabriel moved to the US from Nayarit, Mexico in 1993 when he was 18. Gabriel lives in Fullerton.

- *Paco*, a native of La Piedad, Michoacan, is 30 years old and now lives in Tustin. He is the youngest of six children (four sisters and a brother). Paco's father died three months after he was born. Paco is a legal resident of the United States, although he immigrated illegally in 1990.

- *Roberto* is in his early forties and has lived in the US since migrating from Mexico in 1994. The fourth of five children, he comes from a prestigious and well-to-do family in Nayarit, Mexico. Although never married, Roberto has a teenaged son who lives in Mexico with his mother. Roberto now lives in the San Fernando Valley and works as an AIDS educator for a Latino community organization.

- *Manuel* is 30 years old, identifies as bisexual, and is currently unemployed, although he worked as a registered nurse in Guadalajara, Mexico. He is the third of eight children (seven boys and one girl) and grew up in Tlaquepaque, a town famous for its artisans and now considered part of the Guadalajara metro area. A Jehovah's Witness, he considers himself to be very religious. Due to his HIV status he moved to the US in 1996 to be with his family and is an undocumented immigrant. He lives with his family in Santa Ana, who know of his condition but are not aware of his sexual identity.

- *Carlos* migrated from Guadalajara in 1990 and is currently seeking political asylum in the US based on his sexual orientation. Because Carlos was an active member of the Democratic Revolutionary Party (PRD), an opposition party to Mexico's ruling Institutional Revolutionary Party (PRI), he fears that he may be imprisoned or murdered if he returns to Mexico. He now lives in Los Angeles.

Family Life in Mexico

Social scientists have historically given great focus to the role of *la familia* in Latino culture. Scholarship often points to Latino "familism," defined as the value and preservation of the family over individual concerns (Moore and Pachon 1985; Williams 1990), as the contentious source of both material and emotional support and patriarchal oppression. The stereotype is problematic for a number of reasons, not the least of which is the fact that the same argument could be made of most families regardless of their cultural context. Thus, in this section, while I discuss how the early family lives of Mexican immigrant MSMs influenced migratory processes, my aim is not to reproduce a cultural pathology of *la familia* but, rather, to examine the family as a site where normative constructions of gender and sexuality are reproduced and in which the dynamics of migration are materially embedded.

During my interviews most of the men remembered their lives as children in Mexico fondly. Yet, even when memories of early family life were positive, the daily lessons of normative masculinity which these men learned often resulted in emotional conflicts. I asked them to share with me their memories of family life and educational experiences in order to better understand the processes by which normative gender roles and sexuality are learned. Most early childhood memories were shared with smiles and consisted of generally carefree days; playing typical games and going to school. Most also reported that they were good students who received awards for their scholarship and genuinely seemed to have enjoyed school. However, even men like Paco, who reported that his childhood was "a great time...a very beautiful stage of my life," expressed a sense of inner conflict rooted in normative definitions of masculinity.

These conflicts were even more pronounced for men like Lalo whose memories of early life in Mexico were not good ones. Recounting his childhood Lalo told me:

> As I child I was very mischievous. I was sexually abused when I was seven by the neighbor, a man of forty. It was a childhood experience that affected me greatly. This person continued to abuse me, he would give me money, later I would go looking for him myself and I was like his "boyfriend" until I was nine. I knew what he was doing was wrong so I never told anyone.

Paternostro (1998) reports that child sexual abuse by a family member is a common phenomenon in Latin America (whether it is more prevalent there than in other countries is debatable). In fact Lalo was not the only man I interviewed who was sexually abused as a child, but he was the most forthcoming about the experience. Later in the interview he explained that he was also abused by two older male cousins and when he told his father about the abuse his father's response was to rape him for being a *maricón*.

None of the sexually abused men, including Lalo, remember connecting these experiences to homosexuality at the time of their occurrence; in part because they didn't really know what homosexuality was. Lalo explained that although he had never heard the word "homosexual," words like *maricón* and *joto* were commonly heard in his home. However, Lalo related these terms to effeminate men or *vestidas* like the man in his neighborhood who dressed like a woman. Many informants related similar experiences. As Carlos explained: "Across from us lived the town *maricón*. In every town there is the drunk and the *maricón*, and the *maricón* lived across the street." As children the question of what a *maricón* was remained somewhat of a mystery; although they knew it wasn't anything "good." For instance, it wasn't until later that Lalo started to understand what "homosexual" meant. He explained:

After about the age of twelve or thirteen there was a lot of sexual play among the boys of the *colonia*. We would masturbate one another. There were about twelve of us in the group and we would form a circle and masturbate one another. Later, couples would form and we would penetrate one another. Now they are all grown up and married but there was a lot of sexual play when we were kids.... There were some boys who would refuse to join us, saying, "that's for *maricones*" or "you're going to be a *joto* or a woman." It was then that I started to understand but I never thought that I was going to be like a woman.

Masculine discourse that devalues the feminine and equates homosexuality to the feminine is, of course, not particular to Mexican culture (cf. Fellows 1996; Murray and Roscoe 1998). However, as Lalo explained, homosexuality and femininity are not popularly understood as synonymous. "Being a *joto* is to not be man. Neither a man nor a woman, it is to be an abomination, a curse." Prieur's (1998) recent work on male-to-female transgendered residents of Mexico City supports Lalo's analysis and suggests that class perspectives are an

important dimension of its construction. Thus, the relationship of homosexuality to the feminine is more complex than a synonymous equation implies. Homosexuality is not only the opposite of masculinity, it is a corruption of it, an unnatural form which by virtue of its transgression of the binary male/female order poses a threat that must be contained or controlled.

The liminal/marginal location of homosexuality, perhaps best understood as shaped by what Almaguer (1993) refers to as a sex/gender/power axis, is reproduced through messages in everyday life. Discussing his daily chores at home, Paco said:

My duties at home in particular, well, they were almost never designated to us. I liked very much to sweep, mop, wash the dishes, and when [my mother and sisters] would make cake I always liked to be there when they were preparing it. But only when my mom and my sisters were there, because my brother would often be in the United States. I always liked to help my mom and my sisters, but when my brother would get there, I always had to hide or not do it because he would tell me "You are not a woman to be doing that, that's for the *maricones*." Then, since I was scared of him, I wouldn't do it anymore. But it was what I liked to do, up till now; I like cleaning very much and chores like that. I like to cook very much, I like to have everything clean – I've always liked that.

When I asked Paco to discuss the issue of "women's work" in more detail, he explained:

In Mexico they say "Oh, a homosexual person or a *maricón* or a *joto* are those persons that are dressed like women." They always have a little of that mentality. For example, there were times that a guy named Luis would pass by and he always left his nails long and his hair long like a woman. He had a bag, and he would put on women's pants or a woman's blouse, and he might have put on makeup but not a lot, but obviously he would go around like a woman. Then all the people, well, they said things, but in my family one time I heard my mother call him, she would call them *frescos* [fresh], there goes this *fresco*, there goes that *fresco*, I would hear my mom say that. Then I would get angry when I would hear that, because I would say "Well, I am not like that, but I am attracted to young men."

Armando expressed learning the same type of sex/gender message through child's play. Armando explained that he liked to play with paper dolls and more than anything liked to cut out the clothes, yet he hid when he did so. When I asked him why, Armando replied:

It's the only game I remember playing secretly. I knew my parents wouldn't like it. I thought it was perfectly normal, it was only bad because it was something that little girls do.

The struggle which Paco and Armando relate in attempting to negotiate the perceived contradictions of sex, gender, and sexual identities was a common theme of many of my interviews. Participants expressed a certain sense of isolation or "not belonging" and not wanting to disappoint their families. Even learning to emulate normative gender and sexual performances was not, in itself, sufficient to resolve these conflicts. For some men, these tensions were a catalyst for migration itself.

Leaving Home

One of the questions that I asked immigrant interviewees was what their top three reasons for immigrating were. After analyzing the answers given, it became clear that sexuality was indeed influencing reasons for migration and that "family" dynamics were often linked to these reasons. However, understanding how sexuality actually influenced these decisions was not always as clear cut as having people respond, "it was

my sexuality" – although that sometimes happened. For example, Lalo told me, "Ninety percent of the reason I migrated was because of my sexuality." Such reasons obviously resonate with D'Emilio (1993) and Rubin's (1992) model of rural to urban migration by "gay" men and women seeking greater anonymity and "gay life" in the cities. Yet, in order to understand how sexuality is linked to other socioeconomic dimensions more fully, one must attempt to connect the micro with the meta and macro dimensions of life. That is to say, one cannot separate individual reasons for migration from the larger processes that shape people's everyday lives and perceived "choices." Several themes did arise from the interviews, sometimes from the same source, and are implicated in a queer political economy in different ways.

For example, all of the men I interviewed, in one form or another, gave financial reasons for migrating to the United States. And indeed, immigration scholars have traditionally placed a great deal of emphasis on economic reasons for migration, yet to a great degree their vision of the economic realm is extremely limited. The social inequalities of sexuality, like race and gender, are integrally linked to the economic structures of society. Groups that are marginalized as sexual minorities are constrained by the limits of discrimination and prejudice which may limit their socioeconomic opportunities. Thus, when an immigrant who is part of a sexual minority says that they immigrated for financial reasons, sexuality must be part of the analysis. For instance, even one of the people I interviewed in Mexico who owned his own pesticide and fertilizer business felt the constraints of heterosexism. Business networks, he explained, depend upon having the right image, which means a wife, children, and social events tied to church and school. Clearly as a gay man he was outside this world. His class privilege and the fact that he is his own "boss," however, permits him to remain in Mexico relatively free from some of the pressures that drive others to migrate.

Thus, while men like Lalo clearly migrate to escape a sense of sexual oppression, for others the decision to migrate to the United States is influenced by a combination of sexual liberation and economic opportunities. For example, Gabriel moved to the US from Nayarit, Mexico when he was 18 but explained that he had begun to prepare himself for immigrating at 16. When I asked him why, he explained that he had two major reasons for coming to the US.

> First, I wanted a better level of education. And the second reason was sexuality. I wanted to be able to define myself and have more freedom with respect to that. I wanted to come here to live, not to distance myself from my family but to hide what I already knew I had. I knew I was gay but I thought I might be able to change it. I needed to come here and speak to people, to learn more about it, because in Mexico it's still very taboo. There isn't so much liberation.

Gabriel's experience reveals how the tension of sexual desire versus "not wanting to distance" oneself from family may serve as a migratory "push." Yet while he clearly moved to the United States seeking a more liberal sexual environment it was not just a "personal" matter, it was also because he felt he had limited economic opportunities as a "gay" man in Mexico. Staying in Mexico might very well have meant either attempting to create a heteronormative family or dealing with social and economic discrimination as a gay man.

Sometimes homosexual relationships might have subtle influences such as serving to establish or expand social networks, or they might have a more direct influence driving migration itself. For instance, Roberto explained to me that he was quite happy with his life in Mexico as a civil servant but that people had begun to gossip about his sexual orientation and he feared for his job security, especially since he had

recently learned that he was HIV positive. Roberto had met a man from the United States who was vacationing in Mexico and had maintained a friendly relationship with him. When the American suggested to Roberto that he move to the US to live with him, Roberto took advantage of the opportunity and moved to Los Angeles. Although he is no longer in a relationship with the American, they continue to be friends. In this case, new (transnational) social bonds are created similar to the kinship networks that migration scholars argue facilitate migration, yet these are not "blood-based" but rather based on affiliation – transnational gay networks.

Finding Their Way Home

Adapting to life in the United States is difficult for any migrant, but for immigrants who migrate to the United States expecting a gay utopia like Lalo, the reality of life in the United States can be quite a blow. Indeed Lalo had returned to Mexico for two years after first migrating to the United States because of his disillusionment, but returned when he realized that his prospects as a gay man were limited in Mexico. Thus, for Lalo, "home" was no longer Jalisco. While there are a number of important aspects of an immigrant's experiences adapting to their new "home," in this section I focus on how sexuality might be related to a migrant's adaptation and incorporation. Specifically, I am concerned here with kin networks and the home as mechanisms for adaptation.

In her research on gay and lesbian kin relations, Weston (1991) demonstrates how gays and lesbians construct "chosen" families based on shared affinities and relationships of both material and emotional support. Kinship (biological) plays a central role in migration as a means by which immigrants receive support and acquire important knowledge for survival and adaptation (cf. Chavez 1992). While the Mexican men I interviewed often utilized kinship networks to these ends they also depended upon networks which were similar to those described by Weston. About half of the immigrants I spoke with utilized pre-existing gay networks to migrate to the United States. They were people like Lalo who migrated with the help of a gay compatriot already living in Los Angeles, and like Roberto who came with the help of a gay American. But even some of those who utilized kin networks for initial migration also used gay networks for meeting other gay Latino men, finding gay roommates, job contacts, and other types of information. The existence and use of these alternative networks depended to a large extent on how the men identified sexually, to what extent they were "out of the closet," and to some extent on their ability to speak English (and thus expand their networks into the mainstream gay world).

For instance, although Paco migrated and found his first job using kinship networks, he was soon able to develop a gay network as well.

My second job was in a company where they made pools. I obtained that job through a [gay] friend, an American, who is the person, the third person that I have to thank about my legal status here in this country. He helped me get the job because it was the company of a friend of his. In the morning I would clean the offices and then I would go to the warehouse and take inventory or I would clean the warehouse or cut fiberglass, or things like that. And they paid me well at that time but I worked only a few hours. So after that, since they said "Oh, you clean so well," and they had some very beautiful houses, over in Laguna Beach. Sometimes I would stay over because I could not finish in the weekend. The owners of the company were gay. They would go to San Francisco, or wherever they were going, they always traveled on the weekend, they left me the key. "Here is the stereo and here is the television," and everything like that because I had to sleep over. Then I would go home when they returned on Sundays.

Ironically, Paco is one of the people who assured me that sexuality had not influenced his migratory experiences in the least. This excerpt, however, reveals that gay social networks were an aid for finding work. In addition, Paco shares a home with a lesbian niece and has allowed other gay immigrants to stay with him temporarily until they are able to move on.

Carlos also made use of gay networks in a similar manner. When he migrated to the United States he first lived for two months in Watsonville, California, with a brother and then went to live with his two sisters – who are lesbians – in Milwaukee for two years. He then moved to Los Angeles after meeting and starting a relationship with a gay man. Like Paco, Carlos revealed that his gay friends had helped him find work and even helped him out financially. "Because of my gay friends, I have never gone without," he said.

Both Paco's and Carlos's experiences also point to the fact that sexuality is an important dimension of immigrant household arrangements. While recent immigration literature has discussed the importance of household arrangements as "landing pads" for migrant adaptation (cf. Chavez 1992, 1994), the sexual dimensions of these arrangements are missing from the analyses. For an individual who has migrated to the United States seeking a more liberal sexual environment, it makes little sense to live in a home constrained by heteronormative relations. While about half of the Mexican men I interviewed originally lived with family members when they migrated, most had formed alternative living arrangements as soon as they were able to. Lalo's home exemplifies this alternative type of arrangement.

When I first met Lalo he was living in Santa Ana in an apartment which he shared with three other immigrant men, all gay. Since our first meeting, Lalo has moved twice and has had a number of different roommates, always gay Latino immigrant men. Sometimes the men, especially if they were recent immigrants, would stay only a short time until they found another place to live. It was clear that Lalo's home was a "landing pad," but it was one where Latino men could be openly gay, support one another and share information which was essential for adaptation. Although the men did not explicitly define these relations as "family," they did sometimes refer to each other affectionately as siblings (sometimes as "sisters" and sometimes as "brothers"). Regardless of how these relationships were labeled it was clear that an alternative support system had been created. It is precisely in this type of living arrangement that many men discover the space which transforms the way they think about themselves and their sexual identities.

Migrating Identities

One of the contributions of postmodern and postcolonial literature (including Queer Theory) is that identity is no longer understood as something inherently fixed and stable. Rather, identity is understood as mutable and plural; that is, the subject is the intersection of multiple identities (race/ethnicity, gender, sexuality, etc.) that change and have salience at different moments in time and place. Given the dramatic socio-spatial changes which immigrants experience, their sexual identities therefore cannot be assumed to be stable. As Iain Chambers (1994: 25) puts it, "Identity is formed on the move." The effects of migration upon the sexual identities of Mexican immigrant MSMs are ultimately linked to their emotional and material relationships to their biological families and the degree to which they have been able to resolve the normative sexuality and gender conflicts that fed their desire to migrate.

I asked the men I interviewed if they felt that they had changed at all since migrating to the United States. Nearly all of the men responded with a resounding yes. The changes they described generally centered around racial, gender, sexual, and class identities.

Most of the men inevitably referred to a more liberal sexual environment as a reason for their transformations. Migrating to the United States was for many men one step in a series towards what might be called "a journey to the self." For Gabriel, the desire to live in a place where he could develop his human potential as a "gay man" was a driving force in his decision to immigrate. He adds,

> I have two names, Gabriel Luis, and my family calls me Luis. I've always said that Luis is the person who stayed in Mexico. Once I came here, Gabriel was born. Because, like I've told you, once I was here I defined myself sexually and I've changed a lot emotionally, more than anything emotionally, because I found myself.

This journey of "self-discovery" is intimately linked to resistance to the normative gender and sex regimes described earlier. While earlier scholarship asserted that Mexican male sexual identities were based on the active or passive (*activo/pasivo*) role of the participant (where only the passive was deemed homosexual), more recent research, including my own, finds that Mexican sexual identities are more complex.

Most informants remembered first being aware of their attraction to boys or men in early childhood. Some remembered being attracted to the same sex as young as age four, but the majority of recollections were a bit later. Carlos remembered, "I was around eight years old. I could recognize the beauty of men. But from then on it was an issue of denial." The pressure to conform, or as Lalo described, "la lucha de no querer ser gay" (the struggle of not wanting to be gay) took a toll on most of the men who I interviewed, perhaps most eloquently described by Armando.

Armando explained that he had been tormented by schoolmates after around the fourth grade. They would call him *joto* and *maricon*. He explains,

> But I learned how to hide it better, so it wasn't noticeable. I no longer isolated

myself, instead I would mix with the troublemakers at school so that their reputation would rub-off on me and so no one would tell me anything anymore. A new student arrived who was even more obvious than me and to a certain extent he was my salvation. Everyone focused their attention on him and it was a load off of me. It gave me the opportunity to get closer to the other students and do everything that they did, to act like them, have girlfriends and not be the "good boy" anymore – to take on the heterosexual role.

Armando would later join a seminary in an attempt to escape his sexual feelings and began to lift weights so that his appearance was more masculine. Eventually, however, he realized he needed to face who he "really" was.

> I feel that I lost a lot of my essence as a homosexual during that time. I see it like that now. At that time I only wanted to be part of a group, to be accepted. It's horrible to feel marginalized, in a corner, abnormal. In my attempts to be like everyone else wanted me to be I lost much of my self.

Two months after migrating to the United States seeking the freedom to be a gay man he confessed to a cousin who he was staying with that he was gay. She told him that she accepted and loved him as he was but that he needed to talk to his brothers. Armando told his brothers one by one and they all accepted his homosexuality (although it was by no means easy). He then decided to tell his widowed mother. At the time of our interview it had been five months since he had written his mother a five-page letter explaining his struggle to accept himself. A month later Armando's mother wrote him back asking forgiveness and assuring him that he would have her support and unconditional love. Armando has been able to successfully integrate his calling to service with his desire to be true to himself. He now works as an AIDS educator and program coordinator for an organization that serves gay Latino men.

Like Armando, other men who migrated to the United States also came out to their families and some found acceptance as well. In some of these men's cases it seems that the acceptance is in part tied to a reversal in family roles. Where once they were dependent upon their families for support, now their families are dependent upon them. Thus, while Almaguer (1993) has argued that economic interdependence stifles a gay identity from forming among Latino MSMs, my research reveals that it may actually facilitate familial acceptance. For instance, since migrating to the United States Lalo has also gained acceptance from the family who threw him out of the house. He explained to me that he has sent money to Mexico to have his mother's house repaired and to pay for his brother's tuition and that his family now respects him. Lalo related,

> I'm much more secure now. I'm not afraid to say I'm a homosexual. I'm content being gay and I can help others. I'm stronger and have achieved a lot of things.

Thus the transformation in economic roles and physical separation has allowed Lalo the opportunity to be both gay and "accepted" by his family.

There were, however, a couple of men who I interviewed who were openly gay prior to migrating to the United States. In both cases these men had upper-class backgrounds. The difference which class makes in mitigating the effects of homophobia is significant and needs to be studied more closely. For example, when I asked Roberto about his son he laughed out loud and said:

> Oh my son! My son was the product of an agreement. His mother knew that I was gay. My partner of ten years and I lived together [in Tepic, Nayarit] and she lived in front of us. She knew of my relationship with Alejo and the three of us would go out to dance. In a small town, well, it was known that she was the friend of "the boys." We would go out to dance,

she would come to our home to watch television, listen to music, or have a drink. Then one day she told me flat-out that she wanted to have my baby. Then between the jokes I began to understand and between the jokes we ended up in bed. We had sex for two or three months and one day she called me and told me she was pregnant. I was 23 or 24 and was completely out of the closet with my family and I didn't care about anything.

Without a doubt, Roberto's class privilege allowed him to not "care about anything" as an openly gay man. In all probability it also shaped his gay social networks, which allowed him to migrate to the United States as well.

To be clear, for those men who do not have such privileges in Mexico, migrating to the United States does not necessarily afford them these privileges either. While there may be more space to be "gay" in the United States, migrating has its costs. Carlos lamented,

> Being away from Mexico creates a strong nationalistic feeling with a lot of nostalgia. You begin to notice how different the system is here than in Mexico. An economic system that changes your life completely. A system where one forgets about other things that in Mexico were a priority. Here one lives life from the perspective of money. Working and making enough money to pay your bills is more important than having friends and doing what you like. In Mexico it's very different. It's more important to have friends, one lives less a slave to the clock. One forgets these things and becoming aware of that has made me very sad.

Discovering the virulence of racism in the United States seems to counterbalance any feelings of sexual liberation. I asked the men, in an open-ended manner, if they had ever experienced discrimination (without defining the type). Nearly all of the men responded in ways similar to Carlos: "For being Latino, for not speaking English per-

fectly, for the color of my skin." The irony, of course, is that in their attempts to escape one form of bigotry, most of the Mexican men I interviewed discovered that not only had they not entirely escaped it but they now faced another. As Lalo said, "It wasn't true that homosexuals are free, that they can hold hands or that Americans like Mexicans." Under these circumstances the role of a support system becomes all the more important and for queer Latino immigrant men this often means that new "families" must be created.

Building Family

I was naively surprised by the responses I got when I asked immigrant men about their future plans. I suppose that I had allowed myself to become so immersed in the migration literature that I was expecting to hear something more along the lines of "return to Mexico and start my own business." More common, however, were responses like Paco's.

> I want to be anywhere close to the person I love, to support me. If it's in Mexico, a lot better because I would have my family and that person near me. But, more than anything, right now I worry a lot for my own person and for the partner who I think will be what I wait for in my life. And I see myself in a relationship with a lot of affection, and maybe by then, living with that person, together. And maybe even to get married.
> *Q: So your plans for the future are to have a partner?*
> A stable partner, be happy, and give them all my support, and I would little help that person shine, succeed in anything I could help. I will try to do it all the time. If he accomplishes more than I have it will make me very happy because in that aspect I am not egotistical. And still more things that are positive; get more involved in helping people that need me, in every aspect. Be happy, make my partner happy, above all make myself happy, and my

family, my friends, all the people that like me, and I like.

This type of response does not exclude dreams of material wealth and entrepreneurship, but it centers and gives priority to affective dimensions – to building new families. The desire for stable relationships reflects not only the difficulty of maintaining such relationships in Mexico, but also the isolation that these men feel in the United States. This isolation which gay Mexican immigrant men feel is due in some measure to language difficulties, but racial and class issues also play into it. For instance, Carlos explained to me that although he was in a relationship at the time of our interview he didn't see much of a future in it.

> I don't have many expectations for my relationship because my partner is not Latino. I think that, ideally, for a stable relationship I need to be with a Latino… someone who identifies as Latino. Someone intelligent and a little more cultured. Someone who has the capacity to go to an art or photography exhibit and enjoy it. Someone open-minded, open to learning from other cultures and who is financially independent.

The problem, of course, is that the social location of Mexican immigrant MSMs in the United States is a marginal one. "Stability" is not easily established and "financial independence" may take years to accomplish, if at all. The problem is exacerbated by the fact that there are few public spaces where Latino gay men can openly meet one another. Thus, creating family or even a sense of community depends in no small part upon the ability of queer Latinos to build a new "home" with limited resources and little external support.

Conclusion

"Who do you turn to for support?" I asked the men I interviewed. The standard response was "family and friends." Yet it is clear from my discussions with these men, and the data presented here, that these relationships (whether biological or chosen) were sometimes strained, always evolving, and ultimately negotiated. A queer materialist analysis of the experiences of Mexican immigrant men who have sex with men reveals the ways in which dimensions of family, migration, and sexual identity intersect and are embedded within a political economy. Many of the men interviewed felt marginalized by heteronormative definitions of masculinity reproduced through and embodied in the traditional family. These norms, reproduced in daily activities since childhood, marginalize not only men with "feminine" characteristics but also those able to "pass" who were instilled with a fear of "discovery." Associations of femininity to homosexuality created a sense of confusion in some men who, although they were attracted to men, did not identify as feminine. The economic liability that derived from not creating a heteronormative family unit as an adult also influenced the immigration process. These strict gender/sex regimes were powerful enough to drive many men to migrate to the United States in search of a more liberal environment.

A queer political economy perspective of migration also aids in unveiling how sexuality has shaped processes and strategies for adaptation such as social networks and household arrangements. Alternative relations to biological families are created based on sexual orientation, which serve as systems of support. The members of these "chosen families" assist one another through the trials and tribulations of being a queer Mexican immigrant man. Such assistance takes a variety of forms, including helping with migration itself, sharing knowledge and resources such as job information, and even sharing households.

New economic arrangements mean that some men find that they are empowered to "come out" to their biological families as gay men and maintain a level of acceptance and respect from their loved ones. Shared space is also an important dimension linked to the futures of these gay men. Faced with a sense of isolation and a deep desire to form the stable relationships which they were prevented from having in Mexico, space becomes the base for adaptation, community, and shared futures. Thus, for many men who have come to identify as "gay," new family structures become a means by which dreams may be realized.

Although my focus has been on Mexican immigrant men, there are larger implications that need to be explored. When we understand sexuality as a dimension of power (that intersects with other dimensions such as race, gender, and class) in which certain groups are privileged over others, then these implications become more visible. For instance, Argüelles and Rivero (1993) argue that some immigrant women have migrated in order to flee violent and/or oppressive sexual relationships or marriage arrangements which they contest. Little research has been conducted of Latinas in general, far less exists on the intersections of migration and sexuality (regardless of sexual orientation). While it is clear that biological families reproduce normative constructions of gender and sexuality, the ways in which these norms and power relations influence different groups of people in terms of migration and identity are not understood. The research presented here is, hopefully, a step towards the development of a queer materialist paradigm by which the sexual dimensions of migration can be understood and by which further research may be conducted.

NOTE

This chapter represents part of a larger dissertation research project entitled *Border Crossings: Mexican Men and the Sexuality of Migration*. The author gratefully acknowledges the comments and suggestions of the editors and Nancy Naples, as well as the funding support of the Social Science Research Council's Sexuality Fellowship Program and the Ford Foundation which made this research possible. In addition, the author wishes to express his gratitude to the men who participated in this project.

REFERENCES

Almaguer, Tomás. 1993. "Chicano Men: A Cartography of Homosexual Identity and Behavior" in *The Lesbian and Gay Studies Reader*, edited by Abelove, Barale, and Halperin. New York: Routledge.

Anzaldúa, Gloria. 1987. *Borderlands/La Frontera: The New Mestiza*. San Francisco: Aunt Lute.

Argüelles, Lourdes and Anne M. Rivero. 1993. "Gender/Sexual Orientation Violence and Transnational Migration: Conversations with Some Latinas We Think We Know." *Urban Anthropology*, 22 (3–4): 259–76.

Bennett, James R. 1996. Introduction to "Materialist Queer Theory: A Working Bibliography" in *The Material Queer*, edited by Donald Morton. Boulder, CO: Westview Press.

Cantú, Lionel (Forthcoming) "Entre Hombres/Between Men: Latino Masculinities and Homosexualities" in *Gay Masculinities*, edited by Peter Nardi. Newbury Park, CA: Sage.

Cantú, Lionel. 1999. *Border Crossings: Mexican Men and the Sexuality of Migration*. Dissertation manuscript. University of California, Irvine.

Carrier, Joseph. 1995. *De Los Otros: Intimacy and Homosexuality Among Mexican Men*. New York: Columbia University Press.

Chambers, Iain. 1994. *Migrancy, Culture, Identity*. New York: Routledge.

Chavez, Leo. 1992. *Shadowed Lives: Undocumented Immigrants in American Society*. San Diego, CA: Harcourt Brace Jovanovich College Publishers.

Chavez, Leo. 1994. "The Power of the Imagined Community: The Settlement of Undocumented Mexicans and Central Americans in the United States." *American Anthropologist*, 96 (1): 52–73.

Cousins, Mark and Athar Hussain. 1984. *Michel Foucault*. New York: Macmillan.

D'Emilio, John. 1993 [1983]. "Capitalism and Gay Identity" in *Lesbians, Gay Men, and the Law*, edited by W. B. Rubenstein. New York: New Press.

Donovan, Josephine. 1992. *Feminist Theory*. New York: Continuum.

Engels, Frederick. 1993. *The Origin of the Family, Private Property and the State*. New York: International Publishers.

Fellows, Will (ed.). 1996. *Farm Boys: Lives of Gay Men from the Rural Midwest*. Madison: University of Wisconsin Press.

Foucault, Michel. 1978. *The History of Sexuality: An Introduction*, trans. Robert Hurley. New York: Pantheon.

Gluckman, Amy and Betsy Reed (eds.). 1997. *HomoEconomics: Capitalism, Community, and Lesbian and Gay Life*. New York: Routledge.

Gutmann, Matthew C. 1996. *The Meanings of Macho: Being a Man in Mexico City*. Berkeley: University of California Press.

Hennessy, Rosemary and Chrys Ingraham (eds.). 1997. *Materialist Feminism: A Reader in Class, Difference, and Women's Lives*. New York: Routledge.

Herdt, Gilbert H. 1994 [1981]. *Guardians of the Flutes: Idioms of Masculinity*. New York: McGraw-Hill.

Hondagneu-Sotelo, Pierrette. 1994. *Gendered Transitions: Mexican Experiences of Immigration*. Los Angeles: University of California Press.

Hondagneu-Sotelo, Pierrette and Michael Messner. 1994. "Gender Displays and Men's Power: 'The New Man' and the Mexican Immigrant Man" in *Theorizing Masculinities*, edited by Harry Brod and Michael Kaufman. Thousand Oaks, CA: Sage Publications.

Ingram, Gordon Brent, Anne-Marie Bouthillette, and Yolanda Retter. 1997. *Queers In Space: Communities, Public Places, Sites of Resistance*. Seattle, WA: Bay Press.

Jagose, Annamarie. 1996. *Queer Theory: An Introduction*. New York: New York University Press.

McIntosh, Mary. 1968. "The Homosexual Role." *Social Problems*, 16 (69): 182–92.

Martin, Biddy. 1988. "Feminism, Criticism, and Foucault" in *Feminism and Foucault: Reflections on Resistance*, edited by Irene Diamond and Lee Quinby. Boston, MA: Northeastern University Press.

Massey, Douglas S. and Kristin Espinosa. 1995. "What's Driving Mexico–US Migration? A Theoretical, Empirical, and Policy Analysis." Unpublished paper.

Massey, Douglas S., Joaquin Arango, Graeme Hugo, Ali Kouaouci, Adela Pellegrino, and J. Edward Taylor. 1993. "Theories of International Migration: Review and Appraisal." *Population and Development Review*, 19 (3): 431–67.

Moore, Joan and Harry Pachon. 1985. *Hispanics in the United States*. Englewood Cliffs, NJ: Prentice-Hall.

Morton, Donald (ed.). 1996. *The Material Queer*. Boulder, CO: Westview Press.

Murray, Stephen O. 1995. *Latin American Male Homosexualities*. Albuquerque: University of New Mexico Press.

Murray, Stephen O. and Will Roscoe (eds.). 1998. *Boy-Wives and Female Husbands: Studies in African Homosexualities*. New York: St. Martin's Press.

Paternostro, Silvana. 1998. *In the Land of God and Man: Confronting Our Sexual Culture*. New York: Dutton.

Pedraza, Silvia. 1991. "Women and Migration: The Social Consequences of Gender." *Annual Review of Sociology*, 17: 303–25.

Prieur, Annick. 1998. *Mema's House, Mexico City: On Transvestites, Queens, and Machos*. Chicago, IL: University of Chicago Press.

Rubin, Gayle. 1992 [1984]. "Thinking Sex: Notes for a Radical Theory of the Politics of Sexuality" in *The Lesbian and Gay Studies Reader*, edited by Abelove, Barale, and Halperin. New York: Routledge.

Seidman, Steven (ed.) 1996. *Queer Theory/Sociology*. Cambridge, MA: Blackwell Publishers.

Weeks, Jeffrey. 1977. *Coming Out: Homosexual Politics in Britain from the Nineteenth Century to the Present*. London: Quartet.

Weston, Kath. 1991. *Families We Choose: Lesbians, Gays, Kinship*. New York: Columbia University Press.

Williams, Norma. 1990. *The Mexican American Family: Tradition and Change*. Dix Hills, NY: General Hall Publishers.

Wood, Charles, H. 1982. "Equilibrium and Historical Structural Perspectives on Migration." *International Migration Review*, 16 (2): 298–319.

27 Gay and Lesbian Families Are Here; All Our Families Are Queer; Let's Get Used to It![1]

Judith Stacey

Until but a short time ago, gay and lesbian families seemed quite a queer concept, even preposterous, if not oxymoronic, not only to scholars and the general public, but even to most lesbians and gay men. The grassroots movement for gay liberation that exploded into public visibility in 1969, when gays resisted a police raid at the Stonewall bar in New York City, struggled along with the militant feminist movement of that period to liberate gays and women *from* perceived evils and injustices represented by the family, rather than *for* access to its blessings and privileges. During the early 1970s, marches for gay pride and women's liberation flaunted provocative, countercultural banners, like "Smash The Family" and "Smash Monogamy." Their legacy is a lasting public association of gay liberation and feminism with family subversion. Yet how "queer" such antifamily rhetoric sounds today, when gays and lesbians are in the thick of a vigorous profamily movement of their own.

Gay and lesbian families are indisputably here. In June of 1993, police chief Tom Potter joined his lesbian, police officer daughter in a Portland, Oregon gay pride march for "family values." By the late 1980s an astonishing "gay-by boom" had swelled the ranks of children living with gay and lesbian parents to between six to fourteen million.[2] *Family Values* is the title of a popular 1993 book by and about a lesbian's successful struggle to become a legal second mother to one of these "turkey-baster" babies, the son she and his biological mother have co-parented since his birth.[3] In 1989 Denmark became the first nation in the world to legalize a form of gay marriage, termed "registered partnerships," and its Nordic neighbors Norway and Sweden soon followed suit. In 1993 thousands of gay and lesbian couples participated in a mass wedding ceremony on the Washington Mall during the largest demonstration for gay rights in US history. Three years later, on March 25, 1996, Mayor of San Francisco Willie Brown proudly presided over a civic ceremony to celebrate the domestic partnerships of nearly 200 same-sex couples. "We're leading the way here in San Francisco," the mayor declared, "for the rest of the nation to fully embrace the diversity of people in love, regardless of their gender or sexual orientation."[4] By then thousands of gay and lesbian couples across the nation were eagerly awaiting the outcome of *Baehr v. Lewin*, cautiously optimistic that Hawaii's Supreme Court will soon order the state to become the first in the United States, and in the modern world, to grant full legal marriage rights to same-sex couples. As this book went to press in May 1996, the Republican Party had just made gay marriage opposition a wedge issue in their presidential campaign.

Gay and lesbian families are undeniably here, yet they are not queer, if one uses the term in the sense of "odd" to signify a marginal or deviant population.[5] It is nearly impossible to define this category of families in a manner that could successfully distinguish all of their members, needs, relationships, or even their values, from those of all other families. In fact, it is almost impossible to define this category in a satisfactory, substantive way at all. What should count as a gay or lesbian family? Even if we bracket the thorny matter of how to define an individual as gay or lesbian and rely on self-identification, we still face a jesuitical challenge. Should we count only families in which every single member is gay? Clearly there are not very many, if even any, of these. Or does the presence of just one gay member color a family gay? Just as clearly, there are very many of these, including those of Ronald Reagan, Colin Powell, Phyllis Schlafly, and Newt Gingrich.[6] More to the point, why would we want to designate a family type according to the sexual identity of one or more of its members? No research, as we will see, has ever shown a uniform, distinctive pattern of relationships, structure, or even of "family values," among families that include self-identified gays. Of course, most nongays restrict the term "gay family" to units that contain one or two gay parents and their children. However, even such families that most commonsensically qualify as gay or lesbian are as diverse as are those which do not.

Gay and lesbian families come in different sizes, shapes, ethnicities, races, religions, resources, creeds, and quirks, and even engage in diverse sexual practices. The more one attempts to arrive at a coherent, defensible sorting principle, the more evident it becomes that the category "gay and lesbian family" signals nothing so much as the consequential social fact of widespread, institutionalized homophobia.[7] The gay and lesbian family label marks the cognitive dissonance, and even emotional threat, that much of the nongay public experiences upon recognizing that gays can participate in family life at all. What unifies such families is their need to contend with the particular array of psychic, social, legal, practical, and even physical challenges to their very existence that institutionalized hostility to homosexuality produces. Paradoxically, the label "gay and lesbian family" would become irrelevant if the nongay population could only "get used to it."

In this chapter I hope to facilitate such a process of normalization, ironically, perhaps, to allow the marker "gay and lesbian" as a family category once again to seem queer – as queer, that is, as it now seems to identify a *family*, rather than an individual or a desire, as heterosexual. I conclude my book with an extensive discussion of this historically novel category of family, not only because of its inherent interest, but to suggest how it crystallizes the general processes of family diversification and change that characterize what I have been describing as the postmodern family condition.[8] Gay and lesbian families represent such a new, embattled, visible, and necessarily self-conscious genre of postmodern kinship, that they more readily expose the widening gap between the complex reality of postmodern family forms and the simplistic modern family ideology that still undergirds most public rhetoric, policy, and law concerning families.[9] In short, I hope to demonstrate that the experience of "homosexuals"[10] should be of immense interest to everyone else. Nongay families, family scholars, and policymakers alike can learn a great deal from examining the experience, struggles, conflicts, needs, and achievements of contemporary gay and lesbian families.

A More, or Less, Perfect Union?

Much nearer at hand, however, than most ever dared to imagine has come the momentous prospect of legal gay marriage. The idea of same-sex marriage used to draw nearly as many jeers from gays and lesbians as from nongays. As one lesbian couple recalls, "In 1981, we were a very, very small handful of lesbians who got married. We took a lot of flak from other lesbians, as well as heterosexuals. In 1981, we didn't know any other lesbians, not a single one, who had had a ceremony in Santa Cruz, and a lot of lesbians live in that city. Everybody was on our case about it. They said, What are you doing? How heterosexual. We really had to sell it."[11]

Less than a decade later, gay and lesbian couples could proudly announce their weddings and anniversaries, not only in the gay press, which now includes specialized magazines for gay and lesbian couples, like *Partners Magazine*, but even in such mainstream, Midwestern newspapers as the Minneapolis *Star Tribune*.[12] Jewish rabbis, Protestant ministers, Quaker meetings, and even some Catholic priests regularly perform gay and lesbian wedding or commitment ceremonies. This phenomenon is memorialized in cultural productions within the gay community, like "Chicks In White Satin," a documentary about a Jewish lesbian wedding which won prizes at recent gay film festivals, but it has also become a fashionable pop culture motif. In December 1995 the long-running TV sitcom program *Roseanne* featured a gay male wedding in a much-hyped episode called "December Bride." Even more provocative, however, was a prime-time lesbian wedding that aired one month later on *Friends*, the highest rated sitcom of the 1995–6 television season. Making a cameo appearance on the January 18, 1996 episode, Candice Gingrich, the lesbian half-sister of right-wing Speaker of the House Newt Gingrich, conducted a wedding ceremony which joined the characters who play a lesbian couple on the series "in holy matrimony" and pronounced them "wife and wife."

When the very first social science research collection about gay parents was published in 1987, not even one decade ago, its editor concluded that however desirable such unions might be, "it is highly unlikely that marriages between same-sex individuals will be legalized in any state in the foreseeable future."[13] Yet, almost immediately thereafter, precisely this specter began to exercise imaginations across the political spectrum. A national poll reported by the *San Francisco Examiner* in 1989 found that 86 percent of lesbians and gay men supported legalizing same-sex marriage.[14] However, it is the pending *Baehr v. Lewin* court decision concerning same-sex marriage rights in Hawaii that has thrust this issue into escalating levels of front-page and prime-time prominence. Amidst rampant rumors that thousands of mainland gay and lesbian couples were stocking their hope chests with Hawaiian excursion fares, poised to fly to tropical altars the instant the first gay matrimonial bans falter, right-wing Christian groups began actively mobilizing resistance. Militant antiabortion leader Randall Terry of Operation Rescue flew to Hawaii in February 1996 to fight "queer marriage," and right-wing Christian women's leader and radio broadcast personality Beverly LaHaye urged her "Godly" listeners to fight gay marriage in Hawaii.[15]

Meanwhile, fearing that Hawaii will become a gay marriage mecca, state legislators have rushed to introduce bills that exclude same-sex marriages performed in other states from being recognized in their own, because the "full faith and credit" clause of the US Constitution obligates interstate recognition of legal marriages. While fourteen states had rejected such bills by May 1995, eight others had passed them, and contests were underway in numerous others, including California.[16] On May 8, 1996, gay marriage galloped onto the nation's center political stage when Republicans introduced the Defense of Marriage Act (DOMA) which defines marriage in exclusively heterosexual terms, as "a legal union between one man and one woman as husband and wife."[17] The last legislation that Republican presidential candidate Bob Dole co-sponsored before he resigned from the Senate to pursue his White House bid full throttle, DOMA exploits homophobia to defeat President Clinton and the Democrats in November 1996. With Clinton severely bruised by the political debacle incited by his support for gay rights in the military when he first took office, but still dependent upon the support of his gay constituency, the President indeed found himself "wedged" between a rock and a very hard place. Unsurprisingly, he tried to waffle. Naming this a "time when we need to do things to strengthen the American family," Clinton publicly opposed same-sex marriage at the same time that he tried to reaffirm support for gay rights and to expose the divisive Republican strategy.[18]

Polemics favoring and opposing gay marriage rights now proliferate in editorial pages and legislatures across the nation, and mainstream religious bodies find themselves compelled to confront the issue. In March 1996 the Vatican felt called upon not merely to condemn same-sex marriage as a "moral disorder," but also to warn Catholics that they would themselves risk "moral censure" if they were to support "the election of the candidate who has formally promised to translate into law the homosexual demand."[19] Just one day after the Vatican published this admonition, the Central Conference of American Rabbis, which represents the large, generally liberal wing of Judaism, took a momentous action in direct opposition. The Conference resoundingly endorsed a resolution to "support the right of gay and lesbian couples to share fully and equally in the rights of civil marriage." Unsurprisingly, Orthodox rabbis immediately condemned the action as prohibited in the Bible and "another breakdown in the family unit."[20] One week later, in another historic development, a lead editorial in the *New York Times* strongly endorsed gay marriage.[21]

As with child custody, the campaign for gay marriage clings to legal footholds carved by racial justice pioneers. It is startling to recall how recent it was that the Supreme Court finally struck down antimiscegenation laws. Not until 1967, that is only two years before Stonewall, did the high court, in *Loving vs. Virginia*, find state restrictions on interracial marriages to be unconstitutional. (Twenty states still had such restrictions on the books in 1967, only one state fewer than the twenty-one which currently prohibit sodomy.) A handful of gay couples quickly sought to marry in the

1970s through appeals to this precedent, but until three lesbian and gay male couples sued Hawaii in *Baehr v. Lewin* for equal rights to choose marriage partners without restrictions on gender, all US courts had dismissed the analogy. In a historic ruling in 1993, the Hawaiian state Supreme Court remanded this suit to the state, requiring it to demonstrate a "compelling state interest" in prohibiting same-sex marriage, a strict scrutiny standard that few believe the state will be able to meet. Significantly, the case was neither argued nor adjudicated as a gay rights issue. Rather, just as ERA opponents once had warned and advocates had denied, passage of an equal rights amendment to Hawaii's state constitution in 1972 paved the legal foundation for *Baehr*.[22]

Most gay activists and legal scholars anticipate a victory for gay marriage when *Baehr* is finally decided early in 1997, but they do not all look forward to this prospect with great delight. Although most of their constituents desire the right to marry, gay activists and theorists continue to vigorously debate the politics and effects of this campaign. Refining earlier feminist and socialist critiques of the gender and class inequities of marriage, an articulate, vocal minority seeks not to extend the right to marry, but to dismantle an institution they regard as inherently, and irredeemably, hierarchical, unequal, conservative, and repressive. Nancy Polikoff, one of the most articulate lesbian legal activist-scholars opposed to the marriage campaign, argues that

> Advocating lesbian and gay marriage will detract from, and even contradict, efforts to unhook economic benefits from marriage and make basic health care and other necessities available to all. It will also require a rhetorical strategy that emphasizes similarities between our relationships and heterosexual marriages, values long-term monogamous coupling above all other relationships, and denies the potential of lesbian and gay marriage to transform the gendered nature of marriage for all people. I fear that the very process

of employing that rhetorical strategy for the years it will take to achieve its objective will lead our movement's public representatives, and the countless lesbians and gay men who hear us, to believe exactly what we say.[23]

A second perspective supports legal marriage as one long-term goal of the gay rights movement, but voices serious strategic objections to making this a priority before there is sufficient public support to sustain a favorable ruling in Hawaii or the nation. Such critics fear that a premature victory will prove pyrrhic, because efforts to defend it against the vehement backlash it has already begun to incite are apt to fail, after sapping resources and time better devoted to other urgent struggles for gay rights. Rather than risk a major setback for the gay movement, they advise an incremental approach to establishing legal family status for gay and lesbian kin ties through a multifaceted struggle for family diversity.[24]

However, the largest, and most diverse, contingent of gay activist voices now supports the marriage rights campaign, perhaps because gay marriage can be read to harmonize with virtually every hue on the gay ideological spectrum. Pro-gay marriage arguments range from profoundly conservative to liberal humanist to radical and deconstructive. Conservatives, like those radicals who still oppose marriage, view it as an institution that promotes monogamy, commitment, and social stability, along with interests in private property, social conformity, and mainstream values. They likewise agree that legalizing gay marriage would further marginalize sexual radicals by segregating countercultural gays and lesbians from the "whitebread" gay couples who could then choose to marry their way into Middle America. Radicals and conservatives, in other words, envision the same prospect, but regard it with inverse sentiments.[25]

Liberal gays support legal marriage, of course, not only to affirm the legitimacy of their relationships and help sustain them in

a hostile world, but as a straightforward matter of equal civil rights. As one long-coupled gay man expresses it: "I resent the fact that married people get lower taxes. But as long as there is this institution of marriage and heterosexuals have that privilege, then gay people should be able to do it too."[26] Liberals also recognize that marriage rights provide access to the social advantages of divorce law. "I used to say, 'Why do we want to get married? It doesn't work for straight people,' one gay lawyer comments. 'But now I say we should care: They have the privilege of divorce and we don't. We're left out there to twirl around in pain.'"[27]

Less obvious or familiar, however, are cogent arguments in favor of gay marriage that some feminist and other critical gay legal theorists have developed in response to opposition within the gay community. Nan Hunter, for example, rejects feminist legal colleague Nancy Polikoff's belief that marriage is an unalterably sexist and heterosexist institution. Building upon critical theories that reject the notion that social institutions or categories have inherent, fixed meanings apart from their social contexts, Hunter argues that legalized same-sex marriage would have "enormous potential to destabilize the gendered definition of marriage for everyone."[28]

Evan Wolfson, director of the Marriage Project of the gay legal rights organization Lambda Legal Defense, who has submitted a brief in support of *Baehr*, pursues the logic of "anti-essentialism" even more consistently. The institution of marriage is neither inherently equal nor unequal, he argues, but depends upon an ever-changing cultural and political context.[29] (Anyone who doubts this need only consider such examples as polygamy, arranged marriages, or the same-sex unions in early Western history documented by the late Princeton historian, John Boswell.) Hoping to use marriage precisely to change its context, gay philosopher Richard Mohr argues that access to legal marriage would provide an opportunity to reconstruct its meaning by serving "as a nurturing ground for social marriage, and not (as now) as that which legally defines and creates marriage and so precludes legal examination of it." For Mohr, social marriage represents "the fused intersection of love's sanctity and necessity's demands," and does not necessarily depend upon sexual monogamy.[30]

Support for gay marriage, not long ago anathema to radicals and conservatives, gays and nongays, alike, now issues forth from ethical and political perspectives as diverse, and even incompatible, as these. The cultural and political context has changed so dramatically since Stonewall that it now seems easier to understand why marriage has come to enjoy overwhelming support in the gay community than to grasp the depth of resistance to the institution that characterized the early movement. Still, I take seriously many of the strategic concerns about the costly political risks posed by a premature campaign. Although surveys and electoral struggles suggest a gradual growth in public support for gay rights, that support is tepid, uneven, and fickle, as the debacle over Clinton's attempt to combat legal exclusion of gays from the military made distressingly clear. Thus, while 52 percent of those surveyed in a 1994 *Time* magazine/ CNN poll claimed to consider gay lifestyle acceptable, 64 percent did not want to legalize gay marriages or to permit gay couples to adopt children.[31]

Gay marriage, despite its apparent compatibility with mainstream family values sentiment, raises far more threatening questions than does military service about gender relations, sexuality, and family life. Few contemporary politicians, irrespective of their personal convictions, display the courage to confront this contradiction, even when urged to do so by gay conservatives. In *Virtually Normal: An Argument About Homosexuality*, *New Republic* editor Andrew Sullivan develops the "conservative case for gay marriage" that he earlier published as an op-ed, which stresses the contribution gay marriage could make to a conservative agenda for family and political life. A review of Sullivan's book in the *New Yorker* points out that, "here is where the advocates of gay rights can steal the conservatives' clothes."[32] Jonathan Rauch wrote about the insignificance of the homosexual minority in a *Wall Street Journal* op-ed he wrote to persuade Republicans that they should support legal gay marriage, not only because it is consistent with conservative values, but to guard against the possibility that gay rights advocates will exploit the party's inconsistency on this issue to political advantage.[33]

The logic behind the conservative case for gay marriage strikes me as compelling. Most importantly, gay marriage would strengthen the ranks of those endangered two-parent, "intact," married-couples families whose praises conservative, "profamily" enthusiasts never seem to tire of singing. Unsurprisingly, however, the case has won few nongay conservative converts to the cause. After all, homophobia is a matter of passion and politics, not logic. The religious right regards homosexuality as an abomination, and it has effectively consolidated its influence over the Republican Party. For example, in 1994 Republicans in the Montana state senate went so far as to pass a bill that would require anyone convicted of homosexual acts to register for life as a violent offender. They reversed their vote in response to an outpouring of public outrage.[34] It was not long afterward, however, that Republican presidential contender Robert Dole returned the thousand-dollar campaign contribution from the gay Log Cabin Republicans in the name, of course, of family values. Nor have figures prominent in the centrist, secular neo-family-values campaign or the communitarian movement, whose professed values affirm both communal support for marital commitment and for tolerance, displayed much concern for such consistency. And even when, in the 1995 fall preelection season, President Clinton sought to "shore up" his standing among gays and lesbians by announcing his administration's support of a bill to outlaw employment discrimination against gays, he specifically withheld his support from gay marriage.[35] First Lady Hillary Rodham Clinton's recent book, *It Takes a Village*, ostensibly written to challenge "false nostalgia for family values," fails even to mention gay marriage or gay families, let alone to advocate village rights and resources for children whose parents are gay.[36]

Despite my personal political baptism in the heady, anti-family crucible of early second-wave feminism, I, for one, have converted to the long-term cause. A "post-modern" ideological stew of discordant convictions enticed me to this table. Like Wolfson, Mohr, and Hunter, I have come to believe that legitimizing gay and lesbian marriages would promote a democratic, pluralistic expansion of the meaning, practice, and politics of family life in the United States. This could help to supplant the destructive sanctity of *the family* with respect for diverse and vibrant *families*.

To begin with, the liberal implications of legal gay marriage are far from trivial, as the current rush by the states and Congress to nullify them should confirm. The Supreme Court is certain to have its docket flooded far into the next century with constitutional conflicts that a favourable decision in Hawaii, or elsewhere, will unleash. Under the "full faith and credit" provision of the Constitution, which requires the 50 states to recognize each other's laws, legal gay marriage in one state could begin to threaten anti-sodomy laws in all the others. Policing marital sex would be difficult to legitimate, and differential prosecution of conjugal sex among same-sex couples could violate equal protection legislation. Likewise, if gay marriages were legalized, the myriad state barriers to child custody, adoption, fertility services, inheritance, and other family rights that lesbians and gay men currently suffer could also become subject to legal challenge. Moreover, it seems hard to overestimate the profound cultural implications for the struggle against the pernicious effects of legally condoned homophobia that would ensue were lesbian and gay relationships to be admitted into the ranks of legitimate kinship. In a society that forbids most public school teachers and counselors even the merest expression of tolerance for homosexuality, while lesbian and gay youth attempt suicide at rates three to five times greater than other youth,[37] granting full recognition to even just whitebread lesbian and gay relationships could have dramatic, and salutary, consequences.

Of course, considerations truer to some of my earlier, more visionary feminist convictions also invite me to join the gay wedding procession. For while I share some of Polikoff's disbelief that same-sex marriage can in itself dismantle the patterned gender and sexual injustices of the institution, I do believe it could make a potent contribution to those projects, as the research on gay relationships I discuss below seems to indicate. Moreover, as Mohr suggests, admitting gays to the wedding banquet invites gays and non-gays alike to consider the kinds of place settings that could best accommodate the diverse needs of all contemporary families.

Subjecting the conjugal institution to this sort of heightened democratic scrutiny could help it to assume varied creative forms. If we begin to value the meaning and quality of intimate bonds over their customary forms, there are few limits to the kinds of marriage and kinship patterns people might wish to devise. The "companionate marriage," a much celebrated, but less often realized, ideal of modern sociological lore, could take on new life. Two friends might decide to marry without basing their bond on erotic or romantic attachment, as Dorthe, a prominent Danish lesbian activist who had initially opposed the campaign for gay marriage, fantasized after her nation's parliament approved gay registered partnerships: "If I am going to marry it will be with one of my oldest friends in order to share pensions and things like that. But I'd never marry a lover. That is the advantage of being married to a close friend. Then, you never have to marry a lover!"[38] Or, more radical still, perhaps some might dare to question the dyadic limitations of Western marriage and seek some of the benefits of extended family life through small-group marriages arranged to share resources, nurturance, and labor. After all, if it is true that "The Two-Parent Family Is Better" than a single-parent family, as family-values crusaders like David Popenoe tirelessly proclaim, might not three-, four-, or more-parent families be better yet, as many utopian communards have long believed?

While conservative advocates of gay marriage surely would balk at such radical visions, they correctly realize that putative champions of committed relationships and of two-parent families who oppose gay marriage can be charged with gross hypocrisy on this score. For access to legal marriage not only would promote long-term, committed intimacy among gay couples, but also would afford invaluable protection to the children of gay parents, as well as indirect protection to closeted gay youth who reside with nongay parents. Clearly, only through a process of massive denial of the fact that millions of children living in gay and lesbian families are here, and here to stay, can anyone genuinely concerned with the best interests of children deny their parents the right to marry.

In the face of arguments for legalizing gay marriage as compelling and incongruent as these, it is hard to dispute Evan Wolfson's enthusiastic claim that "The brilliance of our movement's taking on marriage is that marriage is, at once and truly, both conservative and transformative, easily understood in basic human terms of equality and respect, and liberating in its individual and social potential."[39]

If We Could Only Get Used to It

Far from esoteric, the experiences of diverse genres of gay and lesbian "families we choose" bear on many of the most feverishly contested issues in contemporary family politics. They can speak to our mounting cultural paranoia over whether fathers are expendable, to nature–nurture controversies over sexual and gender identities and the gender division of labor, to the meaning and purpose of voluntary marriage, and most broadly, those ubiquitous family values contests over the relative importance for children of family structure or process, of biological or psychological parents.

From the African-American Million Man March in October 1995, the ecstatic mass rallies currently attended by hundreds of thousands of Christian male Promise Keepers, and Blankenhorn's National Fatherhood Initiative pledge campaign, to California governor Pete Wilson's 1996 state of the state address and President Clinton's 1996 state of the union address, the nation seems to be gripped by cultural obsession over the decline of dependable dads. Of course, feminists like myself heartily welcome men's efforts to assume their full share of responsibility for the children they intentionally sire, as well as the ones they acquire.[40] After all, feminists spearheaded struggles coaxing fathers to share equally the drudgery and divinity of child-rearing, at times with paradoxical costs to maternal self-interest.[41] This is quite a different matter, however, from nostalgic, reactionary moves to reify genetic paternity or stereotypical masculinity as crucial to the welfare of children and the nation alike.

Here is where research on lesbian families, particularly on planned lesbian couple families, could prove of no small import. Thus far, as we have seen, such research offers no brief for Blankenhorn's angst over "radically fatherless children," nor does research on other types of families without fathers justify such paternalistic alarm. For example, a careful, comprehensive study of eighth-graders living in single-parent households found that boys derived no benefits from living with fathers rather than mothers: "of the 35 social psychological and educational outcomes studied, we cannot find even one in which both males and females benefit significantly from living with their same-sex parent."[42] Even more challenging to those who seem to believe that the mere presence of a father in a family confers significant benefits on his children are surprising data reported in a recent study of youth and violence conducted by Kaiser Permanente and Children Now. The study of 1,000 11–17-year-olds and of 150 7–10-year-olds found that, contrary to popular belief, 68 percent of the "young people exposed to higher levels of health and safety threats" were from conventional two-parent families. Moreover, rather poignantly, fathers were among the last people that troubled teens would turn to for help, even when they lived in conventional two-parent families. Only 10 percent of the young people in such two-parent families said they would seek their father's advice first, compared with 44 percent who claimed they would turn first to their mothers, and 26 percent who would first seek help from friends. Many more youth were willing to discuss concerns over their health, safety, and sexuality with nurses or doctors.[43] Thus, empirical social science to date, like the historical record, gives us sound cause to regard either fathers or mothers alike as "expendable." It is the quality, commitment, and character of parents, rather than their gender, that truly matter.

Similarly, research on the relationships of gay male and lesbian couples depicts diverse models for intimacy from which others could profit. "Freed" from normative conventions and institutions that govern heterosexual gender and family relationships, self-consciously "queer" couples and families, by necessity, have had to reflect much more seriously on the meaning and purpose of their intimate commitments. Studies that compare lesbian, gay male, and heterosexual couples find intriguing contrasts in their characteristic patterns of intimacy. Gender

seems to shape domestic values and practices more powerfully than sexual identity, so that same-sex couples tend to be more compatible than heterosexual couples. For example, both lesbian and straight women seem to be more likely than either gay or straight men to value their relationships over their work. Yet both lesbian and gay male couples agree that both parties should be employed, while married men are less likely to agree with wives who wish to work. Predictably, same-sex couples share more interests and time together than married couples. Also unsurprising, lesbian couples tend to have the most egalitarian relationships, and married heterosexual couples the least. Lesbian and gay male couples both share household chores more equally and with less conflict than do married couples, but they share them differently. Lesbian couples tend to share most tasks while gay males more frequently assign tasks "to each according to his abilities," schedules, and preferences.[44]

Gender differences in sexuality are particularly striking and intriguing, because in this arena married women may be imposing more of their preferences on their husbands than conventional lore might predict. Gay male couples tend to have much more active, nonexclusive, and casual sex lives than either lesbian or married couples. Nearly two-thirds of the gay male couples studied by sociologists Blumstein and Schwartz in 1983, before AIDS had reached visible epidemic proportions, practiced open relationships, but the clear majority of both lesbian and married couples were monogamous. While sexual frequency was lowest among lesbian couples, they considered themselves more compatible sexually than did either married couples or gay men. Husbands and wives disagreed the most about their sexual compatibility (with husbands claiming greater compatibility than wives reported), but gay men were the least troubled by sexual incompatibility, because they generally invested sex with fewer possessive, romantic, or emotional meanings than did most women or married men.[45]

Each of these modal patterns for intimacy and sexuality has its particular strengths and vulnerabilities. Gender conventions and gender fluidity alike have advantages and limitations, as Blumstein and Schwartz and other researchers have discussed. For example, gay men who seek sexual monogamy can have as much trouble as do many heterosexual men who wish to escape its restrictions.[46] Getting used to queer families would not mean converting to any characteristic patterns of intimacy, but coming to terms with the collapse of a monolithic cultural regime governing our intimate bonds. It would mean embracing a genuinely pluralist understanding that there are diverse, valid ways to form and sustain these which could benefit us all. In the end, Jonathan Rauch may be right in one respect, after all. If we reserve the term "homosexuality" to signify the expression of same-sex desire, it should indeed be of little public concern. "The rest of us," however, share a great interest in becoming so used to the presence of gay and lesbian families among us that the very label will once again come to seem embarrassingly queer.

If there is anything truly distinctive about lesbian and gay families it is how unambiguously the substance of their relationships takes precedence over their form, their emotional and social commitments over genetic claims. Compelled to exercise "good, old-fashioned American" ingenuity in order to fulfill familial desires, gays and lesbians improvisationally assemble a patchwork of blood and intentional relations – gay, straight, and other – into creative, extended kin bonds.[47] Gay communities more adeptly integrate single individuals into their social worlds than does mainstream heterosexual society, a social skill quite valuable in a world in which divorce, widowhood, and singlehood are increasingly normative. Because queer families must continually, self-consciously migrate in and out of the closet,

they also hone bicultural skills particularly suitable for life in a multicultural society.[48] Self-identified queer families serve on the pioneer outpost of the postmodern family condition, confronting most directly its features of improvisation, ambiguity, diversity, contradiction, self-reflection, and flux.

Even the distinctive, indeed the definitional, burden that pervasive homophobia imposes on lesbian and gay families does not fully distinguish them from other contemporary families. Unfortunately, prejudice, intolerance, and disrespect for "different" or "other" families is all too commonplace in the contemporary world, and it diminishes us all. Ethnocentric and intolerant familism harms the families of many immigrants, interracial couples, single mothers (be they unwed or divorced, impoverished or affluent), remarried couples, childless "yuppie" couples, bachelors and "spinsters," house-husbands, and working mothers, the homeless, and it even places that vanishing, once-hallowed breed of full-time homemakers on the ("I'm just-a-housewife") defensive.

Gay and lesbian families simply brave intensified versions of widespread contemporary challenges. Both their plight and their pluck unequivocally expose the dangerous disjuncture between our family rhetoric and policy, on the one hand, and our family and social realities, on the other. Stubbornly denying the complex, pluralist array of contemporary families and kinship, most of our legal and social policies atavistically presume to serve a singular, "normal" family structure – the conventional, heterosexual, married-couple, nuclear family. In the name of children, politicians justify decisions that endanger them, and in the name of The Family, they cause grave harm to our families. It is time to get used to the postmodern family condition we all now inhabit. In the name of our families and democracy, we must move forward, not backward, to address the grave *social* threats that imperil us all.

NOTES

1 With all due credit and apologies to Queer Nation and ACT-UP for adapting their slogan: "We're Here, We're Queer, Get Used to It!"

2 The estimate that at least six million children were living with a gay parent by 1985 appeared in Schulenberg, *Gay Parenting*, and has been accepted or revised upwards by most scholars since then. See, for example, Bozett, 39; Patterson, "Children of Lesbian and Gay Parents"; Allen and Demo, "The Families of Lesbians and Gay Men: A New Frontier in Family Research."

3 Burke, *Family Values: A Lesbian Mother's Fight for Her Son.*

4 Goldenberg, "Virtual Marriages for Same-Sex Couples."

5 Many gay activist groups and scholars, however, have begun to reclaim the term "queer" as a badge of pride, in much the same way that the Black Power movement of the 1960s reclaimed the formerly derogatory term for blacks.

6 Reagan and Schlafly both have gay sons, Powell has a lesbian daughter, and Gingrich has a lesbian half-sister.

7 For a sensitive discussion of the definitional difficulties involved in research on gay and lesbian families, see Allen and Demo, "Families of Lesbians and Gay Men," 112–13.

8 In Stacey, *Brave New Families*, I provide a booklength, ethnographic treatment of postmodern family life in the Silicon Valley.

9 I explain my use of the term "modern" family earlier in this book.

10 Most gay and lesbian scholars and activists reject the term "homosexual" because it originated within a medical model that classified homosexuality as a sexual perversion or disease and because the term emphasizes sexuality as at the core of the individual's identity. In this chapter, I follow the generally preferred contemporary practice of using the terms "lesbians" and "gay men," but I also occasionally employ the term "gay" generically to include both women and men. I also play with the multiple, and currently shifting, meanings of the term "queer," by specifying whether I am using the term in its older pejorative sense, in its newer sense of proudly challenging fixed notions of gender and sexuality, or in its more colloquial sense of simply "odd."

11 Quoted in Sherman, ed., *Lesbian and Gay Marriage*, 191.

12 Ibid., 173.

13 Bozett, epilogue to *Gay and Lesbian Parents*, 232.

14 Cited in Sherman, *Lesbian and Gay Marriage*, 9, n.6. A more recent poll conducted by *The Advocate* suggests that the trend of support for gay marriage is increasing. See Wolfson, "Crossing the Threshold," 583.

15 Terry announced his plans January 24, 1996 on "Randall Terry Live," and LaHaye made her pitch the next day, January 25, 1996 on "Beverly LaHaye Live."

16 Dunlap, "Some States Trying to Stop Gay Marriages before They Start," A18; Dunlap, "Fearing a Toehold for Gay Marriage, Conservatives Rush to Bar the Door," A7; Lockhead, "GOP Bill Targets Same-Sex Marriages," *San Francisco Chronicle*, May 9, 1996, A1, 15.

17 Ibid, A1.

18 Press Briefing by Mike McCurry, White House, May 14, 1996, Office of the Press Secretary.

19 "Vatican Denounces Gay-Marriage Idea," *New York Times*, March 29, 1996, A8.

20 Dunlap, "Reform Rabbis Vote to Back Gay Marriage," *New York Times*, March 29, 1996, A9.

21 "The Freedom to Marry," *New York Times*, April 7, 1996, Editorials/Letters, p. 10.

22 The decision stated that the sexual orientation of the parties was irrelevant, because same-sex spouses could be of any sexual orientation. It was the gender discrimination involved in limiting one's choice of spouse that violated the state constitution. See Wolfson, "Crossing the Threshold," 573.

23 Polikoff, "We Will Get What We Ask For: Why Legalizing Gay and Lesbian Marriage Will Not 'Dismantle the Legal Structure of Gender in Every Marriage'."

24 Law Professor Thomas Coleman, who is executive director of the "Family Diversity Project" in California, expresses these views in Sherman, 128–9.

25 Sullivan, "Here comes the Groom"; Rauch, "A Pro-Gay, Pro-Family Policy."

26 Tede Matthews in Sherman, 57.

27 Kirk Johnson quoted in Wolfson, 567.

28 Hunter, "Marriage, Law, and Gender," 12.
29 Wolfson, "Crossing the Threshold."
30 Mohr, *A More Perfect Union*, 48, 41, 50.
31 "Some Progress Found in Poll on Gay Rights," *San Francisco Chronicle*, June 20, 1994.
32 Ryan, "No Easy Way Out," 90; Sullivan, "Here Comes the Groom."
33 Rauch, "Pro-Gay, Pro-Family Policy."
34 Herscher, "After Reconsidering, Montana Junks Gay Sex Bill," A2.
35 Clinton, according to his senior adviser George Stephanopoulos, "thinks the proper role for the government is to work on the fight against discrimination, but he does not believe we should support (gay) marriage." Quoted in Sandalow and Tuller, "White House Tells Gays It Backs Them," A2.
36 Clinton, *It Takes A Village*, book jacket copy.
37 Remafedi, *Death by Denial*.
38 Quoted in Miller, *Out in the World*, 350.
39 Wolfson, "Crossing the Threshold," 599.
40 See Newton, "A Feminist Among Promise Keepers," A6; Segal, *Slow Motion*; Ehrensaft, *Parenting Together*.
41 Shared parenting between women and men was a favored political goal that many feminists deduced from such 1970s works of feminist theory as Dinnerstein, *The Mermaid and the Minotaur* and Chodorow, *Reproduction of Mothering*. Ehrensaft, *Parenting Together*, provides a balanced treatment of some of the paradoxes, difficulties, and achievements of shared parenting efforts. Joint custody, however, which many feminists first favored, has often been used to reduce child support and financial settlements.
42 Downey and Powell, "Do Children in Single-Parent Households Fare Better Living With Same-Sex Parents?"
43 Fairbank, Maslin, Maullin & Associates, "National Health and Safety Study," pp. 8, 10.
44 Kurdek, "The Allocation of Household Labor in Gay, Lesbian, and Heterosexual Married Couples"; Blumstein and Schwartz, *American Couples*; Peplau, 193.
45 Peplau, 193; Blumstein and Schwartz.
46 Blumstein and Schwartz; Peplau; Laird.
47 See Weston, *Families We Choose*, for an ethnographic treatment of these chosen kin ties.
48 As Allen and Demo suggest, "an aspect of biculturalism is resilience and creative adaptation in the context of minority group oppression and stigma," and this "offers a potential link to other oppressed groups in American society." "The Families of Lesbians and Gay Men," 122.

REFERENCES

Blumstein, Philip and Pepper Schwartz. *American Couples*. New York: William Morrow, 1983.

Bozett, Frederick W., ed. *Gay and Lesbian Parents*. New York: Praeger, 1987.

Burke, Phyllis. *Family Values: A Lesbian Mother's Fight for Her Son*. New York: Random House, 1993.

Chodorow, Nancy. *The Reproduction of Mothering*. Berkeley and Los Angeles: University of California Press, 1978.

Clinton, Hillary Rodham. *It Takes A Village: And Other Lessons Children Teach Us*. New York: Simon & Schuster, 1996.

Dinnerstein, Dorothy. *The Mermaid and the Minotaur: Sexual Arrangements and Human Malaise*. New York: Harper & Row, 1976.

Downey, Douglas B. and Brian Powell. "Do Children in Single-Parent Households Fare Better Living With Same-Sex Parents?" *Journal of Marriage and the Family*, 55 (February 1993): 55–71.

Dunlap, David W. "Some States Trying to Stop Gay Marriages before They Start." *New York Times*, March 15, 1995, A18.

Dunlap, David W. "Fearing a Toehold for Gay Marriage, Conservatives Rush to Bar the Door." *New York Times*, March 6, 1996, A7.

Ehrensaft, Diane. *Parenting Together: Men and Women Sharing the Care of Their Children*. New York: Free Press, 1987.

Fairbank, Maslin, Maullins Associates. "National Health and Safety Study: Summary of Results." Santa Monica and San Francisco, CA: October 1995.

Goldberg, Carey. "Virtual Marriages for Same-Sex Couples." *New York Times*, March 26, 1996, A8.

Herscher, Elaine. "After Reconsidering, Montana Junks Gay Sex Bill." *San Francisco Chronicle*, March 24, 1995.

Hunter, Nan D. "Marriage, Law, and Gender: A Feminist Inquiry." *Law and Sexuality*, 1, n. 1 (1991): 9–30.

Kurdek, Lawrence. "The Allocation of Household Labor in Gay, Lesbian, and Heterosexual Married Couples." *Journal of Social Issues*, 49, n. 3 (1993): 127–39.

Laird, Joan. "Lesbian and Gay Families." In Froma Walsh, ed., *Normal Family Processes*, 2nd edn. New York: Guilford Press, 1993.

Miller, Neil. *Out in the World: Gay and Lesbian Life from Buenos Aires to Bangkok*. New York: Random House, 1992.

Mohr, Richard. *A More Perfect Union: Why Straight America Must Stand Up for Gay Rights*. Boston: Beacon, 1994.

Newton, Judith. "A Feminist Among Promise Keepers." *Davis Enterprise*, 8 October, 1995, A6.

Patterson, Charlotte J. "Children of Lesbian and Gay Parents." *Child Development*, 63 (1992): 1025–42.

Peplau, Letitia. "Research on Homosexual Couples: An Overview." *In Gay Relationships*, John P. De Cecco, ed. New York: Haworth Press, 1988.

Polikoff, Nancy. "We Will Get What We Ask For: Why Legalizing Gay and Lesbian Marriage Will Not 'Dismantle the Legal Structure of Gender in Every Marriage'." *Virginia Law Review*, vol. 79 (1993): 1549–50.

Rauch, Jonathan. "A Pro-Gay, Pro-Family Policy." *Wall Street Journal*, November 29, 1994, A22.

Ryan, Alan. "No Easy Way Out." *New Yorker*, September 11, 1995, p. 90.

Sandalow, Marc and David Tuller. "White House Tells Gays It Backs Them." *San Francisco Chronicle*, October 21, 1995, A2.

Schulenberg, John. *Gay Parenting*. New York: Doubleday, 1985.

Segal, Lynne. *Slow Motion: Changing Masculinities, Changing Men*. London, Virago, 1990.

Sherman, Suzanne, ed. *Lesbian and Gay Marriage: Private Commitments, Public Ceremonies*. Philadelphia: Temple University Press, 1992.

Stacey, Judith. *Brave New Families: Stories of Domestic Upheaval in Late Twentieth Century America*. New York: Basic Books, 1990.

Sullivan, Andrew. "Here Comes the Groom: A (Conservative) Case for Gay Marriage." *New Republic*, vol. 201, no. 9. August 28, 1989, 20–1.

Weston, Kath. *Families We Choose: Lesbians, Gays, Kinship*. New York: Columbia University Press, 1991.

Wolfson, Evan. "Crossing the Threshold: Equal Marriage Rights For Lesbians and Gay Men and the Intra-Community Critique." *Review of Law and Social Change*, 21, n. 3 (1994–5).

28 Social Control, Civil Liberties, and Women's Sexuality

Beth E. Schneider and Valerie Jenness

"Crises and disasters have always held a special fascination for social scientists, at least in part because they expose the fundamental assumptions, institutional arrangements, social linkages, and cleavages that are normally implicit in the social order."[1] The AIDS epidemic is no exception. The biological and medical imperatives associated with HIV have been effectively translated into a moral panic.[2] This panic has in turn uncovered significant social processes and arrangements related to sexuality, gender, and social control.

Not surprisingly, the AIDS epidemic has brought with it repetitive calls that "somebody do something." Historically, epidemics typically evoke demands for some form of managerial response and some mobilized effort to control identifiable, projected, and even unknown hazards.[3] In particular, epidemics inspire new public policy, as well as the reform of extant public policy. Again, the AIDS epidemic has proven to be no exception.

In this essay we focus on several public responses that have emerged purportedly to assist in the control of "the AIDS problem." Specifically, we focus on those responses that have consequences for the expansion of social control mechanisms and the potential denial of civil liberties. Although the AIDS epidemic in the United States has touched every segment of society, it is increasingly becoming an illness of women, as well as of racial, ethnic, and sexual minorities. There is no reason to presume that this trend will reverse as the epidemic continues through the 1990s and into the next century.[4] Thus, our overarching concern is with how public policy responses to the multitude of threats born

of AIDS are structured by gender and sexuality.

The AIDS epidemic has inspired and justified interventionist policies on the part of the state to regulate not only the exchange of bodily fluids, but the social organization of gender and sexuality as well. To illustrate, we focus on public policy surrounding prostitutes and sex education for adolescents, both of which have consequences for the civil liberties of girls and women and the social control of female sexuality through the reinforcement of notions of "good girls" and "bad girls." This particular comparison permits an examination of the complexity of state responses to AIDS and illustrates differing strategies of social control undertaken by two institutions: the legal and the educational.

Some public policies implicitly or explicitly seek to control sexuality and gender; these are our concern in the remainder of the chapter. Different laws and other forms of public policy inspired by the AIDS epidemic operate to interrupt, forbid, and often punish the existence or enactment of particular sexualities. We examine two quite divergent cases – policy surrounding prostitutes in the United States and the policy and practice of AIDS education – for what each reveals about the social control of female sexuality through the construction of "good girls" and "bad girls." We conclude with a discussion of the role that law and other forms of public policy play in redefining social control in general and, more specifically, privacy in light of the "AIDS crisis." We consider what places, spaces, and matters remain private and thus outside the purview of the state, for girls and young women, as well as how processes of protection, intrusion, and redefinition are bound by and reflect the fact that AIDS is structured by race, class, gender, and sexuality.[5]

The AIDS Epidemic as a Disease and as a Moral Panic

The evolution of AIDS resembles the social construction of such diseases as leprosy, syphilis, tuberculosis, and cholera.[6] In each of these epidemics, the evolution and consequences of the disease were tied not only to its biological characteristics, but also to the socially constructed meanings attached to the disease. From the beginning, many interested parties, including some units of the state, have sought to make their interpretations of HIV and AIDS dominant. Scientists, physicians, afflicted groups, government agencies, religious officials, politicians, social workers, and other claims makers concerned with the disease have been and continue to be quick to formulate and disseminate interpretations of the disease.[7]

The melange of meanings surrounding the AIDS epidemic has merged to produce a "moral panic." In simplest terms, a moral panic can be thought of as a widespread feeling on the part of the public – or some relevant public – that something is terribly wrong in society because of the moral failure of a specific group of individuals. The result is that a subpopulation is defined as the enemy. Cohen describes the evolution and consequences of a moral panic:

> A condition, episode, person or group of persons emerges to become defined as a threat to societal values and interests: Its nature is presented in a stylized and stereotypic fashion by the mass media; moral barricades are manned by editors, bishops, politicians, and other right-thinking people; socially accredited experts pronounce their diagnoses and solutions; ways of coping evolve, or (more often) are resorted to.... Sometimes the panic passes

over and is forgotten, except in folklore or collective memory; at other times it has more serious and long-lasting repercussions and might produce such changes as those in legal and social policy.[8]

Such "changes as those in legal and social policy" are necessarily intertwined with the negotiation of power and morality and, by extension, are consequential for major societal processes of social change.

Moral panics are inevitably linked to, and thus consequential for, formal systems of social control. They explicitly or implicitly challenge existing systems of control by defining them as failing or defunct. The consequence is that mandates for reform in legal and social policy are rendered timely and legitimate. Wars, epidemics, and other such moral panic-generating events have, at different points in history, served to justify the expansion of old or the introduction of new mechanisms of social control. These emergent forms of social control often constitute significant incursions on the rights of individuals or groups.

Calls for reform in legal and social policy that are consequential for individual civil liberties are especially pronounced when moral panics are tied, in some real or imagined way, to issues of sexuality.[9] Gayle Rubin, for example, has argued that "it is precisely at times such as these [the era of AIDS], when we live with the possibility of unthinkable destruction, that people are likely to become dangerously crazed about sexuality."[10] As a consequence, regulations emerge to control public and private spaces associated with sexuality and eroticism (such as attempts to close bathhouses frequented by gay men or refusal to perform abortions for HIV-positive women).

The AIDS crisis has generated contemporary discourses in which the social conditions attached to the epidemic serve to rationalize formal and informal social control mechanisms on sexuality and gender, ostensibly in the name of safeguarding the public's health. But this has not been done without historical precedent and without overcoming material and symbolic obstacles.

In an effort to make sense of the variety of ways in which history, culture, and politics frame responses to AIDS, Moerkerk and Aggleton[11] identify four overall approaches that nations in Europe have taken to deal with AIDS. Three of these approaches – the pragmatic, the political, and the biomedical – have particular relevance for our understanding of the mechanisms put in place in the United States to manage female prostitutes and to educate female adolescents. The *pragmatic response* emphasizes provision of crucial education and information, whatever that might be for a group of people, and the need to protect the afflicted. It relies on a cultural consensus and avoids coercive forms of social control. In contrast, the *political response* is based in judgment of what is politically possible and consistent with the beliefs of the nation's leadership. It relies on the law to regulate behavior, and consequently it interprets AIDS prevention as a mechanism for producing behavior it considers desirable. The *biomedical response* is limited; it relies exclusively on medical personnel to determine policy and shows little interest in the involvement of affected groups. As our analyses indicate, each response, often in combination with others, is evident in the United States, especially in the control of young women by educational and legal institutions.

Public Health and Civil Liberties: A Difficult Dilemma

The extension of formal social control mechanisms by the state is not done automatically in times of epidemics because, as Brandt has documented, epidemics marshal two sets of values that are "highly prized by our culture": the fundamental civil liberties of the individual and the role of the state in assuring public welfare.[12] From a public policy point of view, individual civil liberties and public health concerns are generally conceived as values in competition with each other. There is a tension between the extension of social control in the name of "protecting public health" and the prohibition of such extension in the name of "preserving individual civil liberties," especially those related to notions of "privacy" as an aspect of personal liberty protected by the Fourth and Fourteenth Amendments of the US Constitution.[13]

This tension is especially pronounced in situations or contexts where sexuality is salient. For example, the state still interferes in the practice of homosexual sodomy and other sexual acts. However, after providing an extensive review of relevant legislation at state and federal levels, Stoddard and Rieman conclude that, under recent Supreme court decisions, the right to privacy has effectively precluded or sharply limited governmental interference with some personal decisions surrounding sexuality (such as the use of contraception or access to abortion). They warn that this trend is open to reversal in light of the many hazards posed by AIDS: "the government undoubtedly could treat persons who carry the HIV differently from others for some reasons."[14] The same holds for people who are "at risk" for HIV or presumed to be carriers of the virus. Indeed, everything from tattooing on the buttocks to more drastic segregation measures, such as forced quarantining, have been proposed, entertained, and occasionally adopted.[15] As a result, over the course of the epidemic, the rights of the individual have not invariably prevailed and privacy has, at least from a policy point of view, been redefined.[16]

Although it is clear that prostitutes, frequently considered women in need of control, have been particularly susceptible to constraints on their civil liberties, children are rarely understood in these terms. Children's civil liberties are effectively unacknowledged. Indeed, the treatment of children, especially their education and protection, rests far less securely on any right to privacy. Children and adolescents often need, by law, their parents' permission for most of what adults take for granted as sexual – to receive contraceptive devices at school, to attend sex education classes, to seek an abortion. Familial and educational institutions exercise physical and legal control over how young people learn about sexuality and gender. Schools are social control mechanisms that reinforce patriarchal relations of male domination and female submission. In the face of the AIDS epidemic, the ideological apparatus of schools extends social control over its charges by framing, constraining, and ultimately censoring what is thought about AIDS and how it comes to be understood.

Private Spaces, Public Intrusions: The Case of Prostitution

There has been a virtual explosion in the formulation of policy designed to control the spread of HIV and the people who are infected. Laws have been passed by the US Congress and state legislatures; the courts have issued various pronouncements; and businesses, government agencies, prisons, schools, hospitals, and other such public settings have developed workplace policy. Policy proposals with implications for civil liberties in general and privacy in particular include, but certainly are not limited to, requiring blood screening of prisoners or military recruits; banning people with AIDS from being restaurant workers; prohibiting seropositive persons from donating blood; closing gay bathhouses; banning homosexual sodomy; quarantining "suspect" groups, especially prostitutes; dismissing from federal jobs employees suspected of being seropositive; and refusing to care for or provide shelter for PWAs.[17] This list, of course, is not exhaustive of the measures that have been proposed or implemented to control AIDS by restricting liberty and, in some cases, redefining privacy.

Throughout the AIDS epidemic, calls for mass and mandatory testing have been put forth. Initial calls for mass testing and an administrative system developed around testing were expanded in a context of considerable ambiguity over test accuracy, counseling procedures, and the relationship between knowledge of test results and behavior or attitudes. Moreover, these calls seem to point in the direction of quarantining and other forms of detention.[18] However, such calls for testing are not equally applicable to all citizens. They have selectively targeted specific groups – usually gay men, intravenous drug users, prisoners, immigrants, pregnant women, and sex workers.

Implicating female prostitutes in AIDS

Stereotypes about women – especially African-American women, pregnant women, and female prostitutes – have been infused with policy proposals. Perhaps the most obvious case of social and legal policy embedded in gender and sexuality is that surrounding sex work. From the beginning, legislation supporting forced quarantining, reporting, screening, and prosecution of sex workers has been proposed and adopted. The biological characteristics of AIDS, combined with the way in which the disease has been socially constructed, almost guaranteed that prostitutes would be implicated in the social problem of AIDS. In an article entitled "Prostitutes and AIDS: Public Policy Issues," Cohen, Alexander, and Wofsy concluded that "prostitutes have often been held responsible for the spread of AIDS into the heterosexual population in this country."[19] This is not surprising given that AIDS has been conceived of primarily as a sexually transmitted disease and was, at least originally, connected with "promiscuous" sex and "deviant" lifestyles.[20] The historical association of prostitution with venereal disease, unfettered sex, and moral unworthiness remains strong.[21] The prostitute is either dangerous, bad, or both. In short, the historical and contemporary context within which female prostitutes have operated ensured that they would be implicated in the AIDS epidemic, even prior to epidemiological evidence justifying such a focus.[22]

As early as 1984, medical authorities were investigating the possibility that prostitutes could spread AIDS into the heterosexual population. Meanwhile, the media continued to spread suspicion about prostitution as an avenue of transmission for the disease. For example, on an episode of the nationally televised *Geraldo Show* entitled "Have Prostitutes Become the New Typhoid Marys?" the host offered the following introduction to millions of viewers:

> The world's oldest profession may very well have become among its deadliest. A recent study backed by the federal Centers for Disease Control found that one third of New York's prostitutes now carry the AIDS virus. If this study mirrors the national trend, then the implications are as grim as they are clear. Sleeping with a prostitute may have become a fatal attraction....A quick trick may cost you $20, but you may be paying for it with the rest of your life.[23]

Supporting Rivera's introduction, a New York-based AIDS counselor appearing on the show argued:

> A high percentage of prostitutes infected with HIV pass it on to their sexual partners who are johns or the tricks, a lot of whom are married or have sex with a straight woman. I think this is how the AIDS epidemic is passed into the heterosexual population.[24]

He argued further that working prostitutes testing positive for HIV are guilty of manslaughter and/or attempted murder. In a relatively short period of time, claims like this became commonplace. Moreover, claims focusing on prostitution were and still are focused on female prostitutes to the exclusion of male prostitutes, and on female prostitutes but not their customers.

Legislation as social control

Like the media, legislators have turned their attention to female prostitution as an avenue of transmission. In the name of preventing HIV transmission, legislation that intrudes into private, consensual sexual relations has sprung up around the country. A number of proposals have been introduced and adopted that, in one way or another, make it a crime for someone who is antibody positive to engage in sex with anyone else, regardless of the degree to which the behavior is mutually voluntary, the use of condoms, and the failure of the uninfected participant to test seropositive.[25] Luxenburg and Guild have shown that, as early as 1987, more than 140 AIDS-specific laws had been passed across the United States. Approximately a dozen of these criminalized the act of *exposing* another individual to the HIV. In addition to the emergence of new legislation, jurisdictions that have no AIDS-specific criminal laws have begun to rely on traditional criminal laws (attempted murder, aggravated assault, and the like) to prosecute HIV-positive individuals who engage in behaviors that put seronegatives at risk for acquiring the HIV infection – even when the risky contact is conscious and voluntary on the part of the seronegatives.

The introduction of AIDS-related legislation has posed a significant legal threat to female prostitutes. Many governmental and medical establishments have reacted to AIDS with calls for increased regulation of prostitution in the form of registration, mandatory AIDS testing, and prison sentences for those carrying antibodies to the virus.[26] In the mid-1980s and into the 1990s many states considered legislation requiring arrested prostitutes to be tested for HIV infection. By 1988 some states had introduced and passed legislation requiring mandatory testing of arrested prostitutes. Georgia, Florida, Utah, and Nevada were among the first states to legislate the forcible testing of arrested prostitutes; those who test positive can then be subject to arrest on felony charges. These mandatory testing laws in effect create a state registry of infected prostitutes, while the felony charges could create a quarantine situation if prostitutes are kept in isolation while awaiting trial.

Coinciding with the introduction of this legislation, many judges and district attorneys began contemplating and occasionally charging arrested prostitutes who tested positive for HIV with attempted manslaughter and murder. In July 1990, for example, an Oakland, California, prostitute was arrested after *Newsweek* ran a photo of her and quoted her saying that she contracted the deadly virus from contaminated needles but continued to engage in prostitution. According to newspaper reports, Oakland police asked a judge to force the woman to be tested for HIV and pressured the district attorney's office to pursue an attempted manslaughter charge if she tested positive. The arresting officer stated, "I think her actions, with the knowledge that if you're going to get AIDS you're going to die, is a malicious act akin to firing into a crowd or at a passing bus."[27] Although the judge denied the charge, the woman was held for a number of days while the possibility was contemplated. As another example, in Orlando, Florida, an HIV-infected prostitute was charged with manslaughter even though she used a condom with all of her clients and despite the finding that all of her clients who had been tested were negative.[28]

In essence, the AIDS epidemic has led to increased social control of prostitutes, especially in the form of repressive legislation and increasingly punitive legal sanctions. Such changes reflect the commonly held belief that prostitutes constitute a "vector of transmission" for AIDS into the heterosexual population; thus, legislation and increased legal sanctions have been pursued in the name of controlling the spread of AIDS. Female, not male, prostitutes are arrested, even though male prostitutes are much more

likely to be infected.[29] Social policy continues to be used to enforce select moral positions[30] – in this case, the control of female rather than male sexuality. Such laws effectively constitute a social x-ray, one that classifies individuals as mainstream or peripheral, normal or deviant.

Resistance

Some have suggested that the introduction and implementation of AIDS-related statutes and "enhanced penalties" is merely an attempt to mollify public fear of AIDS spreading into the "population at large."[31] Whatever the state's intention, this testing of certain special groups without consent, at both the state and the federal level, has not gone uncontested.[32] The existence of resistance underscores the control of women's sexuality; it is a sign that women are directly experiencing either the reality or the threat of constraints on their sexual practice.

In order to resist the scapegoating of prostitutes, COYOTE and other US prostitute advocacy groups, using scientific studies and research to lend legitimacy to their assessment, went public with two main arguments: (1) that the rate of HIV infection among prostitutes, compared to that among other identifiable groups, is relatively low; and (2) that, regardless of infection rates, it is a violation of prostitutes' civil rights to selectively impose mandatory testing on prostitutes if they are arrested. Additionally, they publicly and persistently explained that sex workers are not at risk from AIDS because of sex work *per se*. As the codirector of the International Committee for Prostitute Rights explained in the late 1980s:

> They [prostitutes] are demanding the same medical confidentiality and choice as other citizens.... They are contesting policies which separate them from other sexually active people, emphasizing that charging money for sex does not transmit disease.[33]

An editorial on this issue by COYOTE's media liaison argues a kind of prostitute exceptionalism:

> Many readers are well aware that prostitutes practice safe sex techniques, using condoms for oral services as well as intercourse, and quite often restricting their activities to manual gratification. Many prostitutes emphasize massage, still others combine fantasy stimulation (S&M, etc.) with minimal physical contact. There is much a "working girl" can do to assure her health and the health of her clients, and we have done it. Most of us followed safe sex practices long before the onset of this epidemic.[34]

These assertions suggest that what separates prostitutes from women in general is higher rates of condom use. In essence, these sex work organizations hold that sex work *per se* is not responsible for the spread of HIV; viruses do not discriminate between those who exchange money for sex and those who do not. When prostitutes are infected, intravenous drug use is the primary cause.

In promoting the notion that prostitutes do not represent a pool of contagion, COYOTE and other sex worker groups regularly distributed public announcements and issued press releases; attended local, state, national, and international conferences on AIDS; and staged protests to oppose legislation requiring the mandatory testing of prostitutes. At legislative hearings they protested mandatory testing of prostitutes for HIV on the grounds that selective testing is discriminatory and a violation of individuals' – in this case prostitutes' – civil rights.

The AIDS epidemic poses a multitude of threats for prostitutes, their organizations, and their movement to decriminalize and legitimate prostitution. It has siphoned personnel and resources from sex work organizations; organizational agendas and activities have shifted in response to the way in which AIDS has been constructed as a social problem implicating sex workers.

But, at the same time, the AIDS epidemic has served to legitimate prostitutes' rights organizations. It has provided prostitutes and their advocates with financial, rhetorical, and institutional resources. The AIDS epidemic has also brought public officials and prostitutes' rights organizations together in direct and indirect ways. As a result of concern over the spread of AIDS into the heterosexual population, government agencies such as state legislatures, the Centers for Disease Control, and local departments of health have turned to prostitutes' rights organizations for assistance.

Those concerned with halting the spread of AIDS have enlisted the help of prostitutes in investigating the role of prostitution in the spread of the disease. For example, COYOTE applied for and received funds to begin an AIDS prevention project for prostitutes. This new entity, the California Prostitutes Education Program (CAL-PEP) is, as its statement of purpose reads:

> an education project developed by members of COYOTE, the prostitutes' rights advocacy organization, to provide educational programs for prostitutes and the interested public on various aspects of prostitution. Our first project is an AIDS prevention project designed and implemented by prostitutes, ex-prostitutes, and prostitutes' rights advocates to help prostitutes to protect themselves and their clients from AIDS.

CAL-PEP outreach workers go into the stroll districts where street prostitutes work and distribute condoms, spermicides, bleach bottles, and educational materials, and talk to prostitutes about how they can work safely. CAL-PEP outreach workers take a van into the stroll districts, and the prostitutes are invited to come into the van, which is fully equipped with HIV-prevention items, to rest and to talk about how to keep themselves and their clients free of AIDS. In addition, CAL-PEP sponsors support groups and monthly workshops in a hotel room in the stroll district for prostitutes and their regular customers, safe-sex workshops at the county jail, and other programs.

This is obviously an outcome replete with contradictions. The state is not dealing with the problem of AIDS and prostitutes in a singular and consistent fashion. It has utilized what Moerkerk and Aggleton call the pragmatic and political responses. Prostitutes are scapegoats and criminals, but also allies with a unique constituency to educate. Women leaders of these organizations, which in certain ways have been made stronger by the struggle around legal control and HIV prevention work, are nevertheless forced to sustain political work at odds with their original intention to free prostitutes from surveillance by health and legal authorities and promote a less constrained sexuality.

Sex Education: To Be or Not To Be, and in What Form?

Unlike prostitutes, other young women face a different set of social control mechanisms. Adolescent girls, even from the most privileged backgrounds, do not have the freedom and resources to organize on their own behalf, and rarely do they have strong advocates. Their families and schools, the primary socializing institutions of children, exercise physical and legal control over what and how they learn about sexuality and accomplish gender. In the face of the AIDS epidemic, the ideological apparatus of schools, which contributes to the perpetuation of race and gender inequality, extends social control over its charges by framing, constraining, and in fact censoring what is thought about AIDS and how it comes to be understood. In that process, it specifies some of the parameters of female sexuality.

Sex education is the vehicle through which children and adolescents learn some portion of what they know about HIV/ AIDS, and that learning has not been accomplished (when it has occurred at all)

unproblematically. Prevention and control of the spread of HIV requires discussions of sexual and drug-using activities, and sex/ health education is a primary institution through which youth are advised whether, as well as how and when, to be sexual beings. In the process, it cues them to what is "safer," "safe," and "risky sex."

Schools respond to AIDS with a hybrid of the political, pragmatic, and biomedical approaches. An examination of how these programs come about in schools reveals a systematic preoccupation with heterosexuality and with the social control of young women's sexuality. These are evident in the multiple discourses of community political struggles over the control of the schools' curricula and over the specific content of prevention materials. Some of these extensions of social control are patently obvious, while others are more implicit. Their limitations are revealed whenever they are resisted, when teenagers provide education for each other in the form of theater, make their own AIDS videos, or join with groups like ACT-UP in the distribution of condoms.

Community struggles, social control, and censorship

AIDS education for young people was initially proposed in a climate of fear that reflected deep social and cultural anxieties about the disease and its transmissibility. Most importantly, homosexuality and its central symbolic attachment to AIDS rendered particularly problematic the matter of the structure and the content of AIDS education in the public schools.[35] School officials anticipated controversy as parents considered the prospects of such programs for their children. The expectations of trouble were not without cause: legislators were publicly unwilling to support mandatory AIDS education packages for children, teachers harbored memories of painful struggles to introduce sex education, and all school administrators wanted to avoid antagonizing community groups who oppose homosexuality and birth control and favor either no sex education programs or teaching of traditional values about sex.[36]

There has not been a consensus about the need for AIDS education programs (nor about their specific content) in the public schools. By the mid-1980s, the Christian Right's campaign to gain control of the nation's school boards was underway. Among the issues around which its efforts to gain control revolve are bilingual education, the teaching of evolution, affirmative action, and the existence or form of AIDS education and condom distribution. For the last decade, conservative parents have been particularly active in banning books and other materials they found offensive.[37] In the 1992–3 New York City struggle over school board membership, traditional values groups, reaching out to the Latino community – usually one of their targets – argued that the city, through its "elite" school board (and its approval of condom distribution and its Rainbow curriculum), intended to turn their children into homosexuals.[38]

This sort of censorship has a chilling effect on the search by women, including young women, to understand their own sexuality. While early twentieth-century censorship shielded women from knowledge of birth control, the current round is preoccupied with gay and lesbian depictions and expressions of women's rebellion.

In spite of the real and anticipated trouble, most school systems have offered some form of AIDS education to their students. They have engaged in complicated debates and a variety of institutional maneuvers to structure a nonproblematic AIDS education curriculum.[39] A recent study by the Sex Information and Education Council of the US reported that, although every state in 1993 required or recommended AIDS education, students were getting incomplete information from unprepared teachers. Only 11 states provided "balanced information

about safe sex" and numerous states prohibited any discussion of homosexuality. Their summary suggests that only three states provided good programs that provided more than biological information, explained sexual orientation, and discussed a range of safe-sex behaviors and strategies.[40]

Our study of a school system in California reveals a variety of these maneuvers, "deflection strategies" taken by accident or design to reduce the probability of criticism and interference.[41] These strategies include special parental permission forms, preview nights for parents, integration of the AIDS materials into already-existing curricula, cooptation of potential student and parent troublemakers, utilizing the "objective" approach in presentations, and avoiding all discussion of homosexuality. Each strategy enhances the influence of parents and diminishes accordingly the power and participation of students. It is the last two strategies that deserve more detailed attention here since they serve very directly to shape the contours and content of the materials presented to young women.

Gender and the biomedical model in sex education

The discourses of expertise position recipients of educational messages in a way that disables their ability to actually apply information to their lives, and leaves them liable for failing to have understood that they were to have appropriately responded to the "danger" of AIDS.[42]

The dominant view of adolescents' sex education and sexuality, heavily influenced by the fields of medicine and psychology, has shaped HIV prevention practice. Adolescents are often understood as "other," as strange beings, with those from racial/ethnic groups viewed as particularly so. The fields of medicine and psychology put forward essentially deterministic models of social behavior that are simply not flexible enough to capture the variation and dynamism of sexuality and social interaction. The supposedly value-free behaviorism that provides information about anatomy, reproductive physiology, contraception, and a limited variety of sexual practices assumes that scientific knowledge about sexuality is nonjudgmental and can be used easily by students in making their own choices about sexual behavior. It conveys the message that heterosexual intercourse is normal behavior that can be engaged in responsibly and calmly with the use of contraception and abortions when birth control fails.

This approach is, or should be, unsatisfactory to feminist parents, educators, and young women themselves. We believe that the limits of the debate about what students should and should not have is premised on the view that they are not capable of critical thinking, emotional self-discipline, and intellectual self-direction. It isolates sexuality from other social relations. It focuses on organs or viruses with little link to humans' relationships to one another or the historical context. It tends to ignore the continued, persistent discrepancies between young women and men regarding attitudes toward birth control, sex, and relationships. As research on classroom interaction continues to indicate, male domination is uncritically accepted as natural, as an important topic but never as one requiring critical discussion or presented as in any way problematic.[43] Hence, most of these efforts ignore the unequal power relations between men and women that structure heterosexuality.

Moreover, the models utilized in public health campaigns teach biomedical safe sex guidelines as the basis of individuals' everyday behavior. But neither of the two prevailing models deals directly with commonsense knowledge about AIDS and its relationship to AIDS prevention. And it is how these youth understand AIDS that is crucial to what they do. For example, Maticka-Tyndale's study shows gender differences in the ways in which young women and men assess the risk of intercourse based on

their views of its consequences. As she describes it:

> For women, coitus, even before AIDS, carried a variety of risks; they commonly cited both risks of pregnancy and emotional hurt. Relative to other risks, HIV was the least likely to occur.... For men, the experience of coitus generally lacked any prior sense of risk. Lacking a concept of risky coitus, men spoke of risk by ranking coitus against other sexual activities [such as anal intercourse].[44]

Finally, in high schools AIDS is seen as an aspect of health and family services, not as a political or historical matter. Public policy issues and historical debates are typically not discussed. Students consequently are shielded from an understanding of what is controversial in what they may be learning or doing and from a more conscious understanding of the political significance of condoms, contraception, and sex. The passive, "objective" stance of most education prevents the expression of opposing or alternative perspectives. The family life-planning classes, though the site of whatever sex education is offered in California high schools, emphasize pregnancy and disease. They are not about sex; indeed, they de-eroticize sexuality. When schools avoid presenting alternative perspectives, including those that incorporate a discussion of eroticism and pleasure, they continue to perpetuate existing class, race, gender, and sexuality hierarchies.

Nevertheless, adolescents have learned the public health information presented to them. Considerable research over the last five years has confidently concluded that adolescents have high levels of knowledge about AIDS and can voice the biomedical position about the role of condoms in AIDS prevention.[45] However, numerous studies show that the major rule they follow to prevent HIV infection is to try not to have sexual intercourse (unprotected and protected) with an infected partner, a determination requiring trust in a specific partner and/or strong faith in one's own ability to judge people based on reputation or appearance.

Gender differences in sexual scripts are also evident. Trust means something different for women and men. Young women expect young men to disclose prior risky sexual activities; men expect that women with whom they are sexual have had no prior sexual activities.[46] That is, they expect them to be "good girls." Since condoms are still seen as primarily for contraception, there are serious gender differences in the ways women and men approach the introduction of condoms. Women, presumed to be using contraception, may be queried about their lack of other birth control and/or about their own or their partners' infection status. Men may introduce condoms in the guise of protecting their partner and in fact be protecting themselves. Young heterosexual women, similar to older women who have been studied in efforts to improve AIDS interventions, fear the regular use of condoms as an insult to their male partner. Most couples – prostitutes with boyfriends included – determine a point in their relationship when they stop using condoms, a point representing deepening trust and commitment. Indeed, the decision to use safe sex is based on perceived HIV status of the partner or on quality of feelings.[47]

AIDS videos and social control

Videos are a major educational tool through which adults bring children AIDS education. In many school systems, a video with an hour or two of discussion may be all the AIDS education students receive.[48] In the best situations, the program around AIDS takes several days, speakers from Planned Parenthood or the local AIDS project appear, and students get to role-play some of what they have learned. But these elaborations on a basic program are rare. The package as a whole usually fosters heterosexism, and every point in the process has its gendered content or outcome.

An examination of four of the commonly used videos available to high schools in the district we studied indicates the variety of ways in which gender inequality and gender difference is reproduced. When given a choice from among these videos, parents tend to select the ones produced by the Red Cross, "A Letter from Brian, and Don't Forget Sherrie," targeted primarily to white students, and "Don't Forget Sherrie," targeted to their African-American counterparts.[49] In each, a young woman or man learns that a former sex partner is HIV-infected and near death. The friends of the just-notified teenager try to figure out what all of them should think and do about their future sexual or drug use behavior in light of the information that one of them might be infected. The two videos carry a long disclaimer on a black screen:

> [This video deals] with teens and others discussing sexual activity and AIDS prevention in frank terms. The film deals with the threat of the disease, AIDS, for teenagers, and how they can avoid getting the disease.

It is followed by the American Red Cross position: Abstinence is highly recommended for young single teenagers, and education regarding sex should be provided within the family with supplementary materials from the schools and community organizations. "Sex education should be based on religious, ethical, legal, and moral foundations."

"Sex, Drugs, and HIV" takes a less apologetic and fearful approach. This video uses popular music, an actress familiar to young people, and an interracial cast. It is divided into three parts: "Relax, AIDS is Hard to Get," a section intended to overcome myths about mosquitoes, touching, and other forms of casual contact; "You Can Get AIDS By Sharing Needles," a brief section whose sole point is that shooting drugs is bad, "so don't shoot up"; and a last section, "AIDS Can Be a Sexually Transmitted Disease."

Each of the videos talks about the "facts" or the "truth" about AIDS. "Sex, Drugs, and HIV," a 19-minute video, goes so far as to conclude with "That's it. That's all you need to know." This is not only simplistic, it is misleading. Most videos take approximately one minute to explain that "AIDS is caused by a virus," one that infects a person and causes the failure of the immune system. And in most videos one confident speaker or the narrator refers to AIDS as a fatal disease.

Even though videos try to use the language of the teenagers to whom they are geared, the language is not believable in its description of risk behaviors. Not only do young girls and boys not use the same language to talk about sex, virtually none call their own practices vaginal, oral, or anal intercourse. Typically only penile–vaginal intercourse "counts" as "going all the way." This is particularly problematic for AIDS education. As Melese-d'Hospital found in her study with adolescents, many are staying "virgins" as a means to avoid HIV. However, the meaning of virginity, what it includes and what it does not, is consequential. The concept is a marker for what is acceptable sexual behavior. For young women, virginity was "located in the vagina" and related to pregnancy, a greater and more visible concern to them than HIV.[50]

Even in those videos that move away from simply telling the facts to more emotion-laden interactions, it is highly unusual to find serious interaction between males and females: males talk to males, females talk to females. "Sex, Drugs, and HIV" has two such scenes. Three girls are stretching in a gymnasium. They are talking about true love, about whether to have sex, about which birth control to use. One suggests that her friend, who has never before had intercourse, should use the pill; the third counters that pills do not protect against disease or AIDS. The young woman without the experience of vaginal intercourse is con-vinced to use a condom but worries about being rejected. The friend with the handy condom responds: "Sit and talk to him. He cares about you. . . . If you can't talk to him about birth control, you shouldn't have sex with him. . . . If you're not sure you want to have sex, you should wait." This enactment, one of the best of its kind in this genre, ignores any direct acknowledgment of the normative context of gender inequality and gendered differences in knowledge about sex.

Conversation among the males in both "Sex, Drugs, and HIV" and "A Letter from Brian" show young men trying to persuade one another to use condoms, with one attempting to best the others by claiming always to have used them. This is a positive and important effort to change the norms of the group. Yet it does not deal directly with the variety of myths surrounding condom use or the interactional and emotional matters at stake in sexual encounters.

The videos are not sex-positive. No other sexual practices are discussed, though adolescents engage in a great many other activities. Consistent with the political approach to the control of AIDS, as described in the Moerkerk and Appleton study, no acknowledgment is made of the possibility of same-sex experience or of the existence of gay and lesbian students. And, in these and other videos, vague use is made of such terms as *love, respect, commitment,* and *monogamy* without any attempt to operationalize them or recognize their multiple meanings. Adolescents are treated as if they are one group, in spite of the strong evidence of diverse and overlapping communities of youth even within similar schools and neighborhoods.[51]

As many women involved in AIDS prevention work have already noted, women are expected to take responsibility for what happens sexually. Many of the videos are addressed to young women, even when they aren't explicitly targeted to them. For example, in the "Brian" video, the US surgeon general offers this confusing statement:

There is another way where you don't need to worry about condoms and that's to have a mutually faithful relationship. In other words, find someone worthy of your love and respect. Give that person both and expect the same from him and remain as faithful to him as he is to you. [If you do this] you will never have to read about AIDS again in your life because it doesn't apply to you.

Aside from the head-in-the-sand attitude, the use of the male pronoun implies that women are the only ones likely to be "good," that they have the burden to make men safe in any relational or sexual situation, and that monogamy protects.

Finally, there are the absences. These videos ignore entrenched fears about homosexuals or unconscious fears about death, though these can surely be said to frame the reception of the facts of AIDS education. With the exception of "Sex, Drugs, and HIV," neither compassion nor "complicity with discrimination"[52] are taught in these and most other HIV-prevention videos. Hence, the strategies of deflection used to shape the content, particularly the avoidance of discussion of homosexuality, highlight the hidden curriculum of schools in their transmission of dominant values and beliefs about heterosexuality. Students are sheltered from the controversial nature of the material presented to them and subsequently rendered politically ignorant.

Working from a feminist framework, a good sex education program would not be simply biological; it would be a political program to change gender relations, free women from emotionally and physically debilitating inequality, and foster positive values about sex. If social relations are bad, so are sexual ones. This kind of sex education would provide what young women need: lessons that women are not just victims of sexuality, that they can construct their own sexual identities and pleasures. This would require a significant restructuring not only of the substance of AIDS education, but also of the organizations responsible for delivering it – the schools. This is no small feat, in that it requires greater recognition of institutionalized gender inequality, including that which is routinely affirmed in the classroom.

Although this sort of sex/AIDS education is not available in any complete form anywhere, some student initiatives are moving in this direction. Students often perceive that part of adults' interest in AIDS education is its potential for containing adolescent sexuality.[53] Young women have been integrally involved in, if not actually leaders of, a number of innovative, usually nonschool-based AIDS prevention programs, such as theater groups supported by local Planned Parenthood organizations and off-campus condom distribution efforts initiated by ACT-UP. At the college level, young women are the major players in most AIDS education efforts.

Discussion

While the cultural and economic implications of the AIDS epidemic are certainly far reaching, so are the consequences for the social organization of sex and gender. Through a logic born of the current epidemic, forms of regulatory intervention that might in other circumstances appear excessive can now be justified in the name of prevention. Such justifications are embedded in, and seemingly cannot be divorced from, larger social systems of gender and sexuality.

The social organization of gender and sexuality is policed by laws and public policy that oversee and regulate our sexual desires, exchanges, images, and identities.[54] The AIDS epidemic strengthens, in legal and educational discourses, the rationale for the extension of social control. Though the special treatment of prostitutes and HIV education of young women in schools may seem wildly divergent, each helps shape the contours of female sexuality, in efforts to contain the "bad girl" and to construct the "good" one. Whether through limits on mutually contracted sex by prostitutes or through limits on balanced information on safe sex for young women, the state is interrupting and forbidding certain sexual practices.

Yet, these processes are not consistent or unidirectional. The combination of political and pragmatic approaches to prostitutes by public health and legal institutions expands social control while legitimizing and in some ways normalizing the existence of prostitutes' organizations. To the extent that prostitutes are organized and in charge of their own HIV education, they are positioned to shape, if not to transform, their own sexuality in their own terms. Still, regulation of this always-suspect group of women continues.

Young women face a different, seemingly more constrained, situation. Schools are forced to confront their own failure to educate, as the rate of new infection in women and adolescents increases in the United States. Because of their use of three approaches to HIV prevention (political, pragmatic, and biomedical), the schools are faced with a continuing series of contradictions. They are the locus of community struggles over the nature and meaning of sexuality. For them, virtually every effort to educate, even in the simple case of supplying just the biological facts, results in challenges to their program, from both interested parties who want more and from those who want less.

Since young women in school are not in charge of their education and are politically disenfranchised, they have severe limits on their privacy and virtually no cultural permission to construct their own sexuality in their own terms. The protection of their "innocence" through the narrowness of the programs presented to them offers some, but rather limited, access to a fuller knowledge of sexuality and the range of sexual options

a young woman might have. Moreover, while the few most expansive programs recognize young women as sexual actors and no longer force them to be chaste and modest, almost all still enforce a femininity centered in presumed heterosexuality in appearance and practice.

It is certainly possible that this crisis has the potential for the adoption of a more positive approach to the sexual in talk and in practice. Nevertheless, it will require the leadership of women of all ages, of all cultural and economic backgrounds, with strong feminist motivations, to counter the emergent forms of social control. Such controls do not stop or slow the epidemic and constitute incursions on the rights of individual and specific groups of women.

NOTES

1   Susan Shapiro, "Policing Trust," in *Private Policing*, ed. Clifford D. Shearing and Philip C. Stenning (Newbury Park, CA: Sage, 1987), 194–220.
2   Watney (p. 43) argues that "we are not, in fact, living through a distinct, coherent and progressing 'moral panic' about AIDS. Rather, we are witnessing the latest variation in the spectacle of the defensive ideological rearguard action which has been mounted on behalf of the 'family' for more than a century." Simon Watney, *Policing Desire: Pornography, AIDS, and the Media* (Minneapolis: University of Minnesota Press, 1987).
3   Allan Brandt, *No Magic Bullet: A Social History of Venereal Disease in the United States Since 1880* (New York: Oxford University Press, 1985); Linda Singer, *Erotic Welfare: Sexual Theory and Politics in the Age of Epidemic* (New York: Routledge, 1993). See also Susan Sontag, *Illness as Metaphor* (New York: Vintage, 1977) and *AIDS and Its Metaphors* (New York: Farrar, Straus and Giroux, 1988).
4   William Darrow, "AIDS: Socioepidemiologic Responses to an Epidemic," in *AIDS and the Social Sciences: Common Threads*, ed. Richard Ulack and William F. Skinner (Lexington: University of Kentucky Press, 1991), 83–99; Samuel V. Duh, *Blacks and AIDS: Causes and*

Origins (Newbury Park, CA: Sage, 1991); Nan D. Hunter, "Complications of Gender: Women and HIV Disease," in *AIDS Agenda: Emerging Issues in Civil Rights*, ed. Nan D. Hunter and William B. Rubenstein (New York: New Press, 1992), 5–39; Beth E. Schneider, "Women, Children, and AIDS: Research Suggestions," in *AIDS and the Social Sciences: Common Threads*, ed. Richard Ulack and William F. Skinner (Lexington: University of Kentucky Press, 1991), 134–48; Beth E. Schneider, "AIDS and Class, Gender, and Race Relations," in *The Social Context of AIDS*, ed. Joan Huber and Beth E. Schneider (Newbury Park, CA: Sage, 1992), 19–43.

5   Duh; Hunter; Schneider 1991, 1992; also Richard Ulack and William F. Skinner, eds., *AIDS and the Social Sciences: Common Threads* (Lexington: University of Kentucky Press, 1991).

6   The history of epidemics is vast. Some of the books and articles most frequently used in discussions of AIDS include, in addition to Brandt 1975, Sontag 1977, and Sontag 1988, Charles E. Rosenberg, *The Cholera Years* (Chicago: University of Chicago Press, 1962) and William H. McNeill, *Plagues and Peoples* (Garden City, NY: Anchor Books, 1976). See also Elizabeth Fee and Daniel M. Fox, eds., *AIDS: The Burdens of History* (Berkeley: University of California Press, 1988) and Ilse J. Volinn, "Health Professionals as Stigmatizers and Destigmatizers of Diseases: Alcoholism and Leprosy as Examples," *Social Science and Medicine* 17 (1983): 385–93.

7   In addition to Watney, see Virginia Berridge, "AIDS: History and Contemporary History," in *The Time of AIDS: Social Analysis, Theory, and Method*, ed. Gilbert Herdt and Shirley Lindenbaum (Newbury Park, CA: Sage, 1992), 41–64 and Cindy Patton, *Inventing AIDS* (New York: Routledge, 1990).

8   Nachman Ben-Yehuda, *The Politics and Morality of Deviance: Moral Panics, Drug Abuse, Deviant Science, and Reversed Stigmatization* (New York: State University of New York Press, 1990); Stanley Cohen, *Folk Devils and Moral Panics* (London: MacGibbon and Kee, 1972).

9   Brandt; Singer.

10 Gayle Rubin, "Thinking Sex: Notes for a Radical Theory of the Politics of Sexuality," in *Pleasure and Danger: Exploring Female Sexuality*, ed. Carole S. Vance (Boston: Routledge and Kegan Paul, 1984).

11 Peter Aggleton, Peter Davies, and Graham Hart (eds.), *AIDS: Individual, Cultural and Policy Dimensions* (London: Falmer Press, 1990), 181–90.

12 Brandt, 195.

13 Larry Gostin, ed., *Civil Liberties in Conflict* (New York: Routledge, 1988); Joel Feinberg, "Harmless Immoralities and Offensive Nuisances," in *AIDS: Ethics and Public Policy*, ed. Christine Pierce and Donald Vande Veer (Belmont, CA: Wadsworth, 1988), 92–102; Thomas B. Stoddard and Walter Rieman, "AIDS and the Rights of the Individual: Toward a More Sophisticated Understanding of Discrimination," in *A Disease of Society: Cultural and Institutional Responses to AIDS*, ed. Dorothy Nelkin, David P. Willis, and Scott V. Parris (Cambridge: Cambridge University Press, 1991), 241–71.

14 Ibid.

15 William Buckley, "Identify All the Carriers," *The New York Times* (March 18, 1986), p. 26; Ronald Elsberry, "AIDS Quarantining in England and the United States," *Hastings International and Comparative Law Journal* 10 (1986): 113–26; Mark H. Jackson, "The Criminalization of HIV," in *AIDS Agenda: Emerging Issues in Civil Rights*, ed. Nan D. Hunter and William B. Rubenstein (New York: New Press, 1992), 239–70.

16 Privacy encompasses "those places, spaces and matters upon or into which others may not intrude without the consent of the person or organization to whom they are designated as belonging" (p. 20); Albert J. Reiss, Jr., "The Legitimacy of Intrusion Into Private Space," in *Private Policing*, ed. Clifford D. Shearing and Philip C. Stenning (Newbury Park, CA: Sage, 1988), 19–44.

17 Jackson; Pierce and Vande Veer.

18 Buckley; Elsberry; Jackson; Stoddard and Rieman.

19 Judith Cohen, Priscilla Alexander, and Constance Wofsy, "Prostitutes and AIDS: Public Policy Issues," *AIDS & Public Policy Journal* 3 (1988): 16–22.

20 Edward Albert, "Illness and/or Deviance: The Response of the Press to Acquired

Immunodeficiency Syndrome," in *The Social Dimensions of AIDS: Method and Theory*, ed. Douglas A. Feldman and Tom Johnson (New York: Praeger, 1986), 163–78; Edward Albert, "AIDS and the Press: The Creation and Transformation of a Social Problem," in *Images of Issues; Typifying Contemporary Social Problems*, ed. Joel Best (New York: Aldine De Gruyter Press, 1989), 39–54. See also Ann Giudici Fettner and William Check, *The Truth About AIDS: The Evolution of an Epidemic* (New York: Holt, 1985); Randy Shilts, *And the Band Played On* (New York: St. Martin's Press, 1988); Harry Schwartz, "AIDS and the Media," in *Science in the Streets* (New York: Priority Press, 1984).

21   For an historical overview see, in addition to Brandt 1985, Beth Bergman, "AIDS, Prostitution, and the Use of Historical Stereotypes to Legislate Sexuality," *The John Marshall Law Review* 211 (1988): 777–830; Barbara Hobson, *Uneasy Virtue: The Politics of Prostitution and the American Reform Tradition* (New York: Basic Books, 1987); Gail Pheterson, *The Whore Stigma: Female Dishonor and Male Unworthiness* (The Netherlands: Dutch Ministry of Social Affairs and Employment, 1986); Gail Sheehy, "The Economics of Prostitution: Who Profits? Who Pays?" in *Sexual Deviance and Sexual Deviants*, ed. Erich Goode and Richard Troiden (New York: William Morrow, 1974), 110–23.

22   Darrow; Joan Luxenburg and Thomas Guild, "Prostitutes and AIDS: What Is All the Fuss About" (paper presented at the annual meetings of the American Society of Criminology in New Orleans, LA, 1992); Valerie Jenness, *Making It Work: The Contemporary Prostitutes' Rights Movement in Perspective* (New York: Aldine de Gruyter, 1993).

23   Geraldo Rivera, "Are Prostitutes the New Typhoid Marys?" The Geraldo Show, 1989, Fox Headquarters, 10201 Pico Boulevard, Los Angeles, California.

24   John Cristallo, "Are Prostitutes the New Typhoid Marys?" The Geraldo Show, 1989, Fox Headquarters, 10201 Pico Boulevard, Los Angeles, California.

25   Jackson; Luxenburg and Guild, 1992; Joan Luxenburg and Thomas Guild, "Coercion,

Criminal Sanctions and AIDS" (paper presented at the annual meetings of the Society for the Study of Social Problems, Washington, DC, 1990).

26   This parallels what happened to prostitutes in the first half of the twentieth century when "physicians and social reformers associated venereal disease, almost exclusively, with the vast population of prostitutes in American cities" (Brandt, p. 31). Perceived threats like these led to the increased social control of prostitution, primarily in the form of state regulation.

27   "No Murder-Try Case for Addicted Hooker," *Sacramento Bee*, 18 July 1990, p. B7.

28   Priscilla Alexander, "A Chronology of Sorts," personal files, 1988.

29   Darrow, p. 94. He observes, "To date, no HIV infections in female prostitutes or their clients can be directly linked to sexual exposure."

30   Lord Patrick Devlin, "Morals and the Criminal Law," in Pierce and Vande Veer, 77–86.

31   Carol Leigh, "AIDS: No Reason For A Witchhunt," *Oakland Tribune* (August 17, 1987), p. 1; Carol Leigh, "Further Violations Of Our Rights," in *AIDS Cultural Analysis, Cultural Activism*, ed. Douglas Crimp (Cambridge, MA: MIT Press, 1988), 177–81.

32   Stoddard and Reiman, 264.

33   Gail Pheterson, *A Vindication of the Rights of Whores* (Seattle: Seal Press, 1989), 28.

34   Leigh 1987, 1.

35   Dennis Altman, *AIDS in the Mind of America* (New York: Anchor, 1987); Paula A. Treichler, "AIDS, Homophobia, and Biomedical Discourse: An Epidemic of Signification," in *AIDS: Cultural Analysis, Cultural Activism*, ed. D. Crimp (Cambridge, MA: MIT Press, 1988), 31–70.

36   Beth E. Schneider, Valerie Jenness, and Sarah Fenstermaker, "Deflecting Trouble: The Introduction of AIDS Education in the Public Schools" (presented at the annual meetings of the Society for the Study of Social Problems, 1991).

37   Michael Granberry, "Besieged by Book Banners," *Los Angeles Times* (May 10, 1993), p. 1ff.

38   Donna Minkowitz, "Wrong Side of the Rainbow," *The Nation* (June 28, 1993), pp. 901–4.

39 Douglas Kirby, "School-Based Prevention Programs: Design, Evaluation, and Effectiveness," in *Adolescents and AIDS: A Generation in Jeopardy,* ed. Ralph DiClemente (Newbury Park, CA: Sage, 1992); David C. Sloane and Beverlie Conant Sloane, "AIDS in Schools: A Comprehensive Initiative," *McGill Journal of Education* 25 (1990): 205–28.

40 John Gallagher, "Why Johnny Can't Be Safe," *The Advocate* 631 (June 15, 1993), pp. 46–7.

41 Schneider, Jenness, and Fenstermaker.

42 Patton, 99.

43 Susan Russell, "The Hidden Curriculum of School: Reproducing Gender and Class Hierarchies," in *Feminism and Political Economy: Women's Work, Women's Struggles,* ed. H. J. Marmey and M. Luxton (Toronto: Methuen, 1987).

44 Eleanor Maticka-Tyndale, "Social Construction of HIV Transmission and Prevention Among Heterosexual Young Adults," *Social Problems* 39 (1992): 238–52.

45 DiClemente, 1992.

46 Maticka-Tyndale.

47 For additional consideration of these issues, see ACT-UP/New York Women and AIDS Book Group, *Women, AIDS and Activism* (Boston: South End Press, 1990); Laurie Wermuth, Jennifer Ham, and Rebecca L. Robbins, "Women Don't Wear Condoms: AIDS Risk Among Sexual Partners of IV Drug Users," in *The Social Context of AIDS,* ed. Joan Huber and Beth E. Schneider (Newbury Park, CA: Sage, 1992), 72–94.

48 Kirby.

49 These videos were produced in 1988. "Sex, Drugs and HIV," referred to in a later discussion, was produced in 1990 after complaints by parents resulted in revisions to an earlier version, "Sex, Drugs and AIDS."

50 Isabelle Melese-d'Hospital, "Still a Virgin: Adolescent Social Constructions of Sexuality and HIV Prevention Education" (paper presented at the annual meetings of the American Sociological Association, Miami, 1993).

51 Benjamin P. Bowser and Gina M. Wingood, "Community Based HIV-Prevention Programs for Adolescents," in DiClemente.

52 Patton 1990, 108.

53 Sloane and Conant Sloane; Schneider, Jenness, and Fenstermaker.

54 Singer; Watney. See also Jeffrey Weeks, *Sexuality and Its Discontents: Meanings, Myths and Modern Sexualities* (New York: Routledge, Kegan Paul, 1985).

Part VIII

Future Directions

The importance modern individuals place upon sexuality and emotional intimacy is relatively new. It is the product of large social changes that have swept modern industrial and post-industrial cultures: the purpose of marriage has shifted from economic necessity to companionship; divorce and "serial monogamy" have become increasingly acceptable; changes in social attitudes and improvements in contraception have allowed individuals to view sexuality as separate from reproduction, as an avenue for self-expression and pleasure. Do these changes represent a "revolution" in sexual norms and behavior? The loosening tie between sexuality and reproduction, and the growth of individual freedom – at least among the middle classes in wealthier nations – has led Anthony Giddens to suggest that intimacy is becoming "democratized." There are signs, according to Steven Seidman, Chet Meeks, and Francie Traschen, that gay stigma is diminishing as well, and along with it the "closet." But lest we become too optimistic about a future of intimate democracy, Lyn Jamieson reminds us about the persistence of gender inequality, and Anne Fausto-Sterling, focusing upon intersexuality, suggests an even more profound (and potentially unsettling) project: the deconstruction of binary conceptions of gender altogether.

29 Beyond the Closet? The Changing Social Meaning of Homosexuality in the United States

Steven Seidman, Chet Meeks, and Francie Traschen

Introduction

In late twentieth-century America, the closet has become a central category for grasping the history and social dynamics of gay life. This concept is intended to capture social patterns of secrecy and sexual self-management that structure the lives of "gay individuals" in societies organized around a norm of heterosexuality.[1] The concept of the closet is linked, perhaps inseparable from, the notion of "coming out." The latter category gives expression to the dramatic quality of privately and publicly coming to terms with a contested social identity. The categories of the closet and coming out have then been foundational to accounts of modern homosexuality.

Moreover, as many social thinkers have argued, concepts and narratives are to be assessed not only by their empirical and conceptual adequacy, but by their social effects – for example, the ways they shape identities, group life, and political movements (Bravman 1997). In this regard, the narrative of coming out of the closet constructs gay individuals as suffering a common fate in a society organized around normative heterosexuality. Gay individuals are said to share an experience of secrecy and social isolation, the ordeal of refashioning a stigmatized identity, and negotiating social inclusion. This narrative shapes a common identity and politicizes it by making homosexuals into unjust social victims.

Despite the analytically and politically productive aspects of the narrative of the closet, we have reservations. Politically speaking, to the extent that this narrative has been linked to identity politics, it shares the strengths and weaknesses of the latter. Rallying around a shared "minority" identity has contributed to gay political empowerment. Yet, there are considerable costs attached to identity politics – for example, the repression of differences among lesbians and gay men, a narrow focus on legitimating same sex preference, the isolation of the gay movement from other movements, and as queer perspectives argue, normalizing a gay identity leaves intact the organization of sexuality around a hetero/homosexual binary. Furthermore, by making the closet into the key focus of gay oppression, coming out and affirming a gay identity is often viewed as the supreme political act – as if mere gay visibility undermines heterosexism. The latter is, however, institutional and cultural, not simply a matter of individual prejudice. Finally, the narrative of coming out of the closet creates divisions between individuals who are "in" and "out" of the closet. The former are stigmatized as living false, unhappy lives and are pressured to be public without considering that the calculus of benefits and costs vary considerably depending on how individuals are socially positioned.

The focus of this article though is less the politics than the sociology of the closet. We argue two main points. First, we defend the analytical value of a concept of the closet but aim to be clear about its historical and sociological meaning. Specifically, we are in broad agreement with the revisionism of Chauncey (1994) who holds that the concept of the closet has unique sociohistorical preconditions – most importantly, the fore-grounding of sexual identity and a system-atic mobilization of social agencies (e.g., the state, medical–scientific institutions, the criminal justice system) aimed at enforcing a norm of heterosexuality. However, we be-lieve that historians such as Chauncey have not questioned a one-sided sociological view that emphasizes the repressive character of the closet. We argue that central to this con-cept is a double life and strategies of every-day sexual self-management. While such practices aim to avoid the risks of unin-tended exposure, they also create a "pro-tected" space that permits individuals to fashion a gay self and facilitates the making of gay social worlds (e.g., gay bars or infor-mal networks). In short, we propose to view the closet as a strategy of accommodation and resistance which both reproduces and contests aspects of a society organized around normative heterosexuality.

Our second argument focuses on emer-gent social patterns that indicate the declin-ing social significance of the closet in contemporary America. Our research sug-gests that many individuals who identify as lesbian, gay, or bisexual have "normalized" (subjectively accepted) and "routinized" (so-cially integrated) their homosexuality. Con-sequently, a double life involving patterns of concealment and sexual self-management is less defining of their lives.

Although our research suggests that many Americans have today fashioned lives "beyond the closet," we are not intending to narrate a one-dimensional story of the pro-gressive social inclusion and equality of gay individuals. First, normalization and routin-ization have been incomplete. Our respond-ents continue to manage their homosexuality in part because of shame, guilt, or fear. In this regard, our point is not that sexual self-man-agement practices are obsolete. Rather, we contend that such practices are more situ-ation-specific than patterning of a whole way of life, as is suggested by the concept of the closet. Second, we distinguish between "interpersonal" and "institutional" routin-ization. The former indicates informal ways individuals integrate homosexuality into their conventional social lives, e.g., disclos-ing to family members or coworkers. Insti-tutional routinization refers to incorporating policies and practices into organizations that do not subordinate nonheterosexuals. We are not convinced that progress at the interper-sonal level has been paralleled at the insti-tutional level. However, the focus of this article is interpersonal routinization.

In 1996–7 we interviewed 25 individuals who identified as lesbian, gay, or bisexual. As other social researchers have argued (e.g., Esterberg 1997; Whisman 1996), a representative sample of homosexually iden-tified individuals is not possible. We sought a sample population that was diverse in terms of gender, race, and class.

Our aim was to interview individuals who have not organized their lives around a gay subculture. We assumed that "subcultu-rally" identified individuals would have nor-malized and routinized their homosexuality. Instead, we sought individuals who would be less subculturally identified and therefore more likely to be "closeted." Although most of our respondents reported a feeling of belonging to a gay community, the extent to which they participated in this commu-nity varied considerably. None were polit-ical activists or organized their lives in relation to a gay subculture.[2]

We have divided this article into three parts. In the first section, we critically exam-ine the way the concept of the closet has been used in folk and expert discourses. We defend a view of the closet which narrows its histor-ical and sociological scope of application. Specifically, we view "closet practices" as a response to repressive strategies aimed at maintaining a norm of heterosexuality by excluding homosexuality from public life. This strategy (roughly inaugurated in the 1940s but intensified in the 1950s and 1960s) created the conditions of the closet – a concept of homosexuality as a distinct sexual identity and a double life. The latter involved intensive and extensive strategies of sexual self-management that created a protected space that allowed individuals to fashion gay selves and to navigate between a straight and gay world. In the second section, we present a series of case studies to make plausible our claim of a trend towards the normalization and the (interpersonal) routinization of homosexuality. We point to social patterns that, though organized by a norm of heterosexuality, are not adequately described by the concept of the closet. In the third section, we consider the implications of these trends for viewing homosexuality as a source of identity, community, and politics. We argue that one effect of normalizing and routinizing trends is the "decentering" of gay identities and communities – that is, homosexuality shifts from being narrated as a core to a partial, more voluntary aspect of identity and basis of community. We conjecture that these social shifts are a source of the "queer" currents in gay culture. In other words, it is the successes, as much as the failures of identity politics, that have contributed to the rise of a queer political culture that is critical of a movement aimed exclusively at normalizing homosexuality.

Rethinking the Sociology of the Closet

Since the Stonewall riots in 1969 the closet has become a core concept for understanding gay life in the US. Our preliminary research indicates that it was initially in the political literature that the closet made its public debut. The major gay liberationist anthology was tellingly entitled *Out of the Closets* (Jay and Young 1972). In her "Introduction" Karla Jay states that this collection was published "in the hope that one day all gay people will be out of the closet" (p. lxii). In Laud Humphreys's (1972) sociology of gay liberationism, he states that the rallying cry of this movement was "Out of the closet, into the streets!" (p. 3). As gay liberationism gave way to a civil rights, pride-based politics in the mid-1970s, and as institutionally elaborated subcultures were created in the 1980s (D'Emilio 1983; Levine 1979; Wolf 1979), the act of coming out, as publicly ritualized in National Coming Out Day and pride marches, became a sacred personal and political event (Herdt 1992; Herrell 1992). The renewal of gay radicalism in the early 1990s, in the form of the politics of outing, underscores the continued significance of the politics of the closet (Gross 1993). Today, political strategies focused on dismantling the closet remain central – whether the site is the classroom (Harbeck 1992), the industrial–media complex (Signorile 1993), corporate America (Woods 1993), the civil service bureaucracy (DeCrescenzo 1997), or the military forces (Cammermayer 1994).

If a political investment underpins a discourse of the closet, this narrative figure was gradually absorbed into the gay mainstream. Between the mid-1980s and the late 1990s, the framing of gay life in terms of the closet and coming out became pervasive. For example, a flourishing industry of self-help literature advises lesbians and gay men, but also their family, friends, and employers, on managing daily life beyond the closet, dealing with the shame and residual homophobia of the closet, and so on (Buxton 1994; Johnson 1997; Kaufman and Raphael 1996). Thus, in Mary Borhek's *Coming Out to Parents* (1993), parents are advised on how to ease their children's exodus from the closet. They are instructed that disclosure by a daughter or son creates closet dynamics for them. For example, the mother must decide who to "come out" to as a parent of a gay child (Hom 1996).

Shifting from "low brow" to "high brow" literary culture, much of what has been canonized as "classic" gay literature has a coming out story as its dramatic center (e.g., Rita Mae Brown's *Rubyfruit Jungle* or Edmund White's *A Boys Own Story*). Consider the memoir as a literary genre that blends folk and literary culture. From Merle Miller's *On Being Different* (1971), *The Original Coming Out Stories* (Penelope and Wolfe 1989), to the testimonies of people of color (Beam 1986; Ramos 1987), the struggle around the closet is the core dramatic motif (see McRuer 1996; Plummer 1995; Zimmerman 1984). For example, Miller's memoir is structured around a shift from a life of passing, which included marriage, to a finale when, unable to countenance his own shame and others' bigotry, he "comes out of the closet" (p. 47). Some twenty years later, Paul Monette (1992) narrates his life story as a "narrow escape from the coffin world of the closet" to the "giddy circle of freedom" that accompanied the public affirmation of his homosexuality.

The concept of the closet has been central in the social scientific literature. In one of the earliest studies in the sociology of homosexuality, Humphreys (1970) analyzes participants in "tearoom trade." The tearoom is a public space where the quest for sexual pleasure is linked to heightened risks of exposure and danger. Humphreys views tearoom participants as exhibiting a "closeted" type of social adaptation. In response to a stigmatized desire, these individuals fashion a double life. Passing in their public life, homosexual expression is confined to furtive sexual encounters involving intense self-management to avoid unwanted exposure. In recent social science, which is often focused on coming out, the closet is typically non-thematized but foundational. For example, Herdt (1992) criticizes views of "coming out as a uniform, ahistorical, stage-driven process." Coming out is approached as an initiation rite marking a transition to an adult gay identity. The dynamics of this rite of passage are complicated by gender or generational difference. The idea of coming out assumes of course an

initial condition involving the secretive management of homosexuality, i.e., the closet. However, whereas coming out is analyzed with attention to sociological and historical complexities, the closet is the taken-for-granted, ahistorical ground of gay life (Jenness 1992; Rust 1993).[3] Although queer perspectives are critical of much of gay culture, the concept of the closet remains foundational. As Sedgwick says, "the gay closet is not a feature only of the lives of gay people. But for many gay people it is still the fundamental feature of social life" (Sedgwick 1990: 68).

One theme that runs through this literature is the claim that the closet always accompanies homosexuality in a normatively heterosexual society. In an early sociological study, Edward Delph wrote:

> An alternative to the "closet" developed after the Stonewall riot gave birth to the gay liberation movement: coming out of their own closets by disclosing secret identities.... If the closet is a result of the fear of stigmatization, it is the major way in which one's social and sexual life is integrated. It has served faithfully for decades and probably centuries as the way to make "sense" out of conflicting demands or expectations of homosexual desires in a heterosexually defined social world. *(Delph 1978: 158–60)*

Theorizing in a very different milieu, Diana Fuss echoes this view. "Paradoxically, the 'ghosting' of homosexuality coincides with its 'birth.' For the historical moment of the first appearance of the homosexual as a 'species' rather than a 'temporary aberration' also marks the moment of the homosexual's disappearance – into the closet" (Fuss 1991: 4).

Recently, Chauncey (1994) has criticized perspectives that apply the concept of the closet to all patterns of homosexual concealment without attention to unique sociohistorical conditions. He argues that the primary cultural division in the early decades of this century in New York City was around gender. The dominant currents of this culture distinguished between "normal" masculine men (who could – and did – have sex with men) and "fairies" or effeminate men (who were thought to be woman-like and to desire sex with "normal" men). Moreover, fairies created a gay world that was public and integrated into at least some (working-class) neighborhoods. Chauncey argues that the homosexual closet is a product of the repression of this working-class gay world. He maintains, moreover, that the notion of a closet assumes that the hetero/homosexual binary, as a framework defining sexual identity by sexual object choice, marginalized the normal/fairy binary – an event that he dates from the 1930s.[4]

We think that Chauncey's argument is persuasive but needs to be amended. He acknowledges that secrecy and self-management were integral to the public gay life created by fairies. Although they were tolerated in some working-class neighborhoods, fairies were also the targets of citizen and state harassment. Chauncey argues that the concealment practices of fairies should not be described by the concept of the closet. He prefers the concept of "double life" because the secretive practices of fairies were not part of a comprehensive pattern of deception and passing, but were strategies to avoid public censure in order to enjoy a public gay life. However, this distinction between the double life (which made possible a positive gay life) and the closet (which repressed a gay life) involves a reductionistic sociological view of the latter as a state of repression.

It is hardly surprising that Chauncey understands the closet as exclusively repressive. This view is pervasive. Consider two contemporary literary and political documents.

In *Becoming a Man* Monette (1992) reverses the conventional coming-of-age narrative. Instead of a story of childhood and adolescence as formative of an adult self, he relates a tale of youth that involved the loss of self to the suffocating logic of the closet. "Until I was 25, I was the only man I knew who had no story at all. I'd long since accepted the fact that nothing had ever happened to me and nothing ever would. That's how the closet feels, once you've made your nest in it and learned to call it home." For Monette, the struggle for self-possession is told as a struggle against the closet which he describes variously as an "internal exile," an "imprisonment," and as "the gutting of all our passions till we are a bunch of eunuchs."

If Monette makes the escape from the closet into the chief act of self-possession, Signorile (1993) makes destroying the closet into the supreme political act. The closet is said to preserve the power of heterosexism by fashioning a "cowering, sad, self-loathing homosexual" (p. 365). It reproduces homosexual oppression by creating a dominated self. "The closeted, as captives, suffer such profound psychological trauma that they develop a relationship to their closets similar to that of hostages to their captors" (p. xviii). To the extent that the closet is viewed as the cornerstone of gay oppression, Signorile defends "outing" as a liberatory political act.

We question whether the concept of the closet is coherent if it refers exclusively to a condition of repression. This view assumes an original, already formed homosexual self who is constrained "in" the closet. This assumption is inconsistent with social constructionist ideas which view gay selves as socially formed and never fully consolidated (Butler 1991; Phelan 1993). From this perspective, the closet would be viewed as not only repressive but productive in a double sense.

First, practices of concealment not only protect the individual from the risks of exposure but create a "protected" psychic space to imaginatively construct a gay self. As Foucault (1980) might say, the self-management practices imposed by normative heterosexuality to suppress homosexuality ironically incite a heightened self-consciousness about such desires. In other words, the prohibition against homosexuality makes it into a preoccupation to the point where the individual may consolidate an identity around this desire.

For example, despite Monette's explicit claim that concealment is only repressive, his autobiographical sketch relates a tale of the formative role of the closet in the making of a gay self. It was in the closet that he began to cultivate his homosexual desires. "I couldn't tell my claque of girls how riveted I'd been on the Prom King's grinding hips – his football hands stroking Connie's bare back up and down" (Monette 1992: 45). Similarly, Paul speaks of struggling to suppress an impulse to stare at the other boys during high school gym. The language he uses to describe this experience suggests only repression. Yet, Paul relates that these boys became part of his fantasy life. "Jerking off every night in the dark thinking about them, summoning them in their nakedness...I was able to picture in stupefying detail a hundred different naked bodies" (ibid: 70–1). It was in the public silence of the closet that these fantasies were elaborated – shaping Paul's gay self and ultimately driving him "out" of the closet: "I had no choice but to keep on looking for the thing I'd never seen: two men in love and laughing. For that was the image in my head...[which] I'd fashioned out of bits of dreams....The vision of the laughing men dogged me and wouldn't be shaken...till I sometimes thought I'd lost my mind – but I also think it kept me alive" (ibid: 178). Thus, while Monette self-consciously tells a story of how heterosexism produced a dominated self, he also narrates a tale of the making of a resisting gay self. The chief drama of his story is that of an inauthentic, unfree self who rebels against the closet in order to recover his true self. If we take the closet as a metaphor only of containment and denial, we cannot explain how a dominated self manages resistance and liberation.

A second sense of the productivity of the closet relates to the making of community.

While some individuals conceal in order to avoid any public exposure, others pass as a strategy to make possible a public gay life. This socially productive aspect of the closet was recognized in a study of lesbian identity and community formation. Barbara Ponse (1978) observes that

> the secrecy around gay life provides a protective milieu for trying on the lesbian identity in a favorable ambience. Once a lesbian identity has been acknowledged and accepted, the lesbian subculture created by the binding and separating powers of secrecy supports and strengthens commitment to that identity, through associations with validating others.

Similarly, Mariana Romo-Carmona underscores the ironic role of the closet in contributing to the making of a Latina lesbian community. While emphasizing the oppression that accompanies practices of silence and secrecy (e.g., misrecognition, invisibility, disenfranchisement), Romo-Carmona remarks that such practices unintentionally create a heightened feeling of difference and solidarity:

> How many daughters, mothers, sisters, Godmothers and grandmothers, aunts, cousins and best friends have lived and died unknown? Each woman's forced silence was a denial of her existence, as if she never loved another woman....Saliendo del closet is ultimately helping to create...a Latina lesbian community. (Ramos 1987: xxiii; cf. Trujillo 1991).

Defining the closet as exclusively repressive assumes moreover that "closeted" individuals reproduce it by internalizing polluted self-images (e.g., Signorile 1993; Vaid 1996). The combination of social and self-hatred is said to inevitably result in personal despair and pathology. Indeed, we have heard many stories of excess with drugs and alcohol, sad tales of depression and loneliness that were linked to a closeted life. For example, Adam, a 40-year-old professional, drank his way through adolescence and early adulthood, through a marriage and a family, in order to manage a life of profound duplicity and shame:

> I was living a lie. I was in a marriage to someone I couldn't stand. I was miserable all the time. I was uncomfortable with myself, but I didn't have the balls to come out of the closet.... In the six months before I came out and got sober, I tried to commit suicide twice. I was just an extremely unhappy individual.

Without minimizing the oppressive aspects of homosexual concealment and self-management, we found that such patterns do not have a uniform psychological and social meaning. For example, some respondents fashioned satisfying lives, despite living with considerable ambivalence.

Phil described himself as "very closeted." He was aware of his desires for men as a youth, but their relation to his self-identity was unclear. Growing up in a small town in the 1940s and 1950s, he was barely exposed to ideas about homosexuality. It was not until Phil was in his thirties and forties (1960s–1970s) that he realized same-sex feelings are often interpreted as indicating a homosexual identity. However, he did not at the time nor does he now define himself as gay, despite acknowledging that his primary desires are for men. He identifies as bisexual as a way to make sense of the fact that his feelings for his deceased wife were real. He does not describe his marriage as a lie or a strategy to pass. "I married because that's what I wanted to do. I wanted that kind of life." Phil's decision to continue to conceal is in part motivated by shame and fear of social disapproval; he also described it as a positive choice to live a publicly heterosexual life. Phil embraces a heterosexual identity in part because of the image he wants those he loves to have of him, in order to maintain the kind of intimacy he now shares with family and friends, and because it is a social life that he has enjoyed,

despite some anguish in having to marginalize his homosexuality.

Jim (born 1967) was aware of his homosexual feelings as a youth though unsure of their meaning. He grew up in a small town and had little exposure to ideas about homosexuality. As late as the 1980s, Jim reports that the only images that made a lasting impression were those heard in church and his family. Homosexuality was said to be immoral and unnatural. Jim says that through adolescence he was unsure of the importance of homosexual feelings in his life. Jim had a girlfriend through high school whom he eventually married. He told his wife about his feelings for men, but he was committed to making the marriage work. After his wife died in an accident Jim chose to publicly identify as gay. Yet, he never reinterpreted his heterosexual past as inauthentic. "I did love my wife; there was a commitment there, and we were best friends. She knew everything about me, there were no secrets, nothing hidden there."

Some respondents were very clear about the meaning of homosexual feelings in their lives. For example, some individuals interpreted their homosexuality as indicating a discredited identity. Their decision to conceal was driven by shame, guilt, and fear. Some married or rigidly conformed to gender stereotypes in order to conceal; others turned to alcohol or drugs.

There is no escaping ambivalent feelings towards homosexuality in a society that makes heterosexuality normative. Yet, some individuals do not interpret homosexual feelings as revealing their true selves. They understand homosexuality as marginal in their psychic economies. They minimize their homosexuality without feeling self-loathing or estrangement. We should not assume that all individuals experience homosexuality as an identity and therefore experience its marginalization as a betrayal of a true self. Moreover, even individuals who interpret their homosexuality as integral to their selves may choose to marginalize it without necessarily surrendering to self-loathing. The presumption that the presence of homosexual feelings marks the individual as a homosexual fails to consider that many individuals experience both homosexual and heterosexual feelings in psychically integral ways. At some point, Phil and Jim made a decision to live heterosexually not simply to avoid social disapproval but because of deeply felt psychological longings for heterosexual intimacy and integration into a conventional social world. Our interviews suggest that not all individuals who identify as gay always distinguish clearly between homosexual and heterosexual feelings, experience them as mutually exclusive, understand them as markers of identity, and describe the suppression of homosexual feelings as necessarily betraying their true selves (Davies 1992; Esterberg 1997; Markowe 1996).

To bring this discussion to a close, we believe that the concept of the closet is analytically useful if its specific sociohistorical scope is clarified. We find plausible Chauncey's claim that the era of the closet began in the 1930s and 1940s. We conjecture that by the 1950s and 1960s the norm of heterosexuality operated by maintaining a symbolic and social separation between a "pure" heterosexuality and a "polluted" homosexuality. Enforcing this social division involved the exclusion of homosexuality from public life. A series of repressive strategies – from censorship to civic disenfranchisement and violence – were deployed. A heterosexist order maintained by a logic of repression created the social practices that have come to be called the closet. Central was a double life – a private life where homosexuality could be acknowledged and expressed in a quasi-public gay world (bars, cruising areas, informal gatherings) and a public life of "passing" as heterosexual (Escoffier 1997). We have argued, moreover, that practices of concealment were not only suppressive and reproductive of domination, but were productive of gay selves and quasi-public worlds.

Case Studies in the (Incomplete) Normalization and Routinization of Homosexuality

The concept of the closet is compelling to the extent that the core areas of an individual's life – work, family, and intimate ties – are structured by practices of managing homosexuality in order to avoid unwanted exposure. The closet refers to a division between a private life where homosexuality can be expressed and a public life where one passes as heterosexual. To the extent that homosexuality continues to be polluted and subject to criminal sanction and civic disenfranchisement, there will be individuals for whom the management of their homosexuality is so intensive and extensive that such practices shape a whole way of life.

In this section, we argue that many Americans have normalized and routinized their homosexuality to a degree that the concept of the closet is less descriptive of their lives. Our thesis is that the behavior of these individuals in the core areas of their lives is not systematically shaped by the need to conceal and manage their homosexuality. The choice for these Americans is no longer between denial or a double life, but how to live a public life that integrates homosexuality while still making decisions about disclosure.

Normalization refers to a subjective condition in which homosexuality is described as natural or normal. Homosexuality is said to make the individual neither inherently inferior nor superior to those who identify as heterosexual. Normalizing homosexuality means that while individuals may still feel some shame or guilt, they describe such feelings as the residues of living in a normatively heterosexual society rather than as judgments about the inherently inferior status of homosexuality. Normalization makes interpersonal routinization possible. This concept refers to individual efforts to integrate homosexuality into the conventional social world. Key indicators of interpersonal routinization would be whether individuals disclose information about their homosexuality to family, close friends, and coworkers, or whether individuals date, form relationships, and make their intimacies public.

We approach normalization and routinization in terms of a continuum. Individuals normalize and routinize their homosexuality to varying degrees over the course of a lifetime. We assume that in a society organized around the norm of heterosexuality, normalization and routinization will be incomplete. This may reflect incomplete normalization (e.g., sustained feelings of shame and guilt around homosexuality), incomplete interpersonal routinization (e.g., intolerance by heterosexuals), or incomplete institutional routinization (institutional practices that subordinate nonheterosexuals).

We describe the lives of some individuals who have normalized and routinized their homosexuality to a considerable extent. Their lives are less plausibly understood by the concept of the closet. Homosexuality does not dictate their lives, e.g., it does not pressure individuals to marry, uncouple sex from one's emotional and social life, or conceal this identity from family or friends. For these individuals, disclosure decisions are less prompted by shame, guilt, or fear than by decisions about drawing boundaries between personal information that is private and public. Despite lives that are "beyond the closet," normalization and routinization are incomplete. Subjective ambivalence and interpersonal and institutional resistance to routinization underscore the continued power of normative heterosexuality in the US.

We present several abbreviated case studies. Aspects of the lives of individuals are sketched with the intent of illustrating a series of positions on a continuum – with one pole indicating a life in the "closet" and the other indicating lives "beyond the closet."

Phil came of age as an adult in the 1950s. He was raised in a working-class, Catholic family in a small rural town. Phil relates the story of his homosexuality in terms of a conventionalized narrative of the closet. Aware of homosexual feelings as a youth, Phil initially denied them and later separated them from the rest of his life. He did what was expected of him – he married and raised a family. His masculine self-presentation and his marital status reduced the risk of exposure. His few homosexual experiences were anonymous or with men who shared his fear of exposure. Nevertheless, Phil was "always concerned that somehow it would be found out." Accordingly, he engaged in intensive daily self-management. He did not associate with gay people, avoided staring at men, was silent in the face of homophobic comments, avoided arguments about homosexuality, maintained a public interest in women, and so on. Even now, widowed for several years, Phil reports that few people know of his homosexuality.

Phil's account of his decision to remain "closeted" is likewise conventionalized. He reported that his family of origin would not have tolerated his homosexuality. His father would have been devastated. His mother would have been very disappointed and it would have strained their intimacy. Similarly, Phil is unsure whether he would have been fired from his job, but his coworkers would certainly have disapproved and made work tense. Once married and having raised a family, the price of integrating his homosexuality into his life became too high. Even now, a widower, economically secure, and his children grown, Phil insists he will never come out. Although his children would probably accept him, Phil wants them to view him in a socially approved way – as heterosexual. The threat of disturbing the rich intimacy of his family stops Phil from living a life which, in his own words, expresses who he is. "[Homosexuality is] very important for my sense of self, but I can't act on it like I wished I could. I can't come out. I have to keep it a secret."

If Phil illustrates the closeted end of the continuum, Clara exemplifies a life that is conducted largely beyond the closet. Clara describes herself as an 18-years-old black lesbian. Clara comes from a large working-class family. Her father and mother were separated when she was a child. She has lived mostly with her mother in a Maryland suburb, but spends some time with her father in Harlem. Clara is a college freshman.

Clara's "coming out" process was remarkably painless. She disclosed her lesbian preference to her mother – and then to her whole family – at the age of 14. Today she is open about her homosexuality to everyone in her family, which she describes as close. The extent to which Clara has normalized and routinized her homosexuality is indicated by the scope of disclosure to her family. "I talk about everything with my mother and my sisters and one brother. They know my lover and everything like that. They know just about everything [about my lesbian life]." Her comments on disclosing to her father, who, as a Jamaican, is described as less understanding, illustrates the extent of Clara's normalizing of her homosexuality: "He had the biggest problem with it but it didn't matter to me, cause I just told him to be telling him. I wasn't telling him for approval."

Clara's description of her social life points to a similar degree of normalization and routinization. She is open with friends, classmates, and teachers. For example, living in a college dorm Clara had to deal quickly with issues of disclosure. She reports the following incident. Invited by dorm mates to a fraternity party, Clara declined: "'I'm not going,' and they were like, 'why?' I'm like, 'I don't do dick.' They were like, 'What do you mean?' I was like, 'I'm a lesbian'." The normalization of homosexuality exhibited in Clara's behavior with family and classmates was stated directly in comments to the effect that her homosexuality was "normal" or her "norm."

Clara describes a life in which her homosexuality has been interpersonally routinized. People who matter to Clara have been accepting. Her dorm mates were surprised at how open she was but they have accepted her. For example:

> When we sit in the dorm room sometimes and we're having conversations about an ex-boyfriend, if I find them talking about something that maybe was similar to something that went on with me I [would say], "oh you know, my ex-girlfriend one time so and so" and they'd be like, "really, they do the same thing like that?"

Similarly, Clara reports the following incident with her dentist: "He [the dentist] knows [about me being a lesbian] because when I went to get my teeth checked … my girlfriend came with me. It wasn't like I sat down and told him, but he asked who she was and I was like, 'oh, that's my girlfriend'." The dentist was very accepting. "Every now and then he'll ask about her, [ask] how she's doing, [and] what she's doing and all of that."

Clara's relatively smooth integration of homosexuality into her life was exceptional. It was more common for our respondents to narrate a shift from a double life to a life beyond the closet.

Bill is a white, 40-year-old, middle-level state worker who comes from a working-class family in a small town close to his present residence in Albany, New York. Bill was aware of his homosexual feelings as a child. These became more vivid between the ages of 10–12 when heterosexual dating began in his peer group. Despite being attracted to men, Bill dated only women in order to conceal his homosexuality. Homosexuals were described by family and peers as "faggots." Bill feared being disowned by family, ridiculed by friends, and condemned by his church. By adolescence Bill had, in his own words, "stepped into the closet." Subsequently, Bill married, joined the marines, and started drinking to manage a closeted life.

His marriage ended in the mid-1980s. Perhaps triggered by a decision to get sober and his abiding loneliness, Bill decided to integrate his homosexuality into his life. He disclosed initially in the gay world of bars and fashioned a gay friendship circle. This social network allowed him to disclose to his mother and eventually to his entire family, friends, coworkers, ex-wife, son, and his hometown: Bill was interviewed by a local newspaper on being gay and Christian.

Bill's relation to his son illustrates the normalizing of his homosexuality. Bill has joint custody of Larry. When his son was 10 years old Bill tried to explain that he was gay. Larry didn't respond. From time to time Bill would reintroduce this topic but Larry remained inattentive. Bill decided to be relaxed about it:

> I would be completely myself in front of him, and that included conversations with gay friends, or talking about gay people or places....I was in a relation and I let him see us hold hands and hug and kiss good-bye....I was just trying to show him that we're a normal gay couple. I kind of hate that word normal but... you know, that it was natural for us.

Bill has, to a significant degree, routinized his homosexuality. For example, Bill has disclosed to his supervisor and his two regular coworkers. "I don't try to hide it in my conversations. I think that most everybody knows." Asked if he talks about the gay aspects of his life (e.g., friends, lovers, social events) with his coworkers in a way that would be similar if he were heterosexual, Bill replied, "Yeah, with two of them, definitely, [because] they're closer friends than the other one." Asked if there was anything important relating to the gay aspects of his life that he conceals with them, he replied "Not at all."

Rachel was born in 1964. She is now completing her Ph.D. thesis. Rachel was married for eight years. She did not become aware of any lesbian feelings until she got involved with a woman in the early 1990s. This surprised and excited her but it was

several years before she would identify as a lesbian. Rachel prefers to identify as a lesbian rather than a bisexual, because she believes that while she chose, out of real needs and feelings to marry, she has subsequently chosen to be with a woman as a life partner.

Rachel initially disclosed to her friends who were very accepting. Disclosure to her family was difficult. She describes her father, with whom she is close, as bigoted. Moreover, her parents pressured her to stay married. Nevertheless, as her marriage ended, and her involvement with Phyllis became serious, Rachel revealed her homosexuality to her family. Although her parents are ambivalent, Rachel insists on integrating the lesbian aspects of her life into her family relations:

> They don't like to talk about that kind of stuff [i.e., lesbian life] but they know about Phyllis. I nudge them every once and awhile when they forget to say something or when they forget to include her... I'm much more sensitive, much more quick to jump on them about it [or] to say something to them.

Phyllis is included in all family events.

Rachel describes a life in which her homosexuality is routinized. She lives with Phyllis in a New England suburb. They bought a home together and both are listed on the mortgage. Their daily lives are conducted publicly as a couple. "When we have contractors to the house, when we go buy furniture..., we make no effort to pretend as if, these are going in my room, or her room. We make every decision as a couple and talk as if we are a couple." In this regard, Rachel says her doctor and dentist know that she is a lesbian. Neighbors also know about her and Phyllis. The disclosure logic here is revealing of Rachel's effort to routinize this practice.

> What I don't think is important is that I put my hand out and say "hello, my name is Rachel and I'm a lesbian." I think that's awkward but... people know that we live

in that house together, and make joint decisions, and our names are on the mailbox. [Also], people when they ask me how I'm doing, [also] say things like, "gee I haven't seen Phyllis around and how is she doing?" So I don't hide it but on the other hand I don't make anybody uncomfortable.

Rachel says that today her homosexuality does not influence her choice of friends (except that they be accepting of her homosexuality), where she lives, the kind of work she does, or the ways she interacts with family, coworkers, neighbors, and service providers. Rachel does not view her life in terms of a division between a straight and gay world.

Albert was born in 1972. He is a middle-class African American. Albert described a strong sense of feeling different throughout growing up. He attended an all-white primary and secondary school. Although Albert grew up in Albany, a capital city, he recalls only negative images of homosexuality through high school (1987–91). Albert managed daily life so as to avoid any risk of exposure.

Albert attempted suicide when he was 18 years old. This prompted a disclosure process. His family was supportive. "My mother loves me for who I am." Albert has boyfriends over to their home, and they are considered "family" by his parents. He admits that there is much about his gay life that is not talked about but this reflects a family culture that excludes personal matters from public discussion. Moreover, while his homosexuality "feels ordinary, it's a little awkward for my mother. She's like, 'I don't have to like it but I accept that's who you are'." Normalizing his homosexuality entailed integrating it into his daily life. Albert disclosed to his high school friends: "It was really good because they were just encountering friends of theirs that they met at school [college] who had come out to them and so it was really very good. They were sorry about what I'd gone through but there was no negative reactions." Albert

says that, so far, "I haven't found any [friend] that hasn't been accepting."

As Albert's suicide attempt indicates, coming to terms with his homosexuality was agonizing. Today, though, "I finally have accepted it for myself, it's who I am and I don't really care what the other person thinks." When asked if there was still anxiety about disclosing, he said, "it's just something that's normal [for me]." Albert is trying to normalize the practice of disclosure. "If someone ask[s] me . . . if I have a girlfriend I say no I have a boyfriend . . . I'm not gonna just come out and tell someone because I don't feel like I have to tell somebody."

Except for two (older) respondents, all of our interviewees have, to a considerable degree, normalized and routinized their homosexuality. Today, concealment and coming out are not their primary concerns. Instead, their (gay) concerns revolve around dating, developing gay friends, gaining legal rights and accompanying social benefits, and social recognition of their relationships. For example, Albert says: "I'm not really focused on coming out of the closet. I've done that already. I guess now I'm dealing with being a gay man who is HIV positive."

To the extent that homosexuality is normalized and interpersonally routinized, we would expect that decisions about disclosure would be prompted less by shame, guilt, or fear. We found that some concealment decisions involved judgments about how to draw boundaries between information about the self that is private – but not necessarily because it is discrediting – and information that is public.

For example, since Mike's marriage ended in 1991 he has lived a publicly gay life. Mike works in a large State agency. He has a picture of his partner (Andy) on his desk. He reports that he talks as openly about his life with Andy as his coworkers talk about their heterosexual partners. For example, "We went to a union ceremony two weeks ago and I brought in all the pictures and showed them to my secretary and the people I'm closest to."

Mike must still make decisions about disclosure. For example, with new clients and coworkers, disclosure "depends on the way the conversation runs. If someone asks me if I'm married...I say that I'm with a man." Mike treats homosexuality as part of a class of "intimate information" that is not routinely shared. He makes disclosure decisions by considering the degree of intimacy established or desired. With most coworkers he does not disclose because "I probably would never have an opportunity to share anything personal with them." Mike's comments on his disclosure practices in relation to his son are similarly revealing of a logic that is not driven by shame or fear. Mike is open to his son (16 years old) who stays with him on weekends. However, when his son invites friends to his home, "Andy and I don't kiss in front of them and we don't sleep in the same bed." Mike's decision to conceal is motivated by respect for his son who has not fully normalized his father's homosexuality. "I think it's sensitivity to my son's relationships with his friends and understanding that it's not easy for everybody to be out, including possibly my son with his friends, being out about me."

Consider the disclosure decisions of Jeff (born 1965). He talks easily about the gay aspects of his life with family, coworkers, and friends, including fraternity brothers. However, Jeff has not disclosed to all his coworkers. "If they don't know it's not because I'm hiding it from them." Jeff says his homosexuality is often irrelevant to his professional life (research scientist). "It just doesn't come up....There is no personal stuff from either side." With regard to his family, Jeff insists that he is as open to them as he would be if he were heterosexual. He brings dates to meet his parents, and his boyfriend has joined his family for holiday gatherings. Yet, Jeff acknowledges that some information linked to his gay life is withheld. For example, Jeff has not told his uncles and aunts that he is gay. "You know if I tell them it will rifle through my family in a second. I couldn't care less [but] I don't know if [my parents are] ready for all our relatives to find out I'm gay." Jeff's decision to accommodate his parents' needs is for him, but perhaps not for his parents, a concealment decision that reflects neither shame nor fear.

Marcia is a 20-year-old college student who is very public about her lesbian identity. However, she does not disclose to everyone, and varies how much she reveals. Two considerations guide her disclosure decisions. First, Marcia considers the timing of disclosure in order to avoid stereotypical reactions. "If I tell a person that I'm queer immediately then they don't really know who I am." Thus, while she has disclosed to most of her coworkers, a new employee does not yet know. "I get the feeling from him that I need to wait a little....He needs to know me, because he seems like the type of person who's going to judge me on my sexuality." Second, Marcia considers the level of intimacy that is socially appropriate or personally desired. Thus, with one coworker "I can talk about anything to her [because we're intimate]," but with others "I don't like to bring my personal life to work....It's none of their business."

As individuals try to make their homosexuality into a routine part of their daily lives, decisions to conceal pivot around considerations other than, or in addition to, fear, shame, or guilt. Individuals withhold information about their homosexuality because it is defined as personal, because disclosure would involuntarily "out" others (e.g., parents or friends), or because they wish to minimize a stereotypical reaction. Today, many individuals disclose not only to gain approval or contest social disapproval, but in order to achieve and sustain intimacy, to avoid misrecognition, to get respect for themselves and their partners, and to integrate their homosexuality into their everyday lives. These are not concealment and disclosure decisions that reflect the social logic of the closet.

In social contexts organized by normative heterosexuality, normalization and routinization will be incomplete. Despite his emphatic rhetoric of self-acceptance, Mike admitted continued ambivalence. Asked to clarify why he has not spoken with his son about what it feels like to conceal when his son has friends in the house, Mike said that "part of it might be that little bit of self-homophobia that I still carry." Or consider Ralph (born 1958), who owns a hairdressing business. Ralph deliberately conceals with middle-aged, working-class male customers because of a "fear of rejection." Similarly, although he is open with his parents, Ralph has not disclosed to his larger kin network because "I fear rejection." Rejection means that family and clients will "say that I'm not as good as anyone else." Ralph is in part vulnerable to self-devaluation because of his own ambivalence towards homosexuality.

Subjective ambivalence is connected to incomplete interpersonal routinization. Thus, perhaps Mike did not press his son because he feared reproducing his estrangement with his parents. Mike's parents have not accepted his being gay. Although they live just a few miles apart, they never call him at home and refuse to meet Andy. Forced to choose between integration into his family of origin and maintaining an integrated, affirmative sense of self and family of choice, Mike has "separated from [his parents]." Similarly, despite normalizing a bisexual identity, Andrea, a college student still financially dependent upon her parents, cannot integrate this identity into her family. Asked how they would react to her disclosure, she commented: "I would be kicked out; I wouldn't even be able to get my stuff from my house. I would not be able to speak to them. My parents are really just like that."

Pressures to self-manage in order to avoid unwanted exposure also underscore a reality of incomplete institutional routinization. Thus, Clara anticipates heightened public self-monitoring as she pursues a career:

> I'm not going to be so loose about it because you do have to watch who you say

something to and that's not...like going back in the closet. I just feel like it's protecting your job, your career, not everybody has to know and when they find out that could cause a problem.

As a doctoral student, Rachel has not experienced workplace discrimination. However, because her partner is a physician who fears loss of patients and collegial support, Rachel and Phyllis engage in intensive sexual self-management. "When we're in more professional situations, and what she [Phyllis] terms as threatening situations, our behavior changes, and it feels like a double life" (on the heterosexist organization of the workplace, see Badgett and King 1997; Friskopp and Silverstein 1995; Schneider 1984; Woods 1993). As these two examples suggest, subjective normalization and interpersonal routinization have not necessarily been paralleled by institutional routinization.

A shift in the social logic of normative heterosexuality in American society is occurring. There has been a considerable relaxing of social repression at the personal and interpersonal levels. Many individuals have fashioned affirmative gay identities; the symbolic and social boundaries between straights and gays have lessened considerably. Many individuals live beyond the closet. It is equally clear, however, that the US remains a nation organized by the institution of heterosexuality. If it operates less through repression, and if it is less directed at regulating individuals at the interpersonal level, it remains embedded at the institutional level as manifested in law, social policy, civic disenfranchisement, institutional practices, and public culture.

The Sociology and Politics of Homosexuality in a Period of the Declining Significance of the Closet

The era of the closet has not passed. Representations continue to typify the homosexual as polluted, and civic and social disenfranchisement and violence structure gay life in the US. As a set of practices responding to the repressive logic of normative heterosexuality, the closet continues to organize the lives of many Americans.

Nevertheless, we have argued that dynamics of normalization and routinization point to the marginalization of the closet in contemporary US. This dynamic has not been analyzed, in part because of the politically mobilizing force of a discourse of the closet. By underscoring lives trapped in the repressive space of the closet, a reality of unjust homosexual oppression is emphasized. We have not denied the continued power of the social conditions producing a politics of the closet. Rather, we have sought to document normalizing and routinizing processes suggesting that accordingly social analysts need to rethink practices of sexual self-management in a way that does not collapse them into a uniform, homogenizing language of the closet.

In this concluding section, we sketch some of the implications of normalization and routinization for issues of identity, community, and politics.

In the course of our interviews, an apparent contradiction surfaced between assertions of the centrality of a gay identity and reported social practices. For example, Mike stated that "being gay is who I am and I don't want anyone to assume otherwise." Yet, Mike hardly participates in gay culture, and his closest friends are heterosexual. He describes a life that revolves around his partner, children, Alcoholics Anonymous, work, and sports. Mike at times invoked a rhetoric of a primary gay identity but his life suggested otherwise. In fact, at one point in the interview he offered an identity description that was more consistent with his practice. "Being out ... doesn't change who I am as a person or as a boss or as a father. Being gay is just another part of me."

We contend that since normalization and routinization involve integrating homosexuality into one's life, this will involve a desire to be publicly recognized as gay. If homo-

sexuality is experienced as an acceptable, integral aspect of oneself, and especially one that is not signaled by the surface of the body and conventional behaviors – and one that individuals normalize in relation to a history of shame and secrecy – we would expect individuals to be deliberate about asserting a public gay identity. At the same time, normalization and routinization prompt individuals to "decenter" or marginalize homosexuality as a basis of personal identity.

Our research suggests that normalization and routinization are paralleled by a shift in the way individuals frame homosexuality in relation to identity. The conditions producing the closet often make homosexuality into a way of life and therefore into a primary (even if discredited) identity. If the "first phase" of normalizing gay identities has typically involved affirming this identity as primary, a "second phase" may occasion decentering homosexuality as a basis of identity. For at least some individuals who have normalized their homosexuality, it is described as a "thread" rather than a core aspect of identity. For example, Jeff says that his homosexuality influences aspects of his life without overdetermining his self-definition. "It's not a separate part of me. It's an overall theme [in my life] ... I guess being gay has a little bit of influence in how I behave at work and a little bit of influence in the way I go shopping, and a little bit of influence in who I'm seeing." Marcia echoes this "decentering" theme. "I wouldn't say that when I think of myself the first thing I think of is a lesbian. Or, I wouldn't say that I think that when people first meet me that's what they need to know. ... Being a lesbian [is] just like being a woman, or being a redhead. These are things that are part of me."

If the conditions of the closet often compel individuals to make their homosexuality into a primary self-identity, normalization gives individuals the latitude to define its relation to identity, and many individuals seem to be choosing to decenter it.

Despite these decentering trends, our respondents expressed an emphatic sense of belonging to a gay community, even though they participate minimally, if at all, in group activities. We conjecture that this collective identification stems in part from the continued nonnormative status of homosexuality. Normalization and routinization have, however, decentering collective effects. To the extent that homosexuality becomes a normalized thread of identity, we would expect a weakening identification of the gay "community" with urban subcultures, as they have typically demanded a "maximum" gay self-identification. In the context of normalizing and routinizing trends, the "gay ghetto" (New York's West Village or San Francisco's Castro) becomes just one form of community, rather than the emblem of the gay community. We anticipate heightened contestation over the question of what the gay community signifies, which collective form represents this gay community, and who speaks for gay people.

Our research points to diverse patterns of group identification and integration. At one extreme are individuals who conceal or disassociate their homosexuality in a systematic (i.e., "closeted") way. They report an abstract identification with a gay community, and exhibit a highly segmented collective involvement. Thus, David, 63 years old and reportedly happily married, expressed a collective identification by self-defining as gay even though his participation in this culture is limited to furtive sexual encounters. At the other extreme are individuals who have normalized and routinized their homosexuality to a considerable degree. They exhibit at least two clear patterns. First, individuals who have chosen to make their homosexuality into a primary identity evidence high levels of community integration. Gordon, an African American in his mid-thirties, found the Black community to be unfriendly towards gay individuals. He substituted a gay identity for the primary Black identity he learned while growing up. His primary group ties are with gay people.

Second, individuals who define homosexuality as an aspect of identity exhibit degrees of collective identification from weak to strong but consistently weak social integration. Despite an emphatic normalizing of a gay identity, Rachel and Jeff publicly signal this identity almost exclusively symbolically – for example, by wearing a "freedom ring" or attaching a rainbow sticker to their cars. For these individuals, homosexuality resembles white European ethnicity in contemporary America. Their link to a gay community is optional, partial, and symbolic. As with white ethnics, there will be an individualizing and symbolic marking of collective identification without extensive social obligations and integration.

We conclude by commenting on some political implications of normalizing and routinizing trends. Gay politics since Stonewall have been predominantly a version of identity politics. The gay movement has sought to legitimate homosexuality. In effect, sexual orientation has been collapsed into gender preference and gay politics into efforts to normalize a gay identity. The closet has served as a marker of the lack of homosexual legitimacy, while coming out has symbolized progress. We recognize that lesbian and gay politics in the post-Stonewall period has been far more varied. For example, gay liberationism was as much about challenging gender roles and capitalism as about legitimating a homosexual identity. Lesbian feminism made the critique of male domination and the institution of the family pivotal to its politics (see Adam 1987). Yet, it has been the politics of normalization and social integration that has dominated mainstream gay politics from the mid-1970s through the 1990s.

Political efforts to normalize a gay identity have had considerable success, despite continued institutional heterosexism, interpersonal intolerance, and subjective ambivalence. Hence, although we are critical of a unidimensional narrative of progress, our research underscores trends towards normalization and social inclusion. An immediate social impetus of these trends has been identity-based political mobilization – from efforts at civic and political legislation to antiviolence and cultural political strategies.

Paradoxically, these very trends have encouraged the decentering of gay identity politics. Specifically, while normalizing gay identities may consolidate a triumphant identity politic, it also encourages political strategies that marginalize such a politic. On the one hand, as gay identities are legitimated, movements organized around other discredited sexual practices such as bisexuality or S/M mobilize as independent sources of sexual identity, community, and politics. On the other hand, normalizing trends encourage a post-identity sexual politics. A gay politics focused exclusively on legitimating a gay identity leaves uncontested norms and practices regulating the ways homosexual and nonhomosexual bodies, pleasures, and intimate practices, including families, are organized.

The rise of queer politics in the 1990s represents a post-identity sexual politic (Seidman 1997). It does not focus on legitimating identities but on challenging the regulatory power of norms of sexual health and normality. Embedded in medical, legal, criminal, familial, psychiatric, and state institutional practices are social norms that control behavior by pathologizing conduct – including consensual adult practices – that deviate from conventional or normalized gender, sexual, and intimate norms, e.g., S/M, phone sex, multiple-partner sex, or nonmarital, noncohabiting forms of "family." Queer political perspectives criticize sexual identity movements to the extent that they freeze identities thereby producing marginalizing and excluding effects, support a narrow range of ways of organizing bodies, pleasures, gendered selves, and intimacies, and do not question medical norms (normality and health) that invest sexual desires with moral significance and therefore legitimate extensive state and social institutional intervention. Queer politics do not signal the end of gay identity

politics. Instead, we imagine an ongoing tension between sexual identity politics and forms of post-identity politics.

NOTES

1 "Homosexual" or "gay" refers to a behavior or an acquired social identity. We do not assume that homosexuality *per se* makes individuals into a distinct personality or social type.

2 The interview was divided into three parts. The first obtained demographic information; the second part focused on concealment decisions at work, with friends and family, and in daily life; and the third part addressed disclosure practices and reactions.

Interviews were transcribed and analyzed. We looked for statements from respondents which were indicative of "normalization" and "interpersonal routinization." An example of the former would be: "I have now accepted my sexuality and if friends or family cannot accept it that's their problem." Interpersonal routinization would be indicated by statements such as, "everyone knows about my sexuality at work because I talk openly about it and even bring my partner to work social functions." We also looked for responses which would highlight the incompleteness of these patterns. The statements included in this article are indicative of what we found throughout the interviews.

Of the 25 respondents, 13 were men, 12 were women; 19 were white, 6 were either Black or Hispanic; 9 could be classified as working or lower middle class, 16 as middle class; 6 respondents were aged 25 years or less, 11 were below 40, and 8 were older than 40.

3 The struggle against the closet is often said to create a shared experience of oppression and desire for freedom associated with coming out. The closet is therefore assumed to be a social fact whose meaning is uniform. However, there are reasons to suspect that social differences complicate this view. For example, some African Americans emphasize unique racial aspects to the social patterns of homosexuality (Beam 1986; Hemphill 1991). The combination of the racism of a white-dominated gay community and the lack of

institutionally elaborated black gay public cultures, along with the reserved public support of black elites, creates distinctive patterns of secrecy, disclosure, and identity formation. Similarly, Latina lesbians describe being situated between the racial worlds of black and white, the worlds of America and their nation of origin or identification, between their heterosexual families, which are solidaristic but homophobic, and lesbian communities that are racist, as shaping a unique social context for experiencing homosexuality (Ramos 1987).

4 Whereas Chauncey argues that a public gay (fairy) culture declined to be replaced by a "closeted" middle-class homosexual culture in the 1950s, the work of Kennedy and Davis (1993) maintains that working-class (butch) lesbians often live outside the closet.

REFERENCES

Adam, Barry (1987) *The Rise of a Gay and Lesbian Movement*. Boston, MA: Twayne.

Altman, Dennis (1971) *Homosexual Oppression and Liberation*. New York: Avon Books.

Badgett, M. V. and King, Mary (1997) "Lesbian and Gay Occupational Strategies," in Amy Gluckman and Betsy Reed (eds.) *Homo Economics*, pp. 73–86. New York: Routledge.

Beam, Joseph, ed. (1986) *In the Life*. Boston, MA: Alyson.

Borhek, Mary (1993) *Coming Out to Parents*. Cleveland, OH: Pilgrim Press.

Bravman, Scott (1997) *Queer Fictions of the Past*. Cambridge: Cambridge University Press.

Butler, Judith (1991) "Imitation and Gender Insubordination," in Diana Fuss (ed.) *Inside/Out*, pp. 13–31. New York: Routledge.

Buxton, Amity (1994) *The Other Side of the Closet*. New York: John Wiley and Sons.

Cain, Roy (1991) "Disclosure and Secrecy Among Gay Men in the United States and Canada: A Shift in Views," in John Fout and Maura Shaw Tantillo (eds.) *American Sexual Politics*, pp. 289–309. Chicago, IL: University of Chicago Press.

Cammermayer, M. (1994) *Serving in Silence*. New York: Penguin.

Chauncey, George (1994) *Gay New York*. New York: Basic Books.

Davies, Peter (1992) "The Role of Disclosure in Coming Out Among Gay Men," in Ken Plummer (ed.) *Modern Homosexualities*, pp. 75–83. London: Routledge.

DeCrescenzo, Teresa, ed. (1997) *The Social Service Closet*. Binghamton, NY: Haworth Press.

Delph, Edward (1978) *The Silent Community*. Beverly Hills, CA: Sage.

D'Emilio, John (1983) *Sexual Politics, Sexual Communities*. Chicago, IL: University of Chicago Press.

Escoffier, Jeff (1997) "The Political Economy of the Closet: Notes Toward an Economic History of Gay and Lesbian Life Before Stonewall," in Amy Gluckman and Betsy Reed (eds.) *Homo Economics*, pp. 123–34. New York: Routledge.

Esterberg, Kristin (1997) *Lesbian and Bisexual Identities*. Philadelphia, PA: Temple University Press.

Foucault, Michel (1980) *The History of Sexuality*, vol. 1. New York: Pantheon.

Friskopp, Annette and Silverstein, Sharon (1995) *Straight Jobs, Gay Lives*. New York: Simon & Schuster.

Fuss, Diana (1991) "Introduction," in *Inside/Out*, pp. 2–10. New York: Routledge.

Gross, Larry (1993) *Contested Closets*. Minneapolis: University of Minnesota Press.

Harbeck, Karen, ed. (1992) *Coming Out of the Classroom Closet*. New York: Haworth Press.

Hemphill, Essex (1991) "Looking for Langston: An Interview with Isaac Julien," in Essex Hemphill and Joseph Beam (eds.) *Brother to Brother*, pp. 174–83. Boston, MA: Alyson.

Herdt, Gilbert (1992) "Coming Out as a Rite of Passage," in Gilbert Herdt (ed.) *Gay Culture in America*, pp. 124–50. Boston, MA: Beacon Press.

Herrell, Richard (1992) "The Symbolic Strategies of Chicago's Gay and Lesbian Pride Day Parade," in Gilbert Herdt, *Gay Culture in America*, pp. 225–52. Boston, MA: Beacon Press.

Hom, Alice (1996) "Stories from the Homefront: Perspectives of Asian-American Parents with Lesbian Daughters and Gay Sons," in Russell Leong (ed.) *Asian American Sexualities*, pp. 37–50. New York: Routledge.

Humphreys, Laud (1970) *Tearoom Trade*. Chicago, IL: Aldine.

Humphreys, Laud (1972) *Out of the Closets*. Englewood Cliffs, NJ: Prentice-Hall.

Jay, Karla and Young, Allen, eds. (1972) "Introduction," in *Out of the Closets and Into the Streets*. New York: Douglas.

Jenness, Valerie (1992) "Coming Out: Lesbian Identities and the Categorization Problem," in Ken Plummer (ed.) *Modern Homosexualities*, pp. 65–74. New York: Routledge.

Johnson, Bret (1997) *Coming Out Every Day*. Oakland, CA: New Harrington Press.

Kaufman, Gershen and Raphael, Lev (1996) *Coming Out of Shame*. New York: Doubleday.

Kennedy, Elizabeth and Davis, Madeline (1993) *Boots of Leather, Slippers of Gold*. New York: Routledge.

Levine, Martin (1979) "Gay Ghetto," in Martin Levine (ed.) *Gay Men*, pp. 182–204. New York: Harper and Row.

McRuer, Robert (1996) "Boys Own Stories and New Spellings of My Name: Coming Out and Other Myths of Queer Positionality," in Carol Siegal and Ann Kibbey (eds.) *Eroticism and Containment*, pp. 260–84. New York: Routledge.

Markowe, Laura (1996) *Redefining the Self*. Cambridge: Polity Press.

Miller, Merle (1971) *On Being Different*. New York: Random House.

Monette, Paul (1992) *Becoming a Man*. New York: HarperCollins.

Penelope, Julia and Wolfe, Susan, eds. (1989) *The Original Coming Out Stories*, 2nd. edn. Freedom, CA: The Crossing Press.

Phelan, Shane (1993) "(Be)Coming Out: Lesbian Identity and Politics," *Signs* 18 (summer): 765–90.

Plummer, Ken (1995) *Telling Sexual Stories*. London: Routledge.

Ponse, Barbara (1978) *Identities in the Lesbian World*. Westport, CT: Greenwood Press.

Ramos, Juanita, ed. (1987) *Companeras*. New York: Routledge.

Rust, Paula (1993) "'Coming Out' in the Age of Social Constructionism: Sexual Identity Formation among Lesbian and Bisexual Women," *Gender & Society* 7 (March): 50–77.

Schneider, Beth (1984) "Peril and Promise: Lesbians' Workplace Participation," in Trudy Darty and Sandee Potter (eds.) *Women-Identified Women*, pp. 21–30. Palo Alto, CA: Mayfield.

Sedgwick, Eve (1990) *The Epistemology of the Closet*. Berkeley: University of California Press.

Seidman, Steven (1997) *Difference Troubles*. Cambridge: Cambridge University Press.

Signorile, Michelangelo (1993) *Queer in America*. New York: Random House.

Trujillo, Carla, ed. (1991) *Chicana Lesbians*. Third Women Press.

Vaid, Urvashi (1996) *Virtual Equality*. New York: Doubleday.

Whisman, Vera (1996) *Queer by Choice*. New York: Routledge.

Wolf, Deborah (1979) *The Lesbian Community*. Berkeley: University of California Press.

Woods, James with Lucas, Jay (1993) *The Corporate Closet*. New York: Free Press.

Zimmerman, Bonnie (1984) "The Politics of Transliteration: Lesbian Personal Narratives," *Signs* 9 (summer): 663–82.

30 Intimacy as Democracy

Anthony Giddens

A democratization of the private sphere is today not only on the agenda, but is an implicit quality of all personal life that comes under the aegis of the pure relationship. The fostering of democracy in the public domain was at first largely a male project – in which women eventually managed, mostly by dint of their own struggle, to participate. The democratization of personal life is a less visible process, in part precisely because it does not occur in the public arena, but its implications are just as profound. It is a process in which women have thus far played the prime role, even if in the end the benefits achieved, as in the public sphere, are open to everyone.

The Meaning of Democracy

First of all it might be worth considering what democracy means, or can mean, in its orthodox sense. There is much debate about the specifics of democratic representation and so forth, but I shall not concern myself with these issues here. If the various approaches to political democracy be compared, as David Held has shown, most have certain elements in common.[1] They are concerned to secure 'free and equal relations' between individuals in such a way as to promote certain outcomes:

1   The creation of circumstances in which people can develop their potentialities and express their diverse qualities. A key objective here is that each individual should respect others' capabilities as well as their ability to learn and enhance their aptitudes.
2   Protection from the arbitrary use of political authority and coercive power. This presumes that decisions can in some sense be negotiated by those they affect, even if they are taken on behalf of a majority by a minority.
3   The involvement of individuals in determining the conditions of their association. The presumption in this case is that individuals accept the authentic and reasoned character of others' judgements.
4   Expansion of the economic opportunity to develop available resources – including here the assumption that when individuals are relieved of the burdens of physical need they are best able to achieve their aims.

The idea of autonomy links these various aspirations. Autonomy means the capacity of individuals to be self-reflective and self-determining: 'to deliberate, judge, choose and act upon different possible courses of action.'[2] Clearly autonomy in this sense could not be developed while political rights and obligations were closely tied to tradition and fixed prerogatives of property. Once these were dissolved, however, a movement towards autonomy became both possible and seen to be necessary. An overwhelming concern with how individuals might best determine and regulate the conditions of their association is characteristic of virtually all interpretations of modern democracy. The aspirations that compose the tendency towards autonomy can be summarized as a general principle, the 'principle of autonomy':

Individuals should be free and equal in the determination of the conditions of their own lives; that is, they should enjoy equal rights (and, accordingly, equal obligations) in the specification of the framework which generates and limits the opportunities available to them, so long as they do not deploy this framework to negate the rights of others.[3]

Democracy hence implies not just the right to free and equal self-development, but also the constitutional limitation of (distributive) power. The 'liberty of the strong' must be restrained, but this is not a denial of all authority – or it only becomes so in the case of anarchism. Authority is justifiable to the degree that it recognizes the principle of autonomy; in other words, to the extent to which defensible reasons can be given as to why compliance enhances autonomy, either now or in the future. Constitutional authority can be understood as an implicit contract which has the same form as conditions of association explicitly negotiated between equals.

It is no good proposing a principle of autonomy without saying something about the conditions of its realization. What are those conditions? One is that there must be equality in influencing outcomes in decision-making – in the political sphere this is usually sought after by the 'one person one vote' rule. The expressed preferences of each individual must have equal ranking, subject in certain instances to qualifications made necessary by the existence of justified authority. There must also be effective participation; the means must be provided for individuals to make their voices heard.

A forum for open debate has to be provided. Democracy means discussion, the chance for the 'force of the better argument' to count as against other means of determining decisions (of which the most important are policy decisions). A democratic order provides institutional arrangements for mediation, negotiation and the reaching of compromises where necessary. The conduct of open discussion is itself a means of democratic education: participation in debate with others can lead to the emergence of a more enlightened citizenry. In some part such a consequence stems from a broadening of the individual's cognitive horizons. But it also derives from an acknowledgement of legitimate diversity – that is, pluralism – and from emotional education. A politically educated contributor to dialogue is able to channel her or his emotions in a positive way: to reason from conviction rather than engage in ill thought through polemics or emotional diatribes.

Public accountability is a further basic characteristic of a democratic polity. In any political system decisions must often be taken on behalf of others. Public debate is normally only possible in relation to certain issues or at particular junctures. Decisions taken, or policies forged, however, must be open to public scrutiny should the need arise. Accountability can never be continuous and therefore stands in tandem with trust. Trust, which comes from accountability and openness, and also protects them, is a thread running through the whole of democratic political order. It is a crucial component of political legitimacy.

Institutionalizing the principle of autonomy means specifying rights and obligations, which have to be substantive, not just formal. Rights specify the privileges which come with membership of the polity but they also indicate the duties which individuals have *vis-à-vis* each other and the political order itself. Rights are essentially forms of empowerment; they are enabling devices. Duties specify the price that has to be paid for the rights accorded. In a democratic polity, rights and duties are negotiated and can never be simply assumed – in this respect they differ decisively from, for example, the medieval *droit de seigneur* or other rights established simply by virtue of an individual's social position. Rights and duties thus have to be made a focus of continual reflexive attention.

Democracy, it should be emphasized, does not necessitate sameness, as its critics have often asserted. It is not the enemy of pluralism. Rather, as suggested above, the principle of autonomy encourages difference – although it insists that difference should not be penalized. Democracy is an enemy of privilege, where privilege is defined as the holding of rights or possessions to which access is not fair and equal for all members of the community. A democratic order does not imply a generic process of 'levelling down', but instead provides for the elaboration of individuality.

Ideals are not reality. How far any concrete political order could develop such a framework in full is problematic. In this sense there are utopian elements in these ideas. On the other hand, it could also be argued that the characteristic trend of development of modern societies is towards their realization. The quality of utopianism, in other words, is balanced by a clear component of realism.[4]

The Democratizing of Personal Life

The possibility of intimacy means the promise of democracy. The structural source of this promise is the emergence of the pure relationship, not only in the area of sexuality but also in those of parent–child relations, and other forms of kinship and friendship. We can envisage the development of an ethical framework for a democratic personal order, which in sexual relationships and other personal domains conforms to a model of confluent love.

As in the public sphere, the distance between ideals and reality is considerable. In the arena of heterosexual relations in particular, as indicated in earlier chapters, there are profound sources of strain. Deep psychological, as well as economic, differences between the sexes stand in the way. Yet utopianism here can again readily be offset by realism. The changes that have helped transform personal environments of action are already well advanced, and they tend towards the realization of democratic qualities.

The principle of autonomy provides the guiding thread and the most important substantive component of these processes. In the arena of personal life, autonomy means the successful realization of the reflexive project of self – the condition of relating to others in an egalitarian way. The reflexive project of self must be developed in such a fashion as to permit autonomy in relation to the past, this in turn facilitating a colonizing of the future. Thus conceived, self-autonomy permits that respect for others' capabilities which is intrinsic to a democratic order. The autonomous individual is able to treat others as such and to recognize that the development of their separate potentialities is not a threat. Autonomy also helps to provide the personal boundaries needed for the successful management of relationships. Such boundaries are transgressed whenever one person uses another as a means of playing out old psychological dispositions, or where a reciprocal compulsiveness, as in the case of co-dependence, is built up.

The second and third conditions of democracy in the public sphere noted above bear very directly upon the democratization of personal life. Violent and abusive relationships are common in the sexual domain and between adults and children. Most such violence comes from men and is directed towards beings weaker than themselves. As an emancipatory ideal of democracy, the prohibition of violence is of basic importance. Coercive influences in relationships, however, obviously can take forms other than physical violence. Individuals may be prone, for example, to engage in emotional or verbal abuse of one another; marriage, so the saying goes, is a poor substitute for respect. Avoidance of emotional abuse is perhaps the most difficult aspect of the equalizing of power in relationship; but the guiding principle is clearly respect for the independent views and personal traits of the other. 'Without respect', as one guide to intimacy puts it, 'ears turn deaf, attitudes sour, and eventually you can't figure out what you're doing living with someone so incompetent, stupid, unreliable, insensitive, ugly, smelly, untidy.... It makes you wonder why you chose your partner in the first place. "I must have been out of my mind." '[5]

'The involvement of individuals in determining the conditions of their association' – this statement exemplifies the ideals of the pure relationship. It expresses a prime difference between traditional and present-day marriage and gets to the heart of the democratizing possibilities of the transformation of intimacy. It applies, of course, not just to the initiation of a relationship, but to the reflexivity inherent in its continuance – or its dissolution. Not just respect for the other, but an opening out to that person, are needed for this criterion to be met. An individual whose real intentions are hidden from a partner cannot offer the qualities needed for a cooperative determination of the conditions of the relationship. Any and every therapeutic text on the subject of relationships will demonstrate why revelation to the other – as a means of communication rather than emotional dumping – is a binding aspiration of democratically ordered interaction.

Rights and obligations: as I have tried to make clear, in some part these define what intimacy actually is. Intimacy should not be understood as an interactional description, but as a cluster of prerogatives and responsibilities that define agendas of practical activity. The importance of rights as means for the achievement of intimacy can easily be seen from the struggle of women to achieve equal status in marriage. The right of women to initiate divorce, to take one instance, which seems only a negative sanction, actually has a major equilibrating effect. Its balancing consequences do more than empower escape from an oppressive relationship, important though this is. They limit the capability of the husband to impose his dominion and thereby contribute to the translation of coercive power into egalitarian communication.

No rights without obligations – this elementary precept of political democracy applies also to the realm of the pure rela-

tionship. Rights help dissolve arbitrary power only in so far as they carry responsibilities towards the other which draw privileges into an equilibrium with obligations. In relationships as elsewhere, obligations have to be treated as revisable in the light of negotiations carried on within them.

What of accountability and its connection to authority? Both accountability and authority – where it exists – in pure relationships are deeply bound up with trust. Trust without accountability is likely to become one-sided, that is, to slide into dependence; accountability without trust is impossible because it would mean the continual scrutiny of the motives and actions of the other. Trust entails the trustworthiness of the other – according 'credit' that does not require continual auditing, but which can be made open to inspection periodically if necessary. Being regarded as trustworthy by a partner is a recognition of personal integrity, but in an egalitarian setting such integrity means also revealing reasons for actions if called upon to do so – and in fact having good reasons for any actions which affect the life of the other.

Authority in pure relationships between adults exists as 'specialization' – where one person has specially developed capabilities which the other lacks. Here one cannot speak of authority over the other in the same sense as in parent–child relations, particularly where very young children are involved. Can a relationship between a parent and young child be democratic? It can, and should be, in exactly the same sense as is true of a democratic political order.[6] It is a right of the child, in other words, to be treated as a putative equal of the adult. Actions which cannot be negotiated directly with a child, because he or she is too young to grasp what is entailed, should be capable of counterfactual justification. The presumption is that agreement could be reached, and trust sustained, if the child were sufficiently autonomous to be able to deploy arguments on an equal basis to the adult.

Mechanisms

In the political sphere democracy involves the creation of a constitution and, normally, a forum for the public debate of policy issues. What are the equivalent mechanisms in the context of the pure relationship? So far as heterosexual relationships go, the marriage contract used to be a bill of rights, which essentially formalized the 'separate but unequal' nature of the tie. The translation of marriage into a signifier of commitment, rather than a determinant of it, radically alters this situation. All relationships which approximate to the pure form maintain an implicit 'rolling contract' to which appeal may be made by either partner when situations arise felt to be unfair or oppressive. The rolling contract is a constitutional device which underlies, but is also open to negotiation through, open discussion by partners about the nature of the relationship.

Here is a 'rule book', drawn up in a self-help manual aimed at helping women to develop more satisfying heterosexual relationships. The individual, the author suggests, should first of all catalogue the problems that have arisen for her in previous relationships – those she sees mainly as her own doing and those perpetrated by her previous lovers. She should share the rule book with her partner, who should develop a convergent set of rules:

Rule 1 When I find myself trying to impress a man I like by talking so much about myself that I'm not asking him any questions, I'll stop performing and focus on whether he is right for me.

Rule 2 I'll express my negative feelings as soon as I become aware of them, rather than waiting until they build up – even if it means upsetting my partner.

Rule 3 I'll work on healing my relationship with my ex-husband by looking at how I set myself up to be hurt, and I won't talk about him as if I'm the victim and he's the villain.

Rule 4 When my feelings are hurt, I'll tell my partner how I'm feeling rather than pouting, getting even, pretending I don't care or acting like a little girl.

Rule 5 When I find myself filling in the blanks ['dead' areas in the relationship], I'll stop and ask myself if my partner has given back much to me lately. If he hasn't, I'll ask him for what I need rather than making things better myself.

Rule 6 When I find myself giving unsolicited advice or treating my partner like a little boy, I'll stop, take a deep breath, and let him figure it out on his own, unless he asks for help.[7]

Such a list appears at first blush, not only embarrassingly naive, but also likely to be quite counter-productive. For stating rules as rules, as Wittgenstein impressed upon us, alters their nature. The making explicit of such prescriptions, it can be argued, might rob them of all chance of having a positive effect, since only if they are taken for granted could a relationship proceed harmoniously. Yet such a view, I think, would miss the point. Differential power, which is sedimented in social life, is likely to stay unchanged if individuals refuse reflexively to examine their own conduct and its implicit justifications. Such rules, however unsophisticated they might seem, if successfully applied help prise the individual's actions away from an unconsciously organized power game. In principle, they serve to generate increased autonomy at the same time as they demand respect from the other.

A rolling contract does not deal in ethical absolutes. This one derives from a specific 'relationship problem list' where there were previously 'negatives'. The individual in question felt that she had been overly concerned to impress men in whom she was interested, was afraid to upset her partner by revealing her fears and needs, tended to mother him and so forth. A 'constitution' of this sort, of course, is only democratic if it is integrated with the other elements mentioned above; it has to reflect a meeting of autonomous and equal persons.

The imperative of free and open communication is the *sine qua non* of the pure relationship; the relationship is its own forum. On this point we come round full circle. Self-autonomy, the break with compulsiveness, is the condition of open dialogue with the other. Such dialogue, in turn, is the medium of the expression of individual needs, as well as the means whereby the relationship is reflexively organized.

Democracy is dull, sex is exciting – although perhaps a few might argue the opposite way. How do democratic norms bear upon sexual experience itself? This is the essence of the question of sexual emancipation. Essentially, such norms sever sexuality from distributive power, above all from the power of the phallus. The democratization implied in the transformation of intimacy includes, but also transcends, 'radical pluralism'. No limits are set upon sexual activity, save for those entailed by the generalizing of the principle of autonomy and by the negotiated norms of the pure relationship. Sexual emancipation consists in integrating plastic sexuality with the reflexive project of self. Thus, for example, no prohibition is necessarily placed on episodic sexuality so long as the principle of autonomy, and other associated democratic norms, are sustained on all sides. On the other hand, where such sexuality is used as a mode of exploitative domination, covertly or otherwise, or where it expresses a compulsiveness, it falls short of the emancipatory ideal.

Political democracy implies that individuals have sufficient resources to participate in an autonomous way in the democratic process. The same applies in the domain of the pure relationship, although as in the political order it is important to avoid economic reductionism. Democratic aspirations do not necessarily mean equality of resources, but they clearly tend in that direction. They do involve including resources within the charter of rights reflexively negotiated as a defining part of the relationship. The importance of this precept within heterosexual relationships is very plain, given the imbalance in economic resources available to men and women and in responsibilities for child care and domestic work. The democratic model presumes equality in these areas; the aim, however, would not necessarily be complete parity so much as an equitable arrangement negotiated according to the principle of autonomy. A certain balance of tasks and rewards would be negotiated which each finds acceptable. A division of labour might be established, but not one simply inherited on the basis of pre-established criteria or imposed by unequal economic resources brought to the relationship.

There are structural conditions in the wider society which penetrate to the heart of the pure relationships; conversely, how such relationships are ordered has consequences for the wider social order. Democratization in the public domain, not only at the level of the nation-state, supplies essential conditions for the democratizing of personal relationships. But the reverse applies also. The advancement of self-autonomy in the context of pure relationships is rich with implications for democratic practice in the larger community.

A symmetry exists between the democratizing of personal life and democratic possibilities in the global political order at the most extensive level. Consider the distinction between positional bargaining and principled negotiation prominent in the analysis of global strategies and conflicts today. In positional bargaining – which can be equated with a personal relationship in which intimacy is lacking – each side approaches negotiation by taking up an extreme stance. Through mutual threats and attrition, one side or other is worn down and an outcome achieved – if the process of negotiation has not by then broken down completely. Global relations ordered in a more democratic manner would move towards principled negotiation. Here the interaction of the parties begins from an attempt to discover each other's underlying concerns and interests, identifying a range of possible options before narrowing down upon a few of them. The problem to be resolved is separated from antagonism towards the other, so that it is possible to be firm about the substance of the negotiation while being supportive of and respectful towards the other party. In sum, as in the personal sphere, difference can become a means of communication.

Sexuality, Emancipation, Life Politics

No one knows whether at the global level a framework of democratic institutions will develop, or whether alternatively world politics will slide into a destructiveness that might threaten the entire planet. Nobody knows if sexual relationships will become a wasteland of impermanent liaisons, marked by emotional antipathy as much as by love, and scarred by violence. There are good grounds for optimism in each case, but in a culture that has given up providentialism futures have to be worked for against a background of acknowledged risk. The open-ended nature of the global project of modernity has a real correlate in the uncertain outcome of the everyday social experiments that are the subject-matter of this book.

What can be said with some certainty is that democracy is not enough. Emancipatory politics is a politics of the internally referential systems of modernity; it is oriented to control of distributive power and cannot confront power in its generative

aspect. It leaves aside most questions posed by the sequestration of experience. Sexuality has the enormous importance it does in modern civilization because it is a point of contact with all that has been forgone for the technical security that day-to-day life has to offer. Its association with death has become for us as bizarre and almost unthinkable as its involvement with life seems obvious. Sexuality has become imprisoned within a search for self-identity which sexual activity itself can only momentarily fulfil. 'Lay your sleeping head, my love / Human on my faithless arm': so much of sexuality is frustrated love, doomed endlessly to seek out difference in the sameness of anatomy and of physical response.

In the tension between the privatizing of passion and the saturation of the public domain by sexuality, as well as in some of the conflicts which today divide men and women, we can see new political agendas. Particularly in its connections with gender, sexuality gave rise to the politics of the personal, a phrase that is misunderstood if tied only to emancipation. What we should rather term life politics[8] is a politics of lifestyle, operating in the context of institutional reflexivity. It is concerned, not to 'politicize', in a narrow sense of that term, lifestyle decisions but to remoralize them – more accurately put, to bring to the surface those moral and existential issues pushed away from everyday life by the sequestration of experience. They are issues which fuse abstract philosophy, ethical ideas and very practical concerns.

The province of life politics covers a number of partially distinct sets of issues. One is that of self-identity as such. In so far as it is focused upon the life-span, considered as an internally referential system, the reflexive project of self is oriented only to control. It has no morality other than authenticity, a modern version of the old maxim 'to thine own self be true'. Today, however, given the lapse of tradition, the question 'Who shall I be?' is inextricably bound up with 'How shall I live?' A host of questions present themselves here, but so far as sexuality is concerned that of sexual identity is the most obvious.

The greater the level of equality achieved between the sexes, one might think, the more pre-existing forms of masculinity and femininity are likely to converge upon an androgynous model of some sort. This may or may not be so, given the revival of difference in current sexual politics; but it is in any case devoid of meaning unless we try to specify the content of androgyny, which is a matter of deciding about values. The dilemmas thus raised were hidden as long as sexual identity appeared to be structured in terms of sexual difference. A binary code of male and female, which admits of virtually no mediating instances, attached gender to sex as though they were the same. Gender attributions were then made in the following way:

1 Every individual was assumed to be male or female, with no one 'in between'.
2 The physical characteristics and traits of behaviour of individuals were interpreted as masculine or feminine according to a dominant gender scheme.
3 Gender cues were routinely weighed and assessed, within the confines of permissible gender status behaviour patterns.
4 Gender differences thus constituted and reconstituted were applied back to concretize sexual identities, with 'cross-gender' elements filtered out.
5 Actors monitored their own appearance and behaviour in accordance with 'naturally given' sexual identity.[9]

The force with which these influences are still felt is indicated by the fact that male transvestism is very commonly stigmatized, even though it is no longer seen in the psychiatric literature as a perversion. More interesting, because it has rather more ambiguity, is the case of women who have or who cultivate the appearance of maleness. Current norms of appearance, demeanour and dress in modern societies permit women a

closer similarity to men in these respects than is normally tolerated the other way around. Yet dualism tends to be enforced: if a person is not 'really' a man then she must be a woman. Women who refuse to look 'feminine' find themselves constantly harassed:

> I won't wear dresses and I won't wear makeup, or carry a purse and act more feminine. My boyfriend told me that's the reason I'm being bugged by people, and I know that it is, but I refuse to do that. I wouldn't feel comfortable wearing a dress. I couldn't sit like I'm sitting now. Like you've got to walk a certain way. And makeup's such a bloody nuisance.[10]

A combination of imbalanced gender power and engrained psychological dispositions keeps dualistic sex divisions quite firmly in place; but in principle matters could be organized quite differently. As anatomy stops being destiny, sexual identity more and more becomes a lifestyle issue. Sex differences will continue for at least the near future to be linked to the mechanics of the reproduction of the species; but there is no longer good reason for them to conform to a clear break in behaviour and attitudes. Sexual identity could become formed through diverse configurations of traits connecting appearance, demeanour and behaviour. The question of androgyny would be settled in terms of what could be justified as desirable conduct – and nothing else.

The issue of sexual identity is a question which demands prolonged debate. It seems very likely, however, that one element might be what John Stoltenberg has called 'refusing to be a man'.[11] Refusing maleness is not the same as embracing femininity. It is again a task of ethical construction, which relates, not only sexual identity, but self-identity more broadly, to the moral concern of care for others. The penis exists; the male sex is only the phallus, the centre of selfhood in masculinity. The idea that there are beliefs and actions that are right for a man and wrong for a woman, or vice versa, is likely to perish with the progressive shrinking of the phallus into the penis.

With the development of modern societies, control of the social and natural worlds, the male domain, became focused through 'reason'. Just as reason, guided by disciplined investigation, was set off from tradition and dogma, so it was also from emotion. As I have said, this presumed not so much a massive psychological process of repression as an institutional division between reason and emotion, a division that closely followed gender lines. The identifying of women with unreason, whether in serious vein (madness), or in seemingly less consequential fashion (women as the creatures of caprice), turned them into the emotional under-labourers of modernity. Along the way emotion, and forms of social relation inspired by it – hate as well as love – became seen as refractory to ethical considerations. Reason cuts away at ethics because of the difficulty of finding empirical arguments to justify moral convictions; it does so also, however, because moral judgements and emotional sentiments come to be regarded as antithetical. Madness and caprice – it needs little effort to see how alien these are to moral imperatives.

Freud rediscovered emotion – through his interpretations of female psychology – but in his thought it remained tied to the dictates of reason, however much cognition was shown to be swayed by the subterranean forces of the unconscious. 'Nothing disturbs feeling...so much as thinking': emotion remains the other side of reason, with its causal power increased. No connection is made between emotion and ethics; perhaps they are pushed even further apart, for the theme 'where id was there ego shall be' suggests that the sphere of the rational can be substantially expanded. If ethical imperatives exist, therefore, they are to be found in the public domain; but there it proves difficult to demonstrate their validity and they stand vulnerable to power.

Passionate love was originally one among other passions, the interpretation of which tended to be influenced by religion. Most emotional dispositions can be passions, but in modern society passion is narrowed down to the sexual realm and once there becomes more and more muted in its expression. A passion is today something admitted to only reluctantly or embarrassedly, even in respect of sexual behaviour itself, partly because its place as a 'compelling force' has been usurped by addiction.

There is no room for passion in the routinized settings which provide us with security in modern social life. Yet who can live without passion, if we see it as the motive-power of conviction? Emotion and motivation are inherently connected. Today we think of motivation as 'rational' – the driving pursuit of profit on the part of the entrepreneur, for example – but if emotion is wholly resistant to rational assessment and ethical judgement, motives can never be appraised except as means to ends, or in terms of their consequences. This is what Weber saw in interpreting the motives of the early industrialists as energized by religious conviction. However, in so doing Weber took for granted, and even elevated to the status of an epistemology, what is distinctly problematic about modernity: the impossibility of evaluating emotion.

Seen as a life-political issue, the problem of the emotions is not one of retrieving passion, but of developing ethical guidelines for the appraisal or justification of conviction. The therapist says, 'Get in touch with your feelings.' Yet in this regard therapy connives with modernity. The precept which lies beyond is 'Evaluate your feelings', and such a demand cannot be a matter of psychological rapport alone. Emotions are not judgements, but dispositional behaviour stimulated by emotional responses is; to evaluate feelings is to ask for the criteria in terms of which such judgements are made.

Emotion becomes a life-political issue in numerous ways with the latter-day development of modernity. In the realm of sexuality, emotion as a means of communication, as commitment to and cooperation with others, is especially important. The model of confluent love suggests an ethical framework for the fostering of non-destructive emotion in the conduct of individual and communal life. It provides for the possibility of a revitalizing of the erotic – not as a specialist skill of impure women, but as a generic quality of sexuality in social relations formed through mutuality rather than through unequal power. Eroticism is the cultivation of feeling, expressed through bodily sensation, in a communicative context; an art of giving and receiving pleasure. Shorn of differential power, it can revive those aesthetic qualities of which Marcuse speaks.

Defined in such a fashion, the erotic stands opposed to all forms of emotional instrumentality in sexual relations. Eroticism is sexuality reintegrated within a wider range of emotional purposes, paramount among which is communication. From the point of view of utopian realism, eroticism is rescued from that triumph of the will which, from de Sade to Bataille, seems to mark out its distinctiveness. Interpreted not as diagnosis but as critique, as was noted earlier, the Sadean universe is an anti-utopia which discloses the possibility of its opposite.

Sexuality and reproduction in the past structured one another. Until it became thoroughly socialized, reproduction was external to social activity as a biological phenomenon; it organized kinship as well as being organized by it, and it connected the life of the individual to the succession of the generations. When directly bound up with reproduction, sexuality was a medium of transcendence. Sexual activity forged a tie with the finitude of the individual, and at the same time carried the promise of its irrelevance; for seen in relation to a cycle

of generations the individual life was part of a more embracing symbolic order. Sexuality for us still carries an echo of the transcendent. Yet given that such is the case, it is bound to be surrounded with an aura of nostalgia and disillusion. A sexually addicted civilization is one where death has become stripped of meaning; life politics at this point implies a renewal of spirituality. From this point of view, sexuality is not the antithesis of a civilization dedicated to economic growth and technical control, but the embodiment of its failure.

NOTES

1 I follow closely Held's thought in the first part of this chapter. See David Held: *Models of Democracy*, Cambridge: Polity Press, 1986.
2 Ibid., p. 270.
3 Ibid., p. 271.
4 Anthony Giddens: *The Consequences of Modernity*, Cambridge: Polity Press, 1990, pp. 154–8.
5 C. Edward Crowther: *Intimacy: Strategies for Successful Relationships*, New York: Dell, 1988, p. 45.
6 Allison James and Alan Prout: *Constructing and Reconstructing Childhood*, Basingstoke: Falmer, 1990. The 'new paradigm' James and Prout suggest for studying childhood relates closely to the ideas developed here.
7 Barbara De Angelis: *Secrets About Men Every Woman Should Know*, London: Thorsons, 1990, p. 274.
8 Anthony Giddens: *Modernity and Self-Identity*, Cambridge: Polity Press, 1991, ch. 7.
9 Holly Devor: *Gender Bending: Confronting the Limits of Duality*, Bloomington: Indiana University Press, 1989, pp. 147–9.
10 Ibid., p. 128.
11 John Stoltenberg: *Refusing to be a Man*, London: Fontana, 1990.

31 Intimacy Transformed? A Critical Look at the 'Pure Relationship'

Lynn Jamieson

Critical Issues

Giddens presents the trends he is identifying as relatively recent. Yet the idea that how personal life is conducted is more intensely intimate, individualized or personalized than ever before, is a long-running theme. For example, eighteenth-century philosophers of the Scottish Enlightenment saw intimate friendship as a 'modern' pattern emerging in their time (Silver 1997). Adam Smith believed that, prior to the development of the impersonal markets of commercial society and the impersonal administration of legal–rational bureaucracies, all friendships tended to have the character of necessity. It was only with the separation of commercial relations and personal life that friendship could become a matter of sympathy and affection devoid of calculation of interest. In more recent sociological writing about marriage and the family, the themes of growing intimacy, privacy and equality date back to at least the 1940s (Burgess and Locke 1945) and are part of the orthodox account of how the 'modern family' developed (Jamieson 1987). In the 1960s Peter Berger and Hans Kellner (1964) laid out theoretically the claim that an intense dialogue between marriage partners (or members of co-resident couples) functions to create a stable sense of the self, screening off a sense of chaos, despite the fragility of a socially constructed world. This prefigured a key strand of Giddens's argument by over twenty years. Giddens is, of course, not the only recent theorist to claim a distinctive late twentieth-century twist. Ulrich Beck (1992; Beck and Beck-Gernsheim 1995), for example, has pro-duced a comparable account. The socio-logical literature of the 1950s–70s, like the more recent contributions, engaged with popular debate about the demise of the family. However, eagerness to counter sim-plistic negative accounts sometimes resulted in over-simplification, underplaying how continued structural inequalities shaped per-sonal life, insufficiently unravelling causality and timing (Harris 1983), failing to distin-guish the experiences of lived lives from views of how they should be lived (Coontz 1992; Finch and Summerfield 1991; Morgan 1991, 1992; Skolnick 1991). All of these issues re-emerge as problems in Giddens's account.

David Morgan (1991, 1992, 1996) has analysed how the twentieth-century story of change in family and marriage 'from institution to relationship', became an ideo-logical simplification of social change par-ticularly promoted by professionals with a vested interest in marital and relationship problems. As Morgan notes, ideological constructions are nevertheless consequen-tial. However, the nature of the fit between the ideological story and everyday relation-ships is not simple. It is possible, for example, for the discourse of 'relationship experts' to infuse everyday talk while other factors modify the parameters of everyday practice. Such issues are not fully explored in *The Transformation of Intimacy*. Despite reference to the reflexive interrelationship between his work, popular culture and therapeutic discourse, Giddens draws rela-tively uncritically on therapeutic literature, as documents about and symptoms of per-sonal and social change (Giddens 1992: 86).

Not surprisingly, his account of 'the pure relationship' fits well with a therapeutic discourse that assumes the value of self-disclosure in therapy and in the relationships which therapy hopes to cure.

In contrast, many academic and popular commentators express concern over individualism 'going too far' and critique the individualizing tendencies of therapy for distorting recognition of social problems and mitigating against collective resistance. Giddens explicitly counters Foucault's discussion of therapy as a mechanism of extending subtle forms of regulation and control (Giddens 1992: 28–34). In the process, Giddens also silently lays aside accounts such as those of Christopher Lasch (1977) and Bauman (1990) which focus on the negativity of dependency on experts for self-direction, self-creativity and unmediated social interaction. Bauman (1991: 205) refers to Richard Sennett's (1977) concept of 'destructive *gemeinschaft*' in asserting that damage is caused to social cohesion by the psychological burdens of incitements to mutual disclosure. There are other earlier warnings in the sociological literature. Georg Simmel (Wolff 1950) argued that total lack of secrets could bankrupt a relationship as there was nothing left to wonder about. In claiming openness as a constructive process, Giddens interleaves his analysis of late modernity with a rather unpacked psychological theory. It is the ontological security of childhood that provides the self-resources for a subsequent creative process of self-disclosure. The starting premise is that a wide range of social circumstances in childhood, anything more caring than suffering violent, sexually abusive or highly neglectful parents, will create the necessary psychological conditions for 'generalized trust' in others and ontological security. This leaves an under-explained biographical contrast between an easily acquired secure sense of self in childhood and an adult who only just escapes doubts about self-authenticity by working hard on a narrative of the self and fragile personal relationships. Given the emphasis Giddens places on the fragility of personal life in a highly self-reflexive late modernity, the exempting of the parent–child relationship from fragility involves resort to a psychology divorced from his own sociological analysis.

The contribution of therapeutic discourse to damaging gender stereotypes is also unremarked, reflecting a more general underplaying of structures of gender inequality in *The Transformation of Intimacy*. Feminist work has documented how women carrying the burdens of systematic gender inequality have been recast by medical and therapeutic experts as pathological individuals (recent accounts are given by Busfield 1996; Dobash and Dobash 1992). Morgan has recently warned that the continued theoretical focus on the relational character of heterosexual partnerships can obscure persisting and institutionalized gender inequalities (Morgan 1996: 77–8). While drawing on particular pieces of feminist work, there is no sustained discussion in *The Transformation of Intimacy* of the feminist scholarship that has subjected the interrelationships between 'private' and 'public', 'personal' and 'political' to intensive theorizing and empirical exploration over the last decades. Yet debate concerning the resilience of gender inequality is centrally relevant to Giddens's case. This is far from a settled matter, but many key players in the debate would declare the undermining of male privilege through transformations in heterosexual intimacy theoretically unlikely. Some would claim the postulated change in heterosexual relationships unlikely in itself; those who accept the possibility are likely to doubt that radical transformation would necessarily follow. It is not clear, for example, that change in the quality of heterosexual relationships would shatter the interconnection of gendered labour markets, gendered distributions of income and wealth, and gendered divisions of domestic labour.

Most theorists who remain committed to the term 'patriarchy' would see difficulties, although not all are as definitive as Christine Delphy and Diana Leonard in the following advice: 'It may be that the family and heterosexuality are not the place to start when trying to change gender relations' (1992: 266). Moreover, it should be noted that many leading theorists of gender and power can envisage gender equality within a heterosexual personal life within and despite patriarchal arrangements. 'Further, if we see patriarchy as referring to properties of a system as a whole rather than to the individual actors who make up the system, it may be possible to find at the more individual or interpersonal level, examples of non-patriarchal [non-oppressive] yet gendered practices' (Morgan 1996: 91). Theorists who prefer speaking in terms of 'doing gender' and different 'gender regimes' to deploying the concept of 'patriarchy' willingly acknowledge the possibility of gender equality in one setting without necessary transformation of another (Connell 1987, 1995). The actual impact of changes within domestic and interpersonal relations on the wider structuring of gender relationships is an empirical matter (Morgan 1996: 80). There is no weighing of either theoretical or empirical states of play by Giddens and *The Transformation of Intimacy* seems strangely cut off from both the wealth of relevant feminist research and his own earlier discussions of the interrelationships of structure and action.

For obvious epistemological and methodological reasons, in examining the empirical evidence of how personal lives are conducted there is no possibility of verifying or disproving Giddens's broad-sweep account. The aim of this essay is necessarily a more modest one of looking for signs concerning the nature of intimacy as it is constructed in everyday relationships and considering how well proximities to and divergences from 'pure relationships' sit with his understanding of social change. In what follows, I mainly focus on research literature that deals with heterosexual couple relationships, as they are the most heavily researched by the key players in the argument. A more general review of personal relationships (Jamieson 1998) suggests that intimacy has more than one dimension, that diversity in the make-up of intimacy is considerable even within one category of relationship such as friendships or mother–child relationships. Moreover, personal interactions, even those of friendships, the least structured of intimate relationships, often reinforce gender, class and ethnic divisions rather than democratize personal life (Allan 1989; Griffiths 1995; Hey 1997; Thorne 1993). Personal relationships are not typically shaped in whatever way gives pleasure without the taint of practical, economic and other material circumstances. Few relationships, even friendships, are mainly simply about mutual appreciation, knowing and understanding.

Couple Relationships

Giddens intimates potential radical shifts in heterosexual practices. If 'pure relationships' are indeed becoming more common, equalization in men and women's interest in and experience of sex and intimacy can be anticipated. Similarly the ascendancy of 'plastic sexuality' will mean greater sexual experimentation and hence an increase in the diversity of sexual practice.

There has undoubtedly been a significant shift in public discourse about sex and sexuality that appears to acknowledge gender equality and show greater tolerance of diversity in sexual practices (Weeks 1995). Greater acceptance of gender equality is typified by the shift in magazines aimed at women and girls. Where once their content retained a coy silence on sex and a strong emphasis on romance, readers now receive acceptance or encouragement of active sexuality and sexual desire (McRobbie 1991, 1994, 1996). However, as Jackson and Scott note, the messages of public discourse remain mixed, reasserting as often as challenging the boundaries of conventional femininity. Incitements to active female sexuality have not undermined the dominant view of 'real sex' as coitus ending in ejaculation. Moreover, 'women and girls are positioned as sexual carers who do the emotional work and police their own emotions to ensure that they do not place excessive demands on men' (Jackson and Scott 1997: 567).

Sexual behaviours, their meanings and significance are notoriously difficult to investigate. Only partial insight can be gleaned from the behavioural measures which surveys offer, such as incidence of 'mutual orgasm'. However, relevant indicators can be found in recent large-scale surveys published in Britain and the United States (Wellings et al. 1994; Lauman et al. 1994). There is modest evidence of departures from conventional forms of sexual activity and of the more varied sexual repertoire implied by 'plastic sexuality'. The British survey found high levels of 'non-penetrative' sex and the US survey of 'oral sex', although it is not possible to know about the meanings and interpersonal dynamics behind these activities. However, there was no clear evidence of gender convergence in sexual behaviour but rather a rediscovery of patterns of gender difference, which appear to have only modestly moderated since Kinsey (1948, 1953). On all measures of sexual activity investigated, ranging from questions on thinking about sex and masturbating (asked only in the United States) to questions on number and type of partners and forms of sexual activity engaged in with them, more men are sexually active than women. The US survey revealed that men are still more likely to experience orgasm during sex than women and the British survey that men think orgasm is more essential to sexual satisfaction than women. Nevertheless, there is some evidence of gender convergence in expectations and ideas about sex. When responding to attitude questions in surveys men and women often say very similar things about the meaning and significance

of sexual behaviour in a couple-relationship. For example, in the British survey, most men and women think that 'companionship and affection are more important than sex in a marriage'.

However, in-depth interview studies continue to uncover a persistent, tenacious and phallocentric view of heterosexual sex as something that men do to women. It is conclusively documented that the early sexual experiences of most young people involve neither the negotiation of mutual pleasure nor a fusion of sex and emotional intimacy (Holland et al. 1991, 1993, 1994, 1998; Thomson and Scott 1991; Tolman 1994; Wight 1994, 1996). Evidence of mutual sexual pleasure, equality and deep intimacy among older heterosexuals is outweighed by sex and gender trouble. In their study of long-term couples, Jean Duncombe and Dennis Marsden (1993, 1995, 1996) find women complaining about lack of intimacy and men about lack of sex. It seems that men are more emotionally withdrawn from the relationship than women and men derive more pleasure from sex in the relationship (see also Mansfield and Collard 1988; Thompson and Walker 1989). Robert Connell's (1995) biographical explorations of masculinities indicate persistent difficulties in reconciling equality, intimacy and sexuality even among 'new men' and 'gay men'.

The Transformation of Intimacy raises the possibility of equality and intimacy in personal life democratizing gender relationships more generally. However, empirical work on heterosexual couples routinely continues to find that men exercise more power than women in the partnerships: for example, having more choice concerning opting in and out of domestic work and child care (Brannen and Moss 1991), and exercising more control of money (Morris 1990; Pahl 1989; Vogler 1994). But at the same time, research continues to find couples exhibiting such inequalities who collaboratively generate a sense of caring, intimate, equal relationships. This was eloquently demonstrated by Kathryn Backett (1982) in the 1970s and her findings continue to be echoed in much more recent work. Couples' carefully constructed sense of each other as good, mutually caring partners, despite unequal sacrifice for their common good, diverges considerably from the 'pure relationship'.

Research suggests that the ways in which couples generate a sense of themselves and their partners as mutually caring often reproduce gender inequality – the creativity and intimacy of couples is not yet typically harnessed to gender transformation. Many couples refer to gendering (i.e. underpinning gender difference) structural factors – the vagaries of employment including men and women's different earnings and prospects in the labour market, the incompatibility of combining the demands of childrearing and full-time employment – as if a traditional division of labour adopted because of such structures beyond their control were therefore exempted from any possible inequality. Many also deploy a variety of gendering but apparently gender-neutral devices to maintain a counterfactual sense of equality ('she happens to be better at cooking', 'he doesn't enjoy cooking as much'). Others continue to make explicit reference to traditional beliefs about manhood and womanhood, sometimes disavowing that this is how life should always be organized, but accepting that it works for them (for example, 'It's how I/he/she was brought up' – see other examples in Brannen and Moss 1991; Hochschild 1990; Mansfield and Collard 1988). This is not to deny the significance of a sense of equality for a sense of intimacy among many couples. There is a general taken-for-granted assumption that a good relationship will be equal and intimate. Rather it is to suggest that creative energy is deployed in disguising inequality, not in undermining it (Bittman and Lovejoy 1993).

Mutual self-disclosure is the basis of intimacy in 'the pure relationship', but empirical evidence suggests this is not the sole

or necessarily the ascendant type of intimacy between couples. Love and care expressed through actions is a very different dimension of intimacy from 'knowing', the mutual disclosure of the 'pure relationship', but it continues to loom large in how many couples view their relationship. For couples who live together, the time, money and effort each devotes to their household often symbolizes love and care for each other. A common traditional rhetoric which couples can and have drawn on when overlooking everyday differences in power and privilege is the visualization of their relationship in terms of complementary gifts – the man's wage as his expression of care for his partner and his family, and the woman's matching gift of housework as expressing her tender loving care (Cheal 1988; Morgan 1991). Many dual-worker households continue to use a slightly modified version of this theme by talking down the woman's wage as supplementary rather than the main earnings and talking up the man's typically relatively limited contributions to domestic work (Brannen and Moss 1991; Hochschild 1990). Tactics also include minimizing the significance of men's lack of practical involvement in the household or child care and maximizing the significance of their role as an emotional support (although discontent is then the consequence when emotional support is perceived as weak). Expressions of interest, concern and reassurance, 'emotional work', can compensate for a lack of practical assistance. Visualizing their relationship as rebalanced in these ways centres on an intimacy that is somewhat removed from the 'pure relationship'. Love and care as expressed by a more practical doing and giving is as much the crux of their relationship, as a process of mutually discovering and enjoying each other.

Couples who achieve a more objective equality are not necessarily any closer to a 'pure relationship'. Empirical research identifies a minority of couples who make painstaking efforts to achieve relatively equal contributions to a joint project of a household. In an Australian study, Goodnow and Bowes (1994) discuss heterosexual couples who have been recruited *because* they do things differently. However, unlike a number of other studies they are not recruited through feminist networks (Haas 1982; Kimball 1983; VanEvery 1995). For these couples, the supposedly gender-neutral 'circumstances', 'competencies' and 'preferences' (Mansfield and Collard 1988) that others use to justify unequal divisions of labour were not good enough reasons if they then produce a situation in which men systematically have more privileges such as free time. Goodnow and Bowes suggest that their respondents were not of a wholly different mind set from more traditional couples, but rather that they focused on the same dimensions of love and care. It was not their assumption that a loving couple would mutually care for each other in practical ways which was distinctive but their thorough analysis of the who, when, where and why of how this was done fairly. This was initiated in the name of fairness towards each other without necessarily adopting any feminist rhetoric, although women had typically prompted the process. These women had talked their way out of co-operating in an enterprise of covering over the gap between an ideal of equality and making more effort in practice to sustain their joint project. The thoroughness of establishing basic principles of fairness ruled out many of the tactics that might otherwise have justified gendered patterns. By the time of interview couples were settled into 'doing things differently', but conflict had often been the initial consequence.

The fact that researchers have identified heterosexual relationships that seem equal and unexploitative does not necessarily make these couples the vanguard of the future but even supposing they are, then something rather different is going on for them than 'the pure relationship'. The couples have applied reflexive awareness of the malleability of the world and themselves to creating a framework of rules. The dialogue that they engage in, reworking what is fair and what is not, is a practical as well as political, sociological and philosophical piece of personal engagement. Any consequent politicization and personal empowerment has not stemmed only from a preoccupation with their own relationship but a more general engagement with the world. While starting from their own situation, their rules of fairness seek universal principles and are not tied to or derived from knowledge of each other's unique qualities. In focusing intense dialogue on practical arrangements and abstract rules, the couple creates projects that inevitably add to the institutionalized framework over and above their relationship. Hence they stand outside of the ideal–typical pure relationship which seeks to bracket off distractions from the intensity of the relationship itself.

Giddens suggests that high rates of dissolution among couples reflect the fragility of the 'pure relationships', which require the psychological balancing act of sustaining mutual trust while knowing the relationship is only 'good until further notice'. However, it seems more plausible to see the fragility of heterosexual couples as a consequence of the tension between strengthening cultural emphasis on intimacy, equality and mutuality in relationships and the structural supports of gender inequalities, which make these ideals difficult to attain. Studies such as Brannen and Moss (1991), Hochschild (1990) and Mansfield and Collard (1988) document how collaborative effort can produce a sense of being equal and intimate, in spite of inequalities. What is important is not an intense process of mutual self-disclosure and exploration but a shared repertoire of cover stories, taboos and self-dishonesty. However, inequalities and asymmetries in parenting, domestic divisions of labour and 'emotion work' sometimes breed simmering discontent which defies the desire to feel equal and intimate. Drawing on Hochschild's work, Duncombe and

Marsden (1993) talk of women 'deep acting' in order to maintain a sense that their relationship is 'ever so happy', but sometimes 'deep acting' gives way to more critically aware and cynical 'shallow acting'. Diane Vaughan (1986) suggests that uncoupling begins with a secret, one partner's unspoken but nurtured feeling of discomfort with the relationship. She theorizes the process of uncoupling as the converse of constructing a sense of self and shared worldview through the marriage dialogue described by Berger and Kellner (1964). Interestingly, her respondents' stories of uncoupling show that while the disaffected partner withdraws from the relationship, the other partner often has no sense of loss until the secret is dramatically announced. Couples did not seem to be seeking to inhabit 'pure relationships' in any of these studies but rather relationships which were intended to last, which couples worked to institutionalize *and* wanted to feel equal and intimate.

Same-sex couples, and particularly lesbians, are identified by Giddens as in the vanguard of developing 'pure relationships' and hence as having a high incidence of relationship breakdown. There is a body of work which suggests that same-sex couples, and particularly lesbians, tend to have and to see themselves as having more equal relationships than heterosexual couples (Dunne 1997; Kurdek 1993; Weeks, Donovan and Heaphy 1998; Weston 1991) and that, moreover, lesbian relationships are particularly characterized by high levels of intimacy and communication (Dunne 1997: 201). However, the empirical evidence does not convince me that either lesbians or gay men typically have 'pure relationships', although Weeks and his colleagues sometimes use the term. Some research indicates that lesbians are wary of treating their partner as the sole source of intimacy but rather carefully maintain a supportive network, a 'chosen family' of friends, ex-lovers and kin (Heaphy, Weeks and Donovan 1998; Weston 1991). Scrutiny of the 'ground rules' Christian gay couples construct reveals a

range of practical devices to protect their relationship, including an understood tactical silence about casual sexual encounters outside the relationship (Yip 1997). As yet the evidence on which to assess the relative fragility of same-sex relationships is rather sparse and tends to stress similarities to heterosexuals rather than difference (Kurdek 1991). Moreover, there are reasons, other than 'the pure relationship', why same-sex relationships may be vulnerable to breakdown. It is clear that if same-sex couples do manage to securely maintain a long-term relationship they do so despite a wider social fabric, which is relatively hostile to its institutionalization.

Couples and Parent–Child Relationships

The processes of having children and making a joint project of their upbringing create structures over and above a relationship and therefore necessarily detract from the purity of 'the pure relationship'. Giddens evades the contradiction he has set up theoretically between parenting and 'the pure relationship' through the assertion that parent–child relationships, like couple relationships, are tending towards 'the pure relationship'. However, he does not then lay claim to the full range of attributes of 'the pure relationship' in the case of parents and children. Unlike couple relationships, this apparently does not render parent–child relationships as fragile, as 'good until further notice', at least not before 'basic trust' and 'ontological security' have typically formed. The research literature suggests that having children can unbalance couples but not primarily because children detract from their pure relationship, but as a consequence of gender inequalities becoming more extreme. Parenting is rarely a gender-neutral activity and often exacerbates inequalities in divisions of labour, free time, disposable income and other privileges. Mothers typically remain much more emotionally and practically involved with their children than fathers.

Unlike his discussion of couple relationships, which more strongly resonates with similar arguments elsewhere, Giddens's claims about 'pure relationships' between parents and children have had little take-up. While empirical research finds parents claiming they want to have closer relationships with their children than they had with their own parents, there is no clear evidence of a trend to democratic 'pure relationships' even among parents and teenage children. The search for a 'pure relationship' with children seems to be an unattainable ideal particularly pursued by white, middle-class mothers. Research into their mothering finds them stressing empathy, understanding and communication with older children (Brannen et al. 1994) and employing reasoning and pseudo-democracy with younger children (Walkerdine and Lucey 1989). Mutually intimate mother–child relationships are not necessarily the consequence, however.

Julia Brannen and her colleagues (1994) document the complex negotiations between London-based parents and their 15- and 16-year-old children. While many fathers were rather shadowy figures in young men's and young women's lives, mothers typically worked hard at trying to maintain a good relationship with their children. However, what a good relationship meant varied by class and ethnicity. Mothers were generally confident that their teenage children knew they continued to love and care for them; but some talked of a 'good relationship' in terms which echoed 'the pure relationship', with particular emphasis on a deeper knowing and understanding of each other. White middle-class mothers were most likely to claim to be very close to their teenage child. They stressed empathy and understanding, being able to 'talk', having 'listened' and 'tried to understand'. However, teenagers did not necessarily experience the practice of 'knowing' in this way. Middle-class mothers were more likely to be constantly

on the lookout for information that would warn them of possible trouble. In doing so they were working against their cherished desire to really *know* their child. Knowing as a means of control interfered with knowing as a dimension of intimacy. What parents consider to be a 'confiding' relationship could be experienced by the teenager as one-sided pressure to make disclosures. Mothers who were attempting to retain some control over their teenager, while being like a friend and equal, could not conceal their precarious balancing act.

Clearly the ideal of the involved and sensitive father has grown in stature in recent years, but research continues to find many men who are content to be providers and background figures (Bjornberg 1992; Brannen and O'Brien 1995; Busfield 1987; Lewis and O'Brien 1987; Russell 1983). The statistics continue to show that many non-custodial fathers lose touch with their children; research indicates that cumulatively, by the end of the second post-divorce year, about half of fathers have faded out of regular contact (Cherlin 1992; Cherlin and Furstenberg 1988). Nevertheless, the ideal of the involved father and equality in mothering and fathering can be highly consequential. For example, Bren Neale and Carol Smart (1997) have found fathers claiming their right to custody of their children following divorce on the grounds that 'everybody's talking about new age man'. Their study revealed that men's interest in custody sometimes reflects a combative approach to their wives rather than their prior relationship with their children. Moreover, men used ideas of gender equality to do their wife down, claiming that because women in general have equality then their wife should forfeit any special claim to children even if she had been a full-time wife and mother. This is a good empirical demonstration of how the ideals of equality and intimacy can feed into consequences that are a negation of 'the pure relationship'.

The significant dimension of intimacy in many parent–child relationships may not be being close by 'knowing' and talking to each other. A sense of unconditional love, trust and acceptance may be sustained with caring actions and relatively few words. Studies suggest that a good relationship between some parents and their growing-up children requires increasing silence on the part of the parents rather than an intense dialogue of mutual disclosure. Just as in couple relationships, silence need not mean an absence of care.

Conclusion

Giddens's work suggests a radical transformation of intimacy is under way with potentially profound consequences for gender politics and the wider social fabric. In order to keep faith with the argument, the much messier and less optimistic picture provided by empirical research has to be seen as the flux and confusion of an uneven transition. Indeed, some commentators seem prepared to give this the benefit of the doubt (Weeks 1995). However, this is a generosity that I balk at on political and theoretical as well as empirical grounds.

Extolling the values of mutual self-disclosure and 'the pure relationship' feeds into a therapeutic discourse that has sometimes been the antithesis of empowering for women and gays. While in *The Transformation of Intimacy* women are treated as the vanguard of the new intimacy, as Stevi Jackson and Sue Scott note 'we should be wary of valorizing what is symptomatic of subordination however tempting it might be to deride men's emotional incompetence' (1997: 568). At the same time as treating women as the vanguard of social change, the book eschews any systematic review of feminist scholarship. It is important to note that feminist-informed work of the last few decades has not typically concluded that if sufficient men and women can live together as equals and intimates then how other institutions, work-places, the state, the street, and the like, 'do gender' will automatically

radically unravel. If anything, the causal arrows point in the other direction to the ways in which efforts within personal life are constantly countered elsewhere. Giddens refers to the diffusion of change from the personal to other arenas without offering a developed sociological explanation of the intervening mechanisms. Ironically, this gives credence to the popular psychology of changing the world by transforming your inner self at the expense of more sociological accounts of social change.

Theoretically, the pure relationship seems to be a near impossibility for domestic partnerships and parent–child relationships that are necessarily embroiled in financial and material matters over and above the relationship. When adults share responsibility for physical space, money and material things, how these are managed cannot but become both symbolic of and reflexively constitutive of the relationship itself. Matters ranging from who last cleaned the toilet to how the insurance claim was spent become means of communicating care or neglect, equality or hierarchy, unity or division. Actions can speak louder than words and perhaps the important words, if men and women are to live together as equals, may be sorting out fair ways to get things done rather than purer forms of mutual self-disclosure.

The current state of play in gender politics remains a matter of debate. No theorist believes that what is happening in everyday gender play can be simply read off from the volume of talk about gender equality and heterosexual or homosexual intimacy. Ideals of equality and intimacy between men and women have been part of public discourse for decades, albeit that the themes have become louder and more diverse, for example, inciting men to become more emotionally expressive, more considerate lovers, communicative partners and sensitive fathers. Unquestionably, this barrage is consequential and must be associated with other changes that are in some sense in this direction. Yet, it is perfectly possible that widely disseminated ideals are, nevertheless, not widely or radically experienced lived realities of the present, nor will they be of the future. Although the evidence suggests most individuals now approach couple relationships with expectations which include mutual emotional support and treating each other like equals, this tells us relatively little concerning how people actually behave towards each other. Empirically, intimacy and inequality continue to coexist in many personal lives. Personal relationships remain highly gendered. Men and women routinely both invoke gender stereotypes or turn a convenient blind eye to gendering processes when making sense of themselves as lovers, partners, mothers, fathers and friends. While agreeing with Giddens's rejection of the more pessimistic account of personal life at the century's end, I note that the creative energies of many social actors are still engaged in coping with or actively sustaining old inequalities rather than transforming them.

REFERENCES

Allan, G. 1989. *Friendship: Developing a Sociological Perspective*. Hemel Hempstead, Harvester Wheatsheaf.

Backett, K. 1982. *Mothers and Fathers*. London, Macmillan.

Bauman, Z. 1990. 'Modernity and Ambivalence.' In M. Featherstone (ed.), *Global Culture: Nationalism, Globalization and Modernity*. London, Sage.

——1991. *Modernity and Ambivalence*. Cambridge, Polity Press.

Beck, U. 1992. *Risk Society: Towards a New Modernity*. London, Sage.

Beck, U. and Beck-Gernsheim, E. 1995. *The Normal Chaos of Love*. Cambridge, Polity Press.

Berger, P. and Kellner, H. 1964. 'Marriage and the Construction of Reality.' *Diogenes*, reprinted in M. Anderson (ed.), *The Sociology of the Family*. Hamondsworth, Penguin, 1980, pp. 302–24.

Bittman, M. and Lovejoy, F. 1993. 'Domestic Power: Negotiating an Unequal Division of Labour within a Framework of Equality.' *Australian and New Zealand Journal of Sociology* 29: 302–21.

Bjornberg, U. (ed.), 1992. *European Parents in the 1990s: Contradictions and Comparisons*. New Brunswick and London, Transaction.

Brannen, J. and Moss, P. 1991. *Managing Mothers: Dual Earner Households after Maternity Leave*. London, Unwin Hyman.

Brannen, J. and O'Brien, M. (eds.), 1995. *Childhood and Parenthood: Proceedings of the ISA Committee for Family Research Conference 1994*. London, Institute of Education, University of London.

Brannen, J., Dodd, K., Oakley, A. and Storey, P. 1994. *Young People, Health and Family Life*. Buckingham, Open University Press.

Burgess, E. W. and Locke, H. J. 1945. *The Family: From Institution to Companionship*. New York, American Book Company.

Busfield, J. 1987. 'Parenting and Parenthood.' In G. Cohen (ed.), *Social Change and the Life Course*. London, Tavistock.

——1996. *Men, Women and Madness: Understanding Gender and Mental Disorder*. London, Macmillan.

Cheal, D. 1988. *The Gift Economy*. London, Routledge.

Cherlin, A. 1992. *Marriage, Divorce, Remarriage*. Cambridge, MA, Harvard University Press.

Cherlin, A. and Furstenberg, F. 1988. 'The Changing European Family: Lessons for the American Reader.' *Journal of Family Issues* 9: 291–7.

Connell, R. W. 1987. *Gender and Power*. London, Allen & Unwin.

——1995. *Masculinities*. Cambridge, Polity Press.

Coontz, S. 1992. *The Way We Never Were: American Families and the Nostalgia Trip*. New York, Basic Books.

Craib, I. 1994. *The Importance of Disappointment*. London, Routledge.

——1997. 'Social Constructionism as a Social Psychosis.' *Sociology* 31: 1–15.

Delphy, C. and Leonard, D. 1992. *Familiar Exploitation: A New Analysis of Marriage in Contemporary Western Societies*. Cambridge, Polity Press.

Dobash, R. E. and Dobash, R. 1992. *Women, Violence and Social Change*. London, Routledge.

Duncombe, J. and Marsden, D. 1993. 'Love and Intimacy: The Gender Division of Emotion and "Emotion Work".' *Sociology* 27: 221–41.

—— 1995. '"Workaholics" and "Whingeing Women": Theorizing Intimacy and Emotion Work: The Last Frontier of Gender Inequality?' *Sociological Review* 43: 150–69.

—— 1996. 'Whose Orgasm is it Anyway? "Sex Work" in Long-Term Heterosexual Couple Relationships.' In J. Weeks and J. Holland (eds), *Sexual Cultures: Communities, Values and Intimacy*. New York, St Martin's Press.

Dunne, G. 1997. *Lesbian Lifestyles: Women's Work and the Politics of Sexuality*. London, Macmillan.

Finch, J. and Summerfield, P. 1991. 'Social Reconstruction and the Emergence of Companionate Marriage.' In D. Clark (ed.), *Marriage, Domestic Life and Social Change: Writings for Jacqueline Burgoyne (1944–88)*. London, Routledge.

Giddens, A. 1990. *The Consequences of Modernity*. Cambridge, Polity Press and Stanford, CA, Stanford University Press.

—— 1991. *Modernity and Self-Identity: Self and Society in the Late Modern Age*. Cambridge, Polity Press.

—— 1992. *The Transformation of Intimacy: Sexuality, Love and Eroticism in Modern Societies*. Cambridge, Polity Press.

—— 1994. 'Living in a Post-Traditional Society.' In U. Beck, A. Giddens and S. Lasch, *Reflexive Modernization: Politics, Tradition and Aesthetics in the Modern Social Order*. Cambridge, Polity Press.

Goodnow, J. and Bowes, J. 1994. *Men, Women and Household Work*. Melbourne, Oxford University Press.

Griffiths, V. 1995. *Adolescent Girls and Their Friends: A Feminist Ethnography*. Aldershot, Avebury.

Haas, L. L. 1982. 'Determinants of Role Sharing Behaviour: A Study of Egalitarian Couples.' *Sex Roles* 8: 747–60.

Harris, C. C. 1983. *The Family and Industrial Society*. London, Allen & Unwin.

Heaphy, B., Weeks, J. and Donovan, C. 1998. '"That's Like my Life": Researching Stories of Non-heterosexual Relationships.' *Sexualities* 1: 453–70.

Hey, V. 1997. *The Company She Keeps: An Ethnography of Girls' Friendships*. Buckingham, Open University Press.

Hochschild, A. 1990. *The Second Shift: Working Parents and the Revolution at Home*. London, Piatkus.

Holland, J., Ramazanoglu, C. and Sharpe, S. 1993. *Wimp or Gladiator: Contradictions in the Acquisition of Masculine Sexuality*. London, Tufnell Press.

—— 1994. 'Power and Desire: The Embodiment of Female Sexuality.' *Feminist Review* 46: 21–38.

Holland, J., Ramazanoglu, C., Sharpe, S. and Thompson, R. 1998. *The Male in the Head: Young People, Heterosexuality and Power*. London, Tufnell Press.

Holland, J., Ramazanoglu, C., Scott, S., Sharpe, S. and Thomson, R. 1991. *Pressure, Resistance, Empowerment: Young Women and the Negotiation of Safer Sex*. London, Tufnell Press.

Jackson, S. and Scott, S. 1997. 'Gut Reactions to Matters of the Heart: Reflections on Rationality, Irrationality and Sexuality.' *Sociological Review* 45: 551–75.

Jamieson, L. 1987. 'Theories of Family Development and the Experience of Being Brought Up.' *Sociology* 21: 591–607.

—— 1998. *Intimacy: Personal Relationships in Modern Societies*. Cambridge, Polity Press.

Kimball, G. 1983. *The 50–50 Marriage*. Boston, MA, Beacon Press.

Kinsey, A. 1948. *Sexual Behaviour in the Human Male*. Philadelphia, W. B. Saunders.

—— 1953. *Sexual Behaviour in the Human Female*. Philadelphia, W. B. Saunders.

Kurdek, L. 1991. 'The Dissolution of Gay and Lesbian Couples.' *Journal of Social and Personal Relationships* 8: 265–78.

—— 1993. 'The Allocation of Household Labour in Gay, Lesbian, and Heterosexual Married Couples.' *Journal of Social Issues* 49: 127–40.

Lasch, C. 1977. *Haven in a Heartless World*. New York, Basic Books.

Laumann, E., Michael R., Michaels, S. and Gagnon, J. 1994. *The Social Organization of Sexuality*. Chicago, University of Chicago Press.

Lewis, C. and O'Brien, M. (eds), 1987. *Reassessing Fatherhood: New Observations on Fathers and the Modern Family*. London, Sage.

McRobbie, A. 1991. *Feminism and Youth Culture: From 'Jackie' to 'Just Seventeen'*. Basingstoke, Macmillan.

—— 1994. *Postmodernism and Popular Culture*. London, Routledge.

—— 1996. '*More!* New Sexualities in Girls' and Women's Magazines.' In J. Curran et al. (eds), *Cultural Studies and Communication*. London, Edward Arnold.

Mansfield, P. and Collard, J. 1988. *The Beginning of the Rest of Your Life: A Portrait of Newly-Wed Marriage*. London, Macmillan.

Morgan, D. 1991. 'Ideologies of Marriage and Family Life.' In D. Clark (ed.), *Marriage, Domestic Life and Social Change: Writings for Jacqueline Burgoyne (1944–88)*. London, Routledge.

—— 1992. 'Marriage and Society.' In J. Lewis, D. Clark and D. Morgan, *Whom God Hath Joined Together: The Work of Marriage Guidance*. London, Tavistock and Routledge.

—— 1996. *Family Connections: An Introduction to Family Studies*. Cambridge, Polity Press.

Morris, L. 1990. *The Workings of the Household*. Cambridge, Polity Press.

Neale, B. and Smart, C. 1997. 'Experiments with Parenthood?' *Sociology* 31: 201–19.

Pahl, J. 1989. *Money and Marriage*. London, Macmillan.

Russell, G. 1983. *The Changing Role of Fathers*. Milton Keynes, Open University Press.

Sennett, R. 1977. 'Destructive Gemeinschaft.' In N. Birnbaum (ed.), *Beyond the Crisis*. Oxford, Oxford University Press.

Silver, A. 1997. '"Two Different Sorts of Commerce", or, Friendship and Strangership in Civil Society.' In J. Weintraub and K. Kumar (eds), *Public and Private in Thought and Practice: Perspectives on the Grand Dichotomy*. Chicago, University of Chicago Press.

Skolnick, A. 1991. *Embattled Paradise: The American Family in an Age of Uncertainty*. New York, Basic Books.

Thompson, L. and Walker, A. 1989. 'Gender in Families: Women and Men in Marriage, Work, and Parenthood.' *Journal of Marriage and the Family* 51: 845–71.

Thomson, R. and Scott, S. 1991. *Learning about Sex: Young Women and the Social Construction of Sexual Identity*. London, Tufnell Press.

Thorne, B. 1993. *Gender Play: Girls and Boys in School*. New Brunswick, NJ, Rutgers University Press, and Milton Keynes, Open University Press.

Tolman, D. L. 1994. 'Doing Desire: Adolescent Girls' Struggle for/with Sexuality.' *Gender & Society* 8: 324–42.

VanEvery, J. 1995. *Heterosexual Women Changing the Family: Refusing to be a 'Wife'*. London, Taylor and Francis.

Vaughan, D. 1986. *Uncoupling: Turning Points in Intimate Relationships*. Oxford, Oxford University Press.

Vogler, C. 1994. 'Money in the Household.' In M. Anderson, F. Bechhofer and J. Gershuny (eds), *The Social and Political Economy of the Household*. Oxford, Oxford University Press.

Walkerdine, V. and Lucey, H. 1989. *Democracy in the Kitchen: Regulating Mothers and Socializing Daughters*. London, Virago.

Weeks, J. 1995. *Invented Moralities: Sexual Values in an Age of Uncertainty*. Cambridge, Polity Press.

Weeks, J., Donovan, C. and Heaphy, B. 1998. 'Everyday Experiments: Narratives of Non-heterosexual Relationships.' In E. Silva and C. Smart (eds), *The 'New' Family?* London, Sage.

Wellings, K., Field, J., Johnson, A. M. and Wadsworth, J. 1994. *Sexual Behaviour in Britain: The National Survey of Sexual Attitudes and Lifestyles*. London, Penguin.

Weston, K. 1991. *Families We Choose: Lesbians, Gays, Kinship*. New York, Columbia University Press.

Wight, D. 1994. 'Boys' Thoughts and Talk about Sex in a Working-Class Locality of Glasgow.' *Sociological Review* 42: 702–37.

—— 1996. 'Beyond the Predatory Male: The Diversity of Young Glaswegian Men's Discourses to Describe Heterosexual Relationships.' In L. Adkins and V. Merchant (eds), *Sexualizing the Social: Power and the Organizing of Sexuality*. London, Macmillan.

Wolff, K. H. 1950. *The Sociology of Georg Simmel*. Glencoe, Free Press.

Yip, A. K. T. 1997. 'Gay Male Christian Couples and Sexual Exclusivity.' *Sociology* 31: 289–306.

32 The Five Sexes: Why Male and Female Are Not Enough

Anne Fausto-Sterling

In 1843 Levi Suydam, a 23-year-old resident of Salisbury, Connecticut, asked the town board of selectmen to validate his right to vote as a Whig in a hotly contested local election. The request raised a flurry of objections from the opposition party, for reasons that must be rare in the annals of American democracy: it was said that Suydam was more female than male and thus (some eighty years before suffrage was extended to women) could not be allowed to cast a ballot. To settle the dispute a physician, one William James Barry, was brought in to examine Suydam. And, presumably upon encountering a phallus, the good doctor declared the prospective voter male. With Suydam safely in their column the Whigs won the election by a majority of one.

Barry's diagnosis, however, turned out to be somewhat premature. Within a few days he discovered that, phallus notwithstanding, Suydam menstruated regularly and had a vaginal opening. Both his/her physique and his/her mental predispositions were more complex than was first suspected. S/he had narrow shoulders and broad hips and felt occasional sexual yearnings for women. Suydam's "feminine propensities, such as a fondness for gay colors, for pieces of calico, comparing and placing them together, and an aversion for bodily labor, and an inability to perform the same, were remarked by many," Barry later wrote. It is not clear whether Suydam lost or retained the vote, or whether the election results were reversed.

Western culture is deeply committed to the idea that there are only two sexes. Even language refuses other possibilities; thus to write about Levi Suydam I have had to invent conventions – s/he and his/her – to denote someone who is clearly neither male nor female or who is perhaps both sexes at once. Legally, too, every adult is either man or woman, and the difference, of course, is not trivial. For Suydam it meant the franchise; today it means being available for, or exempt from, draft registration, as well as being subject, in various ways, to a number of laws governing marriage, the family, and human intimacy. In many parts of the United States, for instance, two people legally registered as men cannot have sexual relations without violating anti-sodomy statutes.

But if the state and the legal system have an interest in maintaining a two-party sexual system, they are in defiance of nature. For biologically speaking, there are many gradations running from female to male; and depending on how one calls the shots, one can argue that along that specterum lie at least five sexes – and perhaps even more.

For some time medical investigators have recognized the concept of the intersexual body. But the standard medical literature uses the term *intersex* as a catch-all for three major subgroups with some mixture of male and female characteristics: the so-called true hermaphrodites, whom I call herms, who possess one testis and one ovary (the sperm- and egg-producing vessels, or gonads); the male pseudohermaphrodites (the "merms"), who have testes and some aspects of the female genitalia but no ovaries; and the female pseudohermaphrodites (the "ferms"), who have ovaries and some aspects of the male genitalia but lack testes. Each of those categories is in itself complex; the percentage of male and female characteristics, for instance, can vary enormously among members of the same subgroup. Moreover, the inner lives of the people in each subgroup – their special needs and their problems, attractions, and repulsions – have gone unexplored by science. But on the basis of what is known about them I suggest that the three intersexes, herm, merm, and ferm, deserve to be considered additional sexes each in its own right. Indeed, I would argue further that sex is a vast, infinitely malleable continuum that defies the constraints of even five categories.

Not surprisingly, it is extremely difficult to estimate the frequency of intersexuality, much less the frequency of each of the three additional sexes: it is not the sort of information one volunteers on a job application. The psychologist John Money of Johns Hopkins University, a specialist in the study of congenital sexual-organ defects, suggests intersexuals may constitute as many as 4 percent of births. As I point out to my students at Brown University, in a student body of about 6,000 that fraction, if correct, implies there may be as many as 240 intersexuals on campus – surely enough to form a minority caucus of some kind.

In reality though, few such students would make it as far as Brown in sexually diverse form. Recent advances in physiology and surgical technology now enable physicians to catch most intersexuals at the moment of birth. Almost at once such infants are entered into a program of hormonal and surgical management so that they can slip quietly into society as "normal" heterosexual males or females. I emphasize that the motive is in no way conspiratorial. The aims of the policy are genuinely humanitarian, reflecting the wish that people be able to "fit in" both physically and psychologically. In the medical community, however, the assumptions behind that wish – that there be only two sexes, that heterosexuality alone is normal, that there is one true model of psychological health – have gone virtually unexamined.

The word *hermaphrodite* comes from the Greek names Hermes, variously known as the messenger of the gods, the patron of music, the controller of dreams or the protector of livestock, and Aphrodite, the goddess of sexual love and beauty. According to Greek mythology, those two gods parented Hermaphroditus, who at age fifteen became half male and half female when his body fused with the body of a nymph he fell in love with. In some true hermaphrodites the testis and the ovary grow separately but bilaterally; in others they grow together within the same organ, forming an ovotestis. Not infrequently, at least one of the gonads functions quite well, producing either sperm cells or eggs, as well as functional levels of the sex hormones – androgens or estrogens. Although in theory it might be possible for a true hermaphrodite to become both father and mother to a child, in practice the appropriate ducts and tubes are not configured so that egg and sperm can meet.

In contrast with the true hermaphrodites, the pseudohermaphrodites possess two gonads of the same kind along with the usual male (XY) or female (XX) chromosomal makeup. But their external genitalia and secondary sex characteristics do not match their chromosomes. Thus merms have testes and XY chromosomes, yet they also have a vagina and a clitoris, and at puberty they often develop breasts. They do not menstruate, however. Ferms have ovaries, two X chromosomes and sometimes a uterus, but they also have at least partly masculine external genitalia. Without medical intervention they can develop beards, deep voices and adult-size penises. . . .

Intersexuality itself is old news. Hermaphrodites, for instance, are often featured in stories about human origins. Early biblical scholars believed Adam began life as a hermaphrodite and later divided into two people – a male and a female – after falling from grace. According to Plato there once were three sexes – male, female, and hermaphrodite – but the third sex was lost with time.

Both the Talmud and the Tosefta, the Jewish books of law, list extensive regulations for people of mixed sex. The Tosefta expressly forbids hermaphrodites to inherit their fathers' estates (like daughters), to seclude themselves with women (like sons), or to shave (like men). When hermaphrodites menstruate they must be isolated from men (like women); they are disqualified from serving as witnesses or as priests (like women), but the laws of pederasty apply to them.

In Europe a pattern emerged by the end of the Middle Ages that, in a sense, has lasted to the present day: hermaphrodites were compelled to choose an established gender role and stick with it. The penalty for transgression was often death. Thus in the 1600s a Scottish hermaphrodite living as a woman was buried alive after impregnating his/her master's daughter.

For questions of inheritance, legitimacy, paternity, succession to title, and eligibility for certain professions to be determined, modern Anglo-Saxon legal systems require that newborns be registered as either male or female. In the US today sex determination is governed by state laws. Illinois permits adults to change the sex recorded on their birth certificates should a physican attest to having performed the appropriate surgery. The New York Academy of Medicine, on the other hand, has taken an opposite view. In spite of surgical alterations of the external genitalia, the academy argued in 1966, the chromosomal sex remains the same. By that measure, a person's wish to conceal his or her original sex cannot outweigh the public interest in protection against fraud.

During this century the medical community has completed what the legal world began – the complete erasure of any form of embodied sex that does not conform to a male–female, heterosexual pattern. Ironically, a more sophisticated knowledge of the complexity of sexual systems has led to the repression of such intricacy.

In 1937 the urologist Hugh H. Young of Johns Hopkins University published a volume titled *Genital Abnormalities, Hermaphroditism and Related Adrenal Diseases*. The book is remarkable for its erudition, scientific insight, and open-mindedness. In it Young drew together a wealth of carefully documented case histories to demonstrate and study the medical treatment of such "accidents of birth." Young did not pass judgment on the people he studied, nor did he attempt to coerce into treatment those intersexuals who rejected that option. And he showed unusual even-handedness in referring to those people who had had sexual experiences as both men and women as "practicing hermaphrodites."

One of Young's more interesting cases was a hermaphrodite named Emma who had grown up as a female. Emma had both a penis-size clitoris and a vagina, which made it possible for him/her to have "normal" heterosexual sex with both men and women. As a teenager Emma had had sex with a number of girls to whom s/he was deeply attracted; but at the age of nineteen s/he had married a man. Unfortunately, he had given Emma little sexual pleasure (though he had had no complaints), and so throughout that marriage and subsequent ones Emma had kept girlfriends on the side. With some frequency s/he had pleasurable sex with them. Young describes his subject as appearing "to be quite content and even happy." In conversation Emma occasionally told him of his/her wish to be a man, a circumstance Young said would be relatively easy to bring about. But Emma's reply strikes a heroic blow for self-interest:

> Would you have to remove that vagina? I don't know about that because that's my meal ticket. If you did that, I would have to quit my husband and go to work, so I think I'll keep it and stay as I am. My husband supports me well, and even though I don't have any sexual pleasure with him, I do have lots with my girlfriends.

Yet even as Young was illuminating inter-sexuality with the light of scientific reason, he was beginning its suppression. For his book is also an extended treatise on the most modern surgical and hormonal methods of changing intersexuals into either males or females. Young may have differed from his successors in being less judgmental and controlling of the patients and their families, but he nonetheless supplied the foundation on which current intervention practices were built.

By 1969, when the English physicians Christopher J. Dewhurst and Ronald R. Gordon wrote *The Intersexual Disorders*, medical and surgical approaches to inter-sexuality had neared a state of rigid uniformity. It is hardly surprising that such a hardening of opinion took place in the era of the feminine mystique – of the post-World War II flight to the suburbs and the strict division of family roles according to sex. That the medical consensus was not quite universal (or perhaps that it seemed poised to break apart again) can be gleaned from the near-hysterical tone of Dewhurst and Gordon's book, which contrasts markedly with the calm reason of Young's founding work. Consider their opening description of an intersexual newborn:

> One can only attempt to imagine the anguish of the parents. That a newborn should have a deformity... [affecting] so fundamental an issue as the very sex of the child... is a tragic event which immediately conjures up visions of a hopeless psychological misfit doomed to live always as a sexual freak in loneliness and frustration.

Dewhurst and Gordon warned that such a miserable fate would, indeed, be a baby's lot should the case be improperly managed; "but fortunately," they wrote, "with correct management the outlook is infinitely better than the poor parents – emotionally stunned by the event – or indeed anyone without special knowledge could ever imagine."

Scientific dogma has held fast to the assumption that without medical care herm-aphrodites are doomed to a life of misery. Yet there are few empirical studies to back up that assumption, and some of the same research gathered to build a case for medical treatment contradicts it. Francies Benton, another of Young's practicing hermaphrodites, "had not worried over his condition, did not wish to be changed, and was enjoying life." The same could be said of Emma, the opportunistic hausfrau. Even Dewhurst and Gordon, adamant about the psychological importance of treating inter-sexuals at the infant stage, acknowledged great success in "changing the sex" of older patients. They reported on twenty cases of children reclassified into a different sex after the supposedly critical age of eighteen months. They asserted that all the reclassifications were "successful," and they wondered then whether reregistration could be "recommended more readily than [had] been suggested so far."

The treatment of intersexuality in this century provides a clear example of what the French historian Michel Foucault has called biopower. The knowledge developed in biochemistry, embryology, endocrinology, psychology, and surgery has enabled physicians to control the very sex of the human body. The multiple contradictions in that kind of power call for some scrutiny. On the one hand, the medical "management" of intersexuality certainly developed as part of an attempt to free people from perceived psychological pain (though whether the pain was the patient's, the parents', or the physician's is unclear). And if one accepts the assumption that in a sex-divided culture people can realize their greatest potential for happiness and productivity only if they are sure they belong to one of only two acknowledged sexes, modern medicine has been extremely successful.

On the other hand, the same medical accomplishments can be read not as progress but as a mode of discipline. Hermaph-rodites have unruly bodies. They do not fall naturally into a binary classification; only a surgical shoehorn can put them there. But why should we care if a "woman," defined as one who has breasts, a vagina, a uterus and ovaries and who menstruates, also has a clitoris large enough to penetrate the vagina of another woman? Why should we care if there are people whose biological equipment enables them to have sex "naturally" with both men and women? The answers seem to lie in a cultural need to maintain clear distinctions between the sexes. Society mandates the control of intersexual bodies because they blur and bridge the great divide. Inasmuch as hermaphrodites literally embody both sexes, they challenge traditional beliefs about sexual difference: they possess the irritating ability to live sometimes as one sex and sometimes the other, and they raise the specter of homosexuality.

But what if things were altogether different? Imagine a world in which the same knowledge that has enabled medicine to intervene in the management of intersexual patients has been placed at the service of multiple sexualities. Imagine that the sexes have multiplied beyond currently imaginable limits. It would have to be a world of shared powers. Patient and physician, parent and child, male and female, heterosexual and homosexual – all those oppositions and others would have to be dissolved as sources of division. A new ethic of medical treatment would arise, one that would permit ambiguity in a culture that had overcome sexual division. The central mission of medical treatment would be to preserve life. Thus hermaphrodites would be concerned primarily not about whether they can conform to society but about whether they might develop potentially life-threatening conditions – hernias, gonadal tumors, salt imbalance caused by adrenal malfunction – that sometimes accompany hermaphroditic development. In my ideal world medical intervention for intersexuals would take place only rarely before the age of reason; subsequent treatment would be a cooperative venture between physician, patient, and other advisers trained in issues of gender multiplicity.

I do not pretend that the transition to my utopia would be smooth. Sex, even the supposedly "normal," heterosexual kind, continues to cause untold anxieties in Western society. And certainly a culture that has yet to come to grips – religiously and, in some states, legally – with the ancient and relatively uncomplicated reality of homosexual love will not readily embrace intersexuality. No doubt the most troublesome arena by far would be the rearing of children. Parents, at least since the Victorian era, have fretted, sometimes to the point of outright denial, over the fact that their children are sexual beings.

All that and more amply explains why intersexual children are generally squeezed into one of the two prevailing sexual categories. But what would be the psychological consequences of taking the alternative road – raising children as unabashed intersexuals? On the surface that tack seems fraught with peril. What, for example, would happen to the intersexual child amid the unrelenting cruelty of the school yard? When the time came to shower in gym class, what horrors and humiliations would await the intersexual as his/her anatomy was displayed in all its nontraditional glory? In whose gym class would s/he register to begin with? What bathroom would s/he use? And how on earth would Mom and Dad help shepherd him/her through the mine field of puberty?

In the past thirty years those questions have been ignored, as the scientific community has, with remarkable unanimity, avoided contemplating the alternative route of unimpeded intersexuality. But modern investigators tend to overlook a substantial body of case histories, most of them compiled between 1930 and 1960, before surgical intervention became rampant. Almost without exception, those reports describe children who grew up knowing they were intersexual (though they did not advertise it) and adjusted to their unusual status. Some of the studies are richly detailed – described at the level of gym-class showering (which most intersexuals avoided without incident); in any event, there is not a psychotic or a suicide in the lot.

Still, the nuances of socialization among intersexuals cry out for more sophisticated analysis. Clearly, before my vision of sexual multiplicity can be realized, the first openly intersexual children and their parents will have to be brave pioneers who will bear the brunt of society's growing pains. But in the long view – though it could take generations to achieve – the prize might be a society in which sexuality is something to be celebrated for its subtleties and not something to be feared or ridiculed.

Index